Henry Alford

The New Testament of Our Lord and Saviour Jesus Christ

after the Authorized version - newly compared with the original Greek, and revised

Henry Alford

The New Testament of Our Lord and Saviour Jesus Christ
after the Authorized version - newly compared with the original Greek, and revised

ISBN/EAN: 9783337313883

Printed in Europe, USA, Canada, Australia, Japan

Cover: Foto ©Lupo / pixelio.de

More available books at **www.hansebooks.com**

THE NEW TESTAMENT

Of our Lord and Saviour Jesus Christ

AFTER THE AUTHORIZED VERSION

Newly compared with the original Greek, and revised

By HENRY ALFORD, D.D.

DEAN OF CANTERBURY

LONDON

DALDY, ISBISTER & CO.

56, LUDGATE HILL

1878

PREFACE

It is necessary to premise a few words regarding the view with which this Revision of the Authorized Version has been undertaken.

It seemed to the Reviser, and to some others, that the time was ripe for an effort to be made to publish the English New Testament in a form more consonant to the now ascertained ancient Greek text, and with corrections of inadequate renderings.

This had been already done in the case of the Gospel of St. John, the Epistles to the Romans, Corinthians, Galatians, Ephesians, Philippians, and Colossians, by "Five Clergymen," of whom the present Reviser was one. The fruit of their joint labours has been kindly placed by his colleagues at his disposal; and those books appear, with the exception of a very few passages in which his own view differed from that of the majority, simply as a reprint from the former Revision.

It seemed desirable that the traditions of our many months' combined labour should not be lost. It was impossible that we could ever meet in council again: and one who inherited those traditions would at all events approach the work at an advantage. For there is no employment in which crude positiveness becomes so mellowed, in which purism has so often to give way before compromise, and rigid uniformity of rendering breaks down before common sense, as in revision of the sacred text. The old story of the scholar who sent King James's translators five reasons in favour of a certain rendering, and was answered that they had fifteen against it, not inaptly represents, in very many cases, the relation between our critics and ourselves. Strictures on our renderings have been advanced, which one sentence or one reference would have sufficed to annihilate. Purisms have been maintained and cast in our teeth, which the next verse of the text would have shewn to be impracticable: and phrases held up to ridicule, of which a word from us would have demonstrated the paramount necessity.

This being so, the present Reviser has simply thrown himself into the gap, that the work might be accomplished at all events on the basis of the experience already acquired. He utterly repudiates for his Revision any aim to be adopted in any place as a substitute for the Authorized Version. It is impossible, to say nothing more, that *one man's work* can ever fulfil the requisites for an accepted Version of the Scriptures. If there was one lesson which the "Five Clergymen" learnt from their sessions, it was that no new rendering is safe until it has gone through many brains, and been thoroughly sifted by differing perceptions and tastes.

His wish mainly is to keep open the great question of an authoritative Revision; to shew the absolute necessity of such a measure sooner or later; and to disabuse men's minds of the fallacies by which the Authorized Version is commonly defended.

At the same time he is not without hope that this Revision may serve the cause of God and His Word by presenting to the English reader the sacred text in a form which, however far from perfection, yet more nearly approaches that in which the faith was once for all delivered to the saints.

It may be well, by the light of experience, to forewarn the reader of some of the criticisms of this Revision which are sure to be made.

It is a common practice with those who do not understand the first principles of textual criticism, if they wish to shew that a reading ought not to have been adopted, to compare it with the *received* reading in point of clearness, of probability, of conformity to usage, and the like. If in these respects it is inferior to the *received*, then, say they, the *received* was better, and ought to have been retained. Now in such reasoning there is not a word of truth. Whether or not a reading is to be adopted, is simply a matter of testimony. If the most ancient authorities concur in it, then we are bound in simple obedience to receive it. Only when ancient authorities are divided can we take such considerations as the above into account; and even then, with precisely the opposite estimate to that of our friend: giving preference, that is, to the harder, the less grammatical, the less probable reading, for this reason,—that, in transcribing, that which was difficult was more likely to be altered to that which was easy, than *vice versâ*.

If it be desired to shew that revision was not worth undertaking, a long passage is chosen from the narrative part of the Gospels, in which perhaps for twenty verses or more there may be hardly any difference between the two texts: and this is paraded as a sample of the work.

If to shew that revision is mischievous in the object, some text is pitched upon in the Authorized Version, on which sound doctrine has relied for proof or confirmation: the same text is quoted from the Revision, and is found to be void of such proof or confirmation. The unhappy Reviser is at once denounced as a heretic, and his work as fostering unsound doctrine. The critic either cannot, or will not, notice that the change was here made simply as an act of honest obedience to truth of testimony, or truth of rendering. Of course it has never dawned upon him that a translator of Holy Scripture must be absolutely colourless; ready to sacrifice the choicest text, and the plainest proof of doctrine, if the words are not those of what he is constrained in his conscience to receive as God's testimony.

The Reviser has only to express his wish and prayer that this work may be as soon as possible rendered useless by the more matured and multifarious labour of a Royal Commission. Such a commission he believes the various sections of the Church in this realm fully able to furnish with members: and he doubts not that its issue would be a new Authorized Version, founded upon the old, but everywhere, by its own weight of excellence, superseding it.

CANTERBURY,
February 12, 1865.

CONTENTS.

	PAGE
THE GOSPEL ACCORDING TO SAINT MATTHEW	1
THE GOSPEL ACCORDING TO SAINT MARK	55
THE GOSPEL ACCORDING TO SAINT LUKE	89
THE GOSPEL ACCORDING TO SAINT JOHN	147
THE ACTS OF THE APOSTLES	190
THE EPISTLE OF PAUL THE APOSTLE TO THE ROMANS	247
THE FIRST EPISTLE OF PAUL THE APOSTLE TO THE CORINTHIANS	270
THE SECOND EPISTLE OF PAUL THE APOSTLE TO THE CORINTHIANS	292
THE EPISTLE OF PAUL THE APOSTLE TO THE GALATIANS	306
THE EPISTLE OF PAUL THE APOSTLE TO THE EPHESIANS	314
THE EPISTLE OF PAUL THE APOSTLE TO THE PHILIPPIANS	322
THE EPISTLE OF PAUL THE APOSTLE TO THE COLOSSIANS	328

CONTENTS.

	PAGE
THE FIRST EPISTLE OF PAUL THE APOSTLE TO THE THESSALONIANS	333
THE SECOND EPISTLE OF PAUL THE APOSTLE TO THE THESSALONIANS	338
THE FIRST EPISTLE OF PAUL THE APOSTLE TO TIMOTHY	341
THE SECOND EPISTLE OF PAUL THE APOSTLE TO TIMOTHY	347
THE EPISTLE OF PAUL TO TITUS	351
THE EPISTLE OF PAUL TO PHILEMON	354
THE EPISTLE TO THE HEBREWS	355
THE GENERAL EPISTLE OF JAMES	372
THE FIRST EPISTLE GENERAL OF PETER	378
THE SECOND EPISTLE GENERAL OF PETER	384
THE FIRST EPISTLE GENERAL OF JOHN	389
THE SECOND EPISTLE OF JOHN	395
THE THIRD EPISTLE OF JOHN	396
THE GENERAL EPISTLE OF JUDE	397
THE REVELATION OF JOHN	399

THE NEW TESTAMENT

THE GOSPEL

ACCORDING TO

SAINT MATTHEW.

CHAPTER I.

THE book of the generation of Jesus Christ the son of David, the son of Abraham.

2 Abraham begat Isaac; and Isaac begat Jacob; and Jacob begat Judah and his brethren;

3 And Judah begat Phares and Zara of Thamar; and Phares begat Esrom; and Esrom begat Aram;

4 And Aram begat Aminadab; and Aminadab begat Naasson; and Naasson begat Salmon;

5 And Salmon begat Boaz of Rachab; and Boaz begat Obed of Ruth; and Obed begat Jesse;

6 And Jesse begat David the king; and David the king begat Solomon of the wife of Uriah;

7 And Solomon begat Rehoboam; and Rehoboam begat Abijah; and Abijah begat Asa;

8 And Asa begat Jehosaphat; and Jehosaphat begat Jehoram; and Jehoram begat Uzziah;

9 And Uzziah begat Jotham; and Jotham begat Ahaz; and Ahaz begat Hezekiah;

10 And Hezekiah begat Manasseh; and Manasseh begat Amon; and Amon begat Josiah;

11 And Josiah begat Jechoniah and his brethren, at the time of the removal to Babylon:

12 And after the removal to Babylon, Jechoniah begat Salathiel; and Salathiel begat Zerubbabel;

13 And Zerubbabel begat Abiud; and Abiud begat Eliakim; and Eliakim begat Azor;

14 And Azor begat Sadoc; and Sadoc begat Achim; and Achim begat Eliud;

15 And Eliud begat Eleazar; and Eleazar begat Matthan; and Matthan begat Jacob;

16 And Jacob begat Joseph the husband of Mary, of whom was born Jesus, who is called Christ.

17 So all the generations from Abraham to David are fourteen generations; and from David until the removal to Babylon are fourteen generations; and from the removal to Babylon unto Christ are fourteen generations.

18 Now the generation of Jesus Christ was on this wise. For when his mother Mary was espoused to Joseph, before they came together, she was found with child of the Holy Ghost.

19 But Joseph her husband, being a just man, and not willing to make her a publick example, was minded to put her away privily.

20 But while he was thus purposed, behold, the angel of

the Lord appeared unto him in a dream, saying, Joseph, thou son of David, fear not to take unto thee Mary thy wife: for that which is conceived in her is of the Holy Ghost.

21 And she shall bring forth a son, and thou shalt call his name JESUS: for HE shall save his people from their sins.

22 Now all this hath come to pass, that it may be fulfilled which was spoken of the Lord by the prophet, saying,

23 Behold, the virgin shall be with child, and shall bring forth a son, and they shall call his name Emmanuel, which being interpreted is, God is with us.

24 And Joseph arose from his sleep, and did as the angel of the Lord had bidden him, and took unto him his wife:

25 And knew her not till she had brought forth ¹a son: and he called his name JESUS.

CHAPTER II.

NOW when Jesus was born in Bethlehem of Judæa in the days of Herod the king, behold, there came ²wise men from the east to Jerusalem,

2 Saying, Where is he that is born King of the Jews? for we have seen his star in the east, and are come to worship him.

3 When Herod the king heard these things, he was troubled, and all Jerusalem with him.

4 And when he had gathered all the chief priests and scribes of the people together, he demanded of them where the Christ should be born.

5 And they said unto him, In Bethlehem of Judæa: for thus it is written by the prophet,

6 And thou Bethlehem, land of Judah, art by no means least among the princes of Judah: for out of thee shall come forth a Governor, one that shall be the Shepherd of my people Israel.

7 Then Herod privily called the ²wise men, and enquired of them diligently what time the star appeared.

8 And he sent them to Bethlehem, and said, Go and search diligently for the young child; and when ye have found him, bring me word again, that I may come and worship him also.

9 When they had heard the king, they departed; and, lo, the star, which they saw in the east, went before them, till it came and stood over where the young child was.

10 When they saw the star, they rejoiced with exceeding great joy.

11 And they came into the house, and saw the young child with Mary his mother, and fell down and worshipped him: and opened their treasures, and presented unto him gifts; gold, and frankincense, and myrrh.

12 And being warned in a dream that they should not return to Herod, they departed into their country another way.

13 And when they were de-

---

¹ *Or*, her first-born son: *but the authority for the reading in the text preponderates.*
² *Literally*, Magi.

parted, behold, an angel of the Lord appeareth to Joseph in a dream, saying, Arise, and take the young child and his mother, and flee into Egypt, and be thou there until I bring thee word: for Herod shall seek the young child to destroy him.

14 And he arose and took the young child and his mother by night, and departed into Egypt:

15 And was there until the death of Herod: that it might be fulfilled which was spoken by the Lord by the prophet, saying, Out of Egypt called I my son.

16 ¶ Then Herod, when he saw that he was mocked by the ¹wise men, was exceeding wroth, and sent forth, and slew all the male children that were in Bethlehem, and in all the borders thereof, from two years old and under, according to the time which he had diligently enquired of the wise men.

17 Then was fulfilled that which was spoken by Jeremiah the prophet, saying,

18 In Rama was there a voice heard, weeping, and great mourning, Rachel weeping for her children, and would not be comforted, because they are not.

19 But when Herod was dead, behold, an angel of the Lord appeareth in a dream to Joseph in Egypt,

20 Saying, Arise, and take the young child and his mother, and go into the land of Israel: for they are dead which sought the young child's life.

¹ Magi.

21 And he arose, and took the young child and his mother, and came into the land of Israel.

22 But when he heard that Archelaus did reign over Judæa in the room of his father Herod, he was afraid to go thither: but, being warned in a dream, he turned aside into the parts of Galilee:

23 And he came and dwelt in a city called Nazareth: that it might be fulfilled which was spoken by the prophets, He shall be called a Nazarene.

CHAPTER III.

NOW in those days cometh John the Baptist, preaching in the wilderness of Judæa,

2 Saying, Repent ye: for the kingdom of heaven is at hand.

3 For this is he that was spoken of by the prophet Isaiah, saying, The voice of one crying in the wilderness, Prepare ye the way of the Lord, make his paths straight.

4 And John himself had his raiment of camel's hair, and a leathern girdle about his loins and his meat was locusts and wild honey.

5 Then went out to him Jerusalem, and all Judæa, and all the region round about Jordan,

6 And were baptized of him in the river Jordan, confessing their sins.

7 But when he saw many of the Pharisees and Sadducees coming to his baptism, he said unto them, O brood of vipers, who warned you to flee from the wrath which is at hand?

8 Bring forth therefore fruit worthy of repentance:

9 And think not to say within yourselves, We have Abraham to our father: for I say unto you, that God is able of these stones to raise up children unto Abraham.

10 But now the axe is laid unto the root of the trees: therefore every tree which bringeth not forth good fruit is hewn down, and cast into the fire.

11 I indeed baptize you with water unto repentance: but he that cometh after me is stronger than I, whose shoes I am not worthy to bear: HE shall baptize you with the Holy Ghost, and with fire:

12 Whose fan is in his hand, and he will throughly purge his floor, and will gather his wheat into the garner; but he will burn up the chaff with unquenchable fire.

13 ¶ Then cometh Jesus from Galilee to the Jordan unto John, to be baptized of him.

14 But John forbad him, saying, I have need to be baptized by thee, and comest thou to me?

15 But Jesus answering said unto him, Suffer it to be so now: for thus it becometh us to fulfil all righteousness. Then he suffereth him.

16 And Jesus, when he was baptized, went up straightway out of the water: and, lo, the heavens were opened unto him, and he saw the Spirit of God descending like a dove, and coming upon him:

17 And lo a voice from heaven, saying, This is my beloved Son, in whom I am well pleased.

CHAPTER IV.

THEN was Jesus led up by the Spirit into the wilderness to be tempted by the devil.

2 And when he had fasted forty days and forty nights, he afterward hungered.

3 And the tempter came to him and said, If thou art the Son of God, command that these stones be made bread.

4 But he answered and said, It is written, Man shall not live upon bread alone, but by every word that proceedeth out of the mouth of God.

5 Then the devil taketh him up into the holy city, and setteth him on the cornice of the temple,

6 And saith unto him, If thou art the Son of God, cast thyself down: for it is written, He shall give his angels charge concerning thee: and in their hands they shall bear thee up, lest at any time thou dash thy foot against a stone.

7 Jesus said unto him, It is written again, Thou shalt not tempt the Lord thy God.

8 Again, the devil taketh him up into an exceeding high mountain, and sheweth him all the kingdoms of the world, and the glory of them;

9 And said unto him, All these things will I give thee, if thou wilt fall down and worship me.

10 Then saith Jesus unto him, Get thee hence, Satan: for it is written, Thou shalt worship

the Lord thy God, and him only shalt thou serve.

11 Then the devil leaveth him, and, behold, angels came and ministered unto him.

12 ¶ Now when he had heard that John was delivered up, he departed into Galilee;

13 And leaving Nazareth, he came and dwelt in Capernaum, which is upon the sea coast, in the borders of Zabulon and Nephthalim:

14 That it might be fulfilled which was spoken by Isaiah the prophet, saying,

15 The land of Zabulon, and the land of Nephthalim, by the way of the sea, beyond Jordan, Galilee of the Gentiles;

16 The people which sat in darkness saw great light; and to them which sat in the region and shadow of death light sprung up.

17 ¶ From that time Jesus began to preach, and to say, Repent: for the kingdom of heaven is at hand.

18 And walking by the sea of Galilee, he saw two brethren, Simon called Peter, and Andrew his brother, casting a net into the sea: for they were fishers.

19 And he saith unto them, Come ye after me, and I will make you fishers of men.

20 And they straightway left their nets, and followed him.

21 And when he had gone on from thence, he saw other two brethren, James the son of Zebedee, and John his brother, in the ship with Zebedee their father, mending their nets; and he called them.

22 And they immediately left the ship and their father, and followed him.

23 ¶ And he went about all Galilee, teaching in their synagogues, and preaching the gospel of the kingdom, and healing every sickness and every disease among the people.

24 And his fame went throughout all Syria: and they brought unto him all sick people that were taken with divers diseases and torments; those which were possessed with devils, and those which were lunatick, and those that had the palsy; and he healed them.

25 And there followed him great multitudes of people from Galilee, and from Decapolis, and from Jerusalem, and from Judæa, and from beyond Jordan.

CHAPTER V.

AND seeing the multitudes, he went up into the mountain: and when he was seated, his disciples came unto him:

2 And he opened his mouth, and taught them, saying,

3 Blessed are the poor in spirit: for theirs is the kingdom of heaven.

4 Blessed are they that mourn: for they shall be comforted.

5 Blessed are the meek: for they shall inherit the earth.

6 Blessed are they which hunger and thirst after righteousness: for they shall be filled.

7 Blessed are the merciful: for they shall obtain mercy.

8 Blessed are the pure in

heart: for they shall see God.

9 Blessed are the peacemakers: for they shall be called sons of God.

10 Blessed are they which are persecuted for righteousness' sake: for theirs is the kingdom of heaven.

11 Blessed are ye, when men shall revile you, and persecute you, and shall say all manner of evil against you falsely, for my sake.

12 Rejoice, and be exceeding glad: for great is your reward in heaven: for so persecuted they the prophets which were before you.

13 ¶ Ye are the salt of the earth: but if the salt have lost its savour, wherewith shall it be salted? it is thenceforth good for nothing, but to be cast out, and to be trodden under foot by men.

14 Ye are the light of the world. A city that lieth on an hill cannot be hid.

15 Neither do men light a candle, and put it under the bushel, but on the candlestick; and it giveth light unto all that are in the house.

16 Even so let your light shine before men: that they may see your good works, and glorify your Father which is in heaven.

17 ¶ Think not that I came to destroy the law, or the prophets: I came not to destroy, but to fulfil.

18 For verily I say unto you, Till heaven and earth pass away, one letter or one stroke shall in no wise pass away from the law, till all be fulfilled.

19 Whosoever therefore shall break one of these least commandments, and shall teach men so, he shall be called least in the kingdom of heaven: but whosoever shall do and teach them, the same shall be called great in the kingdom of heaven.

20 For I say unto you, That except your righteousness shall exceed the righteousness of the scribes and Pharisees, ye shall in no case enter into the kingdom of heaven.

21 ¶ Ye have heard that it was said to them of old time, Thou shalt not kill; and whosoever shall kill shall be in danger of the judgment:

22 But I say unto you, That whosoever is angry with his brother [1][without a cause] shall be in danger of the judgment: and whosoever shall say to his brother, [2] Raca, shall be in danger of the council: and whosoever shall say, [3] Moreh, shall be in danger of hell fire.

23 Therefore if thou bring thy gift to the altar, and there remember that thy brother hath ought against thee;

24 Leave there thy gift before the altar, and go thy way; first be reconciled to thy brother, and then come and offer thy gift.

---

[1] *On the insertion or omission of these words, the ancient authorities are divided.*
[2] *That is,* Vain fellow.
[3] *Perhaps, but not so probably,* Thou fool. Moreh (*i.e.* rebel) *was the word for using which Moses and Aaron were debarred from entering the promised land:* "Hear now, ye rebels." Num. xx. 10

25 Agree with thine adversary quickly, while thou art in the way with him; lest the adversary deliver thee to the judge, and the judge deliver thee to the officer, and thou be cast into prison.

26 Verily I say unto thee, Thou shalt by no means come out thence, till thou hast paid the uttermost farthing.

27 ¶ Ye have heard that it was said, Thou shalt not commit adultery:

28 But I say unto you, That whosoever looketh on a woman in order to lust after her hath committed adultery with her already in his heart.

29 But if thy right eye offendeth thee, pluck it out, and cast it from thee: for it is profitable for thee that one of thy members should perish, and not that thy whole body should be cast into hell.

30 And if thy right hand offendeth thee, cut it off, and cast it from thee: for it is profitable for thee that one of thy members should perish, and not that thy whole body should go to hell.

31 It was said, Whosoever putteth away his wife, let him give her a writing of divorcement:

32 But I say unto you, That every man that putteth away his wife, saving for the cause of fornication, causeth her to commit adultery: and whosoever shall marry her when divorced committeth adultery.

33 ¶ Again, ye have heard that it was said to them of old time, Thou shalt not forswear thyself, but shalt perform unto the Lord thine oaths:

34 But I say unto you, Swear not at all; neither by heaven; for it is God's throne:

35 Nor by the earth; for it is his footstool: neither by Jerusalem; for it is the city of the great King.

36 Neither shalt thou swear by thy head, because thou canst not make one hair white or black.

37 But your manner of speech shall be, Yea, yea; Nay, nay: for whatsoever is more than these cometh of evil.

38 ¶ Ye have heard that it was said, An eye for an eye, and a tooth for a tooth:

39 But I say unto you, That ye resist not evil: but whosoever shall smite thee on thy right cheek, turn to him the other also.

40 And if any man be minded to sue thee at the law, and take away thy coat, let him have thy cloke also.

41 And whosoever shall compel thee to go a mile, go with him two.

42 Give to him that asketh thee, and from him that desireth to borrow of thee turn not thou away.

43 ¶ Ye have heard that it was said, Thou shalt love thy neighbour, and hate thine enemy.

44 But I say unto you, Love your enemies, and pray for them which persecute you;

45 That ye may be sons of your Father which is in heaven: for he maketh his sun to rise on evil men and on good,

and sendeth rain on just and on unjust.

46 For if ye love them which love you, what reward have ye? do not even the publicans so?

47 And if ye salute your brethren only, what do ye more than others? do not even the Gentiles the same?

48 Ye therefore shall be perfect, as your heavenly Father is perfect.

CHAPTER VI.

BUT take heed that ye do not your righteousness before men, to be seen by them: otherwise ye have no [1]reward of your Father which is in heaven.

2 When therefore thou doest alms, do not sound a trumpet before thee, as the hypocrites do in the synagogues and in the streets, that they may have glory from men. Verily I say unto you, They [2]have their reward.

3 But when thou doest alms, let not thy left hand know what thy right hand doeth:

4 That thine alms may be in secret: and thy Father which seeth in secret [3][himself] shall requite thee [3][openly].

5 ¶ And when ye pray, ye shall not be as the hypocrites are: for they love to pray standing in the synagogues and in the corners of the streets, that they may appear unto men. Verily I say unto you, They have their reward.

6 But thou, when thou prayest, enter into thy secret chamber, and shut thy door, and pray to thy Father which is in secret: and thy Father, which seeth in secret, shall requite thee [3][openly].

7 But when ye pray, [4]use not vain repetitions, as the Gentiles do: for they think that they shall be heard for their much speaking.

8 Be not ye therefore like unto them: for your Father knoweth what things ye have need of, before ye ask him.

9 After this manner therefore pray ye: Our Father, which art in heaven, hallowed be thy name,

10 Thy kingdom come, thy will be done, as in heaven, so also on earth:

11 Give us this day our needful bread:

12 And forgive us our debts, as we also have forgiven our debtors:

13 And lead us not into temptation, but deliver us from evil.[5]

14 For if ye forgive men their trespasses, your heavenly Father will also forgive you:

15 But if ye forgive not men their trespasses, neither will

---

[1] *Literally*, hire: *and so in verses* 2, 5, *and* 16.
[2] *Literally*, have in full: *and so in verses* 5 *and* 16.
[3] *Omitted by some of the oldest MSS.*
[4] *Literally (and so rendered in some of the earlier English versions),* babble not.
[5] *The words which follow in the Authorized Version,* For thine is the kingdom, and the power, and the glory, for ever. Amen, *are wanting in all the most ancient MSS., and are not noticed by most of the Greek and Latin Fathers when they expound the prayer.*

your Father forgive your trespasses.

16 ¶ Moreover, when ye fast, be not, as the hypocrites, of a sad countenance: for they disfigure their faces, that they may appear unto men to fast. Verily I say unto you, They have their reward.

17 But thou, when thou fastest, anoint thine head, and wash thy face;

18 That thou appear not unto men to fast, but unto thy Father which is in secret: and thy Father, which seeth in secret, shall requite thee.

19 ¶ Lay not up for yourselves treasures upon earth, where moth and rust doth corrupt, and where thieves break through and steal:

20 But lay up for yourselves treasures in heaven, where neither moth nor rust doth corrupt, and where thieves do not break through nor steal:

21 For where thy treasure is, there will thine heart be also.

22 The light of the body is the eye: if therefore thine eye be single, thy whole body shall be full of light.

23 But if thine eye be evil, thy whole body shall be full of darkness. If therefore the light that is in thee be darkness, how dark is the darkness!

24 No man can serve two masters: for either he will hate the one, and love the other; or else he will hold to the one, and despise the other. Ye cannot serve God and mammon.

25 Therefore I say unto you, Be not careful for your life, what ye shall eat, and what ye shall drink; nor yet for your body, what ye shall put on. Is not the life more than the food, and the body than the raiment?

26 Behold the birds of the air, that they sow not, neither do they reap, nor gather into barns; and your heavenly Father feedeth them. Are ye not much better than they?

27 Which of you by careful thought can add one cubit unto his lifetime?

28 And why are ye careful about raiment? Consider the lilies of the field, how they grow; they toil not, neither do they spin:

29 But I say unto you, That even Solomon in all his glory was not arrayed like one of these.

30 But if God so clothe the grass of the field, which to day is, and to morrow is cast into the oven, shall he not much more clothe you, O ye of little faith?

31 Therefore be not careful, saying, What shall we eat? or, What shall we drink? or, Wherewithal shall we be clothed?

32 For after all these things do the Gentiles seek: for your heavenly Father knoweth that ye have need of all these things.

33 But seek first the kingdom of God, and his righteousness; and all these things shall be added unto you

34 Therefore be not careful for the morrow: for the morrow

shall care for itself. Sufficient unto the day is the evil thereof.

CHAPTER VII.

JUDGE not, that ye be not judged.

2 For with what judgment ye judge, ye shall be judged: and with what measure ye mete, it shall be measured to you again.

3 And why beholdest thou the mote that is in thy brother's eye, but considerest not the beam that is in thine own eye?

4 Or how wilt thou say to thy brother, Let me pull out the mote out of thine eye, and behold, the beam is in thine own eye?

5 Thou hypocrite, pull out first the beam out of thine own eye, and then shalt thou see clearly to pull out the mote out of thy brother's eye.

6 Give not that which is holy unto dogs, neither cast ye your pearls before swine, lest they trample them under their feet, and turn again and rend you.

7 Ask, and it shall be given you: seek, and ye shall find: knock, and it shall be opened unto you.

8 For every one that asketh, receiveth: and he that seeketh, findeth: and to him that knocketh it shall be opened.

9 Or what man is there of you, of whom his son shall ask bread, and he will give him a stone?

10 Or shall ask a fish, and he will give him a serpent?

11 If ye then, being evil, know how to give good gifts unto your children, how much more shall your Father which is in heaven give good things to them that ask him.

12 Therefore all things whatsoever ye would that men should do to you, do ye even so to them: for this is the law and the prophets.

13 ¶ Enter in through the narrow gate: for wide is the gate, and broad is the way, that leadeth to destruction, and many there be which go in thereat:

14 Because narrow is the gate, and straitened is the way, which leadeth unto life, and few there be that find it.

15 But beware of false prophets, such as come to you in sheep's clothing, but inwardly are ravening wolves.

16 By their fruits ye shall know them. Do men gather grapes from thorns, or figs from thistles?

17 Even so every good tree bringeth forth good fruit; but the corrupt tree bringeth forth evil fruit.

18 A good tree cannot bring forth evil fruit, neither can a corrupt tree bring forth good fruit.

19 Every tree that bringeth not forth good fruit is hewn down, and cast into the fire.

20 Wherefore by their fruits ye shall know them.

21 Not every one that saith unto me, Lord, Lord, shall enter into the kingdom of heaven; but he that doeth the will of my Father which is in heaven.

22 Many will say to me in that day, Lord, Lord, did we

not prophesy in thy name? and in thy name cast out devils? and in thy name do many wonderful works?

23 And then will I confess unto them, I never knew you: depart from me, ye that work iniquity.

24 Therefore whosoever heareth these sayings of mine, and doeth them, I will liken him unto a prudent man, which built his house upon the rock:

25 And the rain descended, and the floods came, and the winds blew, and beat upon that house; and it fell not: for its foundation had been laid upon the rock.

26 And every one that heareth these sayings of mine, and doeth them not, shall be likened unto a foolish man, which built his house upon the sand:

27 And the rain descended, and the floods came, and the winds blew, and beat upon that house; and it fell: and great was the fall of it.

28 And it came to pass, when Jesus had ended these sayings, the multitudes were astonished at his teaching:

29 For he taught them as having authority, and not as their scribes.

CHAPTER VIII.

WHEN he was come down from the mountain, great multitudes followed him.

2 And, behold, there came a leper and worshipped him, saying, Lord, if thou wilt, thou canst make me clean.

3 And he put forth his hand, and touched him, saying, I will; be thou clean. And immediately his leprosy was cleansed.

4 And Jesus saith unto him, See thou tell no man; but go thy way, shew thyself to the priest, and offer the gift that Moses commanded, for a testimony unto them.

5 ¶ And when he was entered into Capernaum, there came unto him a centurion, beseeching him,

6 And saying, Lord, my boy lieth at home sick of the palsy, grievously tormented.

7 And he saith unto him, I will come and heal him.

8 The centurion answered and said, Lord, I am not worthy that thou shouldest come under my roof: but speak the word only, and my boy shall be healed.

9 For I also am a man under authority, having soldiers under me: and I say to this man, Go, and he goeth; and to another, Come, and he cometh; and to my servant, Do this, and he doeth it.

10 When Jesus heard it, he marvelled, and said to them that followed, Verily I say unto you, In no man in Israel have I found so great faith.

11 But I say unto you, That many shall come from the east and west, and shall sit down with Abraham, and Isaac, and Jacob, in the kingdom of heaven.

12 But the sons of the kingdom shall be cast out into the darkness without: there

shall be ¹weeping and gnashing of teeth.

13 And Jesus said unto the centurion, Go thy way; as thou hast believed, so be it done unto thee. And the lad was healed in the selfsame hour.

14 ¶ And when Jesus was come into Peter's house, he saw his wife's mother in bed, and sick of a fever.

15 And he touched her hand, and the fever left her: and she arose, and ministered unto him.

16 ¶ When the even was come, they brought unto him many that were possessed with devils: and he cast out the spirits with a word, and healed all that were sick:

17 That it might be fulfilled which was spoken by Isaiah the prophet, saying, Himself took our infirmities, and bare our sicknesses.

18 ¶ Now when Jesus saw great multitudes about him, he gave commandment to depart unto the opposite shore.

19 And a certain scribe came, and said unto him, Master, I will follow thee whithersoever thou goest.

20 And Jesus saith unto him, The foxes have holes, and the birds of the air have nests; but the Son of man hath not where to lay his head.

21 And another of his disciples said unto him, Lord, suffer me first to go and bury my father.

22 But Jesus saith unto him,

¹ *Literally*, the weeping and the gnashing of the teeth.

Follow me; and leave the dead to bury their own dead.

23 ¶ And when he was entered into a ship, his disciples followed him.

24 And, behold, there arose a great tempest in the sea, insomuch that the ship was being covered with the waves: but he was asleep.

25 And his disciples came to him, and awoke him, saying, Lord, save us: we perish.

26 And he saith unto them, Why are ye fearful, O ye of little faith? Then he arose, and rebuked the winds and the sea; and there was a great calm.

27 But the men marvelled, saying, What manner of man is this, that even the winds and the sea obey him?

28 ¶ And when he was come to the other side into the country of the Gadarenes, there met him two possessed with devils, coming out of the tombs, exceeding fierce, so that no man might pass by that way.

29 And, behold, they cried out, saying, What have we to do with thee, thou Son of God? art thou come hither to torment us before the time?

30 And there was a good way off from **them** an herd of many swine feeding.

31 So the devils besought him, saying, If thou cast us out, send us into the herd of swine.

32 And he said unto them, Go. And when they were come out, they departed unto the herd of swine: and, behold, the whole herd of swine ran violently down the cliff into

the sea, and perished in the waters.

33 And they that kept them fled, and went their ways into the city, and told everything, and what was befallen to the possessed with the devils.

34 And, behold, the whole city came out to meet Jesus: and when they saw him, they besought him that he would depart out of their borders.

CHAPTER IX.

AND he entered into a ship, and passed over, and came into his own city.

2 And, behold, they brought to him a man sick of the palsy, lying on a bed: and Jesus seeing their faith said unto the sick of the palsy, Son, be of good cheer; thy sins are forgiven.

3 And, behold, certain of the scribes said within themselves, This man blasphemeth.

4 And Jesus seeing their thoughts said, Wherefore think ye evil in your hearts?

5 For which is easier, to say, Thy sins are forgiven; or to say, Arise, and walk?

6 But that ye may know that the Son of man hath power on earth to forgive sins, (then saith he to the sick of the palsy,) Arise, take up thy bed, and go thy way unto thine house.

7 And he arose, and departed to his house.

8 But when the multitudes saw it, they were afraid, and glorified God, which had given such power unto men.

9 ¶ And as Jesus passed forth from thence, he saw a man, named Matthew, sitting at the receipt of custom; and he saith unto him, Follow me. And he arose, and followed him.

10 And it came to pass, as he sat at meat in the house, behold, many publicans and sinners came and sat down with Jesus and his disciples.

11 And the Pharisees seeing it said unto his disciples, Why eateth your Master with the publicans and sinners?

12 But he heard it, and said, They that are whole need not a physician, but they that are sick.

13 But go ye and learn what that meaneth, I love mercy, and not sacrifice: for I came not to call righteous men, but sinners.

14 ¶ Then come to him the disciples of John, saying, Why do we and the Pharisees fast oft, but thy disciples fast not?

15 And Jesus said unto them, Can the sons of the bridechamber mourn, as long as the bridegroom is with them? but the days will come, when the bridegroom shall be taken from them, and then will they fast.

16 But no one putteth a piece of new cloth upon an old garment, for that which is put in to fill it up taketh from the garment, and a worse rent is made.

17 Neither do they put new wine into old skins: else the skins are burst, and the wine runneth out, and the skins will perish: but they put new wine into new skins, and both are preserved.

18 ¶ While he spake these

things unto them, behold, there came in a ruler, and worshipped him, saying, My daughter just now died : but come and lay thy hand upon her, and she shall live.

19 And Jesus arose, and followed him, and so did his disciples.

20 And, behold, a woman, which had an issue of blood twelve years, came behind him, and touched the border of his garment :

21 For she said within herself, If I may but touch his garment, I shall be ¹made whole.

22 But Jesus, turning himself about, and seeing her, said, Daughter, be of good comfort ; thy faith hath ²made thee whole. And the woman was ¹made whole from that hour.

23 And when Jesus came into the ruler's house, and saw the minstrels, and the multitude making a noise,

24 He said, Give place : for the damsel is not dead, but sleepeth. And they laughed him to scorn.

25 But when the multitude was put forth, he went in, and took her by the hand, and the damsel arose.

26 And the fame hereof went abroad into all that land.

27 ¶ And when Jesus departed thence, two blind men followed him, crying, and saying, Thou son of David, have mercy on us.

28 And when he was come into the house, the blind men came to him : and Jesus saith unto them, Believe ye that I am able to do this ? They say unto him, Yea, Lord.

29 Then touched he their eyes, saying, According to your faith be it done unto you.

30 And their eyes were opened ; and Jesus strictly charged them, saying, See that no one know it.

31 But they went forth, and spread abroad his fame in all that country.

32 ¶ While these were going forth, behold, they brought to him a dumb man possessed with a devil.

33 And when the devil was cast out, the dumb man spake : and the multitudes marvelled, saying, It was never so seen in Israel.

34 But the Pharisees said, By the prince of the devils casteth he out the devils.

35 ¶ And Jesus went about all the cities and the villages, teaching in their synagogues, and preaching the gospel of the kingdom, and healing every sickness and every disease.

36 But seeing the multitudes, he was moved with compassion for them, because they were harassed, and scattered abroad, as sheep not having a shepherd.

37 Then saith he unto his disciples, The harvest truly is plenteous, but the labourers are few ;

38 Pray ye therefore the Lord of the harvest, that he will send forth labourers into his harvest.

¹ *Literally*, saved.
² *Literally*, saved thee.

CHAPTER X.

AND he called unto him his twelve disciples, and gave them power over unclean spirits, to cast them out, and to heal every sickness and every disease.

2 Now the names of the twelve apostles are these: The first, Simon, who is called Peter, and Andrew his brother; James the ¹son of Zebedee, and John his brother;

3 Philip, and Bartholomew; Thomas, and Matthew the publican; James ¹the son of Alphæus, and Lebbæus;

4 Simon the ²Cananæan, and Judas Iscariot, who also ³betrayed him.

5 These twelve Jesus sent forth, and commanded them, saying, Go not forth into the way of the Gentiles, and into any city of the Samaritans enter ye not:

6 But go rather to the lost sheep of the house of Israel.

7 And as ye go, preach, saying, The kingdom of heaven is at hand.

8 Heal the sick, raise the dead, cleanse the lepers, cast out devils: freely ye received, freely give.

9 Provide neither gold, nor silver, nor brass in your ⁴girdles,

10 Nor scrip for your journey, neither two coats, neither shoes, nor yet a staff: for the workman is worthy of his food.

11 And into whatsoever city or village ye shall enter, enquire who in it is worthy; and there abide till ye go thence.

12 And when ye come into an house, salute it.

13 And if the house be worthy, let your peace come upon it: but if it be not worthy, let your peace return to you.

14 And whosoever shall not receive you, nor hear your words, when ye depart out of that house or city, shake off the dust of your feet.

15 Verily I say unto you, It shall be more tolerable for the land of Sodom and Gomorrha in the day of judgment, than for that city.

16 Behold, I send you forth as sheep in the midst of wolves: be ye therefore wise as serpents, and harmless as doves.

17 But beware of men: for they will deliver you up to councils, and they will scourge you in their synagogues;

18 Moreover ye shall be brought before governors and kings for my sake, for a testimony unto them and the Gentiles.

19 But when they deliver you up, be not careful how or what ye shall speak: for it shall be given you in that hour what ye shall speak.

20 For it is not ye that speak,

---

¹ Son *is not expressed in the original*.
² *This word is equivalent, not to "Canaanite," but to "Zelotes" (Luke vi. 15; Acts i. 13), and implies that he had belonged to the sect of the Zealots.*
³ Delivered him up: *the same word as in* ch. iv. 12; *ver.* 17, 19, 21, *&c.*
⁴ *The girdle served for a purse: but the word* purse *must be avoided: see Luke* x. 4.

but the Spirit of your Father which speaketh in you.

21 But brother shall deliver up his brother to death, and the father his child: and children shall rise up against their parents, and shall put them to death.

22 And ye shall be hated by all for my name's sake: but he that hath endured to the end, the same shall be saved.

23 But when they persecute you in one city, flee ye into another: for verily I say unto you, Ye shall not have finished the cities of Israel, till the Son of man be come.

24 The disciple is not above his teacher, nor the servant above his lord.

25 It is enough for the disciple that he be as his teacher, and the servant as his lord. If they called the master of the house Beelzebub, how much more them of his household?

26 Fear them not therefore: for there is nothing covered, that shall not be revealed; and hid, that shall not be known.

27 What I tell you in the darkness, that speak ye in the light: and what ye hear in the ear, that preach ye upon the housetops.

28 And be not afraid of them that kill the body, but are not able to kill the [1]soul: but rather fear him which is able to destroy both [1]soul and body in hell.

29 Are not two sparrows sold for a farthing? and not one of them shall fall on the ground without your Father.

30 But the very hairs of your head are all numbered.

31 Fear ye not therefore, ye are of more value than many sparrows.

32 Whosoever therefore shall confess me before men, him will I confess also before my Father which is in heaven.

33 But whosoever shall deny me before men, him will I deny also before my Father which is in heaven.

34 Think not that I came to send peace upon the earth. I came not to send peace, but a sword.

35 For I came to set a man at variance against his father, and the daughter against her mother, and the daughter in law against her mother in law.

36 And a man's foes shall be they of his own household.

37 He that loveth father or mother more than me is not worthy of me: and he that loveth son or daughter more than me is not worthy of me.

38 And he that taketh not his cross, and followeth after me, is not worthy of me.

39 He that hath found his [2]life shall lose it: and he that hath lost his [2]life for my sake shall find it.

40 He that receiveth you receiveth me, and he that receiveth me receiveth him that sent me.

41 He that receiveth a prophet in the name of a prophet shall receive a prophet's [3]re-

[1] *Or*, life: *see ver*. 39.
[2] *Or*, soul: *the same word as in ver*. 28.
[3] *Or*, hire: *the same word as in ch*. xx. 8.

ward; and he that receiveth a righteous man in the name of a righteous man shall receive a righteous man's ¹reward.

42 And whosoever shall give to drink unto one of these little ones a cup of cold water only in the name of a disciple, verily I say unto you, he shall in no wise lose his ¹reward.

CHAPTER XI.

AND it came to pass, when Jesus had made an end of commanding his twelve disciples, he departed thence to teach and to preach in their cities.

2 ¶ Now when John heard in the prison the works of Christ, he sent by his disciples,

3 And said unto him, Art thou he that should come, or do we look for another?

4 And Jesus answered and said unto them, Go tell John those things which ye do hear and see:

5 The blind receive their sight, and the lame walk, the lepers are cleansed, and the deaf hear, and the dead are raised up, and the poor have ²the gospel preached to them.

6 And blessed is he, whosoever shall not be offended in me.

7 ¶ And as these departed, Jesus began to say unto the multitudes concerning John, What went ye out into the wilderness to ³gaze upon? A reed shaken with the wind?

8 But what went ye out to see? A man clothed in soft raiment? behold, they that wear soft clothing are in kings' houses.

9 But wherefore went ye out? to see a prophet? yea, I say unto you, and more than a prophet.

10 ⁴[For] this is he, of whom it is written, Behold, I send my messenger before thy face, which shall prepare thy way before thee.

11 Verily I say unto you, Among those that are born of women there hath not arisen a greater than John the Baptist: yet he that is least in the kingdom of heaven is greater than he.

12 But from the days of John the Baptist until now the kingdom of heaven is taken by violence, and the violent seize upon it.

13 For all the prophets and the law prophesied until John:

14 And if ye will receive it, this is Elijah, which is to come.

15 He that hath ears, let him hear.

16 But whereunto shall I liken this generation? It is like unto little children sitting in the markets, and calling unto their fellows,

17 And saying, We piped unto you, and ye danced not; we mourned, and ye lamented not.

18 For John came neither eating nor drinking, and they say, He hath a devil.

---

¹ *Or*, hire: *the same word as in ch.* xx. 8.
² *Literally*, the good tidings announced to them.
³ *The word in verses* 8, 9, *is different*.
⁴ For *is omitted, perhaps as not being found in Luke* vii. 27, *by several of the oldest MSS.*

19 The Son of man came eating and drinking, and they say, Behold a man gluttonous, and a winebibber, a friend of publicans and sinners. And yet wisdom was justified at the hands of her children.

20 ¶ Then began he to upbraid the cities wherein most of his mighty works were done, because they repented not:

21 Woe unto thee, Chorazin! woe unto thee, Bethsaida! for if the mighty works, which were done in you, had been done in Tyre and Sidon, they would have repented long ago in sackcloth and ashes.

22 But I say unto you, It shall be more tolerable for Tyre and Sidon in the day of judgment, than for you.

23 And thou, Capernaum, shalt thou be exalted unto heaven? thou shalt be brought down to hell: for if the mighty works, which were done in thee, had been done in Sodom, it would have remained until this day.

24 But I say unto you, That it shall be more tolerable for the land of Sodom in the day of judgment, than for thee.

25 ¶ At that time Jesus answered and said, I confess to thee, O Father, Lord of heaven and earth, that thou hast hid these things from men wise and of understanding, and hast revealed them unto babes.

26 Even so, Father: for thus it seemed good in thy sight.

27 All things are delivered unto me by my Father: and none certainly knoweth the Son, but the Father; neither doth any fully know the Father, but the Son, and he to whomsoever the Son is minded to reveal him.

28 Come unto me, all ye that are weary and heavy laden, and I will give you rest.

29 Take my yoke upon you, and learn from me; for I am meek and lowly in heart: and ye shall find rest unto your souls.

30 For my yoke is easy, and my burden is light.

CHAPTER XII.

AT that time Jesus went on the sabbath day through the corn-fields; and his disciples were hungry, and began to pluck the ears of corn, and to eat.

2 But the Pharisees seeing it said unto him, Behold, thy disciples do that which is not lawful to do upon the sabbath day.

3 But he said unto them, Did ye never read what David did, when he was hungry, and they that were with him;

4 How he entered into the house of God, and did eat the shewbread, which it was not lawful for him to eat, neither for them which were with him, but for the priests alone?

5 Or did ye never read in the law, how that on the sabbath day the priests in the temple profane the sabbath, and are blameless?

6 But I say unto you, That in this place is a greater thing than the temple.

7 But if ye had known what this meaneth, I desire mercy,

and not sacrifice, ye would not have condemned the guiltless.

8 For the Son of man is Lord of the sabbath day.

9 And he departed thence, and went into their synagogue:

10 And, behold, there was a man which had a withered hand. And they asked him, saying, Is it lawful to heal on the sabbath day? that they might accuse him.

11 But he said unto them, What man shall there be among you, that shall have one sheep, and if it fall into a pit on the sabbath day, will he not lay hold on it, and lift it out?

12 How much then is a man better than a sheep! Wherefore it is lawful to do well on the sabbath day.

13 Then saith he to the man, Stretch forth thine hand. And he stretched it forth; and it was restored whole, like as the other.

14 ¶ But the Pharisees went out, and took counsel against him, that they might destroy him.

15 But Jesus knowing it departed thence: and great multitudes followed him, and he healed them all;

16 And charged them that they should not make him known:

17 That it might be fulfilled which was spoken by Isaiah the prophet, saying,

18 Behold my servant, whom I have chosen; my beloved, in whom my soul is well pleased: I will put my Spirit upon him, and he shall proclaim judgment to the Gentiles.

19 He shall not strive, nor cry aloud; neither shall any man hear his voice in the streets.

20 A bruised reed shall he not break, and smoking flax shall he not quench, till he have caused his judgment to issue in victory.

21 And in his name shall the Gentiles hope.

22 ¶ Then was brought unto him one possessed with a devil, blind, and dumb: and he healed him, insomuch that the dumb spake and saw.

23 And all the multitudes were amazed, and said, Is this the Son of David?

24 But the Pharisees heard it, and said, This man doth not cast out the devils, but by Beelzebub the prince of the devils.

25 And he knew their thoughts, and said unto them, Every kingdom divided against itself is brought to desolation; and every city or house divided against itself shall not stand:

26 And if Satan casteth out Satan, he is divided against himself; how shall then his kingdom stand?

27 And if I by Beelzebub cast out the devils, by whom do your sons cast them out? therefore they shall be your judges.

28 But if I by the Spirit of God cast out the devils, then the kingdom of God is come upon you.

29 Or else how can one enter into the strong man's house, and plunder his goods, except he shall have first bound the

strong man? and then he will plunder all his house.

30 He that is not with me is against me; and he that gathereth not with me scattereth.

31 Wherefore I say unto you, All sin and blasphemy shall be forgiven unto [1] [you] men: but the blasphemy against the Spirit shall not be forgiven [1] [unto men].

32 And whosoever shall speak a word against the Son of man, it shall be forgiven him: but whosoever shall speak against the Holy Spirit, it shall not be forgiven him, neither in this world, neither in that which is to come.

33 Either make the tree good, and its fruit good; or else make the tree corrupt, and its fruit corrupt: for by the fruit the tree is known.

34 Ye brood of vipers, how can ye, being evil, speak good things? for out of the abundance of the heart the mouth speaketh.

35 The good man out of his good treasure bringeth forth good things: and the evil man out of his evil treasure bringeth forth evil things.

36 But I say unto you, That every idle word that men shall speak, they shall give account thereof in the day of judgment.

37 For by thy words thou shalt be justified, and by thy words thou shalt be condemned.

38 ¶ Then certain of the scribes and Pharisees answered him, saying, [2]Master, we would see a sign from thee.

39 But he answered and said unto them, An evil and adulterous generation seeketh after a sign; and there shall no sign be given to it, but the sign of the prophet Jonah:

40 For as Jonah was three days and three nights in the belly of the whale; so shall the Son of man be three days and three nights in the heart of the earth.

41 The men of Nineveh shall rise up in the judgment with this generation, and shall condemn it: because they repented at the preaching of Jonah; and, behold, there is more than Jonah here.

42 The queen of the south shall rise up in the judgment with this generation, and shall condemn it: because she came from the uttermost parts of the earth to hear the wisdom of Solomon; and, behold, there is more than Solomon here.

43 But when the unclean spirit is gone out of a man, it goeth through dry places, seeking rest, and findeth none.

44 Then it saith, I will return into my house from whence I came out; and cometh and findeth it empty, swept, and garnished.

45 Then goeth it, and taketh with itself seven other spirits more wicked than itself, and they enter in and dwell there: and the last state of that man becometh worse than the first. Even so shall it be also unto this wicked generation.

---

[1] *The Vatican MS. inserts* you, *and omits* unto men.

[2] *Teacher: see ch.* x. 24, 25.

46 ¶ While he yet talked to the multitudes, behold, his mother and his brethren stood without, desiring to speak with him.

47 And one said unto him, Behold, thy mother and thy brethren stand without, desiring to speak with thee.

48 But he answered and said unto him that told him, Who is my mother? and who are my brethren?

49 And he stretched forth his hand toward his disciples, and said, Behold my mother and my brethren.

50 For whosoever doeth the will of my Father which is in heaven, the same is my brother, and sister, and mother.

CHAPTER XIII.

IN that day went Jesus out of the house, and sat by the sea side.

2 And great multitudes were gathered together unto him, so that he went into a ship, and sat; and the whole multitude stood on the shore.

3 And he spake many things unto them in parables, saying, Behold, a sower went forth to sow;

4 And as he sowed, some seeds fell by the way side, and the birds came and devoured them up.

5 Others fell upon the stony places, where they had not much earth: and forthwith they sprung up, because they had no deepness of earth:

6 And when the sun was up, they were scorched; and because they had no root, they withered away.

7 And others fell upon the thorns; and the thorns grew up, and choked them:

8 But others fell upon the good ground, and yielded fruit, some an hundredfold, some sixty, some thirty.

9 He that hath ears, let him hear.

10 And the disciples came, and said unto him, Why speakest thou unto them in parables?

11 He answered and said unto them, Because unto you it is given to know the mysteries of the kingdom of heaven, but to them it is not given.

12 For whosoever hath, to him shall be given, and he shall have abundance: but whosoever hath not, from him shall be taken away even that he hath.

13 Therefore speak I to them in parables, because seeing they see not; and hearing they hear not, neither do they understand.

14 And the prophecy of Isaiah is being fulfilled unto them, which saith, By hearing ye shall hear, and shall not understand; and seeing ye shall see, and shall not perceive:

15 For this people's heart is waxed gross, and with their ears they have become dull of hearing, and their eyes they have closed; lest at any time they should see with their eyes, and hear with their ears, and should understand with their heart, and should turn, and I should heal them.

16 But blessed are your eyes, for they see : and your ears, for they hear.

17 For verily I say unto you, That many prophets and righteous men desired to see those things which ye behold, and did not see them ; and to hear those things which ye hear, and did not hear them.

18 Hear therefore ye the parable of the sower.

19 When any one heareth the word of the kingdom, and hath not understood it, the wicked one cometh, and catcheth away that which hath been sown in his heart. This is he which was sown by the way side.

20 But he that was sown upon the stony places, this is he that heareth the word, and immediately with joy receiveth it ;

21 Yet hath he not root in himself, but endureth only for a while : and when tribulation or persecution ariseth because of the word, immediately he is offended.

22 But he that was sown among the thorns, this is he that heareth the word, and the care of the world, and the deceitfulness of riches, choke the word, and he becometh unfruitful.

23 But he that was sown upon the good ground, this is he that heareth the word, and understandeth it ; which beareth fruit, and bringeth forth, some an hundredfold, some sixty, some thirty.

24 ¶ Another parable put he forth unto them, saying, The kingdom of heaven is likened unto a man which sowed good seed in his field :

25 But while men slept, his enemy came and sowed tares among the wheat, and went his way.

26 But when the blade was sprung up, and brought forth fruit, then appeared the tares also.

27 So the servants of the householder came and said unto him, Sir, didst not thou sow good seed in thy field ? from whence then hath it tares ?

28 He said unto them, An enemy hath done this. They say unto him, Wilt thou then that we go and gather them up ?

29 But he saith, Nay ; lest while ye gather up the tares, ye root up the wheat with them.

30 Let both grow together until the harvest : and in the time of the harvest I will say to the reapers, Collect together first the tares, and bind them in bundles to burn them : but gather the wheat into my barn.

31 ¶ Another parable put he forth unto them, saying, The kingdom of heaven is like to a grain of mustard seed, which a man took, and sowed in his field :

32 Which indeed is the least of all seeds : but when it is grown, it is the greatest among herbs, and becometh a tree, so that the birds of the air come and lodge in the branches thereof.

33 ¶ Another parable spake he unto them ; The kingdom of heaven is like unto leaven,

which a woman took, and hid in three measures of meal, till the whole was leavened.

34 All these things spake Jesus unto the multitudes in parables; and without a parable spake he nothing unto them:

35 That it might be fulfilled which was spoken by the prophet, saying, I will open my mouth in parables; I will utter things which have been kept secret from the foundation of the world.

36 ¶ Then he sent the multitudes away, and went into the house: and his disciples came unto him, saying, Declare unto us the parable of the tares of the field.

37 He answered and said, He that soweth the good seed is the Son of man;

38 The field is the world; the good seed, these are the sons of the kingdom; but the tares are the sons of the wicked one;

39 The enemy that sowed them is the devil; the harvest is the end of the world; the reapers are the angels.

40 As therefore the tares are collected together and burned with fire; so shall it be in the end of this world.

41 The Son of man shall send forth his angels, and they shall collect together out of his kingdom all things that offend, and them which do iniquity;

42 And shall cast them into the furnace of fire: there shall be ¹wailing and gnashing of teeth.

¹ *Literally*, the wailing and the gnashing of the teeth.

43 Then shall the righteous shine forth as the sun in the kingdom of their Father. He that hath ears, let him hear.

44 ¶ The kingdom of heaven is like unto treasure hidden in the field, which a man found and hid, and for his joy he goeth and selleth all that he hath, and buyeth that field.

45 ¶ Again, the kingdom of heaven is like unto a merchant man, seeking goodly pearls:

46 Who, when he had found one pearl of great price, went and sold all that he had, and bought it.

47 ¶ Again, the kingdom of heaven is like unto a net, that was cast into the sea, and gathered of every kind:

48 Which, when it was full, they drew to shore, and sat down, and gathered the good into vessels, but cast the bad away.

49 So shall it be at the end of the world: the angels shall come forth, and sever the wicked from among the just,

50 And shall cast them into the furnace of fire: there shall be ¹wailing and gnashing of teeth.

51 Have ye understood all these things? They say unto him, Yea.

52 But he said unto them, Therefore every scribe which is instructed unto the kingdom of heaven is like unto a man that is an householder, which bringeth forth out of his treasure things new and old.

53 ¶ And it came to pass, that when Jesus had finished

these parables, he departed thence.

54 And he came into his own country, and taught them in their synagogue, insomuch that they were astonished, and said, Whence hath this man this wisdom, and these mighty works?

55 Is not this the carpenter's son? is not his mother called Mary? and his brethren, James, and Joseph, and Simon, and Judas?

56 And his sisters, are they not all with us? Whence then hath this man all these things?

57 And they were offended at him. But Jesus said unto them, A prophet is not without honour, save in his own country, and in his own house.

58 And he did not many mighty works there because of their unbelief.

CHAPTER XIV.

AT that time Herod the tetrarch heard of the fame of Jesus,

2 And said unto his [1]servants, This is John the Baptist; he is risen from the dead; and therefore the mighty powers work in him.

3 For Herod had laid hold on John, and bound him, and put him in prison for Herodias' sake, his brother's wife.

4 For John was wont to say unto him, It is not lawful for thee to have her.

5 And he wished to put him to death, but feared the multitude, because they counted him as a prophet.

6 But when Herod's birthday was kept, the daughter of Herodias danced before them, and pleased Herod.

7 Whereupon he promised with an oath to give her whatsoever she should ask.

8 And she, being before instructed by her mother, saith, Give me here upon a dish the head of John the Baptist.

9 And the king, though grieved, yet because of his oath, and of them which sat with him at meat, commanded it to be given her.

10 And he sent, and beheaded John in the prison.

11 And his head was brought on a dish, and given to the damsel: and she brought it to her mother.

12 And his disciples came, and took up the body, and buried him, and went and told Jesus.

13 And Jesus, when he heard, departed thence by ship into a desert place apart: and the multitudes heard thereof, and followed him on foot out of the cities.

14 And he went forth, and saw a great multitude, and was moved with compassion toward them, and he healed their sick.

15 ¶ And when it was evening, the disciples came to him, saying, This is a desert place, and the time is now late; send therefore the multitudes away, that they may go into the villages, and buy themselves victuals.

---

[1] *Literally,* lads, *or* young men: *the same word as in ch.* viii. 6, 8, 13.

16 But Jesus said unto them, They need not depart; give ye them to eat.

17 But they say unto him, We have nothing here but five loaves, and two fishes.

18 He said, Bring them hither to me.

19 And he commanded the multitudes to sit down on the grass, and took the five loaves, and the two fishes, and looking up to heaven, he blessed, and brake, and gave the loaves to his disciples, and the disciples gave them to the multitudes.

20 And they did all eat, and were filled: and they took up of the fragments that which remained, twelve baskets full.

21 And they that did eat were about five thousand men, besides women and children.

22 ¶ And straightway he compelled the disciples to get into the ship, and to go before him unto the other side, while he sent the multitudes away.

23 And when he had sent the multitudes away, he went up into the mountain apart to pray: and when the evening was come, he was there alone.

24 But the ship was now in the midst of the sea, tossed with the waves: for the wind was contrary.

25 And in the fourth watch of the night he went unto them, walking over the sea.

26 And when the disciples saw him walking on the sea, they were troubled, saying, It is an apparition; and they cried out for fear.

27 But straightway Jesus spake unto them, saying, Be of good cheer; it is I; be not afraid.

28 But Peter answered him and said, Lord, if it be thou, bid me come unto thee over the water.

29 And he said, Come. And Peter came down out of the ship, and walked over the water, to go to Jesus.

30 But seeing the wind boisterous, he was afraid; and beginning to sink, he cried, saying, Lord, save me.

31 And immediately Jesus stretched forth his hand, and caught him, and saith unto him, Thou of little faith, wherefore didst thou doubt?

32 And when they were come up into the ship, the wind ceased.

33 But they that were in the ship came and worshipped him, saying, Of a truth thou art the Son of God.

34 ¶ And they passed over, and came into the land of Gennesaret.

35 And the men of that place recognised him, and sent out into all that country round about, and brought unto him all that were diseased;

36 And besought him that they might only touch the border of his garment: and as many as touched were made perfectly whole.

CHAPTER XV.

THEN come to Jesus scribes and Pharisees, which were from Jerusalem saying,

2 Why do thy disciples transgress the tradition of the [1]eld-

---

[1] *I.e.* the ancients, *as in Heb.* xi. 2.

ers? for they wash not their hands when they eat bread.

3 But he answered and said unto them, Why do ye also transgress the commandment of God for the sake of your tradition?

4 For God commanded, saying, Honour thy father and thy mother: and, He that curseth father or mother, let him die the death.

5 But ye say, Whosoever shall say to his father or his mother, That from which thou mightest have been profited by me is an offering to God; he shall be exempted from honouring his father or his mother.

6 And ye have made the law of God of none effect for the sake of your tradition.

7 Ye hypocrites, well did Isaiah prophesy of you saying,

8 This people ¹honoureth me with their lips; but their heart is far distant from me.

9 But in vain do they worship me, teaching for doctrines the commandments of men.

10 And he called the multitude, and said unto them, Hear and understand:

11 Not that which goeth into the mouth defileth the man; but that which cometh out of the mouth, this defileth the man.

12 Then came his disciples, and say unto him, Knowest thou that the Pharisees were offended, when they heard this saying?

¹ *The words*, draweth nigh unto me with their mouth, and, *are omitted in nearly all the oldest MSS. They probably were put in from Isa.* xxix. 13.

13 But he answered and said, Every plant, which my heavenly Father did not plant, shall be rooted up.

14 Let them alone: they be blind leaders of blind men. And if a blind man lead a blind man, both shall fall into the ditch.

15 But Peter answered and said unto him, Declare unto us this parable.

16 But he said, Are ye also yet without understanding?

17 Do not ye yet perceive, that whatsoever goeth into the mouth passeth into the belly, and is cast out into the sewer?

18 But those things which proceed out of the mouth come forth from the heart; and they defile the man.

19 For out of the heart proceed evil thoughts, murders, adulteries, fornications, thefts, false witness, blasphemies:

20 These are the things which defile the man: but to eat with unwashen hands defileth not the man.

21 ¶ And Jesus went thence, and withdrew into the parts of Tyre and Sidon.

22 And, behold, a woman of Canaan came out of the same borders, and cried aloud, saying, Have mercy on me, O Lord, thou son of David; my daughter is grievously possessed with a devil.

23 But he answered her not a word. And his disciples came and besought him, saying, Send her away; for she crieth after us.

24 But he answered and said, I was not sent, but unto the

lost sheep of the house of Israel.

25 Nevertheless she came and worshipped him, saying, Lord, help me,

26 But he answered and said, It is not meet to take the bread of the children, and to cast it to the dogs.

27 But she said, Even so, Lord: for the dogs also eat of the crumbs which fall from the table of their masters.

28 Then Jesus answered and said unto her, O woman, great is thy faith: be it unto thee as thou dost desire. And her daughter was made whole from that very hour.

29 ¶ And Jesus departed from thence, and came by the sea of Galilee; and went up into the mountain, and sat down there.

30 And great multitudes came unto him, having with them lame persons, blind, dumb, maimed, and many others; and they cast them down at his feet, and he healed them:

31 Insomuch that the multitude wondered, when they saw the dumb speaking, the maimed whole, and the lame walking, and the blind seeing: and they glorified the God of Israel.

32 ¶ But Jesus called his disciples unto him, and said, I have compassion on the multitude, because they have continued with me now three days, and have nothing to eat: and I am unwilling to send them away fasting, lest they faint in the way.

33 And the disciples say unto him, Whence should we have so many loaves in the wilderness, as to fill so great a multitude?

34 And Jesus saith unto them, How many loaves have ye? And they said, Seven, and a few little fishes.

35 And he commanded the multitudes to sit down on the ground.

36 And he took the seven loaves and the fishes, and gave thanks, and brake them, and gave to the disciples, and the disciples to the multitudes.

37 And they did all eat, and were filled: and they took up of the fragments that which remained, seven wallets full.

38 And they that did eat were four thousand men, beside women and children.

39 And he sent away the multitude, and embarked in the ship, and came into the borders of Magadan.

CHAPTER XVI.

AND the Pharisees and Sadducees came, and tempting desired him that he would shew them a sign from heaven.

2 He answered and said unto them, [1][When it is evening, ye say, It will be fair weather: for the sky is red.

3 And in the morning, It will be foul weather to day: for the sky is red and lowring. Ye know how to discern the face of the sky; but can ye not discern the signs of the times?]

[1] *This passage is omitted by some of our earliest MSS.: possibly as not occurring in the similar place, chap. xii. 38.*

4 A wicked and adulterous generation seeketh after a sign; and there shall no sign be given unto it, but the sign of Jonah. And he left them, and departed.

5 ¶ And when his disciples were come to the opposite shore, they forgot to take bread.

6 But Jesus said unto them, Take heed and beware of the leaven of the Pharisees and Sadducees.

7 And they reasoned among themselves, saying, It is because we took no bread.

8 And Jesus perceiving it said, O ye of little faith, why reason ye among yourselves, because ye took no bread?

9 Do ye not yet perceive, neither remember the five loaves of the five thousand, and how many baskets ye took up?

10 Neither the seven loaves of the four thousand, and how many wallets ye took up?

11 How is it that ye do not perceive that I spake not to you concerning bread? But beware of the leaven of the Pharisees and Sadducees.

12 Then understood they that he bade them not beware of the leaven of bread, but of the teaching of the Pharisees and Sadducees.

13 ¶ And when Jesus came into the parts of Cæsarea Philippi, he asked his disciples, saying, Who do men say that I the Son of man am?

14 And they said, Some say, John the Baptist: some, Elijah; and others, Jeremiah, or one of the prophets.

15 He saith unto them, But who say ye that I am?

16 And Simon Peter answered and said, Thou art the Christ, the Son of the living God.

17 And Jesus answered and said unto him, Blessed art thou, Simon Bar-jona: for flesh and blood revealed it not unto thee, but my Father which is in heaven.

18 And I say also unto thee, That thou art [1]Peter, and upon this rock I will build my church; and the gates of hell shall not prevail against it.

19 And I will give unto thee the keys of the kingdom of heaven: and whatsoever thou shalt bind on earth shall be bound in heaven: and whatsoever thou shalt loose on earth shall be loosed in heaven.

20 Then charged he his disciples that they should tell no man that he was the Christ.

21 ¶ From that time forth began Jesus to shew unto his disciples, how that he must go unto Jerusalem, and suffer many things of the elders and chief priests and scribes, and be killed, and be raised again the third day.

22 And Peter took him, and saith unto him, rebuking him, God forbid it thee, Lord: this shall never be unto thee.

23 But he turned, and said unto Peter, Get thee behind me, Satan: thou art my stumbling block: because thou savourest not the things that be of God, but those that be of men.

24 Then said Jesus unto his

---

[1] *i.e.* a stone, *or* a rock.

disciples, If any man desire to come after me, let him deny himself, and take up his cross, and follow me.

25 For whosoever desireth to save his ¹life shall lose it: and whosoever shall lose his ¹life for my sake shall find it.

26 For what shall a man be profited, if he shall gain the whole world, but lose his ¹life? or what shall a man give in exchange for his ¹life?

27 For the Son of man will come in the glory of his Father with his angels; and then he shall requite unto every man according to his work.

28 Verily I say unto you, There be some standing here, which shall not taste of death, till they have seen the Son of man coming in his kingdom.

CHAPTER XVII.

AND after six days Jesus taketh with him Peter, and James, and John his brother, and bringeth them up into an high mountain apart.

2 And he was transfigured before them: and his face did shine as the sun, and his raiment was white as the light.

3 And, behold, there appeared unto them Moses and Elijah talking with him.

4 And Peter answered, and said unto Jesus, Lord, it is good for us to be here: if thou wilt, I will make here three tabernacles; one for thee, and one for Moses, and one for Elijah.

5 While he yet spake, behold, a bright cloud overshadowed

¹ *Or,* soul: *see chap.* x. 39.

them: and behold a voice out of the cloud, which said, This is my beloved Son, in whom I am well pleased; hear ye him.

6 And when the disciples heard it, they fell on their face, and were sore afraid.

7 And Jesus came and touched them, and said, Arise, and be not afraid.

8 And when they had lifted up their eyes, they saw no one, save Jesus only.

9 And as they came down from the mountain, Jesus charged them, saying, Tell the vision to no man, until the Son of man be risen from the dead.

10 And his disciples asked him, saying, Why then say the scribes that Elijah must first come?

11 And he answered and said unto them, Elijah truly cometh, and shall restore all things.

12 But I say unto you, That Elijah is come already, and they knew him not, but did unto him whatsoever they listed. Thus shall also the Son of man suffer at their hands.

13 Then the disciples understood that he spake unto them of John the Baptist.

14 ¶ And when they were come to the multitude, there came to him a certain man, kneeling down to him, and saying,

15 Lord, have mercy on my son: for he is lunatick, and sore vexed: for ofttimes he falleth into the fire, and oft into the water.

16 And I brought him to thy disciples, and they could not cure him.

17 But Jesus answered and said, O faithless and perverse generation, how long shall I be with you? how long shall I suffer you? bring him hither to me.

18 And Jesus rebuked him, and the devil departed out of him: and the lad was cured from that very hour.

19 Then came the disciples to Jesus apart, and said, Why could not we cast it out?

20 And he saith unto them, Because of your little faith: for verily I say unto you, If ye have faith as a grain of mustard seed, ye shall say unto this mountain, Remove hence to yonder place; and it shall remove; and nothing shall be impossible unto you.

21 ¹[Howbeit this kind goeth not out but by prayer and fasting.]

22 ¶ And while they were in Galilee, Jesus said unto them, The Son of man will be delivered up into the hands of men:

23 And they shall kill him, and the third day he shall be raised up. And they were exceeding sorry.

24 ¶ And when they were come to Capernaum, they that received the ²two drachmas came to Peter, and said, Doth not your master pay the two drachmas?

25 He saith, Yes. And when he was come into the house, Jesus anticipated him, saying, What thinkest thou, Simon? from whom do the kings of the earth take custom or tribute? from their own sons, or from strangers?

26 Peter saith unto him, From strangers. Jesus saith unto him, Then are the sons free.

27 Notwithstanding, lest we should offend them, go thou to the sea, and cast an hook, and take up the fish that first cometh up; and when thou hast opened his mouth, thou shalt find a piece of four drachmas: that take, and give unto them for me and thee.

CHAPTER XVIII.

AT that time came the disciples unto Jesus, saying, Who then is greatest in the kingdom of heaven?

2 And he called a little child unto him, and set it in the midst of them,

3 And said, Verily I say unto you, Except ye be ³converted, and become as the little children, ye shall not enter into the kingdom of heaven.

4 Whosoever therefore shall humble himself as this little child, the same is the greatest in the kingdom of heaven.

5 And whoso shall receive one such little child in my name receiveth me.

6 But whoso shall offend one of these little ones which believe in me, it were better for him that a ⁴great millstone

---

¹ *This verse is omitted in our two oldest MSS., but is found in the other ancient MSS., versions, and Fathers.*

² *Paid annually by every Jew of full age towards the temple. It was not tribute money.*

³ *Literally,* turned.

⁴ *Literally,* a millstone turned by an ass, *as distinguished from the smaller stones of a handmill.*

were hanged about his neck, and that he were drowned in the depth of the sea.

7 Woe unto the world because of offences! for it must needs be that offences come; but woe to that man by whom the offence cometh!

8 But if thy hand or thy foot offendeth thee, cut it off, and cast it from thee: it is good for thee to enter into life halt or maimed, rather than having two hands or two feet to be cast into eternal fire.

9 And if thine eye offendeth thee, pluck it out, and cast it from thee: it is good for thee to enter into life with one eye, rather than having two eyes to be cast into hell fire.

10 Take heed that ye despise not one of these little ones; for I say unto you, That in heaven their angels do always behold the face of my Father which is in heaven.

11 [1][For the Son of man is come to save that which was lost.].

12 How think ye? if a man have an hundred sheep, and one of them be gone astray, will he not leave the ninety and nine on the mountains, and go, and seek that which is going astray?

13 And if so be that he find it, verily I say unto you, he rejoiceth more over it, than over the ninety and nine which were not gone astray.

14 Even so it is not the will [2]of your Father which is in heaven, that one of these little ones should perish.

15 Moreover if thy brother shall trespass [3][against thee], go and tell him his fault between thee and him alone: if he shall hear thee, thou hast gained thy brother.

16 But if he shall not hear, take with thee one or two more, that in the mouth of two or three witnesses every word may be established.

17 But if he shall refuse to hear them, tell it unto the congregation: but if he also refuse to hear the congregation, let him be unto thee as a Gentile man and a publican.

18 Verily I say unto you, What things soever ye shall bind on earth shall be bound in heaven: and what things soever ye shall loose on earth shall be loosed in heaven.

19 Again I say unto you, That if two of you shall agree on earth as touching any thing that they shall ask, it shall be done for them by my Father which is in heaven.

20 For where two or three are gathered together in my name, there am I in the midst of them.

21 Then came Peter and said unto him, Lord, how oft shall my brother sin against me, and I forgive him? till seven times?

22 Jesus saith unto him, I say not unto thee, Until seven times: but, Until seventy times seven.

23 Therefore was the king-

[1] *This verse is not contained in our most ancient MSS.*
[2] *Literally*, in the presence of your Father.
[3] *These words are not found in our two most ancient MSS.*

dom of heaven likened unto a man which was a king, who was minded to take account of his servants.

24 And when he had begun to reckon, one was brought unto him, which owed him ten thousand talents.

25 But forasmuch as he had not to pay, his lord commanded him to be sold, and his wife, and his children, and all that he had, and payment to be made.

26 The servant therefore fell down, and worshipped him, saying, Have patience with me, and I will pay thee all.

27 And the lord of that servant was moved with compassion, and loosed him, and forgave him the debt.

28 But that servant went out, and found one of his fellowservants, which owed him an hundred pence : and he laid hands on him, and took him by the throat, saying, Pay me whatever thou owest.

29 So his fellowservant fell down at his feet, and besought him, saying, Have patience with me, and I will pay thee.

30 But he would not : but went and cast him into prison, till he should pay the debt.

31 When therefore his fellowservants saw what was done, they were very sorry, and came and made known unto their lord all that was done.

32 Then his lord, after that he had called him, saith unto him, O thou wicked servant, I forgave thee all that debt, because thou desirest me :

33 Shouldest not thou also have had compassion on thy fellowservant, even as I had compassion on thee ?

34 And his lord was wroth, and delivered him to the tormentors, till he should pay all that was due.

35 So likewise shall my heavenly Father do unto you, if ye forgive not every one his brother from your hearts.

CHAPTER XIX.

AND it came to pass, that when Jesus had finished these sayings, he departed from Galilee, and came into the borders of Judæa beyond Jordan ;

2 And great multitudes followed him ; and he healed them there.

3 And there came unto him Pharisees, tempting him, and saying, Is it lawful to put away one's wife for any cause ?

4 But he answered and said, Did ye never read, that he which made them from the beginning made them male and female,

5 And said, For this cause shall a man leave his father and his mother, and shall cleave to his wife : and they two shall become one flesh ?

6 So then they are no more two, but one flesh. What therefore God joined together, let not man put asunder.

7 They say unto him, Why did Moses then command to give a writing of divorcement, and to put her away ?

8 He saith unto them, Because Moses in regard to the hardness of your heart suffered

you to put away your wives: but from the beginning it hath not been so.

9 But I say unto you, Whosoever shall put away his wife, except for fornication, and shall marry another, committeth adultery: and whoso marrieth her when put away committeth adultery.

10 ¶ His disciples say unto him, If the case of the man be so with his wife, it is not expedient to marry.

11 But he said unto them, All men cannot receive this saying, but only they to whom it is given.

12 For there are eunuchs, which were so born from their mother's womb: and there are eunuchs, which were made eunuchs by men: and there be eunuchs, which made themselves eunuchs for the kingdom of heaven's sake. He that is able to receive it, let him receive it.

13 ¶ Then were there brought unto him little children, that he should put his hands on them, and pray: but the disciples rebuked them.

14 But Jesus said, Suffer the little children, and forbid them not to come unto me: for of such is the kingdom of heaven.

15 And he laid his hands on them, and departed thence.

16 ¶ And, behold, one came and said unto him, ¹Master, what good thing shall I do, that I may have eternal life?

17 And he said unto him, Why askest thou me concerning good? there is One that is good. But if thou wilt enter into life, keep the commandments.

18 He saith unto him, Which? Jesus said, Thou shalt do no murder, Thou shalt not commit adultery, Thou shalt not steal, Thou shalt not bear false witness,

19 Honour thy father and thy mother: and, Thou shalt love thy neighbour as thyself.

20 The young man saith unto him, All these things have I kept: what lack I yet?

21 Jesus said unto him, If thou wilt be perfect, go and sell thy goods, and give to the poor, and thou shalt have treasure in heaven: and come, follow me.

22 But when the young man heard that saying, he went away sorrowful: for he had great possessions.

23 But Jesus said unto his disciples, Verily I say unto you, That it shall be hard for a rich man to enter into the kingdom of heaven.

24 And again I say unto you, It is easier for a camel to enter in through the eye of a needle, than a rich man into the kingdom of God.

25 And his disciples hearing it were exceedingly amazed, saying, Who then can be saved?

26 But Jesus looked upon them, and said unto them, With men this is impossible; but with God all things are possible.

27 Then answered Peter and said unto him, Behold, we forsook all, and followed thee;

---

¹ *Literally*, Teacher: *see on ch.* x. 24.

what shall we have therefore?

28 But Jesus said unto them, Verily I say unto you, That ye which have followed me, in the regeneration when the Son of man shall sit in the throne of his glory, ye also shall be set upon twelve thrones, judging the twelve tribes of Israel.

29 And every one that hath forsaken brethren, or sisters, or father, or mother, or children, or lands, or houses, for my name's sake, shall receive manifold, and shall inherit eternal life.

30 But many first shall be last; and last first.

CHAPTER XX.

FOR the kingdom of heaven is like unto a man that is an householder, which went out at daybreak to hire labourers into his vineyard.

2 And he agreed with the labourers for a ¹penny a day, and sent them into his vineyard.

3 And he went out about the third hour, and saw others standing idle in the marketplace,

4 And said unto them; Go ye also into the vineyard, and whatsoever is just, I will give you. And they went their way.

5 Again he went out about the sixth and ninth hour, and did likewise.

6 But about the eleventh hour he went out, and found others standing, and saith unto them, Why stand ye here all the day idle?

7 They say unto him, Because no man hath hired us. He saith unto them, Go ye also into the vineyard.

8 So when even was come, the lord of the vineyard saith unto his steward, Call the labourers, and pay them their hire, beginning from the last unto the first.

9 And when they came that were hired about the eleventh hour, they received every man a ¹penny.

10 But when the first came, they supposed that they should have received more; and they likewise ²received every man a ¹penny.

11 And when they had received it, they murmured against the householder,

12 Saying, These last have wrought one hour, and thou hast made them equal unto us, which have borne the burden of the day, and the heat of the sun.

13 But he answered one of them, and said, Friend, I do thee no wrong: didst not thou agree with me for a ¹penny?

14 Take that which is thine, and go thy way: I shall give unto this last, even as unto thee.

15 Is it not lawful for me to do what I will with mine own? Or is thine eye evil, because I am good?

16 Thus the last shall be first, and the first last: ³[for many be called, but few chosen].

---

¹ *i.e. a denarius: in value about eightpence of our money.*

² *Most of the ancient MSS. read, received the penny a man.*

³ *These words are not contained in our most ancient MSS.*

17 ¶ And Jesus going up to Jerusalem took unto him the twelve disciples apart, and said unto them in the way,

18 Behold, we go up to Jerusalem; and the Son of man shall be delivered up unto the chief priests and scribes, and they shall condemn him to death,

19 And shall deliver him up to the Gentiles to mock, and to scourge, and to crucify: and the third day he shall be raised up.

20 ¶ Then came to him the mother of the sons of Zebedee with her sons, worshipping him, and desiring a certain thing of him.

21 And he said unto her, What wilt thou? She saith unto him, Command that these my two sons may sit, one on thy right hand, and one on thy left, in thy kingdom.

22 But Jesus answered and said, Ye know not what ye ask. Are ye able to drink the cup that I am about to drink? They say unto him, We are able.

23 He saith unto them, My cup indeed ye shall drink: but to sit on my right hand, and on my left, this is not mine to give, ¹but it shall be given to them for whom it is prepared of my Father.

24 And when the ten heard it, they were moved with indignation against the two brethren.

25 But Jesus called them and said, Ye know that the princes of the Gentiles exercise lordship over them, and they that are great exercise authority over them.

26 It shall not be so among you: but whosoever will become great among you, let him be your minister;

27 And whosoever will be first among you, let him be your servant:

28 Even as the Son of man came not to be ministered unto, but to minister, and to give his life a ransom for many.

29 ¶ And as they departed from Jericho, a great multitude followed him.

30 And, behold, two blind men sitting by the way side, when they heard that Jesus passed by, cried out, saying, Lord, have mercy on us, thou son of David.

31 And the multitude rebuked them, that they might hold their peace: but they cried the more, saying, Lord, have mercy on us, thou son of David.

32 And Jesus stood still, and called them, and said, What will ye that I shall do unto you?

33 They say unto him, Lord, that our eyes may be opened.

34 And Jesus was moved with compassion, and touched their eyes: and immediately they received sight, and followed him.

CHAPTER XXI.

AND when they drew nigh unto Jerusalem, and came to Bethphage, unto the mount of Olives, then Jesus sent forth two disciples,

2 Saying unto them, Go into

¹ *Or,* except to those for whom.

the village over against you, and straightway ye shall find an ass tied, and a colt with her: loose them, and bring them unto me.

3 And if any man say ought unto you, ye shall say that the Lord hath need of them; and straightway he will send them.

4 All this hath come to pass, that it may be fulfilled which was spoken by the prophet, saying,

5 Tell ye the daughter of Sion, Behold, thy King cometh unto thee, meek, and sitting upon an ass, and upon a colt the foal of an ass.

6 And the disciples went, and did as he commanded them,

7 And brought the ass, and the colt, and put on them their clothes, and he sat thereon.

8 And the greater part of the multitude spread their garmants in the way; but others cut down branches from the trees, and strawed them in the way.

9 And the multitudes that went before him, and that followed, cried, saying, Hosanna to the son of David: Blessed is he that cometh in the name of the Lord; Hosanna in the highest ¹[heavens].

10 And when he was come into Jerusalem, all the city was moved, saying, Who is this?

11 And the multitude said, This is Jesus the prophet, of Nazareth of Galilee.

12 And Jesus went into the temple of God, and cast out all them that sold and bought in the temple, and overthrew the tables of the moneychangers, and the seats of them that sold the doves,

13 And saith unto them, It is written, My house shall be called the house of prayer; but ye are making it a den of thieves.

14 And blind and lame came to him in the temple; and he healed them.

15 And the chief priests and scribes seeing the wonderful things that he did, and the children which cried in the temple, and said, Hosanna to the son of David, were sore displeased,

16 And said unto him, Hearest thou what these say? And Jesus saith unto them, Yea; did ye never read, Out of the mouth of babes and sucklings thou hast perfected praise?

17 And he left them, and went out of the city unto Bethany, and lodged there.

18 ¶ Now in the morning as he returned into the city, he hungered.

19 And seeing one fig tree ²by the way side, he came to it, and found nothing thereon, but leaves only, and saith unto it, Let no fruit grow on thee henceforward for ever. And immediately the fig tree withered away.

20 And the disciples seeing it, marvelled, saying, How immediately is the fig tree withered away!

21 Jesus answered and said unto them, Verily I say unto you, If ye have faith, and

---

¹ *Not expressed in the original.*

² *Literally*, over, *i.e.* hanging over the way.

doubt not, ye shall not only do this which is done to the fig tree, but even if ye shall say unto this mountain, Be thou removed, and be thou cast into the sea ; it shall come to pass.

22 And all things, whatsoever ye shall ask in your prayer, believing, ye shall receive.

23 ¶ And when he was come into the temple, the chief priests and the elders of the people came unto him as he was teaching, and said, With what authority doest thou these things ? and who gave thee this authority ?

24 And Jesus answered and said unto them, I also will ask you one question, which if ye tell me, I also will tell you with what authority I do these things.

25 The baptism of John, whence was it ? of heaven, or of men ? And they reasoned with themselves, saying, If we shall say, Of heaven ; he will say unto us, Why did ye not then believe him ?

26 But if we shall say, Of men ; we fear the multitude ; for all hold John as a prophet.

27 And they answered Jesus, and said, We know not. He also said unto them, Neither do I tell you with what authority I do these things.

28 But what think ye ? A man had two ¹sons ; and he came to the first, and said, ¹Son, go work to day in the vineyard.

29 He answered and said, I will not : but afterward he repented, and went.

30 And he came to the second, and said likewise. And he answered and said, I go, sir : and went not.

31 Which of these two did the will of his father ? They say unto him, The first. Jesus saith unto them, Verily I say unto you, That the publicans and the harlots go into the kingdom of God before you.

32 For John came unto you in the way of righteousness, and ye believed him not : but the publicans and the harlots believed him : and ye, when ye saw it, did not even repent afterwards, that ye might believe him.

33 ¶ Hear another parable : There was a man, an householder, which planted a vineyard, and set an hedge about it, and digged a winepress in it, and built a tower, and let it out to husbandmen, and left the country :

34 And when the time of the fruit drew near, he sent his servants to the husbandmen, that they might receive his fruits.

35 And the husbandmen took his servants, and beat one, and killed another, and stoned another.

36 Again, he sent other servants more than the first : and they did unto them in like manner.

37 But last of all he sent unto them his son, saying, They will reverence my son.

38 But when the husbandmen saw the son, they said

¹ *Literally*, children, *and* Child.

among themselves, This is the heir; come, let us kill him, and let us possess his inheritance.

39 And they took him, and cast him out of the vineyard, and slew him.

40 When therefore the lord of the vineyard shall come, what will he do unto those husbandmen?

41 They say unto him, He will miserably destroy those wicked men, and will let out the vineyard unto other husbandmen, such as shall render him the fruits in their seasons.

42 Jesus saith unto them, Did ye never read in the scriptures, The stone which the builders rejected, the same was made the head of the corner: this was the Lord's doing, and it is marvellous in our eyes?

43 Therefore say I unto you, The kingdom of God shall be taken from you, and shall be given to a nation bringing forth the fruits thereof.

44 And he that falleth on this stone shall be broken: but on whomsoever it shall fall, it will grind him to powder.

45 And when the chief priests and Pharisees had heard his parables, they perceived that he spake of them.

46 And, though they sought to lay hands on him, they feared the multitudes, because they esteemed him as a prophet.

CHAPTER XXII.

AND Jesus answered and spake unto them again in parables, saying,

2 The kingdom of heaven is like unto [1] a king, which made a marriage for his son,

3 And sent forth his servants to call them that were bidden to the wedding: and they would not come.

4 Again, he sent forth other servants, saying, Tell them which are bidden, Behold, I have prepared my dinner: my bulls and my fatlings are killed, and all things are ready: come unto the marriage.

5 But they made light of it, and went their ways, one to his own farm, another to his merchandise:

6 And the rest took his servants, and treated them spitefully, and slew them.

7 But the king was wroth: and sent his armies, and destroyed those murderers, and burned up their city.

8 Then saith he to his servants, The wedding is ready, but they which were bidden were not worthy.

9 Go ye therefore into the meetings of the ways, and as many as ye shall find, bid to the marriage.

10 So those servants went out into the highways, and gathered together all as many as they found, both bad and good: and the wedding was filled with guests.

11 And the king came in to see the guests, and saw there a man which had not on a wedding garment:

12 And he saith unto him, Friend, how camest thou in hither not having a wedding garment? And he was speechless.

[1] *Literally*, a man, a king.

13 Then said the king to the attendants, Bind him hand and foot, and cast him into the darkness without; there shall be ¹weeping and gnashing of teeth.

14 For many are called, but few are chosen.

15 ¶ Then went the Pharisees, and took counsel how they might entangle him in his talk.

16 And they send unto him their disciples with the Herodians, saying, Master, we know that thou art true, and teachest the way of God in truth, neither carest thou for any man: for thou regardest not the person of men.

17 Tell us therefore, What thinkest thou? Is it lawful to give tribute unto Cæsar, or not?

18 But Jesus, knowing their wickedness, said, Why tempt ye me, ye hypocrites?

19 Shew me the coin in which the tribute is paid. And they brought unto him a ²penny.

20 And he saith unto them, Whose is this image and superscription?

21 They say unto him, Cæsar's. Then saith he unto them, Render therefore unto Cæsar the things that are Cæsar's; and unto God the things that are God's.

22 When they heard these words, they marvelled, and left him, and went their way.

23 ¶ In that day came to him Sadducees, saying that there is no resurrection; and they asked him,

24 Saying, Master, Moses said, If a man die, having no children, his brother shall marry his wife, and shall raise up issue unto his brother.

25 Now there were with us seven brethren: and the first married a wife, and died, and, having no issue, left his wife unto his brother:

26 In like manner the second also, and the third, even unto the seven.

27 And last of all the woman died.

28 Therefore in the resurrection whose wife shall she be of the seven? for they all had her.

29 Jesus answered and said unto them, Ye do err, not knowing the scriptures, nor yet the power of God.

30 For in the resurrection they neither marry, nor are given in marriage, but are as angels ³[of God] in heaven.

31 But as touching the resurrection of the dead, did ye never read that which was spoken unto you by God, saying,

32 I am the God of Abraham, and the God of Isaac, and the God of Jacob? God is not God of dead men, but of living.

33 And when the multitudes heard this, they were astonished at his teaching.

34 ¶ But the Pharisees, hearing that he had put the Sadducees to silence, were gathered together.

35 And one of them, which was a lawyer, asked him a

---

¹ *See on chap.* viii. 12.
² *See note at chap.* xx. 2.
³ *These words are not found in several of the most ancient MSS. but are contained in others*

question, tempting him, and saying,

36 ¹Master, which commandment is greatest in the law?

37 He said unto him, Thou shalt love the Lord thy God with all thy heart, and with all thy soul, and with all thy mind.

38 This is the great and first commandment.

39 And the second is like unto it, Thou shalt love thy neighbour as thyself.

40 On these two commandments hang all the law and the prophets.

41 ¶ While the Pharisees were gathered together, Jesus asked them,

42 Saying, What think ye of the Christ? whose son is he? They say unto him, David's.

43 He saith unto them, How then doth David in spirit call him Lord, saying,

44 The LORD said unto my Lord, Sit thou on my right hand, till I put thine enemies under thy feet?

45 If David then calleth him Lord, how is he his son?

46 And no man was able to answer him a word, neither durst any man from that day forth question him any more.

CHAPTER XXIII.

THEN spake Jesus to the multitudes, and to his disciples,

2 Saying, The scribes and the Pharisees sit upon Moses' seat:

3 All things therefore whatsoever they say to you, do and observe; but do not after

¹ *Literal'y,* Teacher.

their works: for they say, and do not.

4 But they bind heavy burdens, and lay them on men's shoulders, and they themselves will not move them with their finger.

5 But all their works they do to be seen of men: for they make broad their phylacteries, and enlarge the borders of their garments,

6 And love the uppermost places at feasts, and the chief seats in the synagogues,

7 And greetings in the markets, and to be called by men, Rabbi, Rabbi.

8 But be not ye called Rabbi: for one is your Teacher; and all ye are brethren.

9 And call none your father upon the earth: for one is your Father, which is in heaven.

10 Neither be ye called leaders: for one is your Leader, even Christ.

11 But he that is greatest among you shall be your servant.

12 And whosoever shall exalt himself shall be humbled; and he that shall humble himself shall be exalted.

13 ¶ But woe unto you, scribes and Pharisees, hypocrites! because ye shut the kingdom of heaven in men's faces; for ye go not in yourselves, neither suffer ye them that are entering to go in.

² 15 Woe unto you, scribes and Pharisees, hypocrites! be-

² *Verse 14 is not contained in any of the most ancient MSS. It has probably been inserted here from Mark* xii. 40, *Luke* xx. 47.

cause ye compass sea and land to make one proselyte, and when he is made, ye make him twofold more the child of hell than yourselves.

16 Woe unto you blind guides, which say, Whosoever shall swear by the temple, it is nothing ; but whosoever shall swear by the gold of the temple, he is a debtor.

17 Ye fools and blind : for which is the greater, the gold, or the temple that hath sanctified the gold ?

18 And, Whosoever shall swear by the altar, it is nothing ; but whosoever sweareth by the gift that is upon it, he is a debtor.

19 Ye blind : for which is the greater, the gift, or the altar that sanctifieth the gift ?

20 He therefore that hath sworn by the altar, sweareth by it, and by all things thereon.

21 And he that hath sworn by the temple, sweareth by it, and by him that hath made his abode therein.

22 And he that hath sworn by heaven, sweareth by the throne of God, and by him that sitteth thereon.

23 Woe unto you, scribes and Pharisees, hypocrites ! because ye tithe mint and anise and cummin, and have omitted the weightier matters of the law, judgment, and mercy, and faith : these ought ye to have done, and not to leave the other undone.

24 Ye blind guides, which strain out the gnat, and swallow down the camel.

25 Woe unto you, scribes and Pharisees, hypocrites ! because ye make clean the outside of the cup and of the platter, but within they are full of extortion and excess.

26 Thou blind Pharisee, cleanse first the inside of the cup, that the outside of it may be clean also.

27 Woe unto you, scribes and Pharisees, hypocrites ! because ye are like unto whited sepulchres, such as indeed appear beautiful outward, but are within full of dead bones, and of all uncleanness.

28 Even so ye also outwardly appear righteous unto men, but within ye are full of hypocrisy and iniquity.

29 Woe unto you, scribes and Pharisees, hypocrites ! because ye build the tombs of the prophets, and garnish the sepulchres of the righteous,

30 And say, If we had been in the days of our fathers, we would not have been partakers with them in the blood of the prophets.

31 So then ye are witnesses unto yourselves, that ye are the sons of them which killed the prophets.

32 Fill ye up then the measure of your fathers.

33 Ye serpents, brood of vipers, how shall ye escape the judgment of hell ?

34 Wherefore, behold, I send unto you prophets, and wise men, and scribes : some of them ye shall kill and crucify ; and some of them shall ye scourge in your synagogues, and persecute from city to city :

35 That upon you may come all the righteous blood shed upon the earth, from the blood of Abel the righteous unto the blood of Zechariah son of Berechiah, whom ye slew between the temple and the altar.

36 Verily I say unto you, All these things shall come upon this generation.

37 O Jerusalem, Jerusalem, thou that killest the prophets, and stonest them which have been sent unto thee, how often have I desired to gather thy children together, even as a hen gathereth her chickens under her wings, and ye would not!

38 Behold, your house is left unto you desolate.

39 For I say unto you, Ye shall not see me henceforth, till ye shall say, Blessed is he that cometh in the name of the Lord.

CHAPTER XXIV.

AND Jesus went out, and departed from the temple: and his disciples came to him to shew him the buildings of the temple.

2 But he answered and said unto them, See ye not all these things? verily I say unto you, There shall not be left here one stone upon another, that shall not be thrown down.

3 ¶ And as he sat upon the mount of Olives, the disciples came unto him privately, saying, Tell us when these things shall be, and what shall be the sign of thy coming, and of the end of the world.

4 And Jesus answered and said unto them, Take heed that no man deceive you.

5 For many shall come in my name, saying, I am Christ; and shall deceive many.

6 And ye will hear of wars and rumours of wars: take heed, be not troubled: for all these things must come to pass, but the end is not yet.

7 For nation shall rise against nation, and kingdom against kingdom: and there shall be famines, and earthquakes, in divers places.

8 But all these are the beginning [1] of sorrows.

9 Then shall they deliver you up to tribulation, and shall kill you: and ye shall be hated by all the nations for my name's sake.

10 And then shall many be offended, and shall deliver up one another, and shall hate one another.

11 And many false prophets shall arise, and shall deceive many.

12 And because iniquity shall abound, the love of the many shall wax cold.

13 But he that hath endured unto the end, the same shall be saved.

14 And this gospel of the kingdom shall be preached in all the world for a witness unto all the nations; and then shall the end come.

15 When ye therefore shall see the abomination of desolation, spoken of by Daniel the prophet, standing in the holy place, (let him that readeth understand:)

[1] *Literally*, of pangs.

16 Then let them which are in Judæa flee into the mountains:

17 Let him which is on the housetop not come down to take the things out of his house:

18 And let him which is in the field not turn back to take his clothes.

19 But woe unto them that are with child, and to them that give suck in those days!

20 But pray ye that your flight be not in the winter, neither on the sabbath day:

21 For then shall be great tribulation, such as hath not been since the beginning of the world to this time, no, nor ever shall be.

22 And if those days had not been shortened, there should no flesh have been saved: but for the elect's sake those days shall be shortened.

23 At that time if any man say unto you, Lo, here is Christ, or there; believe it not.

24 For there shall arise false Christs, and false prophets, and shall shew great signs and wonders, so as to deceive, if it were possible, the very elect.

25 Behold, I have told you before.

26 Wherefore if they say unto you, Behold, he is in the wilderness; go not forth: behold, he is in the secret chambers; believe it not.

27 For even as the lightning cometh out of the east, and shineth as far as the west; so shall the coming of the Son of man be.

28 Wheresoever the carcase is, there will the eagles be gathered together.

29 ¶ But immediately after the tribulation of those days the sun shall be darkened, and the moon shall not give her light, and the stars shall fall from the heaven, and the powers of the heavens shall be shaken:

30 And then shall appear the sign of the Son of man in heaven: and then shall all the tribes of the earth mourn, and they shall see the Son of man coming on the clouds of heaven with power and great glory.

31 And he shall send his angels with a great voice of a trumpet, and they shall gather together his elect from the four winds, from one end of heaven to the other.

32 But learn ye the parable from the fig tree; When now her branch becometh tender, and the leaves spring forth, ye know that summer is nigh:

33 So likewise ye, when ye shall see all these things, know that it is near, even at the doors.

34 Verily I say unto you, This generation shall not pass away, till all these things be fulfilled.

35 Heaven and earth shall pass away, but my words shall never pass away.

36 But of that day and hour knoweth none, no, not the angels of heaven, but my Father only.

37 But even as the days of Noah, so shall the coming of the Son of man be.

38 For as in the days of the

flood they were eating and drinking, marrying and giving in marriage, until the day that Noah entered into the ark,

39 And knew not until the flood came, and took them all away; so shall the coming of the Son of man be.

40 Then shall two be in the field; one is taken, and one is left.

41 Two women shall be grinding at the mill; one is taken, and one is left.

42 Watch therefore: for ye know not on what day your Lord doth come.

43 But know this, that if the master of the house had known in what watch of the night the thief would come, he would have watched, and would not have suffered his house to be broken into.

44 Therefore be ye also ready: for in such an hour as ye think not the Son of man cometh.

45 Who then is that faithful and wise servant, whom his lord hath made ruler over his household, to give them meat in due season?

46 Blessed is that servant, whom his lord when he cometh shall find so doing.

47 Verily I say unto you, That he shall set him over all his goods.

48 But if that evil servant shall say in his heart, My lord delayeth his coming;

49 And shall begin to smite his fellowservants, and eateth and drinketh with the drunken;

50 The lord of that servant shall come in a day when he looketh not for him, and in an hour that he is not aware of,

51 And shall cut him asunder, and appoint him his portion with the hypocrites: there shall be ¹weeping and gnashing of teeth.

CHAPTER XXV.

A T that time shall the kingdom of heaven be likened unto ten virgins, which took their own lamps, and went forth to meet the bridegroom.

2 And five of them were foolish, and five were wise.

3 For the foolish took their lamps, and took with them no oil:

4 But the wise took oil in their vessels with their lamps.

5 And while the bridegroom tarried, they all slumbered and slept.

6 But at midnight there was a cry made, Behold the bridegroom; go ye out to meet him.

7 Then arose all those virgins, and trimmed their own lamps.

8 And the foolish said unto the wise, Give us of your oil; for our lamps are going out.

9 But the wise answered, saying, Not so; lest there be not enough for us and you: go ye rather to them that sell, and buy for yourselves.

10 And while they went away to buy, the bridegroom came; and the virgins that were ready went in with him to the marriage feast: and the door was shut.

11 Afterward come also the

¹ *Literally*, the weeping and the gnashing of the teeth.

other virgins, saying, Lord, Lord, open to us.

12 But he answered and said, Verily I say unto you, I know you not.

13 Watch therefore, for ye know not the day, nor yet the hour.

14 ¶ For it is even as a man leaving his home, who called his own servants, and delivered unto them his goods.

15 And unto one he gave five talents, to another two, and to another one; to every man according to his several ability; and straightway took his journey.

16 But he that received the five talents went and traded with them, and made other five talents.

17 And in like manner he that received the two, he also gained other two.

18 But he that received the one, went away and digged in the earth, and hid his lord's money.

19 But after a long time the lord of those servants cometh, and reckoneth with them.

20 And he that had received the five talents came and brought other five talents, saying, Lord, thou deliveredst unto me five talents: behold, I have gained beside them five other talents.

21 His lord said unto him, Well done, thou good and faithful servant: thou wast faithful over a few things, I will set thee over many things: enter thou into the joy of thy lord.

22 He also that had received the two talents came and said, Lord, thou deliveredst unto me two talents: behold, I have gained beside them two other talents.

23 His lord said unto him, Well done, good and faithful servant; thou wast faithful over a few things, I will set thee over many things: enter thou into the joy of thy lord.

24 Then he also which had received the one talent came and said, Lord, I knew thee that thou art an hard man, reaping where thou didst not sow, and gathering from where thou strawedst not:

25 And I was afraid, and went away and hid thy talent in the earth: lo, thou hast thine own.

26 But his lord answered and said unto him, Thou wicked and slothful servant, thou knewest that I reap where I sowed not, and gather from where I strawed not:

27 Thou oughtest therefore to have put my money to the bankers, and then at my coming I should have received mine own with usury.

28 Take therefore the talent from him, and give it unto him which hath the ten talents.

29 For unto every one that hath shall be given, and he shall have abundance: but from him that hath not shall be taken away even that which he hath.

30 And cast ye the unprofitable servant into the darkness without: there shall be [1] weeping and gnashing of teeth.

31 ¶ But when the Son of

[1] *Literally*, the weeping and the gnashing of the teeth.

man shall have come in his glory, and all the angels with him, then shall he sit upon the throne of his glory:

32 And before him shall be gathered all the nations: and he shall separate them one from another, as the shepherd divideth the sheep from the goats:

33 And he shall set the sheep on his right hand, but the goats on the left.

34 Then shall the King say unto them on his right hand, Come, ye blessed of my Father, inherit the kingdom prepared for you from the foundation of the world:

35 For I was hungry, and ye gave me to eat: I was thirsty, and ye gave me drink: I was a stranger, and ye took me in:

36 Naked, and ye clothed me: I was sick, and ye visited me: I was in prison, and ye came unto me.

37 Then shall the righteous answer him, saying, Lord, when saw we thee hungry, and fed thee? or thirsty, and gave thee drink?

38 When saw we thee a stranger, and took thee in? or naked, and clothed thee?

39 Or when saw we thee sick, or in prison, and came unto thee?

40 And the King shall answer and say unto them, Verily I say unto you, Inasmuch as ye did it unto one of the least of these my brethren, ye did it unto me.

41 Then shall he say also unto them on the left hand, Depart from me, ye cursed, into the eternal fire which is prepared for the devil and his angels:

42 For I was hungry, and ye gave me not to eat: I was thirsty, and ye gave me no drink:

43 I was a stranger, and ye took me not in: naked, and ye clothed me not: sick, and in prison, and ye visited me not.

44 Then shall they also answer, saying, Lord, when saw we thee hungry, or thirsty, or a stranger, or naked, or sick, or in prison, and did not minister unto thee?

45 Then shall he answer them, saying, Verily I say unto you, Inasmuch as ye did it not to one of the least of these, ye did it not to me.

46 And these shall go away into eternal punishment: but the righteous into eternal life.

CHAPTER XXVI.

AND it came to pass, when Jesus had finished all these sayings, he said unto his disciples,

2 Ye know that after two days cometh the passover, and the Son of man is delivered up to be crucified.

3 Then assembled together the chief priests and the elders of the people, unto the palace of the high priest, who was called Caiaphas,

4 And consulted that they might take Jesus by subtilty, and kill him.

5 But they said, Not during the feast, lest there be an uproar among the people.

6 ¶ Now when Jesus was in

Bethany, in the house of Simon the leper,

7 There came unto him a woman having an alabaster box of very precious ointment, and poured it on his head, as he sat at meat.

8 But his disciples seeing it had indignation, saying, To what purpose is this waste?

9 For this might have been sold for much, and given to the poor.

10 But Jesus knowing it said unto them, Why trouble ye the woman? for she wrought a good work upon me.

11 For ye have the poor always with you; but me ye have not always.

12 For in that she poured this ointment on my body, she did it for my burial.

13 Verily I say unto you, Wheresoever this gospel shall be preached in the whole world, this also, that she hath done, shall be spoken of for a memorial of her.

14 ¶ Then one of the twelve, called Judas Iscariot, went unto the chief priests,

15 And said, What will ye give me, and I will deliver him up unto you? And they covenanted with him for thirty pieces of silver.

16 And from that time he sought opportunity to deliver him up.

17 ¶ Now the first day of the unleavened bread the disciples came to Jesus, saying unto him, Where wilt thou that we prepare for thee to eat the passover?

18 But he said, Go into the city to such a man, and say unto him, The Master saith, My time is at hand; I will keep the passover at thy house with my disciples.

19 And the disciples did as Jesus appointed them; and they made ready the passover.

20 Now when it was evening, he sat down with the twelve.

21 And as they did eat, he said, Verily I say unto you, that one of you shall ¹betray me.

22 And they were exceeding sorrowful, and began every one of them to say unto him, Lord, is it I?

23 And he answered and said, He that dippeth his hand with me in the dish, the same shall ¹betray me.

24 The Son of man goeth his way, even as it is written of him: but woe unto that man by whom the Son of man is ²betrayed! it had been good for that man if he had not been born.

25 Then Judas, which ²betrayed him, answered and said, Is it I, Rabbi? He said unto him, Thou saidst it.

26 ¶ And as they were eating, Jesus took the bread, and blessed it, and brake it, and gave it to the disciples, and said, Take, eat; this is my body.

27 And he took the cup, and gave thanks, and gave it to them, saying, Drink ye all of it;

28 For this is my blood of the ³[new] covenant, which is

---

¹ Deliver me up. ² Delivered up.
³ *This word is not contained in several of the ancient MSS.*

shed for many for the remission of sins.

29 But I say unto you, I will not drink henceforth of this fruit of the vine, until the day when I drink it new with you in my Father's kingdom.

30 And when they had sung the hymn, they went out into the mount of Olives.

31 Then saith Jesus unto them, All ye shall be offended because of me this night: for it is written, I will smite the shepherd, and the sheep of the flock shall be scattered abroad.

32 But after I am risen, I will go before you into Galilee.

33 But Peter answered and said unto him, Though all shall be offended because of thee, I will never be offended.

34 Jesus said unto him, Verily I say unto thee, In this night, before the cock crow, thou shalt deny me thrice.

35 Peter saith unto him, Though I should have to die with thee, I will in no wise deny thee. In like manner also said all the disciples.

36 ¶ Then cometh Jesus with them unto a place called Gethsemane, and saith unto the disciples, Sit ye here, while I go and pray yonder.

37 And he took with him Peter and the two sons of Zebedee, and began to be sorrowful and very heavy.

38 Then saith he unto them, My soul is exceeding sorrowful, even unto death: tarry ye here, and watch with me.

39 And he went forward a little, and fell on his face, praying and saying, My Father, if it be possible, let this cup pass from me: nevertheless not as I will, but as thou wilt.

40 And he cometh unto the disciples, and findeth them sleeping, and saith unto Peter, Were ye so unable to watch with me one hour?

41 Watch and pray, that ye enter not into temptation: the spirit indeed is ready, but the flesh is weak.

42 He went away again the second time, and prayed, saying, My Father, if this may not pass away from me, except I drink it, thy will be done.

43 And he came again and found them asleep: for their eyes were heavy.

44 And he left them, and went away again, and prayed, saying the same words.

45 Then cometh he to his disciples, and saith unto them, Sleep on now, and take your rest: behold, the hour is at hand, and the Son of Man is ¹betrayed into the hands of sinners.

46 Rise, let us be going: behold, he is at hand that doth ²betray me.

47 And while he yet spake, lo, Judas, one of the twelve, came, and with him a great multitude with swords and staves, from the chief priests and elders of the people.

48 Now he that ³betrayed him gave them a sign, saying, Whomsoever I shall kiss, that same is he: hold him fast.

¹ Delivered up. ² Deliver me up.
³ Delivered him up.

49 And forthwith he came to Jesus, and said, Hail, Rabbi; and kissed him.

50 And Jesus said unto him, Friend, ¹wherefore art thou come? Then came they, and laid their hands on Jesus, and took him.

51 And, behold, one of them which were with Jesus stretched out his hand, and drew his sword, and struck the servant of the high priest, and smote off his ear.

52 Then saith Jesus unto him, Put up again thy sword into his place: for all they that take the sword shall perish with the sword.

53 Or thinkest thou that I cannot now pray to my Father, and he shall set for my defence more than twelve legions of angels?

54 But how then shall the scriptures be fulfilled, that thus it must be?

55 In that hour said Jesus to the multitudes, Ye are come out as against a thief with swords and staves to take me. I sat daily with you teaching in the temple, and ye laid no hold on me.

56 But all this is done, that the scriptures of the prophets might be fulfilled. Then all the disciples forsook him, and fled.

57 ¶ And they that had laid hold on Jesus led him away to Caiaphas the high priest, where the scribes and the elders were assembled.

58 But Peter followed him afar off, even unto the high priest's palace, and went in, and sat with the servants, to see the end.

59 Now the chief priests, and all the council, sought false witness against Jesus, that they might put him to death;

60 But found none, even though many false witnesses came. At the last came two,

61 And said, This man said, I am able to destroy the temple of God, and to built it in three days.

62 And the high priest arose, and said unto him, Answerest thou not what it is which these witness against thee?

63 But Jesus held his peace. And the high priest answered and said unto him, I adjure thee by the living God, that thou tell us whether thou be the Christ, the Son of God.

64 Jesus saith unto him, Thou saidst it: nevertheless I say unto you, From this time ye shall see the Son of man sitting on the right hand of power, and coming upon the clouds of heaven.

65 Then the high priest rent his clothes, saying, He hath spoken blasphemy; why need we any further witnesses? behold, now ye have heard his blasphemy.

66 What think ye? They answered and said, He is guilty of death.

67 Then did they spit in his face, and smote him with their fists, and others with the palms of their hands.

68 Saying, Prophesy unto us, thou Christ, Who is he that smote thee?

---

¹ *Or*, (execute the purpose) for which thou art come.

60 ¶ Now Peter sat without in the hall: and a damsel came unto him, saying, Thou also wast with Jesus the Galilæan.

70 But he denied before them all, saying, I know not what thou sayest.

71 And when he was gone out into the porch, another maid saw him, and saith unto them that were there, This man was also with Jesus of Nazareth.

72 And again he denied with an oath, I do not know the man.

73 And a little after came unto Peter they that stood by, and said to him, Surely thou also art one of them; for thy speech betrayeth thee.

74 Then began he to curse, and to swear that he knew not the man. And immediately the cock crew.

75 And Peter remembered the word of Jesus, which said, Before the cock crow, thou shalt deny me thrice. And he went out, and wept bitterly.

CHAPTER XXVII.

BUT when the morning was come, all the chief priests and the elders of the people took counsel against Jesus to put him to death:

2 And they bound him, and led him away, and delivered him up to Pontius Pilate the governor.

3 ¶ Then Judas, his betrayer, seeing that he was condemned, repented himself, and brought again the thirty pieces of silver to the chief priests and elders,

4 Saying, I sinned, in betraying the innocent blood. And they said, What is that to us? see thou to that.

5 And he cast down the pieces of silver in the temple, and departed, and went and hanged himself.

6 And the chief priests took the silver pieces, and said, It is not lawful to put them into the treasury, because it is the price of blood.

7 And they took counsel, and bought with them the potter's field, to bury strangers in.

8 Wherefore that field was called, The field of blood, unto this day.

9 Then was fulfilled that which was spoken by the prophet Jeremiah, saying, And they took the thirty pieces of silver, the price of him that was set a value on, whom they of the children of Israel did value;

10 And gave them for the potter's field, as the Lord appointed me.

11 But Jesus stood before the governor: and the governor asked him, saying, Art thou the King of the Jews? And Jesus said unto him, Thou sayest it.

12 And when he was accused by the chief priests and the elders, he answered nothing.

13 Then saith Pilate unto him, Hearest thou not how many things they witness against thee?

14 And he answered him to never a word; insomuch that the governor marvelled greatly.

15 Now at every feast the

governor was wont to release unto the multitude a prisoner, whom they would.

16 And they had then a notable prisoner, called Barabbas.

17 Therefore when they were gathered together, Pilate said unto them, Whom will ye that I release unto you? Barabbas, or Jesus which is called Christ?

18 For he knew that for envy they delivered him up.

19 When he was set down on the judgment seat, his wife sent unto him, saying, Have thou nothing to do with that just man: for I have suffered many things this day in a dream because of him.

20 But the chief priests and the elders persuaded the multitudes that they should ask Barabbas, and destroy Jesus.

21 The governor answered and said unto them, Which of the two will ye that I release unto you? They said, Barabbas.

22 Pilate saith unto them, What shall I do then with Jesus which is called Christ? They all say, Let him be crucified.

23 And he said, Why, what evil hath he done? But they cried out the more, saying, Let him be crucified.

24 When Pilate saw that he could prevail nothing, but that rather a tumult was made, he took water, and washed his hands before the multitude, saying, I am innocent of the blood of this person: see ye to it.

25 And all the people answered, and said, His blood be on us, and on our children.

26 Then released he Barabbas unto them: and when he had scourged Jesus, he delivered him to be crucified.

27 Then the soldiers of the governor took Jesus into the [1]common hall, and gathered unto him the whole band.

28 And they stripped him, and put on him a scarlet robe.

29 And they platted a crown of thorns, and put it upon his head, and a reed in his right hand: and they bowed the knee before him, and mocked him, saying, Hail, King of the Jews!

30 And they spit upon him, and took the reed, and smote him on the head.

31 And after that they had mocked him, they took the robe off from him, and put his own clothes on him, and led him away to crucify him.

32 And as they came out, they found a man of Cyrene, Simon by name: him they compelled to bear his cross.

33 And when they were come unto a place called Golgotha, this is to say, a place of a skull,

34 They gave him vinegar to drink mingled with gall: and when he had tasted thereof, he would not drink.

35 And when they had crucified him, they parted his garments among them, casting lots.[2]

---

[1] *Literally*, the Prætorium. *See Mark* xv. 16.

[2] *What follows here in the Authorized Version, is not contained in*

36 And sitting down they watched him there.

37 And they set up over his head his accusation written, THIS IS JESUS THE KING OF THE JEWS.

38 Then were there two robbers crucified with him, one on the right hand, and another on the left.

39 And they that passed by railed on him, wagging their heads,

40 And saying, Thou that destroyest the temple, and buildest it in three days, save thyself, if thou art the Son of God, come down from the cross.

41 In like manner also the chief priests mocking him, with the scribes and elders, said,

42 He saved others; himself he cannot save. He is the King of Israel; let him now come down from the cross, and we will believe on him.

43 He trusted in God; let him deliver him now, if he will have him: for he said, I am the Son of God.

44 The robbers also, which were crucified with him, reviled him with the same words.

45 Now from the sixth hour there was darkness over all the earth unto the ninth hour.

46 And about the ninth hour Jesus cried out with a loud voice, saying, Eli, Eli, lema sabachthani? that is to say,

any of the most ancient MSS. It has probably been inserted from John xix. 24.

My God, my God, why hast thou forsaken me?

47 Some of them that stood there, when they heard it, said, This man calleth Elijah.

48 And straightway one of them ran, and took a spunge, and filled it with vinegar, and put it on a reed, and gave him to drink.

49 The rest said, Let be, let us see whether Elijah will come to save him.

50 ¶ Jesus, when he had cried again with a loud voice, yielded up his spirit.

51 And, behold, the veil of the temble was rent in twain from the top to the bottom; and the earth did quake, and the rocks were rent;

52 And the graves were opened; and many bodies of the saints which slept arose:

53 And they came out of the graves after his resurrection, and entered into the holy city, and appeared unto many.

54 But when the centurion, and they that were with him watching Jesus, saw the earthquake, and those things that were done, they feared greatly, saying, Truly this was the Son of God.

55 And many women were there beholding afar off, which followed Jesus from Galilee, ministering unto him:

56 Among whom was Mary Magdalene, and Mary the mother of James and Joses, and the mother of the sons of Zebedee.

57 ¶ When the even was come, there came a rich man of Arimathæa, named Joseph,

who also himself was Jesus' disciple:

58 He went to Pilate, and begged the body of Jesus. Then Pilate commanded the body to be delivered.

59 And Joseph took the body, and wrapped it in a clean linen cloth,

60 And laid it in his own new sepulchre, which he had hewn out in the rock: and he rolled a great stone to the door of the sepulchre, and departed.

61 And Mary Magdalene was there, and the other Mary, sitting over against the sepulchre.

62 ¶ But on the next day, which is the day after the preparation, the chief priests and the Pharisees came together unto Pilate,

63 Saying, Sir, we remember that that deceiver said, while he was yet alive, After three days I will rise again.

64 Command therefore that the sepulchre be made sure until the third day, lest his disciples come and steal him away, and say unto the people, He is risen from the dead: and the last error shall be worse than the first.

65 Pilate said unto them, [1] Ye have a guard: go your way, make it as sure as ye can.

66 So they went, and made the sepulchre sure, sealing the stone, and setting the guard.

[1] *Or*, Take [a body of men for] a guard.

CHAPTER XXVIII.

NOW in the end of the sabbath, as it began to dawn toward the first day of the week, came Mary Magdalene and the other Mary to see the sepulchre.

2 And, behold, there was a great earthquake: for an angel of the Lord descended from heaven, and came and rolled back the stone, and sat upon it.

3 His appearance was like lightning, and his raiment white as snow:

4 And for fear of him the keepers did shake, and became as dead men.

5 And the angel answered and said unto the women, Fear not ye: for I know that ye seek Jesus, which hath been crucified.

6 He is not here: for he is risen, as he said. Come, see the place where [2] the Lord lay.

7 And go quickly, and tell his disciples that he is risen from the dead; and, behold, he goeth before you into Galilee; there shall ye see him: lo, I have told you.

8 And they departed quickly from the sepulchre with fear and great joy; and did run to bring his disciples word.

9 ¶ And, behold, Jesus met them, saying, [3] All hail. And they came and held him by the feet, and worshipped him.

10 Then saith Jesus unto

[2] *Our two oldest MSS. have*, he.
[3] *Literally*, Rejoice.

them, Be not afraid: go your way, tell my brethren that they depart into Galilee, and there shall they see me.

11 ¶ Now while they were going, behold, some of the guard came into the city, and told unto the chief priests all the things that were done.

12 And having assembled with the elders, and taken counsel, they gave large money unto the soldiers,

13 Saying, Say ye, His disciples came by night, and stole him away while we slept.

14 And if this come to the governor's ears, we will persuade him, and bear you harmless.

15 So they took the money, and did as they were taught: and this saying is commonly reported among the Jews until this day.

16 ¶ But the eleven disciples went into Galilee, to the mountain where Jesus had appointed them.

17 And when they saw him, they worshipped him: but some doubted.

18 And Jesus came and spake unto them, saying, All power is given unto me in heaven and in earth.

19 ¶ Go ye, make disciples of all the nations, baptizing them into the name of the Father, and of the Son, and of the Holy Ghost:

20 Teaching them to observe all things whatsoever I commanded you: and, lo, I am with you all the days, even unto the end of the world.

THE GOSPEL

ACCORDING TO

SAINT MARK.

CHAPTER I.

THE beginning of the gospel of Jesus Christ, the Son of God.

2 As it is written in Isaiah the prophet, Behold, I send my messenger before thy face, which shall prepare thy way.

3 The voice of one crying in the wilderness, Prepare ye the way of the Lord, make his paths straight.

4 John the Baptist was in the wilderness, preaching the baptism of repentance for the remission of sins.

5 And there went out unto him all the land of Judæa, and all they of Jerusalem, and were baptized by him in the river Jordan, confessing their sins.

6 And John was clothed with camel's hair, and with a leathern girdle about his loins ; and he did eat locusts and wild honey ;

7 And preached, saying, There cometh after me he that is stronger than I, the latchet of whose shoes I am not worthy to stoop down and unloose.

8 I indeed have baptized you with water : but he shall baptize you with the Holy Ghost.

9 And it came to pass in those days, that Jesus came from Nazareth of Galilee, and was baptized by John in the Jordan.

10 And straightway coming up out of the water, he saw the heavens cleaving asunder, and the Spirit like a dove descending upon him :

11 And there came a voice from heaven, saying, Thou art my beloved Son ; in thee I am well pleased.

12 And immediately the Spirit driveth him into the wilderness.

13 And he was in the wilderness forty days, tempted by Satan ; and was with the wild beasts ; and the angels ministered unto him.

14 And after that John was delivered up, Jesus came into Galilee, preaching the gospel of God,

15 Saying, The time is fulfilled, and the kingdom of God is at hand : repent ye, and believe in the gospel.

16 And as he passed by the sea of Galilee, he saw Simon and Andrew the brother of Simon casting a net into the sea : for they were fishers.

17 And Jesus said unto them, Come ye after me, and I will make you to become fishers of men.

18 And they straightway left their nets, and followed him.

19 And when he had gone a little farther, he saw James the [1]son of Zebedee, and John

---

[1] Son *is not expressed in the original.*

his brother, who also were in the ship mending their nets.

20 And straightway he called them: and they left their father Zebedee in the ship with the hired servants, and went away after him.

21 And they go into Capernaum; and straightway on the sabbath day he taught in the synagogue.

22 And they were astonished at his teaching: for he taught them as having authority, and not as the scribes.

23 And straightway there was in their synagogue a man with an unclean spirit; and he cried out,

24 Saying, What have we to do with thee, Jesus of Nazareth? art thou come to destroy us? I know thee who thou art, the Holy One of God.

25 And Jesus rebuked him, saying, Hold thy peace, and come out of him.

26 And the unclean spirit tare him, and cried with a loud voice, and came out of him.

27 And they were all amazed, insomuch that they questioned among themselves, saying, What thing is this? It is a teaching new, and with authority: he commandeth even the unclean spirits, and they obey him.

28 And immediately his fame spread abroad throughout all the surrounding region of Galilee.

29 And forthwith they came out of the synagogue, and entered into the house of Simon and Andrew, with James and John.

30 But Simon's wife's mother lay sick of a fever, and anon they tell him of her.

31 And he came and took her by the hand, and lifted her up; and immediately the fever left her, and she ministered unto them.

32 And at even, when the sun did set, they brought unto him all that were sick, and them that were possessed with devils.

33 And the whole city was gathered together at the door.

34 And he healed many that were sick of divers diseases, and cast out many devils; and suffered not the devils to speak, because they knew him.

35 And in the morning, rising up a great while before day, he went out, and departed into a solitary place, and there prayed.

36 And Simon and they that were with him followed after him.

37 And found him; and they say unto him, All men seek for thee.

38 And he saith unto them, Let us go elsewhere into the neighbouring towns, that I may preach there also: for therefore came I forth.

39 And he remained preaching in their synagogues throughout all Galilee, and casting out devils.

40 And there cometh to him a leper, beseeching him, [1][and kneeling down to him, and] saying unto him, If thou wilt, thou canst make me clean.

41 And Jesus, moved with

[1] *Not contained in many of the older MSS.*

compassion, put forth his hand, and touched him, and saith unto him, I will; be thou clean.

42 And as soon as he had spoken, immediately the leprosy departed from him, and he was cleansed.

43 And he straitly charged him, and forthwith sent him away;

44 And saith unto him, See thou say nothing to any man: but go thy way, shew thyself to the priest, and offer for thy cleansing those things which Moses commanded, for a testimony unto them.

45 But he went out, and began to publish it much, and to blaze abroad the matter, insomuch that he could no more openly enter into the city, but was without in desert places: and they resorted unto him from every quarter.

CHAPTER II.

AND again he entered into Capernaum after some days; and it was heard that he was in the house.

2 And straightway many were gathered together, insomuch that there was no room to receive them, no, not so much as about the door: and he spake the word unto them.

3 And they come unto him, bringing one sick of the palsy, borne by four men.

4 And when they could not come nigh unto him for the multitude, they uncovered the roof where he was: and when they had broken it up, they let down the bed wherein the sick of the palsy lay.

5 And Jesus seeing their faith saith unto the sick of the palsy, Son, thy sins are forgiven.

6 But there were certain of the scribes sitting there, and reasoning in their hearts,

7 Why doth this man thus speak? He blasphemeth: who can forgive sins but God only?

8 And immediately Jesus perceiving in his spirit that they so reasoned within themselves, saith unto them, Why reason ye these things in your hearts?

9 Which is easier, to say to the sick of the palsy, Thy sins are forgiven; or to say, Arise, take up thy bed, and walk?

10 But that ye may know that the Son of man hath power to forgive sins on earth, (he saith to the sick of the palsy,)

11 I say unto thee, Arise, take up thy bed, and go thy way unto thine house.

12 And he arose, and immediately taking up the bed, went forth before them all; insomuch that they were all amazed, and glorified God, saying, We never saw it on this fashion.

13 And he went forth again by the sea side; and all the multitude resorted unto him, and he taught them.

14 And as he passed by, he saw Levi the [1]son of Alphæus sitting at the receipt of custom, and saith unto him, Follow me, And he arose and followed him.

15 And it cometh to pass, that, as he sat at meat in his house, many publicans and

---

[1] Son *is not expressed in the original.*

sinners also sat together with Jesus and his disciples: for there were many, and they followed him about.

16 And the scribes and the Pharisees, seeing him eating with the sinners and publicans, said unto his disciples, He eateth and drinketh with the publicans and the sinners.

17 And Jesus hearing it saith unto them, They that are whole have no need of a physician, but they that are sick : I came not to call righteous men, but sinners.

18 And the disciples of John and of the Pharisees used to fast : and they come and say unto him, Why do the disciples of John and of the Pharisees fast, but thy disciples fast not?

19 And Jesus said unto them, Can the sons of the bridechamber fast, while the bridegroom is with them? as long as they have the bridegroom with them, they cannot fast.

20 But the days will come, when the bridegroom shall be taken away from them, and then will they fast in that day.

21 No one seweth a piece of unfulled cloth on an old garment : else the new piece that filleth it up taketh away from the old, and a worse rent is made.

22 And no one putteth new wine into old skins : else the wine will burst the skins, and the wine perisheth, and the skins also.

23 And it came to pass, that he went on the sabbath day through the corn-fields ; and his disciples began, as they went, to pluck the ears of corn.

24 And the Pharisees said unto him, Behold, why do they on the sabbath day that which is not lawful ?

25 And he said unto them, Did ye never read what David did, when he had need, and was hungry, he, and they that were with him ?

26 How he entered into the house of God in the days of Abiathar the high priest, and did eat the shewbread, which is not lawful to eat but for the priests, and gave also to them which were with him ?

27 And he said unto them, The sabbath was made for the sake of man, and not man for the sake of the sabbath :

28 So that the Son of man is Lord also of the sabbath.

CHAPTER III.

AND he entered again into the synagogue ; and there was a man there which had his hand withered.

2 And they watched him, whether he would heal him on the sabbath day ; that they might accuse him.

3 And he saith unto the man which had the withered hand, Stand forth in the midst.

4 And he saith unto them, Is it lawful to do good on the sabbath day, or to do evil ? to save life, or to kill ? But they held their peace.

5 And when he had looked round about on them with anger, being grieved for the hardness of their hearts, he saith unto the man, Stretch out

thine hand. And he stretched it out: and his hand was restored.

6 And the Pharisees went forth, and straightway took counsel with the Herodians against him, how they might destroy him.

7 And Jesus departed with his disciples to the sea: and a great multitude from Galilee followed him, and from Judæa,

8 And from Jerusalem, and from Idumæa, and beyond the Jordan; and they about Tyre and Sidon, a great multitude, hearing what things he did, came unto him.

9 And he spake to his disciples, that a small boat should wait on him because of the multitude, lest they should throng him.

10 For he had healed many; insomuch that they pressed upon him to touch him, as many as had plagues.

11 And the unclean spirits, whenever they beheld him, fell down before him, and cried, saying, Thou art the Son of God.

12 And he charged them much that they should not make him known.

13 And he goeth up into the mountain, and calleth unto him whom he himself would: and they came unto him.

14 And he appointed twelve, that they should be with him, and that he might send them forth to preach,

15 And to have power to cast out devils:

16 And Simon he surnamed Peter;

17 And James the [1]son of Zebedee, and John the brother of James; and he surnamed them Boanerges, which is, Sons of thunder:

18 And Andrew, and Philip, and Bartholomew, and Matthew, and Thomas, and James the [1]son of Alphæus, and Thaddæus, and Simon the [2]Canaæan,

19 And Judas Iscariot, which also betrayed him. And they go into an house,

20 And the multitude cometh together again, so that they could not so much as eat bread.

21 And when his friends heard of it, they went out to lay hold on him: for they said, He is beside himself.

22 ¶ And the scribes which came down from Jerusalem said, He hath Beelzebub, and by the prince of the devils casteth he out the devils.

23 And he called them unto him, and said unto them in parables, How can Satan cast out Satan?

24 And if a kingdom be divided against itself, that kingdom cannot stand.

25 And if a house be divided against itself, that house will not be able to stand.

26 And if Satan hath risen up against himself, and is divided, he cannot stand, but hath an end.

27 Nay, no one can enter into the strong man's house, and plunder his goods, except

[1] Son *is not expressed in the original.*
[2] *See note on Matt.* x. 4.

he shall first have bound the strong man; and then he will plunder his house.

28 Verily I say unto you, All sins shall be forgiven unto the sons of men, and blasphemies wherewith soever they shall blaspheme:

29 But he that shall blaspheme against the Holy Spirit hath never forgiveness, but is guilty of eternal sin:

30 Because they said, He hath an unclean spirit.

31 ¶ And there come his brethren and his mother, and, standing without, sent unto him, calling him.

32 And the multitude sat about him. And they say unto him, Behold, thy mother and thy brethren [1][and thy sisters] without seek for thee.

33 And answering them, he saith, Who is my mother, or my brethren?

34 And he looked round about on them which sat about him, and saith, Behold my mother and my brethren.

35 Whosoever shall do the things that God willeth, the same is my brother, and sister, and mother.

CHAPTER IV.

AND he began again to teach by the sea side: and there was gathered unto him a very great multitude, so that he entered into a ship, and sat in the sea; and the whole multitude was by the sea on the land.

2 And he taught them many things in parables, and said unto them in his teaching,

3 Hearken; Behold, there went out a sower to sow:

4 And it came to pass, as he sowed, some fell by the way side, and the birds came and devoured it up.

5 And other fell on the stony ground, where it had not much earth; and immediately it sprang up, because it had no depth of earth:

6 And when the sun was up, it was scorched; and because it had no root, it withered away.

7 And other fell among the thorns, and the thorns grew up, and choked it, and it yielded no fruit.

8 And others fell on the good ground, and did yield fruit that grew up and increased; and brought forth, some thirtyfold, and some sixty, and some an hundred.

9 And he said unto them, He that hath ears to hear, let him hear.

10 And when he was alone, they that were about him with the twelve asked of him the parables.

11 And he said unto them, Unto you is given the mystery of the kingdom of God: but unto them that are without, all things are done in parables:

12 That seeing they may see, and not perceive; and hearing they may hear, and not understand; lest at any time they should turn, and be forgiven.

13 And he saith unto them, Know ye not this parable? and how then will ye know all parables?

---

[1] *These words are in some of the ancient MSS. but not in others.*

14 ¶ The sower soweth the word.

15 But these are they by the way side, where the word is sown; and when they have heard, Satan cometh immediately, and taketh away the word that was sown upon them.

16 And these are they in like manner which are sown on the stony places; who, when they have heard the word, immediately with joy receive it;

17 And have no root in themselves, but endure only for a while: afterward, when tribulation or persecution ariseth because of the word, immediately they are offended.

18 And there are others which are sown among the thorns; these are they that have heard the word,

19 And the cares of the world, and the deceitfulness of riches, and the lusts concerning other things entering in, choke the word, and it becometh unfruitful.

20 And these are they which were sown on the good ground; such as hear the word, and receive it, and bring forth fruit, some thirtyfold, some sixty, and some an hundred.

21 ¶ And he said unto them, Is the candle brought to be put under the bushel, or under the bed? and not to be set on the candlestick?

22 For there is nothing hid, except that it should be manifested; neither was any thing kept secret, but that it should come to light.

23 If any man have ears to hear, let him hear.

24 And he said unto them, Take heed what ye hear: with what measure ye mete, it shall be measured to you: and more shall be given unto you.

25 For he that hath, to him shall be given: and he that hath not, from him shall be taken even that which he hath.

26 ¶ And he said, So is the kingdom of God, as if a man should cast his seed upon the ground,

27 And should sleep and rise night and day, and the seed should spring and grow up, he knoweth not how.

28 The earth bringeth forth fruit of herself, first the blade, then the ear; after that the corn is full in the ear.

29 But when the fruit offereth itself, immediately he putteth in the sickle, because the harvest is come.

30 ¶ And he said, How must we liken the kingdom of God? or with what parable must we describe it?

31 It is like a grain of mustard seed, which, when it is sown upon the earth, is less than all the seeds that be upon the earth:

32 And when it is sown, it groweth up, and becometh greater than all the herbs, and shooteth out great branches; so that the birds of the air may lodge under the shadow of it.

33 And with many such parables spake he the word unto them, as they were able to hear it.

34 But without a parable spake he not unto them: and

he expounded all things privately to his own disciples.

35 And in that day, when the even was come, he saith unto them, Let us pass over unto the opposite shore.

36 And when they had sent away the multitude, they take him even as he was in the ship. And there were also with him other ships.

37 And there ariseth a great storm of wind, and the waves beat into the ship, so that the ship was now filling.

38 And he was in the stern, asleep on the cushion: and they awake him, and say unto him, Master, carest thou not that we perish?

39 And being awakened, he rebuked the wind, and said unto the sea, Peace, be still. And the wind ceased, and there was a great calm.

40 And he said unto them, Why are ye so fearful? how is it that ye have no faith?

41 And they feared exceedingly, and said one to another, Who then is this, that even the wind and the sea obey him?

CHAPTER V.

AND they came over unto the other side of the sea, into the country of the Gergesenes.

2 And when he was come out of the ship, immediately there met him out of the tombs a man with an unclean spirit,

3 Who had his dwelling in the tombs; and no man could bind him, no, not with a chain:

4 Because he had been often bound with fetters and chains, and the chains had been plucked asunder by him, and the fetters broken in pieces: neither could any man tame him.

5 And always, night and day, he was in the tombs, and in the mountains, crying, and cutting himself with stones.

6 And seeing Jesus afar off, he ran and worshipped him.

7 And crying with a loud voice, he saith, What have I to do with thee, Jesus, thou Son of the most high God? I adjure thee by God, that thou torment me not.

8 For he was saying unto him, Come out of the man, thou unclean spirit.

9 And he asked him, What is thy name? And he saith unto him, My name is Legion: for we are many.

10 And he besought him much that he would not send them away out of the country.

11 Now there was there nigh unto the mountain a great herd of swine feeding.

12 And they besought him, saying, Send us into the swine, that we may enter into them.

13 And forthwith Jesus gave them leave. And the unclean spirits went out, and entered into the swine: and the herd ran violently down the cliff into the sea, to the number of about two thousand; and were choked in the sea.

14 And they that fed them fled, and told it in the city, and in the country. And they came to see what it was that was done.

15 And they come to Jesus; and they behold him that was

possessed sitting clothed, and in his right mind, even him that had the legion : and they were afraid.

16 And they that saw it told them how it befell to him that was possessed, and also concerning the swine.

17 And they began to pray him to depart out of their borders.

18 And when he was embarking in the ship, he that had been possessed, prayed him that he might be with him.

19 And he suffered him not, but saith unto him, Go home to thy friends, and tell them what things the Lord hath done for thee, and hath had compassion on thee.

20 And he departed, and began to publish in Decapolis what things Jesus had done for him : and all men did marvel.

21 And when Jesus was passed over again by ship unto the opposite shore, a great multitude was gathered unto him : and he was by the sea side.

22 And there cometh one of the rulers of the synagogue, ¹Jairus by name ; and seeing him, he falleth at his feet,

23 And beseecheth him greatly, saying, My little daughter lieth at the point of death : I pray thee, come and lay thy hands on her, that she may be saved, and may live.

24 And he went away with him ; and a great multitude followed him, and thronged him.

25 And a certain woman, which had an issue of blood twelve years,

26 And had suffered many things of many physicians, and had spent all that she had, and was nothing bettered, but rather grew worse,

27 When she had heard of Jesus, came in the crowd behind, and touched his garment.

28 For she said, If I may touch but his garments, I shall be ²made whole.

29 And straightway the fountain of her blood was dried up ; and she knew in her body that she was healed of her plague.

30 And Jesus, immediately knowing in himself the power which had gone forth from him, turned him about in the crowd, and said, Who touched my clothes ?

31 And his disciples said unto him, Thou seest the multitude thronging thee, and sayest thou, Who touched me ?

32 And he looked round about to see her that had done this thing.

33 But the woman fearing and trembling, knowing what had happened unto her, came and fell down before him, and told him all the truth.

34 And he said unto her, Daughter, thy faith hath saved thee ; go in peace, and be whole of thy plague.

35 While he yet spake, there come from the ruler of the synagogue's house certain which said, Thy daughter is dead : why troublest thou the Master any further ?

36 But Jesus immediately, overhearing the word as they were speaking, saith unto the

¹ *Pronounce*, Ja-írus.

² *Literally*, saved.

ruler of the synagogue, Be not afraid, only believe.

37 And he suffered no man to follow with him, save Peter, and James, and John the brother of James.

38 And they come to the house of the ruler of the synagogue, and he beholdeth a tumult, and people weeping and wailing greatly.

39 And when he was come in, he saith unto them, Why make ye this ado, and weep? the child is not dead, but sleepeth.

40 And they laughed him to scorn. But when he had put them all out, he taketh the father of the child, and the mother, and them that were with him, and entereth in where the child was.

41 And taking the hand of the child, he saith unto her, Talitha cooni; which is, being interpreted, Damsel, I say unto thee, arise.

42 And forthwith the damsel arose, and walked; for she was of the age of twelve years. And they were astonished straightway with a great astonishment.

43 And he ordered them many times that none should know this matter; and commanded that something should be given her to eat.

CHAPTER VI.

AND he went out from thence, and cometh into his own country; and his disciples follow him.

2 And when the sabbath day was come, he began to teach in the synagogue: and all that heard him were astonished, saying, From whence hath this man these things? and what wisdom is this which is given unto this man? and whence are such mighty works wrought by his hands?

3 Is not this the carpenter, the son of Mary, and brother of James, and Joses, and Judas, and Simon? and are not his sisters here with us? And they were offended at him.

4 And Jesus said unto them, A prophet is not without honour, except in his own country, and among his own kin, and in his own house.

5 And he could there do no mighty work, save that he laid his hands upon a few sick folk, and healed them.

6 And he marvelled because of their unbelief. And he went round about the villages, teaching.

7 And he calleth unto him the twelve, and began to send them forth by two and two; and gave them power over the unclean spirits;

8 And commanded them that they should take nothing for their journey, save a staff only; no bread, no scrip, no brass in their girdle:

9 But be shod with sandals; and put not on two coats.

10 And he said unto them, Wheresoever ye enter into an house, there abide till ye depart thence.

11 And whatsoever place shall not receive you, nor the people thereof hear you, when ye depart thence, shake off the

dust which is under your feet for a testimony to them.[1]

12 And they went out, and preached that men should repent.

13 And they cast out many devils, and anointed with oil many that were sick, and healed them.

14 And king Herod heard thereof; for his name was spread abroad: and he said, John the Baptist is risen from the dead, and therefore mighty works do shew forth themselves in him.

15 Others said, That it is Elijah. And others said, That it is a prophet, as one of the prophets.

16 But when Herod heard thereof, he said, John, whom I beheaded, is risen from the dead.

17 For Herod himself had sent forth and laid hold upon John, and bound him in prison for Herodias' sake, his brother Philip's wife: for he had married her.

18 For John was wont to say unto Herod, It is not lawful for thee to have thy brother's wife.

19 So Herodias had a quarrel against him, and wished to kill him, but could not:

20 For Herod feared John, knowing that he was a just man and an holy, and kept him safe; and when he heard him, he [2]did many things, and heard him gladly.

[1] *The words which follow in the Authorized Version are wanting in almost all the ancient MSS. and appear to have been inserted from Matt. x. 15.*
[2] *Some MSS. have,* doubted about many things

21 And a convenient day being come, when Herod on his birthday made a supper to his lords, high captains, and chief men of Galilee;

22 And the daughter of the said Herodias having come in, and danced, she pleased Herod and them that sat with him; and the king said unto the damsel, Ask of me whatsoever thou wilt, and I will give it thee.

23 And he sware unto her, Whatsoever thou shalt ask of me, I will give it thee, unto the half of my kingdom.

24 And she went forth, and said unto her mother, What must I ask? And she said, The head of John the Baptist.

25 And she came in straightway with haste unto the king, and asked, saying, I will that thou give me by and by on a dish the head of John the Baptist.

26 And the king was exceeding sorry; yet for his oath's sake, and for their sakes which sat with him, he would not reject her.

27 And immediately the king sent an executioner, and commanded his head to be brought: and he went and beheaded him in the prison,

28 And brought his head on a dish, and gave it to the damsel: and the damsel gave it to her mother.

29 And when his disciples heard of it, they came and took up his corpse, and laid it in a tomb.

30 And the apostles gather themselves together unto Jesus,

and told him all things, both what they had done, and what they had taught.

31 And he saith unto them, Come ye yourselves apart into a desert place, and rest a while : for there were many coming and going, and they had no leisure so much as to eat.

32 And they departed into a desert place in the ship privately.

33 And many saw them departing, and knew him, and ran afoot thither out of all the cities, and outwent them.

34 And he came out, and saw much people, and was moved with compassion toward them, because they were as sheep not having a shepherd : and he began to teach them many things.

35 And when the hour was now late, his disciples came unto him, and said, This is a desert place, and now the hour is late :

36 Send them away, that they may go into the country round about, and into the villages, and buy themselves somewhat to eat.

37 But he answered and said unto them, Give ye them to eat. And they say unto him, Must we go and buy two hundred pennyworth of bread, and shall we thus give them to eat ?

38 He saith unto them, How many loaves have ye? go and see. And when they knew, they say, Five, and two fishes.

39 And he commanded them to make all sit down by companies upon the green grass.

40 And they sat down in ranks, by hundreds, and by fifties.

41 And he took the five loaves and the two fishes, and looking up to heaven, he blessed, and brake the loaves, and gave them to the disciples to set before them ; and the two fishes divided he among them all.

42 And they did all eat, and were filled.

43 And they took up fragments enough to fill twelve baskets ; and what remained of the fishes also.

44 And they that did eat of the loaves were five thousand men.

45 And straightway he constrained his disciples to get into the ship, and to go before him to the other side unto Bethsaida, while he himself sent away the multitude.

46 And when he had dismissed them, he departed into the mountain to pray.

47 And when the evening was come, the ship was in the midst of the sea, and he alone on the land.

48 And seeing them distressed in their rowing—for the wind was contrary unto them— about the fourth watch of the night he cometh unto them, walking upon the sea. And he was purposing to pass by them ;

49 But they, seeing him walking upon the sea, supposed it had been an apparition, and cried out :

50 For they all saw him, and were troubled. And immediately he talked with them, and saith unto them, Be of good cheer : it is I ; be not afraid.

51 And he went up unto them into the ship; and the wind ceased: and they were sore amazed in themselves beyond measure.

52 For they understood not the matter of the loaves: for their heart was hardened.

53 And they passed over, and came into the land of Gennesaret, and drew to the shore.

54 And when they were come out of the ship, straightway the people knew him,

55 And ran through that whole region round about, and began to carry about in beds those that were sick, where they heard he was.

56 And whithersoever he entered, into villages, or into cities, or fields, they laid the sick in the public places, and besought him that they might touch if it were but the border of his garment: and as many as touched him were made whole.

CHAPTER VII.

AND there come together unto him the Pharisees, and certain of the scribes, which came from Jerusalem.

2 And seeing some of his disciples eating their bread with unclean, that is to say, with unwashen hands;

3 (For the Pharisees, and all the Jews, except they carefully wash their hands, eat not, holding the tradition of the [1]elders.

4 And when they come from the market, except they wash, they eat not. And many other things there be, which they

[1] *i. e.* the ancients, *as in Heb.* xi. 2.

have received to hold, washings of cups, and of pots, and of brasen vessels, and of couches.)

5 And the Pharisees and the scribes ask him, Why walk not thy disciples according to the tradition of the [1]elders, but eat their bread with unclean hands?

6 He answered and said unto them, Well did Isaiah prophesy of you hypocrites, as it is written, This people honoureth me with their lips, but their heart is far from me.

7 Howbeit in vain do they worship me, teaching for doctrines the commandments of men.

8 Ye have laid aside the commandment of God, and hold the tradition of men [2][as the washing of pots and cups: and many other such like things ye do].

9 And he said unto them, Full well ye reject the commandment of God, that ye may keep your tradition.

10 For Moses said, Honour thy father and thy mother; and, He that curseth father or mother, let him die the death:

11 But ye say, If a man shall say to his father or mother, That by which thou mightest be profited by me is Corban, that is to say, a gift,

12 Ye suffer him no more to do ought for his father or his mother;

13 Making the word of God of none effect through your

[2] *These words are wanting in several of the most ancient MSS.*

tradition, which ye have delivered : and many such like things ye do.

14 ¶ And he called the multitude again unto him, and said unto them, Hearken unto me, all of you, and understand :

15 There is nothing from without the man, entering into him, that can defile him : but the things which come out of the man, those are they that defile the man.

¹[16 If any man have ears to hear, let him hear.]

17 And when he entered into the house from the multitude, his disciples asked him concerning the parable.

18 And he saith unto them, Are ye so without understanding also ? Do ye not perceive, that whatsoever thing from without entereth into the man, cannot defile him ;

19 Because it entereth not into his heart, but into his belly, and goeth out into the sewer, which carrieth off all the food ?

20 And he said, That which cometh out of the man, that defileth the man.

21 For from within, out of the heart of men, proceed evil thoughts, fornications, thefts, murders, adulteries,

22 Covetousness, wickedness, deceit, lasciviousness, an evil eye, blasphemy, pride, foolishness :

23 All these evil things come forth from within, and defile the man.

¹ *Not contained in some of the oldest MSS.*

24 ¶ And from thence he arose, and departed into the borders of Tyre, and entered into an house, and would have no one know it : and he could not be hid.

25 But a woman, whose young daughter had an unclean spirit, straightway heard of him, and came and fell at his feet :

26 The woman was a Greek, a Syrophenician by nation : and she besought him that he would cast forth the devil out of her daughter.

27 And he said unto her, Let the children first be filled : for it is not meet to take the bread of the children, and to cast it unto the dogs.

28 And she answered and said unto him, Even so, Lord : for the dogs also eat under the table of the children's crumbs.

29 And he said unto her, For this saying go thy way ; the devil is gone out of thy daughter.

30 And she went away unto her house, and found the child laid upon the bed, and the devil gone out.

31 ¶ And again, departing from the borders of Tyre, he came through Sidon unto the sea of Galilee, through the midst of the borders of Decapolis.

32 And they bring unto him one that was deaf, and had an impediment in his speech ; and they beseech him to put his hand upon him.

33 And he took him aside from the multitude, and put

his fingers into his ears, and he spit, and touched his tongue ;

34 And looking up to heaven, he sighed, and saith unto him, Ephphatha, that is, Be thou opened.

35 And his ears were opened, and the string of his tongue was loosed, and he spake plain.

36 And he charged them that they should tell no one: but the more he charged them, so much the more a great deal they published it ;

37 And were beyond measure astonished, saying, He hath done all things well : he maketh both the deaf to hear, and the dumb to speak.

CHAPTER VIII.

IN those days the multitude being again great, and having nothing to eat, he called his disciples unto him, and saith unto them,

2 I have compassion on the multitude, because they have now been continuing three days, and have nothing to eat :

3 And if I shall send them away fasting to their home, they will faint in the way: and some of them are from a distance.

4 And his disciples answered him, From whence can one satisfy these men with bread here in the wilderness?

5 And he asked them, How many loaves have ye? And they said, Seven.

6 And he commandeth the multitude to sit down on the ground : and he took the seven loaves, and gave thanks, and brake, and gave to his disciples to set before them ; and they did set them before the multitude.

7 And they had a few small fishes : and he blessed, and did set them before them.

8 And they did eat, and were filled : and they took up the remnants of the broken meat, seven wallets.

9 And they were about four thousand : and he sent them away.

10 ¶ And straightway he entered into the ship with his disciples, and came into the parts of Dalmanutha.

11 And the Pharisees came forth, and began to question with him, seeking of him a sign from heaven, tempting him.

12 And he sighed deeply in his spirit, and saith, Why doth this generation seek after a sign ? verily I say unto you, There shall no sign be given unto this generation.

13 And he left them, and entering into the ship again departed to the opposite shore.

14 ¶ And they forgot to take bread, neither had they in the ship with them more than one loaf.

15 And he was charging them, saying, Take heed, beware of the leaven of the Pharisees, and the leaven of Herod.

16 And they were reasoning among themselves, because they had no bread.

17 And he, knowing it, saith unto them, Why reason ye, because ye have no bread ?

perceive ye not yet, neither understand? have ye your heart hardened?

18 Having eyes, see ye not? and having ears, hear ye not? and do ye not remember,

19 When I brake the five loaves among five thousand, how many baskets full of fragments took ye up? They say unto him, Twelve.

20 And when the seven among four thousand, how many wallets full of fragments took ye up? And they say unto him, Seven.

21 And he said unto them, Do ye not yet understand?

22 ¶ And they come to Bethsaida; and they bring a blind man unto him, and beseech him to touch him.

23 And he took the hand of the blind man, and brought him out of the town; and when he had spit on his eyes, he put his hands upon him, and asked him if he saw ought.

24 And he looked up, and said, I behold men; for I see them as trees, walking.

25 After that he put his hands again upon his eyes, and he saw clearly: and he was restored, and saw all things plainly.

26 And he sent him away to his house, saying, Neither go into the village, nor tell it to any in the village.

27 ¶ And Jesus went out, and his disciples, into the villages of Cæsarea Philippi: and by the way he asked his disciples, saying unto them, Who do men say that I am?

28 And they spake unto him, saying, John the Baptist: and some, Elijah; and others, that thou art one of the prophets.

29 And he himself asked them, But who say ye that I am? And Peter answereth and saith unto him, Thou art the Christ.

30 And he charged them that they should tell no one of him.

31 And he began to teach them, that the Son of man must suffer many things, and be rejected by the elders, and the chief priests, and the scribes, and be killed, and after three days rise again.

32 And he spake that saying openly. And Peter took him, and began to rebuke him.

33 But he, turning about and looking on his disciples, rebuked Peter, and saith, Get thee behind me, Satan: for thou savourest not the things that be of God, but the things that be of men.

34 And he called the multitude unto him with his disciples, and said unto them, Whosoever desireth to follow after me, let him deny himself, and take up his cross, and follow me.

35 For whosoever desireth to save his [1]life shall lose it; but whosoever shall lose his life for my sake and the gospel's, shall save it.

36 For what doth it profit a man to gain the whole world, and lose his [1]life?

37 For what shall a man give in exchange for his [1]life?

38 For whosoever shall be ashamed of me and of my

[1] *Or,* soul: *see Matt.* x. 39.

words in this adulterous and sinful generation; of him shall also the Son of man be ashamed, when he cometh in the glory of his Father with the holy angels.

CHAPTER IX.

AND he said unto them, Verily I say unto you, That there be some of them that stand here, which shall not taste of death, till they have seen the kingdom of God come with power.

2 ¶ And after six days Jesus taketh with him Peter and James, and John, and bringeth them up into an high mountain apart by themselves: and he was transfigured before them.

3 And his garments became shining, exceeding white; so as no fuller on earth can white them.

4 And there appeared unto them Elijah with Moses: and they were talking with Jesus.

5 And Peter answering saith to Jesus, Rabbi, it is good for us to be here: and let us make three tabernacles; one for thee, and one for Moses, and one for Elijah.

6 For he wist not what to answer; for they were sore afraid.

7 And there came a cloud overshadowing them: and a voice came out of the cloud, saying, This is my beloved Son: hear ye him.

8 And suddenly they looked round about, and saw no one any more, save Jesus only with themselves.

[1] Come *is not here the verb, but the past participle,*=having come.

9 And as they came down from the mountain, he enjoined them that they should tell no one what things they had seen, till the Son of man were risen from the dead.

10 And they kept that saying with themselves, questioning one with another what the rising from the dead should mean.

11 ¶ And they asked him, saying, Why say the scribes that Elijah must first come?

12 But he said unto them, Elijah verily cometh first, and restoreth all things; and how is it written of the Son of man, that he must suffer many things, and be set at nought?

13 Nevertheless I say unto you, That Elijah is indeed come, and they did unto him whatsoever they listed, as it is written concerning him.

14 ¶ And when he came to his disciples, he saw a great multitude about them, and scribes questioning with them.

15 And straightway all the multitude, when they beheld him, were greatly amazed, and running to him saluted him.

16 And he asked them, What question ye with them?

17 And one of the multitude answered him, Master, I brought unto thee my son, which hath a dumb spirit;

18 And wheresoever it taketh him, it teareth him: and he foameth, and gnasheth with his teeth, and is stiffened: and I spake to thy disciples that they should cast it out and they could not.

19 But he answereth and

saith unto them, O faithless generation, how long shall I be with you? how long shall I suffer you? bring him unto me.

20 And they brought him unto him: and when he saw him, straightway the spirit tare him; and he fell on the ground, and wallowed foaming.

21 And he asked his father, How long is it ago since this hath come unto him? And he said, From a child.

22 And ofttimes it hath cast him into the fire, and into waters, to destroy him: but if thou canst do any thing, have compassion on us, and help us.

23 Jesus said unto him, ¹If thou canst believe, all things are possible to him that believeth.

24 Straightway the father of the child cried out, and said,² I believe; help thou mine unbelief.

25 But Jesus, seeing that the people came running together, rebuked the unclean spirit, saying unto it, Thou dumb and deaf spirit, I myself charge thee, come out of him, and enter no more into him.

26 And the spirit cried, and rent him sore, and came out of him: and he was as one dead; insomuch that the more part said, He is dead.

27 But Jesus took him by the hand, and lifted him up; and he arose.

28 And when he was come into the house, his disciples asked him privately, Why could not we cast it out?

29 And he said unto them, This kind can come forth by nothing, but by prayer ³[and fasting].

30 ¶ And they departed thence, and passed on through Galilee; and he would not that any should know it.

31 For he was teaching his disciples, and saying unto them, The Son of man is delivered into the hands of men, and they shall kill him; and when he is killed, he shall rise again after three days.

32 But they were ignorant of the saying, and were afraid to ask him.

33 ¶ And they came to Capernaum: and when he was come into the house he asked them, What disputed ye by the way?

34 But they held their peace: for by the way they had disputed among themselves, who was greatest.

35 And he sat down, and called the twelve, and saith unto them, If any man desireth to be first, he shall be last of all, and minister of all.

36 And he took a little child, and set it in the midst of them: and when he had taken it in his arms, he said unto them,

37 Whosoever shall receive one of such little children in

---

¹ *The ancient MSS. and versions are divided about the reading of this verse. The oldest MSS. have it thus:* Jesus said unto him, If thou canst? All things, &c.

² *The words,* with tears, Lord, *are not found in any of the most ancient MSS.*

³ *These words are not found in the two most ancient MSS.*

my name, receiveth me: and whosoever receiveth me, receiveth not me, but him that sent me.

38 ¶ John spake unto him, saying, Master, we saw one casting out devils in thy name, who followeth not us: and we forbad him, because he followeth not us.

39 But Jesus said, Forbid him not: for there is no man which shall do a miracle in my name, and shall be able ¹lightly to speak evil of me.

40 For he that is not against us is for us.

41 For whosoever shall give you a cup of water to drink in my name, ²because ye belong to Christ, verily I say unto you, he shall in no wise lose his ³ reward.

42 And whosoever shall offend one of these little ones which have faith, it were well for him that a ⁴great millstone were hanged about his neck, and he were cast into the sea.

43 And if thy hand offend thee, cut it off: it is well for thee to enter into life maimed, rather than having thy two hands to go away into hell, into the unquenchable fire:

44 ⁵[Where their worm dieth not, and the fire is not quenched.]

45 And if thy foot offend thee, cut it off: it is well for thee to enter halt into life, rather than having thy two feet to be cast into hell ⁵[into the unquenchable fire]:

46 ⁵[Where their worm dieth not, and the fire is not quenched.]

47 And if thine eye offend thee, pluck it out: it is well for thee to enter into the kingdom of God with one eye, rather than having two eyes to be cast into hell:

48 Where their worm dieth not, and the fire is not quenched.

49 For every one shall be salted with fire, and every sacrifice shall be salted with salt.

50 Salt is good: but if the salt have lost its saltness, wherewith will ye season it? Have salt in yourselves, and be at peace one with another.

CHAPTER X.

AND he arose from thence, and cometh into the borders of Judæa and beyond the Jordan: and the multitudes resort unto him again; and, as he was wont, he taught them again.

2 ¶ And there came to him Pharisees, and asked him, Is it lawful for a man to put away his wife? tempting him.

3 But he answered and said unto them, What did Moses command you?

4 And they said, Moses suffered to write a bill of divorcement, and to put her away.

5 Jesus said unto them, In regard to the hardness of your

---

¹ *Literally*, quickly.
² *Literally*, in the name that, *i.e.* by reason that.
³ *Or*, hire, wages: *see on Matt.* x. 41.
⁴ *See note on Matt.* xviii. 6.
⁵ *These words are wanting in most of the ancient MSS.*

heart he wrote you this commandment.

6 But from the beginning of the creation God made them male and female.

7 For this cause shall a man leave his father and mother, and shall cleave to his wife;

8 And they two shall become one flesh: so then they are no more two, but one flesh.

9 What therefore God joined together, let not man put asunder.

10 And in the house his disciples asked him again of this matter.

11 And he saith unto them, Whosoever shall put away his wife, and marry another, committeth adultery against her.

12 And if she shall put away her husband, and marry another, she committeth adultery.

13 ¶ And they brought little children to him, that he should touch them: but the disciples rebuked those that brought them.

14 But Jesus seeing it, was much displeased, and said unto them, Suffer the little children to come unto me, and hinder them not: for of such is the kingdom of God.

15 Verily I say unto you, Whosoever shall not receive the kingdom of God as a little child shall in no wise enter therein.

16 And he took them up in his arms, and blessed them, putting his hands upon them.

17 ¶ And as he was going forth into the way, there came one running, and kneeled to him, and asked him, Good Master, what shall I do that I may inherit eternal life?

18 And Jesus said unto him, Why callest thou me good? there is none good but God only.

19 Thou knowest the commandments, Do not commit adultery, Do not commit murder, Do not steal, Do not bear false witness, Defraud not, Honour thy father and mother.

20 But he answered and said unto him, Master, all these have I observed from my youth.

21 And Jesus looking upon him loved him, and said unto him, One thing thou lackest: go thy way, sell whatsoever thou hast, and give to the poor, and thou shalt have treasure in heaven: and come, take up the cross, and follow me.

22 And he was vexed at the saying, and went away grieved: for he had great possessions.

23 And Jesus looked round about, and saith unto his disciples, How hard shall it be for them that have riches to enter into the kingdom of God!

24 And the disciples were amazed at his words. But Jesus answereth again, and saith unto them, Children, how hard is it for them that trust in riches to enter into the kingdom of God!

25 It is easier for a camel to go through the eye of a needle, than for a rich man to enter into the kingdom of God.

26 And they were astonished

out of measure, saying among themselves, Who then can be saved?

27 Jesus looking upon them saith, With men it is impossible, but not with God: for with God all things are possible.

28 Peter began to say unto him, Lo, we left all, and have followed thee.

29 Jesus said, Verily I say unto you, There is no man that hath left house, or brethren, or sisters, or mother, or father, or children, or lands, for my sake, and the gospel's,

30 But he shall receive an hundredfold now in this time, houses, and brethren, and sisters, and mothers, and children, and lands, with persecutions; and in the world to come eternal life.

31 But many first shall be last; and the last, first.

32 ¶ And they were in the way going up to Jerusalem; and Jesus was going before them: and they were amazed; and as they followed, they were afraid. And he took unto him again the twelve, and began to tell them what things were about to happen unto him,

33 Saying, Behold, we go up to Jerusalem; and the Son of man shall be delivered up unto the chief priests, and unto the scribes; and they shall condemn him to death, and shall deliver him up to the Gentiles:

34 And they shall mock him, and shall spit upon him, and shall scourge him, and shall kill him: and after three days he shall rise again.

35 ¶ And James and John, the sons of Zebedee, come unto him, saying unto him, Master, we will that thou shouldest do for us whatsoever we shall ask thee.

36 And he said unto them, What will ye that I should do for you?

37 They said unto him, Grant unto us that we may sit, one on thy right hand, and one on thy left hand, in thy glory.

38 But Jesus said unto them, Ye know not what ye ask: can ye drink the cup that I drink? or be baptized with the baptism that I am baptized with?

39 And they said unto him, We can. And Jesus said unto them, The cup that I drink ye shall drink; and with the baptism that I am baptized withal shall ye be baptized:

40 But to sit on my right hand or on my left hand is not mine to give; [1]but it shall be given to them for whom it is prepared.

41 And when the ten heard it, they began to be moved with indignation against James and John.

42 And Jesus called them to him, and saith unto them, Ye know that they which are accounted to rule over the Gentiles exercise lordship over them; and their great ones exercise authority over them.

43 But so is it not among you: but whosoever will become great among you, shall be your minister:

44 And whosoever of you

[1] *Or*, except to those for whom.

will become first, shall be servant of all.

45 For the Son of man also came not to be ministered unto, but to minister, and to give his life a ransom for many.

46 ¶ And they come to Jericho: and as he went out of Jericho with his disciples and a great multitude, Bartimæus, the son of Timæus, a blind beggar, sat by the wayside.

47 And when he heard that it was Jesus of Nazareth, he began to cry out, and say, Jesus, thou son of David, have mercy on me.

48 And many charged him that he should hold his peace: but he cried the more a great deal, Thou Son of David, have mercy on me.

49 And Jesus stood still, and said, Call ye him. And they call the blind man, saying unto him, Be of good comfort, rise; he calleth thee.

50 And he, casting away his garment, leaped up, and came to Jesus.

51 And Jesus answered and said unto him, What wilt thou that I should do unto thee? The blind man said unto him, Rabboni, that I may receive my sight.

52 And Jesus said unto him, Go thy way; thy faith hath saved thee. And immediately he received his sight, and followed him in the way.

CHAPTER XI.

AND when they come nigh to Jerusalem, unto Bethphage and Bethany, at the mount of Olives, he sendeth two of his disciples,

2 And saith unto them, Go your way into the village over against you: and straightway, as ye enter into it, ye shall find a colt tied, whereon never man hath sat; loose him, and bring him.

3 And if any man say unto you, Why do ye this? say ye, The Lord hath need of him; and straightway he will send him hither.

4 And they went their way, and found a colt tied by the door without in the street; and they loose him.

5 And certain of them that stood there said unto them, What do ye, loosing the colt?

6 And they said unto them even as Jesus had commanded: and they let them go.

7 And they bring the colt to Jesus, and cast their garments on him; and he sat upon him.

8 And many spread their garments in the way: and others branches, which they had cut out of the fields.

9 And they that went before, and they that followed, cried, Hosanna; Blessed is he that cometh in the name of the Lord:

10 Blessed is the kingdom of our father David, that cometh: Hosanna in the highest [¹heavens].

11 And he entered into Jerusalem, into the temple: and when he had looked round about upon all things, and now the eventide was come, he went out unto Bethany with the twelve.

¹ *Not expressed in the original.*

12 ¶ And on the morrow, when they had gone out from Bethany, he was hungry:

13 And seeing a fig tree afar off having leaves, he came, if haply he might find any thing thereon: and when he came to it, he found nothing but leaves; [1]for the time of figs was not yet.

14 And he answered and said unto it, No man eat fruit of thee hereafter for ever. And his disciples heard it.

15 ¶ And they come to Jerusalem: and he went into the temple, and began to cast out them that sold and them that bought in the temple, and overthrew the tables of the moneychangers, and the seats of them that sold the doves;

16 And would not suffer that any one should carry a vessel through the temple.

17 And he taught, and said, Is it not written, My house shall be called an house of prayer for all the nations? but ye have made it a den of thieves.

18 And the scribes and the chief priests heard it, and sought how they might destroy him: for they feared him, because all the multitude was astonished at his doctrine.

19 And when even was come, he went out of the city.

20 ¶ And in the morning, as they passed by, they saw the fig tree dried up from the roots.

21 And Peter calling to remembrance saith unto him, Rabbi, behold, the fig tree which thou cursedst is withered away.

[1] *Or*, the season was not one of figs.

22 And Jesus answering saith unto them, Have faith in God.

23 Verily I say unto you, That whosoever shall say unto this mountain, Be thou removed, and be thou cast into the sea; and shall not doubt in his heart, but believeth that those things which he saith shall come to pass; he shall have whatsoever he saith.

24 Therefore I say unto you, All things that ye pray and ask for, believe that ye have received, and ye shall have them.

25 And when ye stand praying, forgive whatever ye have against any: that your Father also which is in heaven may forgive you your trespasses.

[2]26 [But if ye do not forgive, neither will your Father which is in heaven forgive your trespasses.]

27 ¶ And they come again to Jerusalem: and as he was walking in the temple, there come to him the chief priests, and the scribes, and the elders.

28 And they said unto him, With what authority doest thou these things, or who gave thee this authority to do these things?

29 But Jesus said unto them, I will ask of you one question, and answer me, and I will tell you with what authority I do these things.

30 The baptism of John, was it of heaven, or of men? answer me.

31 And they reasoned with themselves, saying, If we shall

[2] *This verse is not found in the two oldest, and in some other MSS*

say, Of heaven; he will say, Why did ye not believe him?

32 But shall we say, Of men? they feared the people: for all men counted John for certain that he was a prophet.

33 And they answering say unto Jesus, We know not. And Jesus saith unto them, Neither do I tell you with what authority I do these things.

CHAPTER XII.

AND he began to speak unto them by parables. A man planted a vineyard, and set an hedge about it, and digged a place for the winefat, and built a tower, and let it out to husbandmen, and left the country.

2 And at the season he sent to the husbandmen a servant, that he might receive from the husbandmen of the fruits of the vineyard.

3 And they took him, and beat him, and sent him away empty.

4 And again he sent unto them another servant; and him they wounded in the head, and treated him shamefully.

5 And he sent another; and him they killed, and many others; beating some, and killing some.

6 He had yet one beloved son; him he sent unto them last of all, saying, They will reverence my son.

7 But those husbandmen said among themselves, This is the heir; come, let us kill him, and the inheritance shall be ours.

8 And they took him, and killed him, and cast him out of the vineyard.

9 What shall the lord of the vineyard do? he will come and destroy the husbandmen, and will give the vineyard unto others.

10 Did ye never even read this scripture; The stone which the builders rejected, the same was made the head of the corner:

11 This was the Lord's doing, and it is marvellous in our eyes?

12 And they sought to lay hold on him; and they feared the multitude: for they knew that he spake the parable against them: and they left him, and went their way.

13 ¶ And they send unto him certain of the Pharisees and of the Herodians, to catch him by his talk.

14 And when they were come, they say unto him, Master, we know that thou art true, and carest for no man: for thou regardest not the person of men, but teachest the way of God in truth. Is it lawful to give tribute to Cæsar, or not?

15 Must we give, or must we not give? But he, knowing their hypocrisy, said unto them, Why tempt ye me? bring me a [1]penny, that I may see it.

16 And they brought it. And he saith unto them, Whose is this image and superscription? And they said unto him, Cæsar's.

17 And Jesus said, Render

[1] *See note on Matt.* xx. 2.

to Cæsar the things that are Cæsar's, and to God the things that are God's. And they marvelled at him.

18 And there come unto him Sadducees, which say there is no resurrection; and they asked him, saying,

19 Master, Moses wrote unto us, If a man's brother die, and leave a wife, and leave no child, that his brother should take his wife, and raise up seed unto his brother.

20 There were seven brethren: and the first took a wife, and dying left no seed.

21 And the second took her, and died, leaving no seed: and the third in like manner.

22 And the seven left no seed: last of all the woman died also.

23 In the resurrection, when they shall rise, whose wife shall she be of them? for the seven had her to wife.

24 Jesus said unto them, Do ye not therefore err, because ye know not the scriptures, nor yet the power of God?

25 For when they shall rise from the dead, they neither marry, nor are given in marriage; but are as the angels which are in heaven.

26 But as touching the dead, that they rise: did ye never read in the book of Moses, in that part concerning the bush, how God spake unto him, saying, I am the God of Abraham, and the God of Isaac, and the God of Jacob?

27 He is not the God of the dead, but of the living: ye do greatly err.

28 ¶ And one of the scribes came near, and having heard them reasoning together, perceiving that he had answered them well, asked him, Which is the first commandment of all?

29 Jesus answered, The first is, Hear, O Israel; the Lord our God is one Lord:

30 And thou shalt love the Lord thy God with all thy heart, and with all thy soul, and with all thy mind, and with all thy strength.

31 The second is this, Thou shalt love thy neighbour as thyself. There is none other commandment greater than these.

32 And the scribe said unto him, Well spoken, Master; thou hast truly said that He is one, and there is none other but he:

33 And to love him with all the heart, and with all the understanding, and with all the soul, and with all the strength, and to love his neighbour as himself, is more than all the whole burnt offerings and sacrifices.

34 And Jesus seeing that he answered discreetly, said unto him, Thou art not far from the kingdom of God. And no one after that durst ask him any question.

35 ¶ And Jesus answered and said, while he taught in the temple, How say the scribes that the Christ is the son of David?

36 David himself said by the Holy Spirit, The LORD said unto my Lord, Sit thou on my right hand, till I put thine enemies beneath thy feet.

37 David himself calleth him Lord; and whence is he then his son? And the great multitude heard him gladly.

38 ¶ And he said unto them in his teaching, Beware of the scribes, which desire to walk in long robes, and greetings in the markets,

39 And chief seats in the synagogues, and uppermost places at feasts:

40 Which devour widows' houses, and for a pretence make long prayers: these shall receive greater condemnation.

41 ¶ And as he sat over against the treasury, he beheld how the multitude cast money into the treasury: and many that were rich cast in much.

42 And there came one poor widow, and she cast in two mites, which make a farthing.

43 And he called unto him his disciples, and saith unto them, Verily I say unto you, that this poor widow hath cast more in, than all they which are casting into the treasury:

44 For all they did cast in of their abundance; but she of her want did cast in all that she had, even all her living.

CHAPTER XIII.

AND as he went out of the temple, one of his disciples saith unto him, Master, see what manner of stones and what buildings are here.

2 And Jesus said unto him, Seest thou these great buildings? there shall not be left one stone upon another, that shall not be thrown down.

3 And as he sat upon the mount of Olives over against the temple, Peter and James and John and Andrew asked him privately,

4 Tell us, when these things shall be; and what shall be the sign when all these things are about to be fulfilled.

5 But Jesus began to say unto them, Take heed lest any deceive you:

6 Many shall come in my name, saying, I am he; and shall deceive many.

7 But when ye hear of wars and rumours of wars, be ye not troubled: they must needs be; but the end shall not be yet.

8 For nation shall rise against nation, and kingdom against kingdom: there shall be earthquakes in divers places, there shall be famines [1][and troubles]: these are the beginnings of sorrows.

9 ¶ But take heed to yourselves: they will deliver you up to councils, and ye shall be beaten in synagogues: and ye shall stand before rulers and kings for my sake, for a testimony unto them.

10 And the gospel must first be published unto all the nations.

11 And when they lead you, and deliver you up, be not careful beforehand what ye shall speak, [2][neither do ye premeditate:] but whatsoever shall be given you in that hour,

[1] *These words are wanting in most of the oldest MSS.*
[2] *These words are wanting in several of the oldest MSS.: but they may have been omitted, as not occurring in Matt. x. 19.*

that speak ye : for it is not ye that speak, but the Holy Spirit.

12 And brother shall deliver up brother to death, and the father the child ; and children shall rise up against parents, and shall put them to death.

13 And ye shall be hated by all for my name's sake : but he that hath endured unto the end, the same shall be saved.

14 ¶ But when ye shall see the abomination of desolation standing where it ought not, (let him that readeth understand,) then let them that are in Judæa flee to the mountains :

15 And let him that is on the housetop not go down into the house, neither enter therein, to take any thing out of his house :

16 And let him that is in the field not turn back again to take his garment.

17 But woe unto them that are with child, and to them that give suck in those days !

18 But pray ye that it come not to pass in the winter.

19 For those days shall be days of affliction, such as hath not been from the beginning of the creation which God created unto this time, and never shall be.

20 And if the Lord had not shortened the days, no flesh should have been saved : but for the elect's sake, whom he chose, he hath shortened the days.

21 And at that time, if any shall say unto you, Lo, here is Christ ; lo, there ; believe it not :

22 For false prophets shall arise, and shall work signs and wonders, to seduce, if it were possible, the elect.

23 But take ye heed : I have foretold you all things.

24 ¶ But in those days, after that tribulation, the sun shall be darkened, and the moon shall not give her light,

25 And the stars shall fall out of the heaven, and the powers that are in the heavens shall be shaken.

26 And then shall they see the Son of man coming in the clouds with great power and glory.

27 And then shall he send his angels, and shall gather together the elect from the four winds, from the uttermost part of the earth to the uttermost part of heaven.

28 But learn ye the parable from the fig-tree ; When now her branch becometh tender, and the leaves spring forth, it is known that summer is near :

29 So likewise ye, when ye shall see these things coming to pass, know that it is near, even at the doors.

30 Verily I say unto you, that this generation shall not pass away, till all these things be done.

31 Heaven and earth shall pass away : but my words shall not pass away.

32 ¶ But of that day or that hour knoweth none, no, not an angel in heaven, nor even the Son, but the Father.

33 Take ye heed, watch : for ye know not when the time is.

34 ¹[It is] as a man taking a journey, who left his house, and gave his authority to his servants, to every man his work, and commanded the porter to watch.

35 Watch ye therefore: for ye know not when the lord of the house cometh, at even, or at midnight, or at the cockcrowing, or in the morning:

36 Lest coming suddenly he find you sleeping.

37 But what I say unto you I say unto all, Watch.

CHAPTER XIV.

NOW after two days was the passover, and the feast of unleavened bread: and the chief priests and the scribes sought how they might take him by craft, and put him to death.

2 For they said, Not during the feast, lest there be an uproar of the people.

3 ¶ And while he was in Bethany in the house of Simon the leper, as he sat at meat, there came a woman having an alabaster box of ointment of ²spikenard very precious; and she brake the box, and poured it on his head.

4 But there were some that had indignation within themselves, saying, Why hath this waste of the ointment been made?

5 For this ointment might have been sold for more than three hundred pence, and have been given to the poor.

¹ *Not expressed in the original.*
² *Literally,* nard pistick: *the meaning of the latter word being quite obscure.*

And they murmured against her.

6 But Jesus said, Let her alone; why trouble ye her? she hath wrought a good work on me.

7 For ye have the poor always with you, and whensoever ye will ye may do them good: but me ye have not always.

8 She did what she could: she anointed my body beforehand for my burial.

9 But verily I say unto you, Wheresoever this gospel shall be preached throughout the whole world, this also that she hath done shall be spoken of, for a memorial of her.

10 ¶ And Judas Iscariot, ³one of the twelve, went unto the chief priests, that he might deliver him up unto them.

11 And when they heard it, they were glad, and promised to give him money. And he sought how he might conveniently deliver him up.

12 ¶ And the first day of unleavened bread, when they killed the passover, his disciples say unto him, Where wilt thou that we go and prepare that thou mayest eat the passover?

13 And he sendeth two of his disciples, and saith unto them, Go into the city, and there shall meet you a man bearing a pitcher of water: follow him.

14 And wheresoever he shall go in, say ye to the owner of the house, The Master saith, Where is my guestchamber,

³ *Literally,* that one; *i. e.* that notorious one.

where I shall eat the passover with my disciples?

15 And he will shew you a large upper room furnished and prepared: and there make ready for us.

16 And his disciples went forth, and came into the city, and found as he said unto them: and they made ready the passover.

17 And when it was evening, he cometh with the twelve.

18 And as they sat and did eat, Jesus said, Verily I say unto you, One of you shall ¹betray me, even he that eateth with me.

19 They began to be sorrowful, and to say unto him one by one, Is it I? and another, Is it I?

20 But he said unto them, It is one of the twelve, that dippeth with me in the dish.

21 For the Son of man indeed goeth his way, as it is written of him: but woe to that man by whom the Son of man is ²betrayed! it had been good for that man if he had not been born.

22 ¶ And as they were eating, he took bread, and blessed it, and brake it, and gave it to them, and said, Take ye it: this is my body.

23 And he took the cup, and gave thanks, and gave it to them: and they all drank of it.

24 And he said unto them, This is my blood of the covenant, which is shed for many.

25 Verily I say unto you, I

¹ Deliver me up.
² Delivered up.

will never drink more of the fruit of the vine, until that day when I drink it new in the kingdom of God.

26 ¶ And when they had sung the hymn, they went out into the mount of Olives.

27 And Jesus saith unto them, Ye shall all be offended, because it is written, I will smite the shepherd, and the sheep shall be scattered abroad.

28 But after I am risen, I will go before you into Galilee.

29 But Peter said unto him, Although all shall be offended, yet will not I.

30 And Jesus saith unto him, Verily I say unto thee, That thou, this day, even in this night, before the cock crow twice, shalt deny me thrice.

31 But he spake the more vehemently, If I should have to die with thee, I will in no wise deny thee. In like manner also said they all.

32 And they come to a place which was named Gethsemane: and he saith to his disciples, Sit ye here, while I shall pray.

33 And he taketh with him Peter and James and John, and began to be sore amazed, and to be very heavy;

34 And saith unto them, My soul is exceeding sorrowful unto death: tarry ye here, and watch.

35 And he went forward a little, and fell on the ground, and prayed that, if it were possible, the hour might pass from him.

36 And he said, Abba, Father, all things are possible unto thee; remove this cup from

me: but not what I will, but what thou wilt.

37 And he cometh, and findeth them sleeping, and saith unto Peter, Simon, sleepest thou? couldest not thou watch one hour?

38 Watch and pray, that ye enter not into temptation. The spirit indeed is willing, but the flesh is weak.

39 And again he went away, and prayed, saying the same words.

40 And when he came again, he found them asleep: for their eyes were heavy, neither wist they what to answer him.

41 And he cometh the third time, and saith unto them, Sleep on now, and take your rest: it is enough, the hour is come; behold, the Son of man is ¹betrayed into the hands of sinners.

42 Rise up, let us go; lo, he that ²betrayeth me is at hand.

43 And immediately, while he yet spake, cometh Judas Iscariot, one of the twelve, and with him a multitude with swords and staves, from the chief priests and the scribes and the elders.

44 And he that ³betrayed him had given them a token, saying, Whomsoever I shall kiss, that same is he; take him, and lead him away safely.

45 And as soon as he was come, he goeth straightway to him, and saith, Rabbi, Rabbi; and kissed him.

46 And they laid their hands on him, and took him.

47 But one of them that stood by drew his sword, and smote the servant of the high priest, and cut off his ear.

48 And Jesus answered and said unto them, Ye are come out, as against a thief, with swords and staves to take me.

49 I was daily with you in the temple teaching, and ye laid no hold on me: but the scriptures must be fulfilled.

50 And they all forsook him, and fled.

51 And there followed with him a certain young man, having a linen cloth cast about his naked body; and they lay hold on him:

52 And he left the linen cloth, and fled from them naked.

53 ¶ And they led Jesus away to the high priest: and there come together unto him all the chief priests and the elders and the scribes.

54 And Peter followed him afar off, even into the hall of the high priest: and he was sitting with the servants, and warming himself at the light ⁴[of the fire].

55 And the chief priests and all the council sought for witness against Jesus to put him to death; and found none.

56 For many bare false witness against him, but their witness agreed not together.

57 And there arose certain, and bare false witness against him, saying,

58 We heard him say, I will destroy this temple that is

¹ Delivered up.
² Delivereth me up.
³ Delivered him up.

⁴ *Not expressed in the original.*

made with hands, and within three days I will build another made without hands.

59 But neither so did their witness agree together.

60 And the high priest stood up in the midst, and asked Jesus, saying, Answerest thou not at all what it is which these witness against thee?

61 But he held his peace, and answered nothing. Again the high priest asked him, and saith unto him, Art thou the Christ, the Son of the Blessed?

62 Jesus said, I am: and ye shall see the Son of man sitting on the right hand of power, and coming with the clouds of heaven.

63 But the high priest rent his clothes, and saith, Why need we any further witnesses?

64 Ye heard his blasphemy: what think ye? And they all condemned him to be guilty of death.

65 And some began to spit on him, and to cover his face, and to smite him with their fists, and to say unto him, Prophesy: and the servants did strike him with the palms of their hands.

66 ¶ And as Peter was beneath in the hall, there cometh one of the maids of the high priest:

67 And seeing Peter warming himself, she looked upon him, and saith, And thou also wast with the Nazarene, with Jesus.

68 But he denied, saying, I know not, neither understand I what thou sayest. And he went out into the porch; and the cock crew.

69 And the maid seeing him, began to say to them that stood by, This is one of them.

70 But he denied it again. And a little after, they that stood by said again to Peter, Surely thou art one of them: for thou art also a Galilæan.

71 But he began to curse, and to swear, saying, I know not this man of whom ye speak.

72 And a second time the cock crew. And Peter called to mind the word that Jesus said unto him, Before the cock crow twice, thou shalt deny me thrice. And when he [1] thought thereon, he wept.

CHAPTER XV.

AND straightway in the morning the chief priests held a consultation with the elders and scribes, and also the whole council, and bound Jesus, and carried him away, and delivered him up to Pilate.

2 And Pilate asked him, Art thou the King of the Jews? And he answering said unto him, Thou sayest it.

3 And the chief priests accused him of many things.

4 And Pilate asked him again, saying, Answerest thou nothing? behold, of how many things they accuse thee.

5 But Jesus yet answered nothing; so that Pilate marvelled.

6 Now at every feast he released unto them one prisoner, whomsoever they desired.

[1] *The word thus rendered is of very uncertain signification. On the whole, the meaning here given is perhaps the best.*

7 And there was one named Barabbas, which lay bound with them that had made insurrection, who had committed murder in their insurrection.

8 And the multitude rising up began to desire him to do as he always did unto them.

9 But Pilate answered them, saying, Will ye that I release unto you the King of the Jews?

10 For he knew that for envy the chief priests had delivered him up.

11 But the chief priests moved the people, that he should rather release Barabbas unto them.

12 And Pilate answered and said again unto them, What will ye then that I shall do unto him whom ye call the King of the Jews?

13 And they cried out again, Crucify him.

14 But Pilate said unto them, Why, what evil hath he done? But they cried out the more, Crucify him.

15 And so Pilate, willing to content the multitude, released Barabbas unto them, and delivered Jesus, when he had scourged him, to be crucified.

16 And the soldiers led him away into the hall, which is the Prætorium; and they call together the whole band.

17 And they clothe him with purple, and plat a crown of thorns, and put it on him,

18 And began to salute him, Hail, King of the Jews!

19 And they smote him on the head with a reed, and did spit upon him, and bowing their knees worshipped him.

20 And when they had mocked him, they took off the purple from him, and put his own clothes on him, and led him out to crucify him.

21 And they compel one Simon a Cyrenian, who passed by, coming out of the country, the father of Alexander and Rufus, to bear his cross.

22 And they bring him unto the place Golgotha, which is, being interpreted, The place of a skull.

23 And they gave him wine mingled with myrrh: but he received it not.

24 And they crucify him, and part his garments among them, casting lots for them, what every man should take.

25 And it was the third hour, and they crucified him.

26 And the superscription of his accusation was written over, THE KING OF THE JEWS.

27 And with him they crucify two robbers; the one on his right hand, and the other on his left.

¹29 And they that passed by railed on him, wagging their heads, and saying, Ah, thou that destroyest the temple, and buildest it in three days,

30 Save thyself, and come down from the cross.

31 In like manner also the chief priests mocking him said among themselves with the scribes, He saved others; himself he cannot save,

¹ *Verse* 28 *is not found in any of the five most ancient MSS. It has probably been inserted from Luke* xxii. 37.

32 The Christ, the King of Israel. Let him now come down from the cross, that we may see and believe. And they that were crucified with him reviled him.

33 And when the sixth hour was come, there was darkness over the whole earth until the ninth hour.

34 And at the ninth hour Jesus cried with a loud voice, saying, Eloi, Eloi, lama sabachthani? which is, being interpreted, My God, my God, why hast thou forsaken me?

35 And some of them that stood by, when they heard it, said, Behold, he calleth Elijah.

36 And one ran and filled a spunge full of vinegar, and put it on a reed, and gave him to drink, saying, Let be; let us see whether Elijah will come to take him down.

37 And Jesus cried with a loud voice, and ¹gave up the ghost.

38 And the veil of the temple was rent in twain from the top to the bottom.

39 But when the centurion, which stood over against him, saw that he so ¹gave up the ghost, he said, Truly this man was the Son of God.

40 There were also women looking on afar off: among whom was Mary Magdalene, and Mary the mother of James the less and of Joses, and Salome;

41 Who also, when he was in Galilee, followed him, and ministered unto him; and many other women which came up with him unto Jerusalem.

42 ¶ And when the even was now come, because it was the preparation, which is the day before the sabbath,

43 Joseph of Arimathæa, an honourable counsellor, who was also himself waiting for the kingdom of God, came, and went in boldly unto Pilate, and begged the body of Jesus.

44 And Pilate marvelled if he were already dead: and calling unto him the centurion, he asked him whether he had been long dead.

45 And when he knew it of the centurion, he gave the corpse to Joseph.

46 And he bought fine linen, and took him down, and wrapped him in the linen, and laid him in a sepulchre which had been hewn out of a rock, and rolled a stone against the door of the sepulchre.

47 And Mary Magdalene and Mary the mother of Joses beheld where he was laid.

CHAPTER XVI.

AND when the sabbath was past, Mary Magdalene, and Mary the ²mother of James, and Salome, bought spices, that they might come and anoint him.

2 And very early in the morning of the first day of the week, they come unto the sepulchre after the rising of the sun.

3 And they said among themselves, Who shall roll us away

---

¹ *Literally*, expired: "breathed his last."

² *This word is not expressed in the original.*

the stone from the door of the sepulchre?

4 And looking up, they saw that the stone was rolled away: for it was very great.

5 And on entering into the sepulchre, they saw a young man sitting on the right side, clothed in a long white garment; and they were sore affrighted.

6 And he saith unto them, Be not affrighted: Ye seek Jesus of Nazareth, which hath been crucified: he is risen; he is not here: behold the place where they laid him.

7 But go your way, tell his disciples and Peter that he goeth before you into Galilee: there shall ye see him, as he said unto you.

8 And they went out, and fled from the sepulchre; for they trembled and were amazed: neither said they any thing to any; for they were afraid.

[1][9 ¶ Now when he was risen early the first day of the week, he appeared first to Mary Magdalene, out of whom he had cast seven devils.

10 She went and told it unto them that had been with him, as they mourned and wept.

11 And they, hearing that he was alive, and had been seen by her, believed not.

12 But after that he appeared in another form unto two of them, as they walked, and went into the country.

13 And they went and told it unto the rest: neither believed they them.

14 Afterward he appeared unto the eleven themselves, as they sat at meat, and upbraided them with their unbelief and hardness of heart, because they believed not them which had seen him after he was risen.

15 And he said unto them, Go ye into all the world, and preach the gospel to the whole creation.

16 He that believeth and is baptized shall be saved; but he that believeth not shall be condemned.

17 And these signs shall follow them that believe; In my name shall they cast out devils; they shall speak with new tongues;

18 They shall take up serpents; and if they drink any deadly thing, it shall not hurt them; they shall lay hands on the sick, and they shall recover.

19 ¶ So then after the Lord had spoken unto them, he was received up into heaven, and sat on the right hand of God.

20 And they went forth, and preached everywhere, the Lord working with them, and confirming the word by the signs that followed.]

---

[1] *The twelve verses which follow are wanting in our two oldest MSS., the Vatican and the Sinaitic; and the passage is stated by the early Fathers not to have existed in the majority of their MSS. Internal evidence also is against St. Mark having been the writer. On the other hand, many ancient MSS. do contain it, and it is cited by some of the primitive Fathers. It probably was an addition, placed here in very early times. Its sources of information are evidently independent of the three Gospels; and it has ever been regarded as possessing the same canonical authority with them.*

THE GOSPEL

ACCORDING TO

SAINT LUKE.

CHAPTER I.

FORASMUCH as many have taken in hand to set forth in order a declaration concerning those things which are surely believed among us,

2 Even as they delivered them unto us, which from the beginning were eyewitnesses, and ministers of the word ;

3 It seemed good to me also, having accurately traced down all things from the very first, to write unto thee in order, most excellent Theophilus,

4 That thou mightest know the certainty of those things, wherein thou wast instructed.

5 ¶ THERE was in the days of Herod, the king of Judæa, a certain priest named Zechariah, of the course of Abijah : and his wife was of the daughters of Aaron, and her name was Elisabeth.

6 And they were both righteous before God, walking in all the commandments and ordinances of the Lord blameless.

7 And they had no child, because Elisabeth was barren, and they both were now advanced [1] in years.

8 And it came to pass, that while he executed the priest's office before God in the order of his course,

9 According to the custom of the priest's office, his lot was to burn incense, going into the temple of the Lord.

10 And the whole multitude of the people were praying without at the time of incense.

11 And there appeared unto him an angel of the Lord standing on the right side of the altar of incense.

12 And when Zechariah saw him, he was troubled, and fear fell upon him.

13 But the angel said unto him, Fear not, Zechariah : for thy prayer is heard ; and thy wife Elisabeth shall bear thee a son, and thou shalt call his name John.

14 And thou shalt have joy and gladness ; and many shall rejoice at his birth.

15 For he shall be great in the sight of the Lord, and shall drink neither wine nor strong drink ; and he shall be filled with the Holy Spirit, even from his mother's womb.

16 And many of the children of Israel shall he turn to the Lord their God.

17 And he himself shall go before him in the spirit and power of Elijah, to turn the hearts of the fathers to the children, and the disobedient to the wisdom of the just ; to make ready a people prepared for the Lord.

18 And Zechariah said unto

---

[1] *Literally,* in their days.

the angel, Whereby shall I know this? for I am an old man, and my wife is advanced ¹ in years.

19 And the angel answering said unto him, I am Gabriel, that stand in the presence of God; and was sent to speak unto thee, and to shew thee these glad tidings.

20 And, behold, thou shalt be silent, and not able to speak, until the day that these things shall be performed, because thou believedst not my words, which shall be fulfilled in their season.

21 And the people were waiting for Zechariah, and marvelled that he tarried so long in the temple.

22 And when he came out, he could not speak unto them: and they perceived that he had seen a vision in the temple: and he beckoned unto them, and remained speechless.

23 And it came to pass, that, as soon as the days of his ministration were accomplished, he departed to his own house.

24 And after those days his wife Elisabeth conceived, and hid herself five months, saying,

25 Thus hath the Lord dealt with me in the days wherein he looked on me, to take away my reproach among men.

26 ¶ But in the sixth month the angel Gabriel was sent from God unto a city of Galilee, named Nazareth,

27 To a virgin espoused to a man whose name was Joseph, of the house of David; and the virgin's name was Mary.

28 And the angel came in unto her, and said, Hail, thou that art highly favoured, the Lord is with thee:

29 But she was troubled at his saying, and cast in her mind what manner of salutation this should be.

30 And the angel said unto her, Fear not, Mary: for thou hast found favour with God.

31 And, behold, thou shalt conceive in thy womb, and bring forth a son, and shalt call his name JESUS.

32 He shall be great, and shall be called the Son of the Highest: and the Lord God shall give unto him the throne of his father David:

33 And he shall reign over the house of Jacob for ever; and of his kingdom there shall be no end.

34 But Mary said unto the angel, How shall this be, seeing I know not a man?

35 And the angel answered and said unto her, The Holy Spirit shall come upon thee, and the power of the Highest shall overshadow thee: therefore also that holy thing which shall be born of thee shall be called the Son of God.

36 And, behold, thy kinswoman Elisabeth, she hath also conceived a son in her old age: and this is the sixth month with her, who is called barren.

37 For with God no word shall be impossible.

38 And Mary said, Behold the handmaid of the Lord; be it unto me according to thy word. And the angel departed from her.

---

¹ *Literally*, in her days.

39 ¶ And Mary arose in those days, and went into the hill country with haste, into ¹a city of Judah;

40 And entered into the house of Zechariah, and saluted Elisabeth.

41 And it came to pass, that, when Elisabeth heard the salutation of Mary, the babe leaped in her womb; and Elisabeth was filled with the Holy Spirit:

42 And she spake out with a great cry, and said, Blessed art thou among women, and blessed is the fruit of thy womb.

43 And whence is this to me, that the mother of my Lord should come to me?

44 For, lo, as soon as the voice of thy salutation sounded in mine ears, the babe leaped in my womb for joy.

45 And blessed is she that believed: for there shall be a performance of those things which were told her from the Lord.

46 And Mary said, My soul doth magnify the Lord,

47 And my spirit hath rejoiced in God my Saviour.

48 For he hath regarded the low estate of his handmaiden: for, behold, from henceforth all generations shall ²count me happy.

49 For he that is mighty hath done to me great things; and holy is his name.

50 And his mercy is ³on them that fear him from generation to generation.

51 He hath wrought strength with his arm; he hath scattered the proud in the imagination of their hearts.

52 He hath put down the mighty from their seats, and exalted them of low degree.

53 He hath filled the hungry with good things; and the rich he hath sent empty away.

54 He hath holpen his servant Israel, in remembrance of his mercy

55 To Abraham, and to his seed for ever, even as he spake unto our fathers.

56 And Mary abode with her about three months, and returned to her own house.

57 Now Elisabeth's full time came that she should be delivered; and she brought forth a son.

58 And her neighbours and her kinsmen heard how the Lord had magnified his mercy toward her; and they rejoiced with her.

59 And it came to pass, that on the eighth day they assembled to circumcise the child; and they were calling him Zechariah, after the name of his father.

60 And his mother answered and said, Not so; but he shall be called John.

61 And they said unto her, There is none of thy kindred that is called by this name.

62 And they made signs to his father how he would have him called.

¹ *Or*, the city of Judah (*Juttah: see Josh.* xxi. 11, 16).

² *See James* v. 11, *where the word is the same. There is no allusion to a* title *to be given to her, as is generally believed, owing to the rendering of the Authorized Version.*

³ *Literally*, on generations and generations to them that fear him.

63 And he asked for a writing table, and wrote, saying, His name is John. And they marvelled all.

64 And his mouth was opened immediately, and his tongue loosed, and he spake, and praised God.

65 And fear came on all that dwelt round about them: and all these sayings were noised abroad throughout all the hill country of Judæa.

66 And all they that heard them laid them up in their heart, saying, What manner of child shall this be! For the hand of the Lord was with him.

67 And his father Zechariah was filled with the Holy Spirit, and prophesied, saying,

68 Blessed be the Lord God of Israel; for he hath visited his people, and hath wrought redemption for them,

69 And hath raised up an horn of salvation for us in the house of his servant David;

70 As he spake by the mouth of his holy prophets, which have been since the world began:

71 Salvation from our enemies, and from the hand of all that hate us;

72 To perform mercy to our fathers, and to remember his holy covenant;

73 The oath which he sware to our father Abraham,

74 That he would grant unto us, that we being delivered out of the hand of our enemies might serve him without fear,

75 In holiness and righteousness before him, all our days.

76 And thou, child, shalt be called the prophet of the Highest: for thou shalt go before the face of the Lord to prepare his ways;

77 To give knowledge of salvation unto his people in the remission of their sins

78 Through the tender mercy of our God; whereby the dayspring from on high hath visited us,

79 To give light to them that sit in darkness and in the shadow of death, to guide our feet into the way of peace.

80 But the child grew, and waxed strong in spirit, and was in the deserts till the day of his shewing unto Israel.

CHAPTER II.

AND it came to pass in those days, that there went out a decree from Cæsar Augustus, that all the world should be enrolled.

2 This enrolling was first made when Cyrenius was governor of Syria.

3 And all went to be enrolled, every one into his own city.

4 And Joseph also went up from Galilee, out of the city of Nazareth, into Judæa, unto the city of David, which is called Bethlehem; because he was of the house and lineage of David:

5 To enroll himself with Mary his espoused, being great with child.

6 And so it was that, while they were there, the days were accomplished that she should be delivered.

7 And she brought forth her firstborn son, and wrapped him in swaddling clothes, and laid

him in a manger; because there was no room for them in the inn.

8 And there were in the same country shepherds abiding in the field, keeping watch over their flock by night.

9 And, lo, an angel of the Lord came upon them, and the glory of the Lord shone round about them: and they [1]were sore afraid.

10 And the angel said unto them, Fear not: for, behold, I bring you good tidings of great joy, which shall be to all the people.

11 For unto you is born this day in the city of David a Saviour, which is Christ the Lord.

12 And this shall be the sign unto you; Ye shall find a babe wrapped in swaddling clothes, and lying in a manger.

13 And suddenly there was with the angel a multitude of the heavenly host praising God, and saying,

14 Glory to God in the highest [2][heavens], and on earth peace [3]among men of good pleasure.

15 And it came to pass, when the angels went away from them into heaven, the shepherds said one to another, Let us now go even unto Bethlehem, and see this saying which is come to pass, which the Lord hath made known unto us.

16 And they came with haste, and found both Mary and Joseph, and the babe lying in the manger.

17 And when they had seen it, they made known the saying which was told them concerning this child.

18 And all they that heard it wondered at those things which were told them by the shepherds.

19 But Mary kept all these sayings, pondering them in her heart.

20 And the shepherds returned, glorifying and praising God for all the things that they had heard and seen, as it was told unto them.

21 And when eight days were accomplished for the circumcising of the child, his name was called JESUS, which was so named of the angel before he was conceived in the womb.

22 And when the days of their purification according to the law of Moses were accomplished, they brought him to Jerusalem, to present him to the Lord;

23 As it is written in the law of the Lord, Every male that openeth the womb shall be called holy to the Lord;

24 And to offer a sacrifice according to that which is said in the law of the Lord, A pair of turtledoves, or two young pigeons.

25 And, behold, there was a man in Jerusalem, whose name was Symeon; and this man was [4]righteous and devout, waiting for the consolation of Israel: and the Holy Spirit was upon him.

---

[1] *Literally*, feared with great fear.
[2] *Not expressed in the original.*
[3] *So all the earliest MSS.*
[4] See chap. i. 6

26 And it had been revealed unto him by the Holy Spirit, that he should not see death, before he had seen the Lord's Christ.

27 And he came in the Spirit into the temple: and when the parents had brought in the child Jesus, that they might do for him after the custom of the law,

28 Then took he him up in his arms, and blessed God, and said,

29 ¹Lord, now lettest thou thy servant depart in peace, according to thy word:

30 For mine eyes have seen thy salvation,

31 Which thou hast prepared before the face of all people;

32 A light to lighten the Gentiles, and the glory of thy people Israel.

33 And his father and his mother marvelled at those things which were spoken concerning him.

34 And Symeon blessed them, and said unto Mary his mother, Behold, he is set for the fall and rising again of many in Israel; and for a sign which shall be spoken against;

35 Yea, a sword shall pierce through thy own soul also: that the thoughts of many hearts may be revealed.

36 And there was one Anna, a prophetess, the daughter of Phanuel, of the tribe of Aser: she was ²of a great age, and had lived with an husband seven years from her virginity;

37 And she had been a widow about fourscore and four years, which departed not from the temple, serving God with fastings and prayers night and day.

38 And coming in at that instant, she gave thanks likewise unto God, and spake of him to all them that looked for ³redemption in Jerusalem.

39 And when they had performed all things that were according to the law of the Lord, they returned into Galilee, to their own city Nazareth.

40 But the child grew, and waxed strong, becoming filled with wisdom: and the grace of God was upon him.

41 And his parents went to Jerusalem every year at the feast of the passover.

42 And when he was twelve years old, they went up after the custom of the feast.

43 And when they had fulfilled the days, as they returned, the child Jesus tarried behind in Jerusalem; and his parents knew not of it.

44 But, supposing him to have been in the company, they went a day's journey, and sought him among their kinsfolk and acquaintance.

45 And when they found him not, they turned back again to Jerusalem, seeking him.

46 And it came to pass, that after three days they found him in the temple, sitting in the midst of the doctors, both hearing them, and asking them questions.

---

¹ *Literally*, Master.
² *Literally*, advanced in many days.
³ *Or*, the redemption of Jerusalem.

47 And all that heard him were astonished at his understanding and answers.
48 And when they saw him, they were exceedingly amazed: and his mother said unto him, Son, why hast thou thus dealt with us? behold, thy father and I have sought thee sorrowing.
49 And he said unto them, How is it that ye sought me? wist ye not that I must be among my Father's matters?
50 And they understood not the saying which he spake unto them.
51 And he went down with them, and came to Nazareth, and was subject unto them: and his mother kept all these sayings in her heart.
52 And Jesus increased in wisdom, as in age, and in favour with God and man.

CHAPTER III.

NOW in the fifteenth year of the reign of Tiberius Cæsar, Pontius Pilate being governor of Judæa, and Herod being tetrarch of Galilee, and his brother Philip tetrarch of Ituræa and of the region of Trachonitis, and Lysanias the tetrarch of Abilene,
2 In the high priesthood of Annas and Caiaphas, the word of God came unto John the son of Zechariah in the wilderness.
3 And he came into all the country about the Jordan, preaching the baptism of repentance for the remission of sins;
4 As it is written in the book of the words of Isaiah the prophet, The voice of one crying in the wilderness, Prepare ye the way of the Lord, make his paths straight.
5 Every valley shall be filled, and every mountain and hill shall be brought low; and the crooked shall be made straight, and the rough ways shall be made smooth;
6 And all flesh shall see the salvation of God.
7 He said therefore to the multitudes that came forth to be baptized of him, O brood of vipers, who hath warned you to flee from the wrath which is at hand?
8 Bring forth therefore fruits worthy of repentance, and begin not to say within yourselves, We have Abraham to our father: for I say unto you, That God is able of these stones to raise up children unto Abraham.
9 And now also the axe is laid unto the root of the trees: every tree therefore which bringeth not forth good fruit is hewn down, and cast into the fire.
10 And the multitudes asked him, saying, What must we do then?
11 He answered and said unto them, He that hath two coats, let him impart to him that hath none; and he that hath food, let him do likewise.
12 There came also publicans to be baptized, and said unto him, ¹Master, what must we do?

- *Literally*, Teacher.

13 And he said unto them, Exact no more than that which is appointed you.

14 And soldiers likewise demanded of him, saying, And what must we do? And he said unto them, Do violence to no man, neither accuse any falsely; and be content with your wages.

15 And as the people were in expectation, and all mused in their hearts concerning John, whether he were the Christ;

16 John answered, saying unto them all, I indeed baptize you with water; but he that is stronger than I cometh, the latchet of whose shoes I am not worthy to unloose: he shall baptize you with the Holy Spirit and with fire:

17 Whose fan is in his hand, and he will throughly purge his floor, and will gather the wheat into his garner; but he will burn up the chaff with unquenchable fire.

18 And many other things in his exhortation ¹preached he unto the people.

19 But Herod the tetrarch, being reproved by him concerning Herodias his brother's wife, and concerning all the evils which Herod had done,

20 Added yet this to all, and shut up John in prison.

21 Now when all the people were baptized, it came to pass, that Jesus also having been baptized, and praying, the heaven was opened,

22 And the Holy Spirit descended in a bodily shape like a dove upon him, and a voice came from heaven, Thou art my beloved Son; in thee I am well pleased.

23 And Jesus himself was about thirty years of age when he began ²[his course], being, as was supposed, the son of Joseph, which was the son of Heli,

24 Which was the son of Matthat, which was the son of Levi, which was the son of Melchi, which was the son of Jannai, which was the son of Joseph,

25 Which was the son of Mattathias, which was the son of Amos, which was the son of Nahum, which was the son of Esli, which was the son of Naggæ,

26 Which was the son of Maath, which was the son of Mattathias, which was the son of Semein, which was the son of Josech, which was the son of Joda,

27 Which was the son of Joanan, which was the son of Rhesa, which was the son of Zorobabel, which was the son of Salathiel, which was the son of Neri,

28 Which was the son of Melchi, which was the son of Addi, which was the son of Cosam, which was the son of Elmodam, which was the son of Er,

29 Which was the son of Jesus, which was the son of Eliezer, which was the son of Jorim, which was the son of Maththat, which was the son of Levi,

¹ *Literally*, evangelized.   ² *Not expressed in the original.*

30 Which was the son of Simeon, which was the son of Juda, which was the son of Joseph, which was the son of Jonam, which was the son of Eliakim,

31 Which was the son of Melea, which was the son of Mennas, which was the son of Mattatha, which was the son of Nathan, which was the son of David,

32 Which was the son of Jesse, which was the son of Obed, which was the son of Boaz, which was the son of Salmon, which was the son of Naasson,

33 Which was the son of Aminadab, which was the son of Admin, which was the son of Arni, which was the son of Esrom, which was the son of Phares, which was the son of Judah,

34 Which was the son of Jacob, which was the son of Isaac, which was the son of Abraham, which was the son of Thara, which was the son of Nachor,

35 Which was the son of Saruch, which was the son of Ragau, which was the son of Phalec, which was the son of Heber, which was the son of Sala,

36 Which was the son of Cainam, which was the son of Arphaxad, which was the son of Sem, which was the son of Noe, which was the son of Lamech,

37 Which was the son of Mathusala, which was the son of Enoch, which was the son of Jared, which was the son of Maleleel, which was the son of Cainan,

38 Which was the son of Enos, which was the son of Seth, which was the son of Adam, which was the Son of God.

CHAPTER IV.

AND Jesus being full of the Holy Spirit returned from Jordan, and was led in the Spirit into the wilderness,

2 Being forty days tempted by the devil. And in those days he did eat nothing: and when they were ended, he hungered.

3 And the devil said unto him, If thou art the Son of God, command this stone that it be made bread.

4 And Jesus answered him, It is written, that man shall not live upon bread alone.

5 And, taking him up, he shewed unto him all the kingdoms of the world in a moment of time.

6 And the devil said unto him, All this power will I give thee, and the glory of them: for that is delivered unto me; and to whomsoever I will I give it.

7 If then thou wilt worship before me, it shall all be thine.

8 And Jesus answered and said unto him, It is written, Thou shalt worship the Lord thy God, and him only shalt thou serve.

9 And he brought him to Jerusalem, and set him on the cornice of the temple, and said unto him, If thou art the Son of God, cast thyself down from hence:

10 For it is written, He shall give his angels charge over thee, to keep thee:

11 And in their hands they shall bear thee up, lest at any time thou dash thy foot against a stone.

12 And Jesus answering said unto him, It is said, Thou shalt not tempt the Lord thy God.

13 And when the devil had ended all the temptation, he departed from him for a season.

14 ¶ And Jesus returned in the power of the Spirit into Galilee : and there went out a fame of him through all the region round about.

15 And he taught in their synagogues, being glorified of all.

16 ¶ And he came to Nazareth, where he had been brought up : and, as his custom was, he went into the synagogue on the sabbath day, and stood up to read.

17 And there was delivered unto him the roll of the prophet Isaiah. And when he had unfolded the roll, he found the place where it was written,

18 The Spirit of the Lord is upon me, because he anointed me to preach the gospel to the poor ; he hath sent me to proclaim deliverance to the captives, and recovering of sight to the blind, to set at liberty them that are bruised,

19 To proclaim the acceptable year of the Lord.

20 And he folded up the roll, and gave it again to the minister, and sat down. And the eyes of all them that were in the synagogue were fastened on him.

21 And he began to say unto them, This day is this scripture fulfilled in your ears.

22 And all bare him witness, and wondered at the gracious words which proceeded out of his mouth, and said, Is not this Joseph's son ?

23 And he said unto them, Ye will surely say unto me this proverb, Physician, heal thyself : whatsoever we have heard done in Capernaum, do also here in thy country.

24 And he said, Verily I say unto you, No prophet is acceptable in his own country.

25 But I tell you of a truth, many widows were in Israel in the days of Elijah, when the heaven was shut up three years and six months, when great famine was over all the earth ;

26 And unto none of them was Elijah sent, save unto Sarepta, a city of Sidon, unto a woman that was a widow.

27 And many lepers were in Israel in the time of Elisha the prophet ; and none of them was cleansed, saving Naaman the Syrian.

28 And all they in the synagogue, when they heard these things, were filled with wrath,

29 And rose up, and thrust him out of the city, and led him unto the brow of the hill whereon their city was built, that they might cast him down headlong.

30 But he passing through the midst of them went his way,

31 And came down to Capernaum, a city of Galilee, and taught them on the sabbath days.

32 And they were exceeding-

ly astonished at his teaching: for his word was with power.

33 ¶ And in the synagogue there was a man, which had a spirit of an unclean devil, and cried out with a loud voice,

34 Let us alone; what have we to do with thee, Jesus of Nazareth? thou art come to destroy us: I know thee who thou art; the Holy One of God.

35 And Jesus rebuked him, saying, Hold thy peace, and come out of him. And the devil, throwing him in the midst, came out of him, and hurt him not.

36 And they were all amazed, and spake among themselves, saying, What word is this, seeing that with authority and power he commandeth the unclean spirits, and they come out?

37 And the fame of him went out into every place of the country round about.

38 ¶ And he arose out of the synagogue, and entered into Simon's house. And Simon's wife's mother was suffering with a great fever; and they besought him for her.

39 And he stood over her, and rebuked the fever; and it left her: and immediately she arose and ministered unto them.

40 ¶ Now when the sun was setting, all they that had any sick with divers diseases brought them unto him; and he laid his hands on every one of them, and healed them.

41 And devils also came out of many, crying out, and saying, Thou art the Son of God. And he rebuking them suffered them not to speak, because they knew that he was the Christ.

42 But when it was day, he departed and went into a desert place: and the multitude sought him diligently, and overtook him, and stayed him, that he should not depart from them.

43 But he said unto them, I must preach the kingdom of God to the rest of the cities also: for therefore was I sent.

44 And he preached in the synagogues of [1]Judæa.

CHAPTER V.

AND it came to pass, that, as the multitude pressed upon him, and were hearing the word of God, he stood by the lake of Gennesaret,

2 And saw two boats standing by the lake: but the fishermen were gone out of them, and were washing their nets.

3 And he entered into one of the boats, which was Simon's, and prayed him that he would thrust out a little from the land. And he sat down, and taught the multitudes out of the boat.

4 And when he had ceased speaking, he said unto Simon, Launch out into the deep, and let down your nets for a draught.

5 And Simon answering said unto him, Master, we have toiled all the night, and have taken nothing: nevertheless at thy word I will let down the net.

6 And when they had this done, they inclosed a great multitude of fishes: and their nets were breaking.

---

[1] *So the great majority of the ancient MSS.* Judæa *was probably altered into* Galilee, *because of the variation from Mark* i. 39.

7 And they beckoned unto their partners in the other boat, that they should come and help them. And they came, and filled both the boats, so that they began to sink.

8 When Simon Peter saw it, he fell down at Jesus' knees, saying, Depart from me; for I am a sinful man, O Lord.

9 For he was astonished, and all that were with him, at the draught of the fishes which they had taken:

10 And so was also James, and John, the sons of Zebedee, which were partners with Simon. And Jesus said unto Simon, Fear not; from henceforth thou shalt catch men.

11 And when they had brought their boats to land, they forsook all, and followed him.

12 ¶ And it came to pass, when he was in a certain city, behold a man full of leprosy: who seeing Jesus fell on his face, and besought him, saying, Lord, If thou wilt, thou canst make me clean.

13 And he put forth his hand, and touched him, saying, I will: be thou clean. And immediately the leprosy departed from him.

14 And he charged him to tell no man: but go shew thyself to the priest, and offer for thy cleansing, according as Moses commanded, for a testimony unto them.

15 But so much the more went there the fame abroad concerning him: and great multitudes came together to hear, and to be healed of their infirmities.

16 And he withdrew himself into the wilderness, and prayed.

17 ¶ And it came to pass on a certain day, as he was teaching, that there were Pharisees and doctors of the law sitting by, which were come out of every town of Galilee, and Judæa, and Jerusalem: and the power of ¹the Lord wrought in him to heal.

18 And, behold, men brought on a bed a man which was taken with a palsy: and they sought means to bring him in, and to lay him before him.

19 And when they could not find by what way they might bring him in because of the multitude, they went upon the housetop, and let him down through the tiling with his couch into the midst before Jesus.

20 And seeing their faith, he said unto him, Man, thy sins are forgiven thee.

21 And the scribes and the Pharisees began to reason, saying, Who is this which speaketh blasphemies? Who can forgive sins, but God alone?

22 But Jesus fully knowing their reasonings answered and said unto them, What reason ye in your hearts?

23 Which is easier, to say, Thy sins are forgiven thee; or to say, Arise and walk?

24 But that ye may know that the Son of man hath power on earth to forgive sins, (he said unto the sick of the palsy,) I say unto thee, Arise, and take up thy couch, and go unto thine house.

¹ *i.e.* of God: of Jehovah.

25 And immediately he rose up before them, and took up that whereon he lay, and departed to his house, glorifying God.

26 And they were all amazed, and they glorified God, and were filled with fear, saying, We have seen strange things to day.

27 ¶ And after these things he went forth, and beheld a publican, named Levi, sitting at the receipt of custom: and said unto him, Follow me.

28 And he left all, rose up, and followed him.

29 And Levi made him a great feast in his house: and there was a great multitude of publicans and of others that sat down with them.

30 And their Pharisees and scribes murmured against his disciples, saying, Why do ye eat and drink with the publicans?

31 And Jesus answering said unto them, They that are whole need not a physician; but they that are sick.

32 I came not to call righteous men, but sinners to repentance.

33 But they said unto him, The disciples of John fast often, and make prayers, and likewise the disciples of the Pharisees; but thine eat and drink.

34 And he said unto them, Can ye make the sons of the bridechamber fast, while the bridegroom is with them?

35 But the days will come, when the bridegroom shall be taken away from them: then will they fast in those days.

36 And he spake also a parable unto them; No one cutteth a piece from a new garment and putteth it upon an old garment; else he both will rend the new, and the piece that was taken out of the new will not agree with the old.

37 And no one putteth new wine into old skins; else the new wine will burst the skins, and it will be spilled, and the skins will perish.

38 But new wine must be put into new skins.

39 No one also having drunk old wine desireth new: for he saith, The old is good.

CHAPTER VI.

AND it came to pass on a [¹second-first] sabbath, that he went through the cornfields; and his disciples plucked the ears of corn, and did eat, rubbing them in their hands.

2 But certain of the Pharisees said, Why do ye that which is not lawful to do on the sabbath day?

3 And Jesus answering them said, Did ye never read so much as this, what David did, when he himself was hungry, and they which were with him;

4 How he entered into the house of God, and did take and eat the shewbread, and gave to them that were with him; which it is not lawful to eat but for the priests alone?

¹ *This word is not found in several of the oldest MSS. and versions. No one knows what it means: but it cannot have the sense given in the Authorized Version. Chrysostom explains it, a sabbath which was also a feast day.*

5 And he said unto them, that the Son of man is Lord also of the sabbath.

6 And it came to pass also on another sabbath, that he entered into the synagogue and taught: and there was a man there, whose right hand was withered.

7 And the scribes and the Pharisees watched him, whether he would heal on the sabbath day; that they might find an accusation against him.

8 But he knew their thoughts, and said to the man which had the withered hand, Rise up, and stand forth in the midst. And he arose and stood forth.

9 And Jesus said unto them, I ask you whether it is lawful on the sabbath days to do good, or to do evil? to save life, or to destroy it?

10 And looking round about upon them all, he said unto him, Stretch forth thy hand. And he did so: and his hand was restored.

11 But they were filled with madness; and communed one with another what they should do to Jesus.

12 ¶ And it came to pass in those days, that he went out into the mountain to pray, and continued all night in prayer to God.

13 And when it was day, he called unto him his disciples: and of them he chose twelve, whom also he named apostles;

14 Simon whom he also named Peter, and Andrew his brother, and James and John, and Philip and Bartholomew,

15 And Matthew and Thomas, and James [1]the son of Alphæus, and Simon called Zelotes,

16 And Judas [2]the brother of James, and Judas Iscariot, who was the traitor.

17 ¶ And he came down with them, and stood on a level place, and a multitude of his disciples, and a great assemblage of the people out of all Judæa and Jerusalem, and the sea coast of Tyre and Sidon, who came to hear him, and to be healed of their diseases;

18 And they that were vexed with unclean spirits were healed.

19 And the whole multitude sought to touch him: for there went power out of him, and healed them all.

20 ¶ And he lifted up his eyes on his disciples, and said, Blessed are ye poor: for yours is the kingdom of God.

21 Blessed are ye that hunger now: for ye shall be filled. Blessed are ye that weep now: for ye shall laugh.

22 Blessed are ye, when men shall hate you, and when they shall separate you from their company, and shall reproach you, and cast out your name as evil, for the Son of man's sake.

23 Rejoice ye in that day, and leap for joy: for, behold, your [3]reward is great in heaven: for after the same manner did their fathers unto the prophets.

[1] The son *is not expressed in the original*.
[2] The brother *is not expressed in the Greek*.
[3] *Or*, wages.

24 But woe unto you that are rich: for ye have received your consolation.

25 Woe unto you that are full now: for ye shall hunger. Woe unto you that laugh now: for ye shall mourn and weep.

26 Woe unto you, when all men shall speak well of you: for after the same manner did their fathers to the false prophets.

27 ¶ But I say unto you which hear, Love your enemies, do good to them which hate you,

28 Bless them that curse you, and pray for them which despitefully use you.

29 And unto him that smiteth thee on the cheek offer also the other; and from him that taketh away thy cloke withhold not thy coat also.

30 Give to every one that asketh of thee; and of him that taketh away thy goods ask them not again.

31 And as ye would that men should do to you, do ye also to them likewise.

32 Moreover, if ye love them which love you, what thank have ye? for sinners also love those that love them.

33 And if ye do good to them which do good to you, what thank have ye? for sinners also do even the same.

34 And if ye lend to them of whom ye hope to receive, what thank have ye? for sinners also lend to sinners, to receive as much again.

35 But love ye your enemies, and do good, and lend, hoping for nothing again; and your [1]reward shall be great, and ye shall be the sons of the Highest: for he is kind unto the unthankful and to the evil.

36 Be ye merciful, even as your Father also is merciful.

37 And judge not, and ye shall not be judged: condemn not, and ye shall not be condemned: forgive, and ye shall be forgiven:

38 Give, and it shall be given unto you; good measure, pressed down, and shaken together, and running over, shall [2]they give into your bosom. For with the same measure that ye mete, it shall be measured to you again.

39 And he spake also a parable unto them, Can a blind man lead a blind man? shall they not both fall into the ditch?

40 The disciple is not above his teacher: but every disciple, when perfected, shall be as his teacher.

41 But why beholdest thou the mote that is in thy brother's eye, but considerest not the beam that is in thine own eye?

42 How canst thou say to thy brother, Brother, let me pull out the mote that is in thine eye, when thou thyself beholdest not the beam that is in thine own eye? Thou hypocrite, pull out first the beam out of thine own eye, and then shalt thou see clearly to pull

[1] *Or*, wages.
[2] Men, *which is supplied in the Authorized Version, tends to mislead. It is not of this world's reward, but of that hereafter, that the Lord is speaking.*

out the mote that is in thy brother's eye.

43 For a good tree bringeth not forth corrupt fruit; neither again doth a corrupt tree bring forth good fruit.

44 For every tree is known by his own fruit. For of thorns men do not gather figs, nor of bramble bush gather they grapes.

45 The good man out of the good treasure of his heart bringeth forth that which is good; and the evil man out of the evil treasure bringeth forth that which is evil: for out of the abundance of the heart his mouth speaketh.

46 ¶ But why call ye me, Lord, Lord, and do not the things which I say?

47 Every one that cometh to me, and heareth my sayings, and doeth them, I will shew you to whom he is like:

48 He is like a man building an house, who digged, and deepened, and laid a foundation on the rock: and when a flood came, the stream beat vehemently upon that house, and could not shake it, because it was well built.

49 But he that heard, and did not, is like a man that without a foundation built an house upon the earth; against which the stream did beat vehemently, and immediately it fell; and the ruin of that house was great.

CHAPTER VII.

NOW when he had ended all his sayings in the audience of the people, he entered into Capernaum.

2 And a certain centurion's servant, who was dear unto him, was sick, and ready to die.

3 And hearing of Jesus, he sent unto him elders of the Jews, beseeching him that he would come and save his servant.

4 And coming to Jesus, they besought him earnestly, saying, That he was worthy for whom he should do this:

5 For he loveth our nation, and at his own expense built us our synagogue.

6 So Jesus went with them. And when he was now not far from the house, the centurion sent friends to him, saying unto him, Lord, trouble not thyself: for I am not worthy that thou shouldest enter under my roof:

7 Wherefore neither thought I myself worthy to come unto thee: but say in a word, and let my servant be healed.

8 For I also am a man set under authority, having under me soldiers, and I say unto one, Go, and he goeth; and to another, Come, and he cometh; and to my servant, Do this, and he doeth it.

9 And Jesus hearing these things marvelled at him, and turned him about, and said unto the multitude that followed him, I say unto you, I have not found so great faith, no, not in Israel.

10 And they that were sent, returning to the house, found the servant whole [1][that had been sick].

11 ¶ And it came to pass

[1] *These words are omitted by some of the oldest MSS.*

afterwards, that he was journeying to a city called Nain; and many of his disciples were journeying with him, and a great multitude.

12 But when he came nigh to the gate of the city, behold, there was a dead man carried out, the only son of his mother, and she was a widow: and much people of the city was with her.

13 And the Lord seeing her had compassion on her, and said unto her, Weep not.

14 And he came and touched the bier: and they that bare it stood still. And he said, Young man, I say unto thee, Arise.

15 And the dead man sat up, and began to speak. And he delivered him to his mother.

16 And there came a fear on all: and they glorified God, saying, That a great prophet is risen up among us; and, That God hath visited his people.

17 And this rumour of him went forth throughout all Judæa, and throughout all the region round about.

18 ¶ And the disciples of John told him of all these things.

19 And calling unto him two of his disciples, John sent them to the Lord, saying, Art thou he that should come? or do we look for another?

20 When the men were come unto him, they said, John the Baptist hath sent us unto thee, saying, Art thou he that should come? or do we look for another?

21 In that same hour he cured many of diseases and plagues, and of evil spirits; and unto many that were blind he gave sight.

22 And he answered and said unto them, Go and tell John what things ye saw and heard; how that the blind see, the lame walk, the lepers are cleansed, the deaf hear, the dead are raised, and the poor have [1]the gospel preached unto them,

23 And blessed is he, whosoever shall not be offended in me.

24 ¶ And when the messengers of John were departed, he began to say unto the multitudes concerning John, What went ye out into the wilderness to gaze upon? A reed shaken with the wind?

25 But what went ye out to see? A man clothed in soft garments? Behold, they which are gorgeously apparelled, and live delicately, are in kings' courts.

26 But what went ye out for to see? A prophet? Yea, I say unto you, and much more than a prophet.

27 This is he, of whom it is written, Behold, I send my messenger before thy face, which shall prepare thy way before thee.

28 I say unto you, Among those that are born of women there is not a greater [2][prophet] than John: but he that is least in the kingdom of God is greater than he.

[1] *Literally*, the good tidings announced to them.
[2] *Omitted by several ancient MSS.*

29 (And all the people, when they heard it, and the publicans, justified God, having been baptized with the baptism of John.

30 But the Pharisees and the lawyers rejected the counsel of God against themselves, not having been baptized of him.)

31 Whereunto then shall I liken the men of this generation? and to what are they like?

32 They are like unto children which sit in the marketplace, and call one to another, saying, We piped unto you, and ye danced not; we mourned to you, and ye wept not.

33 For John the Baptist is come neither eating bread nor drinking wine; and ye say, He hath a devil.

34 The Son of man is come eating and drinking; and ye say, Behold a gluttonous man, and a winebibber, a friend of publicans and sinners.

35 And yet wisdom was justified at the hands of all her children.

36 ¶ And one of the Pharisees desired him that he would eat with him. And he went into the Pharisee's house, and sat down to meat.

37 And, behold, a woman which was in the city, a sinner, when she knew that he sat at meat in the Pharisee's house, brought an alabaster box of ointment,

38 And stood at his feet behind him weeping, and began to wash his feet with the tears, and did wipe them with the hairs of her head, and kissed his feet, and anointed them with the ointment.

39 Now when the Pharisee which had bidden him saw it, he spake within himself, saying, This man, if he were a prophet, would have known who and what manner of woman this is that toucheth him: for she is a sinner.

40 And Jesus answering said unto him, Simon, I have somewhat to say unto thee. And he saith, Master, say on.

41 There were two debtors to a certain creditor: the one owed five hundred pence, and the other fifty.

42 And when they had nothing to pay, he frankly forgave them both. Tell me therefore, which of them will love him most?

43 Simon answered and said, I suppose, he to whom he forgave most. And he said unto him, Thou hast rightly judged.

44 And he turned to the woman, and said unto Simon, Seest thou this woman? I entered into thine house, thou gavest me no water for my feet: but she hath washed my feet with her tears, and wiped them with her hair.

45 Thou gavest me no kiss: but she since the time I came in hath not ceased to kiss my feet.

46 My head with oil thou didst not anoint: but this woman hath anointed my feet with ointment.

47 Wherefore, I say unto thee, her sins, which are many, are forgiven; for she loved

much: but to whom little is forgiven, the same loveth little.

48 And he said unto her, Thy sins are forgiven.

49 And they that sat at meat with him began to say within themselves, Who is this that forgiveth sins also?

50 And he said to the woman, Thy faith hath saved thee; go in peace.

CHAPTER VIII.

AND it came to pass afterward, that he went throughout every city and village, preaching and announcing the glad tidings of the kingdom of God: and the twelve with him,

2 And certain women, which had been healed of evil spirits and infirmities, Mary called Magdalene, out of whom had gone seven devils,

3 And Joanna the wife of Chuza Herod's steward, and Susanna, and many others, which ministered unto them of their substance.

4 ¶ And when much people were gathering together, and were coming to him out of every city, he spake by a parable:

5 A sower went out to sow his seed: and as he sowed, some fell by the way side; and it was trodden down, and the birds of the air devoured it up.

6 And other fell upon the rock; and sprang up and withered away, because it lacked moisture.

7 And other fell among the thorns; and the thorns sprang up with it, and choked it.

8 And other fell on the good ground, and sprang up, and bare fruit an hundredfold. As he said these things, he cried, He that hath ears to hear, let him hear.

9 But his disciples asked him, saying, What might this parable be?

10 And he said, Unto you it is given to know the mysteries of the kingdom of God: but to the rest in parables; that seeing they may not see, and hearing they may not understand.

11 Now the parable is this: The seed is the word of God.

12 Those by the way side are they that hear; then cometh the devil, and taketh away the word from their heart, lest they should believe and be saved.

13 They on the rock are they, which, when they have heard, receive the word with joy; and these have no root, which for a while believe, and in time of temptation fall away.

14 And that which fell among the thorns, these are they, which have heard, and go forth, and are choked with cares and riches and pleasures of life, and bring no fruit to perfection.

15 But that on the good ground, these are they, which in an honest and good heart, having heard the word, ¹retain it, and bring forth fruit with patience.

16 ¶ But no man, when he hath lighted a candle, covereth

---

1 "Keep" *gives the idea of* "observe:" *whereas the word means,* "hold it, do not let it go."

it with a vessel, or putteth it under a bed; but setteth it on a candlestick, that they which enter in may see the light.

17 For nothing is secret, that shall not be made manifest; neither any thing hid, that shall not be known and come abroad.

18 Take heed therefore how ye hear: for whosoever hath, to him shall be given; and whosoever hath not, from him shall be taken even that which he seemeth to have.

19 ¶ And his mother and his brethren came to him, and could not come at him for the crowd.

20 And it was told him by certain which said, Thy mother and thy brethren stand without, desiring to see thee.

21 But he answered and said unto them, My mother and my brethren are these which hear the word of God, and do it.

22 ¶ Now it came to pass on a certain day, that he himself, and his disciples, went into a ship: and he said unto them, Let us go over unto the other side of the lake. And they launched forth.

23 But as they sailed he fell asleep: and there came down a storm of wind on the lake; and they were filling with water, and were in jeopardy.

24 And they came to him, and awoke him, saying, Master, master, we perish. But he, being awakened, rebuked the wind and the raging of the water: and they ceased, and there was a calm.

25 And he said unto them, Where is your faith? But they being afraid wondered, saying one to another, Who then is this, that he commandeth even the winds and the water, and they obey him!

26 ¶ And they arrived at the country of the Gerasenes, which is over against Galilee.

27 And when he went forth to land, there met him a certain man of the city, which had devils long time, and ware no clothes, neither abode in any house, but in the tombs.

28 And seeing Jesus, he cried out, and fell down before him, and with a loud voice said, What have I to do with thee, Jesus, Son of God most high? I beseech thee, torment me not.

29 For he was commanding the unclean spirit to come out of the man. For oftentimes it had seized him: and he was kept bound with chains and in fetters; and he brake the bands, and was driven by the devil into the deserts.

30 And Jesus asked him, saying, What is thy name? And he said, Legion: because many devils were entered into him.

31 And they besought him that he would not command them to go away into the [1]abyss.

32 And there was there an herd of many swine feeding on the mountain: and they besought him that he would suffer them to enter into them. And he suffered them.

[1] *i.e. of hell. See Rev.* ix. 1, 2, 11; xi. 7; xvii. 8; xx. 1, 3, *where the Greek word is the same*

33 And the devils went out of the man, and entered into the swine: and the herd ran violently down the cliff into the lake, and were drowned.

34 When they that fed them saw what was done, they fled, and told it in the city and in the country.

35 So they went out to see what was done; and came to Jesus, and found the man, out of whom the devils were departed, sitting at the feet of Jesus, clothed, and in his right mind: and they were afraid.

36 They also which saw it told them by what means he that was possessed of the devils was healed.

37 Then the whole multitude of the country of the Gerasenes round about besought him to depart from them; for they were taken with great fear: and he entered into a ship, and returned back again.

38 And the man out of whom the devils were departed besought him that he might be with him: but Jesus sent him away, saying,

39 Return to thine house, and tell how great things God hath done unto thee. And he departed, publishing throughout the whole city how great things Jesus had done unto him.

40 ¶ And it came to pass that, when Jesus was returned, the multitude gladly received him: for they were all waiting for him.

41 And, behold, there came a man named [1]Jairus, and he was ruler of the synagogue: and he fell down at Jesus' feet, and besought him that he would come into his house:

42 For he had one only daughter, about twelve years of age, and she was dying. And it came to pass that, as he went, the multitudes thronged him.

43 And a woman having an issue of blood twelve years, which had spent all her living upon physicians, neither could be healed by any,

44 Came behind him, and touched the border of his garment: and immediately her issue of blood stanched.

45 And Jesus said, Who touched me? When all denied, Peter and they that were with him said, Master, the multitudes throng thee and press thee, and sayest thou, Who touched me?

46 But Jesus said, Somebody touched me: for I perceive that power is gone forth from me.

47 And the woman, seeing that she was not hid, came trembling, and falling down before him, she declared unto him before all the people for what cause she touched him, and how she was healed immediately.

48 And he said unto her, Daughter, thy faith hath [2]made thee whole; go in peace.

49 While he yet spake, there cometh one from the ruler of the synagogue's house, saying to him, Thy daughter is dead; trouble not the Master.

---

[1] *Pronounce*, Ja-ĭrus.

[2] *Literally*, saved thee.

50 But Jesus, hearing it, answered him, saying, Be not afraid: believe only, and she shall be ¹made whole.

51 And when he came into the house, he suffered no man to go in with him, save Peter, and John, and James, and the father and the mother of the maiden.

52 And all wept, and bewailed her: but he said, Weep not; she is not dead, but sleepeth.

53 And they laughed him to scorn, knowing that she was dead.

54 And he took her by the hand, and called, saying, Maid, arise.

55 And her spirit came again, and she arose straightway: and he commanded to give her to eat.

56 And her parents were astonished: but he charged them that they should tell no one what was done.

CHAPTER IX.

AND he called his twelve disciples together, and gave them power and authority over all devils, and to cure diseases.

2 And he sent them to preach the kingdom of God, and to heal.

3 And he said unto them, Take nothing for your journey, neither staff, nor scrip, neither bread, neither money; neither have two coats apiece.

4 And into whatsoever house ye shall enter, there abide, and thence go forth.

¹ *Literally*, saved.

5 And whosoever receive you not, when ye go out of that city, shake off the dust from your feet for a testimony against them.

6 And they went forth, and journeyed through the towns, preaching the gospel, and healing every where.

7 ¶ Now Herod the tetrarch heard of all that was doing: and he was perplexed, because it was said by some, John was risen from the dead;

8 And by some, that Elijah had appeared; and by others, that one of the old prophets was risen again.

9 And Herod said, John I beheaded: but who is this, of whom I hear such things? And he sought to see him.

10 ¶ And the apostles returned and told him all that they had done. And he took them, and went aside privately to the city called Bethsaida.

11 But the multitudes knew it, and followed him: and he received them, and spake unto them of the kingdom of God, and healed them that had need of healing.

12 And the day began to decline: and the twelve came, and said unto him, Send the multitude away, that they may go into the villages and country round about, and lodge, and get victuals: for we are here in a desert place.

13 But he said unto them, Give ye them to eat. But they said, We have no more than five loaves and two fishes; except we should go and buy food for all this people.

14 For they were about five thousand men. And he said to his disciples, Make them sit down by companies of about fifty each.

15 And they did so, and made them all sit down.

16 But he took the five loaves and the two fishes, and looking up to heaven, he blessed them, and brake, and gave to the disciples to set before the multitude.

17 And they did eat, and were all filled: and there was taken up that which remained to them, twelve baskets of fragments.

18 ¶ And it came to pass, as he was alone praying, his disciples were with him: and he asked them, saying, Who do the multitudes say that I am?

19 They answering said, John the Baptist; but some say, Elijah; and others say, that one of the old prophets is risen again.

20 He said unto them, But who say ye that I am? Peter answering said, The Christ of God.

21 And he charged them, and commanded them to tell no man that thing;

22 Saying, The Son of man must suffer many things, and be rejected by the elders and chief priests and scribes, and be slain, and rise again the third day.

23 And he said to them all, If any desire to come after me, let him deny himself, and take up his cross daily, and follow me.

24 For whosoever desireth to save his [1]life shall lose it: but whosoever shall lose his [1]life for my sake, the same shall save it,

25 For what is a man profited, if he gain the whole world, and destroy or lose himself?

26 For whosoever shall be ashamed of me and of my words, of him shall the Son of man be ashamed, when he shall come in his glory, and in the glory of his Father, and in the glory of the holy angels.

27 But I tell you of a truth, there be some of them that stand here, who shall not taste of death, till they shall see the kingdom of God.

28 ¶ And it came to pass about eight days after these sayings, he took with him Peter and John and James, and went up into the mountain to pray.

29 And as he prayed, the fashion of his countenance was altered, and his raiment became white and glistering.

30 And, behold, there talked with him two men, which were Moses and Elijah:

31 Who appeared in glory, and spake of his decease which he was about to accomplish at Jerusalem.

32 But Peter and they that were with him were heavy with sleep: but they kept awake, and saw his glory, and the two men that stood with him.

33 And it came to pass, as they departed from him, Peter said unto Jesus, Master, it is good for us to be here: and

[1] *Or,* soul.

let us make three tabernacles; one for thee, and one for Moses, and one for Elijah: not knowing what he said.

34 While he thus spake, there came a cloud, and overshadowed them: and they feared as they entered into the cloud.

35 And there came a voice out of the cloud, saying, This is my Son, whom I have chosen: hear ye him.

36 And when the voice was past, Jesus was found alone. And they kept it close, and told no man in those days any of those things which they had seen.

37 ¶ And it came to pass, that on the next day, when they were come down from the hill, a great multitude met him.

38 And, behold, a man from the multitude cried out, saying, Master, I beseech thee, look upon my son: for he is mine only child.

39 And, lo, a spirit taketh him, and he suddenly crieth out; and it teareth him with foaming, and bruising him hardly departeth from him.

40 And I besought thy disciples to cast it out; and they could not.

41 And Jesus answering said, O faithless and perverse generation, how long shall I be with you, and suffer you? Bring thy son hither.

42 And as he was yet coming, the devil rent him, and tare him. But Jesus rebuked the unclean spirit, and healed the lad, and delivered him again to his father.

43 And they were all exceedingly amazed at the mighty power of God. But while they wondered every one at all things which he did, he said unto his disciples,

44 Let these sayings sink down into your ears: for the Son of man is about to be delivered into the hands of men.

45 But they knew not this saying, and it was hid from them, that they might not perceive it: and they feared to ask him of this saying.

46 ¶ But there arose a reasoning among them, which of them should be greatest.

47 And Jesus, perceiving the thought of their heart, took a little child, and set it by him,

48 And said unto them, Whosoever shall receive this little child in my name receiveth me: and whosoever shall receive me receiveth him that sent me: for he that is least among you all, the same is great.

49 ¶ And John answered and said, Master, we saw one casting out devils in thy name; and we forbad him, because he followeth not with us.

50 And Jesus said unto him, Forbid him not: for he that is not against us is for us.

51 ¶ And it came to pass, when the days were accomplishing that he should be received up ¹[into heaven], he stedfastly set his face to go to Jerusalem,

52 And sent messengers before his face: and having set forth, they entered into a village of the Samaritans, to make ready for him.

¹ *Not expressed in the original.*

53 And they did not receive him, because his face was as though he would go to Jerusalem.

54 And when his disciples James and John saw this, they said, Lord, wilt thou that we command fire to come down from heaven, and consume them, even as Elijah did?

55 But he turned, and rebuked them ¹[, *and said, Ye know not what manner of spirit ye are of.*

56 *For the Son of man came not to destroy men's lives, but to save them*]. And they went to another village.

57 ¶ And as they were going in the way, a certain man said unto him, Lord, I will follow thee whithersoever thou goest.

58 And Jesus said unto him, The foxes have holes, and the birds of the heaven have nests; but the Son of man hath not where to lay his head.

59 And he said unto another, Follow me. But he said, Lord, suffer me first to go and bury my father.

60 But he said unto him, Leave the dead to bury their own dead: but go thou and declare abroad the kingdom of God.

61 And another also said, Lord, I will follow thee; but let me first go bid them farewell, which are at home at my house.

62 And Jesus said unto him, No man, having put his hand to the plough, and looking back, is fitted for the kingdom of God.

CHAPTER X.

AFTER these things the Lord appointed others also, seventy in number, and sent them two and two before his face into every city and place, whither he himself was about to come.

2 And he said unto them, The harvest is great, but the labourers are few: pray ye therefore the Lord of the harvest, that he would send forth labourers into his harvest.

3 Go your ways: behold, I send you forth as lambs in the midst of wolves.

4 Carry neither purse, nor scrip, nor shoes: and salute no man by the way.

5 And into whatsoever house ye shall enter, first say, Peace be to this house.

6 And if the son of peace be there, your peace shall rest upon it: but if not, it shall turn to you again.

7 And in that house remain, eating and drinking such things as they give: for the labourer is worthy of his hire. Go not from house to house.

8 And into whatsoever city ye enter, and they receive you, eat such things as are set before you:

9 And heal the sick that are therein, and say unto them, The kingdom of God is come nigh unto you.

---

¹ *These words, as far as the end of verse* 55, *are not found in the five oldest MSS.; and verse* 56 *is wanting in the six oldest. On the other hand, they are contained in many of the oldest versions and fathers. Their genuineness must remain therefore an undecided question.*

10 But into whatsoever city ye shall enter, and they receive you not, go out into its streets, and say,

11 Even the very dust of your city, which cleaveth to us on our feet, we do wipe off against you : notwithstanding, be ye sure of this, that the kingdom of God is come nigh.

12 I say unto you, that it shall be more tolerable in that day for Sodom, than for that city.

13 Woe unto thee, Chorazin ! woe unto thee, Bethsaida ! for if the mighty works which were done in you had been done in Tyre and Sidon, they would have a great while ago repented, sitting in sackcloth and ashes.

14 But it shall be more tolerable for Tyre and Sidon in the judgment, than for you.

15 And thou, Capernaum, shalt thou be exalted to heaven ? Thou shalt be thrust down to hell.

16 He that heareth you heareth me ; and he that despiseth you despiseth me ; and he that despiseth me despiseth him that sent me.

17 ¶ And the seventy returned again with joy, saying, Lord, even the devils are subject unto us through thy name.

18 And he said unto them, I beheld Satan as lightning fall from heaven.

19 Behold, I have given unto you authority to tread on serpents and scorpions, and over all the power of the enemy : and nothing shall by any means hurt you.

20 Notwithstanding in this rejoice not, because the spirits are subject unto you ; but rejoice, because your names are written in heaven.

21 ¶ In that hour he rejoiced in the Holy Spirit, and said, I confess to thee, O Father, Lord of heaven and earth, that thou hast hid these things from the wise and prudent, and hast revealed them unto babes : even so, Father ; for thus it seemed good in thy sight.

22 [1] [And turning to his disciples, he said,] All things are delivered to me by my Father: and none knoweth who the Son is, but the Father ; and who the Father is, but the Son, and he to whomsoever the Son is minded to reveal him.

23 And turning unto his disciples, he said privately, Blessed are the eyes which see the things that ye see :

24 For I tell you, that many prophets and kings wished to see those things which ye see, and did not see them ; and to hear those things which ye hear, and did not hear them.

25 ¶ And behold, a certain lawyer stood up, tempting him, saying, Master, what shall I do to inherit eternal life ?

26 He said unto him, What is written in the law ? how readest thou ?

27 And he answering said, Thou shalt love the Lord thy God with all thy heart, and with all thy soul, and with all

[1] *These words are omitted by several MSS., but contained in two of the oldest and several others, and in the oldest versions.*

thy strength, and with all thy mind; and thy neighbour as thyself.

28 And he said unto him, Thou hast answered right: this do, and thou shalt live.

29 But he, willing to justify himself, said unto Jesus, And who is my neighbour?

30 And Jesus answering said, A certain man went down from Jerusalem to Jericho, and fell among thieves, which stripped him of his raiment, and beat him, and departed, leaving him half dead.

31 And by chance there came down a certain priest by that way: and he saw him, and passed by on the other side.

32 And likewise a Levite, arriving at the place, came and saw him, and passed by on the other side.

33 But a certain Samaritan, as he journeyed, came where he was: and saw him, and had compassion on him,

34 And went to him, and bound up his wounds, pouring in oil and wine, and set him on his own beast, and brought him to an inn, and took care of him.

35 And on the morrow [1] [when he departed], he took out two pence, and gave them to the host, and said unto him, Take care of him; and whatsoever thou spendest more, when I come again, I will repay thee.

36 Which of these three, thinkest thou, was neighbour unto him that fell among the thieves?

[1] *These words are not found in several of the old MSS.*

37 And he said, He that shewed mercy on him. Then said Jesus unto him, Go, and do thou likewise.

38 ¶ Now it came to pass, as they went, that he entered into a certain village: and a certain woman named Martha received him into her house.

39 And she had a sister called Mary, which also sat at the feet of the Lord, and heard his word.

40 But Martha was cumbered about much serving, and came in, and said, Lord, dost thou not care that my sister hath left me to serve alone? bid her therefore that she help me.

41 And Jesus answered and said unto her, Martha, Martha, thou art anxious and troublest thyself about many things:

42 But one thing is needful: and Mary hath chosen the good portion, which shall not be taken away from her.

CHAPTER XI.

AND it came to pass, that, as he was praying in a certain place, when he ceased, one of his disciples said unto him, Lord, teach us to pray, as John also taught his disciples.

2 And he said unto them, When ye pray, say, Father, Hallowed be thy name. Thy kingdom come.

3 Give us day by day our needful bread.

4 And forgive us our sins; for we also forgive every one that is indebted to us. And lead us not into temptation.

5 And he said unto them Which of you shall have a

friend, and shall go unto him at midnight, and say unto him, Friend, lend me three loaves;

6 For a friend of mine in his journey is come to me, and I have nothing to set before him?

7 And he from within shall answer and say, Trouble me not: the door is now shut, and my children are with me in bed; I cannot rise and give thee.

8 I say unto you, Though he will not rise and give him, because he is his friend, yet because of his importunity he will rise and give him as many as he needeth.

9 And I say unto you, Ask, and it shall be given you; seek, and ye shall find; knock, and it shall be opened unto you.

10 For every one that asketh receiveth; and he that seeketh findeth; and to him that knocketh it shall be opened.

11 Which of you that is a father, if his son shall ask bread, will give him a stone? or if he ask a fish, will he for a fish give him a serpent?

12 Or if he shall ask an egg, will he give him a scorpion?

13 If ye then, being evil, know how to give good gifts unto your children: how much more shall your Father from heaven give the Holy Spirit to them that ask him?

14 ¶ And he was casting out a devil, and it was dumb. And it came to pass, when the devil was gone out, the dumb spake; and the multitudes wondered.

15 But some of them said, By Beelzebub the chief of the devils casteth he out the devils.

16 And others, tempting him, sought of him a sign from heaven.

17 But he, knowing their thoughts, said unto them, Every kingdom divided against itself is brought to desolation; and a house divided against a house falleth.

18 If Satan also hath been divided against himself, how shall his kingdom stand? because ye say that I cast out the devils by Beelzebub.

19 And if I by Beelzebub cast out the devils, by whom do your sons cast them out? therefore they shall be your judges.

20 But if I by the finger of God cast out the devils, then the kingdom of God is come upon you.

21 When the strong man armed keepeth his palace, his goods are in peace:

22 But when a stronger than he shall come upon him, and overcome him, he taketh from him his armour wherein he had trusted, and divideth his spoils.

23 He that is not with me is against me: and he that gathereth not with me scattereth.

24 When the unclean spirit is gone out of a man, it goeth through dry places, seeking rest; and finding none, it saith, I will return unto my house whence I came out;

25 And cometh, and findeth it swept and garnished.

26 Then goeth it, and taketh to it seven other spirits more wicked than itself; and they enter in, and dwell there: and the last state of that man becometh worse than the first.

27 ¶ And it came to pass, as he spake these things, a certain woman from among the crowd lifted up her voice, and said unto him, Blessed is the womb that bare thee, and the paps which thou hast sucked.

28 But he said, Yea rather, blessed are they that hear the word of God, and keep it.

29 ¶ And when the multitudes were gathering thick together, he began to say, This generation is an evil generation: it seeketh a sign; and there shall no sign be given it, but the sign of Jonah.

30 For as Jonah was a sign unto the Ninevites, so shall also the Son of man be to this generation.

31 The queen of the south shall rise up in the judgment with the men of this generation, and condemn them: because she came from the utmost parts of the earth to hear the wisdom of Solomon; and, behold, there is more than Solomon here.

32 The men of Nineve shall rise up in the judgment with this generation, and shall condemn it: because they repented at the preaching of Jonah; and, behold, there is more than Jonah here.

33 No man, when he hath lighted a candle, putteth it in a secret place, neither under the bushel, but on the candlestick, that they which come in may see the light.

34 The light of the body is thine eye: when thine eye is single, thy whole body also is full of light; but when thine eye is evil, thy body also is dark.

35 Take heed therefore that the light which is in thee is not darkness.

36 If thy whole body therefore be full of light, having no part dark, the whole shall be full of light, as when a candle with its shining doth give thee light.

37 ¶ And as he spake, a certain Pharisee asketh him to dine with him: and he went in, and sat down to meat.

38 And when the Pharisee saw it, he marvelled that he did not first wash before dinner.

39 And the Lord said unto him. Now do ye Pharisees make clean the outside of the cup and the platter; but your inward part is full of extortion and wickedness.

40 Ye fools, did not he that made that which is without make that which is within also?

41 But give alms ¹of such things as ye have; and, behold, all things are clean unto you.

42 But woe unto you, Pharisees! because ye tithe mint and rue and every herb, and pass over judgment and the love of God: these ought ye to have done, and not to leave the other undone.

43 Woe unto you, Pharisees! because ye love the uppermost

¹ *Literally*, of the contents, *i.e. of the vessel.*

seats in the synagogues, and greetings in the markets.

44 Woe unto you, because ye are as graves which appear not, and the men that walk over them are not aware of them.

45 But one of the lawyers answered, and saith unto him, Master, thus saying thou reproachest us also.

46 But he said, Woe unto you also, ye lawyers! because ye lade men with burdens grievous to be borne, and ye yourselves touch not the burdens with one of your fingers.

47 Woe unto you! because ye build the sepulchres of the prophets, and your fathers killed them.

48 Therefore ye bear testimony to and allow the deeds of your fathers: for they indeed killed them, and ye build.

49 For this cause said also the wisdom of God, I will send unto them prophets and apostles, and some of them they shall slay and persecute:

50 That the blood of all the prophets, which was shed from the foundation of the world, may be required of this generation;

51 From the blood of Abel unto the blood of Zechariah, which perished between the altar and the temple: verily I say unto you, It shall be required of this generation.

52 Woe unto you, lawyers! because ye took away the key of knowledge: ye entered not in yourselves, and them that were entering in ye hindered.

53 And when he was gone out thence, the scribes and the Pharisees began to urge him vehemently, and to provoke him to speak of many things:

54 Laying wait for him, and seeking to catch something out of his mouth.

CHAPTER XII.

IN the mean time, when the multitude was gathered together in myriads, insomuch that they trode one upon another, he began to say unto his disciples first of all, Take heed to yourselves of the leaven of the Pharisees, which is hypocrisy.

2 For there is nothing covered up, that shall not be revealed; and hid, that shall not be known.

3 Therefore whatsoever ye have spoken in the darkness shall be heard in the light; and that which ye have spoken in the ear in the secret chambers shall be proclaimed upon the housetops.

4 But I say unto you my friends, Be not afraid of them that kill the body, and after that have no more that they can do.

5 But I will forewarn you whom ye shall fear: Fear him, which after he hath killed hath power to cast into hell; yea, I say unto you, Fear him.

6 Are not five sparrows sold for two farthings? and not one of them is forgotten before God.

7 But even the very hairs of your head are all numbered. Fear not: ye are of more value than many sparrows.

8 But I say unto you, Whosoever shall confess me before men, him shall the Son of man also confess before the angels of God:

9 But he that hath denied me before men shall be denied before the angels of God.

10 And whosoever shall speak a word against the Son of man, it shall be forgiven him: but unto him that hath blasphemed against the Holy Spirit it shall not be forgiven.

11 And when they bring you before the synagogues, and magistrates, and the powers, take not anxious thought how or what thing ye shall answer, or what ye shall say:

12 For the Holy Spirit shall teach you in that hour what ye ought to say.

13 ¶ And one from among the multitude said unto him, Master, speak to my brother, that he divide the inheritance with me.

14 But he said unto him, Man, who made me a judge or a divider over you?

15 And he said unto them, Take heed, and beware of all covetousness: for not, because a man hath abundance, doth his life consist in the things which he possesseth.

16 And he spake a parable unto them, saying, The ground of a certain rich man brought forth plentifully:

17 And he thought within himself, saying, What shall I do, because I have no room where to bestow my fruits?

18 And he said, This will I do: I will pull down my barns, and build greater; and there will I bestow all my fruits and my goods.

19 And I will say to my [1]soul, Soul, thou hast much goods laid up for many years; take thine ease, eat, drink, and be merry.

20 But God said unto him, Thou fool, this night [2]thy soul shall be required of thee: then whose shall those things be, which thou hast provided?

21 So is he that layeth up treasure for himself, and is not rich toward God.

22 And he said unto his disciples, Therefore I say unto you, Be not careful for your life, what ye shall eat; neither for your body, what ye shall put on.

23 The life is more than the food, and the body than the raiment.

24 Consider the ravens, that they neither sow nor reap; which neither have storehouse nor barn; and God feedeth them: how much more are ye better than the birds?

25 And which of you by careful thought can add to his age one cubit?

26 If ye then be not able to do that thing which is least, why take ye thought for the rest?

27 Consider the lilies, how they neither spin nor weave; and yet I say unto you, that not even Solomon in all his glory was arrayed like one of these.

[1] *Or*, life. *It is the same word as that rendered* life *in ver.* 22.
[2] *Literally*, they demand thy soul (*or*, life) of thee.

28 But if God so clotheth the grass, which is to day in the field, and to morrow is cast into the oven; how much more will he clothe you, O ye of little faith?

29 And seek not ye what ye shall eat, or what ye shall drink, neither be ye of doubtful mind.

30 For all these things do the nations of the world seek after: but your Father knoweth that ye have need of these things.

31 But seek ye his kingdom, and these things shall be added unto you.

32 Fear not, little flock; for it is your Father's good pleasure to give you the kingdom.

33 Sell that ye have, and give alms; provide yourselves bags which wax not old, a treasure in the heavens that faileth not, where no thief approacheth, neither moth corrupteth.

34 For where your treasure is, there will your heart be also.

35 Let your loins be girded about, and your lights burning;

36 And ye yourselves like unto men that wait for their lord, when he will return from the wedding; that when he cometh and knocketh, they may open unto him immediately.

37 Blessed are those servants, whom the lord when he cometh shall find watching: verily I say unto you, that he will gird himself, and make them to sit down to meat, and will come and serve them.

38 And if he shall come in the second watch, or come in the third watch, and find them so, blessed are those servants.

39 But this know, that if the master of the house had known what hour the thief would come, he would have watched, and not have suffered his house to be broken into.

40 Be ye therefore ready also: for the Son of man cometh at an hour when ye think not.

41 But Peter said unto him, Lord, speakest thou this parable with regard to us, or also to all?

42 And the Lord said, Who then is that faithful, that wise steward, whom his lord shall set over his household, to give them their portion of meat in due season?

43 Blessed is that servant, whom his lord when he cometh shall find so doing.

44 Of a truth I say unto you, that he will set him over all that he hath.

45 But if that servant say in his heart, My lord delayeth his coming; and shall begin to beat the menservants and maidens, and to eat and drink, and to be drunken;

46 The lord of that servant will come in a day when he looketh not for him, and at an hour when he is not aware, and will cut him in sunder, and will appoint him his portion with the unbelievers.

47 And that servant, which knew his lord's will, and prepared not himself, neither did according to his will, shall be beaten with many stripes.

48 But he that knew not, and did commit things worthy of

stripes, shall be beaten with few stripes. For unto whomsoever much is given, of him shall be much required: and to whom men have committed much, of him they will ask the more.

49 ¶ I came to send fire on the earth; and what will I? would that it were already kindled!

50 But I have a baptism to be baptized with; and how am I straitened till it be accomplished!

51 Suppose ye that I came to give peace on the earth? I tell you, Nay; but rather division;

52 For from henceforth there shall be five in one house divided; three shall be divided against two, and two against three,

53 Father against son, and son against father; mother against daughter, and daughter against the mother; mother in law against her daughter in law, and daughter in law against the mother in law.

54 ¶ And he said also to the multitudes, When ye see the cloud rising out of the west, straightway ye say, There cometh a shower; and so it is.

55 And when ye see the south wind blow, ye say, There will be heat; and it cometh to pass.

56 Ye hypocrites, ye know how to discern the face of the earth and of the sky; but how is it that ye do not discern this time?

57 Yea, and why even of yourselves judge ye not what is right?

58 For while thou goest with thine adversary to the magistrate, give diligence in the way that thou mayest be delivered from him; lest he hale thee to the judge, and the judge shall deliver thee to the officer, and the officer shall cast thee into prison.

59 I tell thee, thou shalt by no means depart thence, till thou hast paid the very last mite.

CHAPTER XIII.

AND there came at that season some telling him of the Galilæans, whose blood Pilate had mingled with their sacrifices.

2 And he answering said unto them, Suppose ye that these Galilæans were sinners above all the Galilæans, because they suffered such things?

3 I tell you, Nay: but, except ye repent, ye shall all perish in like manner.

4 Or those eighteen, upon whom the tower in Siloam fell, and slew them, think ye that they were [1]sinners above all men that dwelt in Jerusalem?

5 I tell you, Nay: but, except ye repent, ye shall all perish even thus.

6 But he spake this parable; A certain man had a fig tree planted in his vineyard; and he came seeking fruit thereon, and found none.

7 So he said unto his vinedresser, Behold, these three

[1] *Literally,* debtors.

years I come seeking fruit on this fig tree, and find none: cut it down; why moreover cumbereth it the ground?

8 But he answering said unto him, Lord, let it alone this year also, till I shall dig about it, and cast in manure:

9 And if it bear fruit hereafter, well: and if not, thou shalt cut it down.

10 ¶ And he was teaching in one of the synagogues on the sabbath.

11 And, behold a woman which had a spirit of infirmity eighteen years; and she was bowed together, and could in no wise lift up herself.

12 And Jesus seeing her, called her to him, and said unto her, Woman, thou art loosed from thine infirmity.

13 And he laid his hands on her: and immediately she was made straight, and glorified God.

14 And the ruler of the synagogue answered with indignation, because that Jesus had healed on the sabbath day, and said unto the multitude, There are six days in which men ought to work: in them therefore come and be healed, and not on the sabbath day.

15 But the Lord answered him, and said, Ye hypocrites, doth not each one of you on the sabbath loose his ox or his ass from the stall, and lead him away and water him?

16 And ought not this woman, being a daughter of Abraham, whom Satan hath bound, lo, these eighteen years, to be loosed from this bond on the sabbath day?

17 And while he said these things, all his adversaries were ashamed: and all the multitude rejoiced for all the glorious things that were done by him.

18 He said therefore, Unto what is the kingdom of God like? and whereunto shall I resemble it?

19 It is like a grain of mustard seed, which a man took, and cast into his garden; and it grew, and waxed a great tree; and the birds of the air lodged in the branches of it.

20 And again he said, Whereunto shall I liken the kingdom of God?

21 It is like leaven, which a woman took and hid in three measures of meal, till the whole was leavened.

22 ¶ And he went through the cities and villages, teaching, and journeying toward Jerusalem.

23 And one said unto him, Lord, are there few that be saved? And he said unto them,

24 Strive to enter in through the narrow door: for many, I say unto you, will seek to enter in, and shall not be able.

25 When once the master of the house is risen up, and hath shut to the door, and ye begin to stand without, and to knock at the door, saying, Lord, open unto us; and he shall answer and say unto you, I know you not whence ye are:

26 Then shall ye begin to say, We ate and drank in thy

presence, and thou didst teach in our streets.

27 And he shall say, I tell you, I know you not whence ye are; depart from me, all ye workers of iniquity.

28 ¹There shall there be ² weeping and gnashing of teeth, when ye shall see Abraham, and Isaac, and Jacob, and all the prophets, in the kingdom of God, and you yourselves being thrust out.

29 And they shall come from the east, and west, and from the north, and south, and shall sit down in the kingdom of God.

30 And, behold, there are last which shall be first, and there are first which shall be last.

31 ¶ At that time there came certain of the Pharisees, saying unto him, Get thee out, and depart hence: for Herod desireth to kill thee.

32 And he said unto them, Go ye, and tell that fox, Behold, I cast out devils, and I perfect cures to day and to morrow, and the third day I shall be completed.

33 Nevertheless I must walk to day, and to morrow, and the day following: for it cannot be that a prophet perish outside of Jerusalem.

34 O Jerusalem, Jerusalem, which killest the prophets, and stonest them that have been sent unto thee; how often would I have gathered thy children together, as a hen doth gather her brood under her wings, and ye would not!

35 Behold, your house is left unto you: but I say unto you, Ye shall not see me, until the time come when ye shall say, Blessed is he that cometh in the name of the Lord.

CHAPTER XIV.

AND it came to pass, when he had gone into the house of one of the chief Pharisees to eat bread on the sabbath day, that they were watching him.

2 And, behold, there was a certain man before him which had the dropsy.

3 And Jesus answering spake unto the lawyers and Pharisees, saying, Is it lawful on the sabbath day to heal, or not?

4 But they held their peace. And he took him, and healed him, and let him go;

5 And answered them, saying, Among yourselves, whose son, or whose ox, shall fall into a pit, and he will not straightway pull him out on the sabbath day?

6 And they could not answer again to these things.

7 ¶ And he spoke a parable to those which were bidden, when he marked how they chose out the chief seats; saying unto them,

8 When thou art bidden by any one to a wedding, sit not down in the highest seat; lest a more honourable man than thou have been bidden by him;

9 And he that bade thee and

---

¹ *The first* "there" *is local, which is lost sight of in the Authorized Version.*

² *Literally,* the weeping and the gnashing.

him shall come and say to thee, Give this man place; and then shalt thou begin with shame to take the lowest place.

10 But when thou art bidden, go and sit down in the lowest place, that when he that hath bidden thee cometh, he may say unto thee, Friend, go up higher: then shalt thou have honour in the presence of them that sit at meat with thee.

11 Because whosoever exalteth himself shall be humbled; and he that humbleth himself shall be exalted.

12 Moreover he said to him that bade him, When thou makest a dinner or a supper, call not thy friends, neither thy brethren, nor yet thy kinsmen, nor even thy rich neighbours; lest they also bid thee again, and a recompence be made thee.

13 But when thou makest a feast, call the poor, the maimed, the lame, the blind:

14 And thou shalt be blessed; because they cannot recompense thee: for recompence shall be made thee at the resurrection of the just.

15 ¶ And when one of them that sat at meat with him heard these things, he said unto him, Blessed is he that shall eat bread in the kingdom of God.

16 But he said unto him, A certain man made a great supper, and bade many:

17 And sent his servant at supper time to say to them that were bidden, Come; for all things are now ready.

18 And they all with one consent began to make excuse. The first said unto him, I have bought a piece of ground, and I must needs go forth and see it: I pray thee have me excused.

19 And another said, I have bought five yoke of oxen, and I go to prove them: I pray thee have me excused.

20 And another said, I have married a wife, and therefore I cannot come.

21 So the servant came, and told his lord these things. Then the master of the house being angry said to his servant, Go out quickly into the streets and lanes of the city, and bring in hither the poor, and maimed, and blind, and lame.

22 And the servant said, Lord, it is done as thou commandedst, and yet there is room.

23 And the lord said unto the servant, Go out into the highways and hedges, and compel them to come in, that my house may be filled.

24 For I say unto you, That not one of those men which have been bidden shall taste of my supper.

25 ¶ And there went great multitudes with him: and he turned, and said unto them,

26 If any cometh to me, and hateth not his father, and his mother, and his wife, and his children, and his brethren, and his sisters, yea, and his own life also, he cannot be my disciple.

27 And whosoever doth not bear his own cross, and come after me, cannot be my disciple.

28 For which of you, wish-

ing to build a tower, sitteth not down first, and counteth the cost, whether he have sufficient to finish it?

29 Lest haply, after he hath laid the foundation, and is not able to finish it, all that behold it begin to mock him,

30 Saying, This man began to build, and was not able to finish.

31 Or what king, going forth to make war against another king, sitteth not down first, and consulteth whether he is able with ten thousand to meet him that cometh against him with twenty thousand?

32 Or else, while he is yet a great way off, he sendeth an ambassage, and desireth conditions of peace.

33 So likewise, whosoever he be of you that biddeth not farewell to all that he hath, he cannot be my disciple.

34 Salt therefore is good: but if even the salt have lost his savour, wherewith shall it be seasoned?

35 It is neither fit for the land, nor for the dunghill; but men cast it out. He that hath ears to hear, let him hear.

CHAPTER XV.

AND all the publicans and sinners were drawing near unto him to hear him.

2 And both the Pharisees and the scribes murmured, saying, This man receiveth sinners, and eateth with them.

3 ¶ But he spake this parable unto them, saying,

4 What man of you, having an hundred sheep, and having lost one of them, doth not leave the ninety and nine in the wilderness, and go after that which is lost, until he find it?

5 And when he hath found it, he layeth it on his shoulders, rejoicing.

6 And when he is come home, he calleth together his friends and neighbours, saying unto them, Rejoice with me; for I have found my sheep which was lost.

7 I say unto you, that even thus there shall be joy in heaven over one sinner that repenteth, more than over ninety and nine just persons, which need no repentance.

8 ¶ Either what woman having ten [1] pieces of silver, if she lose one piece, doth not light a candle, and sweep the house, and seek diligently till she find it?

9 And when she hath found it, she calleth her friends and neighbours together, saying, Rejoice with me; for I have found the [1] piece which I had lost.

10 Even thus, I say unto you, there is joy in the presence of the angels of God over one sinner that repenteth.

11 ¶ And he said, A certain man had two sons:

12 And the younger of them said to his father, Father, give me the portion of goods that falleth to me. And he divided unto them his living.

13 And not many days after the younger son gathered all together, and took his journey into a far country, and there

[1] *Literally*, drachmæ *and* drachma

wasted his substance with reckless living.

14 And when he had spent all, there arose a mighty famine in that land; and he began to be in want.

15 And he went and joined himself to one of the citizens of that country; and he sent him into his fields to feed swine.

16 And he would fain have filled his belly with the husks that the swine did eat: and no man gave unto him.

17 But he came to himself, and said, How many hired servants of my father's have bread enough and to spare! but I perish here with hunger.

18 I will arise and go to my father, and will say unto him, Father, I have sinned against heaven, and before thee:

19 I am no more worthy to be called thy son: make me as one of thy hired servants.

20 And he arose, and came to his father. But when he was yet a great way off, his father saw him, and had compassion, and ran, and fell on his neck, and kissed him.

21 And the son said unto him, Father, I have sinned against heaven, and in thy sight: I am no more worthy to be called thy son.

22 But the father said to his servants, Bring forth quickly the best robe, and clothe him; and put a ring on his hand, and shoes on his feet:

23 And bring hither the fatted calf, and kill it; and let us eat, and be merry:

24 For this my son was dead, and is alive again; he was lost, and is found. And they began to be merry.

25 But his elder son was in the field: and as he came and drew nigh to the house, he heard musick and dancing.

26 And he called one of the young men, and asked what these things meant.

27 And he said unto him, Thy brother is come; and thy father hath killed the fatted calf, because he hath received him safe and sound.

28 And he was angry, and would not go in: but his father came out, and intreated him.

29 And he answering said to his father, Lo, these many years do I serve thee, and never transgressed thy commandment: and thou never gavest me a kid, that I might make merry with my friends:

30 But as soon as this thy son was come, which hath devoured thy living with harlots, thou hast killed for him the fatted calf.

31 But he said unto him, [1]Son, thou art ever with me, and all that I have is thine.

32 It was meet that we should make merry, and be glad: for this thy brother was dead, and is alive; and was lost, and is found.

CHAPTER XVI.

AND he said also unto the disciples, There was a certain rich man, which had a steward; and the same was accused unto him that he was wasting his goods.

[1] *Literally*, Child.

2 And he called him, and said unto him, How is it that I hear this of thee? give thine account of thy stewardship; for thou mayest be no longer steward.

3 Then the steward said within himself, What shall I do, seeing that my lord taketh away from me the stewardship? I cannot dig; to beg I am ashamed.

4 I am resolved what I will do, that, when I am put out of the stewardship, they may receive me into their houses.

5 So he called every one of his own lord's debtors unto him, and said unto the first, How much owest thou unto my lord?

6 And he said, An hundred measures of oil. And he said unto him, Take thy bill, and sit down quickly, and write—fifty.

7 Then said he to another, And how much owest thou? And he said, An hundred measures of wheat. And he said unto him, Take thy bill, and write—fourscore.

8 And his lord commended the unjust steward, because he had done wisely: for the sons of this world are in their generation wiser than the sons of light.

9 And I say unto you, Make to yourselves friends of the mammon of unrighteousness; that, when it shall fail, they may receive you into the eternal tabernacles.

10 He that is faithful in that which is least is faithful also in much: and he that is unjust in the least is unjust also in much.

11 If therefore ye have not been faithful in the unrighteous mammon, who will commit to your trust the true ¹[riches]?

12 And if ye have not been faithful in that which is another's, who shall give you that which is your own?

13 ¶ No servant can serve two lords: for either he will hate the one, and love the other; or else he will hold to the one, and despise the other. Ye cannot serve God and mammon.

14 And the Pharisees also, who were covetous, heard all these things: and they derided him.

15 And he said unto them, Ye are they which justify yourselves before men; but God knoweth your hearts: because that which is ²highly esteemed among men is abomination in the sight of God.

16 The law and the prophets were until John: since that time the kingdom of God is ³preached, and every one presseth into it.

17 But it is easier for heaven and earth to pass, than for one stroke of the law to fail.

18 Whosoever putteth away his wife, and marrieth another, committeth adultery: and whosoever marrieth her that is put away from her husband committeth adultery.

19 But there was a certain rich man, and he was clothed

---

¹ *Not expressed in the original*
² *Literally*, lofty.
³ *Literally*, evangelized.

in purple and fine linen, and ¹fared sumptuously every day :

20 And a certain beggar named Lazarus had been laid at his gate, full of sores,

21 And longing to be fed with the crumbs which fell from the rich man's table : moreover the dogs came and licked his sores.

22 And it came to pass, that the beggar died, and he was carried by the angels into Abraham's bosom : the rich man also died, and was buried ;

23 And in hell he lift up his eyes, being in torments, and seeth Abraham afar off, and Lazarus in his bosom.

24 And he cried and said, Father Abraham, have mercy on me, and send Lazarus, that he may dip the tip of his finger in water, and cool my tongue ; for I am tormented in this flame.

25 But Abraham said, ²Son, remember that thou in thy lifetime receivedst thy good things, and in like manner Lazarus evil things : but now he is comforted here, and thou art tormented.

26 And beside all this, between us and you there is a great gulf fixed : so that they which would pass from hence to you cannot ; neither can they pass to us, that would come from thence.

27 Then he said, I pray thee therefore, father, that thou wouldest send him to my father's house :

28 For I have five brethren ; that he may testify unto them, lest they also come into this place of torment.

29 Abraham saith unto him, They have Moses and the prophets ; let them hear them.

30 And he said, Nay, father Abraham : but if one go unto them from the dead, they will repent.

31 And he said unto him, If they hear not Moses and the prophets, neither will they be persuaded, even if one rise from the dead.

CHAPTER XVII.

AND he said unto his disciples, It is impossible but that offences will come : but woe unto him, through whom they come !

2 It were better for him that a millstone were hanged about his neck, and he cast into the sea, than that he should offend one of these little ones.

3 Take heed to yourselves : If thy brother sin, rebuke him ; and if he repent, forgive him.

4 And if he sin against thee seven times in a day, and seven times turn again to thee, saying, I repent ; thou shalt forgive him.

5 And the apostles said unto the Lord, Give us more faith.

6 But the Lord said, If ye have faith as a grain of mustard seed, ye might say unto this sycamine tree, Be thou plucked up by the root, and be thou planted in the sea ; and it should obey you.

7 But which of you, having a servant plowing or tending cattle, will say unto him, when

---

¹ *Or*, made merry splendidly.
² *Literally*, Child.

he is come from the field, Come straightway, and sit down to meat?

8 And will not rather say unto him, Make ready wherewith I may sup, and gird thyself, and serve me, till I have eaten and drunken ; and afterward thou shalt eat and drink?

9 Doth he thank that servant because he did the things that were commanded him?

10 So likewise ye, when ye shall have done all those things which are commanded you, say, We are unprofitable servants : we have done that which was our duty to do.

11 ¶ And it came to pass, as he went to Jerusalem, that he passed through the midst of Samaria and Galilee.

12 And as he entered into a certain village, there met him ten men that were lepers, which stood afar off :

13 And they lifted up their voice, and said, Jesus, Master, have mercy on us.

14 And seeing them, he said unto them, Go shew yourselves unto the priests. And it came to pass, that, as they went, they were cleansed.

15 But one of them, seeing that he was healed, turned back, with a loud voice glorifying God,

16 And fell down on his face at his feet, giving him thanks : and he was a Samaritan.

17 And Jesus answering said, Were not the ten cleansed? but where are the nine?

18 Were there found none that returned to give glory to God, save this stranger?

19 And he said unto him, Arise, go thy way : thy faith hath saved thee.

20 ¶ And he was asked by the Pharisees, when the kingdom of God should come ; and he answered them and said, The kingdom of God cometh not with observation :

21 Neither shall they say, See here, or there ; for, behold, the kingdom of God is among you.

22 And he said unto the disciples, The days will come, when ye shall long to see one of the days of the Son of man, and ye shall not see it.

23 And they shall say to you, See here, see there : go not after them, nor follow them.

24 For as the lightning, that lighteneth out of the one part under heaven, shineth unto the other part under heaven ; so shall the Son of man be in his day.

25 But first must he suffer many things, and be rejected of this generation.

26 And as it was in the days of Noah, so shall it be also in the days of the Son of man.

27 They did eat, they drank, they married wives, they were given in marriage, until the day that Noah entered into the ark, and the flood came, and destroyed them all.

28 In like manner also as it was in the days of Lot ; they did eat, they drank, they bought, they sold, they planted, they builded ;

29 But the same day that Lot went out of Sodom it rained fire and brimstone from

heaven, and destroyed them all.

30 Even thus shall it be in the day when the Son of man is revealed.

31 In that day, he which shall be upon the housetop, and his stuff in the house, let him not come down to take it away: and he that is in the field, let him in like manner not return back.

32 Remember Lot's wife.

33 Whosoever shall seek to save his [1]life shall lose it; and whosoever shall lose his [1]life shall quicken it into life.

34 I tell you, in that night there shall be two men in one bed; the one shall be taken, and the other shall be left.

35 Two women shall be grinding together; the one shall be taken, and the other left.[2]

37 And they answering say unto him, Where, Lord? And he said unto them, Where the body is, there will also the eagles be gathered together.

CHAPTER XVIII.

AND he spake a parable unto them to this end, that they ought always to pray, and not to faint;

2 Saying, There was in a city a certain judge, which feared not God, neither regarded man:

3 And there was a widow in that city; and she came unto him, saying, Avenge me of mine adversary.

4 And he would not for a while: but afterward he said within himself, Though I fear not God, nor regard man;

5 Yet because this widow troubleth me, I will avenge her, [3]lest by her continual coming she weary me.

6 And the Lord said, Hear what the unjust judge saith.

7 And shall not God avenge his elect, which cry day and night unto him, and he is long-suffering over them?

8 I tell you that he will avenge them speedily. Nevertheless when the Son of man cometh, shall he find faith on the earth?

9 And he spake also this parable regarding certain which trust in themselves that they are righteous, and despise others:

10 Two men went up to the temple to pray; the one a Pharisee, and the other a publican.

11 The Pharisee stood and prayed thus with himself, God, I thank thee, that I am not as the rest of men, extortioners, unjust, adulterers, or even as this publican.

12 I fast twice in the week, I give tithes of all my increase.

13 And the publican, standing afar off, would not lift up so much as his eyes unto heaven, but smote upon his breast, saying, God be merciful to me [4]a sinner.

14 I tell you, this man went down to his house justified rather than the other: for every one that exalteth himself shall be humbled; and he that humbleth himself shall be exalted.

[1] *Or*, soul.
[2] *Verse 36 is not contained in any of the oldest MSS.*
[3] *Or*, lest at the last she come and smite me.
[4] *Literally*, the sinner.

15 ¶ And they brought unto him also their infants, that he might touch them: but the disciples seeing it rebuked them.

16 But Jesus called them unto him, and said, Suffer the little children to come unto me, and hinder them not: for of such is the kingdom of God.

17 Verily I say unto you, Whosoever shall not receive the kingdom of God as a little child shall in no wise enter therein.

18 ¶ And a certain ruler asked him, saying, Good Master, what shall I do to inherit eternal life?

19 And Jesus said unto him, Why callest thou me good? There is none good, but God only.

20 Thou knowest the commandments, Do not commit adultery, Do not commit murder, Do not steal, Do not bear false witness, Honour thy father and thy mother.

21 But he said, All these have I kept from my youth up.

22 And Jesus hearing it said unto him, Yet lackest thou one thing: sell all that thou hast, and distribute unto the poor, and thou shalt have treasure in heaven: and come, follow me.

23 And when he heard this, he was exceeding sorrowful: for he was very rich.

24 And Jesus looked on him and said, How hard is it for them that have riches to enter into the kingdom of God!

25 For it is easier for a camel to enter in through the eye of a needle, than for a rich man to enter into the kingdom of God.

26 And they that heard it said, Who then can be saved?

27 But he said, The things which are impossible with men are possible with God.

28 And Peter said, Lo, we left our own, and followed thee.

29 And he said unto them, Verily I say unto you, There is no man that hath left house, or wife, or brethren, or parents, or children, for the kingdom of God's sake,

30 Who shall not receive manifold more in this present time, and in the world to come life eternal.

31 ¶ Then he took unto him the twelve, and said unto them, Behold, we go up to Jerusalem, and all things that are written by the prophets concerning the Son of man shall be accomplished.

32 For he shall be delivered up unto the Gentiles, and shall be mocked, and spitefully entreated, and spitted on:

33 And they shall scourge him, and kill him: and the third day he shall rise again.

34 And they understood none of these things: and this saying was hid from them, and they knew not the things which were spoken.

35 ¶ And it came to pass, that as he was coming nigh unto Jericho, a certain blind man sat by the way side begging:

36 And hearing the multitude pass by, he asked what it meant.

37 And they told him, that Jesus of Nazareth passeth by.

38 And he cried out, saying, Jesus, thou son of David, have mercy on me.

39 And they which went before rebuked him, that he should hold his peace: but he cried so much the more, Thou son of David, have mercy on me.

40 And Jesus stood, and commanded him to be brought unto him: and when he was come near, he asked him,

41 Saying, What wilt thou that I shall do unto thee? And he said, Lord, that I may receive my sight.

42 And Jesus said unto him, Receive thy sight: thy faith hath saved thee.

43 And immediately he received his sight, and followed him, glorifying God: and all the people, seeing it, gave praise unto God.

CHAPTER XIX.

AND he entered and passed through Jericho.

2 And, behold, a man named Zacchæus, and he was the chief among the publicans, and he was rich.

3 And he sought to see Jesus who he was; and could not for the multitude, because he was little of stature.

4 And he ran before, and climbed up into a sycomore tree to see him: for he was to pass that way.

5 And when Jesus came to the place, he looked up, and saw him, and said unto him, Zacchæus, make haste, and come down; for to day I must abide at thy house.

6 And he made haste, and came down, and received him joyfully.

7 And when they saw it, they all murmured, saying that he was gone to be guest with a man that is a sinner.

8 And Zacchæus stood, and said unto the Lord; Behold, Lord, the half of my goods I give to the poor; and whatever I have wrongfully exacted of any man, I restore fourfold.

9 And Jesus said unto him, This day is salvation come to this house, forsomuch as he also is a son of Abraham.

10 For the Son of man came to seek and to save that which was lost.

11 And as they heard these things, he added and spake a parable, because he was nigh to Jerusalem, and because they thought that the kingdom of God was about immediately to appear.

12 He said therefore, A certain nobleman went into a far country to receive for himself a kingdom, and to return.

13 And he called ten of his servants, and delivered them ten [1]pounds, and said unto them, Trade, until come.

14 But his citizens hated him, and sent a message after him, saying, We will not have this man to reign over us.

15 And it came to pass, that when he was returned, having received the kingdom, he commanded these servants to be called unto him, to whom he had given the money, that he

[1] *In the Greek*, minæ. *A mina was equal to about £3 of our money*

might know how much every man had gained by trading.

16 Then came the first, saying, Lord, thy pound hath gained ten pounds.

17 And he said unto him, Well done, thou good servant: because thou hast been faithful in a very little, have thou authority over ten cities.

18 And the second came, saying, Lord, thy pound hath made five pounds.

19 And he said likewise to him, Be thou also over five cities.

20 And the other came, saying, Lord, behold, here is thy pound, which I have kept laid up in a napkin:

21 For I feared thee, because thou art an austere man: thou takest up that which thou layedst not down, and reapest that which thou didst not sow.

22 He saith unto him, Out of thine own mouth will I judge thee, thou wicked servant. Thou knewest that I am an austere man, taking up that which I laid not down, and reaping that which I did not sow:

23 Wherefore then gavest not thou my money into a bank, that at my coming I might have required it with usury?

24 And he said unto them that stood by, Take from him the pound, and give it to him that hath the ten pounds.

25 And they said unto him, Lord, he hath ten pounds already.

26 I say unto you, That unto every one which hath shall be given; but from him that hath not, even that he hath shall be taken away from him.

27 But those mine enemies, which would not that I should reign over them, bring hither, and slay them before me.

28 ¶ And when he had thus spoken, he went before, ascending up to Jerusalem.

29 And it came to pass, when he came nigh to Bethphagé and Bethany, at the mount called the mount of Olives, he sent two of his disciples,

30 Saying, Go your way into the village over against you; in the which at your entering ye shall find a colt tied, whereon yet never man sat: loose him, and bring him hither.

31 And if any one ask you, Why do ye loose him? thus shall ye say unto him, that the Lord hath need of him.

32 And they that were sent went their way, and found even as he had said unto them.

33 And as they were loosing the colt, the owners thereof said unto them, Why loose ye the colt?

34 And they said that the Lord hath need of him.

35 And they brought him to Jesus: and they cast their garments upon the colt, and they sat Jesus thereon.

36 And as he went, they spread their clothes in the way.

37 And when he was drawing nigh, even now at the descent of the mount of Olives, the whole multitude of the disciples began to rejoice and praise God with a loud voice for all the mighty works that they had seen;

38 Saying, Blessed is the King that cometh in the name of the Lord : peace in heaven, and glory in the highest places.

39 And some of the Pharisees from among the multitude said unto him, Master, rebuke thy disciples.

40 And he answered and said, I tell you that, if these shall hold their peace, the stones will cry out.

41 ¶ And when he drew near, he beheld the city, and wept over it,

42 Saying, If thou hadst known, even thou, at least in this thy day, the things which belong unto thy peace! but now they are hid from thine eyes.

43 For the days shall come upon thee, that thine enemies shall cast a trench about thee, and compass thee round, and keep thee in on every side,

44 And shall lay thee even with the ground, and thy children within thee; and they shall not leave in thee one stone upon another; because thou knewest not the time of thy visitation.

45 And he went into the temple, and began to cast out them that sold,

46 Saying unto them, It is written, And my house shall be an house of prayer: but ye have made it a den of robbers.

47 And he taught daily in the temple. But the chief priests and the scribes and the chief of the people sought to destroy him,

48 And could not find what they might do: for all the people hung upon him, listening.

CHAPTER XX.

AND it came to pass, on one of the days, as he taught the people in the temple, and preached the gospel, the priests and the scribes came upon him with the elders,

2 And said unto him, Tell us, with what authority doest thou these things? or who is he that gave thee this authority?

3 And he answered and said unto them, I will also ask you one question; and answer me:

4 The baptism of John, was it of heaven, or of men?

5 And they reasoned with themselves, saying, If we shall say, Of heaven; he will say, Why believed ye him not?

6 But if we shall say, Of men; all the people will stone us: for they be persuaded that John was a prophet.

7 And they answered, that they knew not whence it was.

8 And Jesus said unto them, Neither do I tell you with what authority I do these things.

9 And he began to speak to the people this parable; A man planted a vineyard, and let it out to husbandmen, and left the country for a long time.

10 And at the season he sent a servant to the husbandmen, that they should give him of the fruit of the vineyard: but the husbandmen beat him, and sent him away empty.

11 And again he sent another

servant: and they beat him also, and treated him shamefully, and sent him away empty.

12 And again he sent a third: and they wounded him also, and cast him out.

13 And the lord of the vineyard said, What shall I do? I will send my beloved son: it may be they will reverence him when they see him.

14 But when the husbandmen saw him, they reasoned among themselves, saying, This is the heir: let us kill him, that the inheritance may be ours.

15 So they cast him out of the vineyard, and killed him. What therefore shall the lord of the vineyard do unto them?

16 He will come and destroy these husbandmen, and will give the vineyard to others. And when they heard it, they said, [1]God forbid.

17 And he looked upon them, and said, What is this then that is written, The stone which the builders rejected, the same was made the head of the corner?

18 Whosoever hath fallen upon that stone shall be broken; but on whomsoever it shall fall, it will grind him to powder.

19 And the scribes and the chief priests the same hour sought to lay hands on him; and they feared the people: for they perceived that he had spoken this parable against them.

20 And they watched him, and sent forth spies, which should feign themselves just men, that they might take hold of him by some saying, so as to deliver him unto the power and authority of the governor.

21 And they asked him, saying, Master, we know that thou sayest and teachest rightly, neither respectest thou persons, but teachest the way of God truly:

22 Is it lawful for us to give tribute unto Cæsar, or no?

23 But he perceived their craftiness, and said unto them,

24 Shew me a [2]penny. Whose image and superscription hath it? They answered and said, Cæsar's.

25 And he said unto them, Render therefore unto Cæsar the things that are Cæsar's, and unto God the things that are God's.

26 And they could not take hold of him for that saying before the people: and they marvelled at his answer, and held their peace.

27 ¶ But certain of the Sadducees, which deny that there is any resurrection, came to him, and asked him,

28 Saying, Master, Moses wrote unto us, If any man's brother die, having a wife, and he be without children, that his brother should take the wife, and raise up seed unto his brother.

29 There were therefore seven brethren: and the first took a wife, and died without children.

30 And the second and the third took her;

31 And in like manner the

---

[1] *Literally,* Let it not be

[2] *See note on Matt.* xx. 2.

seven also left no children, and died.

32 Last of all the woman died also.

33 Therefore in the resurrection whose wife of them shall the woman be? for the whole seven had her to wife.

34 And Jesus said unto them, The children of this world marry, and are given in marriage:

35 But they which shall be accounted worthy to obtain that world, and the resurrection from the dead, neither marry, nor are given in marriage:

36 For neither can they die any more: for they are equal unto the angels; and are the sons of God, being the sons of the resurrection.

37 But that the dead are raised, even Moses shewed in the history of the bush, when he calleth the Lord the God of Abraham, and the God of Isaac, and the God of Jacob.

38 For God is not God of the dead, but of the living: for all live unto him.

39 And certain of the scribes answering said, Master, thou hast well said.

40 For after that they durst not ask him any question at all.

41 But he said unto them, How say they that the Christ is David's son?

42 And David himself saith in the book of Psalms, The LORD said unto my Lord, Sit thou on my right hand,

43 Till I make thine enemies thy footstool.

44 David therefore calleth him Lord: and how is he his son?

45 ¶ Then in the hearing of all the people he said unto them,

46 Beware of the scribes, which desire to walk in long robes, and love greetings in the markets, and chief seats in the synagogues, and uppermost places at feasts;

47 Which devour widows' houses, and for a pretence make long prayers: these shall receive greater condemnation.

CHAPTER XXI.

AND he looked up, and saw the rich men which cast their gifts into the treasury.

2 And he saw also a certain poor widow casting in thither two mites.

3 And he said, Of a truth I say unto you, that this poor widow cast in more than they all:

4 For all these of their abundance cast in unto the gifts: but she of her want cast in all the living that she had.

5 ¶ And as some spake of the temple, that it was adorned with goodly stones and gifts, he said,

6 As for these things which ye behold, the days will come, in the which there shall not be left one stone upon another, that shall not be thrown down.

7 And they asked him, saying, Master, when then shall these things be? and what shall be the sign when these things are about to come to pass?

8 And he said, Take heed

that ye be not deceived: for many shall come in my name, saying, I am he; and, The time draweth near: go ye not after them.

9 But when ye shall hear of wars and commotions, be not terrified: for these things must first come to pass; but the end is not immediately.

10 Then said he unto them, Nation shall rise up against nation, and kingdom against kingdom:

11 And great earthquakes shall be in divers places, and pestilences, and famines; and fearful sights shall there be and great signs from heaven.

12 But before all these things, they shall lay their hands on you, and persecute you, delivering you up to synagogues, and into prisons, being brought before kings and rulers for my name's sake.

13 But it shall turn to you for a testimony.

14 Settle it therefore in your hearts, not to meditate before what ye shall answer.

15 For I will give you a mouth and wisdom, which all your adversaries shall not be able to gainsay nor resist.

16 Moreover ye shall be delivered up by parents, and brethren, and kinsfolks, and friends; and some of you shall they cause to be put to death.

17 And ye shall be hated by all men for my name's sake.

18 And yet there shall not an hair of your head perish.

19 By your patience ye shall save your souls.

¹ *Literally,* acquire.

20 But when ye shall see Jerusalem compassed with armies, then know that her desolation is nigh.

21 Then let them which are in Judæa flee to the mountains; and let them which are in the midst of her depart out; and let not them that are in the fields enter into her.

22 For these are the days of vengeance, that all things which are written may be fulfilled.

23 Woe unto them that are with child, and to them that give suck in those days! for there shall be great distress upon the earth, and wrath upon this people.

24 And they shall fall by the edge of the sword, and shall be led away captive into all the nations: and Jerusalem shall be trodden down by the Gentiles, until the times of the Gentiles be fulfilled.

25 ¶ And there shall be signs in the sun, and the moon, and the stars; and upon the earth distress of nations, with despair, for the roaring of the sea and the waves,

26 Men's hearts failing them for fear, and for expectation of those things which are coming on the earth: for the powers of the heavens shall be shaken.

27 And then shall they see the Son of man coming in a cloud with power and great glory.

28 And when these things begin to come to pass, look up, and lift up your heads; for your redemption draweth nigh.

29 And he spake to them a parable; Behold the fig tree, and all the trees;

30 When they now shoot forth, ye know of your own selves, when ye see it, that summer is now nigh at hand.

31 So likewise ye, when ye see these things coming to pass, know ye that the kingdom of God is nigh at hand.

32 Verily I say unto you, This generation shall not pass away, till all be fulfilled.

33 Heaven and earth shall pass away: but my words shall never pass away.

34 But take heed to yourselves, lest at any time your hearts be overcharged with surfeiting, and drunkenness, and cares of life, and that day come upon you unawares as a snare.

35 For it shall come on all them that [1]dwell on the face of the whole earth.

36 But watch ye, praying always that ye may be [2]able to escape all these things that shall come to pass, and to stand before the Son of man.

37 And in the day time he was teaching in the temple; but at night he went out, and abode in the mount that is called the mount of Olives.

38 And all the people came early in the morning to him in the temple, for to hear him.

CHAPTER XXII.

NOW the feast of unleavened bread drew nigh, which is called the Passover.

[1] *Literally,* sit.
[2] *So the two oldest MSS.*

2 And the chief priests and the scribes sought how they might kill him; for they feared the people.

3 But Satan entered into Judas surnamed Iscariot, being of the number of the twelve.

4 And he went his way, and communed with the chief priests and captains, how he might deliver him up unto them.

5 And they were glad, and covenanted to give him money.

6 And he promised, and sought opportunity to deliver him up unto them in the absence of the multitude.

7 ¶ And the day of unleavened bread came, when the passover must be killed.

8 And he sent Peter and John, saying, Go and prepare us the passover, that we may eat.

9 And they said unto him, Where wilt thou that we prepare?

10 And he said unto them, Behold, when ye are entered into the city, there shall meet you a man, bearing a pitcher of water; follow him into the house where he entereth in.

11 And ye shall say unto the owner of the house, The Master saith unto thee, Where is the guestchamber, where I shall eat the passover with my disciples?

12 And he will shew you a large upper room furnished: there make ready.

13 And they went, and found as he had said unto them: and they made ready the passover.

14 And when the hour was come, he sat down, and the apostles with him.

15 And he said unto them, With desire I desired to eat this passover with you before I suffer:

16 For I say unto you, I will not any more eat it, until it be fulfilled in the kingdom of God.

17 And he took a cup, and gave thanks, and said, Take this, and divide it among yourselves:

18 For I say unto you, I will not henceforth drink of the fruit of the vine, until the kingdom of God shall come.

19 And he took bread, and gave thanks, and brake it, and gave it unto them, saying, This is my body which is given for you: this do in remembrance of me.

20 And in like manner the cup after supper, saying, This cup is the new covenant in my blood, which is shed for you.

21 But behold, the hand of him that [1]betrayeth me is with me on the table.

22 And truly the Son of man goeth according to that which hath been determined: but woe unto that man by whom he is [2]betrayed!

23 And they began to enquire among themselves, which of them it was that should do this thing.

24 And there was also a strife among them, which of them should be accounted the greatest.

25 But he said unto them, The kings of the Gentiles exercise lordship over them; and they that exercise authority upon them are called benefactors.

26 But ye shall not be so: but he that is greatest among you, let him be as the younger; and he that is chief, as he that doth serve.

27 For which is greater, he that sitteth at meat, or he that serveth? is not he that sitteth at meat? but I am among you as he that serveth.

28 Ye are they which have continued with me in my temptations.

29 And I appoint unto you a kingdom, even as my Father hath appointed unto me;

30 That ye may eat and drink at my table in my kingdom, and sit on thrones judging the twelve tribes of Israel.

31 Simon, Simon, behold, Satan hath prevailed to have you all, that he may sift you as wheat:

32 But I have prayed for thee, that thy faith fail not: and when thou art converted, strengthen thy brethren.

33 And he said unto him, Lord, I am ready to go with thee, both into prison, and to death.

34 And he said, I tell thee, Peter, the cock shall not crow this day, before that thou hast thrice denied that thou knowest me.

35 And he said unto them, When I sent you without purse, and scrip, and shoes, lacked ye any thing? And they said, Nothing.

36 He said therefore unto them, But now, he that hath a purse, let him take it, and in

---

[1] Delivereth me up.
[2] Delivered up.

like manner a scrip: and he that hath no sword, let him sell his garment, and buy one.

37 For I say unto you, that this that is written must yet be accomplished in me, And he was reckoned among the transgressors: for the matter concerning me hath an end.

38 And they said, Lord, behold, here are two swords. And he said unto them, It is enough.

39 ¶ And he came out, and went, as he was wont, to the mount of Olives; and his disciples also followed him.

40 And when he was at the place, he said unto them, Pray that ye enter not into temptation.

41 And he withdrew himself from them about a stone's cast, and kneeled down, and prayed,

42 Saying, Father, if thou be willing to remove this cup from me,—nevertheless not my will, but thine, be done.

¹43 And there appeared an angel unto him from heaven, strengthening him.

44 And being in an agony he prayed more earnestly: and his sweat was as it were great drops of blood falling down to the ground.

45 And when he rose up from his prayer, he came to the disciples, and found them sleeping for sorrow,

46 And said unto them, Why sleep ye? arise and pray that ye enter not into temptation.

47 While he yet spake, behold a multitude, and he that was called Judas, one of the twelve, went before them, and drew near unto Jesus to kiss him.

48 But Jesus said unto him, Judas, ²betrayest thou the Son of man with a kiss?

49 When they which were about him saw what would follow, they said unto him, Lord, shall we smite with the sword?

50 And a certain one of them smote the servant of the high priest, and cut off his right ear.

51 But Jesus answered and said, ³Suffer ye thus far. And he touched his ear, and healed him.

52 And Jesus said unto the chief priests, and captains of the temple, and elders, which were come against him, Ye are come out, as against a thief, with swords and staves.

53 When I was daily with you in the temple, ye stretched not forth your hands against me: but this is your hour, and the power of darkness.

54 ¶ And when they had taken him, they led him, and brought him into the high priest's house. And Peter followed afar off.

55 And when they had kindled a fire in the midst of the hall, and were set down together, Peter sat down among them.

56 But a certain maid saw

---

¹ *Verses* 43, 44 *are not found in some of the oldest MSS.; but they are contained in the greater number, and in the earliest versions, and are quoted by the primitive Fathers, Justin, Irenæus, and Hippolytus.*

² Deliverest thou up.
³ *i.e.* Give me thus much liberty: *viz.*, to stretch out His arm and touch the man's ear.

him as he sat in the light of the fire, and earnestly looked upon him, and said, This man was also with him.

57 But he denied ¹[him], saying, Woman, I know him not.

58 And after a little while another saw him, and said, Thou art also of them. But Peter said, Man, I am not.

59 And about the space of one hour after another confidently affirmed, saying, Of a truth this man also was with him: for he is a Galilæan.

60 And Peter said, Man, I know not what thou sayest. And immediately, while he yet spake, the cock crew.

61 And the Lord turned, and looked upon Peter. And Peter remembered the word of the Lord, how he said unto him, Before the cock crow this day, thou shalt deny me thrice.

62 And Peter went out, and wept bitterly.

63 ¶ And the men that held him mocked him, and smote him.

64 And when they had blindfolded him, they asked him, saying, Prophesy, who is it that smote thee?

65 And many other things blasphemously spake they against him.

66 ¶ And when it was day, the assembly of elders of the people, both chief priests and scribes, was gathered together, and they led him into their council, saying,

67 If thou art the Christ, tell us. But he said unto them, If I tell you, ye will not believe:

¹ *Many ancient MSS. omit* him.

68 And if I ask you questions, ye will not answer me ²[nor let me go].

69 Henceforth shall the Son of man be seated on the right hand of the power of God.

70 But they all said, Art thou then the Son of God? And he said unto them, Ye say that I am.

71 And they said, Why need we any further witness? for we ourselves heard from his own mouth.

CHAPTER XXIII.

AND the whole multitude of them arose, and led him unto Pilate.

2 And they began to accuse him, saying, We found this man perverting our nation, and forbidding to give tribute to Cæsar, and saying that he himself is Christ a King.

3 And Pilate asked him, saying, Art thou the King of the Jews? And he answered him and said, Thou sayest it.

4 But Pilate said to the chief priests, and to the multitudes, I find no fault in this man.

5 But they were the more fierce, saying, He stirreth up the people, teaching throughout all Judæa, beginning from Galilee to this place.

6 When Pilate heard of Galilee, he asked whether the man were a Galilæan.

7 And as soon as he knew that he belonged unto Herod's jurisdiction, he sent him to Herod, who himself also was at Jerusalem at that time.

² *Omitted in several of the oldest MSS.*

8 And when Herod saw Jesus, he was exceeding glad: for he was desirous to see him of a long season, because he had heard of him; and he hoped to have seen some miracle done by him.

9 And he questioned with him in many words; but he answered him nothing.

10 And the chief priests and the scribes stood and vehemently accused him.

11 And Herod with his troops set him at nought, and mocked him, and arrayed him in a gorgeous robe, and sent him again to Pilate.

12 And the same day Pilate and Herod were made friends together: for before they were at enmity between themselves.

13 ¶ And Pilate called together the chief priests and the rulers and the people,

14 And said unto them, Ye have brought this man unto me, as one that perverteth the people: and, behold, I have examined him before you, and have found no fault in this man touching those things whereof ye accuse him:

15 No, nor yet Herod: for I sent you to him; and, lo, nothing worthy of death hath been done by him.

16 I will therefore chastise him, and release him.

¹[17 For of necessity he must release one unto them at the feast.]

18 But they cried out all at once, saying, Away with this man, and release unto us Barabbas:

19 Who for a certain sedition made in the city, and for murder, was cast into prison.

20 But Pilate, willing to release Jesus, spake again to them.

21 But they continued crying, saying, Crucify him, crucify him.

22 And he said unto them the third time, Why, what evil hath he done? I have found no cause of death in him: I will therefore chastise him, and let him go.

23 And they were urgent with loud voices, requiring that he might be crucified. And the voices of them and of the chief priests prevailed.

24 And Pilate gave sentence that it should be as they required.

25 And he released unto them him that for sedition and murder was cast into prison, whom they desired; but he delivered up Jesus to their will.

26 And as they led him away, they laid hold upon one Simon, a Cyrenian, coming out of the country, and on him they laid the cross, that he might bear it after Jesus.

27 ¶ And there followed him a great company of the people, and of women, which also bewailed and lamented him.

28 But Jesus turning unto them said, Daughters of Jerusalem, weep not for me, but weep for yourselves, and for your children.

29 For behold, the days are coming, in which they shall

---

¹ *This verse is omitted in several of the early MSS.: but is contained in others.*

CH. XXIII.]   GOSPEL OF ST. LUKE.   141

say, Blessed are the barren, and the wombs that never bare, and the paps which never gave suck.

30 Then shall they begin to say to the mountains, Fall on us ; and to the hills, Cover us.

31 For if they do these things ¹ to the green tree, what shall be done ¹ to the dry ?

32 And there were also two other malefactors led with him to be put to death.

33 And when they were come to the place, which is called A skull, there they crucified him, and the malefactors, one on the right hand, and the other on the left.

34 But Jesus said, Father, forgive them ; for they know not what they do. And parting his garments among them, they cast lots.

35 And the people stood beholding. And the rulers also derided him, saying, He saved others ; let him save himself, if this man is the Christ of God, his chosen.

36 And the soldiers also mocked him, coming near and offering him vinegar,

37 And saying, If thou art the king of the Jews, save thyself.

38 And a superscription also was written over him ² [in letters of Greek, and Latin, and Hebrew], THIS IS THE KING OF THE JEWS.

39 And one of the malefactors which were hanged railed on him, saying, Art not thou the Christ? Save thyself and us.

40 But the other answering rebuked him, saying, Dost not even thou fear God, seeing thou art in the same condemnation ?

41 And we indeed justly ; for we receive the due reward of our deeds : but this man hath done nothing amiss.

42 And he said, Jesus, remember me when thou comest in thy kingdom.

43 And he said unto him, Verily I say unto thee, To day shalt thou be with me in Paradise.

44 And it was now about the sixth hour, and there was darkness over all the earth until the ninth hour.

45 And the sun was darkened, and the veil of the temple was rent in the midst.

46 And Jesus cried with a loud voice, and said, Father, into thy hands I commend my spirit : and having said thus, he ³ gave up the ghost.

47 But when the centurion saw what was done, he glorified God, saying, Certainly this man was ⁴ innocent.

48 And all the multitudes that came together to that sight, when they beheld the things which were done, turned back, smiting upon their breasts.

49 And all his acquaintance, and the women that followed him from Galilee, stood afar off, beholding these things.

¹ *Literally*, in the case of.
² *These words are omitted in several of the early MSS., but inserted in others, and in the earliest versions. See John xix. 20.*

³ *Literally*, expired : " breathed his last."
⁴ *Literally*, righteous.

50 ¶ And, behold, a man named Joseph, being a counsellor, was a good man, and a just,

51 (The same had not consented to the counsel and deed of them;) of Arimathæa, a city of the Jews, who also himself waited for the kingdom of God;

52 This man went unto Pilate, and begged the body of Jesus.

53 And he took it down, and wrapped it in linen, and laid it in a sepulchre that was hewn in stone, wherein never man before was laid.

54 And that day was the preparation, and the sabbath drew on.

55 And the women also, which had come with him from Galilee, followed after, and beheld the sepulchre, and how his body was laid.

56 And they returned, and prepared spices and ointments. And on the sabbath indeed, they rested according to the commandment;

CHAPTER XXIV.

BUT upon the first day of the week, [1] when it was just beginning to dawn, they came unto the sepulchre, bringing the spices which they had prepared.

2 And they found the stone rolled away from the sepulchre.

3 But on entering in, they found not the body of the Lord Jesus.

4 And it came to pass, as they were perplexed thereabout, behold, two men stood by them in shining garments:

5 And as they were afraid, and bowed down their faces to the earth, they said unto them, Why seek ye the living among the dead?

6 He is not here, but is risen: remember how he spake unto you when he was yet in Galilee,

7 Saying, The Son of man must be delivered up into the hands of sinful men, and be crucified, and the third day rise again.

8 And they remembered his words,

9 And returned from the sepulchre, and told all these things unto the eleven, and to all the rest.

10 It was Mary Magdelene, and Joanna, and Mary the mother of James, and the other women with them, which told these things unto the apostles.

11 And these words seemed to them as idle tales, and they believed them not.

12 But Peter arose, and ran unto the sepulchre; and stooping down, he beheld the linen clothes lying by themselves, and departed to his own home, wondering at that which was come to pass.

13 ¶ And, behold, two of them were journeying that same day to a village called Emmaus, which was distant from Jerusalem threescore furlongs.

14 And they talked together of all these things which had happened.

15 And it came to pass, that, while they talked together and

---

[1] *Literally*, at deep dawn.

reasoned, Jesus himself drew near, and went with them.

16 But their eyes were holden that they should not know him.

17 And he said unto them, What manner of communications are these that ye have one to another, as ye walk? ¹And they stood still, and were sad.

18 And one of them, whose name was Cleopas, answering said unto him, Dost thou lodge alone in Jerusalem, and hast not known the things which are come to pass there in these days?

19 And he said unto them, What things? And they said unto him, Concerning Jesus of Nazareth, which was a prophet mighty in deed and word before God and all the people:

20 And how the chief priests and our rulers delivered him to be condemned to death, and crucified him.

21 But we hoped that it had been he which should have redeemed Israel: and beside all this, to day is the third day since these things were done.

22 Yea, and certain women also of our company made us astonished, which were early at the sepulchre;

23 And when they found not his body, they came, saying, that they had also seen a vision of angels, which said that he was alive.

24 And certain of them which were with us went to the sepulchre, and found it even so as the women had said: but him they saw not.

25 And he said unto them, O fools, and slow of heart to believe all that the prophets spake:

26 Ought not the Christ to have suffered these things, and to enter into his glory?

27 And beginning at Moses and at all the prophets, he expounded unto them in all the scriptures the things concerning himself.

28 And they drew nigh unto the village, whither they were going: and he made as though he would go further.

29 And they constrained him, saying, Abide with us: for it is toward evening, and the day is now far spent. And he went in to tarry with them.

30 And it came to pass, as he sat at meat with them, he took the bread, and blessed it, and brake, and gave to them.

31 And their eyes were opened, and they knew him; and he vanished out of their sight.

32 And they said one to another, Did not our heart burn within us, while he talked with us by the way, while he opened to us the scriptures?

33 And they rose up the same hour, and returned to Jerusalem, and found the eleven gathered together, and them that were with them,

34 Saying, The Lord is risen indeed, and hath appeared to Simon.

35 And they told what things were done in the way, and how

---

¹ *There is great difference of reading here. We have followed the two oldest MSS., the Vatican and the Sinaitic.*

he was known to them in breaking of bread.

36 ¶ And as they thus spake, he himself stood in the midst of them, and saith unto them, Peace be unto you.

37 But they were terrified and affrighted, and supposed that they saw a spirit.

38 And he said unto them, Why are ye troubled? and why do doubts arise in your hearts?

39 Behold my hands and my feet, that it is I myself: handle me, and see; for a spirit hath not flesh and bones, as ye see me have.

40 And when he had thus spoken, he shewed them his hands and his feet.

41 And while they yet believed not for joy, and wondered, he said unto them, Have ye here any food?

42 And they gave him a piece of a broiled fish, and of an honeycomb.

43 And he took it, and did eat before them.

44 And he said unto them, These are my words which I spake unto you, while I was yet with you, that all things must be fulfilled, which are written in the law of Moses, and in the prophets, and in the psalms, concerning me.

45 Then opened he their understanding, that they might understand the scriptures,

46 And said unto them, Thus it is written, and thus it behoved the Christ to suffer, and to rise from the dead the third day:

47 And that repentance and remission of sins should be preached in his name among all the nations, beginning at Jerusalem.

48 Ye are witnesses of these things.

49 And behold, I send the promise of my Father upon you: but tarry ye in the city,[1] until ye be clothed with power from on high.

50 ¶ And he led them out as far as to Bethany, and he lifted up his hands, and blessed them.

51 And it came to pass, while he blessed them, he was parted from them, and carried up into heaven.

52 And they worshipped him, and returned to Jerusalem with great joy:

53 And were continually in the temple, praising and blessing God.

[1] Of Jerusalem *is omitted in all the oldest MSS.*

THE GOSPEL
ACCORDING TO
SAINT JOHN.

CHAPTER I.

IN the beginning was the Word, and the Word was with God, and the Word was God.

2 The same was in the beginning with God.

3 All things were made by him; and without him was not any thing made that hath been made.

4 In him was life; and the life was the light of men.

5 And the light shineth in the darkness; and the darkness comprehended it not.

6 There was a man sent from God, whose name was John.

7 The same came for witness, to bear witness of the Light, that all men through him might believe.

8 He was not the Light, but [came] to bear witness of the Light.

9 The true Light, which lighteneth every man, came into the world.

10 He was in the world, and the world was made by him, and the world knew him not.

11 He came unto his own possessions, and his own people received him not.

12 But as many as received him, to them gave he power to become children of God, even to them that believe in his name:

13 Which were born, not of blood, nor of the will of the flesh, nor of the will of man, but of God.

14 And the Word became flesh, and [1]dwelt among us, (and we beheld his glory, glory as of the only-begotten from the Father,) full of grace and truth.

15 John beareth witness of him, and crieth, saying, This was he of whom I said, He that cometh after me [2]taketh place before me: because he was before me.

16 And out of his fulness all we received, and grace for grace.

17 Because the law was given through Moses; grace and truth came through Jesus Christ.

18 No man hath seen God at any time; the only-begotten [3]Son, which is in the bosom of the Father, he declared him.

19 And this is the testimony of John, when the Jews sent priests and Levites from Jerusalem to ask him, Who art thou?

20 And he confessed, and denied not; and he confessed, I am not the Christ.

[1] *Literally*, had his tabernacle.
[2] *Literally*, is become.
[3] *Many ancient MSS. and authorities have*, the only-begotten God.

21 And they asked him, What then? Art thou Elijah? And he saith, I am not. Art thou the prophet? And he answered, No.

22 They said therefore unto him, Who art thou? that we may give an answer to them that sent us. What sayest thou of thyself?

23 He said, I am the voice of one crying in the wilderness, Make straight the way of the Lord, as said Isaiah the prophet.

24 And they had been sent by the Pharisees.

25 And they asked him, and said unto him, Why baptizest thou then, if thou art not the Christ, nor Elijah, neither the prophet?

26 John answered them, saying, I baptize with water: but in the midst of you there standeth one whom ye know not.

27 This is he that cometh after me, who [1]taketh place before me, the thong of whose shoe I am not worthy to unloose.

28 These things were done in [2]Bethany beyond Jordan, where John was baptizing.

29 ¶ The next day he seeth Jesus coming unto him, and saith, Behold the Lamb of God, which taketh away the sin of the world.

30 This is he of whom I said, After me cometh a man which [1]taketh place before me: because he was before me.

See on ver. 15.
[2] *So all the oldest MSS.*

31 And I knew him not: but that he should be made manifest to Israel, for this cause came I baptizing with water.

32 And John bare witness, saying, I have beheld the Spirit descending as a dove from heaven, and it remained upon him.

33 And I knew him not: but he that sent me to baptize with water, the same said unto me, Upon whomsoever thou shalt see the Spirit descending, and remaining upon him, the same is he which baptizeth with the Holy Spirit.

34 And I have seen, and have borne witness that this is the Son of God.

35 ¶ Again the next day John was standing, and two of his disciples;

36 And looking upon Jesus as he walked, he saith, Behold the Lamb of God!

37 And the two disciples heard him speak; and they followed Jesus.

38 But Jesus turned, and beheld them following, and saith unto them, What seek ye? They said unto him, Rabbi, (which is to say, being interpreted, Master,) where abidest thou?

39 He saith unto them, Come and see. They came and saw where he abode, and remained with him that day: it was about the tenth hour.

40 One of the two which heard John speak, and followed him, was Andrew, Simon Peter's brother.

41 He first findeth his own

brother Simon, and saith unto him, We have found the Messias (which is, being interpreted, Christ).

42 And he brought him to Jesus. Jesus looked on him and said, Thou art Simon the son of [1]Jonas : thou shalt be called Cephas (which is by interpretation, Peter).

43 ¶ The next day Jesus was minded to go forth into Galilee, and findeth Philip, and saith unto him, Follow me.

44 Now Philip was from Bethsaida, of the city of Andrew and Peter.

45 Philip findeth Nathanael, and saith unto him, We have found him of whom Moses in the law, and the prophets, did write, Jesus, the son of Joseph, which is from Nazareth.

46 And Nathanael said unto him, Can any good thing come out of Nazareth? Philip saith unto him, Come and see.

47 Jesus saw Nathanael coming to him, and saith of him, Behold an Israelite indeed, in whom is no guile!

48 Nathanael saith unto him, Whence knowest thou me? Jesus answered and said unto him, Before Philip called thee, when thou wast under the fig tree, I saw thee.

49 Nathanael answered him, Rabbi, thou art the Son of God; thou art the King of Israel.

50 Jesus answered and said unto him, Because I said unto thee, I saw thee under the fig tree, believest thou? thou shalt see greater things than these.

51 And he saith unto him, Verily, verily, I say unto you, Ye shall see the heaven opened, and the angels of God ascending and descending upon the Son of man.

CHAPTER II.

AND the third day there was a marriage in Cana of Galilee ; and the mother of Jesus was there.

2 And Jesus also was bidden, and his disciples, to the marriage.

3 And when wine failed, the mother of Jesus saith unto him, They have no wine.

4 Jesus saith unto her, Woman, what have I to do with thee? mine hour is not yet come.

5 His mother saith unto the servants, Whatsoever he saith unto you, do it.

6 Now there were set there six waterpots of stone, after the manner of the purifying of the Jews, holding two or three firkins apiece.

7 Jesus saith unto them, Fill the waterpots with water. And they filled them up to the brim.

8 And he saith unto them, Draw out now, and bear unto the ruler of the feast. And they bare it.

9 But when the ruler of the feast tasted the water now become wine, and knew not whence it was : (but the servants which had drawn the

---

[1] *Most of the ancient MSS., here and in chap.* xxi. 15—17, *have for Jonas,* John. *But, the same name being apparently represented, I have made no change in the English.*

water knew;) the ruler of the feast calleth the bridegroom,

10 And saith unto him, Every man setteth on the good wine first; and when men are drunken, then that which is worse : thou hast kept the good wine until now.

11 This beginning of his miracles did Jesus in Cana of Galilee, and manifested his glory; and his disciples believed in him.

12 After this he went down to Capernaum, he, and his mother, and his brethren, and his disciples : and there they continued not many days.

13 And the passover of the Jews was at hand, and Jesus went up to Jerusalem.

14 And he found in the temple those that sold oxen and sheep and doves, and the changers of money sitting :

15 And when he had made a scourge of small cords, he drove all out of the temple, both the sheep and the oxen; and poured out the changers' money, and overthrew their tables;

16 And to them that sold the doves, he said, Take these things hence; make not my Father's house an house of merchandise.

17 And his disciples remembered that it is written, My zeal for thine house shall eat me up.

18 The Jews therefore answered and said unto him, What sign shewest thou unto us, seeing that thou doest these things?

19 Jesus answered and said unto them, Destroy this temple, and in three days I will raise it up.

20 Then said the Jews, Forty and six years was this temple in building, and wilt thou raise it in three days?

21 But he spake of the temple of his body.

22 When therefore he was risen from the dead, his disciples remembered that he had said this; and they believed the scripture, and the word which Jesus had spoken.

23 Now when he was in Jerusalem at the passover, at the feast, many believed in his name, beholding his miracles which he did.

24 Yet Jesus did not trust himself to them, because he knew all men,

25 And because he needed not that any one should testify of man : for of himself he knew what was in man.

CHAPTER III.

BUT there was a man of the Pharisees, named Nicodemus, a ruler of the Jews :

2 The same came to him by night, and said unto him, Rabbi, we know that thou art a teacher come from God : for no man can do these miracles that thou doest, except God be with him.

3 Jesus answered and said unto him, Verily, verily, I say unto thee, Except a man be born [1]anew, he cannot see the kingdom of God.

[1] *Or*, from above.

4 Nicodemus saith unto him, How can a man be born when he is old? can he enter the second time into his mother's womb, and be born?

5 Jesus answered, Verily, verily, I say unto thee, Except a man be born of water and the Spirit, he cannot enter into the kingdom of God.

6 That which hath been born of the flesh is flesh; and that which hath been born of the Spirit is spirit.

7 Marvel not that I said unto thee, Ye must be born [1]anew.

8 The wind bloweth where it will, and thou hearest the sound thereof, but knowest not whence it cometh, and whither it goeth: so is every one that hath been born of the Spirit.

9 Nicodemus answered and said unto him, How can these things be?

10 Jesus answered and said unto him, Art thou the teacher of Israel, and understandest not these things?

11 Verily, verily, I say unto thee, We speak that which we know, and testify that which we have seen; and ye receive not our testimony.

12 If I have told you earthly things, and ye believe not, how shall ye believe, if I tell you heavenly things?

13 And no one hath ascended into heaven, but he that came down from heaven, [even] the Son of man which is in heaven.

14 And as Moses lifted up the serpent in the wilderness, even so must the Son of man be lifted up:

[1] *Or,* from above.

15 That whosoever believeth in him may not perish, but may have eternal life.

16 For God so loved the world, that he gave his only-begotten Son, that whosoever believeth in him might not perish, but might have eternal life.

17 For God sent not his Son into the world that he might judge the world; but that the world through him might be saved.

18 He that believeth in him cometh not into judgment: but he that believeth not hath been judged already, because he hath not believed in the name of the only-begotten Son of God.

19 And this is the judgment, that the light is come into the world, and men loved the darkness rather than the light; for their works were evil.

20 For every one that doeth evil hateth the light, and cometh not to the light, lest his works should be detected.

21 But he that doeth the truth cometh to the light, that his works may be made manifest, that they are wrought in God.

22 ¶ After these things came Jesus and his disciples into the land of Judæa; and there he tarried with them, and baptized.

23 But John also was baptizing in Ænon near to Salim, because there was much water there: and they came, and were baptized.

24 For John was not yet cast into prison.

25 Then there arose a question on the part of John's disciples with [1] a Jew about purifying.

26 And they came unto John, and said unto him, Rabbi, he that was with thee beyond Jordan, to whom thou hast borne witness, behold, the same baptizeth, and all men come to him.

27 John answered and said, A man can receive nothing, except it have been given him from heaven.

28 Ye yourselves bear me witness, that I said, I am not the Christ, but that I am sent before him.

29 He that hath the bride is the bridegroom: but the friend of the bridegroom, which standeth and heareth him, rejoiceth with joy because of the bridegroom's voice: this my joy therefore is fulfilled.

30 He must increase, but I must decrease.

31 He that cometh from above is above all: he that is of the earth is of the earth, and speaketh of the earth: he that cometh from heaven is above all;

32 What he hath seen and heard, that he testifieth; and his testimony no man receiveth.

33 He that hath received his testimony hath set his seal that God is true.

34 For he whom God sent speaketh the words of God: for God giveth not the Spirit by measure.

35 The Father loveth the

Son, and hath given all things into his hand.

36 He that believeth in the Son hath eternal life, but he that believeth not the Son shall not see life, but the wrath of God abideth on him.

CHAPTER IV.

WHEN therefore [2] the Lord knew that the Pharisees had heard that Jesus made and baptized more disciples than John,

2 (Howbeit Jesus himself baptized not, but his disciples,)

3 He left Judæa, and departed again into Galilee.

4 Now he must needs go through Samaria.

5 He cometh therefore to a city of Samaria, called Sychar, near to the parcel of ground that Jacob gave to his son Joseph.

6 Now Jacob's well was there. Jesus therefore, being wearied with his journey, was sitting thus by the well. It was about the sixth hour.

7 There cometh a woman of Samaria to draw water: Jesus saith unto her, Give me to drink.

8 For his disciples were gone away unto the city to buy food.

9 The Samaritan woman therefore saith unto him, How is it that thou, being a Jew, askest drink of me, which am a Samaritan woman? for Jews have no dealings with Samaritans.

10 Jesus answered and said

[1] *So most of the oldest MSS.*

[2] *Some of the earliest MSS. and authorities have, instead of* the Lord, Jesus.

GOSPEL OF ST. JOHN.

unto her, If thou knewest the gift of God, and who it is that saith to thee, Give me to drink; thou wouldest have asked of him, and he would have given thee living water.

11 The woman saith unto him, Sir, thou hast nothing to draw with, and the well is deep: from whence then hast thou that living water?

12 Art thou greater than our father Jacob, which gave us the well, and drank thereof himself, and his sons, and his cattle?

13 Jesus answered and said unto her, Every one that drinketh of this water shall thirst again:

14 But whosoever shall drink of the water that I shall give him shall not thirst for evermore; but the water that I shall give him shall become in him a fountain of water springing up into eternal life.

15 The woman saith unto him, Sir, give me this water, that I thirst not, neither come all the way hither to draw.

16 He saith unto her, Go, call thy husband, and come hither.

17 The woman answered and said, I have not a husband. Jesus saith unto her, Thou saidst well, I have not a husband:

18 For thou hast had five husbands; and now he whom thou hast is not thy husband: in this thou hast spoken truth.

19 The woman saith unto him, Sir, I perceive that thou art a prophet.

20 Our fathers worshipped in this mountain; and ye say, that in Jerusalem is the place where men ought to worship.

21 Jesus saith unto her, Woman, believe me, an hour cometh, when neither in this mountain, nor in Jerusalem, shall ye worship the Father.

22 Ye worship that which ye know not: we worship that which we know; because salvation cometh of the Jews.

23 Howbeit an hour cometh, and now is, when the true worshippers shall worship the Father in spirit and truth: for such the Father also seeketh them that worship him to be.

24 God is a Spirit: and they that worship him must worship in spirit and truth.

25 The woman saith unto him, I know that Messias cometh, which is called Christ: when he shall come, he will tell us all things.

26 Jesus saith unto her, I that speak unto thee am he.

27 And upon this came his disciples, and marvelled that he was talking with a woman: yet no one said, What seekest thou? or, Why talkest thou with her?

28 The woman then left her waterpot, and went away into the city, and saith to the men,

29 Come, see a man, which told me all things that ever I did: is this the Christ?

30 They went out of the city, and were coming to him.

31 In the mean while his disciples prayed him, saying, Rabbi, eat.

32 But he said unto them, I

have meat to eat that ye know not of.

33 Therefore said the disciples one to another, Hath any man brought him ought to eat?

34 Jesus saith unto them, My meat is that I should do the will of him that sent me, and should finish his work.

35 Say not ye, There are yet four months, and then cometh harvest? lo, I say unto you, Lift up your eyes, and behold the fields, that they are white to harvest already.

36 He that reapeth receiveth wages, and gathereth fruit unto eternal life; that both the sower and the reaper may rejoice together.

37 For herein is [fulfilled] that true saying, One is the sower and another the reaper.

38 I sent you to reap that whereon ye have bestowed no labour: others have laboured, and ye are entered into their labours.

39 Now many of the Samaritans of that city believed in him for the saying of the woman, which testified, He told me all things that ever I did.

40 When therefore the Samaritans came unto him, they besought him to tarry with them: and he tarried there two days.

41 And many more believed because of his word;

42 And said unto the woman, No longer do we believe because of thy story; for we have heard for ourselves, and know that this is indeed [1]the Saviour of the world.

43 ¶ Now after two days he departed thence into Galilee.

44 For Jesus himself testified, that a prophet hath no honour in his own country.

45 When therefore he came into Galilee, the Galilæans received him, having seen all the things that he did in Jerusalem at the feast: for they also went unto the feast.

46 So he came again unto Cana of Galilee, where he made the water wine. And there was a certain nobleman whose son was sick at Capernaum.

47 The same, when he heard that Jesus was come out of Judæa into Galilee, went unto him, and besought him to come down, and heal his son: for he was at the point of death.

48 Then said Jesus unto him, Except ye see signs and wonders, ye will never believe.

49 The nobleman saith unto him, Lord, come down ere my child die.

50 Jesus saith unto him, Go thy way; thy son liveth. The man believed the word that Jesus spake unto him, and went his way.

51 But as he was now going down, his servants met him, and brought tidings, saying, Thy child liveth.

52 He inquired therefore of them the hour in which he began to amend. So they said unto him, Yesterday in the

[1] *The Christ is omitted by most of the oldest MSS.*

seventh hour the fever left him.

53 The father knew therefore that it was in that hour, in the which Jesus said unto him, Thy son liveth: and himself believed, and his whole house.

54 This again, a second miracle, did Jesus, when he was come out of Judæa into Galilee.

CHAPTER V.

AFTER these things there was a feast of the Jews; and Jesus went up to Jerusalem.

2 Now there is in Jerusalem by the sheep-gate a pool, which is called in the Hebrew tongue Bethesda, having five porches.

3 In these lay a multitude of the sick, of blind, halt, withered.[1]

5 And there was a certain man there, which had been thirty and eight years in his infirmity.

6 When Jesus saw him lying, and knew that he had been now a long time in that case, he saith unto him, Desirest thou to be made whole?

7 The sick man answered him, Sir, I have no man, when the water is troubled, to put me into the pool: but while I am coming, another goeth down before me.

[1] *The words which follow in the received text*, waiting for the moving of the water. For an angel went down at certain seasons into the pool, and troubled the water: he therefore who first went in after the troubling of the water was made whole, with whatsoever disease he was afflicted, *are not found in the great majority of the ancient MSS.*

8 Jesus saith unto him, Rise, take up thy bed, and walk.

9 And immediately the man was made whole, and took up his bed, and walked. Now on that day was the sabbath.

10 The Jews therefore said unto him that was cured, It is the sabbath day: it is not lawful for thee to take up thy bed.

11 He answered them, He that made me whole, the same said unto me, Take up thy bed, and walk.

12 They asked him, Who is the man which said unto thee, Take up,[2] and walk?

13 But he that was healed wist not who it was: for Jesus escaped his notice, a multitude being in the place.

14 Afterward Jesus findeth him in the temple, and said unto him, Behold, thou art made whole: sin no more, lest some worse thing befall thee.

15 The man departed, and brought the Jews word that it was Jesus which made him whole.

16 And for this cause the Jews persecuted Jesus,[3] because he did these things on the sabbath day.

17 But Jesus answered them, My Father worketh even until now, and I work.

18 For this cause therefore the Jews sought the more to kill him, because he not only broke the sabbath, but also called God his own Father, making himself equal with God.

19 Jesus answered therefore

[2] *So the majority of the ancient MSS.*
[3] *So the oldest MSS.*

and said unto them, Verily, verily, I say unto you, The Son can do nothing of himself, save what he seeth the Father doing: for what things soever he doeth, these also doeth the Son in like manner.

20 For the Father loveth the Son, and sheweth him all things that himself doeth: and greater works than these will he shew him, that ye may marvel.

21 For like as the Father raiseth up the dead, and quickeneth them; even so the Son also quickeneth whom he will.

22 For neither doth the Father judge any one, but hath committed judgment altogether unto the Son:

23 That all may honour the Son, even as they honour the Father. He that honoureth not the Son honoureth not the Father which sent him.

24 Verily, verily, I say unto you, He that heareth my word, and believeth him that sent me, hath eternal life, and cometh not into judgment, but hath passed out of death into life.

25 Verily, verily, I say unto you, An hour cometh, and now is, when the dead shall hear the voice of the Son of God: and they that hear shall live.

26 For like as the Father hath life in himself; even so gave he to the Son also to have life in himself;

27 And gave him authority to execute judgment, because he is the Son of man.

28 Marvel not at this: for an hour cometh, in which all that are in the graves shall hear his voice,

29 And shall come forth; they that have done good, unto the resurrection of life; and they that have done evil, unto the resurrection of judgment.

30 I can of mine own self do nothing: as I hear, I judge: and my judgment is just; because I seek not mine own will, but the will of him that sent me.

31 If I bear witness concerning myself, my witness is not true.

32 It is another that beareth witness of me; and I know that the witness which he witnesseth of me is true.

33 Ye have sent unto John, and he hath borne witness unto the truth.

34 Yet the witness which I receive is not from man: but these things I say, that ye may be saved.

35 He was the lamp that burneth and shineth: and ye were willing to rejoice for a while in his light.

36 But the testimony which I have is greater than John: for the works which the Father gave me to finish, the very works that I am doing, bear witness of me, that the Father hath sent me.

37 And the Father which sent me, himself hath borne witness of me. Ye have neither heard his voice at any time, nor have seen his shape.

38 And ye have not his word abiding in you: for whom he sent, him ye believe not.

39 ¹Search the scriptures: because ye think that in them ye have eternal life: and they are they which testify of me;

40 And yet ye are not willing to come unto me, that ye may have life.

41 I receive not glory from men.

42 But I know you, that ye have not the love of God in you.

43 I am come in my Father's name, and ye receive me not: if another shall come in his own name, him ye will receive.

44 How can ye believe, which receive glory one of another, and seek not the glory which is from the only God?

45 Do not think that I will accuse you to the Father: there is one that accuseth you, even Moses, in whom ye hope.

46 For had ye believed Moses, ye would believe me: for he wrote of me.

47 But if ye believe not his writings, how shall ye believe my words?

CHAPTER VI.

AFTER these things Jesus went away over the sea of Galilee, which is the sea of Tiberias.

2 And a great multitude followed him, because they beheld the miracles which he did on them that were sick.

3 And Jesus went up into the mountain, and there he sat with his disciples.

4 And the passover, the feast of the Jews, was nigh.

5 Jesus then lifting up his eyes,

¹ *Or, but less probably,* Ye search.

and seeing that a great multitude cometh unto him, saith unto Philip, Whence are we to buy bread, that these may eat?

6 But this he said proving him: for he himself knew what he was about to do.

7 Philip answered him, Two hundred pennyworth of bread is not sufficient for them, that every one of them may take a little.

8 One of his disciples, Andrew, Simon Peter's brother, saith unto him,

9 There is a little lad here, which hath five barley loaves, and two fishes: but what are they among so many?

10 Jesus said, Make the people sit down. Now there was much grass in the place. So the men sat down, in number about five thousand.

11 Jesus therefore took the loaves; and when he had given thanks, he distributed to ²them that were sat down; and in like manner of the fishes as much as they would.

12 Now when they were filled, he saith unto his disciples, Gather up the fragments that remain over, that nothing be lost.

13 So they gathered them together, and filled twelve baskets with fragments of the five barley loaves, which remained over unto them that had eaten.

14 The men therefore, seeing the miracle that he did, said, This is of a truth the prophet that is to come into the world.

² *So the oldest MSS. and versions.*

15 Jesus therefore, knowing that they would come and take him by force that they might make him a king, withdrew again into the mountain himself alone.

16 But when even was come, his disciples went down unto the sea,

17 And entered into a ship, and were going over the sea toward Capernaum. And darkness had now come on, and Jesus was not yet come to them.

18 And the sea was rising, for a strong wind was blowing.

19 When then they had rowed about five and twenty or thirty furlongs, they behold Jesus walking on the sea, and drawing nigh unto the ship: and they were afraid.

20 But he saith unto them, It is I; be not afraid.

21 They were willing therefore to receive him into the ship: and immediately the ship was at the land whither they were going.

22 The day following, the multitude which stood on th other side of the sea saw that there was none other boat there, save one,[1] and that Jesus went not together with his disciples into the ship, but that his disciples went away alone;

23 (Yet other boats came from Tiberias nigh unto the place where they ate the bread when the Lord had given thanks :)

24 When the multitude therefore saw that Jesus was not there, neither his disciples,

[1] *So the oldest MSS.*

they themselves entered into the boats and came to Capernaum, seeking for Jesus.

25 And when they had found him on the other side of the sea, they said unto him, Rabbi, when camest thou hither?

26 Jesus answered them and said, Verily, verily, I say unto you, Ye seek me, not because ye saw miracles, but because ye ate of the loaves, and were filled.

27 Work not for the meat which perisheth, but for the meat which endureth unto eternal life, which the Son of man shall give unto you: for him the Father sealed, even God.

28 They said therefore unto him, What must we do, that we may work the works of God?

29 Jesus answered and said unto them, This is the work of God, that ye should believe in him whom he sent.

30 They said therefore unto him, What doest thou then as a sign, that we may see, and may believe thee? what dost thou work?

31 Our fathers ate the manna in the wilderness; as it is written, He gave them bread from heaven to eat.

32 Jesus therefore said unto them, Verily, verily, I say unto you, Moses gave you not the bread from heaven; but my Father giveth you the true bread from heaven.

33 For the bread of God is that which cometh down from heaven, and giveth life unto the world.

34 They said therefore unto

him, Lord, evermore give us this bread.

35 Jesus said unto them, I am the bread of life: he that cometh to me shall not hunger; and he that believeth in me shall never thirst.

36 But I said unto you that ye have even seen me, and believe not.

37 All which the Father giveth me shall come unto me; and him that cometh to me I will in no wise cast out;

38 For I am come down from heaven, not to do mine own will, but the will of him that sent me.

39 And this is the will of him that sent me, that of all which he hath given me I should lose nothing, but should raise it up at the last day.

40 For this is the will of my Father, that every one which looketh on the Son, and believeth in him, should have eternal life, and that I should raise him up at the last day.

41 The Jews therefore murmured at him, because he said, I am the bread which came down from heaven:

42 And they said, Is not this Jesus, the son of Joseph, whose father and mother we know? how then doth he say, I am come down from heaven?

43 Jesus answered and said unto them, Murmur not among yourselves.

44 No one can come to me, except the Father which sent me draw him, and I raise him up in the last day.

45 It is written in the prophets, And they shall be all taught of God. Every man therefore that heareth from the Father, and learneth, cometh unto me.

46 Not that any man hath seen the Father, save he which is from God, he hath seen the Father.

47 Verily, verily, I say unto you, He that believeth [1]in me hath eternal life.

48 I am the bread of life.

49 Your fathers ate the manna in the wilderness, and died.

50 This is the bread which cometh down from heaven, that a man may eat thereof, and not die.

51 I am the living bread which came down from heaven: if a man eat of this bread, he shall live for ever: yea, and the bread that I will give is my flesh, [2]for the life of the world.

52 The Jews therefore contended among themselves, saying, How can this man give us his flesh to eat?

53 Jesus therefore said unto them, Verily, verily, I say unto you, Except ye eat the flesh of the Son of man, and drink his blood, ye have no life in you.

54 He that eateth my flesh, and drinketh my blood, hath eternal life; and I will raise him up at the last day.

55 For my flesh is meat indeed, and my blood is drink indeed.

56 He that eateth my flesh,

[1] *The words* in me *are omitted by several of the oldest MSS., but inserted by the rest, and by the ancient versions.*

[2] *The words* which I will give *are omitted by all the oldest MSS.*

and drinketh my blood, dwelleth in me, and I in him.

57 As the living Father sent me, and I live by reason of the Father: even so he that eateth me, he also shall live by reason of me.

58 This is the bread which came down from heaven: not as the fathers ate,[1] and died: he that eateth this bread shall live for ever.

59 These things said he in the synagogue, as he taught in Capernaum.

60 Many therefore of his disciples, when they heard this, said, This saying is hard; who can hear it?

61 But Jesus knowing in himself that his disciples were murmuring at this, said unto them, Doth this offend you?

62 What then if ye should behold the Son of man ascending up where he was before?

63 It is the spirit that giveth life; the flesh profiteth nothing: the words that I have spoken unto you are spirit, and are life.

64 But there are some of you that believe not. For Jesus knew from the beginning who they were that believed not, and who it was that should [2]betray him.

65 And he said, For this cause have I said unto you, that no man can come unto me, except it be given unto him of my Father.

66 ¶ Upon this many of his disciples went back, and walked no more with him.

67 Therefore said Jesus unto the twelve, Do ye also wish to go away?

68 Simon Peter answered him, Lord, to whom shall we go? thou hast the words of eternal life.

69 And we have believed and know that thou art the [3]Holy One of God.

70 Jesus answered them, Did I not choose you twelve, and one of you is a devil?

71 He spake of Judas the son of [4]Simon Iscariot: for it was he that was about to [2]betray him, being one of the twelve.

CHAPTER VII.

AND after these things Jesus walked in Galilee: for he would not walk in Judæa, because the Jews sought to kill him.

2 Now the Jews' feast of tabernacles was at hand.

3 His brethren therefore said unto him, Depart hence, and go into Judæa, that thy disciples also may behold thy works which thou doest.

4 For no man doeth any thing in secret, and seeketh himself to be known openly. If thou doest these things, manifest thyself to the world.

5 For even his brethren did not believe in him.

6 Jesus therefore saith unto them, My time is not yet come: but your time is alway ready.

7 The world cannot hate you; but me it hateth, be-

---

[1] *So all the oldest MSS.*
[2] Deliver him up.

[3] *So all the early MSS.*
[4] *So most of the early MSS.*

cause I testify of it, that the works thereof are evil.

8 Go ye up unto the feast: I go not up ¹yet unto this feast; because my time is not yet full come.

9 And when he had said these words unto them, he remained in Galilee.

10 But when his brethren were gone up unto the feast, then went he also up, not openly, but as in secret.

11 The Jews therefore sought him at the feast, and said, Where is he?

12 And there was much murmuring among the multitudes concerning him: some said, He is a good man: others said, Nay; but he deceiveth the multitude.

13 Howbeit no man spake openly of him for fear of the Jews.

14 But when it was now the midst of the feast, Jesus went up into the temple, and taught.

15 The Jews therefore marvelled, saying, How knoweth this man letters, having never learned?

16 Jesus therefore answered them, and said, My teaching is not mine, but his that sent me.

17 If any man be willing to do his will, he shall know concerning the teaching, whether it is of God, or whether I speak from myself.

18 He that speaketh from himself seeketh his own glory: but he that seeketh the glory

of him that sent him, the same is true, and no unrighteousness is in him.

19 Did not Moses give you the law, and yet none of you keepeth the law? Why seek ye to kill me?

20 The multitude answered and said, Thou hast a devil: who seeketh to kill thee?

21 Jesus answered and said unto them, I did one work, and ye all marvel.

22 For this cause hath Moses given you circumcision, not that it is of Moses, but of the fathers; and ye on the sabbath day circumcise a man.

23 If a man on the sabbath day receiveth circumcision, that the law of Moses may not be broken; are ye angry at me, because I made a man whole every whit on the sabbath day?

24 Judge not according to appearance, but judge righteous judgment.

25 Then said some of them of Jerusalem, Is not this he, whom they seek to kill?

26 And, lo, he speaketh boldly, and they say nothing unto him. Have the rulers come to know indeed that this man is the Christ?

27 Howbeit we know this man whence he is: but when the Christ cometh, no man knoweth whence he is.

28 Therefore cried Jesus, teaching in the temple, and saying, Ye both know me, and ye know whence I am: and I am not come of myself, but he that sent me is true, whom ye know not.

¹ Yet *is omitted by some of the most ancient MSS., but inserted by others, and by the early versions.*

29 I know him: because I am from him, and he sent me.

30 Therefore sought they to take him: and yet no man laid his hand on him, because his hour was not yet come.

31 But many of the multitude believed in him, and said, When the Christ shall come, will he do more miracles than these which this man hath done?

32 The Pharisees heard the multitude murmuring these things concerning him; and the chief priests and the Pharisees sent officers to take him.

33 Jesus said therefore, Yet a little while am I with you, and I go unto him that sent me.

34 Ye shall seek me, and shall not find me: and where I am, ye cannot come.

35 The Jews therefore said among themselves, Whither will this man go, that we shall not find him? will he go unto the dispersed among the Greeks, and teach the Greeks?

36 What is this saying that he said, Ye shall seek me, and shall not find me: and where I am, ye cannot come?

37 Now in the last day, the great day of the feast, Jesus stood and cried, saying, If any man thirst, let him come unto me, and drink.

38 He that believeth in me, as the scripture saith, out of his belly shall flow rivers of living water.

39 But this spake he of the Spirit, which they that believe in him were about to receive: for the [1] Holy Spirit was not yet: because Jesus was not yet glorified.

40 Some of the multitude therefore, when they heard these sayings, said, Of a truth this is the Prophet.

41 Others said, This is the Christ. But others said, Doth the Christ then come out of Galilee?

42 Hath not the scripture said, That the Christ cometh of the seed of David, and from Bethlehem, the town where David was?

43 So there was a division among the multitude because of him.

44 And some of them were minded to take him; nevertheless no man laid his hands on him.

45 The officers therefore came to the chief priests and Pharisees; and they said unto them, Why have ye not brought him?

46 The officers answered, [2] Never man spake like this man.

47 Then answered them the Pharisees, Are ye also deceived?

48 Hath any of the rulers believed in him, or of the Pharisees?

49 But this multitude which knoweth not the law are cursed.

50 Nicodemus saith unto them, (he that came to him before, being one of them,)

51 Doth our law judge a man, except it first hear from him, and learn what he doeth?

---

[1] Holy *is omitted by some of the ancient MSS.*

[2] *Several of the early MSS. have only,* Never man spake thus.

52 They answered and said unto him, Art thou also of Galilee? Search, and see: for out of Galilee ariseth no prophet.

[1][53 And every man went unto his own house.

CHAPTER VIII.

BUT Jesus went unto the mount of Olives.

2 But early in the morning he came again into the temple, and all the people came unto him.

3 But the scribes and the Pharisees bring a woman taken in sin; and when they had set her in the midst,

4 The priests say unto him, tempting him, that they might have to accuse him, Master, this woman hath been taken in adultery, in the very act.

5 Now Moses in the law commanded to stone such: but now what sayest thou?

6 But Jesus stooped down, and with his finger wrote on the ground.

7 But when they continued asking, he lifted up himself, and said unto them, He that is without sin among you, let him first cast a stone at her.

8 And again he stooped down, and wrote with his finger on the ground.

9 But each of the Jews went out, beginning at the elders, so that all went out: and he was left alone, and the woman in the midst.

10 And when Jesus had lifted up himself, he said unto the woman, Where are they? did no man condemn thee?

11 And she said unto him, No man, Lord. And he said, Neither do I condemn thee: go, henceforth sin no more.]

12 Jesus therefore spake again unto them, saying, I am the light of the world: he that followeth me shall in no wise walk in the darkness, but shall have the light of life.

13 The Pharisees therefore said unto him, Thou art bearing witness concerning thyself; thy witness is not true.

14 Jesus answered and said unto them, Though I bear witness concerning myself, my witness is true; because I know whence I came, and whither I go: but ye know not whence I come or whither I go.

15 Ye judge after the flesh; I judge no man.

16 Yea and if I should judge, my judgment is true: because I am not alone, but I and the Father that sent me.

17 Moreover it is written in your law, that the testimony of two men is true.

18 I am he that beareth witness concerning myself, and the Father that sent me beareth witness of me.

19 They said therefore unto him, Where is thy father? Jesus answered, Ye know neither me, nor my Father: if ye had known me, ye would know my Father also.

---

[1] *The passage*, vii. 53—viii. 11, *enclosed within brackets, is wanting in the best ancient manuscripts. The version here given is from the Cambridge MS., the only at all early one that contains it. In the later MSS. all sorts of variations occur in the text.*

20 These words spake he in the treasury, as he was teaching in the temple: and no man laid hands on him; because his hour was not yet come.

21 Therefore said he again unto them, I go away, and ye shall seek me, and shall die in your sin: whither I go, ye cannot come.

22 The Jews therefore said, Will he kill himself? because he saith, Whither I go, ye cannot come.

23 And he said unto them, Ye are from beneath; I am from above: ye are of this world; I am not of this world.

24 I said therefore unto you, that ye shall die in your sins: for if ye believe not that I am he, ye shall die in your sins.

25 Therefore said they unto him, Who art thou? And Jesus said unto them, In very deed, that same which I also speak unto you.

26 I have many things to say and to judge of you: howbeit he that sent me is true; and the things which I heard from him, these speak I unto the world.

27 They understood not that he was speaking to them of the Father.

28 Jesus therefore said, When ye have lifted up the Son of man, then shall ye know that I am he, and that I do nothing of myself; but according as the Father taught me, I speak these things.

29 And he that sent me is with me: the Father hath not left me alone; because I do always those things that are pleasing to him.

30 As he spake these words, many believed in him.

31 Jesus therefore said to those Jews which had believed him, If ye continue in my word, ye are my disciples indeed;

32 And ye shall know the truth, and the truth shall make you free.

33 They answered him, We be Abraham's seed, and have never been in bondage to any man: how sayest thou, Ye shall be made free?

34 Jesus answered them, Verily, verily, I say unto you, Every one that committeth sin is the bondman of sin.

35 Now the bondman abideth not in the house for ever: the Son abideth for ever.

36 If then the Son shall make you free, ye shall be free indeed.

37 I know that ye are Abraham's seed; nevertheless ye seek to kill me, because my word gaineth no ground in you.

38 I speak that which I have seen with my Father: and ye likewise do that which ye have seen from your father.

39 They answered and said unto him, Abraham is our father. Jesus saith unto them, If ye were Abraham's children, ye would do the works of Abraham.

40 But now ye seek to kill me, a man that hath spoken unto you the truth, which I heard from God: this did not Abraham.

41 Ye do the works of your father. They said to him, We were not born of fornication; we have one Father, even God.

42 Jesus said unto them, If God were your Father, ye would love me: for I proceeded forth and am come from God; for neither am I come of myself, but he sent me.

43 Why do ye not understand my speech? because ye cannot hear my word.

44 Ye are of your father the devil, and the lusts of your father ye love to do. He was a murderer from the beginning, and standeth not in the truth, because there is no truth in him. When he speaketh a lie, he speaketh of his own: because he is a liar, and the father thereof.

45 But because I speak the truth, ye believe me not.

46 Which of you convicteth me of sin? If I speak truth, why do ye not believe me?

47 He that is of God heareth the words of God: for this cause ye hear them not, because ye are not of God.

48 The Jews answered and said unto him, Say we not well that thou art a Samaritan, and hast a devil?

49 Jesus answered, I have not a devil; but I honour my Father, and ye do dishonour me.

50 But I seek not mine own glory: there is one that seeketh and judgeth.

51 Verily, verily, I say unto you, If a man keep my word, he shall never see death.

52 Then said the Jews unto him, Now we know that thou hast a devil. Abraham died, and the prophets; and thou sayest, If a man keep my word, he shall never taste death.

53 Art thou greater than our father Abraham, which died? and the prophets died: whom makest thou thyself?

54 Jesus answered, If I glorify myself, my glory is nothing: it is my Father that glorifieth me; of whom ye say, He is our God:

55 And ye have not known him; but I know him: and if I should say, I know him not, I shall be a liar like unto you: but I know him, and keep his word.

56 Your father Abraham rejoiced to see my day: and he saw it, and was glad.

57 The Jews therefore said unto him, Thou art not yet fifty years old, and hast thou seen Abraham?

58 Jesus said unto them, Verily, verily, I say unto you, Before Abraham was made, I am.

59 Therefore took they up stones to cast at him: but Jesus hid himself, and went out of the temple.[1]

CHAPTER IX.

AND as he was passing by, he saw a man blind from his birth.

2 And his disciples asked him, saying, Rabbi, who sinned, this

---

[1] *The words*, going through the midst of them, and so passed by, *are not found in the most ancient MSS.*

man, or his parents, that he should be born blind?

3 Jesus answered, Neither did this man sin, nor his parents: but that the works of God should be made manifest in him.

4 I must work the works of him that sent me, while it is day: the night cometh, when no man can work.

5 When I am in the world, I am the light of the world.

6 When he had thus spoken, he spat on the ground, and made clay of the spittle, and spread the clay upon his eyes,

7 And said unto him, Go, wash in the pool of Siloam, (which is interpreted, Sent.) He went his way therefore, and washed, and came seeing.

8 The neighbours therefore, and they which before had seen him that he was a beggar, said, Is not this he that sitteth and beggeth?

9 Some said, This is he: others said, Nay, but he is like him. He said, I am he.

10 Therefore said they unto him, How were thine eyes opened?

11 He answered, A man that is called Jesus made clay, and anointed mine eyes, and said unto me, Go to Siloam, and wash. I went therefore and washed, and received sight.

12 They said unto him, Where is the man? He saith, I know not.

13 They bring to the Pharisees him that aforetime was blind.

14 Now it was the sabbath, on the day when Jesus made the clay, and opened his eyes.

15 Therefore again the Pharisees also asked him how he received his sight. He said unto them, He put clay upon mine eyes, and I washed, and do see.

16 Therefore said some of the Pharisees, This man is not from God, because he keepeth not the sabbath day. Others said, How can a man that is a sinner do such miracles? And there was a division among them.

17 They say therefore unto the blind man again, What sayest thou of him, seeing that he hath opened thine eyes? He said, He is a prophet.

18 The Jews therefore did not believe concerning him, that he had been blind, and received his sight, until they called the parents of him that had received his sight,

19 And asked them, saying, Is this your son, who ye say was born blind? how then doth he now see?

20 His parents answered and said, We know that this is our son, and that he was born blind:

21 But by what means he now seeth, we know not; or who opened his eyes, we know not: ask him: he is of age; he will speak for himself.

22 These things said his parents, because they feared the Jews: for the Jews had agreed already, that if any man should acknowledge him as Christ, he should be put out of the synagogue.

23 For this cause his parents said, He is of age; ask him.

24 So they called the second time the man that had been blind, and said unto him, Give glory to God: we know that this man is a sinner.

25 He therefore answered, Whether he is a sinner, I know not: one thing I know, that I, a blind man, now see.

26 They said therefore to him, What did he to thee? how opened he thine eyes?

27 He answered them, I have told you already, and ye did not hear: wherefore would ye hear again? would ye also become his disciples?

28 They reviled him, and said, Thou art his disciple; but we are disciples of Moses.

29 We know that God hath spoken unto Moses: but as for this man, we know not from whence he is.

30 The man answered and said unto them, Why herein is a marvellous thing, that ye know not from whence he is, and yet he opened mine eyes.

31 We know that God heareth not sinners: but if any man be a worshipper of God, and do his will, him he heareth.

32 Since the world began it was never heard that any one opened the eyes of a man born blind.

33 If this man were not from God, he could do nothing.

34 They answered and said unto him, Thou wast wholly born in sins, and dost thou teach us? And they cast him out.

35 Jesus heard that they had cast him out; and he found him and said unto him, Dost thou believe in the Son of God?

36 He answered and said, And who is he, Lord, that I may believe in him?

37 Jesus said unto him, Thou hast both seen him, and he that talketh with thee is he.

38 And he said, I believe, Lord: and worshipped him.

39 And Jesus said, For judgment came I into this world, that they which see not may see; and that they which see may become blind.

40 And those of the Pharisees which were with him heard these things, and said unto him, Are we also blind?

41 Jesus said unto them, If ye were blind, ye would not have sin: but now ye say, We see. Your sin remaineth.

CHAPTER X.

VERILY, verily, I say unto you, He that entereth not through the door into the sheepfold, but climbeth up some other way, the same is a thief and a robber.

2 But he that entereth in through the door is shepherd of the sheep.

3 To him the porter openeth; and the sheep hear his voice: and he calleth his own sheep by name, and leadeth them out.

4 When he hath put forth all his own, he goeth before them; and the sheep follow him, because they know his voice.

5 But a stranger they will

not follow, but will flee from him: because they know not the voice of strangers.

6 This parable spake Jesus unto them: but they understood not what things they were which he spake unto them.

7 Therefore said Jesus again, Verily, verily, I say unto you, I am the door of the sheep.

8 All that ever came before me are thieves and robbers: but the sheep did not hear them.

9 I am the door: through me if any man enter in, he shall be saved, and shall go in and out, and shall find pasture.

10 The thief cometh not, but for to steal, and to kill, and to destroy: I came that they might have life, and that they might have it abundantly.

11 I am the good shepherd: the good shepherd layeth down his life for the sheep.

12 But he that is an hireling, and not the shepherd, whose own the sheep are not, beholdeth the wolf coming, and leaveth the sheep, and fleeth: and the wolf teareth them, and scattereth the sheep;

13 Because he is an hireling, and careth not for the sheep.

14 I am the good shepherd; and I know mine own, and am known of mine.

15 Even as the Father knoweth me, and I know the Father: and I lay down my life for the sheep.

16 And other sheep I have, which are not of this fold: them also must I bring, and they shall hear my voice; and they shall become one flock, one shepherd.

17 For this cause doth the Father love me, because I lay down my life, that I may take it again.

18 None taketh it from me, but I lay it down of myself. I have power to lay it down, and I have power to take it again. This commandment received I from my Father.

19 ¶ There was a division therefore again among the Jews because of these sayings.

20 For many of them said, He hath a devil, and is mad; why hear ye him?

21 Others said, These are not the words of him that hath a devil. Can a devil open the eyes of the blind?

22 ¶ Now it was the feast of the dedication at Jerusalem. It was winter,

23 And Jesus was walking in the temple, in Solomon's porch.

24 The Jews therefore came round about him, and said unto him, How long dost thou hold our mind in suspense? If thou art the Christ, tell us plainly.

25 Jesus answered them, I told you, and ye believe not. The works that I do in my Father's name, these bear witness of me:

26 Nevertheless ye believe not: for ye are not of my sheep, ¹[as I said unto you].

27 My sheep hear my voice, and I know them, and they follow me:

---

¹ *These words are omitted by many of the ancient MSS.: perhaps on account of their difficulty*

28 And I give unto them eternal life; and they shall never perish, and none shall tear them out of my hand.
29 My Father, which hath given them to me, is greater than all; and none is able to tear them out of my Father's hand.
30 I and the Father are one.
31 The Jews therefore took up stones again to stone him.
32 Jesus answered them, Many good works have I shewed you from the Father; for which of these works do ye stone me?
33 The Jews answered him, saying, For a good work we stone thee not; but for blasphemy; and because thou, being a man, makest thyself God.
34 Jesus answered them, Is it not written in your law, I said, Ye are gods?
35 If he called them gods, unto whom the word of God came, and the scripture cannot be made void;
36 Say ye of him, whom the Father sanctified, and sent into the world, Thou blasphemest; because I said, I am the Son of God?
37 If I do not the works of my Father, believe me not.
38 But if I do them, though ye believe not me, believe the works: that ye may know, and understand, that the Father is in me, and I in the Father.
39 Therefore they sought again to take him: and he passed out of their hand,
40 And went away again beyond the Jordan into the place where John at first baptized; and there he tarried.
41 And many came unto him, and said, John indeed did no miracle: but all things whatsoever John spake of this man were true.
42 And many believed in him there.

CHAPTER XI.

NOW there was a certain man sick, named Lazarus, from Bethany, of the town of Mary and her sister Martha.
2 It was that Mary which anointed the Lord with ointment, and wiped his feet with her hair, whose brother Lazarus was sick.
3 The sisters therefore sent unto him, saying, Lord, behold he whom thou lovest is sick.
4 But when Jesus heard it, he said, This sickness is not unto death, but for the glory of God, that the Son of God may be glorified thereby.
5 Now Jesus loved Martha, and her sister, and Lazarus.
6 When therefore he heard that he was sick, at that time he continued two days in the place where he was.
7 Then after this he saith to the disciples, Let us go into Judæa again.
8 The disciples say unto him, Rabbi, the Jews were but now seeking to stone thee; and goest thou thither again?
9 Jesus answered, Are there not twelve hours in the day? If any man walk in the day, he stumbleth not, because he seeth the light of this world.

10 But if a man walk in the night, he stumbleth, because the light is not in him.

11 These things said he : and after this he saith unto them, Our friend Lazarus is fallen asleep ; but I go, that I may awake him out of sleep.

12 Therefore said his disciples, Lord, if he is fallen asleep, he will recover.

13 Howbeit Jesus spake of his death : but they thought that he was speaking of the taking of rest in sleep.

14 Then said Jesus therefore unto them plainly, Lazarus is dead.

15 And I am glad for your sakes that I was not there, to the intent ye may believe ; nevertheless let us go unto him.

16 Thomas therefore, which is called Didymus, said unto his fellow-disciples, Let us also go, that we may die with him.

17 When therefore Jesus came, he found that he had lain in the grave four days already.

18 Now Bethany was nigh unto Jerusalem, about fifteen furlongs off:

19 And many of the Jews had come to Martha and Mary, to comfort them concerning their brother.

20 Then Martha, when she heard that Jesus was coming, went to meet him : but Mary was sitting in the house.

21 Martha then said unto Jesus, Lord, if thou hadst been here, my brother had not died.

22 And even now I know, that whatsoever thou shalt ask of God, God will give unto thee.

23 Jesus saith unto her, Thy brother shall rise again.

24 Martha saith unto him, I know that he shall rise again in the resurrection at the last day.

25 Jesus said unto her, I am the resurrection, and the life : he that believeth in me, though he die, yet shall he live :

26 And every one that liveth and believeth in me shall not die for evermore. Believest thou this ?

27 She said unto him, Yea, Lord : I have believed that thou art the Christ, the Son of God, which is to come into the world.

28 And when she had so said, she went away, and called Mary her sister secretly, saying, The Master is here, and calleth thee.

29 When she heard that, she arose quickly, and came to him.

30 Now Jesus was not yet come into the town, but was still in the place where Martha met him.

31 The Jews therefore which were with her in the house, and were comforting her, when they saw Mary, that she rose up hastily and went out, followed her, thinking that she was going to the grave to weep there.

32 Mary therefore, when she came where Jesus was, and saw him, fell down at his feet, saying unto him, Lord, if thou hadst been here, my brother had not died.

33 Jesus therefore, when he saw her weeping, and the Jews also weeping which came with her, was greatly moved in his spirit, and troubled himself,

34 And said, Where have ye laid him? They say unto him, Lord, come and see.

35 Jesus wept.

36 The Jews therefore said, Behold how he loved him!

37 But some of them said, Could not this person, which opened the eyes of the blind man, have caused also that this man should not have died?

38 Jesus therefore again greatly moved within himself cometh to the grave. Now it was a cave, and a stone lay against it.

39 Jesus saith, Take ye away the stone. Martha, the sister of him that was dead, saith unto him, Lord, by this time he stinketh: for he hath been four days.

40 Jesus saith unto her, Said I not unto thee, If thou believe, thou shalt see the glory of God?

41 So they took away the stone. And Jesus lifted his eyes upward, and said, Father, I thank thee that thou heardest me.

42 Yet I knew that thou hearest me always: but for the sake of the multitude which stand around I said it, that they may believe that thou hast sent me.

43 And when he had thus spoken, he cried out with a loud voice, Lazarus, come forth.

44 And the dead man came forth, bound hand and foot with graveclothes: and his face was bound about with a napkin. Jesus saith unto them, Loose him, and let him go.

45 Many therefore of the Jews which had come to Mary, and beheld the things which he did, believed in him.

46 But some of them went away to the Pharisees, and told them what things Jesus had done.

47 Therefore gathered the chief priests and the Pharisees a council, and said, What are we doing, seeing that this man doeth many miracles?

48 If we let him thus alone, all men will believe in him: and the Romans will come and take away both our place and nation.

49 And a certain one of them, Caiaphas, being high priest that year, said unto them, Ye know nothing at all,

50 Nor do ye consider that it is expedient for us, that one man should die for the people, and that the whole nation perish not.

51 Now this he spake not of himself: but being high priest that year, he prophesied that Jesus was about to die for the nation;

52 And not for the nation only, but also that he might gather together into one the children of God that are scattered abroad.

53 Therefore from that day forth they took counsel together to put him to death.

54 Jesus therefore walked no more openly among the Jews; but departed thence into the country near the wilderness, to a city called Ephraim, and there tarried with his disciples.

55 ¶ Now the passover of the Jews was nigh: and many went up out of the country to Jerusalem before the passover, to purify themselves.

56 So they sought for Jesus, and said among themselves, as they stood in the temple, What think ye? that he will not come to the feast?

57 Now the chief priests and the Pharisees had given commandment, that, if any man knew where he was, he should shew it, that they might take him.

CHAPTER XII.

JESUS then six days before the passover came to Bethany, where Lazarus was which had been dead, whom Jesus raised from the dead.

2 So they made him a supper there; and Martha served: but Lazarus was one of them that sat at the table with him.

3 Then took Mary a pound of ointment of pure ¹spikenard, very costly, and anointed the feet of Jesus, and wiped his feet with her hair: and the house was filled with the odour of the ointment.

4 Then saith Judas Iscariot, Simon's son, one of his disciples, which was about to ²betray him,

5 Why was not this ointment sold for three hundred pence, and given to the poor?

6 This he said, not because he cared for the poor; but because he was a thief, and kept the bag, and took away what was put therein.

7 Then said Jesus, Let her alone, that she may keep it against the day of my burying.

8 For the poor ye have always with you; but me ye have not always.

9 Much people of the Jews therefore knew that he was there: and they came not on account of Jesus only, but that they might see Lazarus also, whom he had raised from the dead.

10 But the chief priests took counsel that they might put Lazarus also to death;

11 Because that by reason of him many of the Jews were going away, and believing in Jesus.

12 ¶ On the next day much people which were come to the feast, having heard that Jesus was coming into Jerusalem,

13 Took branches of the palm trees, and went forth to meet him, and cried, Hosanna: Blessed is he that cometh in the name of the Lord, the King of Israel.

14 But Jesus, having found a young ass, sat thereon; as it is written,

15 Fear not, daughter of Sion: behold, thy King cometh, sitting on an ass's colt.

16 These things understood not his disciples at the first:

---

¹ *See note on Mark* xiv. 3.
² *Deliver him up.*

but when Jesus was glorified, then remembered they that these things were written of him, and that they had done these things unto him.

17 The multitude therefore that was with him when he called Lazarus out of the grave, and raised him from the dead, bare witness.

18 For this cause the multitude also went to meet him, for that they heard that he had done this miracle.

19 The Pharisees therefore said among themselves, Perceive ye that ye prevail nothing? behold, the world is gone away after him.

20 ¶ Now there were certain Greeks among those that came up to worship at the feast:

21 The same came therefore to Philip, which was from Bethsaida of Galilee, and prayed him, saying, Sir, we would see Jesus.

22 Philip cometh and telleth Andrew: Andrew and Philip come and tell Jesus.

23 But Jesus answered them, saying, The hour is come, that the Son of man should be glorified.

24 Verily, verily, I say unto you, Except a grain of wheat fall into the ground and die, it abideth by itself alone: but if it die, it bringeth forth much fruit.

25 He that loveth his ¹soul shall lose it; and he that hateth his ¹soul in this world shall keep it unto life eternal.

26 If any man serve me, let him follow me; and where

¹ *Or*, life.

I am, there shall also my servant be: if any man serve me, him will the Father honour.

27 Now is my soul troubled; and what shall I say? Father, save me from this hour: but yet for this cause came I unto this hour.

28 Father, glorify thy name. Then came there a voice from heaven, I have both glorified it, and will glorify it again.

29 The multitude therefore, that stood by, and heard it, said that it had thundered: others said, An angel hath spoken to him.

30 Jesus answered and said, This voice came not for my sake, but for your sakes.

31 Now is the judgment of this world: now shall the prince of this world be cast out.

32 And I, if I be lifted up from the earth, will draw all men unto myself.

33 This he said, signifying by what manner of death he was about to die.

34 The multitude therefore answered him, We have heard out of the law that the Christ abideth for ever: and how sayest thou, The Son of man must be lifted up? who is this Son of man?

35 Jesus therefore said unto them, Yet a little while is the light with you. Walk while ye have the light, that darkness overtake you not: and he that walketh in the darkness knoweth not whither he goeth.

36 While ye have the light,

believe in the light, that ye may become sons of light. These things spake Jesus, and he departed, and did hide himself from them.

37 But though he had done so many miracles before them, yet they believed not in him:

38 That the saying of Isaiah the prophet might be fulfilled, which he spake, Lord, who hath believed our report? and to whom hath the arm of the Lord been revealed?

39 For this cause they could not believe, for that Isaiah said again,

40 He hath blinded their eyes, and hardened their heart; that they should not see with their eyes, and understand with their heart, and be converted, and I should heal them.

41 These things said Isaiah, when he saw his glory; and he spake of him.

42 Nevertheless even of the rulers many believed in him; but because of the Pharisees they confessed it not, that they might not be put out of the synagogue:

43 For they loved the glory that is of men more than the glory that is of God.

44 But Jesus cried and said, He that believeth in me, believeth not in me, but in him that sent me.

45 And he that beholdeth me beholdeth him that sent me.

46 I am come a light into the world, that whosoever believeth in me may not remain in the darkness.

47 And if a man hear my words, and keep them not, I judge him not: for I came not that I might judge the world, but that I might save the world.

48 He that rejecteth me, and receiveth not my words, hath one that judgeth him: the word that I spake, the same shall judge him in the last day.

49 Because I spake not of myself; but the Father which sent me, he gave me commandment, what I should say, and what I should speak.

50 And I know that his commandment is eternal life: whatsoever I speak therefore, even as the Father hath said unto me, so I speak.

CHAPTER XIII.

NOW before the feast of the passover, Jesus, knowing that his hour was come that he should depart out of this world unto the Father, having loved his own which were in the world, loved them unto the end.

2 And when supper was begun, the devil having now put into the heart of Judas Iscariot, Simon's son, to betray him;

3 Knowing that the Father had given him all things into his hands, and that he came forth from God, and was going to God;

4 He riseth from the supper, and layeth aside his garments; and took a towel, and girded himself.

5 After that he poureth water into the bason, and began to wash the disciples' feet, and

GOSPEL OF ST. JOHN.

to wipe them with the towel wherewith he was girded.

6 He cometh therefore to Simon Peter: and Peter saith unto him, Lord, dost **thou** wash **my** feet?

7 Jesus answered and said unto him, What I do thou knowest not now; but thou shalt understand afterwards.

8 Peter saith unto him, Never shalt thou wash my feet. Jesus answered him, If I wash thee not, thou hast no part with me.

9 Simon Peter saith unto him, Lord, not my feet only, but also my hands and my head.

10 Jesus saith to him, He that hath been bathed hath no need save to wash his feet, but is clean every whit: and ye are clean, yet not all.

11 For he knew him that was betraying him; for this cause said he, Ye are not all clean.

12 So after he had washed their feet, and had taken his garments, and had sat down again, he said unto them, Know ye what I have done to you?

13 Ye call me Master and Lord: and ye say well; for so I am.

14 If I then, your Lord and Master, have washed your feet; ye also ought to wash one another's feet.

15 For I gave you an example, that ye also should do according as I did to you.

16 Verily, verily, I say unto you, There is no servant greater than his lord, nor apostle greater than he that sent him.

17 If ye know these things, blessed are ye if ye do them.

18 I speak not of you all: I know whom I chose: but that the scripture may be fulfilled, He that eateth bread with me lifted up his heel against me.

19 From this time I tell you before it come to pass, that, when it is come to pass, ye may believe that I am he.

20 Verily, verily, I say unto you, He that receiveth whomsoever I send receiveth me; and he that receiveth me receiveth him that sent me.

21 When Jesus had thus said, he was troubled in his spirit, and testified, and said, Verily, verily, I say unto you, that one of you shall ¹betray me.

22 The disciples looked one on another, being in doubt of whom he spake.

23 There was reclining at meat in Jesus' bosom one of his disciples, whom Jesus loved.

24 Simon Peter therefore maketh a sign to him, and saith unto him, Tell us who it is of whom he speaketh.

25 He then leaning back thus on Jesus' breast saith unto him, Lord, who is it?

26 Jesus therefore answereth, He it is, for whom I shall dip the sop, and give it to him. And when he had dipped the sop, he taketh it and giveth it to Judas Iscariot, the son of Simon.

27 And after the sop, then Satan entered into him. Jesus therefore saith unto him, What thou doest, do quickly.

28 Now no man at the table knew for what intent he spake unto him.

¹ **Deliver me up.**

29 For some thought, because Judas kept the bag, that Jesus said unto him, Buy the things that we have need of against the feast; or, that he should give something to the poor.

30 He then having received the sop went immediately out; and it was night.

31 Therefore, when he was gone out, Jesus saith, Now is the Son of man glorified, and God is glorified in him.

32 [1][If God is glorified in him,] God also shall glorify him in himself, and shall straightway glorify him.

33 Little children, yet a little while I am with you. Ye shall seek me: and as I said unto the Jews, Whither I go, ye cannot come; so now I say to you.

34 A new commandment I give unto you, That ye love one another; even as I loved you, that ye also love one another.

35 Herein shall all men perceive that ye are my disciples, if ye have love one to another.

36 Simon Peter saith unto him, Lord, whither goest thou? Jesus answered him, Whither I go, thou canst not follow me now; but thou shalt follow me afterwards.

37 Peter saith unto him, Lord, why cannot I follow thee now? I will lay down my life for thee.

38 Jesus answered him, Wilt thou lay down thy life for me? Verily, verily, I say unto thee, The cock shall not crow, till thou hast denied me thrice.

CHAPTER XIV.

LET not your heart be troubled; [2]believe in God, believe also in me.

2 In my Father's house are many mansions; if it were not so, I would have told you; for I go to prepare a place for you.

3 And if I go and prepare a place for you, I will come again, and will receive you unto myself; that where I am, ye may be also.

4 And whither I go ye know the way.

5 Thomas saith unto him, Lord, we know not whither thou goest; and how do we know the way?

6 Jesus saith unto him, I am the way, and the truth, and the life: no man cometh unto the Father, but through me.

7 If ye had known me, ye would have known my Father also: from henceforth ye know him, and have seen him.

8 Philip saith unto him, Lord, shew us the Father, and it sufficeth us.

9 Jesus saith unto him, Have I been so long time with you, and yet dost thou not know me, Philip? he that hath seen me hath seen the Father; and how sayest thou, Shew us the Father?

10 Believest thou not that I am in the Father, and the Father in me? the words that I speak unto you I speak not

---

[1] *These words are omitted by most of the oldest MSS.: probably by a common mistake of the copyists, occasioned by the similar endings of this and the preceding clause.*

[2] *Or,* ye believe.

of myself: but the Father that dwelleth in me doeth ¹his works.

11 Believe me that I am in the Father, and the Father in me: or else believe me for the very works' sake.

12 Verily, verily, I say unto you, He that believeth in me, the works that I do shall he do also; and greater works than these shall he do; because I go unto the Father.

13 And whatsoever ye shall ask in my name, that will I do, that the Father may be glorified in the Son.

14 If ye shall ask any thing in my name, I will do it.

15 If ye love me, keep my commandments.

16 And I will pray the Father, and he shall give you another Comforter, that he may be with you for ever;

17 Even the Spirit of truth; whom the world cannot receive, because it beholdeth him not, neither knoweth him. Ye know him: because he dwelleth with you, and is in you.

18 I will not leave you orphans: I will come to you.

19 Yet a little while, and the world beholdeth me no more; but ye behold me: because I live, ye shall live also.

20 In that day ye shall know that I am in my Father, and ye in me, and I in you.

21 He that hath my commandments, and keepeth them,

---

¹ There is much variety here among the ancient MSS.: this is the reading of the Vatican, Sinaitic, and Cambridge MSS.

he it is that loveth me: and he that loveth me shall be loved by my Father, and I will love him, and will manifest myself to him.

22 Judas saith unto him, not Iscariot, Lord, how is it that thou wilt manifest thyself unto us, and not unto the world?

23 Jesus answered and said unto him, If a man love me, he will keep my word: and my Father will love him, and we will come unto him, and make our abode with him.

24 He that loveth me not keepeth not my words: and the word which ye hear is not mine, but the Father's which sent me.

25 These things have I spoken unto you, while yet abiding with you.

26 But the Comforter, even the Holy Spirit, whom the Father will send in my name, he shall teach you all things, and bring to your remembrance all things which I spake unto you.

27 Peace I leave with you, my peace I give unto you: not as the world giveth, give I unto you. Let not your heart be troubled, neither let it be afraid.

28 Ye heard how I said unto you, I go away, and come again unto you. If ye loved me, ye would have rejoiced that I go unto the Father; for my Father is greater than I.

29 And now I have told you before it come to pass, that, when it is come to pass, ye may believe.

30 I will no more talk much with you: for the prince of the world cometh, and hath nothing in me.

31 But that the world may know that I love the Father; and as the Father gave me commandment, even so I do. Arise, let us go hence.

CHAPTER XV.

I AM the true vine, and my Father is the husbandman.

2 Every branch in me that beareth not fruit he taketh away: and every branch that beareth fruit, he cleanseth, that it may bear more fruit.

3 Ye are clean already by reason of the word which I have spoken unto you.

4 Abide in me, and I in you. Even as the branch cannot bear fruit of itself, except it abide in the vine, so neither can ye, except ye abide in me.

5 I am the vine, ye are the branches: He that abideth in me, and I in him, the same beareth much fruit; for apart from me ye can do nothing.

6 If a man abide not in me, he is cast forth as a branch, and is withered; and they gather them, and cast them into the fire, and they burn.

7 If ye abide in me, and my words abide in you, ask whatsoever ye will, and it shall be done unto you.

8 Herein is my Father glorified, that ye bear much fruit, and become my disciples.

9 As the Father hath loved me, so have I loved you: abide ye in my love.

10 If ye keep my commandments, ye shall abide in my love; even as I have kept my Father's commandments, and abide in his love.

11 These things have I spoken unto you, that my joy may be in you, and that your joy may be full.

12 This is my commandment, That ye love one another, as I loved you.

13 Greater love hath no man than this, that a man lay down his life for his friends.

14 Ye are my friends, if ye do the things which I command you.

15 I call you no longer servants; because the servant knoweth not what his lord doeth: but I have called you friends; because I made known unto you all things that I heard from my Father.

16 Ye did not choose me, but I chose you, and appointed you, that ye should go and bear fruit, and that your fruit should remain: that whatsoever ye ask of the Father in my name, he may give it you.

17 These things I command you, that ye love one another.

18 If the world hateth you, ¹know that it hath hated me before you.

19 If ye were of the world, the world would love his own: but because ye are not of the world, but I have chosen you out of the world, therefore the world hateth you.

20 Remember the word that I said unto you, There is no servant greater than his lord. If they persecuted me, they

¹ *Or,* ye know.

will also persecute you; if they keep my word, they will keep yours also.

21 Howbeit all these things will they do unto you for my name's sake, because they know not him that sent me.

22 If I had not come and spoken unto them, they would not have sin: but now they have no excuse for their sin.

23 He that hateth me hateth my Father also.

24 If I had not done among them the works which none other man did, they would not have sin: but now have they both seen and hated both me and my Father.

25 But ¹[this cometh to pass,] that the word may be fulfilled that is written in their law, They hated me without a cause.

26 But when the Comforter is come, whom I will send unto you from the Father, even the Spirit of truth, which proceedeth from the Father, he shall bear witness of me:

27 And ye also are witnesses, because ye have been with me from the beginning.

CHAPTER XVI.

THESE things have I spoken unto you, that ye should not be offended.

2 They shall put you out of the synagogues: yea, an hour cometh, that every man that killeth you will think that he offereth a service unto God.

3 And these things will they do, because they have not known the Father, nor me.

¹ *Not expressed in the original.*

4 Nevertheless these things have I spoken unto you, that when their hour is come, ye may remember them. But these things I told you not at the beginning, because I was with you.

5 But now I go my way to him that sent me; and none of you asketh me, Whither goest thou?

6 Yet because I have spoken these things unto you, sorrow hath filled your heart.

7 Nevertheless I tell you the truth; It is expedient for you that I depart: for if I depart not, the Comforter will not come unto you; but if I go, I will send him unto you.

8 And when he is come, he will convict the world of sin, and of righteousness, and of judgment:

9 Of sin, because they believe not in me:

10 Of righteousness, because I go to my Father, and ye behold me no more;

11 Of judgment, because the prince of this world hath been judged.

12 I have yet many things to say unto you, but ye cannot bear them now.

13 Howbeit when he, the Spirit of truth, is come, he shall guide you into all the truth: for he shall not speak of himself; but whatsoever he shall hear, that shall he speak: and he shall tell you the things to come.

14 He shall glorify me; for he shall receive of mine, and shall tell it unto you.

15 All things that the Father

hath are mine: for this cause said I, that he receiveth of mine, and shall tell it unto you.

16 A little while, and ye behold me no longer; and again, a little while, and ye shall see me.[1]

17 Therefore said some of his disciples one to another, What is this that he saith unto us, A little while, and ye behold me not; and again, a little while, and ye shall see me: and because I go to the Father?

18 They said therefore, What is this that he saith, this little while? we know not of what he speaketh.

19 Jesus knew that they were desirous to ask him, and he said unto them, Do ye inquire of this among yourselves, because I said, A little while, and ye behold me not; and again, a little while, and ye shall see me?

20 Verily, verily, I say unto you, Ye shall weep and lament, but the world shall rejoice: ye shall be sorrowful, but your sorrow shall be turned into joy.

21 A woman when she is in travail hath sorrow, because her hour is come: but as soon as she is delivered of the child, she remembereth no more the anguish, for her joy that a man is born into the world.

22 So ye also now have sorrow. but I will see you again, and your heart shall rejoice, and your joy no man shall take from you.

[1] *The words that follow,* because I go to the Father, *are omitted by the great majority of early MSS.*

23 And in that day ye shall ask me nothing. Verily, verily, I say unto you, Whatsoever ye shall ask of the Father, he will give it you in my name.

24 Hitherto have ye asked nothing in my name: ask, and ye shall receive, that your joy may be made full.

25 These things have I spoken unto you in parables: but an hour cometh, when I shall no more speak unto you in parables, but I shall tell you plainly concerning the Father.

26 In that day ye shall ask in my name: and I say not unto you, that I will pray the Father for you:

27 For the Father himself loveth you, because ye have loved me, and have believed that I came forth from the Father.

28 I came forth from the Father, and am come into the world: again, I leave the world, and go to the Father.

29 His disciples say unto him, Lo, now speakest thou plainly, and speakest no parable.

30 Now know we that thou knowest all things, and needest not that any man should ask thee: by this we believe that thou camest forth from God.

31 Jesus answered them, Ye do now believe:

32 Behold, an hour cometh, yea, is now come, that ye shall be scattered, every man to his own, and shall leave me alone: and yet I am not alone, because the Father is with me.

33 These things I have

spoken unto you, that in me ye may have peace. In the world ye have tribulation: but be of good cheer; I have overcome the world.

CHAPTER XVII.

THESE words spake Jesus, and lifted up his eyes to heaven, and said, Father, the hour is come; glorify thy Son, that thy Son also may glorify thee:

2 According as thou gavest him power over all flesh, that whatsoever thou hast given him, to them he should give eternal life.

3 And this is eternal life, to know thee the only true God, and him whom thou didst send, even Jesus Christ.

4 I glorified thee on the earth [1]by finishing the work which thou hast given me to do.

5 And now, O Father, glorify thou me with thine own self with the glory which I had with thee before the world was.

6 I manifested thy name unto the men which thou hast given me out of the world: thine they were, and thou hast given them unto me; and they have kept thy word.

7 Now they know that all things whatsoever thou hast given me are from thee.

8 For I have given unto them the words which thou gavest unto me; and they received them, and knew surely that I came forth from thee, and believed that thou didst send me.

9 I am praying for them: I am not praying for the world, but for them which thou hast given me; for they are thine:

10 And all things that are mine are thine, and thine are mine; and I am glorified in them.

11 And I am no more in the world, and these are in the world, and I come to thee. Holy Father, keep them in thy name which thou hast given me, that they may be one, even as we are.

12 While I was with them, I kept them in thy name which thou hast given me, and guarded them; and not one of them perished, but the son of perdition; that the scripture may be fulfilled.

13 But now come I to thee; and these things I speak in the world, that they may have my joy fulfilled in themselves.

14 I have given them thy word; and the world hated them, because they are not of the world, even as I am not of the world.

15 I pray not that thou shouldest take them out of the world, but that thou shouldest keep them from the evil.

16 They are not of the world, even as I am not of the world.

17 Sanctify them in the truth: thy word is truth.

18 As thou didst send me into the world, even so I also sent them into the world.

19 And for their sakes I sanctify myself, that they also may be sanctified in truth.

20 Yet not for these alone do I pray, but for them also

---

[1] *So all the earliest MSS.*

that ¹believe in me through their word;

21 That they all may be one; even as thou, Father, in me, and I in thee, that they also may be ²[one] in us: that the world may believe that thou didst send me.

22 And the glory which thou hast given me I have given them: that they may be one, even as we are one:

23 I in them, and thou in me, that they may be made perfect in one, that the world may know that thou didst send me, and lovedst them, even as thou lovedst me.

24 Father, I will that³ what thou hast given me, even they may be with me where I am; that they may behold my glory, which thou hast given me, because thou lovedst me before the foundation of the world.

25 O righteous Father, the world knew thee not; but I knew thee, and these knew that thou didst send me.

26 And I made known unto them thy name, and will make it known; that the love wherewith thou lovedst me may be in them, and I in them.

CHAPTER XVIII.

WHEN Jesus had spoken these words, he went forth with his disciples over the brook Kedron, where was a garden, into the which he entered, and his disciples.

2 Now Judas also, which ⁴betrayed him, knew the place: because Jesus ofttimes resorted thither with his disciples.

3 Judas then, having received the band of men, and officers from the chief priests and Pharisees, cometh thither with lanterns and torches and weapons.

4 Jesus therefore, knowing all things that were coming upon him, went forth, and said unto them, Whom seek ye?

5 They answered him, Jesus of Nazareth. Jesus saith unto them, I am he. Now Judas also, which ⁴betrayed him, was standing with them.

6 As soon then as he said unto them, I am he, they went backward, and fell to the ground.

7 He asked them therefore again, Whom seek ye? And they said, Jesus of Nazareth.

8 Jesus answered, I told you that I am he: if therefore ye seek me, let these go their way:

9 That the saying might be fulfilled, which he spake, Of them which thou hast given me I lost none.

10 Then Simon Peter having a sword, drew it, and smote the high priest's servant, and cut off his right ear. The servant's name was Malchus.

11 Jesus therefore said unto Peter, Put up thy sword into the sheath: the cup which my Father hath given me, shall I not drink it?

12 So the band and the captain, and the officers of the Jews, took Jesus, and bound him,

13 And led him away to

¹ *So all the ancient MSS.*
² *Omitted in several of the ancient MSS.*
³ *So the majority of the early MSS.*
⁴ *Delivered him up.*

Annas first; for he was father in law to Caiaphas, which was high priest that same year.

14 Now Caiaphas was he, which gave counsel to the Jews, that it was expedient that one man should die for the people.

15 And Simon Peter followed Jesus, and so did the other disciple: that disciple was known unto the high priest, and went in with Jesus into the palace of the high priest.

16 But Peter stood at the door without. Then went out the other disciple, which was known unto the high priest, and spake unto her that kept the door, and brought in Peter.

17 Then saith the damsel that kept the door unto Peter, Art thou also one of this man's disciples? He saith, I am not.

18 Now the servants and the officers were standing there, having made a fire of coals, because it was cold, and were warming themselves: and Peter stood with them, and warmed himself.

19 The high priest then asked Jesus of his disciples, and of his doctrine.

20 Jesus answered him, I have spoken openly to the world; I ever taught in the synagogue, and in the temple, whither the Jews always resort; and in secret spake I nothing.

21 Why askest thou me? ask them which have heard me, what I spake unto them: behold, these know what I said.

22 And when he had thus said, one of the officers who was standing by struck Jesus with the palm of his hand,[1] saying, Answerest thou the high priest so?

23 Jesus answered him, If I spoke evil, bear witness of the evil: but if well, why smitest thou me?

24 Annas therefore sent him bound unto Caiaphas the high priest.

25 ¶ And Simon Peter was standing and warming himself. They said unto him, Art thou also one of his disciples? He denied, and said, I am not.

26 One of the servants of the high priest, being a kinsman of him whose ear Peter cut off, saith, Did not I see thee in the garden with him?

27 So Peter denied again: and immediately the cock crew.

28 They lead Jesus therefore from Caiaphas unto [2]the palace of the governor: and it was early; and they themselves went not into [2]the palace, that they might not be defiled, but that they might eat the passover.

29 Pilate therefore went out unto them, and said, What accusation bring ye against this man?

30 They answered and said unto him, If he were not a malefactor, we would not have delivered him up unto thee.

31 Pilate therefore said unto them, Take him yourselves, and judge him according to your law. The Jews said unto him, It is not lawful for us to put any man to death:

[1] *Or,* with a rod.
[2] *Literally,* the prætorium.

32 That the saying of Jesus might be fulfilled, which he spake, signifying what manner of death he should die.

33 Pilate therefore entered into ¹the palace again, and called Jesus, and said unto him, Art thou the King of the Jews?

34 Jesus answered him, Sayest thou this of thyself, or did others tell it thee concerning me?

35 Pilate answered, Am I a Jew? Thine own nation and the chief priests delivered thee unto me: what hast thou done?

36 Jesus answered, My kingdom is not of this world: if my kingdom were of this world, my servants would fight, that I should not be delivered to the Jews: but now is my kingdom not from hence.

37 Pilate therefore said unto him, Art thou a king then? Jesus answered, Thou sayest; for I am a king.² To this end have I been born, and to this end am I come into the world, that I may bear witness unto the truth. Every one that is of the truth heareth my voice.

38 Pilate saith unto him, What is truth? And when he had said this, he went out again unto the Jews, and saith unto them, I find no fault in him.

39 But ye have a custom, that I should release unto you one at the passover: will ye therefore that I release unto you the King of the Jews?

40 Then they all cried out again, saying, Not this man, but Barabbas. Now Barabbas was a robber.

CHAPTER XIX.

THEN Pilate therefore took Jesus, and scourged him.

2 And the soldiers platted a crown of thorns, and put it on his head, and they clothed him with a purple robe,

3 And they ³kept coming unto him, and saying, Hail, King of the Jews! and they smote him with their hands.

4 And Pilate went forth again, and saith unto them, Behold, I bring him forth to you, that ye may know that I find no fault in him.

5 Jesus therefore came forth, wearing the crown of thorns, and the purple robe. And he saith unto them, Behold the man!

6 When the chief priests therefore and the officers saw him, they cried out, saying, Crucify him, crucify him. Pilate saith unto them, Take him yourselves, and crucify him: for I find no fault in him.

7 The Jews answered him, We have a law, and by the law he ought to die, because he made himself the Son of God.

8 When Pilate therefore heard this saying, he was the more afraid;

9 And went into the palace again, and saith unto Jesus, Whence art thou? But Jesus gave him no answer.

---

¹ *Literally*, the prætorium.
² *Or*, Thou sayest that I am a king.
³ *So nearly all the ancient MSS.*

10 Pilate therefore saith unto him, Speakest thou not unto me? knowest thou not that I have power to release thee, and have power to crucify thee?

11 Jesus answered, Thou wouldest have no power against me, except it were given thee from above: for this cause he that delivereth me unto thee hath the greater sin.

12 Upon this Pilate sought to release him: but the Jews cried, saying, If thou let this man go, thou art not Cæsar's friend: every one that maketh himself a king speaketh against Cæsar.

13 When Pilate therefore heard these words, he brought Jesus forth, and sat down upon the judgment seat in a place called the Pavement, but in Hebrew, Gabbatha.

14 Now it was the preparation of the passover. It was about the sixth hour, when he saith unto the Jews, Behold your King!

15 They cried out therefore, Away with him, away with him, crucify him. Pilate saith unto them, Shall I crucify your King? The chief priests answered, We have no king but Cæsar.

16 Then delivered he him therefore unto them to be crucified. And they took Jesus, ¹[and led him away.]

17 And he bearing his cross went forth unto the place called the place of a skull, which is called in Hebrew Golgotha:

18 Where they crucified him, and two others with him, on either side one, and Jesus in the midst.

19 Moreover Pilate wrote a title, and put it on the cross. And there was written, JESUS OF NAZARETH THE KING OF THE JEWS.

20 This title then read many of the Jews, because the place where Jesus was crucified was nigh to the city: and it was written in Hebrew, and in Greek, and in Latin.

21 Therefore said the chief priests of the Jews to Pilate, Write not, The King of the Jews; but that he said, I am the King of the Jews.

22 Pilate answered, What I have written I have written.

23 The soldiers therefore, when they had crucified Jesus, took his garments, and made four parts, to every soldier a part; and also his coat: now the coat was without seam, woven from the top throughout.

24 They said therefore one to another, Let us not rend it, but cast lots for it, whose it shall be: that the scripture might be fulfilled, which saith, They parted my garments among them, and for my vesture they did cast lots. These things therefore the soldiers did.

25 Now there stood by the cross of Jesus his mother, and his mother's sister, Mary the ²[wife] of Clopas, and Mary Magdalene.

---

¹ *These words are wanting, or otherwise read, in many of the ancient MSS.*

² *Not expressed in the original.*

26 Jesus therefore seeing his mother, and the disciple standing by, whom he loved, saith unto his mother, Woman, behold thy son!

27 And then saith he to the disciple, Behold thy mother! And from that hour the disciple took her unto his own home.

28 After this, Jesus knowing that all things were now finished, that the scripture might be accomplished, saith, I thirst.

29 Now there was set a vessel full of vinegar: and they filled a spunge with vinegar, and fixed it upon hyssop, and put it to his mouth.

30 When Jesus therefore had received the vinegar, he said, It is finished: and he bowed his head, and gave up the ghost.

31 The Jews therefore, since it was the preparation, that the bodies might not remain upon the cross on the sabbath day, (for that sabbath day was an high day,) besought Pilate that their legs might be broken, and that they might be taken away.

32 So the soldiers came, and brake the legs of the first, and of the other which was crucified with him.

33 But when they came to Jesus, and when they saw that he was dead already, they brake not his legs:

34 Nevertheless one of the soldiers with a spear pierced his side, and forthwith there came out blood and water.

35 And he that saw it hath borne witness, and his witness is true: and he knoweth that he saith true, that ye may believe.

36 For these things came to pass, that the scripture might be fulfilled, A bone of him shall not be broken.

37 And again another scripture saith, They shall look on him whom they pierced.

38 And after these things Joseph of Arimathæa, being a disciple of Jesus, though in secret for fear of the Jews, besought Pilate that he might take away the body of Jesus: and Pilate gave him leave. He came therefore, and took away his body.

39 And there came Nicodemus also, which at the first came to him by night, bringing a mixture of myrrh and aloes, about an hundred pound weight.

40 They took therefore the body of Jesus, and wound it in linen clothes with the spices, as is the manner of the Jews to bury.

41 Now in the place where he was crucified there was a garden; and in the garden a new sepulchre, wherein was never man yet laid.

42 There therefore, by reason of the Jews' preparation day, because the sepulchre was nigh at hand, they laid Jesus.

CHAPTER XX.

NOW on the first day of the week cometh Mary Magdalene early, while it was yet dark, unto the sepulchre, and seeth the stone taken away from the sepulchre.

2 Then she runneth, and cometh to Simon Peter, and to the other disciple, whom Jesus loved, and saith unto them, They have taken away the Lord out of the sepulchre, and we know not where they have laid him.

3 Peter therefore went forth, and the other disciple, and they went toward the sepulchre.

4 And they ran both together: and the other disciple did outrun Peter, and came first to the sepulchre.

5 And stooping down and looking in, he seeth the linen clothes lying; yet went he not in.

6 Then cometh Simon Peter following him, and went into the sepulchre, and beholdeth the linen clothes lying,

7 And the napkin, that was on his head, not lying with the linen clothes, but wrapped together in a place by itself.

8 Then went in therefore the other disciple also, which came first to the sepulchre, and he saw, and believed.

9 For as yet they knew not the scripture, that he must rise again from the dead.

10 So the disciples went away again unto their own home.

11 But Mary stood without at the sepulchre weeping: and as she wept, she stooped down and looked into the sepulchre,

12 And beholdeth two angels in white sitting, one at the head, and the other at the feet, where the body of Jesus had lain.

13 And they say unto her, Woman, why weepest thou? She saith unto them, Because they have taken away my Lord, and I know not where they have laid him.

14 And having thus said, she turned herself back, and beholdeth Jesus standing, and knew not that it was Jesus.

15 Jesus saith unto her, Woman, why weepest thou? whom seekest thou? She, supposing that it was the gardener, saith unto him, Sir, if thou hast borne him hence, tell me where thou hast laid him, and I will take him away.

16 Jesus saith unto her, Mary. She turned herself, and saith unto him, Rabboni; which is to say, Master.

17 Jesus saith unto her, Touch me not; for I am not yet ascended to my Father: but go to my brethren, and say unto them, I ascend unto my Father and your Father, and my God and your God.

18 Mary Magdalene cometh and bringeth tidings to the disciples that she had seen the Lord, and that he had said these things unto her.

19 When it was evening therefore, on that same day, being the first day of the week, the doors being shut where the disciples were assembled for fear of the Jews, came Jesus and stood in the midst, and saith unto them, Peace be unto you.

20 And when he had so

said, he shewed unto them both his hands and his side. The disciples therefore were glad, when they saw the Lord.

21 So then Jesus said to them again, Peace be unto you: as the Father hath sent me, even so send I you.

22 And when he had said this, he breathed on them, and saith unto them, Receive ye the Holy Spirit:

23 Whose soever sins ye remit, they are remitted unto them; whose soever ye retain, they are retained.

24 But Thomas, one of the twelve, called Didymus, was not with them when Jesus came.

25 The other disciples therefore said unto him, We have seen the Lord. But he said unto them, Except I see in his hands the print of the nails, and put my finger into the print of the nails, and put my hand into his side, I will not believe.

26 And after eight days again his disciples were within, and Thomas with them. Jesus cometh, the doors being shut, and stood in the midst, and said, Peace be unto you.

27 And then he saith to Thomas, Reach hither thy finger, and behold my hands; and reach hither thy hand, and put it into my side: and be not faithless, but believing.

28 Thomas answered and said unto him, My Lord and my God.

29 Jesus saith unto him, Because thou hast seen me, thou hast believed: blessed are they that have not seen, and yet have believed.

30 Many other signs truly did Jesus in the presence of his disciples, which are not written in this book:

31 But these are written, that ye may believe that Jesus is the Christ, the Son of God; and that believing ye may have life in his name.

CHAPTER XXI.

AFTER these things he manifested himself again to the disciples at the sea of Tiberias; and he manifested himself on this wise.

2 There were together Simon Peter, and Thomas called Didymus, and Nathanael of Cana in Galilee, and the sons of Zebedee, and two other of his disciples.

3 Simon Peter saith unto them, I go a fishing. They say unto him, We also come with thee. They went forth, and entered into the ship; and that night they caught nothing.

4 But when morning was now come, Jesus stood on the shore: howbeit the disciples knew not that it was Jesus.

5 Jesus therefore saith unto them, Children, have ye any fish? They answered him, No.

6 And he said unto them, Cast the net on the right side of the ship, and ye shall find. They cast therefore, and now they were not able to draw it for the multitude of the fishes.

7 Therefore that disciple whom Jesus loved saith unto Peter, It is the Lord. Simon Peter then, hearing that it was

the Lord, girt his fisher's coat about him, (for he was naked,) and cast himself into the sea.

8 But the other disciples came in the boat; (for they were not far from land, but about two hundred cubits off,) dragging the net with the fishes.

9 As soon then as they went on shore, they see a fire of coals there, and fish lying thereon, and bread.

10 Jesus saith unto them, Bring of the fish which ye have now caught.

11 Simon Peter went aboard, and drew the net to land full of great fishes, an hundred and fifty and three: and for all there were so many, the net was not rent.

12 Jesus saith unto them, Come and dine. Now none of his disciples durst ask him, Who art thou? knowing that it was the Lord.

13 Jesus cometh, and taketh the bread, and giveth them, and the fish likewise.

14 This third time now was Jesus manifested to his disciples, after that he was risen from the dead.

15 ¶ So when they had dined, Jesus saith to Simon Peter, Simon, son of [1]Jonas, lovest thou me more than these? He saith unto him, Yea, Lord; thou knowest that I love thee. He saith unto him, Feed my lambs.

16 He saith to him again the second time, Simon, son of Jonas, lovest thou me? He saith unto him, Yea, Lord; thou knowest that I love thee.

[1] *See note on chap.* i. 42.

He saith unto him, Keep my sheep.

17 He saith unto him the third time, Simon, son of Jonas, lovest thou me? Peter was grieved because he said unto him the third time, Lovest thou me? And he said unto him, Lord, thou knowest all things; thou knowest that I love thee. Jesus saith unto him, Feed my sheep.

18 Verily, verily, I say unto thee, When thou wast young, thou girdedst thyself, and walkedst whither thou wouldest: but when thou art old, thou shalt stretch forth thy hands, and another shall gird thee, and shall carry thee whither thou wouldest not.

19 This spake he, signifying by what manner of death he should glorify God. And when he had spoken this, he saith unto him, Follow me.

20 Peter, turning about, seeth the disciple whom Jesus loved following; which also leaned on his breast at the supper, and said, Lord, which is he that betrayeth thee?

21 Peter therefore seeing him saith to Jesus, Lord, and what shall this man do?

22 Jesus saith unto him, If I will that he tarry till I come, what is that to thee? Do **thou** follow **me**.

23 This saying therefore went abroad among the brethren, that that disciple was not to die: and yet Jesus said not unto him, that he was not to die; but, If I will that he tarry till I come, what is that to thee?

24 This is the disciple whi*

testifieth of these things, and wrote these things, and we know that his testimony is true.

25 Moreover there are many other things which Jesus did, the which, if they should be written every one, I suppose that even the world itself could not contain the books that should be written.

THE ACTS OF THE APOSTLES.

CHAPTER I.

THE former treatise I made, O Theophilus, of all that Jesus began both to do and to teach,

2 Until the day in which he was taken up, after that he through the Holy Spirit had given commandments unto the apostles whom he had chosen:

3 To whom also he shewed himself alive after his passion by many proofs, appearing to them during forty days, and speaking of the things pertaining to the kingdom of God:

4 And, being assembled together with them, commanded them that they should not depart from Jerusalem, but wait for the promise of the Father, which, saith he, ye heard from me.

5 For John truly baptized with water; but ye shall be baptized with the Holy Spirit not many days hence.

6 They therefore came together, and asked him, saying, Lord, wilt thou at this time restore again the kingdom to Israel?

7 But he said unto them, It is not for you to know the times or the seasons, which the Father placed in his own authority.

8 But ye shall receive power by the Holy Spirit coming upon you: and ye shall be my witnesses both in Jerusalem, and in all Judæa, and in Samaria, and unto the uttermost part of the earth.

9 And when he had spoken these things, while they beheld, he was lifted up; and a cloud received him out of their sight.

10 And while they looked stedfastly toward heaven as he went, behold, two men stood by them in white apparel;

11 Which also said, Ye men of Galilee, why stand ye gazing into heaven? this same Jesus, which was taken up from you into heaven, shall so come

[CH. II.] THE ACTS. 191

in like manner as ye beheld him going into heaven.

12 Then returned they unto Jerusalem from the mount called the mount of Olives, which is near to Jerusalem, being a sabbath day's journey.

13 And when they were come in, they went up into the upper room where they abode ; both Peter, and John, and James, and Andrew, Philip, and Thomas, Bartholomew, and Matthew, James the [1]son of Alphæus, and Simon Zelotes, and Judas the [1]brother of James.

14 These all continued with one accord in prayer, with the women, and with Mary the mother of Jesus, and his brethren.

15 ¶ And in these days Peter stood up in the midst of the brethren, and said, (the number of names together were about an hundred and twenty,)

16 Brethren, this scripture must needs have been fulfilled, which the Holy Spirit by the mouth of David spake before concerning Judas, which was guide to them that took Jesus.

17 Because he was numbered with us, and had obtained his lot in this ministry.

18 Now this man purchased a field with the wages of his iniquity ; and falling headlong, he burst asunder in the midst, and all his bowels gushed out.

19 And it was known unto all the dwellers at Jerusalem ; insomuch as that field is called in their proper dialect, Aceldama, that is, The field of blood.

20 For it is written in the book of Psalms, Let his habitation be desolate, and let no man dwell therein : and, His office let another take.

21 Wherefore of these men which have companied with us all the time that the Lord Jesus went in and out among us,

22 Beginning from the baptism of John, unto that same day that he was taken up from us, must one become a witness with us of his resurrection.

23 And they appointed two, Joseph called Barsabas, who was surnamed Justus, and Matthias.

24 And they prayed, and said, Thou, Lord, which knowest the hearts of all men, appoint one of these two, him whom thou hast chosen,

25 To receive the place of this ministry and apostleship, from which Judas by transgression fell, that he might go to his own place.

26 And they cast lots for them ; and the lot fell upon Matthias ; and he was numbered with the eleven apostles.

CHAPTER II.

AND while the day of Pentecost was being fulfilled, they were all together in one place.

2 And suddenly there came a sound from heaven as of a rushing mighty wind, and it filled all the house where they were sitting.

---

[1] Son *and* brother *are not expressed in the original.*

3 And there appeared unto them cloven tongues like as of fire, and it sat upon each of them.

4 And they were all filled with the Holy Spirit, and began to speak with other tongues, even as the Spirit gave them utterance.

5 And there were dwelling at Jerusalem Jews, devout men, out of every nation under heaven.

6 Now when this sound took place, the multitude came together, and were confounded, because that every man heard them speak in his own language.

7 And they were amazed and marvelled, saying, Behold, are not all these which speak Galilæans?

8 And how hear we every man in our own language, wherein we were born?

9 Parthians, and Medes, and Elamites, and the dwellers in Mesopotamia, and in Judæa, and Cappadocia, in Pontus, and Asia,

10 Phrygia, and Pamphylia, in Egypt, and in the parts of Libya about Cyrene, and the Romans in Jerusalem, Jews and proselytes,

11 Cretans and Arabians, we do hear them speaking in our tongues the wonderful works of God.

12 And they were all amazed, and were in doubt, saying one to another, What may this be?

13 But others mocking said, that they were full of sweet wine.

14 ¶ But Peter, standing up with the eleven, lifted up his voice, and said unto them, Ye Jews, and all that dwell at Jerusalem, be this known unto you, and hearken to my words:

15 For these are not drunken, as ye suppose, seeing it is but the third hour of the day.

16 But this is that which is spoken by the prophet [1][Joel];

17 It shall come to pass in the last days, saith God, I will pour out of my Spirit upon all flesh: and your sons and your daughters shall prophesy, and your young men shall see visions, and your old men shall dream dreams:

18 Moreover on my servants and on my handmaidens I will pour out in those days of my Spirit; and they shall prophesy:

19 And I will shew wonders in heaven above, and signs on the earth beneath; blood, and fire, and vapour of smoke:

20 The sun shall be turned into darkness, and the moon into blood, before that great and notable day of the Lord come:

21 And it shall come to pass, that whosoever shall call on the name of the Lord shall be saved.

22 Ye men of Israel, hear these words; Jesus of Nazareth, a man proved by God unto you by miracles and wonders and signs, which God did by him in the midst of you, as ye yourselves know:

23 Him, being delivered ac-

---

[1] *Probably this word ought to be omitted.*

cording to the determinate counsel and foreknowledge of God, ye by the hand of ¹heathen men nailed to a cross and slew :

24 Whom God raised up, having loosed the ²pains of death : because it was not possible that he should be holden by it.

25 For David speaketh concerning him, I foresaw the Lord always before my face, for he is on my right hand, that I may not be moved :

26 Therefore did my heart rejoice, and my tongue was glad ; moreover also my flesh shall rest in hope :

27 Because thou wilt not leave my life in the grave, neither wilt thou suffer thine Holy One to see corruption.

28 Thou madest known to me the ways of life ; thou shalt make me full of joy with thy countenance.

29 Brethren, I may freely speak unto you of the patriarch David, that he both died and was buried, and his sepulchre is amongst us unto this day.

30 Therefore being a prophet, and knowing that God had sworn with an oath to him, that of the fruit of his loins he would ³set one upon his throne ;

31 He foreseeing spake of the resurrection of Christ, that he was not left in the grave, neither did his flesh see corruption.

32 This Jesus God raised up, whose witnesses are we all.

33 Therefore being by the right hand of God exalted, and having received from the Father the promise of the Holy Spirit, he hath shed forth this, which ye see and hear.

34 For David ascended not into the heavens : but he saith himself, The LORD said unto my Lord, Sit thou on my right hand,

35 Until I make thy foes ⁴thy footstool.

36 Therefore let all the house of Israel know assuredly, that God hath made him both Lord and Christ, even that same Jesus whom ye crucified.

37 ¶ But when they heard this, they were pricked in their heart, and said unto Peter and to the rest of the apostles, Brethren, what must we do ?

38 Peter said unto them, Repent, and be baptized every one of you in the name of Jesus Christ for the remission of sins, and ye shall receive the gift of the Holy Spirit.

39 For the promise is unto you, and to your children, and to all that are afar off, whomsoever the Lord our God shall call unto him.

40 And with many other words did he testify and exhort them, saying, Be ye saved from this crooked generation.

41 ¶ They therefore that gladly received his word were baptized : and the same day there were added unto them about three thousand souls.

42 And they continued sted-

---

¹ *Literally*, men without law: *see* 1 *Cor.* ix. 21.
² *Literally*, birth-pangs.
³ *So all the oldest authorities.*
⁴ *Literally*, a footstool of thy feet.

fastly in the teaching of the apostles and their fellowship, in their breaking of the bread, and their prayers.

43 And fear came upon every soul: and many wonders and signs were done by the apostles.

44 And all that believed were together, and had all things common;

45 And sold their possessions and their goods, and parted them to all, as any one had need.

46 And they, continuing daily with one accord in the temple, and breaking bread at home, did eat their meat with gladness and singleness of heart,

47 Praising God, and having favour with all the people. And the Lord added to their number day by day them that were in the way of salvation.

CHAPTER III.

NOW Peter and John were going up into the temple at the hour of prayer, being the ninth hour.

2 And a certain man lame from his mother's womb was being carried, whom they laid daily at the gate of the temple which is called Beautiful, to ask alms of them that entered into the temple;

3 Who seeing Peter and John about to go into the temple asked an alms.

4 But Peter, fastening his eyes upon him with John, said, Look on us.

5 And he gave heed unto them, expecting to receive something from them.

6 But Peter said, Silver and gold have I none; but what I have, that give I thee: In the name of Jesus Christ of Nazareth [1][rise up and] walk.

7 And he took him by the right hand, and lifted him up: and immediately his feet and ancle bones received strength.

8 And he leaping up stood, and walked, and entered with them into the temple, walking, and leaping, and praising God.

9 And all the people saw him walking and praising God:

10 And they knew him well, that it was he which sat for alms at the Beautiful gate of the temple: and they were filled with wonder and amazement at that which had happened unto him.

11 And as [2]he held Peter and John, all the people ran together unto them in the porch that is called Solomon's, greatly wondering.

12 And Peter seeing it answered unto the people, Ye men of Israel, why marvel ye at this man? or why look ye earnestly on us, as though by our own power or godliness we had made him to walk?

13 The God of Abraham, and of Isaac, and of Jacob, the God of our fathers, glorified his Servant Jesus; whom ye delivered up, and denied him in the presence of Pilate, when he had determined to let him go.

14 But ye denied the Holy

---

[1] *These words are omitted by three of the most ancient MSS.*
[2] *So all the ancient MSS. and versions.*

One and the Just, and desired a murderer to be granted unto you;

15 And killed the Prince of life, whom God raised from the dead; whose witnesses we are.

16 And his name through faith in his name hath made this man strong, whom ye see and know: yea, the faith which is by him hath given him this perfect soundness in the presence of you all.

17 And now, brethren, I know that in ignorance ye did it, as did also your rulers.

18 But those things, which God before announced by the mouth of all the prophets, that his Christ should suffer, he hath so fulfilled.

19 Repent ye therefore, and turn you, that your sins may be blotted out, that the times of refreshing may come from the presence of the Lord;

20 And that he may send the Christ foreordained unto you, even Jesus;

21 Whom the heaven must receive until the times of restoration of all things, concerning which times God spake by the mouth of all his holy prophets since the world began.

22 Moses indeed said, A prophet shall the Lord your God raise up unto you from among your brethren, like unto me; him shall ye hear in all things whatsoever he shall say unto you.

23 And it shall come to pass, that every soul, which shall not hear that prophet, shall be destroyed from among the people.

24 Yea, and all the prophets from Samuel and those that follow after, as many as spake, likewise foretold of these days.

25 Ye are the sons of the prophets, and of the covenant which God made with your fathers, saying unto Abraham, And in thy seed shall all the families of the earth be blessed.

26 Unto you first God, having raised up his Servant Jesus, sent him to bless you, in turning away every one of you from your iniquities.

CHAPTER IV.

AND as they spake unto the people, the priests, and the captain of the temple, and the Sadducees, came upon them,

2 Being grieved that they taught the people, and preached, by the example of Jesus, the resurrection from the dead.

3 And they laid hands on them, and put them in custody until the next day: for it was now eventide.

4 Howbeit many of them which heard the word believed; and the number of the **men** was about five thousand.

5 ¶ And it came to pass on the morrow, that their rulers, and elders, and scribes were gathered together at Jerusalem,

6 And Annas the high priest, and Caiaphas, and John, and Alexander, and as many as were of the kindred of the high priest.

7 And when they had set them in the midst, they asked, In what power, or in what name, have ye done this?

8 Then Peter, filled with the Holy Spirit, said unto them, Ye rulers of the people, and elders ¹[of Israel],

9 If we this day are examined concerning the good deed done to this impotent man, by what means he is made whole;

10 Be it known unto you all, and to all the people of Israel, that in the name of Jesus Christ of Nazareth, whom ye crucified, whom God raised from the dead, even by him doth this man stand here before you whole.

11 This is the stone which was set at nought by you builders, which is become the head of the corner.

12 And there is no salvation in any other: for neither is there any other name under heaven given among men, whereby we must be saved.

13 Now beholding the boldness of Peter and John, and being aware that they were unlearned and ignorant men, they marvelled; and they recognised them, that they had been with Jesus.

14 And beholding the man which was healed standing with them, they could say nothing against it.

15 But when they had commanded them to go aside out of the council, they conferred among themselves,

16 Saying, What must we do

Omitted by the three oldest MSS.

to these men? for that indeed a notable miracle hath been done by them is manifest to all them that dwell in Jerusalem; and we cannot deny it.

17 But that it spread no further among the people, let us straitly threaten them, that they speak henceforth to no man in this name.

18 And they called them, and commanded them not to speak at all nor teach in the name of Jesus.

19 But Peter and John answered and said unto them, Whether it is right in the sight of God to hearken unto you more than unto God, judge ye.

20 For **we** cannot but speak the things which we saw and heard.

21 So when they had further threatened them, they let them go, finding nothing how they might punish them, because of the people: for all glorified God for that which was done.

22 For the man was above forty years old, on whom this miracle of healing had been wrought.

23 ¶ And being let go, they came unto their own company, and reported all that the chief priests and elders had said unto them.

24 And when they heard that, they lifted up their voice to God with one accord, and said, Lord, thou art God, which hast made the heaven, and the earth, and the sea, and all that in them is:

25 Who by the mouth of our

father thy servant David hast said by the Holy Spirit, Why did the heathen rage, and the people imagine vain things?

26 The kings of the earth stood up, and the rulers were gathered together against the Lord, and against ¹his Christ.

27 For of a truth against thy holy Servant Jesus, whom thou didst anoint, both Herod, and Pontius Pilate, with the Gentiles, and the people of Israel, were gathered together,

28 To do whatsoever thy hand and thy counsel determined before to be done.

29 And now, Lord, behold their threatenings: and grant unto thy servants, that with all boldness they may speak thy word,

30 ²By stretching forth thine hand to heal; and that signs and wonders may be done by the name of thy holy Servant Jesus.

31 And when they had prayed, the place was shaken where they were assembled together; and they were all filled with the Holy Spirit, and they spake the word of God with boldness.

32 And the multitude of them that believed were of one heart and of one soul: neither said any of them that ought of the things which he possessed was his own; but they had all things common.

33 And with great power gave the apostles their witness of the resurrection of the Lord Jesus: and great grace was upon them all.

34 For neither was there any among them that lacked: for as many as were possessors of lands or houses sold them and brought the prices of the things that were sold,³

35 And laid them down at the apostles' feet: and distribution was made unto each according as any had need.

36 And Joseph, who by the apostles was surnamed Barnabas, (which is, being interpreted, The son of ⁴exhortation,) a Levite, and a Cyprian by birth,

37 Having land, sold it, and brought the money, and laid it at the apostles' feet.

CHAPTER V.

BUT a certain man named Ananias, with Sapphira his wife, sold a possession,

2 And kept back part of the price, his wife also being privy to it, and brought a certain part, and laid it at the apostles' feet.

3 But Peter said, Ananias, why did Satan fill thine heart to lie to the Holy Spirit, and to keep back part of the price of the land?

4 While it remained, was it not thine? and after it was sold, was it not in thy power? why

---

¹ *Or*, his Anointed.
² *Two of the most ancient MSS. save*, By thy stretching forth.
³ *The original implies that a general sale took place, and that while the things were being offered for sale, they brought the prices as they were received. This cannot well be expressed in English.*
⁴ *Or, but less probably*, consolation. *See chap.* xi. 23, *where the cognate verb is used.*

didst thou conceive this thing in thine heart? thou liedst not unto men, but unto God.

5 And Ananias hearing these words fell down, and [1]gave up the ghost. And great fear came on all them that heard it.

6 And the young men arose, wrapped him up, and carried him out, and buried him.

7 And it came to pass, after the space of about three hours, that his wife, not knowing what had been done, came in.

8 Peter answered unto her, Tell me whether ye sold the land for so much? And she said, Yea, for so much.

9 But Peter said unto her, How is it that ye agreed together to tempt the Spirit of the Lord? behold, the feet of them which buried thy husband are at the door, and shall carry thee out.

10 And she fell down straightway at his feet, and [2]gave up the ghost: and the young men came in, and found her dead, and, carrying her forth, buried her by her husband.

11 And great fear came upon all the church, and upon as many as heard these things.

12 And by the hands of the apostles were many signs and wonders wrought among the people. And they were all with one accord in Solomon's porch:

13 And of the rest durst no man join himself to them: but the people magnified them.

14 And believers were the more added to the Lord,

multitudes both of men and women.

15 Insomuch that they brought forth the sick into the streets, and laid them on beds and couches, that, when Peter should come, at the least his shadow might overshadow [3]some of them.

16 Moreover also the multitude belonging to the cities round about Jerusalem were flocking together, bringing sick folks, and them which were vexed with unclean spirits: and these were all being healed.

17 But the high priest rose up, and all they that were with him, which is the sect of the Sadducees, and were filled with indignation,

18 And laid their hands on the apostles, and put them in public custody.

19 But an angel of the Lord by night opened the prison doors, and brought them forth, and said,

20 Go, stand and speak in the temple to the people all the words of this life.

21 And when they heard that, they entered at break of day into the temple, and taught. But the high priest came, and they that were with him, and called the council together, and all the senate of the children of Israel, and sent to the prison to have them brought.

22 But the officers which came found them not in the prison: and they returned, and told,

23 Saying, The prison truly

[1] *Literally*, breathed his last.
[2] *Literally*, breathed her last.
[3] *Literally*, some one.

found we shut with all safety, and the keepers standing before the doors; but when we had opened, we found no man within.

24 Now when both the captain of the temple and the chief priests heard these words, they doubted concerning them, whereunto this would grow.

25 But one came and told them, Behold, the men whom ye put in the prison are in the temple, standing and teaching the people.

26 Then went the captain with the officers, and brought them without violence: for they feared the people, lest they should be stoned.

27 And when they had brought them, they set them before the council: and the high priest asked them,

28 Saying, We straitly commanded you that ye should not teach in this name: and, behold, ye have filled Jerusalem with your teaching, and intend to bring this man's blood upon us.

29 But Peter and the apostles said, It is right to obey God rather than men.

30 The God of our fathers raised up Jesus, whom ye hanged on a tree and slew.

31 Him God exalted with his right hand as a Prince and a Saviour, to give repentance to Israel, and remission of sins.

32 And we are his witnesses of these words; and so is also the Holy Spirit, whom God hath given to them that obey him.

33 When they heard that, they were cut to the heart, and took counsel to slay them.

34 But a certain man stood up in the council, a Pharisee, named Gamaliel, a doctor of the law, had in reputation among all the people, and commanded to put the men out for a little time;

35 And said unto them, Ye men of Israel, take heed to yourselves what ye intend to do as touching these men.

36 For before these days rose up Theudas, boasting himself to be somebody; to whom a number of men, about four hundred, joined themselves: who was slain; and all, as many as obeyed him, were scattered, and came to nought.

37 After this man rose up Judas of Galilee in the days of the taxing, and drew away people after him: he also perished; and all, as many as obeyed him, were dispersed.

38 And now I say unto you, Refrain from these men, and let them alone: for if this counsel or this work be of men, it will be overthrown:

39 But if it be of God, ye cannot overthrow it; lest haply ye be found even to fight against God.

40 And to him they agreed: and when they had called the apostles, and beaten them, they commanded them not to speak in the name of Jesus, and let them go.

41 ¶ So they departed rejoicing from the presence of the council, because they were

counted worthy to suffer shame for ¹that Name.

42 And every day, in the temple and at home, they ceased not teaching and ²preaching that Jesus is the Christ.

CHAPTER VI.

BUT in those days, when the number of the disciples was multiplying, there arose a murmuring of the Grecian Jews against the Hebrews, because their widows were neglected in the daily ministration.

2 But the twelve called the multitude of the disciples unto them, and said, It ³seemeth not good that we should leave the word of God, and serve tables.

3 Wherefore, brethren, look ye out among you seven men of honest report, full of the Spirit and of wisdom, whom we will appoint over this business.

4 But we will give ourselves continually to prayer, and to the ministry of the word.

5 ¶ And the saying pleased the whole multitude: and they chose Stephen, a man full of faith and of the Holy Spirit, and Philip, and Prochorus, and Nicanor, and Timon, and Parmenas, and Nicolaüs a proselyte of Antioch:

6 Whom they set before the apostles: and when they had prayed, they laid their hands on them.

7 And the word of God increased; and the number of the disciples multiplied in Jerusalem greatly; and a great multitude of the priests were obedient to the faith.

8 Now Stephen, full of grace and power, did great wonders and miracles among the people.

9 But there arose certain of them of the synagogue which is called the synagogue of the Libertines, and Cyrenians, and Alexandrians, and of them of Cilicia and of Asia, disputing with Stephen.

10 And they were not able to resist the wisdom and the spirit by which he spake.

11 Then they suborned men to say, We have heard him speak blasphemous words against Moses and against God.

12 And they stirred up the people, and the elders, and the scribes, and came upon him, and seized him, and brought him to the council,

13 And set up false witnesses, saying, This man ceaseth not to speak blasphemous words against this holy place, and the law:

14 For we have heard him say, that this Jesus of Nazareth shall destroy this place, and shall change the customs which Moses delivered us.

15 And all that sat in the council, looking stedfastly on him, saw his face as it had been the face of an angel.

CHAPTER VII.

AND the high priest said, Are these things so?

2 But he said, Brethren and fathers, hearken; The God of glory appeared unto our

---

¹ *Literally,* the Name.
² *Literally,* evangelizing.
³ *Literally,* is not pleasing.

father Abraham, when he was in Mesopotamia, before he dwelt in Charran,

3 And said unto him, Get thee out of thy country, and from thy kindred, and come into the land which I shall shew thee.

4 Then came he out of the land of the Chaldæans, and dwelt in Charran: and from thence, when his father was dead, he removed him into this land, wherein ye now dwell.

5 And he gave him none inheritance in it, no, not so much as to set his foot on: and he promised that he would give it to him for a possession, and to his seed after him, although he had no child.

6 And God spake on this wise, That his seed should sojourn in a strange land; and that they should bring them into bondage, and ill treat them four hundred years.

7 And the nation to whom they shall be in bondage will I judge, said God: and after that shall they come forth, and they shall serve me in this place.

8 And he gave him the covenant of circumcision: and so he begat Isaac, and circumcised him the eighth day; and Isaac begat Jacob; and Jacob begat the twelve patriarchs.

9 And the patriarchs, envying Joseph, sold him into Egypt: but God was with him.

10 And delivered him out of all his afflictions, and gave him favour and wisdom in the sight of Pharaoh king of Egypt; and he made him governor over Egypt and all his house.

11 Now there came a famine over all Egypt and Canaan, and great affliction: and our fathers found no sustenance.

12 But when Jacob heard that there was corn in Egypt, he sent out our fathers first.

13 And at the second time Joseph was made known to his brethren; and Joseph's kindred was made known unto Pharaoh.

14 And Joseph sent, and called his father Jacob to him, and all his kindred, seventy and five souls.

15 And Jacob went down into Egypt, and died, he, and our fathers.

16 And were carried to Sychem, and laid in the sepulchre that Abraham bought for a sum of money of the sons of Emmor [1][the father] of Sychem.

17 But as the time of the promise drew nigh, which God ratified to Abraham, the people grew and multiplied in Egypt,

18 Till another king arose, which knew not Joseph.

19 The same dealt subtilly with our kindred, and ill treated our fathers, so that they exposed their young children, in order that they might not live.

20 In which time Moses was born, and was [2]fair in the sight of God. And he was nourished

[1] *Not expressed in the original.*
[2] *That is, as the Authorized Version,* exceeding fair: *but the original expression must be kept.*

up in his father's house three months:

21 But when he was exposed, Pharaoh's daughter took him up, and nourished him for herself as a son.

22 And Moses was instructed in all the wisdom of the Egyptians, and was mighty in his words and deeds.

23 But when he was full forty years old, it came into his heart to visit his brethren the children of Israel.

24 And seeing one of them suffer wrong, he defended him, and avenged him that was oppressed, and smote the Egyptian:

25 For he supposed his brethren would have understood how that God by his hand would give them ¹deliverance: but they understood not.

26 And the next day he shewed himself unto them as they strove, and set them at peace, saying, Ye are brethren; why do ye wrong one to another?

27 But he that did his neighbour wrong thrust him away, saying, Who made thee a ruler and a judge over us?

28 Wilt thou kill me, as thou killedst the Egyptian yesterday?

29 But Moses fled at this saying, and was a stranger in the land of Madian, where he begat two sons.

30 And when forty years were expired, there appeared to him in the wilderness of mount Sinai an angel in a flame of fire ²in a bush.

31 When Moses saw it, he wondered at the vision: and as he drew near to behold it, the voice of the Lord came unto him,

32 Saying, I am the God of thy fathers, the God of Abraham, and of Isaac, and of Jacob. And Moses trembled, and durst not behold.

33 But the Lord said to him, Put off thy shoes from thy feet: for the place where thou standest is holy ground.

34 I have seen, I have seen the ill-treatment of my people which is in Egypt, and I have heard their groaning, and am come down to deliver them. And now come, I will send thee into Egypt.

35 This Moses whom they refused, saying, Who made thee a ruler and a judge? the same hath God sent as a ruler and a deliverer with the help of the angel which appeared to him in the bush.

36 This ³[Moses] brought them out, working wonders and signs in the land of Egypt, and in the Red sea, and in the wilderness forty years.

37 This is that Moses, which said unto the children of Israel, A prophet shall God raise up unto you from among your brethren, like unto me.⁴

38 This is he that was in the congregation in the wilderness with the angel which spake to him in the mount Sinai, and with our fathers: who received

---

¹ *Literally*, salvation.
² *Literally*, of a bush.

³ *Not expressed in the original.*
⁴ *The words* him shall ye hear *(Deut.* xviii. 15) *are not found in the oldest MSS.*

the lively oracles to give unto us:

39 To whom our fathers would not obey, but thrust him from them, and in their hearts turned back again into Egypt,

40 Saying unto Aaron, Make us gods which shall go before us: for as for this Moses, which brought us out of the land of Egypt, we wot not what is become of him.

41 And they made a calf in those days, and offered sacrifice unto the idol, and rejoiced in the works of their hands.

42 Then God turned, and gave them up to worship the host of heaven; as it is written in the book of the prophets, O ye house of Israel, did ye offer to me slain beasts and sacrifices for forty years in the wilderness,

43 And did ye take the tabernacle of Moloch, and the star of your god Rephan, the figures which ye made to worship them? Yea, I will carry you away beyond Babylon.

44 Our fathers had the tabernacle of witness in the wilderness, as he appointed who spake unto Moses, that he should make it according to the fashion that he had seen.

45 Which also our fathers inheriting, brought in with [1]Joshua, when they took possession of the nations which God drave out before the face of our fathers, unto the days of David;

46 Who found favour before God, and prayed that he might find a tabernacle for the God of Jacob.

47 But Solomon built him an house.

48 Howbeit the most High dwelleth not in houses made with hands; even as the prophet saith,

49 Heaven is my throne, and earth is my footstool: what house will ye build me? saith the Lord: or what is the place of my rest?

50 Did not my hand make all these things?

51 ¶ Ye stiffnecked and uncircumcised in heart and ears, ye do always resist the Holy Spirit: as your fathers did, so do ye.

52 Which of the prophets did not your fathers persecute? and they slew them which predicted concerning the coming of the Just One; of whom ye have been now betrayers and murderers:

53 Ye who received the law at the injunction of angels, and kept it not.

54 ¶ When they heard these things, they were cut to the heart, and they gnashed their teeth upon him.

55 But he, being full of the Holy Spirit, looked up stedfastly into heaven, and saw the glory of God, and Jesus on the right hand of God,

56 And said, Behold, I see the heavens opened, and the Son of man standing on the right hand of God.

57 But they cried out with a loud voice, and stopped their ears, and ran upon him with one accord,

---

[1] *In the original,* Jesus, *which is the Greek form of* Joshua.

58 And cast him out of the city, and stoned him: and the witnesses laid down their clothes at a young man's feet, whose name was Saul.

59 And they stoned Stephen, praying, and saying, Lord Jesus, receive my spirit.

60 And he kneeled down, and cried with a loud voice, Lord, lay not this sin to their charge. And when he had said this, he fell asleep.

CHAPTER VIII.

AND Saul was consenting unto his death. And in that day there was a great persecution against the church which was at Jerusalem; and they were all scattered abroad throughout the regions of Judæa and Samaria, except the apostles.

2 And devout men carried Stephen to his burial, and made great lamentation over him.

3 But Saul made havock of the church, entering into every house, and haling men and women committed them to prison.

4 So then they that were scattered abroad went every where ¹preaching the word.

5 And Philip went down to a city of Samaria, and preached Christ unto them.

6 And the people with one accord gave heed unto those things which Philip spake, hearing and seeing the miracles which he did.

7 For ²unclean spirits, crying out with loud voice, came forth from many that were possessed with them: and many taken with palsies, and that were lame, were healed.

8 And there was great joy in that city.

9 But there was beforetime in the city a certain man, called Simon, which used sorcery, and bewitched the people of Samaria, giving out that himself was some great one:

10 To whom they all gave heed, from the least to the greatest, saying, This man is the so-called great power of God.

11 And to him they had regard, because that of long time he had bewitched them with his sorceries.

12 But when they believed Philip ¹preaching the things concerning the kingdom of God, and the name of Jesus Christ, they were baptized, both men and women.

13 And Simon himself believed also: and when he was baptized, he continued with Philip, and wondered, beholding the signs and great miracles which were done.

14 Now when the apostles which were at Jerusalem heard that Samaria had received the word of God, they sent unto them Peter and John:

15 Who, when they were come down, prayed for them, that they might receive the Holy Spirit:

16 (For as yet he was fallen upon none of them: only

---

¹ *Literally*, evangelizing.
² *Literally*, in the case of many who had unclean spirits, they, crying out with a loud voice, came forth

they had been baptized into the name of the Lord Jesus.)

17 Then laid they their hands on them, and they received the Holy Spirit.

18 But when Simon saw that through the laying on of the apostles' hands the Holy Spirit was given, he offered them money,

19 Saying, Give me also this power, that on whomsoever I lay hands, he may receive the Holy Spirit.

20 But Peter said unto him, Thy money perish with thee, because thou thoughtest to purchase with money the gift of God.

21 Thou hast neither part nor lot in this matter: for thy heart is not right in the sight of God.

22 Repent therefore of this thy wickedness, and pray the Lord, if perhaps the thought of thine heart may be forgiven thee.

23 For I perceive that thou art in the gall of bitterness, and in the bond of iniquity.

24 Then answered Simon, and said, Pray ye to the Lord for me, that none of these things which ye have spoken come upon me.

25 So they, when they had finished their testimony and had spoken the word of the Lord, returned to Jerusalem, and ¹preached the gospel in many villages of the Samaritans.

26 And an angel of the Lord spake unto Philip, saying, Arise, and go toward the south unto the way that goeth down from Jerusalem unto Gaza, ²which is desert.

27 And he arose and went: and, behold, a man of Ethiopia, an eunuch of great authority under ³Candace queen of the Ethiopians, who had the charge of all her treasure, and had come to Jerusalem to worship,

28 Was returning, and sitting in his chariot, and read Isaiah the prophet.

29 And the Spirit said unto Philip, Go near, and join thyself to this chariot.

30 And Philip ran thither, and heard him read the prophet Isaiah, and said, Understandest thou what thou readest?

31 And he said, How can I, except some one should guide me? And he desired Philip that he would come up and sit with him.

32 Now the place of the scripture which he was reading was this, He was led as a sheep to the slaughter; and like a lamb dumb before his shearer, so openeth he not his mouth:

33 In his humiliation his judgment was taken away: and who shall declare his generation? for his life is taken from the earth.

34 And the eunuch answered Philip, and said, I pray thee, of whom speaketh the prophet this? of himself, or of some other man?

² *i.e. most probably*, which way. *There were two ways.*
³ *Pronounce* Cándacé.

¹ Preached the gospel in *is literally* evange'ized.

35 And Philip opened his mouth, and began at the same scripture, and ¹preached unto him Jesus.

36 And as they went on the way, they came unto a certain water: and the eunuch said, See, here is water; what doth hinder me to be baptized?²

38 And he commanded the chariot to stand still: and they went down both into the water, both Philip and the eunuch; and he baptized him.

39 And when they were come up out of the water, the Spirit of the Lord caught away Philip, that the eunuch saw him no more: for he went on his way rejoicing.

40 But Philip was found at Azotus: and passing through he ³preached in all the cities, till he came to Cæsarea.

CHAPTER IX.

BUT Saul, yet breathing out threatenings and slaughter against the disciples of the Lord, went unto the high priest,

2 And desired of him letters to Damascus to the synagogues, that if he found any of this way, whether they were men or women, he might bring them bound unto Jerusalem.

3 And as he journeyed, it came to pass that he drew near Damascus: and suddenly there shined round about him a light from heaven:

4 And he fell to the earth, and heard a voice saying unto him, Saul, Saul, why persecutest thou me?

5 And he said, Who art thou, Lord? And he said, I am Jesus whom thou persecutest.⁴

6 But arise, and go into the city, and it shall be told thee what thou must do.

7 And the men which journeyed with him stood speechless, hearing the voice, but seeing no man.

8 And Saul arose from the earth; and when his eyes were opened, he saw no man: but they led him by the hand, and brought him into Damascus.

9 And he was three days without sight, and neither did eat nor drink.

10 And there was a certain disciple at Damascus, named Ananias; and to him said the Lord in a vision, Ananias. And he said, Behold, I am here, Lord.

11 And the Lord said unto him, Arise, and go into the street which is called Straight, and enquire in the house of Judas for one called Saul, of Tarsus: for, behold, he prayeth,

12 And hath seen in a vision a man named Ananias coming in, and putting his hand on him, that he might receive his sight.

13 But Ananias answered,

---

¹ *Literally,* evangelized.
² *The words which follow here as verse 37 are not found in any of the ancient MSS. They were probably inserted to suit the baptismal liturgies.*
³ *Literally,* he evangelized all the cities.
⁴ *The words which follow in the common text are without any authority whatever from the Greek MSS. They were put in here by Erasmus.*

Lord, I have heard from many of this man, how much evil he did to thy saints at Jerusalem:

14 And here he hath authority from the chief priests to bind all that call on thy name.

15 But the Lord said unto him, Go thy way: for he is a vessel of my choice, to bear my name before Gentiles, and kings, and the children of Israel:

16 For I will shew him how great things he must suffer for my name's sake.

17 And Ananias went his way, and entered into the house; and putting his hands on him said, Brother Saul, the Lord hath sent me, even Jesus, that appeared unto thee in the way by which thou camest, that thou mightest receive thy sight, and be filled with the Holy Spirit.

18 And immediately there fell from his eyes as it had been scales: and he received sight, and arose, and was baptized.

19 And when he had received food, he was strengthened. And he was certain days with the disciples which were at Damascus.

20 And straightway he preached Christ in the synagogues, that he is the Son of God.

21 But all that heard him were amazed, and said; Is not this he that destroyed in Jerusalem them which called on this name? And he was come hither for that intent, that he might bring them bound unto the chief priests.

22 But Saul increased more and more in strength, and confounded the Jews which dwelt at Damascus, proving that he is Christ.

23 ¶ And after many days were fulfilled, the Jews took counsel to kill him:

24 But their conspiracy was known to Saul. And they even watched the gates day and night to kill him.

25 But the disciples took him by night, and let him down by the wall in a basket.

26 And when he was come to Jerusalem, he assayed to join himself to the disciples: and they were all afraid of him, not believing that he was a disciple.

27 But Barnabas took him, and brought him to the apostles, and declared unto them how he had seen the Lord in the way, and that he had spoken to him, and how he had preached boldly at Damascus in the name of Jesus.

28 And he was with them, coming in and going out at Jerusalem.

29 And he preached boldly in the name of the Lord, and spake and disputed against the Grecian Jews: but they endeavoured to slay him.

30 Which when the brethren knew, they brought him down to Cæsarea, and sent him forth to Tarsus.

31 So then the church throughout all Judæa and Galilee and Samaria had peace, being built up, and walking in the fear of the Lord: and by the exhortation of the Holy Spirit was multiplied.

32 And it came to pass, as Peter passed through, visiting all, he came down also to the saints which dwelt at Lydda.

33 And there he found a certain man named ¹Æneas, which had kept his bed eight years, and was sick of the palsy.

34 And Peter said unto him, Æneas, Jesus, the Christ, maketh thee whole: arise, and make thy bed. And he arose immediately.

35 And all that dwelt at Lydda and Saron saw him; which also turned to the Lord.

36 ¶ Now there was at Joppa a certain disciple named Tabitha, which by interpretation is called ²Dorcas: this woman was full of good works and almsdeeds which she did.

37 And it came to pass in those days, that she was sick, and died: whom when they had washed, they laid in an upper chamber.

38 And forasmuch as Lydda was nigh to Joppa, the disciples, hearing that Peter was there, sent unto him two men, desiring him that he would not delay to come to them.

39 So Peter arose and went with them. When he was come, they brought him into the upper chamber: and all the widows stood by him weeping, and shewing the coats and garments which Dorcas made, while she was with them.

40 But Peter put them all forth, and kneeled down, and prayed; and turning to the body said, Tabitha, arise. And she opened her eyes: and when she saw Peter, she sat up.

41 And he gave her his hand, and lifted her up, and when he had called the saints and the widows, presented her alive.

42 And it was known throughout all Joppa; and many believed on the Lord.

43 And it came to pass, that he tarried many days in Joppa with one Simon a tanner.

CHAPTER X.

THERE was a certain man in Cæsarea called Cornelius, a centurion of the band called the Italian band,

2 A devout man, and one that feared God with all his house, which gave much alms to the people, and prayed to God alway.

3 He saw in a vision evidently about the ninth hour of the day an angel of God coming in to him, and saying unto him, Cornelius.

4 And when he looked on him, he was afraid, and said, What is it, Lord? And he said unto him, Thy prayers and thine alms are come up for a memorial before God.

5 And now send men to Joppa, and call for one Simon, whose surname is Peter:

6 He lodgeth with one Simon a tanner, whose house is by the sea side: he shall tell thee what thou oughtest to do.

7 And when the angel which spake unto him was departed, he called two of his household

---

¹ *Pronounce* Æneas.
² *i.e. a hind, or gazelle: which also is the meaning of* Tabitha.

servants, and a devout soldier of them that waited on him continually;

8 And when he had declared all these things unto them, he sent them to Joppa.

9 ¶ On the morrow, as they went on their journey, and drew nigh unto the city, Peter went up upon the housetop to pray about the sixth hour:

10 And he became very hungry, and would have eaten: but while they made ready, he fell into a trance,

11 And saw heaven opened, and a certain vessel descending, as it had been a great sheet suspended by four ropes, and let down to the earth:

12 Wherein were all fourfooted and creeping things of the earth, and birds of the air.

13 And there came a voice to him, Rise, Peter; kill, and eat.

14 But Peter said, Not so, Lord; for I have never eaten any thing that is common or unclean.

15 And the voice spake unto him again the second time, What God cleansed, that call not thou common.

16 This was done thrice: and the vessel was received up again into heaven.

17 Now while Peter doubted in himself what this vision which he had seen should mean, behold, the men which were sent from Cornelius had made enquiry for Simon's house, and stood before the gate,

18 And called, and asked whether Simon, which was surnamed Peter, were lodged there.

19 While Peter thought on the vision, the Spirit said unto him, Behold men seeking thee.

20 But arise, and get thee down, and go with them, doubting nothing: for I have sent them.

21 Then Peter went down to the men, and said, Behold, I am he whom ye seek: what is the cause wherefore ye are come?

22 And they said, Cornelius a centurion, a just man, and one that feareth God, and of good report among all the nation of the Jews, was warned by an holy angel to send for thee into his house, and to hear words from thee.

23 Then called he them in, and lodged them. And on the morrow he rose up, and went forth with them, and certain of the brethren from Joppa accompanied him.

24 And the morrow they entered into Cæsarea. And Cornelius was waiting for them, and had called together his kinsmen and near friends.

25 And as Peter was coming in, Cornelius met him, and fell down at his feet, and worshipped him.

26 But Peter took him up, saying, Stand up; I myself also am a man.

27 And as he talked with him, he went in, and findeth many come together.

28 And he said unto them, Yourselves know, that it is an unlawful thing for a man that is a Jew to keep company with, or come unto one of another nation; and me also God hath

shewed that I should not call any man common or unclean.

29 Therefore also came I without gainsaying, as soon as I was sent for: I ask therefore for what intent ye have sent for me?

30 And Cornelius said, Four days ago [1]I was fasting until this hour; and at the ninth hour I was praying in my house, and, behold, a man stood before me in bright clothing,

31 And said, Cornelius, thy prayer is heard, and thine alms are had in remembrance in the sight of God.

32 Send therefore to Joppa, and call hither Simon, whose surname is Peter; he is lodged in the house of one Simon a tanner by the sea side: [2][who, when he cometh, shall speak unto thee.]

33 Immediately therefore I sent to thee; and thou hast well done that thou art come. Now therefore are we all here present before [3]God, to hear all things that are commanded thee of God.

34 ¶ Then Peter opened his mouth, and said, Of a truth I perceive that God is no respecter of persons:

35 But in every nation he that feareth him, and worketh righteousness, is accepted with him;

36 The word which God sent unto the children of Israel, preaching peace by Jesus Christ: he is Lord of all.

37 Yourselves know the word which went throughout all Judæa, beginning from Galilee, after the baptism which John preached;

38 Even concerning Jesus of Nazareth, how God anointed him with the Holy Spirit and with power: who went about doing good, and healing all that were oppressed by the devil; for God was with him.

39 And we are witnesses of all things which he did both in the land of the Jews, and in Jerusalem; whom also they slew, hanging him on a tree:

40 Him God raised up the third day, and granted that he should appear;

41 Not to all the people, but unto witnesses chosen before by God, even to us, who did eat and drink with him after he rose from the dead.

42 And he commanded us to preach unto the people, and to testify that it is he which is appointed by God the Judge of quick and dead.

43 To him give all the prophets witness, that through his name whosoever believeth in him shall receive remission of sins.

44 ¶ While Peter yet spake these words, the Holy Spirit fell on all them which heard the word.

45 And they of the circumcision which believed were astonished, as many as came with Peter, because that on the

---

[1] *The four most ancient MSS. have,* I was until this hour keeping the ninth hour of prayer: *omitting was* fasting.

[2] *These words are not found in the three oldest MSS.*

[3] *One early MS. has* before thee, *which perhaps is the right reading.*

Gentiles also was poured out the gift of the Holy Spirit.

46 For they heard them speak with tongues, and magnify God. Then answered Peter,

47 Can any man forbid the water, that these should not be baptized, which have received the Holy Spirit as well as we?

48 And he commanded them to be baptized in the name of the Lord. Then prayed they him to tarry certain days.

CHAPTER XI.

AND the apostles and brethren that were in Judæa heard that the Gentiles also had received the word of God.

2 But when Peter was come up to Jerusalem, they that were of the circumcision contended with him,

3 Saying, Thou wentest in to men uncircumcised, and didst eat with them.

4 But Peter expounded the matter by order unto them from the beginning, saying,

5 I was in the city of Joppa praying: and in a trance I saw a vision, A certain vessel descend, as it had been a great sheet, let down from heaven by four ropes; and it came even to me:

6 Upon the which when I had fastened mine eyes, I considered, and saw the four-footed beasts of the earth, and the wild beasts, and the creeping things, and the fowls of the air.

7 And I also heard a voice saying unto me, Rise, Peter; kill and eat.

8 But I said, Not so, Lord: for nothing common or unclean hath at any time entered into my mouth.

9 But the voice answered me again from heaven,. What God cleansed, that call not thou common.

10 And this was done three times: and all were drawn up again into heaven.

11 And, behold, immediately there were three men already come unto the house where I was, sent from Cæsarea unto me.

12 And the Spirit bade me go with them. Moreover these six brethren accompanied me, and we entered into the man's house:

13 And he told us how he had seen an angel in his house, which stood and said unto him, Send to Joppa, and call for Simon, whose surname is Peter;

14 Who shall speak unto thee words, whereby thou shalt be saved, and all thy house.

15 And as I began to speak, the Holy Spirit fell on them, as on us at the beginning.

16 And I remembered the word of the Lord, how that he said, John indeed baptized with water; but ye shall be baptized with the Holy Spirit.

17 Forasmuch then as God gave them the like gift as he did unto us upon belief on the Lord Jesus Christ; what was I, that I could withstand God?

18 When they heard these things, they held their peace, and glorified God, saying, Then hath God also to the Gentiles granted repentance unto life.

19 ¶ So then they which were scattered abroad upon the persecution that arose about Stephen travelled as far as Phenicé, and Cyprus, and Antioch, speaking the word to none but unto the Jews only.

20 And some of them were men of Cyprus and Cyrene, which, when they were come to Antioch, spake unto the Greeks, ¹preaching the Lord Jesus.

21 And the hand of the Lord was with them: and a great number which believed turned unto the Lord.

22 And tidings of these things came unto the ears of the church which was in Jerusalem: and they sent forth Barnabas, that he should go as far as Antioch.

23 Who, when he came, and had seen the grace of God, was glad, and exhorted them all, that with purpose of heart they would cleave unto the Lord.

24 For he was a good man, and full of the Holy Spirit and of faith: and much people was added unto the Lord.

25 And he departed to Tarsus, to seek Saul:

26 And when he had found him, he brought him unto Antioch. And it came to pass, that a whole year they assembled themselves in the church, and taught much people. And the disciples were called Christians first in Antioch.

27 ¶ And in these days came prophets from Jerusalem unto Antioch.

¹ *Literally*, evangelizing.

28 And there stood up one of them named Agabus, and signified by the Spirit that there should be a great famine throughout all the world: which came to pass in the days of Claudius Cæsar.

29 And the disciples, every man according to his ability, determined to send relief unto the brethren which dwelt in Judæa:

30 Which also they did, and sent it to the elders by the hands of Barnabas and Saul.

CHAPTER XII.

NOW about that time Herod the king laid his hands upon certain of the church, to vex them.

2 And he killed James the brother of John with the sword.

3 And when he saw it pleased the Jews, he proceeded further to take Peter also. Then were the days of unleavened bread.

4 And when he had apprehended him, he put him in prison, delivering him to four quaternions of soldiers to keep him; intending after the passover to bring him forth to the people.

5 Peter therefore was kept in the prison: but prayer was made without ceasing by the church unto God for him.

6 And when Herod was about to bring him forth, the same night Peter was sleeping between two soldiers, bound with two chains: and the keepers before the door kept the prison.

7 And, behold, an angel of

the Lord came upon him, and a light shined in the cell: and he smote Peter on the side, and raised him up, saying, Arise up quickly. And his chains fell off from his hands.

8 And the angel said unto him, Gird thyself, and bind on thy sandals. And he did so. And he saith unto him, Cast thy garment about thee, and follow me.

9 And he went out, and followed him; and wist not that it was true which was done by the angel; but thought he saw a vision.

10 When they were past the first watch, and the second, they came unto the iron gate that leadeth unto the city; which opened to them of its own accord: and they went out, and passed on through one street; and forthwith the angel departed from him.

11 And when Peter was come to himself, he said, Now I know of a surety, that the Lord sent his angel, and delivered me out of the hand of Herod, and from all the expectation of the people of the Jews.

12 And when he was aware of it, he came to the house of Mary the mother of John, whose surname was Mark; where many were gathered together and praying.

13 And as he knocked at the door of the gate, a damsel came to hearken, named Rhoda.

14 And she, knowing Peter's voice, opened not the gate for gladness, but ran in, and told that Peter stood before the gate.

15 And they said unto her, Thou art mad. But she constantly affirmed that it was even so. Then said they, It is his angel.

16 But Peter continued knocking: and when they had opened the door, they saw him, and were astonished.

17 But he, beckoning unto them with the hand to hold their peace, declared unto them how the Lord had brought him out of the prison. And he said, Go report these things unto James, and to the brethren. And he departed, and went into another place.

18 Now as soon as it was day, there was no small stir among the soldiers, what was become of Peter.

19 And when Herod had sought for him, and found him not, he examined the keepers, and commanded that they should be put to death. And he went down from Judæa to Cæsarea, and there abode.

20 ¶ And Herod was highly displeased with them of Tyre and Sidon: but they came with one accord to him, and, having made Blastus the king's chamberlain their friend, desired peace; because their country was nourished by the king's country.

21 And upon a set day Herod, arrayed in royal apparel, sat upon his throne, and made an oration unto them.

22 And the people gave a shout, saying, It is the voice of a god, and not of a man.

23 And immediately an an-

gel of the Lord smote him, because he gave not God the glory: and he was eaten of worms, and gave up the ghost.

24 But the word of God grew and multiplied.

25 And Barnabas and Saul returned from Jerusalem, when they had fulfilled their ministry, bringing with them also John, whose surname was Mark.

CHAPTER XIII.

NOW there were in the church that was at Antioch prophets and teachers; as Barnabas, and Symeon that was called Niger, and Lucius of Cyrene, and Manaen, the foster-brother of Herod the tetrarch, and Saul.

2 And as they ministered to the Lord, and fasted, the Holy Spirit said, Separate me forthwith Barnabas and Saul for the work whereunto I have called them.

3 Then they fasted and prayed, and laid their hands on them, and sent them away.

4 So they, being sent forth by the Holy Spirit, went down unto Seleucia; and from thence they sailed away to Cyprus.

5 And when they were at Salamis, they preached the word of God in the synagogues of the Jews: and they had also John as their minister.

6 And when they had gone through the isle unto Paphos, they found a certain magician, a false prophet, a Jew, whose name was Bar-jesus:

7 Which was with the proconsul, Sergius Paulus, a prudent man; who called for Barnabas and Saul, and desired to hear the word of God.

8 But Elymas the magician (for so is his name by interpretation) withstood them, seeking to turn away the proconsul from the faith.

9 Then Saul, (who also is called Paul,) filled with the Holy Spirit, fixed his eyes on him,

10 And said, O full of all subtilty and all mischief, thou son of the devil, thou enemy of all righteousness, wilt thou not cease to pervert the straight ways of the Lord?

11 And now, behold, the hand of the Lord is upon thee, and thou shalt be blind, not seeing the sun for a season. And immediately there fell on him a mist and a darkness; and he felt about seeking some to lead him by the hand.

12 Then the proconsul, when he saw what was done, believed, being astonished at the teaching of the Lord.

13 ¶ Now Paul and his company put to sea from Paphos, and came to Perga in Pamphylia: and John departing from them returned to Jerusalem.

14 But they went on from Perga, and came to Antioch in Pisidia, and went into the synagogue on the sabbath day, and sat down.

15 And after the reading of the law and the prophets the rulers of the synagogue sent unto them, saying, Brethren, if ye have any word of exhor-

[CH. XIII.] THE ACTS. 215

tation for the people, say on.

16 And Paul stood up, and beckoning with his hand said, Men of Israel, and ye that fear God, give audience.

17 The God of this people Israel chose our fathers, and exalted the people when they dwelt as strangers in the land of Egypt, and with an high arm brought he them out of it.

18 And for about the time of forty years carried he them as a nurse in the wilderness.

19 And he destroyed seven nations in the land of Canaan, and divided their land to them by lot.

20 And after that he gave unto them judges about the space of four hundred and fifty years, until Samuel the prophet.

21 And from that time they desired a king: and God gave unto them Saul the son of Kish, a man of the tribe of Benjamin, for the space of forty years.

22 And he removed him, and raised up unto them David to be their king; to whom also he gave testimony, and said, I have found David the son of Jesse, a man after mine own heart, which shall fulfil all my will.

23 Of this man's seed hath God according to his promise raised unto Israel a Saviour, Jesus:

24 When John had first preached ¹before his coming

the baptism of repentance to all the people of Israel.

25 And as John fulfilled his course, he said, What think ye that I am? I am not he: but behold, there cometh one after me, whose shoes of his feet I am not worthy to loose.

26 Brethren, sons of the stock of Abraham, and whosoever among you feareth God, to you was the word of this salvation sent.

27 For they that dwell at Jerusalem, and their rulers, because they knew him not, nor yet the voices of the prophets which are read every sabbath day, they fulfilled them in their judgment of him.

28 And when they found no cause of death in him, they desired Pilate that he should be slain.

29 And when they had fulfilled all that was written of him, they took him down from the tree, and laid him in a sepulchre.

30 But God raised him from the dead:

31 And he was seen many days by them which came up with him from Galilee to Jerusalem, those men who now are his witnesses unto the people.

32 And we declare unto you glad tidings, how that the promise which was made unto the fathers,

33 God hath perfectly fulfilled the same unto our children, in that he hath raised up Jesus again; as it is also

¹ *Literally*, before the face of his coming.

written in the second psalm, Thou art my Son, this day have I begotten thee.

34 And as concerning that he raised him up from the dead, no more to return to corruption, he said on this wise, I will give you the sure mercies of David.

35 Wherefore he saith also in another psalm, Thou shalt not suffer thine Holy One to see corruption.

36 For David, after he had served his own generation by the will of God, fell asleep, and was gathered unto his fathers, and saw corruption:

37 But he, whom God raised again, saw no corruption.

38 Be it known unto you therefore, brethren, that through him is proclaimed unto you forgiveness of sins:

39 And in him every one that believeth is justified from all things from which ye could not be justified under the law of Moses.

40 Beware therefore, lest that come upon you, which is spoken of in the prophets;

41 Behold, ye despisers, and wonder, and perish: for I work a work in your days, a work which ye shall in no wise believe, though a man declare it unto you.

42 And as they were going out, they besought that these words might be preached to them the next sabbath.

43 But when the synagogue was broken up, many of the Jews and religious proselytes followed Paul and Barnabas: who, speaking to them, persuaded them to continue in the grace of God.

44 And the next sabbath day came almost the whole city together to hear the word of God.

45 But when the Jews saw the multitudes, they were filled with envy, and contradicted those things which were spoken by Paul, ¹[contradicting and] blaspheming.

46 And Paul and Barnabas waxed bold, and said, It was necessary that the word of God should first have been spoken to you: but seeing ye put it from you, and judge yourselves unworthy of everlasting life, lo, we turn to the Gentiles.

47 For so hath the Lord commanded us; I have set thee to be a light of the Gentiles, that thou shouldest be for salvation unto the end of the earth.

48 And when the Gentiles heard this, they were glad, and glorified the word of the Lord: and as many as were disposed to eternal life believed.

49 And the word of the Lord was published throughout all the region.

50 But the Jews stirred up the devout women of rank, and the chief men of the city, and raised persecution against Paul and Barnabas, and expelled them out of their borders.

51 But they shook off the dust of their feet against them, and came unto Iconium.

52 And the disciples were

¹ *These words are omitted by most of the ancient MSS.*

filled with joy, and with the Holy Spirit.

CHAPTER XIV.

AND it came to pass in Iconium, that they went both together into the synagogue of the Jews, and so spake, that a great multitude both of the Jews and also of the Greeks believed.

2 But the unbelieving Jews stirred up and embittered the minds of the Gentiles against the brethren.

3 Long time therefore abode they speaking boldly in the Lord, which gave testimony unto the word of his grace, granting signs and wonders to be done by their hands.

4 And the multitude of the city was divided: and part held with the Jews, and part with the apostles.

5 And when there was an assault made both of the Gentiles, and also of the Jews with their rulers, to use them despitefully, and to stone them,

6 They were aware of it, and fled unto Lystra and Derbe, cities of Lycaonia, and unto the region that lieth round about:

7 And there they remained preaching the gospel.

8 And there sat a certain man at Lystra, impotent in his feet, being a cripple from his mother's womb, who never had walked.

9 The same was listening to Paul as he spake: who fixing his eyes on him, and perceiving that he had faith to be healed,

10 Said with a loud voice, Stand upright on thy feet. And he leaped and walked.

11 And when the people saw what Paul had done, they lifted up their voices, saying in the speech of Lycaonia, The gods are come down to us in the likeness of men.

12 And they called Barnabas, Jupiter; and Paul, Mercury, because he was the chief speaker.

13 And the priest of Jupiter which was before their city brought oxen and garlands unto the doors of the house, and wanted to do sacrifice with the people.

14 Which when the apostles, Barnabas and Paul, heard of, they rent their clothes, and ran in among the multitude, crying out,

15 And saying, Sirs, why do ye these things? We also are men of like passions with you, and [1]preach unto you that ye should turn from these vanities unto the living God, which made the heaven, and the earth, and the sea, and all things that are therein:

16 Who in generations gone by suffered all the nations to walk in their own ways.

17 Nevertheless he left not himself without witness, in that he did good, and gave us rain from heaven, and fruitful seasons, filling our hearts with food and gladness.

18 And with these sayings scarce restrained they the multitudes, that they had not done sacrifice unto them.

19 ¶ And there came thither

[1] *Literally*, evangelize.

certain Jews from Antioch and Iconium, who persuaded the multitudes, and stoned Paul, and drew him out of the city, supposing he had been dead.

20 Howbeit, as the disciples stood round about him, he rose up, and came into the city: and the next day he departed with Barnabas to Derbe.

21 And when they had [1]preached the gospel to that city, and had made many disciples, they returned again to Lystra, and to Iconium, and to Antioch,

22 Confirming the souls of the disciples, exhorting them to continue in the faith, and that we must through many tribulations enter into the kingdom of God.

23 And when they had elected for them elders in every church, and had prayed with fasting, they commended them to the Lord, in whom they believed.

24 And they passed throughout Pisidia, and came to Pamphylia.

25 And they preached the word in Perga, and went down into [2]Attalia:

26 And thence sailed away to Antioch, from whence they had been recommended to the grace of God for the work which they fulfilled.

27 And when they were come, and had gathered the church together, they rehearsed all that God had done with them, and how he had opened the door of faith unto the Gentiles.

28 And there they abode no little time with the disciples.

CHAPTER XV.

AND certain men had come down from Judæa, and were teaching the brethren, Except ye have been circumcised after the manner of Moses, ye cannot be saved.

2 When therefore Paul and Barnabas had no small dissension and disputation with them, they determined that Paul and Barnabas, and certain others of them, should go up to Jerusalem unto the apostles and elders about this question.

3 So they, being brought on their way by the church, passed through Phenice and Samaria, declaring the conversion of the Gentiles: and they caused great joy unto all the brethren.

4 And when they were come to Jerusalem, they were received by the church, and by the apostles and the elders, and they declared all things that God had done with them.

5 But there rose up certain of the sect of the Pharisees which believed, saying, That it was needful to circumcise them, and to command them to keep the law of Moses.

6 ¶ And the apostles and the elders came together to consider of this matter.

7 And when there had been much disputing, Peter rose up, and said unto them, Brethren, ye yourselves know how that [3]a good while ago God made choice among us, that the Gentiles by my mouth should hear

---

[1] *Literally,* evangelized that city.
[2] *Pronounce* Attalĭa.

[3] *Literally,* from ancient days.

the word of the gospel, and believe.

8 And God, which knoweth the hearts, bare them witness, giving them the Holy Spirit, even as unto us;

9 And put no difference between us and them, purifying their hearts by the faith.

10 Now therefore why tempt ye God, to put a yoke upon the neck of the disciples, which neither our fathers nor we were able to bear?

11 Nay, we believe that through the grace of the Lord Jesus Christ we are saved, even as also they.

12 So all the multitude kept silence, and gave audience to Barnabas and Paul, declaring what signs and wonders God had wrought among the Gentiles by them.

13 And after they had held their peace, James answered, saying, Brethren, hearken unto me:

14 [1]Symeon hath declared how God at the first did visit the Gentiles, to take out of them a people for his name.

15 And to this agree the words of the prophets; as it is written,

16 After this I will return, and will build again the tabernacle of David, which is fallen down; and I will build again the ruins thereof, and I will set it up:

17 That the residue of men may seek after the Lord, and all the Gentiles, upon whom my name is called, saith the Lord, who [2]maketh all these things known from the beginning.

19 Wherefore my sentence is, that we trouble not them, which from among the Gentiles are turning to God:

20 But that we command them, that they abstain from pollutions of idols and from fornication, and from things strangled, and from blood.

21 For Moses from of old hath in every city them that preach him, being read in the synagogues every sabbath day.

22 Then pleased it the apostles and elders, with the whole church, to choose out men of their own company, and send them to Antioch with Paul and Barnabas; namely, Judas surnamed Barsabbas, and Silas, chief men among the brethren:

23 And they wrote letters by them after this manner; The apostles, and brethren which are elders, send greeting unto the brethren which are of the Gentiles in Antioch and Syria and Cilicia:

24 Forasmuch as we heard, that certain which went out from us troubled you with words, subverting your souls,[3] to whom we gave no commandment:

25 It seemed good unto us, being assembled with one ac-

---

[1] *i.e.* Peter: *see* 2 *Pet.* i. 1.

[2] *The reading here is in great confusion. Various explanatory insertions have been made in the later MSS. The reading adopted is that of the three oldest MSS.*

[3] *The words which follow in the Authorized Version,* saying, Ye must be circumcised, and keep the law, *are not contained in the most ancient MSS.*

cord, to choose out and send men unto you with our beloved Barnabas and Paul,

26 Men that have hazarded their lives for the name of our Lord Jesus Christ.

27 We have sent therefore Judas and Silas, who shall also tell you the same things by word of mouth.

28 For it seemed good to the Holy Spirit, and to us, to lay upon you no greater burden than these necessary things;

29 That ye abstain from meats offered to idols, and from blood, and from things strangled, and from fornication: from which if ye keep yourselves, ye shall do well. Fare ye well.

30 So when they were dismissed, they came down to Antioch: and when they had gathered the multitude together, they delivered the epistle:

31 Which when they had read, they rejoiced for the consolation.

32 And Judas and Silas, being prophets also themselves, exhorted the brethren with many words, and confirmed them.

33 And after they had tarried there a space, they were let go in peace from the brethren unto ¹them that had sent them forth.

35 But Paul and Barnabas continued in Antioch, teaching

¹ *So all the ancient MSS. Verse 34 is not found in the most ancient MSS. and many others: and in those which do contain it, is read with great variations. It was probably inserted to explain verse 40.*

and preaching the word of the Lord, with many others also.

36 And after some days Paul said unto Barnabas, Let us now go again and visit our brethren in every city where we have preached the word of the Lord, and see how they do.

37 And Barnabas was minded to take with them John, who was called Mark.

38 But Paul thought not good to take him with them, who departed from them from Pamphylia, and went not with them to the work.

39 And there arose a sharp contention, so that they departed asunder one from the other: and Barnabas took Mark, and sailed forth unto Cyprus;

40 And Paul chose Silas, and departed, being recommended by the brethren unto the grace of God.

41 And he went through Syria and Cilicia, confirming the churches.

CHAPTER XVI.

AND he came to Derbe and Lystra: and, behold, a certain disciple was there, named Timotheus, the son of a certain woman, which was a Jewess, and believed; but his father was a Greek:

2 Which was well reported of by the brethren that were at Lystra and Iconium.

3 Him would Paul have to go forth with him; and took and circumcised him because of the Jews which were in those quarters: for they knew all that his father was a Greek.

4 And as they went through the cities, they delivered them the decrees to keep, that were ordained by the apostles and elders which were at Jerusalem.

5 And so the churches were established in the faith, and increased in number daily.

6 And they went throughout Phrygia and the region of Galatia; and being forbidden by the Holy Spirit to preach the word in Asia,

7 After they were come to Mysia, they assayed to go into Bithynia: but the Spirit [1]of Jesus suffered them not.

8 And passing by Mysia they came down to Troas.

9 And a vision appeared to Paul in the night; a certain man of Macedonia standing, and praying him, saying, Come over into Macedonia, and help us.

10 And after he had seen the vision, immediately we endeavoured to go into Macedonia, assuredly gathering that the Lord had called us to preach the gospel unto them.

11 Therefore loosing from Troas, we came with a straight course to Samothrace, and the next day to Neapolis;

12 And from thence to Philippi, which is the first Macedonian city of the district, and a colony: and we were in that city abiding certain days.

13 And on the sabbath we went out of the city by a river side, where prayer was wont to be made; and we sat down,

[1] *So all the ancient MSS. and versions.*

and spake unto the women which resorted thither.

14 ¶ And a certain woman named Lydia, a seller of purple, of the city of Thyatira, which worshipped God, heard us: whose heart the Lord opened, that she attended unto the things which were spoken by Paul.

15 And when she was baptized, and her household, she besought us, saying, If ye have judged me to be faithful to the Lord, come into my house, and abide there. And she constrained us.

16 ¶ And it came to pass, as we went forth to the place of prayer, a certain damsel possessed with a spirit of divination met us, which brought her masters much gain by soothsaying:

17 The same followed Paul and us, and cried, saying, These men are the servants of the most high God, which tell unto us the way of salvation.

18 And this did she many days. But Paul, being grieved, turned and said to the spirit, I command thee in the name of Jesus Christ to come out of her. And he came out the same hour.

19 And when her masters saw that the hope of their gains was gone, they caught Paul and Silas, and drew them into the marketplace unto the rulers,

20 And brought them to the magistrates, saying, These men, being Jews, do exceedingly trouble our city,

21 And teach customs, which are not lawful for us to receive,

neither to observe, being Romans.

22 And the multitude rose up together against them: and the magistrates rent off their clothes, and commanded to beat them.

23 And when they had laid many stripes upon them, they cast them into prison, charging the jailor to keep them safely:

24 Who, having received such a charge, thrust them into the inner prison, and made their feet fast in the stocks.

25 And at midnight Paul and Silas prayed, and sang praises unto God: and the prisoners heard them.

26 And suddenly there was a great earthquake, so that the foundations of the prison were shaken: and immediately all the doors were opened, and every one's bands were loosed.

27 And the jailor awaking out of his sleep, and seeing the prison doors open, drew his sword, and was about to kill himself, supposing that the prisoners had been fled.

28 But Paul cried with a loud voice, saying, Do thyself no harm: for we are all here.

29 Then he called for lights, and sprang in, and came trembling, and fell down before Paul and Silas,

30 And brought them out, and said, Sirs, what must I do to be saved?

31 And they said, Believe on the Lord Jesus,[1] and thou shalt be saved, and thy house.

32 And they spake unto him the word of the Lord, and to all that were in his house.

33 And he took them the same hour of the night, and [2]washed their stripes; and was baptized, he and all his, straightway.

34 And when he had brought them up into his house, he set meat before them, and rejoiced, believing in God with all his house.

35 And when it was day, the magistrates sent the serjeants, saying, Let those men go.

36 And the jailor told this saying to Paul, The magistrates have sent to let you go: now therefore depart, and go in peace.

37 But Paul said unto them, They beat us openly uncondemned, being Romans, and cast us into prison; and now do they thrust us out privily? nay verily; but let them come themselves and fetch us out.

38 And the serjeants told these words unto the magistrates: and they feared, when they heard that they were Romans,

39 And came and besought them, and brought them out, and desired them to depart out of the city.

40 And they went out of the prison, and entered into the house of Lydia: and when they had seen the brethren, they exhorted them, and departed.

CHAPTER XVII.

NOW when they had passed through Amphipolis and

---

[1] Christ *is omitted in the most ancient MSS.*

[2] *Literally,* washed them from their stripes.

Apollonia, they came to Thessalonica, where was the synagogue of the Jews:

2 And Paul, as his manner was, went in unto them, and three sabbath days reasoned with them out of the scriptures,

3 Opening and alleging, that Christ must needs have suffered, and risen again from the dead; and that this Jesus, whom I preach unto you, is Christ.

4 And some of them were persuaded, and consorted with Paul and Silas; and of the devout Greeks a great multitude, and of the chief women not a few.

5 But the Jews being base, moved with envy, took unto them certain fellows out of the streets, and gathered a mob, and set the city on an uproar, and assaulted the house of Jason, and sought to bring them out to the people.

6 And when they found them not, they drew Jason and certain brethren unto the [1]rulers of the city, crying, These that have turned the world upside down are come hither also;

7 Whom Jason hath received: and these all do contrary to the decrees of Cæsar, saying that there is another king, one Jesus.

8 And they troubled the people and the rulers of the city, when they heard these things.

9 And when they had taken security of Jason, and of the other, they let them go.

10 ¶ And the brethren immediately sent away Paul and Silas by night unto Berœa: who, as soon as they arrived, went into the synagogue of the Jews.

11 These were more noble than those in Thessalonica, in that they received the word with all readiness of mind, searching the scriptures daily, whether those things were so.

12 Therefore many of them believed; also of honourable women which were Greeks, and of men, not a few.

13 But when the Jews of Thessalonica had knowledge that the word of God was preached by Paul at Berœa likewise, they came, stirring up and troubling the people there also.

14 And then immediately the brethren sent away Paul to go towards the sea: and Silas and Timotheus abode there still.

15 ¶ And they that conducted Paul brought him unto Athens: and receiving a commandment unto Silas and Timotheus, to come to him with all speed, they departed.

16 And while Paul waited for them at Athens, his spirit was stirred in him, when he saw the city wholly given to idolatry.

17 Therefore disputed he in the synagogue with the Jews, and with the devout persons, and in the market daily with them that met with him.

18 Certain also of the Epicurean and of the Stoic philosophers encountered him. And some said, What will this babbler say? and others, He seemeth to be a setter forth of

---

[1] *Literally*, politarchs—*the title of the magistrates at Thessalonica.*

strange gods: because he preached unto them Jesus, and the resurrection.

19 And they took him, and brought him unto Mars' hill, saying, May we know what this new doctrine, whereof thou speakest, is?

20 For thou bringest certain strange things to our ears: we would know therefore what these things mean.

21 Now all the Athenians and strangers which were there spent their time in nothing else, but either to tell, or to hear some new thing.

22 ¶ Then Paul stood in the midst of Mars' hill, and said, Ye men of Athens, I perceive that in all things ye are very religious.

23 For as I passed by, and beheld your objects of worship, I found an altar with this inscription, TO AN UNKNOWN GOD. What therefore ye ignorantly reverence, that declare I unto you.

24 God that made the world and all things therein, seeing that he is Lord of heaven and earth, dwelleth not in temples made with hands;

25 Neither is served with men's hands, as though he needed any thing, seeing he giveth to all life, and breath, and all things;

26 And made all nations of men, (created) of one [1]blood, to dwell on all the face of the earth, and determined the times appointed, and the bounds of their habitation;

[1] *This word is not found in the three most ancient MSS.*

27 That they should seek God, if haply they might feel after him, and find him, though he is not far from every one of us:

28 For in him we live, and move, and have our being; as certain also of your own poets have said, For we are also his offspring.

29 Forasmuch then as we are the offspring of God, we ought not to think that the Godhead is like unto gold, or silver, or stone, graven by art and man's device.

30 And the times of this ignorance God overlooked: but now commandeth all men every where to repent:

31 Because he hath appointed a day, in the which he will judge the world in righteousness by the man whom he hath ordained; whereof he hath given assurance unto all men, in that he hath raised him from the dead.

32 And when they heard of the resurrection of the dead, some mocked: but others said, We will hear thee again of this matter.

33 And thus Paul departed from among them.

34 Howbeit certain men clave unto him, and believed: among the which was Dionysius the Areopagite, and a woman named Damaris, and others with them.

CHAPTER XVIII.

AFTER these things Paul departed from Athens, and came to Corinth;

2 And finding a certain Jew

named Aquila, born in Pontus, lately come from Italy, and Priscilla his wife (because that Claudius had commanded all Jews to depart from Rome), he came unto them.

3 And because he was of the same craft, he abode with them, and worked : for by their occupation they were tent-makers.

4 And he reasoned in the synagogue every sabbath, and persuaded the Jews and the Greeks.

5 But when Silas and Timotheus came from Macedonia, Paul was earnestly occupied ¹in discoursing, testifying to the Jews that Jesus was the Christ.

6 And when they opposed themselves, and blasphemed, he shook his raiment, and said unto them, Your blood be upon your own heads ; I shall henceforth with a pure conscience go unto the Gentiles.

7 And he departed thence, and entered into a certain man's house, named Justus, one that worshipped God, whose house joined close to the synagogue.

8 But Crispus, the chief ruler of the synagogue, believed on the Lord with all his house ; and many of the Corinthians, when they heard it, believed, and were baptized.

9 And the Lord spake unto Paul in the night by a vision, Be not afraid, but speak, and hold not thy peace :

10 For I am with thee, and no man shall set on thee to hurt thee : for I have much people in this city.

11 And he continued there a year and six months, teaching the word of God among them.

12 ¶ And when Gallio was the proconsul of Achaia, the Jews made insurrection with one accord against Paul, and brought him to the judgment seat,

13 Saying, This man persuadeth men to worship God contrary to the law.

14 And when Paul was now about to open his mouth, Gallio said unto the Jews, If it were any matter of wrong or wicked lewdness, O ye Jews, I should reasonably have borne with you :

15 But if it is a question of words and names, and of your law, ye yourselves must look to it ; I will be no judge of such matters.

16 And he drave them from the judgment seat.

17 Then ² they all took Sosthenes, the chief ruler of the synagogue, and beat him before the judgment seat. And Gallio cared for none of those things.

18 But Paul tarried yet many days, and then took his leave of the brethren, and sailed thence to Syria, and with him Priscilla and Aquila ; having shorn his head in ³ Kenchreæ : for he had a vow.

19 And he came to Ephesus, and left them there : but he himself entered into the synagogue, and reasoned with the Jews.

¹ *So all the ancient MSS.*
² *Thus the three most ancient MSS.*
³ *Pronounce* Kénchrĕæ.

20 But when they desired him to tarry longer time, he consented not;

21 But bidding them farewell, and saying,[1] I will return again unto you, if God will, he sailed from Ephesus.

22 And when he had landed at Cæsarea, and [2] gone up, and saluted the church, he went down to Antioch.

23 And after he had spent some time there, he departed, and went over the country of Galatia and Phrygia in order, confirming all the disciples.

24 ¶ And a certain Jew named Apollos, an Alexandrian by descent, an eloquent man, came to Ephesus, being mighty in the scriptures.

25 This man had been instructed in the way of the Lord; and being fervent in his spirit, he spake and taught accurately the things [3]concerning Jesus, knowing only the baptism of John.

26 And he began to speak boldly in the synagogue: whom when Aquila and Priscilla had heard, they took him unto them, and expounded unto him the Way[4] more accurately.

27 And when he was disposed to pass into Achaia, the brethren wrote, exhorting the disciples to receive him: who, when he was come, helped them much which had believed through grace:

28 For he continued powerfully confuting the Jews in public, shewing by the scriptures that Jesus was the Christ.

CHAPTER XIX.

AND it came to pass that, while Apollos was at Corinth, Paul having passed through the upper regions came to Ephesus: and finding certain disciples,

2 He said unto them, Did ye receive the Holy Spirit when ye believed? And they said unto him, We did not so much as hear whether there were any Holy Spirit.

3 And he said unto them, Unto what then were ye baptized? And they said, Unto John's baptism.

4 Then said Paul, John baptized with the baptism of repentance, saying unto the people, that they should believe in him which should come after him, that is, on Jesus.

5 When they heard this, they were baptized into the name of the Lord Jesus.

6 And when Paul had laid his hands upon them, the Holy Spirit came on them; and they spake with tongues, and prophesied.

7 And all the men were about twelve.

8 And he went into the synagogue, and spake boldly for the space of three months, disputing and persuading the things concerning the kingdom of God.

---

[1] *The words,* I must by all means keep this feast that cometh in Jerusalem, *are not found in the most ancient MSS., and vary much in those which contain them.*

[2] *i.e.* to Jerusalem.

[3] *So all the ancient MSS.*

[4] *The words* of God *are very variously read by those MSS. which insert them: and it is therefore probable that one ancient MS., which does not contain them, is right.*

9 But when some were hardened, and believed not, but spake evil of the Way before the multitude, he departed from them, and separated the disciples, disputing daily in the school of Tyrannus.

10 And this continued for the space of two years; so that all they which dwelt in Asia heard the word of the Lord Jesus, both Jews and Greeks.

11 And God wrought by the hands of Paul miracles of no common sort:

12 So that from his body were brought unto the sick handkerchiefs or aprons, and the diseases departed from them, and the evil spirits went out of them.

13 ¶ But certain of the vagabond Jews, exorcists, took upon them to name over them which had evil spirits the name of the Lord Jesus, saying, I adjure you by Jesus whom Paul preacheth.

14 And there were certain men, seven sons of Sceva, a Jew, chief of the priests, which did so.

15 But the evil spirit answered and said unto them, Jesus I know, and Paul I know; but who are ye?

16 And the man in whom the evil spirit was leaped on them, and overcame them ¹both, and prevailed against them, so that they fled out of that house naked and wounded.

17 And this became known to all the Jews and Greeks also which dwelt at Ephesus; and fear fell on them all, and the name of the Lord Jesus was magnified.

18 And many that believed came, and confessed, and made known their deeds.

19 Many of them also which used curious arts brought their books together, and burned them before all men: and they counted the price of them, and found it fifty thousand pieces of silver.

20 So mightily grew the word of God and prevailed.

21 ¶ But after these things were ended, Paul purposed in the spirit, when he had passed through Macedonia and Achaia, to go to Jerusalem, saying, After I have been there, I must also see Rome.

22 So he sent into Macedonia two of them that ministered unto him, Timotheus and Erastus; but he himself stayed in Asia for a season.

23 And about that time there arose no small stir concerning the Way.

24 For a certain man named Demetrius, a silversmith, which made silver shrines for Diana brought no small gain unto the craftsmen;

25 Whom he called together with the workmen of like occupation, and said, Sirs, ye know that by this craft we have our wealth.

26 And ye see and hear, that not alone at Ephesus, but almost throughout all Asia, this Paul hath persuaded and turned away much people, saying

¹ *So all the ancient MSS. There seem to have been two only of the seven engaged in this particular act.*

that they be no gods, which are made with hands:

27 So that not only this our business is in danger to be set at nought; but also that the temple of the great goddess Diana will be despised, and her magnificence destroyed, whom all Asia and the world worshippeth.

28 And when they heard, they were filled with wrath, and cried out, saying, Great is Diana of the Ephesians.

29 And the whole city was filled with the confusion: and having seized Gaius and Aristarchus, men of Macedonia, Paul's companions in travel, they rushed with one accord into the theatre.

30 And when Paul would have entered in unto the people, the disciples suffered him not.

31 And certain of the ¹chief of Asia, which were his friends, sent unto him, desiring him that he would not adventure himself into the theatre.

32 Some therefore cried one thing, and some another: for the assembly was confused; and the more part knew not wherefore they were come together.

33 And they brought forth Alexander out of the multitude, the Jews putting him forward. And Alexander beckoned with the hand, and would have made a defence unto the people.

34 But when they knew that he was a Jew, all with one voice about the space of two hours cried out, Great is Diana of the Ephesians.

35 And when the townclerk had appeased the multitude, he said, Ye men of Ephesus, what man is there that knoweth not how that the city of the Ephesians is guardian of the temple of the great Diana, and of the image which fell down from Jupiter?

36 Seeing then that these things cannot be spoken against, ye ought to be quiet, and to do nothing rashly.

37 For ye have brought hither these men, which are neither robbers of temples, nor yet blasphemers of your goddess.

38 Wherefore if Demetrius, and the craftsmen which are with him, have a matter against any man, there are assizes held, and there are appointed judges: let them implead one another.

39 But if ye enquire any thing concerning other matters, it shall be determined in the lawful assembly.

40 For we are in danger to be called in question for this day's uproar, there being no cause whereby we may give an account of this concourse.

41 And when he had thus spoken, he dismissed the assembly.

CHAPTER XX.

AND after the uproar was ceased, Paul called unto him the disciples, and ²exhort-

¹ *Literally,* Asiarchs: *officers so named.*

² *So all the ancient MSS*

ed them, and ¹embraced them, and departed to go into Macedonia.

2 And when he had gone over those parts, and had given them much exhortation, he came into Greece,

3 And there abode three months. And when the Jews laid wait for him, as he was about to sail into Syria, he purposed to return through Macedonia.

4 And there accompanied him as far as Asia, Sopater ²[the son] of Pyrrhus, a Berœan; and of the Thessalonians, Aristarchus and Secundus; and Gaius of Derbe, and Timotheus; and of Asia, Tychicus and Trophimus.

5 These going before tarried for us at Troas.

6 But we sailed away from Philippi after the days of unleavened bread, and came unto them to Troas in five days; where we abode seven days.

7 And upon the first day of the week, when ³we came together to break bread, Paul preached unto them, intending to depart on the morrow; and continued his speech until midnight.

8 And there were many lights in the upper chamber, where we were gathered together.

9 And a certain young man named Eutychus, who was sitting in the window, fell into a deep sleep: and as Paul was long preaching, he sunk down in his sleep, and fell from the third story, and was taken up dead.

10 And Paul went down, and fell on him, and embracing him said, Trouble not yourselves; for his life is in him.

11 When he therefore was come up again, and had broken the bread, and eaten, and talked a long while, even till break of day, so he departed.

12 And they brought the young man alive, and were not a little comforted.

13 And we went before to the ship, and sailed unto Assos, there intending to take in Paul: for so had he appointed, minding himself to go afoot.

14 And when he met with us at Assos, we took him in, and came to Mitylene.

15 And we sailed thence, and came the next day over against Chios; and the next day we put in at Samos, and tarried at Trogyllium; and the next day we came to Miletus.

16 For Paul had determined to sail by Ephesus, because he would not spend time in Asia; for he hasted, if it were possible for him, to be at Jerusalem the day of Pentecost.

17 But from Miletus he sent to Ephesus, and summoned the elders of the church.

18 And when they were come to him, he said unto them, Ye yourselves know, from the first day that I came into Asia, after what manner I was with you the whole time,

19 Serving the Lord with all humility of mind, and with

---

¹ *Literally*, saluted them.
² *So all the ancient MSS.:* the son being, as usual, implied.
³ *So all the ancient MSS.*

¹tears, and temptations, which befell me by the lyings in wait of the Jews:

20 How I kept back nothing that was profitable unto you, but shewed you, and taught you publicly, and from house to house,

21 Testifying both to Jews, and also to Greeks, repentance toward God, and faith toward our Lord Jesus.

22 And now, behold, I go bound in the spirit unto Jerusalem, not knowing the things that shall befall me there:

23 Save that the Holy Spirit witnesseth in every city, saying that bonds and afflictions abide me.

24 But ²I count my life of no value unto myself, so that I may finish my course, and the ministry which I received from the Lord Jesus, to testify the gospel of the grace of God.

25 And now, behold, I know that ye all, among whom I have gone preaching the kingdom of God, shall see my face no more.

26 Wherefore I take you to witness this day, that I am pure from the blood of all men.

27 For I did not shun to declare unto you all the counsel of God.

28 Take heed therefore unto yourselves, and to all the flock, over the which the Holy Spirit hath made you bishops, to feed the church of ³God, which he purchased with his own blood.

29 For I know this, that after my departing shall grievous wolves enter in among you, not sparing the flock.

30 Also of your own selves shall men arise, speaking perverse things, to draw away the disciples after them.

31 Therefore watch, and remember, that for the space of three years I ceased not to warn every one night and day with tears.

32 And now I commend you to God, and to the word of his grace, which is able to build you up, and to give you the inheritance among all them which are sanctified.

33 I have coveted no man's silver, or gold, or apparel.

34 Ye yourselves know, that these hands have ministered unto my necessities, and to them that were with me.

35 I shewed you in all things, how that so labouring ye ought to support the weak, and to remember the words of the Lord Jesus, that he said, It is more blessed to give than to receive.

36 ¶ And when he had thus spoken, he kneeled down, and prayed with them all.

37 And they all wept sore, and fell on Paul's neck, and kissed him,

38 Sorrowing most of all for the word which he spake, that they should see his face no more. And they accompanied him unto the ship.

---

¹ Many *is not found in any of the ancient MSS.*
² *So the most ancient MSS.*
³ *Some ancient MSS. have the* Lord: *but the two earliest, the Vatican and Sinaitic, read as in the text.*

CHAPTER XXI.

AND when at last we had parted from them, and had set sail, we came with a straight course unto Coos, and the day following unto Rhodes, and from thence unto ¹Patara:

2 And finding a ship sailing over unto Phenicia, we went aboard, and set forth.

3 Now when we had discovered Cyprus, we left it on the left hand, and sailed into Syria, and landed at Tyre: for there the ship was to unlade her burden.

4 And having sought out disciples, we tarried there seven days: who said to Paul through the Spirit, that he should not go up to Jerusalem.

5 And when we had accomplished those days, we departed and went our way; and they all brought us on our way, with wives and children, till we were out of the city: and when we had kneeled down on the shore, and prayed,

6 We took our leave one of another, and embarked in the ship; and they returned home again.

7 And having ended our voyage, we came from Tyre to Ptolemais, and saluted the brethren, and abode with them one day.

8 And on the morrow we that were of Paul's company departed, and came unto Cæsarea: and we entered into the house of Philip the evangelist, which was one of the seven; and abode with him.

¹ *Pronounce* Pátăra.

9 And he had four daughters, virgins, which did prophesy.

10 And as we tarried there many days, there came down from Judæa a certain prophet, named Agabus.

11 And he came unto us, and taking Paul's girdle, he bound his own hands and feet, and said, Thus saith the Holy Spirit, So shall the Jews at Jerusalem bind the man that owneth this girdle, and shall deliver him into the hands of the Gentiles.

12 And when we heard these things, both we, and they of that place, besought him not to go up to Jerusalem.

13 Then Paul answered, What do ye, weeping and breaking mine heart? for I am ready not to be bound only, but also to die at Jerusalem for the name of the Lord Jesus.

14 And when he would not be persuaded, we ceased, saying, The will of the Lord be done.

15 And after those days we made ready our baggage, and went up to Jerusalem.

16 There went with us also certain of the disciples of Cæsarea, to introduce us to one Mnason of Cyprus, an old disciple, with whom we should lodge.

17 And when we were come to Jerusalem, the brethren received us gladly.

18 And the day following Paul went in with us unto James; and all the elders were present.

19 And when he had saluted them, he declared particularly

what things God had wrought among the Gentiles by his ministry.

20 And when they heard it, they glorified the Lord, and said unto him, Thou seest, brother, how many thousands of Jews there are which believe; and they are all zealous of the law:

21 And they are informed of thee, that thou teachest all the Jews which are among the Gentiles to forsake Moses, saying that they ought not to circumcise their children, neither to walk after the customs.

22 What is it therefore? a multitude must needs come together: for they will hear that thou art come.

23 Do therefore this that we say to thee: We have four men which have a vow on them;

24 Them take, and purify thyself with them, and bear their charges, that they may shave their heads: and all shall know that those things, whereof they were informed concerning thee, are nothing; but that thou thyself also walkest orderly, and keepest the law.

25 As touching the Gentiles which believe, we have given command, judging that they observe no such thing, save only that they keep themselves from things offered to idols, and from blood, and from strangled, and from fornication.

26 Then Paul took the men, and the next day purifying himself with them entered into the temple, giving notice of the accomplishment of the days of purification, until that the offering was offered for every one of them.

27 And when the seven days were almost ended, the Jews which were of Asia, when they saw him in the temple, stirred up all the multitude, and laid hands on him,

28 Crying out, Men of Israel, help: This is the man, that teacheth all men every where against the people, and the law, and this place: and he further brought Greeks also into the temple, and hath polluted this holy place.

29 For they had seen before with him in the city Trophimus the Ephesian, whom they supposed that Paul had brought into the temple.

30 And all the city was moved, and the people ran together: and they took Paul, and drew him out of the temple: and forthwith the doors were shut.

31 And as they were seeking to kill him, tidings came unto the chief captain of the band, that all Jerusalem was in an uproar.

32 Who immediately took soldiers and centurions, and ran down unto them: and when they saw the chief captain and the soldiers, they left off beating Paul.

33 Then the chief captain came near, and took him, and commanded him to be bound with two chains; and demanded who he was, and what he had done.

34 And some cried one thing.

some another, among the multitude: and when he could not know the certainty for the tumult, he commanded him to be carried into the castle.

35 And when he came upon the stairs, so it was, that he was carried by the soldiers, because of the violence of the people.

36 For the multitude of the people followed after, crying, Away with him.

37 And as Paul was about to be brought into the castle, he said unto the chief captain, May I speak unto thee? Who said, Dost thou know Greek?

38 Art not thou that Egyptian, which before these days madest an uproar, and leddest out into the wilderness those four thousand men that were murderers?

39 But Paul said, I am a man which am a Jew of Tarsus, a citizen of no mean city in Cilicia: and, I beseech thee, suffer me to speak unto the people.

40 And when he had given him licence, Paul stood on the stairs, and beckoned with the hand unto the people. And when there was made a great silence, he spake unto them in the Hebrew tongue, saying,

CHAPTER XXII.

BRETHREN and fathers, hear ye my defence which I make now unto you.

2 And when they heard that he spake in the Hebrew tongue to them, they kept the more silence: and he saith,

3 I am [1] a man which am a Jew, born in Tarsus of Cilicia, yet brought up in this city at the feet of Gamaliel, taught according to the strict manner of the law of the fathers: and I was zealous toward God, as ye all are this day.

4 And I persecuted this Way unto the death, binding and delivering into prisons both men and women.

5 As also the high priest doth bear me witness, and all the council of the elders: from whom also I received letters unto the brethren, and went to Damascus, to bring them which were there bound unto Jerusalem, to be punished.

6 And it came to pass, that, as I made my journey, and was coming nigh unto Damascus, about noon suddenly there shone from heaven a great light round about me.

7 And I fell unto the ground, and heard a voice saying unto me, Saul, Saul, why persecutest thou me?

8 And I answered, Who art thou, Lord? And he said unto me, I am Jesus of Nazareth, whom thou persecutest.

9 And they that were with me saw indeed the light, [2][and were afraid;] but they heard not the voice of him that spake to me.

10 And I said, What shall I do, Lord? And the Lord said unto me, Arise, and go into Damascus; and there it shall

[1] Verily *is omitted in all the ancient MSS.*
[2] *These words are omitted in several of the oldest MSS.*

be told thee of all things which are appointed for thee to do.

11 And when I could not see for the glory of that light, being led by the hand of them that were with me, I came into Damascus.

12 And one Ananias, a devout man according to the law, having a good report of all the Jews which dwelt there,

13 Came unto me, and stood, and said unto me, Brother Saul, receive thy sight. And the same hour I looked up upon him.

14 And he said, The God of our fathers chose thee, that thou shouldest know his will, and see the Just One, and shouldest hear the voice of his mouth.

15 For thou shalt be his witness unto all men of what thou hast seen and heard.

16 And now why tarriest thou? arise, and be baptized, and wash away thy sins, calling on his name.

17 And it came to pass, that, when I was come again to Jerusalem, and was praying in the temple, I was in a trance ;

18 And saw him saying unto me, Make haste, and get thee quickly out of Jerusalem : for they will not receive thy testimony concerning me.

19 And I said, Lord, they themselves know that I was wont to imprison and beat in every synagogue them that believe on thee :

20 And when the blood of thy [1] martyr Stephen was shed, I also was standing by, and consenting, and keeping the raiment of them that slew him.

21 And he said unto me, Depart : for I will send thee far hence unto the Gentiles.

22 And they gave him audience unto this word, and then lifted up their voices, and said, Away with such a fellow from the earth : for it is not fit that he should live.

23 And as they were crying out, and shaking their clothes, and throwing dust into the air,

24 The chief captain commanded him to be brought into the castle, and bade that he should be examined by scourging ; that he might know wherefore they cried so against him.

25 And as they bound him down with the thongs, Paul said unto the centurion that stood by, Is it lawful for you to scourge a man that is a Roman, and uncondemned ?

26 When the centurion heard that, he went and told the chief captain, saying, What art thou doing? for this man is a Roman.

27 Then the chief captain came, and said unto him, Tell me, art thou a Roman? He said, Yea.

28 The chief captain answered, With a great sum obtained I this freedom of a citizen. And Paul said, But I was free born.

29 Then straightway they departed from him which should have examined him : and the

---

[1] *Perhaps* witness, *the original signification of* martyr. *But the word* had its present meaning in apostolic times.

chief captain also was afraid, knowing that he was a Roman, and that he had bound him.

30 On the morrow, desiring to know the certainty wherefore he was accused by the Jews, he loosed him, and commanded the chief priests and all the council to assemble, and brought Paul down, and set him before them.

CHAPTER XXIII.

AND Paul, fixing his eyes upon the council, said, Brethren, I have lived in all good conscience before God until this day.

2 And the high priest Ananias commanded them that stood by him to smite him on the mouth.

3 Then said Paul unto him, God shall smite thee, thou whited wall: for sittest thou to judge me after the law, and commandest me to be smitten contrary to the law?

4 And they that stood by said, Revilest thou God's high priest?

5 Then said Paul, I wist not, brethren, that it was the high priest: for it is written, Thou shalt not speak evil of the ruler of thy people.

6 But when Paul perceived that the one part were Sadducees, and the other Pharisees, he cried out in the council, Brethren, I am a Pharisee, the son of Pharisees: concerning the hope and the resurrection of the dead I am called in question.

7 And when he had so said, there arose a dissension between the Pharisees and the Sadducees: and the multitude was divided.

8 For Sadducees say that there is no resurrection, neither angel, nor spirit: but Pharisees confess both.

9 And there arose a great cry: and some of the scribes that were of the Pharisees' part arose, and strove, saying, We find no evil in this man: what if a spirit hath spoken to him,[1] or an angel?

10 And when there arose a great dissension, the chief captain, fearing lest Paul should have been pulled in pieces by them, commanded the troop to go down, and to take him by force from among them, and to bring him into the castle.

11 And the night following the Lord stood by him, and said, Be of good cheer: for as thou hast testified of me in Jerusalem, so must thou bear witness also at Rome.

12 And when it was day, the Jews banded together, and bound themselves under a curse, saying that they would neither eat nor drink till they had killed Paul.

13 And they were more than forty which had made this conspiracy.

14 And they came to the chief priests and elders, and said, We have bound ourselves under a curse, that we will taste nothing until we have slain Paul.

---

[1] *The words* let us not fight against God *are not in any of the most ancient MSS. They were probably inserted from ch.* v. 39.

15 Now therefore ye with the council signify to the chief captain that he bring him down unto you, as though ye would determine his matter more regularly: and we, before ever he come near, are ready to kill him.

16 And Paul's sister's son heard of their lying in wait, and came and entered into the castle, and told Paul.

17 And Paul called one of the centurions unto him, and said, Bring this young man unto the chief captain: for he hath a certain thing to tell him.

18 So he took him, and brought him to the chief captain, and said, Paul the prisoner called me unto him, and prayed me to bring this young man unto thee, for that he hath something to say unto thee.

19 And the chief captain took him by the hand, and went aside privately, and asked him, What is that thou hast to tell me?

20 And he said, The Jews have agreed to desire thee that thou wouldest bring down Paul to morrow into the council, as though thou wouldest enquire somewhat concerning him more accurately.

21 Do thou therefore not yield unto them: for there lie in wait for him of them more than forty men, which have bound themselves with an oath, that they will neither eat nor drink till they have killed him: and now are they ready, looking for this promise from thee.

22 So the chief captain let the young man depart, and charged him, Tell no man that thou hast shewed these things to me.

23 And he called unto him two centurions, saying, Make ready two hundred soldiers to go to Cæsarea, and horsemen threescore and ten, and [1] spearmen two hundred, at the third hour of the night;

24 And provide them beasts, that they may set Paul on, and bring him safe unto Felix the governor.

25 And he wrote a letter after this manner:

26 Claudius Lysias unto the most excellent governor Felix, greeting.

27 This man was taken by the Jews, and would have been killed by them: then came I with my troop, and rescued him, having understood that he was a Roman.

28 And when I desired to know the cause wherefore they accused him, I brought him down into their council:

29 Whom I perceived to be accused of questions of their law, but to have nothing laid to his charge worthy of death or of bonds.

30 And when it was told me that a conspiracy was preparing against the man, I sent him straightway to thee, and gave commandment to his accusers also to say before thee what they had against him.

31 So then the soldiers, as it was commanded them, took

[1] *The exact meaning of the word is uncertain.*

Paul, and brought him by night to Antipatris.

32 And on the morrow they left the horsemen to go with him, and returned to the castle:

33 Who, when they came to Cæsarea, and delivered the epistle to the governor, presented Paul also before him.

34 And when the governor had read the letter, and had asked of what province he was, and understood that he was of Cilicia;

35 I will hear thee, said he, when thine accusers are also come. And he commanded him to be kept in Herod's palace.

CHAPTER XXIV.

AND after five days Ananias the high priest came down with certain elders, and with a certain orator named Tertullus: and these informed the governor against Paul.

2 And when he was called forth, Tertullus began to accuse him, saying, Seeing that by thee we enjoy great quietness, and that very worthy deeds are done unto this nation by thy providence,

3 We accept it always, and in all places, most noble Felix, with all thankfulness.

4 Notwithstanding, that I be not further tedious unto thee, I pray thee that thou wouldest hear us of thy clemency a few words.

5 For we have found this man a pestilent fellow, and a mover of sedition among all the Jews who are scattered throughout the world, and a ringleader of the sect of the Nazarenes:

6 Who also hath attempted to profane the temple: whom we took, [1][and would have judged according to our law.

7 But the chief captain Lysias came, and with great violence took him away out of our hands,

8 Commanding his accusers to come unto thee:] by examining of whom thyself mayest take knowledge of all these things, whereof we accuse him.

9 And the Jews also assented, saying that these things were so.

10 And Paul, after that the governor had beckoned unto him to speak, answered, Forasmuch as I know that thou hast been for many years a judge unto this nation, I cheerfully answer for myself:

11 Because that thou mayest understand, that there are yet but twelve days since I went up to Jerusalem for to worship.

12 And they neither found me in the temple disputing with any man, neither raising up the multitude, neither in the synagogues, nor in the city:

13 Nor are they able to prove the things whereof they now accuse me.

14 But this I confess unto thee, that after the way which they call heresy, so worship I

[1] *These words are not found in any of the most ancient MSS. They are contained in one MS. of the seventh century, and in some of the very early versions. The question respecting their authenticity is exceedingly difficult.*

the God of my fathers, believing all things which are written in the law and in the prophets:

15 And have hope toward God, which they themselves also allow, that there shall be a resurrection of the dead, both of the just and unjust.

16 And herein do I exercise myself, to have always a conscience void of offence toward God, and toward men.

17 Now after many years I came to bring alms to my nation, and offerings.

18 [1]Whereupon certain Jews from Asia found me purified in the temple, not with multitude, nor yet with tumult.

19 Who ought to have been here before thee, and to accuse me, if they had ought against me.

20 Or else let these same here say what evil doing they found in me, while I stood before the council,

21 Except it be for this one voice, that I cried standing among them, Touching the resurrection of the dead I am called in question by you this day.

22 And Felix having perfect knowledge of the Way, deferred them, and said, When Lysias the chief captain shall come down, I will adjudge your matter.

23 And he commanded a centurion to keep him, and to let him have liberty, and that he should forbid none of his own people to minister or come unto him.

24 And after certain days Felix came with his wife Drusilla, which was a Jewess, and sent for Paul, and heard him concerning the faith in Christ.

25 And as he reasoned of righteousness, and temperance, and the judgment which is to come, Felix [2]was afraid, and answered, Go thy way for this time; when I have a convenient season, I will call for thee.

26 He hoped also that money should have been given him by Paul:[3] wherefore he sent for him the oftener, and communed with him.

27 But after two years Felix was succeeded by Porcius Festus: and Felix, willing to shew the Jews a pleasure, left Paul bound.

CHAPTER XXV.

FESTUS then, being come into the province, after three days went up from Cæsarea to Jerusalem.

2 And the high priest and the chief of the Jews informed him against Paul, and besought him,

3 And desired favour against him, that he would send for him to Jerusalem, laying wait to kill him in the way.

4 So Festus answered, that Paul should be kept at Cæsarea, and that he himself would depart shortly thither.

---

[1] *The original is somewhat involved, and is literally:* Amidst which (offerings) they found me purified in the temple, not with multitude, nor yet with tumult, but certain Jews from Asia, who, &c.

[2] *There is nothing whatever about trembling in the text.*

[3] *That he might loose him is not in any of the ancient MSS.*

5 Let therefore, said he, the men of weight among you go down with me, and accuse this man, if there be any wickedness in him.

6 And when he had tarried among them not more than ¹eight or ten days, he went down unto Cæsarea; and the next day sitting on the judgment seat commanded Paul to be brought.

7 And when he was come, the Jews which were come down from Jerusalem stood round about him, bringing many and grievous charges, which they could not prove.

8 While Paul answered for himself, Neither against the law of the Jews, neither against the temple, nor yet against Cæsar, have I offended any thing at all.

9 But Festus, willing to do the Jews a pleasure, answered Paul, and said, Wilt thou go up to Jerusalem, and there be judged of these things before me?

10 Then said Paul, I am standing at Cæsar's judgment seat, where I ought to be judged: to the Jews have I done no wrong, as thou very well knowest.

11 If now I be an offender, or have committed any thing worthy of death, I refuse not to die: but if there be none of these things whereof these accuse me, no man may deliver me unto them. I appeal unto Cæsar.

12 Then Festus, when he had conferred with the council,

¹ *So all the most ancient MSS.*

answered, Thou hast appealed unto Cæsar; unto Cæsar shalt thou go.

13 And after certain days king Agrippa and Bernice came unto Cæsarea to salute Festus.

14 And when they had been there many days, Festus declared Paul's cause unto the king, saying, There is a certain man left in bonds by Felix:

15 About whom, when I was at Jerusalem, the chief priests and the elders of the Jews informed me, desiring to have judgment against him.

16 To whom I answered, It is not the manner of the Romans to deliver over any man, before that he which is accused have the accusers face to face, and have licence to answer for himself concerning the crime laid against him.

17 Therefore, when they were come hither, without any delay on the morrow I sat on the judgment seat, and commanded the man to be brought forth.

18 And when the accusers stood up round about him, they brought no evil accusation of such things as I supposed:

19 But had certain questions against him of their own superstition, and of one Jesus, which was dead, whom Paul affirmed to be alive.

20 And because I doubted of such manner of questions, I asked him whether he would go to Jerusalem, and there be judged of these matters.

21 But when Paul had ap-

pealed to be reserved unto the hearing of Augustus, I commanded him to be kept till I might send him to Cæsar.

22 Then Agrippa said unto Festus, I would also hear the man myself. To morrow, said he, thou shalt hear him.

23 And on the morrow, when Agrippa was come, and Bernice, with great pomp, and they were entered into the place of hearing, with the chief captains, and principal men of the city, at Festus' commandment Paul was brought forth.

24 And Festus said, King Agrippa, and all men which are here present with us, ye see this man, about whom all the multitude of the Jews have been urgent with me, both at Jerusalem, and also here, crying that he ought not to live any longer.

25 But I found that he had committed nothing worthy of death ; and, as he himself had appealed to Augustus, I determined to send him.

26 Of whom I have no certain thing to write unto my lord. Wherefore I have brought him forth before you, and specially before thee, O king Agrippa, that, after examination had, I might have somewhat to write.

27 For it seemeth to me unreasonable to send a prisoner, and not withal to signify the crimes laid against him.

CHAPTER XXVI.

AND Agrippa said unto Paul, Thou art permitted to speak for thyself. Then Paul stretched forth the hand, and answered for himself :

2 I think myself happy, king Agrippa, that I am to answer for myself this day before thee touching all the things whereof I am accused by the Jews :

3 Especially as thou art expert in all customs and questions which are among the Jews : wherefore I beseech thee to hear me patiently.

4 My manner of life from my youth, which was at the first among mine own nation and in Jerusalem, know all the Jews ;

5 Which know me from the beginning, if they would testify, that after the straitest sect of our religion I lived a Pharisee.

6 And now I stand and am judged for the hope of the promise made by God unto our fathers :

7 Unto which promise our twelve tribes, earnestly serving God day and night, hope to come. Concerning which hope I am accused of the Jews, O king.

8 Why should it be thought a thing incredible with you, if God raiseth the dead ?

9 I verily thought with myself, that I ought to do many things contrary to the name of Jesus of Nazareth.

10 Which thing I also did in Jerusalem : and many of the saints did I shut up in prison, having received the necessary authority from the chief priests ; and when they were put to death, I gave my vote against them.

11 And I punished them oft in every synagogue, and com-

pelled them to blaspheme; and being exceedingly mad against them, I persecuted them even unto strange cities.

12 Whereupon as I went to Damascus with authority and commission from the chief priests,

13 At midday, O king, I saw in the way a light from heaven, above the brightness of the sun, shining round about me and them which journeyed with me.

14 And when we were all fallen to the earth, I heard a voice speaking unto me, and saying in the Hebrew tongue, Saul, Saul, why persecutest thou me? it is hard for thee to kick against the pricks.

15 And I said, Who art thou, Lord? And the Lord said, I am Jesus whom thou persecutest.

16 But rise, and stand upon thy feet: for I have appeared unto thee for this purpose, to appoint thee a minister and a witness both of these things which thou hast seen, and of those things in the which I will appear unto thee;

17 Delivering thee from the people, and from the Gentiles, unto whom [1]I send thee,

18 To open their eyes, that they may turn them from darkness to light, and from the power of Satan unto God, that they may receive forgiveness of sins, and inheritance among them which are sanctified by faith that is in me.

19 Whereupon, O king Agrippa, I was not disobedient unto the heavenly vision:

20 But shewed first unto them in Damascus, and Jerusalem, and throughout all the country of Judæa, and to the Gentiles, that they should repent and turn to God, doing works worthy of their repentance.

21 For these causes the Jews caught me in the temple, and sought to kill me.

22 Having therefore obtained the help which is from God, I continue unto this day, witnessing both to small and great, saying nothing besides those things which the prophets and Moses did say should come:

23 To wit, that Christ is to suffer, and be the first out of the resurrection from the dead to proclaim light unto the people, and to the Gentiles.

24 And as he thus spake for himself, Festus said with a loud voice, Paul, thou art beside thyself; thy much learning doth make thee mad.

25 But he said, I am not mad, most excellent Festus; but am speaking forth the words of truth and soberness.

26 For the king knoweth of these things, before whom also I speak boldly: for I am persuaded that none of these things are hidden from him; for this thing hath not been done in a corner.

27 King Agrippa, believest thou the prophets? I know that thou believest.

28 Then Agrippa said unto Paul, [2]Lightly art thou per-

[1] Now *has no authority whatever.*

[2] *The reading of the Authorized Version is against the most ancient MSS.; and even of that reading the rendering is incorrect.*

suading thyself that thou canst make me a Christian.

29 And Paul said, I would to God, that, whether lightly or with pains, not only thou, but also all that hear me this day, might become such as I am, except these bonds.

30 And the king rose up, and the governor, and Bernice, and they that sat with them:

31 And they went aside, and talked between themselves, saying, This man doeth nothing worthy of death or of bonds.

32 And Agrippa said unto Festus, This man might have been set at liberty, if he had not appealed unto Cæsar.

CHAPTER XXVII.

AND when it was determined that we should sail into Italy, they delivered Paul and certain other prisoners unto one named Julius, a centurion of Augustus' band.

2 And we embarked in a ship of Adramyttium, which was to sail to the coasts of Asia, and put to sea; Aristarchus, a Macedonian of Thessalonica, being with us.

3 And the next day we touched at Sidon. And Julius courteously entreated Paul, and gave him liberty to go unto his friends to refresh himself.

4 And we put off from thence, and sailed under Cyprus, because the winds were contrary.

5 And when we had sailed over the sea which is off Cilicia and Pamphylia, we came to Myra in Lycia.

6 And there the centurion found a ship of Alexandria sailing into Italy; and he put us therein.

7 And sailing slowly many days, and with difficulty coming over against Cnidus, the wind not suffering us, we sailed under Crete, over against [1]Salmoné;

8 And, with difficulty passing it, came unto a place which is called The fair havens; nigh whereunto was the city of Lasæa.

9 Now when much time was spent, and when the voyage was now dangerous, because the fast was now already past, Paul admonished them,

10 And said unto them, Sirs, I perceive that this voyage will be with hurt and much damage, not only of the lading and ship, but also of our lives.

11 Nevertheless the centurion believed the master of the ship, and the owner, more than those things which were spoken by Paul.

12 And because the haven was not commodious to winter in, the more part advised to depart thence also, if by any means they might attain to Phenice to winter; which is an haven of Crete, and looketh in the direction of the south-west and north-west winds.

13 And when the south wind blew softly, supposing that they had obtained their purpose, loosing thence, they sailed close by Crete.

14 But not long after there blew from the shore a tem-

[1] *Pronounce* Salmóné.

pestuous wind, called ¹Euroclydon.

15 And when the ship was caught, and could not bear up against the wind, we let her drive.

16 And running under a certain island which is called ²Clauda, we had much work to come by the boat:

17 Which when they had taken up, they used helps, undergirding the ship; and, fearing lest they should fall into ³the quicksand, lowered our top-gear, and so were driven.

18 And we being exceedingly tossed with the tempest, the next day they lightened the ship;

19 And the third day we cast out with our own hands the furniture of the ship.

20 And when neither sun nor stars for many days appeared, and no small tempest lay on us, all hope that we should be saved was then taken away.

21 But when there had been long abstinence from food, then Paul stood forth in the midst of them, and said, Sirs, ye should have hearkened unto me, and not have loosed from Crete, and have spared this harm and loss.

22 And now I exhort you to be of good cheer: for there shall be no loss of any life among you, but only of the ship.

23 For there stood by me this night an angel of God, whose I am, and whom I serve,

24 Saying, Fear not, Paul; thou must be brought before Cæsar: and, lo, God hath given thee all them that sail with thee.

25 Wherefore, sirs, be of good cheer: for I believe God, that it shall be even as it hath been told me.

26 Howbeit we must be cast upon a certain island.

27 But when the fourteenth night was come, as we were driven up and down in ⁴Adria, about midnight the shipmen deemed that they drew near to some country;

28 And sounded, and found it twenty fathoms: and when they had gone a little further, they sounded again, and found it fifteen fathoms.

29 And fearing lest we should have fallen upon rocks, they cast four anchors out of the stern, and wished for the day.

30 And as the shipmen were seeking to flee out of the ship, when they had let down the boat into the sea, under colour as though they would have cast anchors out of the foreship,

31 Paul said to the centurion and to the soldiers, Except these abide in the ship, ye cannot be saved.

32 Then the soldiers cut off the ropes of the boat, and let her fall off.

33 And while the day was coming on, Paul besought them all to take food, saying,

---

¹ *The three most ancient MSS. have* Eurakylon.
² *More probably* Cauda; *the present* Gozzo.
³ *The great quicksand called the* Syrtis, *on the African coast*.
⁴ *Not what is now called the Adriatic, but the sea south of Greece and Italy*

This day is the fourteenth day that ye have tarried and continued fasting, having taken nothing.

34 Wherefore I pray you to take some food : for this is for your health : for there shall not an hair fall from the head of any of you.

35 And when he had thus spoken, he took bread, and gave thanks to God in presence of them all : and when he had broken it, he began to eat.

36 Then were they all of good cheer, and they also took food.

37 And we were in all in the ship two hundred and seventy-six souls.

38 And when they had eaten enough, they lightened the ship, casting out the wheat into the sea.

39 And when it was day, they knew not the land : but they discovered a certain creek with a shore, into the which they were minded, if it were possible, to run the ship aground.

40 And when they had cut away the anchors, they left them in the sea, and loosed the rudder bands, and hoised up the foresail to the wind, and made toward shore.

41 And falling into a place where two seas met, they ran the ship aground; and the forepart stuck fast, and remained unmovable, but the hinder part was broken with the violence of the waves.

42 And the soldiers' counsel was to kill the prisoners, lest any of them should swim out, and escape.

43 But the centurion, willing to save Paul, kept them from their purpose ; and commanded that they which could swim should cast themselves first into the sea, and get to land :

44 And the rest, some on boards, and some on broken pieces of the ship. And so it came to pass, that they escaped all safe to land.

CHAPTER XXVIII.

AND when we were escaped, then we knew that the island was called Melita.

2 And the [1]natives shewed us no common kindness : for they kindled a fire, and received us every one, because of the present rain, and because of the cold.

3 And when Paul had gathered a bundle of sticks, and laid them on the fire, there came a viper out of the heat, and fastened on his hand.

4 And when the natives saw the beast hanging on his hand, they said among themselves, No doubt this man is a murderer, whom, though he hath escaped the sea, yet vengeance suffereth not to live.

5 So then he shook off the beast into the fire, and felt no harm.

6 Howbeit they looked when he should have swollen, or fallen down dead suddenly : but when they looked a great while, and saw no harm come to him, they changed their

[1] *Literally*, barbarians: *the common name for all who were not Greeks, but used here in speaking of the inhabitants of an unknown or new place.*

minds, and said that he was a god.

7 In the same quarters were possessions of the chief man of the island, whose name was Publius; who received us, and lodged us three days courteously.

8 And it came to pass, that the father of Publius lay sick of a fever and of a bloody flux: to whom Paul entered in, and prayed, and laid his hands on him, and healed him.

9 So when this was done, the rest also, which had diseases in the island, came, and were healed:

10 Who also honoured us with many honours; and when we were departing, they laded us with such things as we needed.

11 And after three months we departed in a ship of Alexandria, which had wintered in the isle, whose sign was Castor and Pollux.

12 And landing at Syracuse, we tarried there three days.

13 And from thence we made a circuit, and came to Rhegium: and after one day, the south wind arising, we came in two days to Puteoli:

14 Where we found brethren, and were desired to tarry with them seven days: and so we went toward Rome.

15 And from thence, when the brethren heard of our arrival, they came to meet us as far as Appii forum, and The three taverns: whom when Paul saw, he thanked God, and took courage.

16 And when we came to Rome,[1] Paul was suffered to dwell by himself with the soldier that kept him.

17 And it came to pass, that after three days Paul called the chief of the Jews together: and when they were come together, he said unto them, I, brethren, though I committed nothing against the people, or customs of our fathers, yet was delivered prisoner from Jerusalem into the hands of the Romans.

18 Who, when they had examined me, were willing to let me go, because there was no cause of death in me.

19 But when the Jews spake against it, I was compelled to appeal unto Cæsar; not that I had ought to accuse my nation of.

20 For this cause therefore have I called for you, to see you, and to speak with you: for on behalf of the hope of Israel I am bound with this chain.

21 And they said unto him, We neither ourselves received letters out of Judæa concerning thee, neither any of the brethren that came shewed or spake any harm of thee.

22 But we desire to hear of thee what thou thinkest: for as concerning this sect, we know that every where it is spoken against.

23 And they appointed him a day, and came in numbers to him into his lodging; to whom he expounded and testified the

[1] *The words which follow here in the Authorized Version,* the centurion delivered the prisoners to the captain of the guard: but, *are not found in any of the oldest MSS.*

kingdom of God, persuading them concerning Jesus, both out of the law of Moses, and out of the prophets, from morning till evening.

24 And some believed the things which were spoken, and some believed not.

25 And when they agreed not among themselves, they departed, after that Paul had spoken one word, Well spake the Holy Spirit by Isaiah the prophet unto our fathers,

26 Saying, Go unto this people, and say, Hearing ye shall hear, and shall not understand; and seeing ye shall see, and not perceive:

27 For the heart of this people is waxed gross, and their ears are dull of hearing, and their eyes have they closed; lest they should see with their eyes, and hear with their ears, and understand with their heart, and should turn, and I should heal them.

28 Be it known therefore unto you, that this salvation of God is sent unto the Gentiles: and they will hear it.[1]

30 And he dwelt two whole years in his own hired house, and received all that came in unto him,

31 Preaching the kingdom of God, and teaching those things which concern the Lord Jesus Christ, with all confidence, no man forbidding him.

[1] *Verse* 29, And when he had said these words, the Jews departed, and had great reasoning among themselves, *is not contained in any of the ancient MSS., nor in the old Syriac version.*

THE EPISTLE OF PAUL THE APOSTLE

TO THE

ROMANS.

CHAPTER I.

PAUL, a servant of Jesus Christ, called to be an apostle, set apart unto the gospel of God,

2 Which he promised before by his prophets in the holy scriptures,

3 Concerning his Son, which was born of the seed of David according to the flesh,

4 Which was with power declared to be the Son of God, according to the Spirit of holiness, by the resurrection of the dead, even Jesus Christ our Lord;

5 Through whom we received grace and apostleship, unto obedience of faith among all the nations, for his name's sake:

6 Among whom ye also are called by Jesus Christ:

7 To all that be in Rome, beloved of God, called to be saints: Grace be unto you and peace from God our Father, and the Lord Jesus Christ.

8 First, I thank my God through Jesus Christ for you all, that your faith is published throughout the whole world.

9 For God is my witness, whom I serve in my spirit in the gospel of his Son, how unceasingly I make mention of you, always in my prayers

10 Making request, if by any means now at length I shall have a way opened by the will of God to come unto you.

11 For I long to see you, that I may impart unto you some spiritual gift, to the end that ye may be established;

12 That is, that I with you may be comforted among you, each by the faith which is in the other, both yours and mine.

13 But I would not have you ignorant, brethren, that oftentimes I purposed to come unto you, (but was hindered hitherto,) that I might have some fruit in you too, even as also in the rest of the Gentiles.

14 I am debtor both to Greeks and to Barbarians; both to wise and to foolish.

15 So, as much as in me lieth, I am ready to preach the gospel to you also that are in Rome.

16 For I am not ashamed of the gospel: for it is the power of God unto salvation to every one that believeth; to the Jew first, and also to the Greek.

17 For the righteousness of God is therein revealed from faith unto faith: even as it is written, But [1]the righteous shall live by faith.

18 For the wrath of God is revealed from heaven against

[1] *Or*, the righteous by faith shall live.

all ungodliness and unrighteousness of men, who hold down the truth in unrighteousness;

19 Because that which is known of God is manifest in them; for God manifested it unto them:

20 For from the creation of the world his invisible things, even his eternal power and divinity, are plainly seen, being perceived by means of the things that are made: so that they are without excuse:

21 Because though they knew God, they glorified him not as God, neither gave thanks; but were brought to vanity in their reasonings, and their heart being without understanding was darkened.

22 Professing themselves to be wise, they were made fools,

23 And changed the glory of the uncorruptible God for the likeness of an image of corruptible man, and of birds, and fourfooted beasts, and creeping things.

24 Wherefore God also gave them up in the desires of their heart to uncleanness, to dishonour their bodies among themselves:

25 Inasmuch as they changed the truth of God for a lie, and worshipped and served the creature rather than the Creator, who is blessed for ever. Amen.

26 For this cause God gave them up unto shameful passions: for even their women changed the natural use into that which is against nature:

27 And in like manner the men also, leaving the natural use of the woman, burned in their lust one toward another; men with men working unseemliness, and receiving in themselves the recompence of their error, which was meet.

28 And even as they did not choose to retain God in their knowledge, God gave them up to a reprobate mind, to do the things which are not fit to be done:

29 Being filled with all unrighteousness, wickedness, covetousness, maliciousness; full of envy, murder, strife, deceit, malignity; whisperers,

30 Slanderers, hated of God, insolent, proud, boasters, devisers of evil things, disobedient to parents,

31 Without understanding, covenant breakers, without natural affection, unmerciful:

32 Men who knowing well the righteous judgment of God, that they which do such things are worthy of death, not only commit the same, but also consent unto them that do them.

CHAPTER II.

WHEREFORE thou art without excuse, O man, whosoever thou art that judgest: for wherein thou judgest thy neighbour, thou condemnest thyself; for thou that judgest doest the same things.

2 Now we know that the judgment of God is according to truth against them which do such things.

3 And reckonest thou this, O man, that judgest them which

do such things, and committest the same, that thou shalt escape the judgment of God?

4 Or despisest thou the riches of his goodness and his forbearance and his longsuffering; not knowing that the goodness of God is leading thee to repentance;

5 And after thy hardness and impenitent heart art treasuring up for thyself wrath in the day of wrath and of the revelation of the righteous judgment of God;

6 Who will render to every one according to his works:

7 To them who by patience in well doing seek for glory and honour and incorruption, eternal life:

8 But to them that seek their own, and do not obey the truth, but obey unrighteousness, [1][shall there be] indignation and wrath,

9 Tribulation and distress, upon every soul of man that worketh evil, of the Jew first, and also of the Greek;

10 But glory, and honour, and peace, to every man that worketh good, to the Jew first, and also to the Greek:

11 For there is no respect of persons with God.

12 For as many as have sinned without law shall also perish without law: and as many as have sinned under the law shall be judged by the law;

13 For not the hearers of the law are righteous before God, but the doers of the law shall be justified:

[1] *Not expressed in the original*

14 For when Gentiles, which have not the law, do by nature the things of the law, these, though they have not the law, are the law unto themselves;

15 Inasmuch as they shew the work of the law written in their hearts, their conscience bearing witness thereto, and their thoughts among one another accusing or else excusing:

16 In the day when God shall judge the secrets of men by Jesus Christ according to my gospel.

17 But if thou art called a Jew, and restest upon the law, and makest thy boast in God,

18 And knowest his will, and approvest the things that are more excellent, being instructed out of the law;

19 And art confident that thou thyself art a guide of the blind, a light of them which are in darkness,

20 An instructor of the foolish, a teacher of babes, possessing the model of knowledge and of the truth in the law;

21 Thou then which teachest another, dost thou not teach thyself? thou that preachest men should not steal, dost thou steal?

22 Thou that forbiddest to commit adultery, dost thou commit adultery? thou that abhorrest idols, dost thou rob temples?

23 Thou that makest thy boast in the law, dost thou by thy transgression of the law dishonour God?

24 For the name of God is blasphemed among the Gen-

tiles because of you, even as it is written.

25 For circumcision indeed is profitable, if thou do the law; but if thou be a transgressor of the law, thy circumcision is become uncircumcision.

26 If then the uncircumcision keep the ordinances of the law, shall not his uncircumcision be reckoned for circumcision?

27 And the uncircumcision which is by nature, if it fulfil the law, shall judge thee, who through the letter and circumcision art a transgressor of the law.

28 For he is not a Jew, which is one outwardly; neither is that circumcision, which is outward in the flesh:

29 But he is a Jew, which is one inwardly; and circumcision is of the heart, in the spirit, not in the letter; whose praise is not of men, but of God.

CHAPTER III.

WHAT then is the advantage of the Jew? or what is the benefit of circumcision?

2 Much every way: first indeed, that they were entrusted with the oracles of God.

3 For what if some were unfaithful? shall their unfaithfulness make void the faithfulness of God?

4 ¹God forbid: nay, let God be true, and every man a liar; as it is written, That thou mayest be justified in thy words, and mayest overcome when thou art judged.

5 But if our unrighteousness establisheth the righteousness of God, what shall we say? Is God unrighteous who inflicteth his wrath? (I speak as a man.)

6 ¹God forbid: for then how shall God judge the world?

7 For if by my lie the truth of God abounded unto his glory; why am I still to be judged as a sinner?

8 And ²[why should we] not ²[say], as we be slanderously reported, and as some affirm that we say, Let us do evil, that good may come? whose condemnation is just.

9 What then? do we excel them? No, in no wise: for we before brought the charge against both Jews and Greeks, that they are all under sin;

10 As it is written, There is none righteous, no, not one:

11 There is none that understandeth, there is none that seeketh after God.

12 They are all gone out of the way, they are together become unprofitable; there is none that doeth good, no, not so much as one.

13 Their throat is an open sepulchre; with their tongues they have used deceit; the poison of asps is under their lips:

14 Whose mouth is full of cursing and bitterness:

15 Their feet are swift to shed blood:

16 Destruction and misery are in their ways:

---

¹ *Literally,* Let it not be.   ² *Not expressed in the original.*

17 And the way of peace have they not known.

18 There is no fear of God before their eyes.

19 Now we know that what things soever the law saith, it speaketh to them who are under the law; in order that every mouth may be stopped, and that all the world may be brought under the judgment of God.

20 Because by the works of the law shall no flesh be justified in his sight: for through the law cometh the knowledge of sin.

21 But now apart from the law the righteousness of God hath been manifested, being witnessed by the law and the prophets;

22 Even the righteousness of God through faith of Jesus Christ unto all and upon all that believe: for there is no distinction:

23 For all have sinned, and fall short of the glory of God;

24 Being justified freely by his grace through the redemption that is in Christ Jesus:

25 Whom God set forth as a propitiation through faith by his blood, for the shewing forth of his righteousness, because of the passing over of the former sins, in the forbearance of God;

26 For the shewing forth of his righteousness in this present time, that he may be just and the justifier of him which is of faith in Jesus.

27 Where is our boasting then? It is excluded. By what manner of law? of works? Nay: but by the law of faith.

28 For we reckon that a man is justified by faith apart from the works of the law.

29 Is God [1][the God] of the Jews only? is he not also of the Gentiles? Yes, of the Gentiles also:

30 Seeing that God is one, which shall justify the circumcision by faith, and the uncircumcision through faith.

31 Do we then make void the law through faith? [2]God forbid: nay, we establish the law.

CHAPTER IV.

WHAT then shall we say that Abraham our father hath found as pertaining to the flesh?

2 For if Abraham was justified by works, he hath ground of boasting. But he hath none before God:

3 For what saith the scripture? And Abraham believed God, and it was reckoned unto him for righteousness.

4 Now to him that worketh, his reward is not reckoned in the way of grace, but of debt;

5 But to him that worketh not, but believeth on him that justifieth the ungodly, his faith is reckoned for righteousness.

6 Even as David also declareth the man blessed, unto whom God reckoneth righteousness apart from works,

7 [1][Saying,] Blessed are they whose iniquities are forgiven, and whose sins are covered.

[1] *Not expressed in the original.*
[2] *Literally,* Let it not be.

8 Blessed is the man to whom the Lord will not reckon sin.

9 Is this blessing then pronounced upon the circumcision, or upon the uncircumcision also? for we say that faith was reckoned to Abraham for righteousness.

10 How then was it reckoned? when he was in circumcision, or in uncircumcision? Not in circumcision, but in uncircumcision.

11 And he received the sign of circumcision, a seal of the righteousness of the faith which he had while in his uncircumcision: in order that he might be the father of all in uncircumcision that believe; that the righteousness might be reckoned unto them also:

12 And the father of the circumcision to them who are not only of the circumcision, but to them also who walk in the steps of the faith of our father Abraham, which he had while in uncircumcision.

13 For it was not through the law that the promise was given to Abraham or to his seed that he should be the heir of the world, but through the righteousness of faith.

14 For if they which are of the law be the heirs, faith is made void, and the promise is made of none effect:

15 For the law worketh wrath: but where there is no law, neither is there transgression.

16 For this cause it was of faith, that it might be by grace; in order that the promise may be sure to all t¹ seed, not only to that which is of the law, but to that also which is of the faith of Abraham; who is the father of us all,

17 (As it is written, A father of many nations have I made thee,) before God, in whose sight he believed, who quickeneth the dead, and calleth those things which be not as though they were:

18 Who against hope believed in hope, that he might become the father of many nations, according to that which was spoken, So shall thy seed be.

19 And not being weak in faith, he considered ¹[not] his own body, now become dead, being about an hundred years old, and the deadness of Sarah's womb:

20 He staggered not at the promise of God through unbelief; but was made strong in faith, giving glory to God,

21 And being fully persuaded that what he hath promised he is able also to perform.

22 Wherefore also it was reckoned unto him for righteousness.

23 Now it was not written for his sake alone, that it was reckoned unto him;

24 But for our sake also, to whom it shall be reckoned, who believe on him that raised Jesus our Lord from the dead:

25 Who was delivered up for our offences, and was raised for our justification.

¹ *Omitted by many of the oldest authorities.*

CHAPTER V.

BEING then justified by faith, ¹let us have peace with God through our Lord Jesus Christ;

2 Through whom we have also had our access ²[by faith] into this grace wherein we stand; and we glory in the hope of the glory of God.

3 And not only so, but ³we even glory in our tribulations: knowing that tribulation worketh endurance;

4 And endurance, approval; and approval, hope:

5 And hope maketh not ashamed; because God's love hath been poured forth in our hearts by the Holy Spirit which was given unto us.

6 For when we were yet without strength, in due season Christ died for the ungodly.

7 For scarcely for a righteous man will any one die: yet for a good man peradventure some one may even dare to die.

8 But ⁴he giveth proof of his own love toward us, in that, while we were yet sinners, Christ died for us.

9 Much more then, having been now justified by his blood, shall we be saved through him from the wrath ⁵[to come].

10 For if, being enemies, we were reconciled to God through the death of his Son, much more, having been reconciled, shall we be saved by his life:

11 And not only so, but also glorying in God through our Lord Jesus Christ, through whom we have now received our reconciliation.

12 For this cause, as through one man sin entered into the world, and through sin, death; and thus death spread through unto all men, for that all sinned:

13 For until the law there was sin in the world: but sin is not imputed where there is no law.

14 Nevertheless death reigned from Adam to Moses, even over them that sinned not after the likeness of the transgression of Adam, who is a type of him that is to come.

15 Howbeit not as the trespass, so also is the gift of grace. For if by the trespass of the one the many died, much more did the grace of God and his free gift abound unto the many by the grace of the one man Jesus Christ.

16 And not as ⁶[it was] through one that sinned, so is the gift: for the judgment came of one unto condemnation, but the gift of grace came of many trespasses unto justification.

17 For if by the trespass of the one death reigned through the one, much more shall they which receive the abundance of the grace and of the free gift of righteousness reign in life

---

¹ *So all the ancient MSS. and earliest versions.*
² *Omitted, or variously read, in our oldest authorities.*
³ *Literally*, even glorying.
⁴ *So our oldest MS.* God *has apparently been an explanation.*
⁵ *Not expressed in the original, which has simply* the wrath. *We might supply* [of God].

⁶ *Not expressed in the original.*

through the one, even Jesus Christ.

18 Therefore as through one trespass ¹[the issue was] unto all men to condemnation; even so through one righteous act ¹[the issue was] unto all men to justification of life.

19 For as through the disobedience of the one man the many were made sinners, even so through the obedience of the one shall the many be made righteous.

20 Now the law came in besides, that the trespass might be multiplied. But where sin was multiplied, grace did beyond measure abound:

21 In order that as sin reigned in death, even so grace may reign through righteousness unto eternal life through Jesus Christ our Lord.

CHAPTER VI.

WHAT then shall we say? Are we to continue in sin, that grace may be multiplied?

2 ²God forbid. We who died unto sin, how shall we live any longer therein?

3 Or know ye not, that all we who were baptized into Jesus Christ were baptized into his death?

4 We were buried therefore with him through our baptism into his death: that like as Christ was raised from the dead through the glory of the Father, so we also might walk in newness of life.

5 For if we have become united to the likeness of his death, surely we shall be also to the likeness of his resurrection:

6 Knowing this, that our old man was crucified with him, that the body of sin might be destroyed, in order that we might no longer be in bondage to sin.

7 For he that hath died hath been ³set free from sin.

8 Now if we died with Christ, we believe that we shall also live with him:

9 Knowing that Christ being raised from the dead dieth no more; death hath dominion over him no more.

10 For the death that he died, he died unto sin once: but the life that he liveth, he liveth unto God.

11 Even so reckon ye yourselves to be dead unto sin, but alive unto God in Christ Jesus.⁴

12 Let not sin then reign in your mortal body, that ye should obey⁵ the lusts thereof.

13 Neither yield ye your members as instruments of unrighteousness unto sin; but yield yourselves up to God as those that were dead and are alive, and your members as instruments of righteousness unto God.

14 For sin shall not have dominion over you: for ye are not under the law, but under grace.

15 What then? are we to sin, because we are not under the

---

¹ *Not expressed in the original.*
² *Literally,* Let it not be.
³ *Literally,* justified.
⁴ Our Lord *is omitted in almost all our oldest copies.*
⁵ It in *is omitted in all our oldest copies.*

law, but under grace? ¹God forbid.

16 Know ye not, that to whomsoever ye yield yourselves ²servants to obey, his servants ye are whom ye obey; whether it be of sin unto death, or of obedience unto righteousness?

17 But thanks be to God, that ye were [once] ²servants of sin, but ye obeyed from the heart the form of doctrine whereunto ye were delivered;

18 And being made free from sin, ye were made ²servants to righteousness.

19 I speak after the manner of men because of the infirmity of your flesh: for as ye yielded your members ²servants to uncleanness and to iniquity unto iniquity; so now yield your members ²servants to righteousness unto sanctification.

20 For when ye were ²servants of sin, ye were free in regard of righteousness.

21 What fruit then had ye at that time? Things whereof ye are now ashamed: for the end of those things is death.

22 But now being made free from sin, and made ²servants to God, ye have your fruit unto sanctification, and the end everlasting life.

23 For the wages of sin is death; but the gift of God is eternal life in Jesus Christ our Lord.

CHAPTER VII.

KNOW ye not, brethren, (for I am speaking to men that know the law,) how that the law hath dominion over a man for so long time as he liveth?

2 For the woman which hath an husband is bound by the law to her husband while he liveth; but if her husband die, she is loosed from the law of the husband.

3 Therefore, while her husband liveth, she shall be called an adulteress, if she be joined to another man: but if her husband die, she is free from the law; so that she is no adulteress, though she be joined to another man.

4 So then, my brethren, ye also were made dead to the law through the body of Christ; that ye might be joined to another, even to him who was raised from the dead, to the intent that we should bring forth fruit unto God.

5 For when we were in the flesh, the stirrings of sins, which were through the law, were active in our members so as to bring forth fruit unto death.

6 But now we have been loosed from the law, having died unto that wherein we were held; so that we serve in the newness of the spirit, and not in the oldness of the letter.

7 What then shall we say? Is the law sin? ³God forbid. Nevertheless, I had not known sin, except through the law: for I had not known coveting, if the law had not said, Thou shalt not covet.

8 But sin, having found an occasion, through the commandment wrought in me all

---

¹ *Literally*, Let it not be.
² *Literally*, slaves, *or* bondmen.

³ *Literally*, Let it not be.

manner of coveting. For without the law sin is dead.

9 And I was alive without the law once: but when the commandment came, sin came to life, and I died;

10 And the very commandment, which was for life, I found to be for death.

11 For sin, having found an occasion, through the commandment deceived me, and through it slew me.

12 So that the law is holy, and the commandment is holy, and righteous, and good.

13 Did then that which is good become death unto me? God forbid: but sin ¹[became death unto me], to the end that it might be shewn to be sin, working death to me through that which is good; that through the commandment sin might become exceeding sinful.

14 For we know that the law is spiritual: but I am carnal, sold into the power of sin.

15 For what I perform, that I know not: for not what I desire, that do I; but what I hate, that I do.

16 But if I do that which I desire not, I consent unto the law that it is good.

17 So now it is no longer I that perform it, but sin that dwelleth in me.

18 For I know that there dwelleth not in me, that is, in my flesh, any good: for to desire is present with me; but to perform that which is good is not.

19 For the good that I desire I do not: but the evil which I desire not, that I do.

20 But if I do that I desire not, it is no longer I that perform it, but the sin that dwelleth in me.

21 I find therefore this law, that, when I desire to do that which is good, evil is present with me.

22 For I delight in the law of God after the inward man:

23 But I see a different law in my members, warring against the law of my mind, and bringing me into captivity to the law of sin which is in my members.

24 O wretched man that I am! who shall deliver me from the body of this death?

25 Thanks be to God through Jesus Christ our Lord. So then I myself with the mind serve the law of God; but with the flesh the law of sin.

CHAPTER VIII.

THERE is therefore now no condemnation to them which are in Christ Jesus.²

2 For the law of the Spirit of life in Christ Jesus set me free from the law of sin and of death.

3 For what the law could not do, in that it was weak through the flesh, God sending his own Son in the likeness of the flesh of sin, and for sin, condemned sin in the flesh:

4 That the righteous demand of the law might be fulfilled in us, who walk not after the flesh, but after the Spirit.

¹ *Not expressed in the original.*

² *The words,* who walk not after the flesh, but after the Spirit, *are omitted by all the most ancient MSS.*

5 For they that are after the flesh do mind the things of the flesh; but they that are after the Spirit the things of the Spirit.
6 For the mind of the flesh is death; but the mind of the Spirit is life and peace.
7 Because the mind of the flesh is enmity against God: for it doth not submit itself to the law of God, neither indeed can it:
8 And they that are in the flesh cannot please God.
9 But ye are not in the flesh, but in the Spirit, if the Spirit of God dwelleth in you. But if any man hath not the Spirit of Christ, he is none of his.
10 Now if Christ is in you, the body indeed is dead by reason of sin; but the spirit is life by reason of righteousness.
11 But if the Spirit of him that raised up Jesus from the dead dwelleth in you, he that raised up Christ from the dead shall quicken even your mortal bodies [1]by reason of his Spirit that dwelleth in you.
12 So then, brethren, we are debtors, not to the flesh, that we should live after the flesh.
13 For if ye live after the flesh, ye must die: but if by the Spirit ye mortify the deeds of the body, ye shall live.
14 For as many as are led by the Spirit of God, they are sons of God.
15 For ye did not receive the spirit of bondage [2][leading] back unto fear; but ye received the Spirit of adoption, wherein we cry, Abba, Father.
16 The Spirit itself beareth witness to our spirit, that we are children of God:
17 And if children, then heirs; heirs of God, and joint-heirs with Christ; if we are suffering with him, to the end that we may also be glorified with him.
18 For I reckon that the sufferings of this present time are of no account in comparison of the glory which is to be revealed [3]in us.
19 For the earnest expectation of the creation is waiting for the revelation of the sons of God.
20 For the creation was made subject to vanity, not of its own will, but by reason of him who made it subject, [4]in hope:
21 Because even the creation itself shall be set free from the bondage of corruption into the liberty of the glory of the children of God.
22 For we know that the whole creation groaneth and travaileth in pain together until now:
23 And not only so, but even ourselves, having the firstfruit of the Spirit, even we ourselves groan within ourselves, waiting for the end of the adoption, to wit, the redemption of our body.
24 For in hope were we saved: but hope that is seen is not hope: for what a man seeth, why doth he also hope for?
25 But if we hope for what

---

[1] *Or*, by means of, through: *the ancient MSS. are divided.*
[2] *Not expressed in the original.*
[3] *Literally*, toward, *or* in regard to, us.
[4] *Some render*, in hope that even the creation, &c

we see not, we wait for it with patience.

26 In like manner doth the Spirit also help our weakness: for we know not what we should pray for as we ought: but the Spirit itself maketh intercession ¹[for us] with groanings which cannot be uttered:

27 But he that searcheth the hearts knoweth what is the mind of the Spirit, ²because he maketh intercession for the saints according to ¹[the will of] God.

28 Moreover we know that to them that love God all things work together for good, ¹[even] to them who are called according to ¹[his] purpose.

29 Because whom he foreknew, them he also foreordained to bear the likeness of the image of his Son, that he might be the firstborn among many brethren:

30 And whom he foreordained, them he also called: and whom he called, them he also justified: and whom he justified, them he also glorified.

31 What then shall we say to these things? If God is for us, who shall be against us?

32 He that spared not his own Son, but delivered him up for us all, how shall he not also with him freely give us all things?

33 Who shall bring any charge against God's elect? Shall God that justifieth?

34 Who is he that condemneth? Is it Christ that died, yea more, that is also risen again, who is also at the right hand of God, who also maketh intercession for us?

35 Who shall separate us from the love of Christ? shall tribulation, or distress, or persecution, or famine, or nakedness, or peril, or sword?

36 Even as it is written, For thy sake are we being killed all the day long; we were accounted as sheep for the slaughter.

37 Nay, in all these things we are more than conquerors through him that loved us.

38 For I am persuaded, that neither death, nor life, nor angels, nor principalities, nor things present, nor things to come, nor powers,

39 Nor height, nor depth, nor any other created thing, shall be able to separate us from the love of God, which is in Christ Jesus our Lord.

CHAPTER IX.

I SAY the truth in Christ, I lie not, my conscience bearing me witness of the same in the Holy Spirit,

2 That I have great sorrow and unceasing anguish in my heart:

3 For I could wish that I myself were accursed from Christ on behalf of my brethren, my kinsmen according to the flesh:

4 Who are Israelites; to whom belongeth the adoption, and the glory, and the covenants, and the giving of the law, and the service [of the sanctuary], and the promises;

---

¹ *Not expressed in th. original.* Or, that.

5 Whose are the fathers, and of whom as concerning the flesh is Christ, who is God over all, blessed for ever. Amen.

6 Not as though the word of God hath fallen to the ground. For not all they which are of Israel, are Israel:

7 Nor yet, because they are Abraham's seed, are they all children: but, In Isaac shall thy seed be called.

8 That is, Not they which are the children of the flesh, are the children of God: but the children of the promise are reckoned for seed.

9 For this word was of promise, According to this time I will come, and Sarah shall have a son.

10 And not only so; but when Rebecca also had conceived by one, even by our father Isaac;

11 For when ¹the children were not yet born, and had not done anything good or evil, to the end that the purpose of God according to election may stand, not depending on works, but on him that calleth;

12 It was said unto her, The elder shall serve the younger:

13 Even as it is written, Jacob I loved, but Esau I hated.

14 What then shall we say? Is there unrighteousness with God? ²God forbid.

15 For he saith to Moses, I will have mercy on whomsoever I have mercy, and I will have compassion on whomsoever I have compassion.

16 Therefore it is not of him that willeth, nor yet of him that runneth, but of God that hath mercy.

17 For the scripture said unto Pharaoh, For this very purpose did I raise thee up, that I may shew forth my power in thee, and that my name may be published abroad in all the earth.

18 Therefore he hath mercy on whom he will, and whom he will he hardeneth.

19 Thou wilt say then unto me, Why then doth he yet find fault? For who resisteth his will?

20 Nay but, O man, who art thou that repliest against God? Shall the thing formed say to him that formed it, Why didst thou make me thus?

21 Or hath not the potter power over the clay, out of the same lump to make one vessel unto honour, and another unto dishonour?

22 What if God, purposing to shew forth his wrath, and to make his power known, endured with much longsuffering vessels of wrath fitted for destruction:

23 And to the end that he might make known the riches of his glory on the vessels of mercy, which he before prepared unto glory,

24 Whom he also called, even us, not from among the Jew only, but also from among th Gentiles?

25 As he saith also in Hosea, I will call them my people, which were not my people; and her beloved, which was not beloved.

---

¹ *The original has only*, when they were not yet born.
² *Literally*, Let it not be.

26 And it shall be, that in the place where it was said unto them, Ye are not my people; there shall they be called sons of the living God.

27 Moreover Isaiah crieth concerning Israel, Though the number of the sons of Israel be as the sand of the sea, the remnant shall be saved:

28 For he is finishing the reckoning, and cutting it short in righteousness: because a short reckoning will the Lord make upon the earth.

29 And as Isaiah hath said before, Except the Lord of Sabaoth had left us a seed, we had become as Sodom, and had been made like unto Gomorrah.

30 What then shall we say? That the Gentiles, which pursue not after righteousness, attained to righteousness, even the righteousness which is of faith.

31 But Israel, pursuing after the law of righteousness, arrived not at the law.

32 Wherefore? Because ¹[pursuing after it] not by faith, but as by the works of the law, they stumbled against the stone of stumbling.

33 Even as it is written, Behold, I lay in Sion a stone of stumbling and rock of offence: and he that believeth thereon shall not be put to shame.

CHAPTER X.

BRETHREN, my heart's desire and my supplication to God on their behalf is for salvation.

¹ *Not expressed in the original.*

2 For I bear them witness that they have a zeal for God, but not according to knowledge.

3 For not knowing the righteousness of God, and seeking to set up their own righteousness, they have not submitted themselves unto the righteousness of God.

4 For Christ is the end of the law unto righteousness to every one that believeth.

5 For Moses describeth the righteousness which is of the law, ¹[saying,] The man which hath done them shall live in it.

6 But the righteousness which is of faith speaketh on this wise, Say not in thine heart, Who shall ascend into heaven? that is, to bring Christ down:

7 Or, Who shall descend into the deep? that is, to bring Christ up from the dead:

8 But what saith it? The word is nigh unto thee, in thy mouth, and in thy heart: that is, the word of faith, which we preach;

9 Because if thou shalt confess with thy mouth the Lord Jesus, and shalt believe in thine heart that God raised him from the dead, thou shalt be saved.

10 For with the heart man believeth unto righteousness; and with the mouth confession is made unto salvation.

11 For the scripture saith, Whosoever believeth on him shall not be put to shame.

12 For there is no distinction between Jew and Greek: for the same Lord over all is rich

unto all them that call upon him:

13 For every one whosoever shall call upon the name of the Lord shall be saved.

14 How then can they call on him in whom they have not believed? and how can they believe in him of whom they have not heard? and how can they hear without a preacher?

15 And how can they preach, except they be sent? as it is written, How beautiful are the feet of them that bring glad tidings of peace, that bring glad tidings of good things!

16 Howbeit they did not all hearken to the glad tidings. For Isaiah saith, Lord, who hath believed our report?

17 So then faith cometh of report, and the report is through the word of Christ.

18 But I say, Did they not hear? Nay verily, Their voice went out into all the earth, and their words unto the ends of the world.

19 But I say, Did Israel not know? First Moses saith, I will provoke you to jealousy against that which is not a nation, against a nation that hath no understanding will I anger you.

20 But Isaiah is very bold and saith, I was found by them that sought me not; I became manifest unto them that asked not after me.

21 But in regard of Israel he saith, All the day long did I stretch forth my hands unto a disobedient and gainsaying people.

CHAPTER XI.

I SAY then, Did God cast away his people? [1]God forbid. For I also am an Israelite, of the seed of Abraham, of the tribe of Benjamin.

2 God did not cast away his people which he foreknew. Know ye not what the scripture saith in [2][the history of] Elijah? how he pleadeth with God against Israel,

3 Lord, they have killed thy prophets, they have digged down thine altars; and I only am left, and they seek my life.

4 Nevertheless what saith the answer of God unto him? I have reserved to myself seven thousand men, who have not bowed the knee to Baal.

5 Even so then in this present time also there is a remnant according to the election of grace.

6 Now if it is by grace, it is no more of works: for otherwise grace becometh no more grace. [3] But if it is of works, it is no more grace: for otherwise work is no more work.]

7 What then? That which Israel seeketh for, he found not; but the election found it, and the rest were hardened

8 According as it is written, God gave them a spirit of stupor, eyes that they should not see, and ears that they

[1] *Literally,* Let it not be.
[2] *Not expressed in the original.*
[3] *Omitted by most of the ancient MSS., but contained in the oldest MS. of all, and in the ancient Syriac version.*

should not hear; unto this very day.

9 And David saith, Let their table be made a snare, and a trap, and a stumblingblock, and a recompence unto them:

10 Let their eyes be darkened, that they may not see, and their back bow thou down always.

11 I say then, Did they stumble in order that they should fall? God forbid: but by their trespass salvation is come unto the Gentiles, in order to provoke them to jealousy.

12 But if their trespass is the riches of the world, and their diminishing the riches of the Gentiles; how much more their fulness?

13 But I am speaking to you Gentiles: inasmuch therefore as I am the apostle of the Gentiles, I glorify mine office,

14 If by any means I may provoke to jealousy mine own flesh, and may save some of them.

15 For if the casting away of them be the reconciling of the world, what shall the receiving of them be, but life from the dead?

16 Moreover if the firstfruit be holy, so also is the lump: and if the root be holy, so also are the branches.

17 But if some of the branches were broken off, and thou, being a wild olive, wast grafted in among them, and wast made partaker of the root of the fatness of the olive tree;

18 Boast not against the branches. But if thou boastest against them, it is not thou that bearest the root, but the root thee.

19 Thou wilt say then, The branches were broken off, that I might be grafted in.

20 Well; because of their unbelief they were broken off, and thou standest by thy faith. Be not highminded, but fear:

21 For if God spared not the natural branches, take heed lest he spare not thee also.

22 Behold therefore the goodness and severity of God: toward them which fell, severity; but toward thee, God's goodness, if thou continue in his goodness; for [1][otherwise] thou also shalt be cut off.

23 Yea and they, if they continue not in their unbelief, shall be grafted in: for God is able to graft them in again.

24 For if thou wast cut off from the olive tree which is by nature wild, and wast grafted contrary to nature into a good olive tree: how much more shall these, which are the natural branches, be grafted into their own olive tree?

25 For I would not, brethren, that ye should be ignorant of this mystery, lest ye should be wise in your own conceits; that hardness is come upon Israel in part, until the fulness of the Gentiles come in:

26 And thus all Israel shall be saved: even as it is written, Out of Zion shall come the Deliverer; he shall turn away ungodlinesses from Jacob:

27 And this is the covenant

[1] *Not expressed in the original: but the construction implies it.*

from me unto them, when I take away their sins.

28 As touching the gospel, they are enemies for your sakes: but as touching the election, they are beloved for the fathers' sakes:

29 For the gifts and the calling of God cannot be repented of.

30 For as ye in times past were disobedient to God, yet now by the disobedience of these have obtained mercy:

31 Even so have these also now been disobedient, that by the mercy shewn to you they also may obtain mercy.

32 For God shut up all men in disobedience, that he may have mercy upon all men.

33 O the depth of the riches and wisdom and knowledge of God! how unsearchable are his judgments, and his ways past finding out!

34 For who hath known the mind of the Lord? or who hath been his counsellor?

35 Or who hath first given to him, and shall have recompence made unto him again?

36 For of him, and through him, and unto him, are all things: to him be glory for ever. Amen.

CHAPTER XII.

I BESEECH you therefore, brethren, by the mercies of God, to present your bodies a living sacrifice, holy, wellpleasing unto God, which is your rational service;

2 And not to be conformed to this world, but to be transfigured in the renewing of your mind, that ye may discern what is the will of God, good and wellpleasing, and perfect.

3 For I say, through the grace given unto me, to every man that is among you, not to be highminded above that which he ought to be, but to be minded so as to be soberminded, according as God hath dealt to each his measure of faith.

4 For as in one body we have many members, but the members have not all the same office:

5 So we, being many, are one body in Christ, and severally members one of another;

6 And having gifts differing according to the grace given to us, whether [1][we have] prophecy, [1][let us prophesy] according to the proportion of our faith;

7 Or ministry, [1][let us be occupied] in our ministry: or he that teacheth, in his teaching;

8 Or he that exhorteth, in his exhortation: he that giveth, [1][let him do it] with liberality; he that ruleth, with diligence; he that sheweth mercy, with cheerfulness.

9 Let your love be unfeigned. Abhor that which is evil; cleave to that which is good.

10 In love of the brethren, be affectionate one to another; in giving honour, outdoing one another;

11 In diligence, not slothful; in spirit, fervent; serving the Lord;

12 In hope, rejoicing; in tri-

[1] *Not expressed in the original.*

bulation, patient; in prayer, persevering.

13 Communicating to the necessities of the saints; given to hospitality.

14 Bless them which persecute you: bless, and curse not.

15 Rejoice with them that do rejoice; weep with them that weep:

16 Being of the same mind one toward another: not minding high things, but ¹condescending to men of low estate. Be not wise in your own conceits.

17 Recompense to no man evil for evil. Provide things honourable in the sight of all men.

18 If it be possible, as much as dependeth on you, be at peace with all men.

19 Avenge not yourselves, dearly beloved, but give place unto wrath: for it is written, Vengeance is mine; I will repay, saith the Lord.

20 Nay rather, if thine enemy hunger, feed him; if he thirst, give him drink: for by so doing thou shalt heap coals of fire on his head.

21 Be not overcome by evil, but overcome evil with good.

CHAPTER XIII.

LET every soul submit himself to the authorities that are above him: for there is no authority except from God: those that be have been ordained by God.

2 So that he which setteth himself against the authority, resisteth the ordinance of God:

¹ *Or*, inclining unto the.

and they that resist shall receive to themselves condemnation.

3 For rulers are not a terror to the good work, but to the evil. Dost thou desire not to be afraid of the authority? do that which is good, and thou shalt have praise from the same:

4 For he is God's minister unto thee for good. But if thou do that which is evil, be afraid; for he weareth not the sword in vain: for he is God's minister, an avenger for wrath unto him that doeth evil.

5 Wherefore ye must needs submit yourselves, not only because of the wrath, but also for your conscience sake.

6 For for this cause ye also pay tribute: for they are ministers of God, attending continually to this very thing.

7 Render to all their dues: tribute to whom tribute is due; custom to whom custom; fear to whom fear; honour to whom honour.

8 Owe no man any thing, except to love one another: for he that loveth his neighbour hath fulfilled the law.

9 For this, Thou shalt not commit adultery, Thou shalt not kill, Thou shalt not steal,² Thou shalt not covet; and if there be any other commandment, it is briefly comprehended in this saying, namely, Thou shalt love thy neighbour as thyself.

10 Love worketh no ill to

² Thou shalt not bear false witness *is not found in the majority of the oldest MSS*

his neighbour: love therefore is the fulfilment of the law.

11 And this, knowing the time, that now it is high time for us to awake out of sleep: for now is salvation nearer to us than when we ¹[first] believed.

12 The night is far spent, the day is at hand: let us therefore cast off the works of darkness, and let us put on the armour of light.

13 Let us walk seemly, as in the day; not in revelling and drunkenness, not in chambering and wantonness, not in strife and envying.

14 But put ye on the Lord Jesus Christ, and take no forethought for the flesh, ²to fulfil the lusts thereof.

CHAPTER XIV.

HIM that is weak in the faith receive ye, ³[yet] not for the deciding of doubts.

2 One man believeth that he may eat all things: but he that is weak eateth herbs.

3 Let not him that eateth despise him that eateth not: neither let him that eateth not judge him that eateth: for God hath received him.

4 Who art thou that judgest the servant of another? to his own lord he standeth or falleth. But he shall be made to stand: for the Lord is able to make him stand.

5 One man esteemeth one day above another: another esteemeth every day. Let each be fully persuaded in his own mind.

6 He that regardeth the day, regardeth it to the Lord; ⁴[and he that regardeth not the day, to the Lord he doth not regard it.] He that eateth, eateth to the Lord, for he giveth thanks unto God; and he that eateth not, to the Lord he eateth not, and giveth thanks unto God.

7 For none of us liveth to himself, and none dieth to himself.

8 For whether we live, we live unto the Lord; and whether we die, we die unto the Lord: whether we live therefore, or die, we are the Lord's.

9 For to this end Christ died, and ⁵lived, that he might be Lord both of the dead and of the living.

10 But thou, why judgest thou thy brother? And again, thou, why despisest thou thy brother? for we shall all stand before the judgment seat of God.

11 For it is written, As I live, saith the Lord, every knee shall bow to me, and every tongue shall make confession to God.

12 So then each one of us shall give account concerning himself to God.

13 Therefore let us not judge

---

¹ *Not expressed, but implied, in the original.*
² *Literally,* in the direction, *or* for the purpose, *of lusts.*
³ *Not expressed in the original.*
⁴ *This clause is omitted in all the most ancient MSS.: probably from its ending in the original with the same word as the preceding one. It is contained in the ancient Syriac version.*
⁵ *So all our most ancient MSS.,* again *not being expressed.*

one another any more : but let this rather be your judgment, not to put a stumblingblock or an occasion of falling in a brother's way.

14 I know, and am persuaded in the Lord Jesus, that nothing is unclean of itself : only to him that accounteth anything unclean, to him it is unclean.

15 For if because of meat thy brother is grieved, thou art no longer walking according to love. Destroy not by thy meat him for whom Christ died.

16 Let not then your good be evil spoken of :

17 For the kingdom of God is not eating and drinking, but righteousness, and peace, and joy in the Holy Spirit.

18 For he that herein serveth Christ is wellpleasing to God, and approved of men.

19 Let us therefore follow after the things of peace, and the things which pertain unto mutual edification.

20 Do not for the sake of meat undo the work of God. All things indeed are clean; nevertheless it is evil to the man who eateth with offence.

21 It is good not to eat flesh, nor to drink wine, nor ¹[to do] any thing wherein thy brother stumbleth, or is offended, or is weak.

22 The faith which thou hast, have it to thyself before God. Blessed is he that judgeth not himself in that which he alloweth.

23 But he that doubteth is condemned if he eat, because

¹ Not expressed in the original.

¹[he eateth] not of faith : but whatsoever is not of faith is sin.

CHAPTER XV.

MOREOVER we that are strong ought to bear the infirmities of the weak, and not to please ourselves.

2 Let every one of us please his neighbour for his good with a view to edification.

3 For Christ also pleased not himself; but, as it is written, The reproaches of them that reproached thee fell on me.

4 For whatsoever things were written aforetime were written for our instruction, that through the patience and the comfort of the scriptures we might have our hope.

5 And may the God of patience and comfort grant you to be of the same mind one toward another according to Christ Jesus :

6 That with one accord ye may with one mouth glorify the God and Father of our Lord Jesus Christ.

7 Wherefore receive ye one another, as Christ also received ²you, to the glory of God.

8 For I say that Christ hath been made a minister of the circumcision, for the sake of God's truth, in order to confirm the promises made unto the fathers :

9 And that the Gentiles glorified God for [his] mercy ; as it is written, For this cause I will give thanks unto thee among the Gentiles, and will sing unto thy name.

² So most of our ancient authorities.

10 And again he saith, Rejoice, ye Gentiles, with his people.

11 And again, Praise the Lord, all ye Gentiles; and laud him, all ye people.

12 And again, Isaiah saith, There shall be the root of Jesse, and he that riseth to rule over the Gentiles; in him shall the Gentiles hope:

13 And may the God of hope fill you with all joy and peace in believing, that ye may abound in hope, by the power of the Holy Spirit.

14 Now I am persuaded, my brethren, even I myself, concerning you, that ye also yourselves are full of goodness, filled with all knowledge, able also to admonish one another.

15 Howbeit I have written more boldly unto you, brethren, in some measure, as putting you in mind, because of the grace given to me by God,

16 That I should be a minister of Christ Jesus unto the Gentiles, ministering as a priest in the gospel of God, that the offering up of the Gentiles may be acceptable, being sanctified by the Holy Spirit.

17 I have then my boasting in Christ Jesus in the things which pertain to God.

18 For I will not dare to speak [1]at all save of those things which Christ wrought by me, in order to the obedience of the Gentiles, by word and deed,

19 In the power of signs and wonders, in the power of the Holy Spirit; so that from Jerusalem and round about, as far as Illyricum, I have fully preached the gospel of Christ;

20 Yet on this wise making it my ambition to preach the gospel, not where Christ was already named, that I might not build upon another man's foundation:

21 But according as it is written, They to whom no tidings of him came shall see: and they that have not heard shall understand.

22 For which cause also these many times I have been hindered from coming to you.

23 But now I have no more place in these parts, and have had these many years a longing to come unto you,

24 Whensoever I take my journey into Spain:[2] for I hope to see you as I pass through, and to be set forward on my journey thither by you, if first I be in some measure filled with your company.

25 But now I go unto Jerusalem, ministering unto the saints.

26 For Macedonia and Achaia have thought good to make a certain contribution for the poor among the saints which are at Jerusalem.

27 They have thought it good, and they are their debtors. For if the Gentiles have been

---

[1] *Literally*, of any of those things which Christ did not work.

[2] *The words* I will come to you, *inserted here in the received text, are wanting in all our most ancient authorities.*

partakers in their spiritual things, they ought in their turn to minister unto them in carnal things.

28 When therefore I have performed this, and have secured to them this fruit, I will return by you into Spain.

29 And I know that, when I come unto you, I shall come in the fulness of the blessing¹ of Christ.

30 Now I beseech you, brethren, by our Lord Jesus Christ, and by the love of the Spirit, to strive together with me in your prayers for me to God ;

31 That I may be delivered from them that are disobedient in Judæa ; and that my ministration which is for Jerusalem may prove acceptable to the saints ;

32 That I may come unto you in joy by the will of God, and may with you find rest.

33 Now the God of peace be with you all. Amen.

CHAPTER XVI.

I COMMEND unto you Phebe our sister, which is a deaconess of the church which is at ²Kenchreæ :

2 That ye receive her in the Lord so as becometh saints, and that ye assist her in whatsoever business she may have need of you : for she too hath been a succourer of many, and of myself also.

3 Salute Prisca and Aquila my fellow-labourers in Christ Jesus :

4 Who for my life laid down their own necks : unto whom not only I give thanks, but also all the churches of the Gentiles.

5 Likewise salute the church that is in their house. Salute ³Epænetus my wellbeloved, who is the firstfruits of Asia unto Christ.

6 Salute Mary, which bestowed much labour on us.

7 Salute ⁴Andronicus and Junias, my kinsmen, and my fellow-prisoners, which are of note among the apostles, which also were in Christ before me.

8 Salute Amplias my beloved in the Lord.

9 Salute Urbanus, our fellow-labourer in Christ, and Stachys my beloved.

10 Salute Apelles the approved in Christ. Salute them that be of the household of ⁵Aristobulus.

11 Salute Herodion my kinsman. Salute them of the household of Narcissus, which are in the Lord.

12 Salute Tryphena and Tryphosa, who labour in the Lord. Salute Persis the beloved, which laboured much in the Lord.

13 Salute Rufus the elect in the Lord, and [her who is] his mother and mine.

14 Salute ⁶Asyncritus, Phlegon, Hermes, ⁷Patrobas, Her-

---

¹ Of the gospel *is omitted by all the ancient MSS.*
² *Pronounce* Kénchreæ.

³ *Pronounce* Epænĕtus.
⁴ *Pronounce* Andronícus.
⁵ *Pronounce* Aristobúlus.
⁶ *Pronounce* Asýncrĭtus.
⁷ *Pronounce* Pátrŏbas.

mas, and the brethren which are with them.

15 Salute Philologus, and Julia, Nereus, and his sister, and Olympas, and all the saints which are with them.

16 Salute one another with an holy kiss. ¹All the churches of Christ salute you.

17 Now I beseech you, brethren, to mark them which cause divisions and offences contrary to the doctrine which ye learned ; and avoid them.

18 For they that are such serve not our Lord Christ, but their own belly ; and by their good words and fair speeches deceive the hearts of the simple.

19 For your obedience is come abroad unto all men. I rejoice therefore over you : yet I would have you wise unto that which is good, and harmless unto that which is evil.

20 And the God of peace shall bruise Satan under your feet shortly. The grace of our Lord Jesus Christ be with you.

21 Timotheus my fellow-labourer saluteth you, and Lucius, and Jason, and ²Sosipater, my kinsmen.

22 I Tertius, who wrote the epistle, salute you in the Lord.

23 Gaius mine host, and ³[the host] of the whole church, saluteth you. Erastus the treasurer of the city saluteth you, and Quartus our brother.

24 The grace of our Lord Jesus Christ be with you all. Amen.

25 Now to him that is able to stablish you according to my gospel and the preaching of Jesus Christ, according to the revelation of the mystery, which hath been kept in silence during eternal ages,

26 But now is made manifest, and by the scriptures of the prophets, according to the commandment of the eternal God, is made known to all the nations unto obedience of faith :

27 To the only wise God through Jesus Christ ; to whom be the glory for ever. Amen.

¹ *So all the ancient MSS.*

² *Pronounce* Sosípăter.
³ *Not expressed in the original.*

THE FIRST EPISTLE OF PAUL THE APOSTLE
TO THE
CORINTHIANS.

CHAPTER I.

PAUL, called [to be] an apostle of Christ Jesus through the will of God, and Sosthenes our brother,

2 Unto the church of God which is in Corinth, men sanctified in Christ Jesus, called [to be] saints, together with all that call upon the name of our Lord Jesus Christ in every place, both theirs and ours:

3 Grace be unto you, and peace, from God our Father and the Lord Jesus Christ.

4 I thank my God always concerning you, for the grace of God which was given you in Christ Jesus;

5 That in every thing ye were made rich in him, in all teaching and all knowledge:

6 According as the testimony of Christ was firmly established in you:

7 So that ye come not behind in any gift; waiting for the revealing of our Lord Jesus Christ:

8 Who shall also stablish you until the end, unblameable in the day of our Lord Jesus Christ.

9 God is faithful, by whom ye were called into the fellowship of his Son Jesus Christ our Lord.

10 Now I beseech you, brethren, by the name of our Lord Jesus Christ, that ye all speak the same thing, and that there be no divisions among you; but that ye be made perfect in the same mind and in the same judgment.

11 For it hath been declared unto me concerning you, my brethren, by them [1][which are of the house] of Chloe, that there are contentions among you.

12 I mean this, that each one of you saith, I am of Paul; and I of Apollos; and I of Cephas; and I of Christ.

13 Is Christ divided? was Paul crucified for you, or were ye baptized into the name of Paul?

14 I thank God that I baptized none of you, save only Crispus and Gaius;

15 That no man should say that I baptized into mine own name.

16 And I baptized also the household of Stephanas: further, I know not whether I baptized any other.

17 For Christ did not send me to baptize, but to preach the gospel: not in wisdom of speech, lest the cross of Christ should be made of none effect.

18 For the preaching of the cross is to them that are perishing foolishness; but to us which

---

[1] *Not expressed in the original*

are being saved it is the power of God.

19 For it is written, I will destroy the wisdom of the wise, and the understanding of the understanding ones will I bring to nothing.

20 Where is the wise? where is the scribe? where is the disputer of this world? did not God make foolish the wisdom of the world?

21 For when in the wisdom of God the world through its wisdom knew not God, God was pleased through the foolishness of preaching to save them that believe.

22 Seeing that Jews ask for signs, and Greeks seek after wisdom:

23 But we preach Christ crucified, unto Jews a stumblingblock, and unto Gentiles foolishness;

24 But unto them which are the called, both Jews and Greeks, Christ the power of God, and the wisdom of God.

25 Because the foolishness of God is wiser than men; and the weakness of God is stronger than men.

26 For consider your calling, brethren, how that not many ¹[of you] are wise after the flesh, not many mighty, not many noble.

27 Nay, God chose the foolish things of the world that he might put to shame the wise men; and God chose the weak things of the world that he might put to shame the things which are strong.

¹ *Not expressed, but implied, in the original.*

28 And the base things of the world, and the things which are despised, did God choose, the things which are not, that he might bring to nought the things that are:

29 That no flesh should glory before God.

30 But of him are ye in Christ Jesus, who was made wisdom unto us from God, both righteousness and sanctification, and redemption:

31 That, according as it is written, He that glorieth, let him glory in the Lord.

CHAPTER II.

AND I, brethren, when I came to you, came declaring unto you the testimony of God, not with excellency of speech or of wisdom.

2 For I determined not to know any thing among you, save Jesus Christ, and him crucified.

3 And I was with you in weakness, and in fear, and in much trembling.

4 And my speech and my preaching was not with persuasive words of [man's] wisdom, but with demonstration of the Spirit and of power.

5 To the end that your faith may not stand in the wisdom of men, but in the power of God.

6 Yet we speak wisdom among the perfect: but a wisdom not of this world, nor of the rulers of this world, that are coming to nought:

7 But we speak God's wisdom in a mystery, even the hidden wisdom, which God foreordain-

ed before the worlds unto our glory.

8 Which none of the rulers of this world knoweth: for had they known it, they would not have crucified the Lord of glory.

9 But as it is written, Things which eye hath not seen and ear hath not heard, and which have not entered into the heart of man, things which God hath prepared for them that love him,

10 God revealed unto us through his Spirit: for the Spirit searcheth all things, yea even the deep things of God.

11 For who among men knoweth the things of a man, save the spirit of the man which is in him? so also the things of God knoweth none, save only the Spirit of God.

12 And we received, not the spirit of the world, but the Spirit which is from God; that we might know the things freely given to us by God.

13 Which things also we speak, not in words taught by man's wisdom, but in words taught by the Spirit, interpreting spiritual things to the spiritual.

14 But the natural man receiveth not the things of the Spirit of God: for they are foolishness unto him: and he cannot know them, because they are spiritually discerned.

15 But he that is spiritual discerneth all things, yet he himself is discerned by none.

16 For who hath known the mind of the Lord, that he shall instruct him? But we have the mind of Christ.

CHAPTER III.

AND I, brethren, was not able to speak unto you as unto spiritual men, but as unto men of flesh, even as unto babes in Christ.

2 I fed you with milk, and not with meat: for ye were not yet able [1][to bear it]; nay, nor even now are ye able.

3 For ye are yet carnal: for whereas there is among you envying, and strife, and divisions, are ye not carnal, and walking after the manner of men?

4 For when one saith, I am of Paul; and another, I am of Apollos; are ye not [1][as] men?

5 Who then is Apollos, and who is Paul? ministers, through whom ye believed, even as the Lord gave to each.

6 I planted, Apollos watered; but God gave the growth.

7 So then neither is he that planteth any thing, nor he that watereth; but God that giveth the growth.

8 And he that planteth and he that watereth are **one**: but each shall receive his own reward according to his own labour.

9 For we are God's fellow-labourers: ye are God's tillage, God's building.

10 According to the grace of God which was given unto me, as a wise masterbuilder, I have laid a foundation, and another buildeth thereon. But let each man take heed how he buildeth thereupon.

11 For other foundation can

[1] *Not expressed in the original.*

no man lay than that which is laid, which is Jesus Christ.

12 But if any man buildeth upon this foundation gold, silver, costly stones, wood, hay, straw;

13 The work of each man shall be made manifest: for the day shall declare it, because it is to be revealed in fire; and each man's work, of what sort it is, the fire itself shall prove.

14 If any man's work shall endure which he hath built thereupon, he shall receive wages.

15 If any man's work shall be burned up, he shall suffer loss: but he himself shall be saved; yet so as through fire.

16 Know ye not that ye are the temple of God, and that the Spirit of God dwelleth in you?

17 If any man destroyeth the temple of God, him shall God destroy; for the temple of God is holy, the which[1] are ye.

18 Let no man deceive himself. If any man seemeth to be wise among you in this world, let him become a fool, that he may become wise.

19 For the wisdom of this world is foolishness with God. For it is written, He that taketh the wise in their craftiness.

20 And again, The Lord knoweth the reasonings of the wise, that they are vain.

21 So then let no man glory in men. For all things are yours;

22 Whether Paul, or Apollos, or Cephas, or the world, or life, or death, or things present,

i.e. holy

or things to come; all are yours;

23 And ye are Christ's; and Christ is God's.

CHAPTER IV.

LET a man so account of us, as ministers of Christ, and stewards of the mysteries of God.

2 Moreover it is required in stewards [2]here, that a man be found faithful.

3 But with me it is a very small thing that I should be judged by you, or by the day of man's judgment: nay, I do not even judge mine own self.

4 For I know nothing against myself: yet am I not hereby justified; but he that judgeth me is the Lord.

5 So then judge not any thing before the time, until the Lord come, who shall both bring to light the hidden things of darkness, and make manifest the counsels of the hearts: and then shall each man have his praise from God.

6 Now these things, brethren, have I transferred in a figure to myself and Apollos for your sakes; that in us ye may learn the lesson, not to go beyond what is written, that ye be not puffed up each for one against another.

7 For who distinguisheth thee [3][above another]? and what hast thou that thou didst not receive? but if thou didst receive it, why dost thou glory, as if thou hadst not received it?

[2] *i.e.* here on earth. *So the ancient MSS.*
[3] *Not expressed in the original.*

T

8 Already ye are filled full, already ye are rich, ye reign as kings without us : and I would indeed that ye did reign, that we also might reign with you.

9 For methinks God hath set forth us the apostles last, as men sentenced to death : for we are made a spectacle unto the world, to angels, and to men.

10 We are fools for Christ's sake, but ye are wise in Christ ; we are weak, but ye are strong ; ye are in honour, but we are despised.

11 Even unto this present hour we both hunger, and thirst, and are naked, and are buffeted, and have no certain dwelling-place ;

12 And labour, working with our own hands : being reviled, we bless ; being persecuted, we endure :

13 Being defamed, we intreat : we are become as the filth of the world, the offscouring of all things unto this day.

14 I write not these things to shame you, but as my beloved children I admonish you.

15 For though ye may have ten thousand schoolmasters in Christ, yet have ye not many fathers : for in Christ Jesus I begat you through the gospel.

16 I beseech you therefore, be ye imitators of me.

17 For this cause have I sent unto you Timothy, who is my child, beloved and faithful in the Lord, who shall remind you of my ways in Christ, according as I teach every where in every church.

18 Now some are puffed up, as though I were not coming to you.

19 But I will come to you shortly, if the Lord will, and will know, not the words of them which are puffed up, but the power.

20 For the kingdom of God is not in word, but in power.

21 What will ye? shall I come unto you with a rod, or in love, and the Spirit of meekness ?

CHAPTER V.

IT is actually reported that there is fornication among you, and such fornication as is not even among the Gentiles, so that one [1][of you] hath his father's wife.

2 And ye are puffed up, and did not rather mourn, that he that did this deed might be removed from among you.

3 For I verily, being absent in body, but present in spirit, have judged already, as though I were present, concerning him that hath so done this deed,

4 In the name of our Lord Jesus, ye being gathered together, and my spirit, with the power of our Lord Jesus Christ,

5 To deliver such an one unto Satan for the destruction of his flesh, that his spirit may be saved in the day of the Lord.

6 Your glorying is not good. Know ye not that a little leaven leaveneth the whole lump ?

7 Purge out the old leaven, that ye may be a new lump, according as ye are unleavened. For our passover also hath been sacrificed, even Christ :

[1] *Not expressed in the original.*

8 So then let us keep the feast, not with the old leaven, neither with the leaven of malice and wickedness; but with the unleavened bread of sincerity and truth.

9 I wrote unto you in my letter not to company with fornicators:

10 Not absolutely with the fornicators of this world, or with the covetous, and extortioners, or idolaters; for then must ye needs go out of the world.

11 But, as it is, I wrote unto you not to company with him, if any man called a brother be a fornicator, or covetous, or an idolater, or a reviler, or a drunkard, or an extortioner; with such an one no not to eat.

12 For what have I to do with judging them that are without? do not ye judge them that are within?

13 But them that are without God judgeth. ¹Put away from among yourselves the wicked man.

CHAPTER VI.

DARE any of you, having a matter against his brother, go to law before the unjust, and not before the saints?

2 What? know ye not that the saints shall judge the world? and if the world is to be judged by you, are ye unworthy of ²[judging] the smallest judgments?

---
¹ *The* therefore, *in the Authorized Version, has absolutely no authority in its favour. All the ancient authorities read as our text.*
² *Not expressed in the original.*

3 Know ye not that we shall judge angels? surely then things that pertain to this life.

4 If then ye have judgments of things pertaining to this life, set them to judge who are of no esteem in the church.

5 I speak this to your shame. Is it so, that there is not even one wise man among you, that shall be able to decide between his brethren?

6 Nay, brother goeth to law with brother, and that before unbelievers.

7 Now therefore it is altogether a fault in you, that ye go to law one with another. Why do ye not rather take wrong? why do ye not rather suffer yourselves to be defrauded?

8 Nay, ye do wrong, and defraud, and that your brethren.

9 What? know ye not that doers of wrong shall not inherit the kingdom of God? Be not deceived: neither fornicators, nor idolaters, nor adulterers, nor effeminate, nor abusers of themselves with men,

10 Nor thieves, nor covetous, nor drunkards, nor revilers, nor extortioners, shall inherit the kingdom of God.

11 And such things were some of you: but ye washed them off, but ye were sanctified, but ye were justified in the name of the Lord Jesus, and in the Spirit of our God.

12 All things are lawful unto me, but not all things are expedient: all things are lawful for me, but I will not be

brought under the power of any thing.

13 Meats for the belly, and the belly for meats: but God shall bring to an end both it and them. The body however is not for fornication, but for the Lord; and the Lord for the body.

14 And God both raised the Lord, and will also raise up us by his power.

15 Know ye not that your bodies are members of Christ? shall I then take away the members of Christ, and make them members of an harlot? ¹God forbid.

16 What? know ye not that he which is joined to an harlot is one body? for the two, saith he, shall be one flesh.

17 But he that is joined unto the Lord is one spirit.

18 Flee fornication. Every sin whatsoever that a man doeth is outside the body; but he that committeth fornication sinneth against his own body.

19 What? know ye not that your body is the temple of the Holy Spirit which is in you, which ye have from God, and that ye are not your own?

20 For ye were bought with a price: glorify therefore God in your body.²

CHAPTER VII.

NOW concerning the things whereof ye wrote unto me: It is good for a man not to touch a woman.

2 But because of fornications, let each man have his own wife, and let each woman have her own husband.

3 Let the husband render unto the wife ³her due: and in like manner the wife also unto the husband.

4 The wife hath not power over her own body, but the husband: and in like manner the husband also hath not power over his own body, but the wife.

5 Defraud ye not one the other, except it be by agreement for a time, that ye may be free for ⁴prayer, and may ³be together again, in order that Satan tempt you not owing to your incontinency.

6 But this I say by way of allowance, not by way of commandment.

7 Yet I would that all men were even as I myself. Nevertheless each hath his proper gift from God, one after this manner, and another after that.

8 Now to the unmarried and to the widows I say, It is good for them if they abide even as I:

9 Yet if they have not continency, let them marry: for it is better to marry than to burn.

10 But unto the married I command, yet not I, but the Lord, that the wife be not separated from her husband:

11 But if she be actually separated, let her remain unmarried, or let her be recon-

---

¹ *Literally*, Let it not be.
² *The words*, and in your spirit, which are God's, *are wanting in almost all our earliest authorities.*

³ *So all our most ancient MSS.*
⁴ *The words* fasting and *are wanting in all our principal oldest authorities.*

ciled unto her husband: and that the husband leave not his wife.

12 But to the rest say I, not the Lord: If any brother hath a wife that believeth not, and she too is content to dwell with him, let him not leave her.

13 And any woman which hath an husband that believeth not, and he too is content to dwell with her, let her not leave her husband.

14 For the unbelieving husband is sanctified in the wife, and the unbelieving wife is sanctified in the [1][believing] [2]brother: else are your children unclean; but now are they holy.

15 But if the unbelieving separateth himself, let him be separated. A brother or a sister is not put under bondage in such cases: but God hath called us in peace.

16 For how knowest thou, O wife, whether thou shalt save thy husband? or how knowest thou, O man, whether thou shalt save thy wife?

17 Only as the Lord distributed to each, as God hath called each, so let him walk. And so ordain I in all the churches.

18 Was any man called being circumcised; let him not become uncircumcised. Hath any been called in uncircumcision? let him not be circumcised.

19 Circumcision is nothing, and uncircumcision is nothing, but the keeping of the commandments of God [1][is every thing].

20 Let each abide in the same calling wherein he was called.

21 Wast thou called being a slave? care not for it: nay, even if thou canst be made free, use it rather.

22 For the slave who was called in the Lord, is the Lord's freedman: in like manner he that was called being free, is the slave of Christ.

23 Ye were bought with a price; be not slaves of men.

24 Brethren, [in that state] wherein each was called, therein let him abide with God.

25 Now concerning virgins I have no commandment of the Lord: but I give my judgment, as having received mercy from the Lord to be faithful.

26 I consider then that this is good by reason of the present necessity, that it is good for a man so to be.

27 Art thou bound unto a wife? seek not to be loosed. Art thou loosed from a wife? seek not a wife.

28 But and if thou marry, thou hast not sinned; and if a virgin marry, she hath not sinned. Yet such shall have affliction in the flesh: and I desire to spare you.

29 But this I say, brethren, the time henceforth is shortened; in order that both they that have wives be as if they had none;

30 And they that weep, as weeping not; and they that rejoice, as rejoicing not; and

---

[1] *Not expressed in the original.*
[2] *So the most ancient MSS.*

they that buy, as not possessing;

31 And they that use this world, as not using it to the full: for the fashion of this world is passing away.

32 But I would have you to be free from cares. He that is unmarried careth for the things of the Lord, how he shall please the Lord:

33 But he that is married careth for the things of the world, how he shall please his wife.

34 There is difference also between a wife and a virgin. The unmarried woman careth for the things of the Lord, that she may be holy both in body and spirit: but she that is married careth for the things of the world, how she shall please her husband.

35 And this I speak for your own profit; not that I may cast a snare upon you, but with a view to what is seemly, and that ye may attend upon the Lord without distraction.

36 But if any man thinketh that he is behaving himself unseemly toward his virgin daughter, in case she should pass the flower of her age, and if it must needs be so, let him do what he will; he sinneth not: let them marry.

37 But he that standeth stedfast in his heart, having no necessity, and hath power in respect of his own will, and hath determined this in his own heart that he will keep his own virgin daughter, shall do well.

38 So then both he that giveth his own virgin daughter in marriage doeth well; and he that giveth her not in marriage shall do better.

39 A wife is bound as long as her husband liveth; but if her husband die, she is at liberty to be married to whom she will; only in the Lord.

40 But she is more blessed if she so abide, after my judgment: and I think that I also have the Spirit of God.

CHAPTER VIII.

NOW concerning the things sacrificed to idols, we know that we all have knowledge. Knowledge puffeth up, but love edifieth.

2 If any man thinketh that he knoweth any thing, he knoweth it not yet as he ought to know:

3 But if any man loveth God, the same is known by him.

4 As concerning then the eating of things sacrificed to idols, we know that there is no idol in the world, and that there is no God but one.

5 For even if there are gods so called, whether in heaven or on earth, (as there are gods many, and lords many,)

6 Yet to us there is one God, the Father, of whom are all things, and we unto him; and one Lord Jesus Christ, by whom are all things, and we by him.

7 Howbeit there is not in all men this knowledge: but some from conscience of the idol, even until now, eat it as a thing sacrificed unto an idol;

and their conscience being weak is defiled.

8 But meat shall not be reckoned to us before God : for neither, if we eat, are we the better ; neither, if we eat not, are we the worse.

9 But take heed lest by any means this liberty of yours become a stumblingblock to the weak.

10 For if any man see thee which hast knowledge sitting at meat in an idol's temple, will not his conscience, seeing he is weak, be emboldened to eat things sacrificed unto idols ;

11 And he that is weak perisheth by thy knowledge, the brother for whom Christ died ?

12 But when thus ye sin against the brethren, and wound their weak conscience, ye sin against Christ.

13 Wherefore, if meat is a stumblingblock to my brother, I will eat no flesh for evermore, that I be not a stumblingblock to my brother.

CHAPTER IX.

AM I not free ? am I not an apostle ? have I not seen Jesus Christ our Lord ? are not ye my work in the Lord ?

2 If I am not an apostle unto others, yet doubtless I am to you : for the seal of mine apostleship are ye in the Lord.

3 This is my defence to them that do examine me.

4 Have we not liberty to eat and to drink ?

5 Have we not liberty to take about with us a [1][believing]

[1] *Not expressed, but implied, in the original.*

sister as a wife, as well as the other apostles, and as the brethren of the Lord, and Cephas ?

6 Or have I only and Barnabas no liberty to forbear working ?

7 Who ever serveth as a soldier at his own charges ? who planteth a vineyard, and eateth not the fruit thereof ? or who feedeth a flock, and eateth not of the milk of the flock ?

8 Am I speaking these things as a man ? or doth not the law also say these things ?

9 For it is written in the law of Moses, Thou shalt not muzzle the ox when he treadeth out the corn. Is it for the oxen that God careth ?

10 Or doth he say it altogether for our sakes ? Yea, for our sakes it was written : because he that ploweth ought to plow in hope ; and he that thresheth [2][ought to thresh] in hope of partaking.

11 If we sowed for you the things that are spiritual, is it a great thing if we shall reap your carnal things ?

12 If others partake of this power over you, do not we still more ? Nevertheless we used not this power ; but we bear all things, that we may not cause any hindrance to the gospel of Christ.

13 Do ye not know that they which minister about the holy things eat of the temple ? and they which wait at the altar share with the altar ?

14 Thus also did the Lord appoint unto them which

[2] *Not expressed in the original.*

preach the gospel, to live of the gospel.

15 But I have used none of these things: yet I have not written these things, that it should be so done unto me: for it were good for me to die, rather than that any man should make my glorying void.

16 For if I should ¹preach the gospel, I have nothing to glory of: for necessity is laid upon me; for woe is unto me, if I ¹preach not ¹the gospel!

17 For if I do this thing willingly, I have a reward: but if I do it unwillingly, I have a stewardship entrusted to me.

18 What then is my reward, that, in ¹preaching the gospel, I may make the gospel without charge, that I use not to the full my power in the gospel?

19 Yea, being free from all men, yet made I myself servant unto all, that I might gain the greatest number.

20 And unto the Jews I became as a Jew, that I might gain Jews; to them that are under the law as under the law, not being myself under the law, that I might gain them that are under the law;

21 To them that are without law as without law, (not being without law to God, but under the law to Christ,) that I might gain them that are without law.

22 To the weak became I as weak, that I might gain the weak: I am become all things to all men, that I may by all means save some.

23 And all things I do for the gospel's sake, that I may become a partaker thereof with them.

24 Know ye not that they which run in a race run all, but one receiveth the prize? In this manner run ye, that ye may obtain.

25 And every man that contendeth in the games is temperate in all things. Now they do it to obtain a corruptible crown; but we an incorruptible.

26 I therefore so run, as not uncertainly; so fight I, as not beating the air:

27 But I ²chastise my body, and bring it into subjection: lest that by any means, when I have preached to others, I myself should be a castaway.

CHAPTER X.

FOR I would not, brethren, that ye should be ignorant, that our fathers were all under the cloud, and all passed through the sea;

2 And were all baptized unto Moses in the cloud and in the sea;

3 And all ate the same spiritual meat;

4 And all drank the same spiritual drink; for they drank of the spiritual Rock accompanying them: but the Rock was Christ.

5 Howbeit with the more part of them God was not well pleased: for they were overthrown in the wilderness.

6 But these things came to pass as our examples, to the

---

¹ *The words are literally*, evangelize *and* evangelizing

² *Literally*, bruise.

intent that we should not lust after evil things, as they also lusted.

7 Neither be ye idolaters, as were some of them; as it is written, The people sat down to eat and drink, and rose up to play.

8 Neither let us commit fornication, as some of them committed, and fell in one day three and twenty thousand.

9 Neither let us tempt the Lord, as some of them tempted, and were destroyed by the serpents.

10 Neither murmur ye, as some of them murmured, and were destroyed by the destroyer.

11 But all these things happened unto them by way of example: and they were written for our admonition, upon whom the ends of the world are come.

12 Wherefore let him that thinketh he standeth take heed lest he fall.

13 There hath no temptation taken you but such as is common to man: but God is faithful, who will not suffer you to be tempted above that ye are able; but will with the temptation make also the way to escape, that ye may be able to bear it.

14 Wherefore, my beloved, flee from idolatry.

15 I speak as to wise men; judge ye what I say.

16 The cup of blessing which we bless, is it not the participation of the blood of Christ? The bread which we break, is it not the participation of the body of Christ?

17 Because we being many are one bread, one body: for we all partake of that one bread.

18 Behold Israel after the flesh: are not they which eat the sacrifices partakers with the altar?

19 What do I say then? that that which is sacrificed to idols is any thing, or that an idol is any thing?

20 Nay; but that the things which they sacrifice, they sacrifice to devils, and not to God: and I would not that ye should be partakers with devils.

21 Ye cannot drink the cup of the Lord, and the cup of devils: ye cannot partake of the Lord's table, and of the table of devils.

22 What? do we provoke the Lord to jealousy? are we stronger than he?

23 All things are lawful, but not all things are expedient: all things are lawful, but not all things edify.

24 Let no man seek his own, but his neighbour's good.

25 Whatever is sold in the shambles, eat, asking no question, for conscience sake:

26 For the earth is the Lord's, and the fulness thereof.

27 If any of the unbelievers inviteth you, and ye are disposed to go; whatever is set before you, eat, asking no question, for conscience sake.

28 But if any man say unto you, This hath been offered in sacrifice, eat not, for his sake

that shewed it, and for conscience sake.[1]

29 Conscience, I say, not thine own, but the other man's; for why is my liberty to be judged by another conscience [than mine own]?

30 If I partake thankfully, why am I to be evil spoken of for that for which I give thanks?

31 Whether then ye eat, or drink, or do any thing whatsoever, do all to the glory of God.

32 Give none occasion of stumbling, neither to Jews, nor to Gentiles, nor to the church of God:

33 Even as I also please all men in all things, not seeking mine own profit, but that of the many, that they may be saved.

CHAPTER XI.

BE ye followers of me, even as I also am of Christ.

2 ¶ But I praise you, brethren, that ye remember me in all things, and keep the traditions, according as I delivered them to you.

3 Now I would have you know, that the head of every man is Christ; and the head of the woman is the man; and the head of Christ is God.

4 Every man praying or prophesying, having his head covered, dishonoureth his head.

5 But every woman praying or prophesying with her head uncovered dishonoureth her head: for it is one and the same thing as if she were shaven.

6 For if a woman is not covered, let her also be shorn: but if it be a shame for a woman to be shorn or shaven, let her be covered.

7 For a man indeed ought not to cover his head, forasmuch as he is the image and glory of God: but the woman is the glory of the man.

8 For the man is not from the woman; but the woman from the man.

9 For neither was the man created for the woman's sake; but the woman for the man's.

10 For this cause ought the woman to have [2][the token of] power on her head because of the angels.

11 Nevertheless neither is the man without the woman, neither the woman without the man, in the Lord.

12 For even as the woman is from the man, so also is the man by the woman; but all things from God.

13 Judge in your own selves: is it seemly for a woman to pray unto God uncovered?

14 Doth not even nature itself teach you, that, if a man have long hair, it is a disgrace unto him,

15 But if a woman have long hair, it is a glory to her? for her hair is given her for a covering.

16 But if any man seemeth to be contentious, we have no such custom, nor yet the churches of God.

17 ¶ Now this precept I give unto you not praising you; because ye come together not for the better, but for the worse.

18 For in the first place, when

---

[1] *The quotation, which is in the Authorized Version repeated here, is omitted in all the ancient authorities.*

[2] *Not expressed in the original.*

ye come together in assembly, I hear that divisions exist among you; and I partly believe it.

19 For there must also be heresies among you, that they [also] which are approved may be made manifest among you.

20 When then ye come together to one place, ¹there is no eating of the Lord's Supper.

21 For in eating each one taketh before another his own supper: and one is hungry, and another is drunken.

22 What? have ye not houses to eat and to drink in? or despise ye the church of God, and put them to shame that have not? What am I to say to you? shall I praise you in this? I praise you not.

23 For I received from the Lord that which I also delivered unto you, That the Lord Jesus in the night in which he was betrayed took bread:

24 And having given thanks, he brake it, and said, ²This is my body, which is ³for you: this do in remembrance of me.

25 After the same manner the cup also, after they had supped, saying, This cup is the new covenant in my blood: this do, as oft as ye drink it, in remembrance of me.

26 For as often as ye eat this bread, and drink ⁴the cup, ye declare the Lord's death till he come.

27 Wherefore whosoever eateth ⁴the bread, or drinketh the cup of the Lord, unworthily, shall be guilty of the body and the blood of the Lord.

28 But let a man examine himself, and so let him eat of the bread, and drink of the cup.

29 For he that eateth and ⁵drinketh, eateth and drinketh judgment to himself, if he discern not the ⁶body.

30 For this cause many are weak and sickly among you, and many fall asleep.

31 But if we duly discerned ourselves, we should not be judged.

32 But when we are judged, we are chastened by the Lord, that we may not be condemned with the world.

33 Wherefore, my brethren, when ye come together to eat, tarry one for another.

34 If any man be hungry, let him eat at home; that ye come not together unto judgment. And the rest will I set in order when I come.

CHAPTER XII.

NOW concerning spiritual gifts, brethren, I would not have you ignorant.

2 Ye know that ⁷when ye were Gentiles, ye were carried away unto the dumb idols, even as ye might be led.

---

¹ *Or*, it is not to eat.
² Take, eat, *is omitted by all the most ancient MSS.*
³ *Some MSS. supply* given, some broken: *but the most ancient have no word.*
⁴ *So all the most ancient MSS.*
⁵ *The word* unworthily *is spurious, not occurring in the most ancient MSS., and having found its way into the text by repetition from verse* 27.
⁶ *The word* Lord's *is omitted by the most ancient MSS.*
⁷ *Such is the reading of all the most ancient MSS.*

3 Wherefore I give you to understand that no man speaking in the Spirit of God saith Jesus is accursed: and no man is able to say Jesus is the Lord, but in the Holy Spirit.

4 Now there are diversities of gifts, but the same Spirit.

5 And there are diversities of ministrations, and the same Lord.

6 And there are diversities of operations, and the same God which worketh all in all men.

7 But to each is given the manifestation of the Spirit for profit.

8 For to one is given through the Spirit the word of wisdom; to another the word of knowledge according to the same Spirit;

9 To another faith, in the same Spirit; to another gifts of healings in the ¹one Spirit;

10 To another operations of miraculous powers; to another prophecy; to another discernings of spirits; to another divers kinds of tongues; to another interpretation of tongues;

11 But all these worketh the one and selfsame Spirit, dividing severally to each man as he willeth.

12 For even as the body is one, and hath many members, and all the members of the ²body, though they be many, are one body: so also is Christ.

13 For in one Spirit also we were all baptized into one body, whether Jews or Greeks, whether bondmen or free; and were all made to drink of one Spirit.

14 For the body also is not one member, but many.

15 If the foot should say, Because I am not a hand, I am not of the body; is it therefore not of the body?

16 And if the ear should say, Because I am not an eye, I am not of the body; is it therefore not of the body?

17 If the whole body were an eye, where were the hearing? If the whole were hearing, where were the smelling?

18 But now hath God set the members each of them severally in the body, as he pleased.

19 And if they all were one member, where were the body?

20 But now are there many members, yet but one body.

21 And the eye cannot say unto the hand, I have no need of thee: nor again the head to the feet, I have no need of you.

22 Nay, much more those members of the body which seem to be more feeble, are necessary:

23 And those which we think to be less honourable parts of the body, upon them we bestow more abundant honour; and our uncomely parts have more abundant comeliness;

24 But our comely parts have no need. Howbeit God hath tempered the body together, giving more abundant honour to the part which lacketh:

25 That there should be no schism in the body; but that the members should have the same care one in behalf of another.

---

¹ *So the principal oldest MSS.*
² *One is omitted by almost all the most ancient MSS.*

26 And if one member suffereth, all the members suffer with it; or one member is honoured, all the members rejoice with it.

27 Now ye are the body of Christ, and severally members thereof.

28 And God hath set some in the church, first apostles, secondly prophets, thirdly teachers, then miraculous powers, then gifts of healings, helpings, governings, divers kinds of tongues.

29 Are all apostles? are all prophets? are all teachers? are all [1][workers of] miracles?

30 Have all gifts of healings? do all speak with tongues? do all interpret?

31 But desire earnestly the greatest gifts: and moreover I shew unto you [2]a more excellent way.

CHAPTER XIII.

THOUGH I speak with the tongues of men and of angels, yet have not love, I am become as sounding brass, or a tinkling cymbal.

2 And though I have the gift of prophecy, and understand all mysteries, and all knowledge; and though I have all faith, so as to remove mountains, yet have not love, I am nothing.

3 And though I give away all my goods in food, and though I give up my body [3]that I may be burned, yet have not love, it profiteth me nothing.

[1] *Not expressed in the original.*
[2] *Literally*, an eminently excellent way.
[3] *Or* that I may boast.

4 Love is long suffering, is kind; love envieth not; love vaunteth not itself, is not puffed up,

5 Doth not behave itself unseemly, seeketh not its own, is not easily provoked, imputeth not the evil;

6 Rejoiceth not at unrighteousness, but rejoiceth with the truth;

7 Beareth all things, believeth all things, hopeth all things, endureth all things.

8 Love never faileth: but whether there be prophesyings, they shall be done away; whether there be tongues, they shall cease; whether there be knowledge, it shall be done away.

9 For we know in part, and we prophesy in part.

10 But when that which is perfect is come, that which is in part shall be done away.

11 When I was a child, I spake as a child, I thought as a child, I reasoned as a child: now that I am become a man, I have done away the things of the child.

12 For now we see in a glass, obscurely; but then face to face: now I know in part; but then I shall know fully even as also I was fully known.

13 But now there abideth faith, hope, love, these three; and the greatest of these is love.

CHAPTER XIV.

FOLLOW after love, yet desire earnestly spiritual gifts, but chiefly that ye may prophesy.

2 For he that speaketh in an [unknown]¹ tongue speaketh not unto men, but unto God : for no one understandeth [him], but in the spirit he speaketh mysteries.

3 But he that prophesieth speaketh unto men edification, and exhortation, and comfort.

4 He that speaketh in a tongue edifieth himself ; but he that prophesieth edifieth the church.

5 Howbeit I wish you all to speak with tongues, but rather that ye should prophesy : for greater is he that prophesieth than he that speaketh with tongues, except he interpret, that the church may receive edification.

6 But now, brethren, if I come unto you speaking with tongues, what shall I profit you, except I shall speak to you either in revelation, or in knowledge, or in prophesying, or in teaching ?

7 And things without life giving sound, whether pipe or harp, yet if they give no distinction in the sounds, how shall that be known which is piped or harped ?

8 For if the trumpet also give an uncertain sound, who shall prepare himself for war ?

9 So likewise ye, if ye utter not by the tongue words easy to be understood, how shall that be known which is spoken ? for ye will be speaking into the air.

10 There are, it may be, so many kinds of voices in the world, and none is without signification.

11 If then I know not the meaning of the voice, I shall be unto him that speaketh a barbarian, and he that speaketh shall be a barbarian unto me.

12 Even so ye, forasmuch as ye are earnestly desirous of spiritual gifts, seek them, that ye may abound in them, to the edification of the church.

13 Wherefore let him that speaketh in a tongue pray that he may interpret.

14 For if I pray in a tongue, my spirit prayeth, but my understanding is unfruitful.

15 What is it then ? I will pray with my spirit, but I will pray with my understanding also : I will sing with my spirit, but I will sing with my understanding also.

16 Else if thou shalt bless with the spirit, how shall he that is in the situation of a private person say the Amen at thy giving of thanks, seeing he knoweth not what thou sayest ?

17 For thou verily givest thanks well, but the other is not edified.

18 I thank ²God, I speak in ³a tongue more than ye all :

19 Yet in the assembly I had rather speak five words with my understanding, that I may instruct others also, than ten thousand words in a tongue.

20 Brethren, be not children

¹ *Not expressed in the original.*
² *My is omitted by all the most ancient authorities.*
³ *The oldest MSS. are divided here: but the reading in the text is the most probable.*

in your understanding: howbeit in malice be as babes, but in your understanding be full grown men.

21 In the law it is written, With men of other tongues and with lips of ¹others will I speak unto this people; and yet for all that will they not hear me, saith the Lord.

22 So then the tongues are for a sign, not to them that believe, but to unbelievers: but prophesying is not for unbelievers, but for them that believe.

23 If therefore the whole church be met together, and all speak with tongues, and there come in private persons, or unbelievers, will they not say that ye are mad?

24 But if all prophesy, and there come in an unbeliever or a private person, he is convicted by all: he is judged by all:

25 ²The secrets of his heart are made manifest; and so falling down on his face he will worship God, declaring that God is in you of a truth.

26 How is it then, brethren? whenever ye come together, each one of you hath a psalm, hath a doctrine, hath a revelation, hath a tongue, hath an interpretation. Let all things be done unto edification.

27 If any speaketh in a tongue, let it be by two, or at the most by three, and that in turn; and let one interpret.

28 But if there be no interpreter, let him keep silence in the church; and let him speak to himself, and to God.

29 Of prophets let two or three speak, and let the others judge.

30 But if a revelation be made to another sitting by, let the first hold his peace.

31 For ye can all prophesy one by one, that all may learn, and all may be comforted.

32 Moreover the spirits of prophets are subject to the prophets.

33 For God is not a God of confusion, but of peace, as in all the churches of the saints.

34 ¶ Let your women keep silence in the churches: for it is not permitted unto them to speak, but to be in subjection, as the law also saith.

35 And if they wish to learn any thing, let them ask their own husbands at home: for it is a shame for ³a woman to speak in the church.

36 ¶ What? did the word of God come forth from you? or came it unto you alone?

37 If any man thinketh himself to be a prophet, or spiritual, let him acknowledge that the things that I write unto you are the Lord's ⁴commandment.

38 But if any man is ignorant, let him be ignorant.

39 Wherefore, brethren, earnestly desire to prophesy, and forbid not to speak with tongues.

40 But let all things be done decently and in order.

---

¹ *So the oldest MSS.*
² *And thus is omitted by all the oldest authorities.*
³ *So the principal oldest MSS.*
⁴ *So the principal oldest MSS.: some omit* commandment.

CHAPTER XV.

NOW I make known unto you, brethren, the gospel which I preached unto you, which also ye received, wherein also ye stand;

2 By which also ye are being saved, if ye hold fast the words in which I preached it unto you, unless ye believed in vain.

3 For I delivered unto you first of all that which I also received, that Christ died for our sins according to the scriptures;

4 And that he was buried, and that he is risen the third day according to the scriptures:

5 And that he appeared to Cephas, then to the twelve:

6 After that, he appeared to above five hundred brethren at once; of whom the greater part remain unto this present, but some are fallen asleep.

7 After that, he appeared to James; then to all the apostles.

8 And last of all he appeared to me also, as to the one born ¹out of due time.

9 For I am the least of the apostles, that am not meet to be called an apostle, because I persecuted the church of God.

10 But by the grace of God I am what I am: and his grace which was ²[shewed] toward me was not in vain; but I laboured more abundantly than they all: yet not I, but the grace of ³God with me.

11 Whether then it were I or they, so we preach, and so ye believed.

12 But if Christ is preached that he is risen from the dead, how say some among you that there is no resurrection of the dead?

13 But if there is no resurrection of the dead, then neither is Christ risen:

14 But if Christ is not risen, then vain is also ³our preaching, vain also is your faith.

15 Yea, and we are found false witnesses of God; because we testified concerning God that he raised up ⁴Christ: whom he raised not, if so be that the dead rise not.

16 For if the dead rise not, then neither is Christ risen:

17 And if Christ is not risen, your faith is to no purpose; ye are yet in your sins.

18 Then they also which fell asleep in Christ perished.

19 If only in this life we have had hope in Christ, we are of all men most to be pitied.

20 But now is Christ risen from the dead, ⁵the firstfruits of them that sleep.

21 For since by man is death, by man is also the resurrection of the dead.

22 For even as in Adam all die, so also in Christ shall all be made alive.

23 But each in his own order: the firstfruits Christ; afterward they that are Christ's, at his coming.

24 Then cometh the end, when he delivereth up the kingdom to God and the Father: when he shall have done away

---

¹ *Or,* abortively.
² *Not expressed in the original.*
³ *So the oldest MSS.*
⁴ *The Sinaitic MS. reads* his Christ.
⁵ *And* become *is omitted by all the oldest MSS.*

all rule and all authority and power.

25 For he must reign, till he hath put all his enemies under his feet.

26 The last enemy that is to be done away is death.

27 For, He hath put all things in subjection under his feet. But when he shall declare, that all things are put in subjection, it is manifest that [1][it is] with the exception of him, which did make all things subject unto him.

28 And when all things shall be subject unto him, then shall the Son also himself be subject unto him that made all things subject unto him, that God may be all in all.

29 Else what shall they do which are baptized on behalf of the dead? If the dead rise not at all, why are they then baptized for them?

30 Why do we also stand in jeopardy every hour?

31 Day by day I die; yea, by the glorying which I have of you in Christ Jesus our Lord!

32 If after the manner of men I fought with wild beasts at Ephesus, what doth it profit me? If the dead rise not, Let us eat and drink; for to-morrow we die.

33 Be not deceived: " Evil communications corrupt good manners."

34 Awake to soberness righteously, and sin not; for some are in ignorance of God: I speak this to your shame.

35 But some man will say, How are the dead to rise? and with what kind of body are they to come?

36 Thou fool, that which thou thyself sowest is not quickened, except it die:

37 And that which thou sowest, thou sowest not the body that shall be, but a bare grain of wheat, it may be, or of some other [grain]:

38 But God giveth it a body according as he pleased, and to each kind of seed a body of its own.

39 All flesh is not the same flesh: but there is one flesh of men, another flesh of beasts, another flesh of birds, and another of fishes.

40 There are also celestial bodies, and bodies terrestrial: but the glory of the celestial is one, and the glory of the terrestrial is another.

41 There is one glory of the sun, and another glory of the moon, and another glory of the stars: for star differeth from star in glory.

42 So also is the resurrection of the dead. It is sown in corruption; it riseth in incorruption:

43 It is sown in dishonour; it riseth in glory: it is sown in weakness; it riseth in power:

44 It is sown a natural body; it riseth a spiritual body. [2]If there is a natural body, there is also a spiritual.

45 So also it is written, The first man Adam was made a living soul; the last Adam, a lifegiving spirit.

46 Howbeit the spiritual is

[1] *Not expressed in the original.*
[2] *If is inserted by all the oldest MSS., and* body *omitted.*

not first, but the natural; and afterward the spiritual.

47 The first man is of the earth, earthy: the second man is ¹from heaven.

48 As is the earthy, such are they also that are earthy: and as is the heavenly, such are they also that are heavenly.

49 And even as we bore the image of the earthy, ²we shall also bear the image of the heavenly.

50 But this I say, brethren, that flesh and blood cannot inherit the kingdom of God; neither doth corruption inherit incorruption.

51 Behold, I tell you a mystery; ³We shall not all sleep, but we shall all be changed,

52 In a moment, in the twinkling of an eye, at the last trump: for the trumpet shall sound, and the dead shall be raised incorruptible, and we shall be changed.

53 For this corruptible must put on incorruption, and this mortal must put on immortality.

54 But when this corruptible shall have put on incorruption, and this mortal shall have put on immortality, then shall be brought to pass the saying that is written, Death is swallowed up in victory.

55 O death, where is thy sting? O ⁴death, where is thy victory?

56 Now the sting of death is sin; and the strength of sin is the law.

57 But thanks be to God, which giveth us the victory through our Lord Jesus Christ.

58 Wherefore, my beloved brethren, be ye stedfast, unmoveable, always abounding in the work of the Lord, knowing that your labour is not vain in the Lord.

CHAPTER XVI.

NOW concerning the collection for the saints, as I gave order to the churches of Galatia, even so do ye also.

2 Upon the first day of the week let each one of you lay by him in store whatsoever he be prospered in, that there be no collections when I come.

3 And when I am come, whomsoever ye shall approve, them will I send with letters to carry your liberality unto Jerusalem.

4 But if it be worth while that I go also, they shall go with me.

5 Now I will come unto you, when I shall have passed through Macedonia; for I pass through Macedonia:

6 But it may be that I shall abide, or even winter with you, that ye may set me forward on my journey whithersoever I go.

7 For I do not wish to see

---

¹ The Lord *is omitted by the oldest MSS.*

² *Most of the ancient MSS. read* let us also bear; *but the Vatican MS. and ancient Syriac version read as in the text.*

³ *There is great variation of reading here. Several of the most ancient MSS., including the Sinaitic, read,* We shall all sleep, but we shall not all be changed. *But the Vatican MS. and the ancient Syriac version read as in our text.*

⁴ *So all the oldest MSS.*

you now in passing; ¹for I hope to tarry some time with you, if the Lord permit.

8 But I shall tarry at Ephesus until Pentecost.

9 For a great and effectual door is opened unto me, and there are many adversaries.

10 But if Timothy come, see that he be with you without fear: for he worketh the work of the Lord, even as I.

11 Let no man therefore despise him: but set him forward in peace, that he may come unto me: for I look for him with the brethren.

12 But as touching our brother Apollos, I much besought him to come unto you with the brethren; and it was not at all his will to come now; but he will come when he shall have convenient time.

13 Watch ye, stand fast in the faith, quit you like men, be strong.

14 Let all you do be done in love.

15 Now I beseech you, brethren, (ye know the house of Stephanas, that it is the firstfruits of Achaia, and that they have set themselves to minister unto the saints,)

16 That ye also submit yourselves unto such, and to eveiy one that helpeth in the work, and laboureth.

17 I am glad of the coming of Stephanas and Fortunatus and Achaicus: for that which was lacking on your part they supplied.

18 For they refreshed my spirit and yours: acknowledge therefore them that are such.

19 The churches of Asia salute you. Aquila and Priscilla salute you much in the Lord, together with the church that is in their house.

20 All the brethren salute you. Salute ye one another with an holy kiss.

21 The salutation of me Paul with mine own hand.

22 If any man loveth not the ²Lord, let him be Anathema. ³The Lord cometh.

23 The grace of the ⁴Lord Jesus be with you.

24 My love be with you all in Christ Jesus. Amen.

¹ *So all the most ancient authorities.*

² *The words* Jesus Christ *are omitted by the oldest MSS.*

³ *This is expressed in the original, not in Greek, but in Hebrew (Aramaic), by* Maran Atha.

⁴ *The word* Christ *is omitted by the two oldest MSS*

THE SECOND EPISTLE OF PAUL THE APOSTLE
TO THE
CORINTHIANS.

CHAPTER I.

PAUL, an apostle of Jesus Christ through the will of God, and Timothy our brother, unto the church of God which is in Corinth, together with all the saints which are in all Achaia:

2 Grace be unto you and peace from God our Father, and the Lord Jesus Christ.

3 Blessed is the God and Father of our Lord Jesus Christ, the Father of mercies, and God of all comfort:

4 Who comforteth us in all our tribulation, that we may be able to comfort them which are in any tribulation, by the comfort wherewith we ourselves are comforted by God.

5 Because as the sufferings of Christ abound unto us, even so through Christ aboundeth also our comfort.

6 But whether we be in tribulation, it is for your comfort and salvation, which worketh in the endurance of the same sufferings which we also suffer (and our hope is stedfast for you); or whether we be comforted, it is for your comfort and salvation:

7 Knowing, that as ye are partakers of the sufferings, so are ye of the comfort also.

8 For we would not, brethren, have you ignorant of our tribulation which happened to us in Asia, that we were oppressed exceedingly, above [our] strength, insomuch that we despaired even of life:

9 Yea, we have had within our own selves the sentence of death, that we should not trust in ourselves, but in God which raiseth the dead:

10 Who delivered us from so great a death, and [1]will deliver us: in whom we trust that he will also yet deliver us;

11 Ye also helping together on our behalf by your supplication, that for the mercy bestowed upon us by means of many persons thanks may be given by many on our behalf.

12 For our glorying is this, the testimony of our conscience, that in [2]holiness and sincerity of God, not in fleshly wisdom, but in the grace of God, we had our conversation in the world, and more abundantly towards you.

13 For we write none other things unto you, than what ye read or even acknowledge, and I trust will acknowledge even to the end;

14 Even as also ye did acknowledge us in part, that we are your boast, even as ye also

[1] *So the principal most ancient MSS.*
[2] *So all the most ancient MSS.*

are ours, in the day of the Lord Jesus.

15 And in this confidence I was minded to come unto you before, that ye might have a second benefit ;

16 And by you to pass into Macedonia, and from Macedonia to come again unto you, and by you to be brought on my way toward Judæa.

17 When therefore I was thus minded, did I act with lightness of mind ? or the things that I purpose, do I purpose according to the flesh, that with me there should be the yea yea, and the nay nay?

18 But God is faithful, that our word unto you [1]is not yea and nay.

19 For the Son of God, Jesus Christ, who was preached among you by us, by me and Silvanus and Timothy, was not yea and nay, but is made yea in him.

20 For how many soever be the promises of God, in him is the yea ; [2]wherefore through him is the Amen, for glory unto God by us.

21 Now he which stablisheth us with you in Christ, and anointed us, is God ;

22 Who also sealed us, and gave the earnest of the Spirit in our hearts.

23 But I call God for a witness upon my soul, that to spare you I forbore coming unto Corinth.

24 Not that we exercise dominion over your faith, but are helpers of your joy : for by faith ye stand.

CHAPTER II.

BUT I determined this with myself, that I would not come again to you in sorrow.

2 For if I make you sorry, who then is he that maketh me glad, but the same which is made sorry by me ?

3 And this same thing wrote I unto you, in order that when I came, I might not have sorrow from them of whom I ought to have joy ; having confidence in you all, that my joy is the joy of you all.

4 For out of much tribulation and anguish of heart I wrote unto you with many tears ; not that ye should be made sorry, but that ye might know the love which I have more abundantly unto you.

5 But if any hath caused sorrow, he hath not caused sorrow to me, but in part (that I press not too heavily) to you all.

6 Sufficient to such a man is this punishment, which was inflicted by the more part [of you].

7 So that contrariwise ye ought rather to forgive and comfort him, lest by any means such an one should be swallowed up with the increase of sorrow.

8 Wherefore I beseech you to confirm your love toward him.

9 For to this end also did I write, that I might know the proof of you, whether ye be obedient in all things.

---

[1] *So all the most ancient MSS.*
[2] *So the chief most ancient MSS.*

10 To whom ye forgive any thing, I forgive also: for indeed what I have forgiven, if I have forgiven any thing, for your sakes forgave I it in the person of Christ;

11 That no advantage be gained over us by Satan: for we are not ignorant of his devices.

12 Furthermore, when I came to Troas for the gospel of Christ, and a door was opened unto me in the Lord,

13 I had no rest for my spirit, because I found not Titus my brother: but taking my leave of them, I went forth into Macedonia.

14 But thanks be unto God, which at all times leadeth us in triumph in Christ, and maketh manifest by us in every place the savour of the knowledge of him.

15 Because we are unto God a sweet savour of Christ, among them that are being saved, and among them that are perishing:

16 To the one a savour of death unto death; to the other a savour of life unto life. And for these things who is sufficient?

17 For we are not as the many, adulterating the word of God: but as of sincerity, but as of God, in the sight of God speak we in Christ.

CHAPTER III.

ARE we beginning again to recommend ourselves? or need we, as some others, epistles of recommendation to you, or from you?

2 Ye are our epistle written in our hearts, known and read of all men:

3 Being manifestly shewn to be an epistle of Christ ministered by us, written not with ink, but with the Spirit of the living God; not on tables of stone, but on fleshly tables, [your] ¹hearts.

4 Such confidence have we through Christ toward God.

5 Not that we are sufficient to think any thing of ourselves as from ourselves; but our sufficiency is from God;

6 Who also made us sufficient as ministers of the new covenant; not of the letter, but of the spirit: for the letter killeth, but the spirit giveth life.

7 But if the ministration of death, [written] in letters, engraven on stones, was in glory, so that the children of Israel could not look stedfastly on the face of Moses for the glory of his countenance, a glory which was to be done away:

8 How shall not the ministration of the spirit still more be in glory?

9 For if the ministration of condemnation was glory, much more doth the ministration of righteousness abound in glory.

10 For indeed that which hath been made glorious hath not been made glorious in this respect, by reason of the superior glory.

11 For if that which is being done away was with glory, much more that which abideth is in glory.

12 Seeing then that we have

¹ *So all the most ancient MSS*

such an hope, we use great openness of speech:

13 And not as Moses put a vail over his face, that the children of Israel might not look stedfastly upon the end of that which was being done away.

14 But their understandings were hardened: for until this very day, at the reading of the old covenant, the same vail remaineth, it not being discovered that it is done away in Christ.

15 But even unto this day, when Moses is read, a vail lieth upon their heart.

16 But whensoever it turneth to the Lord, the vail is taken away.

17 Now the Lord is the Spirit: and where the Spirit of the Lord is, there is liberty.

18 But we all, with unvailed face beholding in a mirror the glory of the Lord, are being transfigured into the same image from glory to glory, even as by the Lord the Spirit.

CHAPTER IV.

FOR this cause, seeing we have this ministry even as we received mercy, we [1]shrink not back;

2 But have renounced the hidden things of shame, not walking in craftiness, nor handling the word of God deceitfully; but by the manifestation of the truth recommending ourselves to every man's conscience in the sight of God.

3 And even if our gospel is vailed, it is vailed to them that are perishing:

4 In whom the god of this world hath blinded the understandings of the unbelieving, that the illumination of the gospel of the glory of Christ, who is the image of God, should not shine [2]forth.

5 For we preach not ourselves, but Christ Jesus as Lord; and ourselves as your servants for Jesus' sake.

6 Because it is God, who [3]said Out of darkness light shall shine, that shined in our hearts, to give the light of the knowledge of the glory of God in the face of Christ.

7 But we have this treasure in earthen vessels, that the exceeding greatness of the power may be God's, and not of us;

8 Being troubled on every side, yet not distressed; perplexed, yet not in despair;

9 Persecuted, yet not forsaken; struck down, yet not destroyed;

10 Always bearing about in the body the dying of [4]Jesus, that the life also of Jesus may be made manifest in our body.

11 For we which live are alway being delivered unto death for Jesus' sake, that the life also of Jesus may be made manifest in our mortal flesh.

12 So then death worketh in us, but life in you.

13 But having the same spirit of faith, according to that

---

[1] *So most of the oldest MSS.: the others having as in A.V. It is a difference of one letter only in the Greek.*

[2] *Unto them is omitted in all the most ancient MSS.*

[3] *So most of the oldest MSS.*

[4] *The Lord is omitted in all the most ancient authorities*

which is written, I believed, and therefore did I speak ; we also believe, and therefore also speak ;

14 Knowing that he which raised up the Lord Jesus shall raise up us also ¹with Jesus, and shall present us with you.

15 For all things are for your sakes, that grace, being multiplied by means of the greater number, may make the thanksgiving abound unto the glory of God.

16 Wherefore we ²shrink not back ; but though our outward man is decaying, yet our inward man is being renewed day by day.

17 For our present light affliction worketh for us more and more exceedingly an eternal weight of glory ;

18 While we look not at the things which are seen, but at the things which are not seen : for the things which are seen are for a time ; but the things which are not seen are eternal.

CHAPTER V.

FOR we know that if the earthly tabernacle wherein we dwell be dissolved, we have a building from God, a dwelling not made with hands, eternal in the heavens.

2 For in this we groan, longing to clothe ourselves with our house which is from heaven :

3 Seeing that we shall verily be found clothed, not naked.

4 For also we that are in this tabernacle do groan, being burdened : because we desire not to be unclothed, but clothed upon, that what is mortal may be swallowed up of life.

5 But he that wrought us unto this very thing is God, who ³gave unto us the earnest of the Spirit.

6 Being then always confident, and knowing that, whilst we are in our home in the body, we are away from our home in the Lord,

7 (For we walk by faith, not by appearance,)

8 We are still confident, and well content rather to go from our home in the body, and to come to our home with the Lord.

9 Wherefore also it is our aim, that, whether present or absent, we may be well pleasing unto him.

10 For we must all be made manifest before the judgment seat of Christ ; that each one may receive the things [done] in the body, according to the things that he did, whether it were good or bad.

11 Knowing then the fear of the Lord, we persuade men, but unto God we are already made manifest ; and I hope that we are made manifest in your consciences also.

12 ⁴We are not recommending ourselves again unto you, but are giving you occasion of glorying on our behalf, that ye may have it against them which glory in face, and not in heart.

13 For whether we have been

---

¹ *So all the oldest MSS.*
² *See on ver. 1.*
³ Also *is omitted by all the oldest authorities.*
⁴ For *is omitted in all the oldest MSS.*

beside ourselves, it was for God: or whether we be of sound mind, it is for you.

14 For Christ's love constraineth us, having judged this, that one died for all, therefore all died:

15 And he died for all, that they which live should live no longer unto themselves, but unto him which died and rose again for them.

16 So that we henceforth know no man after the flesh: if even we have known Christ after the flesh, yet now know we him no more.

17 So that if any man is in Christ, [he is] a new creature: the old things are passed away; behold, ¹they are become new.

18 And all things are of God, who reconciled us to himself through Christ, and gave unto us the ministration of the reconciliation;

19 To wit, that God was reconciling the world unto himself in Christ, not reckoning unto them their trespasses; and put into our hands the word of the reconciliation.

20 On Christ's behalf then we are ambassadors, as though God were intreating by us: we pray on Christ's behalf, Be reconciled to God.

21 ²Him who knew not sin he made [to be] sin for us; that we might become the righteousness of God in him.

CHAPTER VI.

AND as workers together with him, we also intreat

¹ *So all the oldest MSS.*
² *For is omitted in all the oldest MSS.*

that ye receive not the grace of God in vain.

2 (For he saith, I heard thee in an accepted time, and in a day of salvation did I succour thee: behold, now is the well-accepted time; behold, now is the day of salvation.)

3 Giving no cause of offence in any thing, that the ministry be not blamed:

4 But as God's ministers recommending ourselves in every thing, in much patience, in tribulations, in necessities, in distresses,

5 In stripes, in imprisonments, in tumults, in labours, in watchings, in fastings;

6 In pureness, in knowledge, in longsuffering, in kindness, in the Holy Ghost, in love unfeigned,

7 In the word of truth, in the power of God, through the weapons of righteousness on the right hand and on the left,

8 Through glory and dishonour, through evil report and good report: as deceivers, and true;

9 As unknown, and well known; as dying, and, behold, we live; as chastened, and not killed;

10 As sorrowful, yet alway rejoicing; as poor, yet making many rich; as having nothing, and possessing all things.

11 Our mouth is open unto you, O Corinthians, our heart is enlarged.

12 Ye are not straitened in us, but ye are straitened in your own hearts.

13 Now as a recompence in the same kind, (I speak as unto

my children,) be ye enlarged also yourselves.

14 Be not yoked unequally with unbelievers: for what fellowship is there between righteousness and iniquity? or what communion hath light with darkness?

15 And what concord hath Christ with Belial? or what part hath a believer with an unbeliever?

16 And what agreement hath the temple of God with idols? for ye are the temple of the living God; even as God said, I will dwell in them, and will walk among them; and I will be their God, and they shall be to me a people.

17 Wherefore come ye out from among them, and be separated, saith the Lord, and touch not any thing unclean; and I will receive you,

18 And I will be unto you a Father, and ye shall be unto me sons and daughters, saith the Lord Almighty.

CHAPTER VII.

HAVING therefore these promises, dearly beloved, let us cleanse ourselves from every pollution of flesh and spirit, perfecting holiness in the fear of God.

2 Receive us; we wronged no man, we ruined no man, we defrauded no man.

3 I speak it not for condemnation: for I have said before, that ye are in our hearts to die with you and to live with you.

4 Great is my confidence toward you, great is my boasting on your behalf: I am filled with comfort, I overflow with joy in all our tribulation.

5 For indeed, when we came into Macedonia, our flesh had no rest, but we were troubled on every side; without [were] fightings, within [were] fears.

6 Nevertheless he that comforteth those that are cast down, even God, comforted us in the coming of Titus;

7 And not in his coming only, but also in the comfort wherewith he was comforted in you, telling us your longing desire, your lamentation, your zeal for me; so that I rejoiced the more.

8 Because though I made you sorry with my letter, I do not repent it, though I did repent it: for I perceive that that letter did make you sorry, though it was but for a season.

9 Now I rejoice, not that ye were made sorry, but that ye were made sorry unto repentance: for ye were made sorry after a godly manner, to the end that ye might in nothing receive damage from us.

10 For godly sorrow worketh repentance unto salvation never to be regretted: but the sorrow of the world worketh out death.

11 For behold this selfsame thing, that ye were made sorry after a godly manner, what carefulness it wrought in you, yea, what clearing of yourselves, yea, what indignation, yea, what fear, yea, what longing desire, yea, what zeal, yea, what exacting of punishment! In every thing ye approved yourselves to be pure in the matter.

12 Wherefore, though I wrote unto you, [I wrote] not for his cause that did the wrong, nor for his cause that suffered wrong, but that your ¹earnest care for us might be made manifest unto you in the sight of God.

13 For this cause we have been comforted: but in ²our comfort we joyed the more exceedingly for the joy of Titus, because his spirit hath found refreshment from you all.

14 For if I have boasted at all to him of you, I was not put to shame; but as we spake all things to you in truth, even so our boasting before Titus was found to be truth.

15 And his affection is more abundantly toward you, whilst he remembereth the obedience of you all, how with fear and trembling ye received him.

16 I rejoice that in every thing I am of good courage concerning you.

CHAPTER VIII.

MOREOVER, brethren, we make known unto you the grace of God which hath been bestowed on the churches of Macedonia;

2 How that in much trial of affliction the abundance of their joy and their deep poverty abounded unto the riches of their liberality.

3 For according to their power, I bear witness, yea, and beyond their power of their own accord,

4 Praying of us with much ³intreaty the grace and the participation in the ministering unto the saints:

5 And not as we expected, but their own selves gave they first to the Lord and to us by the will of God.

6 Insomuch that we exhorted Titus, that as he had before begun, so he would also complete among you this grace also.

7 But, as ye abound in every thing, in faith, and word, and knowledge, and all diligence, and in your love to us, see that ye abound in this grace also.

8 I speak not by way of command, but by means of the forwardness of others proving the sincerity of your love also.

9 For ye know the grace of our Lord Jesus Christ, that, though he was rich, yet for your sakes he became poor, that ye by his poverty might become rich.

10 And herein I give my opinion: for this is expedient for you, seeing that ye began before them, a year ago, not only to do, but also to be forward.

11 But now complete the doing also; that as there was the readiness of will, so also there may be the completion according to your means.

12 For if there is first the willing mind, it is favourably accepted according to that which ⁴it may have, not ac-

---

¹ *So all the most ancient authorities.*
² *So all the oldest MSS.*
³ *The sentence stands thus in all the ancient authorities.*
⁴ *A man is omitted by all the most ancient authorities.*

cording to that which it hath not.

13 For [it is] not that other men may be relieved, and ye burdened:

14 But that, by the rule of equality, at this present time your abundance may be a supply for their want, in order that their abundance also may be a supply for your want: that there may be equality:

15 As it is written, He that gathered much had nothing over; and he that gathered little had no lack.

16 But thanks be to God, which putteth the same earnest care for you into the heart of Titus:

17 In that he accepted indeed our exhortation; but being himself full of zeal, of his own accord he set forth unto you.

18 And together with him we sent the brother, whose praise in the gospel is throughout all the churches;

19 And not only so, but who was also chosen by the churches to be our fellow-traveller with this gift, which is administered by us; to the glory of the ¹Lord, and the furtherance of ¹our zeal:

20 Being careful of this, that no man should blame us in the matter of this abundance which is administered by us:

21 For we provide things honourable not only in the sight of the Lord, but also in the sight of men.

22 And we sent with them

¹ *Thus in all the oldest MSS.*

our brother, whom we have many times in many things proved to be diligent, but now much more diligent through the great confidence which he hath toward you.

23 Whether concerning Titus,—he is my partner and fellow-worker toward you: or our brethren,—they are apostles of the churches, and the glory of Christ.

24 Continue then to show unto them, in the face of the churches, the proof of your love, and of our boasting on your behalf.

CHAPTER IX.

FOR as touching the ministration for the saints, it is superfluous for me to write to you:

2 For I know your forwardness of mind, for which I boast of you to them of Macedonia, that Achaia hath been prepared a year ago; and your zeal stirred up very many of them.

3 Yet I sent the brethren, that our boast of you may not be made void in this respect; that, as I said, ye may be ready:

4 Lest haply, if any Macedonians come with me, and find you unprepared, we (not to say, ye) should be put to shame in this same confidence.²

5 I thought it necessary therefore to exhort the brethren, that they should go before unto you, and make up beforehand your promised blessing,

² *Of boasting is omitted by the principal most ancient MSS.*

that it may be ready, as matter of blessing, and not as matter of covetousness.

6 But [remember] this, He which soweth sparingly shall reap also sparingly; and he which soweth with blessings shall reap also with blessings.

7 Each man according as he purposeth in his heart; not grudgingly, or of necessity; for God loveth a cheerful giver.

8 And God is able to make every grace abound unto you; that ye, always having all sufficiency in every thing, may abound to every good work:

9 As it is written, He dispersed abroad; he gave to the poor: his righteousness remaineth for ever.

10 But he that supplieth seed to the sower and bread for eating, shall supply and multiply your seed sown, and increase the fruits of your righteousness;

11 Being enriched in every thing unto all liberality, which worketh through us thanksgiving to God.

12 Because the ministration of this service is not only supplying the wants of the saints, but is abounding also through many thanksgivings unto God;

13 While by the experience of this ministration they glorify God for the subjection of your confession unto the gospel of Christ, and for the liberality of your contribution unto them, and unto all;

14 Themselves also with prayer for you longing after you, by reason of the exceeding grace of God in you.

15 Thanks be unto God for his unspeakable gift.

CHAPTER X.

NOW I Paul myself intreat you by the meekness and gentleness of Christ, who in presence am lowly among you, but being absent am bold toward you:

2 But I beseech you, that I may not when I am present be bold with that confidence, wherewith I think to be bold against some, which think of us as if we were walking according to the flesh.

3 For though we walk in the flesh, we do not war according to the flesh:

4 (For the weapons of our warfare are not fleshly, but mighty before God to the casting down of strongholds;)

5 Casting down reasonings, and every high thing that is lifted up against the knowledge of God, and bringing every intent into captivity to the obedience of Christ;

6 And being in readiness to exact punishment for all disobedience, when your obedience shall be fulfilled.

7 Do ye look on things after the outward appearance? If any man trusteth to himself that he is Christ's, let him of himself again consider this, that even as he is Christ's, so also are we.[1]

8 For even if I should boast somewhat more abundantly of our authority, which the Lord gave us for building you up

[1] Christ's *is omitted in all the men ancient authorities.*

and not for casting you down, I shall not be ashamed:

9 That I may not seem as if I would terrify you by my letters.

10 For his letters, saith one, are weighty and strong; but his bodily presence is weak, and his speech contemptible.

11 Let such an one consider this, that, such as we are in word by letters, when we are absent, such are we also in deed when we are present.

12 For we make not bold to number ourselves or compare ourselves with some of them that commend themselves: but they measuring themselves among themselves, and comparing themselves with themselves, are not wise.

13 But we will not boast without measure, but according to the measure of the line which God apportioned to us as a measure to reach even unto you.

14 For we are not stretching ourselves beyond ¹[our measure], as if we reached not unto you: for even as far as unto you did we come in the gospel of Christ:

15 Not boasting without measure in other men's labours; but having hope, as your faith increaseth, to be enlarged among you according to our rule unto great abundance,

16 So as to preach the gospel in the regions beyond you, not to boast in another man's line of things made ready to our hand.

¹ *Not expressed in the original.*

17 But he that boasteth, let him boast in the Lord.

18 For not he that commendeth himself is approved, but he whom the Lord commendeth.

CHAPTER XI.

I WOULD that ye could bear with me a little in folly: but indeed ye do bear with me.

2 For I am jealous over you with a jealousy of God: for I betrothed you to one husband, to present you as a pure virgin to Christ.

3 But I fear, lest by any means, as the serpent beguiled Eve by his subtilty, so your minds should be corrupted from the ²simplicity and the purity that is toward Christ.

4 For if indeed he that cometh is preaching another Jesus, whom we preached not, or if ye are receiving another spirit, which ye received not, or another gospel, which ye accepted not, ye with reason ³bear with him.

5 For I reckon that I am not a whit behind those overmuch apostles.

6 But though I be a common man in my speech, yet am I not in my knowledge; but in every thing ⁴ did we make things manifest unto you before all men.

7 Did I commit an offence in abasing myself that ye might

² *So the majority of the most ancient MSS.*
³ *So the Vatican MS.: the reading varies.*
⁴ *So the two oldest MSS. The others differ widely.*

be exalted, in that I preached unto you the gospel of God without charge?

8 I robbed other churches, taking wages ¹[of them], that I might minister unto you.

9 And when I was present with you, and was in want, I was a burden to no man: for the brethren coming from Macedonia supplied my wants; and in every thing I kept myself from being burdensome unto you, and so will I keep myself.

10 The truth of Christ is in me, that this boasting shall not be shut ²against me in the regions of Achaia.

11 Wherefore? because I love you not? God knoweth.

12 But what I do, that I will do, that I may cut off the occasion of those who desire an occasion; that wherein they boast, they may be found even as we.

13 For such men are false apostles, deceitful workmen, transforming themselves into apostles of Christ.

14 And no marvel; for even Satan transformeth himself into an angel of light.

15 It is no great thing then if his ministers also transform themselves as ministers of righteousness; whose end shall be according to their works.

16 I say again, Let no man think me a fool; but if ye will think so, yet even as a fool receive me, that I too may boast myself a little.

¹ *Not expressed in the original.*
² *So all the great MSS.*

17 That which I speak, I speak not after the Lord, but as in foolishness, in this confidence of boasting.

18 Seeing that many boast after the flesh, I will boast also.

19 For ye bear with fools gladly, being ¹[yourselves] wise.

20 For ye bear with them, if a man bringeth you into bondage, if a man devoureth you, if a man seizeth you, if a man exalteth himself, if a man smiteth you on the face.

21 By way of disparagement I assume that we were weak. Howbeit whereinsoever any is bold, (I speak in foolishness,) I am bold also.

22 Are they Hebrews? so am I. Are they Israelites? so am I. Are they Abraham's seed? so am I.

23 Are they ministers of Christ? (I speak as beside myself) I am more; in labours more ²abundantly, in prisons more abundantly, in stripes above measure, in deaths oft.

24 Of the Jews five times received I forty stripes save one.

25 Thrice was I beaten with rods, once was I stoned, thrice I suffered shipwreck, a night and a day have I spent in the deep;

26 By journeyings often, by perils of rivers, by perils of robbers, by perils from my countrymen, by perils from the Gentiles, by perils in the city, by perils in the wilderness, by perils in the sea, by perils among false brethren;

² *So the oldest MSS.*

27 By weariness and painfulness, in watchings often, in hunger and thirst, in fastings often, in cold and nakedness.

28 Omitting what is besides, ¹my care day by day, my anxiety for all the churches.

29 Who is weak, and I am not weak? who is offended, and I myself burn not?

30 If I must needs boast, I will boast of the things which concern mine infirmities.

31 The God and Father of the Lord Jesus Christ, which is blessed for evermore, knoweth that I lie not.

32 In Damascus the governor under Aretas the king kept watch over the city of the Damascenes to apprehend me:

33 And through a window was I let down in a basket by the wall, and escaped his hands.

CHAPTER XII.

I ²MUST needs boast, though it is not expedient: but I will come to visions and revelations of the Lord.

2 I know a man in Christ, above fourteen years ago (whether in the body, I know not; or whether out of the body, I know not: God knoweth;) such an one caught up even unto the third heaven.

3 And I know such a man, (whether in the body, or apart from the body, I know not: God knoweth;)

4 That he was caught up into paradise, and heard unspeakable words, which it is not lawful for a man to utter.

5 Of such an one will I boast: but of myself I will not boast, save in my weaknesses.

6 For if I should desire to boast, I shall not be a fool; for I shall say the truth: but I forbear, lest any man should esteem of me above that which he seeth me to be, or heareth perchance from me.

7 And that I might not through the exceeding greatness of the revelations be exalted overmuch, there was given to me a thorn in my flesh, an angel of Satan, that he may buffet me, that I might not be exalted overmuch.

8 Concerning this I thrice besought the Lord, that he might depart from me.

9 And he said unto me, My grace is sufficient for thee: for ³[my] power is made perfect in weakness. Most gladly therefore will I rather boast in my infirmities, that the power of Christ may rest upon me.

10 Wherefore I am well content in infirmities, in insults, in necessities, in persecutions, in distresses, for Christ's sake: for when I am weak, then am I strong.

11 I am become a ⁴fool; ye compelled me: for I ought to have been commended by you: for in nothing came I behind those overmuch apostles, even though I am nothing.

---

¹ *So the most ancient MSS.*
² *So, or nearly so, the most ancient MSS.: but the reading is in great confusion.*
³ *Not expressed in the original.*
⁴ *In glorying is omitted by all the oldest MSS.*

12 Truly the signs of an apostle were wrought among you in all patience, in signs, and wonders, and mighty deeds.

13 For what is there wherein ye were inferior to the other churches, except that I myself was not a burden to you? forgive me this wrong.

14 Behold, the third time I am ready to come to you; and I will not be a burden to you: for I seek not yours, but you: for the children ought not to lay up for the parents, but the parents for the children.

15 Yet I very gladly will spend and be spent for your souls; though while I love you more abundantly, I am less loved.

16 But be it so, I myself did not burden you: nevertheless, being crafty, I caught you with guile.

17 Did I take advantage of you by any of them whom I have sent unto you?

18 I entreated Titus [1][to come unto you], and with him I sent our brother. Did Titus take any advantage of you? walked we not in the same Spirit? [1][walked we] not in the same steps?

19 Ye have been long [2]thinking that we are excusing ourselves unto you. We speak before God in Christ: but all we do, dearly beloved, is for your edifying.

20 For I fear, that, when I come, I may find you not such as I would, and that I may be found by you such as ye would not; lest there be strifes, envyings, wraths, self-seekings, slanderings, whisperings, swellings, tumults:

21 Lest, when I come again, my God will humble me among you, and I shall bewail many of those which have sinned already, and repented not of the uncleanness and fornication and lasciviousness which they committed.

CHAPTER XIII.

THIS third time I am coming to you. In the mouth of two witnesses and three shall every word be established.

2 I have said already, and now say beforehand, as when [I was] present the second time, so also now [3]in my absence to them which have sinned heretofore, and to all the rest, that, if I come again, I will not spare:

3 Since ye seek a proof of Christ that speaketh in me, who to you-ward is not weak, but is powerful in you.

4 For [4]indeed he was crucified from weakness, yet he liveth from the power of God. For we also are weak in him, yet we shall live with him from the power of God toward you.

5 Try your own selves, whether ye are in the faith; prove your own selves. Do ye not know your own selves, that Jesus Christ is in you? except indeed ye be reprobates.

[1] *Not expressed in the original.*
[2] *So the most ancient MSS.*
[3] I write *is omitted in all the most ancient MSS.*
[4] Though *is omitted by the most ancient MSS.*

6 But I trust that ye shall know that we are not reprobates.

7 Yet [1]we pray to God that ye do no evil; not that we should appear approved, but that ye should do that which is honest, though we be as reprobates.

8 For we can do nothing against the truth, but for the truth.

9 For we rejoice, when we are weak, and ye are strong: we also pray for this, even your perfection.

10 For this cause write I these things being absent, that I may not when present use sharpness, according to the power which the Lord hath given me for building up, and not for casting down.

11 Finally, brethren, rejoice, be made perfect, take comfort, be of one mind, be at peace; and the God of love and peace shall be with you.

12 Salute one another with an holy kiss.

13 All the saints salute you.

14 The grace of the Lord Jesus Christ, and the love of God, and the communion of the Holy Spirit, be with you all.[2]

[1] Thus all the most ancient MSS.
[2] Amen *is omitted by all the most ancient MSS.*

THE EPISTLE OF PAUL THE APOSTLE
TO THE
GALATIANS.

CHAPTER I.

PAUL, an apostle, not from men, neither by man, but by Jesus Christ, and God the Father, who raised him from the dead;

2 And all the brethren which are with me, unto the churches of Galatia:

3 Grace be unto you and peace from God the Father, and our Lord Jesus Christ,

4 Who gave himself for our sins, that he might deliver us out of the present evil world, according to the will of God and our Father:

5 To whom be the glory for ever and ever. Amen.

6 I marvel that ye are so soon removing from him that called you in the grace of Christ unto a different gospel:

7 Which is not another; only there be some that trouble you, and desire to pervert the gospel of Christ.

8 But even though we, or an angel from heaven, should preach unto you any gospel other than that which we preached unto you, let him be accursed.

9 As we have said before, even so now I say again, If

any man preacheth unto you any gospel other than that which ye received, let him be accursed.

10 For am I now persuading men, or God? or do I seek to please men? If I were still pleasing men, I should not be Christ's servant.

11 ¹But I certify you, brethren, concerning the gospel which was preached by me, that it is not after man.

12 For neither did I myself receive it from man, nor was I taught it ²[by man], but by revelation of Jesus Christ.

13 For ye heard of my former way of life in the Jewish religion, how that beyond measure I persecuted the church of God, and was destroying it.

14 And I made progress in the Jewish religion beyond many of mine own age among my countrymen, being more exceedingly zealous for the traditions of my fathers.

15 But when it pleased God, who set me apart from my mother's womb, and called me by his grace,

16 To reveal his Son in me, that I might preach him among the Gentiles; immediately I conferred not with flesh and blood:

17 Neither went I away to Jerusalem to them which were apostles before me; but I went away into Arabia, and returned back again unto Damascus.

¹ *Many of the ancient MSS. read* For.
² *Not expressed in the original, but implied by the construction.*

18 Then after three years I went up to Jerusalem to visit Cephas, and tarried with him fifteen days.

19 But other of the apostles saw I none, save James the brother of the Lord.

20 Now the things which I write unto you, behold, before God, I lie not.

21 Afterwards I came into the regions of Syria and Cilicia;

22 And I was unknown by face unto the churches of Judæa which were in Christ:

23 But they heard only, That our former persecutor is now preaching the faith which before he was destroying.

24 And they glorified God in me.

CHAPTER II.

THEN after fourteen years I went up again to Jerusalem with Barnabas, taking Titus also with me.

2 But I went up by revelation, and communicated unto them the gospel which I preach among the Gentiles, but privately to them which were of reputation, lest by any means I should be running, or have run, in vain.

3 Howbeit not even Titus, my companion, though he was a Greek, was compelled to be circumcised:

4 And that because of the false brethren secretly brought in, who came in by stealth to spy out our liberty which we have in Christ Jesus, that they might bring us into bondage:

5 To whom we did not give way by subjection, no, not for

an hour; that the truth of the gospel might abide with you.

6 But from these who seemed to be somewhat, whatsoever they were, it maketh no matter to me: God respecteth no man's person: they, I say, who seemed ¹[to be somewhat], imparted nothing unto me:

7 But on the contrary, when they saw that I was entrusted with the gospel of the uncircumcision, even as Peter was with the gospel of the circumcision;

8 (For he that wrought for Peter unto the apostleship of the circumcision, the same wrought for me also unto the Gentiles:)

9 And perceiving the grace that was given unto me, James, and Cephas, and John, who seemed to be pillars, gave to me and Barnabas the right hands of fellowship; that we ¹[should be apostles] unto the Gentiles, and they unto the circumcision.

10 Only that we should remember the poor; which very thing I was also forward to do.

11 But when ²Cephas came to Antioch, I withstood him to the face, because he was condemned.

12 For before that certain men came from James, he ate with the Gentiles: but when they came, he withdrew and separated himself, fearing them which were of the circumcision.

13 And the rest of the Jews also joined in his hypocrisy; insomuch that even Barnabas was carried away with them in their hypocrisy.

14 But when I saw that they were not walking uprightly according to the truth of the gospel, I said unto Cephas before them all, If thou, being a Jew, livest as a Gentile, and not as a Jew, ³how is it that thou compellest the Gentiles to keep the customs of the Jews?

15 We are Jews by nature, and not sinners of the Gentiles:

16 Knowing nevertheless that a man is not justified by the works of the law, save ¹[only] through faith in Jesus Christ, we also believed in Christ Jesus, that we might be justified by faith in Christ, and not by the works of the law: seeing that by the works of the law shall no flesh be justified.

17 But if, seeking to be justified in Christ, we ourselves also were found sinners, is not Christ a minister of sin? God forbid.

18 For if I build up again the very things which I destroyed, I prove myself a transgressor.

19 For I myself through the law died unto the law, that I might live unto God.

20 I have been crucified with Christ: and it is no longer I that live, but Christ that liveth in me: yea, the life which I now live in the flesh I live in the faith of the Son of God, who loved me, and gave himself for me.

---

¹ *Not expressed in the original.*
² *So all the oldest authorities, and in ver. 14 also.*
³ *So all the oldest authorities*

21 I do not make void the grace of God: for if righteousness be by the law, then Christ died without cause.

CHAPTER III.

O FOOLISH Galatians, who hath bewitched you,[1] before whose eyes Jesus Christ was evidently set forth, [1]crucified?

2 This only would I learn of you, Was it from the works of the law that ye received the Spirit, or from the hearing of faith?

3 Are ye so foolish? having begun in the Spirit, are ye now being made perfect in the flesh?

4 Did ye suffer so many things in vain? if it be indeed in vain.

5 He then that supplieth unto you the Spirit, and worketh mighty works in you, doeth he it from the works of the law, or from the hearing of faith?

6 Even as Abraham believed God, and it was reckoned to him for righteousness.

7 Ye know therefore that they which are of faith, these are sons of Abraham.

8 Moreover the scripture, foreseeing that God would justify the Gentiles by faith, proclaimed beforehand the gospel unto Abraham, [saying,] In thee shall all the Gentiles be blessed.

9 So then they which be of faith are blessed together with faithful Abraham.

10 For as many as are of the works of the law are under a curse: for it is written, Cursed is every one that continueth not in all the things which are written in the book of the law to do them.

11 But that in the law no man is justified before God, it is evident: because, The just by faith shall live.

12 Now the law is not of faith: but, The man that hath done them shall live in them.

13 Christ redeemed us from the curse of the law, having become a curse for us: for it is written, Cursed is every one that hangeth on a tree:

14 To the end that upon the Gentiles the blessing of Abraham might come in Christ Jesus; that we might receive the promise of the Spirit through faith.

15 Brethren, I speak after the manner of men; Even a man's covenant, when it hath been ratified, none setteth aside, or addeth thereunto.

16 Now to Abraham were the promises spoken, and to his seed. He saith not, And to seeds, as of many; but as of one, And to thy seed, which is Christ.

17 Now this is what I say; The covenant already ratified by God,[2] the law, which was four hundred and thirty years after, doth not disannul, so as to make the promise of none effect.

18 For if the inheritance is of the law, it is no more of

---

[1] That ye should not obey the truth *and* among you *are omitted by* nearly all the oldest authorities.

[2] In *or* unto Christ *is omitted by* nearly all the ancient authorities.

promise: but to Abraham hath God given it by promise.

19 Wherefore then serveth the law? It was added because of transgressions, till the seed should come to whom the promise is made; being ordained by means of angels, by the hand of a mediator.

20 Now a mediator cannot be of one, but God is one.

21 Is the law then against the promises of God? ¹God forbid: for if a law had been given which could give life, verily righteousness would have been by the law.

22 Howbeit the scripture shut up all under sin, that the promise by faith of Jesus Christ might be given to them that believe.

23 But before faith came, we were kept in ward, shut up under the law unto the faith which was afterwards to be revealed.

24 So that the law hath become our schoolmaster to guide us unto Christ, that we may be justified by faith.

25 But now that faith is come, we are no longer under a schoolmaster.

26 For ye are all sons of God through the faith in Christ Jesus.

27 For all ye who were baptized into Christ did put on Christ.

28 There is neither Jew nor Greek, there is neither bond nor free, there is not male and female: for ye all are one ²[man] in Christ Jesus.

29 And if ye be Christ's, then are ye Abraham's seed, ³heirs according to promise.

CHAPTER IV.

NOW I say, That the heir, as long as he is a child, differeth nothing from a bondservant, though he be lord of all;

2 But is under guardians and stewards until the time appointed by the father.

3 Even so we, when we were children, were kept in bondage under the rudiments of the world:

4 But when the fulness of the time came, God sent forth his Son, born of a woman, born under the law,

5 That he might redeem them that were under the law, that we might receive the adoption of sons.

6 And because ye are sons, God sent forth into ⁴our hearts the Spirit of his Son, crying, Abba, Father.

7 So then thou art no longer a bondservant, but a son; and if a son, then an heir ⁵through God.

8 Howbeit at that time, not knowing God, ye served ⁶gods which by nature exist not.

9 But now that ye know God, or rather are known of God, how is it that ye turn back again to the weak and beggarly rudiments, whereunto ye desire

---

³ And *is omitted by all the oldest MSS.*
⁴ *So all the oldest MSS.*
⁵ *So in almost all the oldest authorities.*
⁶ *So all the oldest authorities.*

¹ *Literally,* Let it not be.
² *Not expressed, but implied by one being in the masculine gender.*

from the beginning again to be in bondage? 10 Ye are observing days, and months, and times, and years. 11 I am afraid of you, lest haply I have bestowed upon you labour in vain. 12 Brethren, I beseech you, be as I am; for I am as ye are. Ye did me no wrong. 13 Ye know that because of an infirmity of my flesh I preached the gospel unto you at the first. 14 And [1]your temptation which was in my flesh ye despised not, nor rejected; but ye received me as an angel of God, even as Christ Jesus. 15 Where then is the blessedness ye boasted of? for I bear you witness that, if it had been possible, ye would have plucked out your own eyes, and have given them to me. 16 Am I then become your enemy by telling you the truth? 17 They zealously court you, but not well; nay, they desire to shut you out, that ye may court them. 18 But it is good to be zealously courted in a good cause at all times, and not only when I am present with you. 19 My little children, of whom I am again in travail until Christ be formed in you, 20 Yea, I could desire to be present with you now, and to change my voice; for I am perplexed about you. 21 Tell me, ye that desire to be under the law, do ye not hear the law?

22 For it is written, that Abraham had two sons, one by the bondmaid, and one by the freewoman. 23 Howbeit he who was of the bondmaid was born after the flesh; but he of the freewoman was by the promise. 24 Which things have another meaning: for these women are [2]two covenants; one from Mount Sinai, bearing children unto bondage, which is Hagar. 25 For the word Hagar is in Arabia Mount Sinai; and she answereth to the Jerusalem which now is, for she is in bondage with her children. 26 But Jerusalem which is above is free, which is [1]our mother. 27 For it is written, Rejoice, thou barren that bearest not; break forth and shout, thou that travailest not: for many are the children of the desolate more than of her which hath an husband. 28 Now [3]we, brethren, like Isaac, are children of promise. 29 But as then he that was born after the flesh persecuted him [that was born] after the Spirit, even so it is now. 30 Nevertheless what saith the scripture? Cast out the bondmaid and her son: for the son of the bondmaid must not inherit with the son of the freewoman. 31 Wherefore, brethren, we

[1] *So all the oldest MSS.*

[2] *The insertion of the is against the testimony of all the MSS., ancient and later.*

[3] *Many of the ancient MSS. read* ye.

are not children of a bondmaid, but of the freewoman.

CHAPTER V.

¹ IN liberty Christ hath made us free. Stand fast therefore, and be not entangled again in the yoke of bondage.

2 Behold, I Paul say unto you, that if ye should be circumcised, Christ shall profit you nothing.

3 Yea, I testify again to every man that is circumcised, that he is a debtor to do the whole law.

4 Christ is become of no effect unto you, whosoever of you would be justified in the law; ye are fallen from grace.

5 For we by the Spirit wait for the hope of righteousness by faith.

6 For in Christ Jesus neither circumcision availeth any thing, nor uncircumcision; but faith working by love.

7 Ye were running well; who hindered you from obeying the truth?

8 This persuasion cometh not from him that calleth you.

9 A little leaven leaveneth the whole lump.

10 I have confidence as regards you in the Lord, that ye will be none otherwise minded: but he that troubleth you shall bear his judgment, whosoever he be.

11 But I, brethren, if I am still preaching circumcision, why am I still persecuted? in that case the offence of the cross is done away.

12 Would that they which unsettle you would even cut themselves off!

13 For ye, brethren, were called unto liberty; only turn not your liberty into an occasion for the flesh, but by your love be servants one of another.

14 For the whole law is fulfilled in one saying, even in this; Thou shalt love thy neighbour as thyself.

15 But if ye bite and devour one another, take heed that ye be not consumed one of another.

16 But I say, Walk ²by the Spirit, and ye shall not fulfil the lust of the flesh.

17 For the flesh lusteth against the Spirit, and the Spirit against the flesh: for these are contrary the one to the other, that ye may not do the things that ye would.

18 But if ye are led by the Spirit, ye are not under the law.

19 Now the works of the flesh are manifest, such as, ³fornication, uncleanness, wantonness,

20 Idolatry, sorcery, hatreds, strife, jealousy, wrath, self-seeking, divisions, heresies,

21 Envyings, murders, drunkenness, revellings, and such like: of the which I forewarn you, as I also forewarned you before, that they which do

---

¹ *This is the reading best attested by the most ancient authorities. It is difficult to decide between the varieties.*

² *So the most ancient MSS.*

³ Adultery *is omitted by all the most ancient authorities.*

such things shall not inherit the kingdom of God.

22 But the fruit of the Spirit is love, joy, peace, longsuffering, kindness, goodness, faithfulness,

23 Meekness, temperance: against such things there is no law.

24 And they that are ¹Jesus Christ's crucified the flesh together with its passions and lusts.

25 If we live by the Spirit, by the Spirit let us also walk.

26 Let us not become vainglorious, provoking one another, envying one another.

CHAPTER VI.

BRETHREN, if a man even be overtaken in any transgression, ye which are spiritual restore such an one in the spirit of meekness; considering thyself, lest thou also be tempted.

2 Bear ye one another's burdens, and so fulfil the law of Christ.

3 For if a man thinketh himself to be something, when he is nothing, he deceiveth himself.

4 But let each man prove his own work, and then shall he have his boasting in regard to himself alone, and not in regard to another.

5 For each man shall bear his own burden.

6 But let him that is taught in the word share with him that teacheth in all good things.

7 Be not deceived; God is not mocked: for whatsoever a man soweth, that shall he also reap.

8 For he that soweth unto his own flesh shall of the flesh reap corruption; but he that soweth unto the Spirit shall of the Spirit reap everlasting life.

9 But let us not be weary in well doing: for in due season we shall reap, if we faint not.

10 Therefore as we have opportunity, let us work that which is good unto all men, especially unto them who belong to the faith.

11 See in how large letters I have written unto you with mine own hand.

12 As many as desire to make a fair show in the flesh, the same constrain you to be circumcised; only that they may not be persecuted for the cross of Christ.

13 For even they who receive circumcision do not themselves keep the law; but they wish you to be circumcised, that they may glory in your flesh.

14 But ²God forbid that I should glory, save in the cross of our Lord Jesus Christ, through whom the world hath been crucified unto me, and I unto the world.

15 For in Christ Jesus neither circumcision ³is any thing, nor uncircumcision, but a new creature.

16 And as many as walk by this rule, peace be on them, and mercy, and upon the Israel of God.

---

¹ *So all the oldest MSS.*

² *Literally*, to me let it not be to glory, &c.

³ *So all the oldest authorities.*

17 Henceforth let no man trouble me: for I bear in my body the marks of ¹Jesus.

18 The grace of our Lord Jesus Christ be with your spirit, brethren. Amen.

¹ *Most of the oldest MSS. have the Lord Jesus.*

THE EPISTLE OF PAUL THE APOSTLE

TO THE

EPHESIANS.

CHAPTER I.

PAUL, an apostle of Jesus Christ through the will of God, to the saints which are ¹[in Ephesus], and the faithful in Christ Jesus:

2 Grace be unto you, and peace, from God our Father, and the Lord Jesus Christ.

3 Blessed be the God and Father of our Lord Jesus Christ, who blessed us in all spiritual blessing in the heavenly places in Christ:

4 Even as he chose us in him before the foundation of the world, that we should be holy and blameless before him in love:

5 Having foreordained us unto adoption through Jesus Christ unto him, according to the good pleasure of his will,

6 To the praise of the glory of his grace, ²which he freely bestowed upon us in the beloved One.

7 In whom we have our redemption through his blood, the forgiveness of our transgressions, according to the riches of his grace;

8 Which he made to abound toward us in all wisdom and prudence;

9 Having made known unto us the mystery of his will, according to his good pleasure which he purposed in himself,

10 Unto the dispensation of the fulness of the times, to gather up together all things in Christ, the things which are in the heavens, and the things which are on the earth; even in him,

11 In whom we were also made his inheritance, having been foreordained according to the purpose of him who worketh all things after the counsel of his will:

12 That we should be unto the praise of his glory, we who before have hoped in Christ.

13 In whom are ye also, having heard the word of truth, the gospel of your salvation: in whom also ye hav-

¹ *The words* in Ephesus *are omitted by the two most ancient MSS.*
² *So all the oldest authorities.*

ing believed were sealed by the Spirit of the promise, even the holy ¹[Spirit],

14 ²Who is the earnest of our inheritance for the redemption of the purchased possession, unto the praise of his glory.

15 For this cause I also, having heard of the faith in the Lord Jesus which is among you, and ³[the love which ye have] unto all the saints,

16 Cease not to give thanks for you, making mention of you in my prayers;

17 That the God of our Lord Jesus Christ, the Father of glory, would give unto you the spirit of wisdom and revelation in full knowledge of him:

18 Having the eyes of your ⁴heart enlightened; that ye may know what is the hope of his calling, ⁵what the riches of the glory of his inheritance in the saints,

19 And what the exceeding greatness of his power to usward who believe, according to the working of the might of his strength,

20 Which he ⁶hath wrought in Christ, by raising him from the dead, and he made him sit at his right hand in the heavenly places,

21 Above all rule, and authority, and power, and lordship, and every name that is named, not only in this world, but also in that which is to come:

22 And put all things in subjection under his feet, and gave him to be head over all things to the church,

23 Which is his body, the fulness of him that filleth all things in all.

CHAPTER II.

YOU also, who were dead by reason of your trespasses and your sins;

2 Wherein ye once walked according to the course of this world, according to the prince of the powers of the air, of the spirit that now worketh in the sons of disobedience:

3 Among whom we also all had our way of life in times past in the lusts of our flesh, performing the desires of our flesh and of our thoughts; and we were by nature children of wrath, even as the rest.

4 But God, being rich in mercy, because of his great love wherewith he loved us,

5 Even when we were dead in our trespasses, quickened us together with Christ, (by grace ye have been saved;)

6 And raised us up together with him, and made us sit together with him in the heavenly places in Christ Jesus:

7 That he might shew forth in the ages which are to come the exceeding riches of his grace in kindness toward us in Christ Jesus.

8 For by grace have ye been

---

¹ *Not expressed in the original.*
² *Several of the oldest MSS. read* which.
³ *The three oldest MSS. omit these words.*
⁴ *So, and not* understanding, *all the ancient MSS. of every kind.*
⁵ And *is omitted by the oldest authorities.*
⁶ *So some of the most ancient MSS.*

saved through faith ; and that not of yourselves : of God is the gift :

9 Not of works, in order that no man should boast.

10 For we are his handiwork, having been created in Christ Jesus for good works, which God before prepared that we should walk in them.

11 Wherefore remember, that ¹aforetime ye being Gentiles in the flesh, who are called the Uncircumcision by that which is called the Circumcision in the flesh wrought by hands ;

12 That ye were at that time separate from Christ, being alienated from the commonwealth of Israel, and strangers to the covenants of the promise, having no hope, and without God in the world :

13 But now in Christ Jesus ye who aforetime were far off have been brought nigh in the blood of Christ.

14 For he is our peace, who made both one, and brake down the middle wall of the partition,

15 To wit, the enmity, in his flesh ; abolishing the law of the commandments ²[consisting] in ordinances ; that he might make the two into one new man in himself, so making peace ;

16 And might reconcile them both in one body unto God through his cross, having slain the enmity thereby :

17 And he came and brought glad tidings of peace to you which were afar off, and ³of peace to them that were nigh.

18 Because through him we both have our access in one Spirit unto the Father.

19 So then ye are no longer strangers and sojourners, but ⁴are fellow-citizens with the saints, and of the household of God ;

20 Built up upon the foundation of the apostles and prophets, Christ Jesus himself being the chief corner stone ;

21 In whom all the building fitly framed together is growing unto an holy temple in the Lord :

22 In whom ye also are being builded together for an habitation of God in the Spirit.

CHAPTER III.

FOR this cause I Paul, the prisoner of Christ Jesus in behalf of you the Gentiles,

2 If indeed ye heard of the dispensation of the grace of God which was given me to you-ward :

3 That by revelation was ⁵the mystery made known unto me ; as I wrote afore in few words,

4 Whereby, when ye read, ye can perceive my understanding in the mystery of Christ ;

5 Which in other generations was not made known unto the sons of men, as it hath now been revealed unto his holy apostles and prophets in the Spirit ;

6 That the Gentiles are joint-

---

¹ *So the oldest MSS.*
² *Not expressed in the original.*
³ *Thus all the oldest authorities.*
⁴ *So all the oldest MSS.*
⁵ *So all the oldest authorities.*

heirs, and joined in the same body, and joint-partakers of ¹the promise in Christ ²Jesus through the gospel:

7 Whereof I was made a minister, according to the gift of the grace of God, which was given unto me according to the working of his power.

8 Unto me, who am less than the least of all saints, was this grace given, to bring ³to the Gentiles the glad tidings of the unsearchable riches of Christ;

9 And to enlighten all men what is the ⁴dispensation of the mystery, which from the beginning of the world hath been hidden in God, who created ⁵all things:

10 To the intent that now unto the principalities and to the powers in the heavenly places may be made known through the church the manifold wisdom of God,

11 According to the eternal purpose which he purposed in the Christ, even Jesus our Lord:

12 In whom we have our boldness and our access in confidence through the faith of him.

13 Wherefore I intreat you not to faint at my tribulations on your behalf, seeing that they are your glory.

14 For this cause I bow my knees unto the ⁶Father,

---
¹ *So all the oldest authorities.*
² *So the oldest MSS.*
³ *So, and not* among, *the oldest MSS.*
⁴ *So, and not* fellowship, *all the most ancient authorities of every kind.*
⁵ *By* Jesus Christ *is omitted in all the oldest authorities.*
⁶ *So all the oldest MSS.*

15 From whom every family in heaven and on earth is named,

16 That he would grant you, according to the riches of his glory, to be strengthened with might through his Spirit towards the inner man;

17 So that Christ may dwell in your hearts by your faith, [ye] having been rooted and grounded in love,

18 That ye may be fully able to comprehend with all the saints what is the breadth, and length, and depth, and height;

19 And to know the love of Christ, which surpasseth knowledge, that ye may be filled up unto all the fulness of God.

20 But unto him that is able above all things to do exceeding abundantly above what we ask or think, according to the power that worketh in us,

21 Unto him be the glory in the church ⁶and in Christ Jesus to all the generations of eternal ages. Amen.

CHAPTER IV.

I BESEECH you therefore, I the prisoner in the Lord, that ye walk worthy of the calling wherewith ye were called,

2 With all lowliness and meekness, with longsuffering, forbearing one another in love;

3 Earnestly striving to maintain the unity of the Spirit in the bond of peace.

4 There is one body, and one Spirit, as ye were also called in one hope of your calling;

5 One Lord, one faith, one baptism,

6 One God and Father of all, who is over all, and through all, and ¹in all.

7 But unto each one of us was the grace given according to the measure of the gift of Christ.

8 Wherefore he saith, When he ascended up on high, he led captives captive, and gave gifts unto men.

9 But that he ascended, what is it but that he also descended ²into the lower parts of the earth?

10 He that descended is the same also that ascended up above all the heavens, that he might fill all things.

11 And he gave some to be apostles; and some, prophets; and some, evangelists; and some, pastors and teachers;

12 Unto the perfecting of the saints, for the work of ministration, for the building up of the body of Christ:

13 Till we all attain unto the unity of the faith and of the perfect knowledge of the Son of God, unto the fullgrown man, unto the measure of the stature of the fulness of Christ:

14 That we be no longer children, tossed as waves and carried about by every wind of teaching, in the sleight of men, in craftiness that leadeth to the system of error;

15 But being followers of truth in love may grow up into him in all things, which is the head, even Christ:

16 From whom the whole body being fitly framed together and compacted by means of every joint of the supply, according to the working in the measure of each several part, maketh the growth of the body unto the building up of itself in love.

17 This therefore I say, and testify in the Lord, that ye no longer walk as ³also the Gentiles walk, in the vanity of their mind,

18 Being darkened in their understanding, alienated from the life of God because of the ignorance that is in them, because of the hardening of their heart:

19 Who being past feeling gave themselves up unto wantonness, in order to the working of uncleanness of every kind in greediness.

20 But not so did ye learn Christ;

21 If indeed it was He that ye heard, and in him that ye were taught, according as is truth in Jesus:

22 That as concerneth your former way of life ye put off the old man, which is corrupting according to the lusts of deceit,

23 And be renewed by the Spirit of your mind;

24 And that ye put on the new man, which hath been created after God's image in righteousness and holiness of the truth.

25 Wherefore having put a-

---

¹ You *is not read in any of the old MSS.: some read* us; *but the chief entirely omit any pronoun.*

² First *is omitted by the majority of the oldest MSS.*

³ *So all the oldest MSS*

way falsehood, speak ye truth each one with his neighbour : because we are members of one another.

26 Be angry, and sin not : let not the sun go down upon your wrath :

27 Neither give occasion to the devil.

28 Let him that stealeth steal no longer : but rather let him labour, working with his own hands that which is good, that he may be able to impart to him that hath need.

29 Let no corrupt communication proceed out of your mouth, but whatever is good for the building up of the need, that it may give grace unto the hearers.

30 And grieve not the holy Spirit of God, in whom ye were sealed unto the day of redemption.

31 Let all bitterness, and wrath, and anger, and clamour, and evil speaking, be put away from you, with all malice :

32 And be ye kind one to another, tenderhearted, forgiving each other, even as God also in Christ forgave you.

CHAPTER V.

BE ye therefore followers of God, as beloved children ;

2 And walk in love, even as Christ also loved [1]us, and gave himself up for [2]us an offering and a sacrifice to God for an odour of a sweet smell.

3 But fornication, and all uncleanness, or covetousness, let it not be even named among you, as becometh saints ;

4 Neither filthiness, nor foolish talking, or jesting, things which are not becoming ; but rather giving of thanks.

5 For of this ye are sure, [3]knowing that no whoremonger, nor unclean person, nor covetous man, [4]which is an idolater, hath any inheritance in the kingdom of Christ and God.

6 Let no man deceive you with empty words : for because of these things the wrath of God cometh upon the sons of disobedience.

7 Be not therefore partakers with them.

8 For once ye were darkness, but now are ye light in the Lord : walk as children of light :

9 For the fruit of the [5]light is in all goodness and righteousness and truth ;

10 Proving what is wellpleasing unto the Lord.

11 And have no fellowship with the unfruitful works of darkness, but rather even reprove them.

12 For the things which are done by them in secret it is a shame even to speak of.

13 But all things when they are reproved are made manifest by the light : for every thing that is made manifest is light.

14 Wherefore he saith, Up ! thou that sleepest, and arise from the dead, and Christ shall shine upon thee.

---

[1] *Two of the oldest MSS. read you.*
[2] *One of the oldest MSS. reads you.*
[3] *So all the most ancient authorities.*
[4] *So the most ancient M.*
[5] *So all the oldest MS.*

15 Take heed then how ye walk strictly, not as unwise men, but as wise,

16 Buying up opportunities, because the days are evil.

17 Therefore be ye not foolish, but [1]understand what is the will of the Lord.

18 And be not drunken with wine, wherein is profligacy; but be ye filled with the Spirit;

19 Speaking to one another in psalms and hymns and [2][spiritual] songs, singing and making melody in your heart to the Lord;

20 Giving thanks always for all things unto God and the Father in the name of our Lord Jesus Christ;

21 Submitting yourselves one to another in the fear of [3]Christ;

22 Ye wives, [4]unto your own husbands, as unto the Lord.

23 Because an husband is the head of his wife, as Christ also is the head of the church, [5]himself the saviour of the body.

24 Nevertheless as the church is subject unto Christ, so let the wives also be to their [6]husbands in every thing.

25 Husbands, love your wives, even as Christ also loved the church, and gave himself for her;

26 That he might sanctify her, cleansing her by the laver of the water in the word,

27 That he might [3]himself present unto himself the church glorious, not having spot, or wrinkle, or any such thing; but that she might be holy and without blemish.

28 So ought husbands [1]also to love their own wives as their own bodies. He that loveth his own wife loveth himself.

29 For no man ever hated his own flesh; but nourisheth and cherisheth it, even as Christ [3]also doth the church:

30 Because we are members of his body, [7][being of his flesh, and of his bones.]

31 For this cause shall a man leave father and mother, and shall be joined unto his wife, and the two shall be one flesh.

32 This mystery is a great one: but I say it in regard to Christ and to the church.

33 Nevertheless do ye also severally each one of you so love his wife as himself; and [let] the wife [see] that she reverence her husband.

CHAPTER VI.

CHILDREN, obey your parents [8][in the Lord]: for this is right.

2 Honour thy father and thy mother; which is the first commandment with promise;

3 That it may be well with thee, and thou mayest live long on the earth.

---

[1] *So the oldest MSS.*
[2] *Spiritual is omitted by one of the oldest MSS.*
[3] *So all the oldest MSS.*
[4] *So the oldest MSS., and, by the testimony of Jerome, the Greek MSS. in his time. The other MSS. fill up in different ways: a sure sign that the shorter reading is the genuine one.*
[5] *Thus all the oldest MSS.*
[6] *Own is omitted by the oldest MSS.*
[7] *Omitted by the three oldest MSS.*
[8] *In the Lord is omitted by some of the oldest MSS.*

4 And, ye fathers, fret not your children to anger; but bring them up in the discipline and admonition of the Lord.

5 Bondmen, be obedient unto your masters according to the flesh, with fear and trembling, in simplicity of your heart, as unto Christ;

6 Not with eyeservice, as menpleasers; but as bondmen of Christ, doing the will of God;

7 From the heart with good will doing service, as to the Lord, and not to men:

8 Knowing that [1]each man, if he shall have done any good thing, shall receive the same from the Lord, whether he be bondman or free.

9 And, ye masters, do the same things unto them, forbearing your threatening: knowing that [2]their Master and yours is in heaven; and that there is no respect of persons with him.

10 [3]Henceforth be ye strengthened in the Lord, and in the power of his might.

11 Put on the whole armour of God, that ye may be able to stand against the wiles of the devil.

12 For our wrestling is not against flesh and blood, but against the principalities, against the powers, against the worldrulers of this present darkness,[4] against the spiritual hosts of wickedness in the heavenly places.

13 Wherefore take up the whole armour of God, that ye may be able to withstand in the evil day, and having accomplished all, to stand.

14 Stand therefore, having girt your loins about with truth, and having put on the breastplate of righteousness;

15 And having shod your feet with the readiness of the gospel of peace;

16 [5]Besides all, taking up the shield of faith, wherewith ye shall be able to quench all the fiery darts of the evil one.

17 And receive the helmet of salvation, and the sword of the Spirit, which is the word of God:

18 Praying at all times in the Spirit with all prayer and supplication, and watching thereunto in all perseverance and supplication for all the saints;

19 And on my behalf, that utterance may be given unto me, in the opening of my mouth, to make known in boldness the mystery of the gospel,

20 For the sake of which I am an ambassador in chains: that therein I may speak boldly, as I ought to speak.

21 But that ye also may know the things concerning me, how I fare, Tychicus, the beloved brother and faithful minister in the Lord, shall make all known to you:

22 Whom I have sent unto

[1] *So the majority of the oldest MSS.*
[2] *So all the oldest MSS.*
[3] *So, and omitting* my brethren, *all the oldest MSS.*
[4] *Of this world is omitted by all the oldest MSS.*
[5] *The two oldest MSS. read* In all things.

you for this very purpose, that ye may know our affairs, and that he may comfort your hearts.

23 Peace be to the brethren, and love with faith, from God the Father and the Lord Jesus Christ.

24 Grace be with all them that love our Lord Jesus Christ in incorruption. Amen.

THE EPISTLE OF PAUL THE APOSTLE
TO THE
PHILIPPIANS.

CHAPTER I.

PAUL and Timothy, servants of ¹Christ Jesus, to all the saints in Christ Jesus which are at Philippi, with the bishops and deacons:

2 Grace be unto you, and peace, from God our Father, and the Lord Jesus Christ.

3 I thank my God in all my remembrance of you,

4 Always in every prayer of mine making my prayer for you all with joy,

5 For your fellowship in regard to the gospel from the first day until now;

6 Being confident of this very thing, that he which began a good work in you will perfect it up to the day of Jesus Christ:

7 Even as it is just for me to be thus minded for you all, because you have me in your heart, both in my bonds, and in my defence and confirmation of the gospel, being partakers of my grace.

8 For God is my witness, how I long after you all in the tender heart of ¹Christ Jesus.

9 And this I pray, that your love may abound yet more and more in knowledge and all perception;

10 So that ye may discern the things that are more excellent; that ye may be sincere and without offence unto the day of Christ;

11 Being filled with the ²fruit of righteousness, which is through Jesus Christ, unto the glory and praise of God.

12 But I would have you know, brethren, that the things concerning me have fallen out rather unto the furtherance of the gospel;

13 So that my bonds became manifest in Christ in all the palace, and to all others;

14 And that most of the brethren in the Lord, waxing

---

¹ *So the oldest MSS.*   ² *So all the oldest MSS.*

confident by my bonds, are more abundantly bold to speak the word without fear.

15 Some indeed are preaching Christ even for envy and strife; and some also for good will:

16 [1]These indeed out of love, knowing that I am set for the defence of the gospel:

17 But the others out of self-seeking proclaim Christ, not sincerely, thinking to [2]raise up tribulation to my bonds.

18 What then? notwithstanding, every way, whether in pretence, or in truth, Christ is proclaimed; and therein I do rejoice, yea, and I shall rejoice;

19 For I know that this shall fall out to me unto salvation through your prayer, and supply of the Spirit of Jesus Christ,

20 According to my expectation and hope, that in nothing I shall be ashamed, but that with all boldness, as always, so now also Christ shall be magnified in my body, whether by life or by death.

21 For to me to live is Christ, and to die is gain.

22 But if to live in the flesh, [3][if] this be to me fruit of my labour, then what I shall choose I know not.

23 But I am in a strait betwixt the two, having my desire for departing, and being with Christ; for it is very far better:

24 Yet to abide in my flesh is more necessary for your sake.

25 And being confident of this, I know that I shall abide and shall continue with you all for your furtherance and joy in your faith;

26 That in me your matter of boasting may abound in Christ Jesus, through my presence with you again.

27 Only conduct yourselves worthily of the gospel of Christ: that whether I come and see you, or be absent, I may hear of your state, that ye are standing fast in one spirit, with one soul striving together for the faith of the gospel;

28 And not being terrified in any thing by your adversaries: the which is to them an evidence of perdition, but of [4]your salvation, and that from God.

29 Because unto you it hath been given, in the behalf of Christ not only to believe in him, but also to suffer in his behalf.

30 Having the same conflict as ye saw in me, and now hear of in me.

CHAPTER II.

IF then there be any exhortation in Christ, if any comfort of love, if any communion of the Spirit, if any tenderness and compassions,

2 Make ye my joy full, that ye be of the same mind, having the same love, with united souls being of one mind,

---

[1] *So these two verses are arranged and read in all the most ancient authorities.*
[2] *So all the oldest MSS.*
[3] *Not expressed in the original.*
[4] *So the oldest MSS.: some very ancient ones reading* to us of salvation.

3 In nothing following self-seeking nor vainglory; but through your lowliness of mind esteeming each other better than yourselves.

4 Not looking each of you on his own things, but each of you on the things of others also.

5 ¹Have this mind in you, which was also in Christ Jesus:

6 Who, being in the form of God, deemed not his equality with God a thing to grasp at,

7 But emptied himself, taking upon him the form of a servant, being made in the likeness of men:

8 And being found in fashion as a man, he humbled himself, becoming obedient even unto death, and that the death of the cross.

9 Wherefore God also exalted him exceedingly, and bestowed on him ¹the name which is above every name:

10 That in the name of Jesus every knee should bend, of things in heaven and on earth and under the earth;

11 And that every tongue should confess that Jesus Christ is Lord, to the glory of God the Father.

12 So then, my beloved, even as ye were always obedient, not as in my presence only, but now much more in my absence, carry out with fear and trembling your own salvation.

13 For it is God which worketh in you both to will and to work for his good pleasure.

¹ *So all the oldest MSS.*

14 Do all things without murmurings and disputings:

15 That ye may be blameless and harmless, children of God, without reproach, amidst a crooked and perverse generation, among whom ye shine as lights in the world;

16 Holding forth the word of life, for a boast to me against the day of Christ, that I have not run in vain, neither laboured in vain.

17 Yea, if I am even being poured out upon the sacrifice and ministration of your faith, I joy, and congratulate you all.

18 And in like manner do ye also joy, and congratulate me.

19 But I hope in the Lord Jesus to send Timothy shortly unto you, that I also may be of good courage, when I know your state.

20 For I have no man likeminded, who will naturally be careful about your state.

21 For they all seek their own things, not the things of Christ Jesus.

22 But ye know the proof of him, that, as a child [serveth] a father, he hath served with me unto the gospel.

23 Him therefore I hope to send presently, so soon as I see how it will go with me.

24 But I trust in the Lord that I myself also shall come shortly.

25 Yet I thought it necessary to send to you Epaphroditus, my brother, and fellow-labourer, and fellow-soldier, but your apostle, and minister to my need:

26 Since he was longing after

you all, and was full of heaviness, because ye had heard that he was sick.

27 For indeed he was sick nigh unto death: yet God had mercy on him; and not on him only, but on me also, that I might not have sorrow upon sorrow.

28 I sent him therefore the more anxiously, that, when ye see him, ye may rejoice again, and that I may be the less sorrowful.

29 Receive him therefore in the Lord with all gladness; and hold such men in honour:

30 Because for the work [1][of Christ] he came nigh unto death, hazarding his life that he might supply what was lacking on your part in your ministration toward me.

CHAPTER III.

FINALLY, my brethren, rejoice in the Lord. To write the same things to you, to me indeed is not irksome, but for you it is safe.

2 Beware of the dogs, beware of the evil workers, beware of the concision.

3 For we are the circumcision, who worship by the Spirit of God, and glory in Christ Jesus, and trust not in the flesh.

4 Though I myself have confidence also in the flesh. If any other man thinketh to trust in the flesh, I still more:

5 Circumcised the eighth day, of the stock of Israel, of the tribe of Benjamin, an Hebrew, of Hebrews; as touching the law, a Pharisee;

6 As touching zeal, persecuting the church; as touching the righteousness which is in the law, having lived blameless.

7 Howbeit, what things were gain to me, those for Christ's sake have I counted loss.

8 Nay more, and I still count [them] all but loss for the sake of the excellency of the knowledge of Christ Jesus my Lord: for whose sake I suffered the loss of all things, and count them but dung, that I may gain Christ,

9 And be found in him, not having mine own righteousness, which is of the law, but that which is through the faith of Christ, the righteousness which is from God upon my faith:

10 That I may know him, and the power of his resurrection, and the fellowship of his sufferings, being conformed to the likeness of his death;

11 If by any means I may attain unto the resurrection [2]from the dead.

12 Not that I have already obtained, or am already made perfect: but I press on, if so be that I may lay hold on that for which also I was laid hold on by [3]Christ.

13 Brethren, I count not myself to have laid hold: but one thing [4][I do], forgetting the things which are behind, and stretching forth unto the things which are before,

---

[1] *Omitted by one of the oldest MSS. and variously read by others.*
[2] *So all the oldest authorities.*
[3] *So most of the ancient MSS.*
[4] *Not expressed in the original.*

14 I press toward the mark for the prize of the heavenly calling of God in Christ Jesus.

15 Let us then, as many as be perfect, be thus minded: and if in any thing ye be otherwise minded, even this shall God reveal unto you.

16 Nevertheless, whereunto we have attained, walk on by the same ¹path.

17 Brethren, be followers together of me, and mark them which are walking so as ye have us for an ensample.

18 For many walk, of whom I often told you, and now tell you even weeping, that they are the enemies of the cross of Christ:

19 Whose end is perdition, whose god is their belly, and their glory is in their shame, who mind earthly things.

20 For our country is in the heavens; from whence also we look for a Saviour, the Lord Jesus Christ:

21 Who shall change the body of our humiliation, ²[that it may be] conformed unto the body of his glory, according to the working of his power whereby he is able even to subdue all things unto him.

CHAPTER IV.

WHEREFORE, my brethren beloved and longed for, my joy and crown, so stand ye fast in the Lord, my beloved.

2 I beseech Euodia, and I beseech ³Syntyche, to be of the same mind in the Lord.

3 Yea, I entreat thee also, true yokefellow, help them, inasmuch as they laboured with me in the gospel, with Clement also,—and my other fellow-labourers, whose names are in the book of life.

4 Rejoice in the Lord alway: again I will say it, Rejoice.

5 Let your moderation be known unto all men. The Lord is at hand.

6 Be anxious about nothing; but in every thing by your prayer and your supplication with thanksgiving let your requests be made known unto God.

7 And the peace of God, which surpasseth all understanding, shall guard your hearts and your thoughts in Christ Jesus.

8 Finally, brethren, whatsoever things are true, whatsoever things are seemly, whatsoever things are right, whatsoever things are pure, whatsoever things are lovely, whatsoever things are of good report; whatever virtue there is, and whatever praise, think on these things.

9 The things, which ye also learned, and received, and heard, and saw in me; these do, and the God of peace shall be with you.

10 But I rejoiced in the Lord greatly, that now at last ye have revived again in your care for me; wherein ye were also careful, but lacked opportunity.

---

¹ *So the three most ancient MSS.: others variously.*

² *These words are omitted by the most ancient MSS.*

³ *Pronounce* Sýntўché. *The two names are those of women.*

11 Not that I speak in respect of want: for I learned, in the state in which I am, therein to be content.

12 I know also how to be in low estate, I know also how to abound: in each and in all things have I been instructed both how to be full and to be hungry, both how to abound and to be in want.

13 I have strength for all things in him[1] which giveth me power.

14 Yet ye did well in communicating with my affliction.

15 But ye Philippians yourselves also know that in the beginning of the gospel, when I departed from Macedonia, no church communicated with me in an account of giving and receiving, but ye only.

16 Since even in Thessalonica ye sent once and again unto my need.

17 Not that the gift is what I seek: but I seek the fruit that aboundeth to your account.

18 But I have all things, and more than enough: I am filled full, having received from Epaphroditus the things which were sent from you, an odour of a sweet smell, a sacrifice acceptable, wellpleasing to God.

19 And my God shall fully supply every need of yours, according to his riches in glory in Christ Jesus.

20 But unto our God and Father be the glory for ever and ever. Amen.

21 Salute every saint in Christ Jesus. The brethren which are with me salute you.

22 All the saints salute you, chiefly they that are of Cæsar's household.

23 The grace of our Lord Jesus Christ be with [2]your spirit.

[1] Christ *is omitted in the oldest MSS.*

[2] *So all the oldest MSS., most of them also omitting* Amen.

THE EPISTLE OF PAUL THE APOSTLE

TO THE

COLOSSIANS.

CHAPTER I.

PAUL, an apostle of ¹Christ Jesus through the will of God, and Timothy our brother,

2 To the saints and faithful brethren in Christ at Colossæ: Grace be unto you, and peace, from God our Father and the Lord Jesus Christ.

3 We give thanks to God ²the Father of our Lord Jesus Christ, praying always for you,

4 Having heard of your faith in Christ Jesus, and of the love which ye have to all the saints,

5 Because of the hope which is laid up for you in the heavens, whereof ye heard before in the word of the truth of the gospel;

6 Which is present among you, as in all the world; ³it is bringing forth fruit ⁴and growing, even as it doth in you also, since the day ye heard it, and came to know the grace of God in truth:

7 As ye ⁵learned from Epaphras our beloved fellow-servant, who is a faithful minister of Christ on ⁶our behalf;

8 Who also declared unto us your love in the Spirit.

9 For this cause we also, since the day we heard it, do not cease praying for you, and making request that ye may be filled with the knowledge of his will in all wisdom and spiritual understanding,

10 So as to walk worthy of the Lord unto all pleasing, bringing forth fruit in every good work, and growing ¹by the knowledge of God;

11 Being strengthened with all strength, according to the might of his glory, unto all patience and longsuffering with joy;

12 Giving thanks unto the Father, which made us meet for the portion of the inheritance of the saints in light:

13 Who delivered us out of the power of darkness, and translated us into the kingdom of the Son of his love:

14 In whom we have our redemption,⁷ even the remission of our sins:

15 Who is the image of the invisible God, the firstborn of all creation:

---

¹ *So all the oldest MSS.*
² And *is omitted by two of the oldest MSS. and the most ancient version.*
³ And *is omitted in all the oldest MSS.*
⁴ *Thus all the oldest authorities.*
⁵ Also *is omitted by all the oldest authorities.*
⁶ *Thus most of the oldest MSS.*
⁷ Through his blood *is omitted in all the ancient authorities. It has been supplied here from* Eph. i. 7.

16 Because in him were all things created, the things in the heavens, and the things on the earth, things visible and things invisible, whether they be thrones, or dominions, or principalities, or powers: all things have been created by him and for him:

17 And he is before all things, and in him all things subsist.

18 And he is the head of the body, the church: who is the beginning, the firstborn from the dead; that in all things he may be the first.

19 Because he was well pleased that in him should all the fulness dwell;

20 And through him to reconcile all things unto himself; having made peace through the blood of his cross; through him ¹[I say], whether they be the things on the earth, or the things in the heavens.

21 And you that once were alienated and enemies in your mind by your wicked works, yet now hath he reconciled

22 In the body of his flesh through his death, to present you holy and blameless and unreproveable in his sight:

23 Provided that ye abide in the faith grounded and settled, and be not moved away from the hope of the gospel, which ye heard, which was preached in all creation which is under heaven; whereof I Paul was made a minister.

24 I now rejoice in my sufferings on your behalf, and fill up what remaineth behind of the afflictions of Christ in my flesh for his body's sake, which is the church:

25 Whereof I was made a minister, according to the stewardship of God which was given to me for you, to fulfil the word of God;

26 Even the mystery which hath been hidden from the ages and from the generations, but now hath been manifested unto his saints:

27 To whom God was pleased to make known what is the riches of the glory of this mystery among the Gentiles; which is Christ among you, the hope of the glory:

28 Whom we proclaim, warning every man, and teaching every man in all wisdom; that we may present every man perfect in ²Christ:

29 Whereunto I labour also, earnestly contending according to his working, which worketh in me mightily.

CHAPTER II.

FOR I would have you know how great a contention I have for you, and those at Laodicea, and as many as have not seen my face in the flesh;

2 That their hearts may be confirmed, they being knit together in love, and unto all the riches of the full assurance of the understanding, unto the thorough knowledge of the mystery of ³God,

---

¹ *Not expressed in the original.*

² Jesus *is omitted by all the oldest MSS.*

³ *It is almost impossible to say what was the original reading. The Vatican MS. has*, of God [even] Christ: *the Sinaitic*, of God, Father of Christ: *the Alexandrine*

3 Wherein are all the hidden treasures of wisdom and knowledge.

4 But this I say, lest any man should beguile you with enticing words.

5 For though I am absent in the flesh, yet in the spirit I am with you, joying and beholding your good order, and the firm foundation of your faith in Christ.

6 As therefore ye received Christ Jesus the Lord, so walk in him:

7 Rooted and being builded up in him, and stablished in the faith, even as ye were taught, abounding therein with thanksgiving.

8 Beware lest there shall be any man that leadeth you captive through his philosophy and vain deceit, according to the tradition of men, according to the rudiments of the world, and not according to Christ.

9 Because in him dwelleth all the fulness of the Godhead bodily.

10 And ye are filled full in him, which is the head of all principality and power:

11 In whom ye were also circumcised with a circumcision not wrought with hands, in the putting off of the body[1] of the flesh in the circumcision of Christ:

and Parisian MSS., of God, Father of the Christ: the Claromontane, of God, which is Christ: the ancient Syriac version, of God [the] Father, and of Christ. The received reading, as A. V., has no very ancient authority.

[1] *Of the sins is omitted by all the oldest MSS*

12 Having been buried with him in your baptism, wherein ye were also raised with him through the faith in the operation of God, who raised him from the dead.

13 And you, being dead in your trespasses and the uncircumcision of your flesh, he quickened together with him, having forgiven [2]us all our trespasses;

14 Blotting out the handwriting in ordinances that was against us, which was contrary to us, and he hath taken it out of the way, nailing it to the cross;

15 [And] stripping off from himself the principalities and the powers, he made a shew of them openly, triumphing over them in him.

16 Let no man therefore judge you in eating, or in drinking, or in respect of a feast day, or of the new moon, or of sabbath days:

17 Which are a shadow of the things to come; but the body is of Christ.

18 Let no one of purpose defraud you of your prize, in lowliness of mind and worshipping of the angels, [3]insisting on things which he hath seen, vainly puffed up by the mind of his flesh,

19 And not holding fast the Head, from whom all the body by means of the joints and bands having nourishment ministered, and knit together, groweth with the increase of God.

[2] *So all the oldest authorities.*
[3] *So the majority of the oldest MSS.*

20 ¹If ye died with Christ from the rudiments of the world, why, as though living in the world, are ye being prescribed to,
21 Handle not, nor taste, nor touch;
22 (Which things are all to perish with the using;) according to the commandments and teachings of men?
23 Such as have indeed a shew of wisdom in voluntary worship, and lowliness of mind, and not sparing of the body, not in any honour, to the satisfying of the flesh.

CHAPTER III.

IF then ye were raised together with Christ, seek the things above, where Christ is, sitting on the right hand of God.
2 Set your mind on the things above, not on the things on the earth.
3 For ye died, and your life is hidden with Christ in God.
4 When Christ, who is our life, is manifested, then shall ye also with him be manifested in glory.
5 Make dead therefore your members which are upon the earth; fornication, uncleanness, lustful passion, evil concupiscence, and covetousness, for it is idolatry,
6 ²On which account cometh the wrath of God:
7 In the which ye also once walked, when ye lived in these things.
8 But now lay ye also aside the whole; anger, wrath, malice, reviling, foul language out of your mouth.
9 Lie not one unto another, seeing that ye have put off the old man with his deeds;
10 And have put on the new man, which is being renewed unto perfect knowledge after the image of him that created him:
11 Wherein there is no such thing as Greek and Jew, circumcision and uncircumcision, Barbarian, Scythian, bondman, freeman: but Christ is all, and in all.
12 Put on therefore, as God's elect, holy and beloved, an heart of ³pity, kindness, lowliness of mind, meekness, longsuffering;
13 Forbearing one another, and forgiving each other, if any man have a complaint against any: even as ⁴the Lord forgave you, so also ye.
14 But over all these things put on love, which is the bond of perfectness.
15 And let the peace of ⁵Christ rule in your hearts, to the which ye were also called in one body; and be ye thankful.
16 Let the word of Christ dwell in you richly; in all wisdom teaching and admonishing each other with ⁶psalms,

---

¹ Wherefore *is omitted by all the most ancient authorities.*
² *This verse is thus read in some of the oldest MSS. It has in others of them, and in the later MSS., been conformed to Eph.* v. 6.
³ *So nearly all the ancient MSS.*
⁴ *So most of the oldest MSS.*
⁵ *So all the most ancient authorities.*
⁶ *So most of the ancient MSS.*

hymns, spiritual songs, in grace singing in your hearts to ¹God.

17 And every thing whatsoever ye do in word or in deed, do all in the name of the Lord Jesus, giving thanks to God² the Father through him.

18 Wives, submit yourselves unto your³ husbands, as it is fit in the Lord.

19 Husbands, love your wives, and be not embittered against them.

20 Children, obey your parents in all things: for this is wellpleasing ⁴in the Lord.

21 Fathers, irritate not your children, that they be not disheartened.

22 Servants, obey in all things your masters according to the flesh; not with eyeservice, as menpleasers; but in simplicity of heart, fearing ⁵the Lord:

23 ⁶Whatsoever ye do, work at it heartily, as unto the Lord, and not unto men;

24 Knowing that of the Lord ye shall receive the recompence of the inheritance: ⁷serve ye the Lord Christ.

25 ¹For he that doeth wrong shall receive back the wrong which he did: and there is no respect of persons.

---

¹ So all the oldest *MSS.*
² And *is omitted by most of the earliest authorities.*
³ Own *is omitted by all the early authorities. See Eph.* v. 22.
⁴ So all the ancient authorities.
⁵ So all the earliest authorities.
⁶ And every thing *is omitted by the earliest MSS.*
⁷ So, omitting for, *all the oldest MSS.*

CHAPTER IV.

MASTERS, render unto your servants justice and equality; knowing that ye also have a Master in heaven.

2 Persevere in prayer, watching therein with thanksgiving;

3 Withal praying for us also, that God would open unto us a door for the word, to speak the mystery of Christ, for which I am also in bonds:

4 That I may make it manifest, as I ought to speak.

5 Walk in wisdom toward them that are without, buying up opportunities.

6 Let your speech be alway in grace, seasoned with salt, that ye may know how ye ought to answer every man.

7 All my state shall Tychicus make known unto you, the beloved brother, and faithful minister and fellow-servant in the Lord:

8 Whom I have sent unto you for this very purpose, that ⁸he may know your state, and comfort your hearts;

9 Together with Onesimus, the faithful and beloved brother, who is one of you. They shall make known unto you all the things here.

10 Aristarchus my fellow-prisoner saluteth you, and Mark, the cousin of Barnabas, touching whom ye received commandments: if he come unto you, receive him;

11 And Jesus, which is called Justus, who are of the circum-

⁸ *Several of the oldest MSS. have* that ye may know our state: *from Eph.* vi. 22.

cision. These only are my fellow-workers unto the kingdom of God, men that proved a comfort unto me.

12 Epaphras, who is one of you, a servant of Christ ¹Jesus, saluteth you, always striving earnestly for you in his prayers, that ye may stand perfect and ²fully assured in all the will of God.

13 For I bear him witness, that he hath much ¹labour for you, and those at Laodicea, and those at Hierapolis.

14 Luke, the beloved physician, saluteth you, and Demas.

¹ *So most of the oldest MSS.*
² *So all the oldest MSS.*

15 Salute the brethren at Laodicea, and Nymphas, and the church in his house.

16 And when this epistle is read among you, cause that it be read in the church of the Laodiceans also; and that ye likewise read the epistle from Laodicea.

17 And say to Archippus, Look to the ministry which thou receivedst in the Lord, that thou fulfil it.

18 The salutation by the hand of me Paul. Remember my bonds. Grace be with you.³

³ *Most of the oldest MSS. omit Amen.*

THE FIRST EPISTLE OF PAUL THE APOSTLE
TO THE
THESSALONIANS.

CHAPTER I.

PAUL, and Silvanus, and Timothy, unto the church of Thessalonians in God the Father and the Lord Jesus Christ. Grace unto you, and peace.¹

2 We give thanks to God always for you all, making mention of you in our prayers unceasingly,

3 Remembering the work of your faith, and the labour of your love, and the patience of your hope of our Lord Jesus Christ, before God and our Father;

4 Knowing, brethren beloved by God, your election.

5 Because our gospel came not unto you in word only, but also in power, and in the Holy Spirit, and in much confidence; even as ye know what manner of men we

¹ *The words which follow here in the A. V. are retained in some of the oldest MSS., but are omitted by the Vatican MS. and ancient Syriac version. They have probably been inserted here from other and later Epistles: see* 1 Cor. i. 3; 2 Cor. i. 2, &c.

proved among you for your sakes.

6 And ye became imitators of us, and of the Lord, receiving the word in much affliction, with joy of the Holy Spirit:

7 So that ye became an example to all that believe in Macedonia and Achaia.

8 For from you hath sounded out the word of the Lord not only in Macedonia and Achaia, but in every place your faith which is toward God is gone forth; so that we need not to speak any thing.

9 For they themselves report concerning us what manner of entering in we had unto you, and how ye turned to God from your idols to serve the living and true God;

10 And to wait for his Son from the heavens, whom he raised from the dead, even Jesus, who delivereth us from the wrath which is to come.

CHAPTER II.

FOR yourselves know, brethren, our entering in unto you, that it hath not been in vain:

2 Nay, after that we had suffered before, and had been shamefully treated, as ye know, at Philippi, we were bold in our God to speak unto you the gospel of God in much conflict.

3 For our exhortation springeth not from deceit, nor yet from impurity, nor yet is it in guile:

4 But according as we have been approved of God to be put in trust with the gospel, even so we speak; not as pleasing men, but God, which proveth our hearts.

5 For neither at any time did we practise words of flattery, as ye know, nor a pretext of covetousness; God is witness:

6 Nor of men sought we glory, either from you, or from others, though we might have been burdensome, as apostles of Christ.

7 But we proved gentle among you, like as when a nursing mother cherisheth her own children:

8 Thus being affectionately desirous of you, we were willing to impart unto you, not only the gospel of God, but also our own lives, because ye became very dear unto us.

9 For ye remember, brethren, our labour and toil: working night and day, that we might not burden any of you, we proclaimed unto you the gospel of God.

10 Ye are witnesses, and God also, how holily and justly and unblameably we behaved ourselves toward you that believe:

11 Even as ye know, exhorting and comforting every one of you, as a father his own children, and charging you,

12 That ye might walk worthily of God, who calleth you into his own kingdom and glory.

13 And for this cause we also thank God unceasingly, because, when ye received God's word by hearing it from us, ye accepted, not the word of men, but as it is in truth, the word of God, which worketh also in you that believe.

14 For ye became imitators,

brethren, of the churches of God which are in Judæa in Christ Jesus: because ye also suffered like things of your own countrymen, even as they suffered of the Jews:

15 Who both killed Jesus the Lord, and the prophets, and drove out us; and please not God, and are contrary to all men,

16 Forbidding us to speak to the Gentiles that they may be saved; to the end that they may fill up their sins alway. But the wrath ¹[of God] came upon them to the uttermost.

17 But we, brethren, when we had been separated from you for a short time in presence, not in heart, endeavoured the more abundantly to see your face with great desire.

18 Wherefore we would fain have come unto you, even I Paul, both once and again; and Satan hindered us.

19 For what is our hope, or joy, or crown of boasting? Are not even ye, in the presence of our Lord Jesus² at his coming?

20 For ye are our glory and joy.

CHAPTER III.

WHEREFORE being no longer able to forbear, we thought it good to be left behind alone in Athens;

2 And we sent Timothy, our brother, and ³fellow-worker with God in the gospel of Christ, to establish you, and to exhort you on behalf of your faith:

3 That no one might be disquieted in these afflictions: for yourselves know that we are appointed thereunto.

4 For even when we were with you, we told you before that we are to suffer tribulation; even as it also came to pass, and ye know.

5 For this cause I also, when I could no longer forbear, sent in order to know your faith, lest haply the tempter have tempted you, and our labour prove in vain.

6 But Timothy having just now come unto us from you, and brought us good tidings of your faith and love, and that ye have good remembrance of us always, longing to see us, as we also to see you:

7 For this cause we were comforted, brethren, over you in all our distress and affliction by your faith:

8 Since now we live, if ye stand fast in the Lord.

9 For what thanksgiving can we render again to God for you, for all the joy wherewith we rejoice for your sakes before our God;

10 Night and day praying very exceedingly that we may see your faces, and may fill up the defects of your faith?

---

¹ *Not expressed in the original.*
² Christ *is omitted in all the oldest authorities.*
³ *The readings are in some confusion. That adopted in the text was probably the original, and the alterations took place from the expression seeming objectionable. The Sinaitic and Alexandrian MSS. have only* minister of God; *the Vatican, only and* fellow-worker: *the Claromontane, as in text.*

11 But may God himself and our Father, and our Lord ¹Jesus, direct our way unto you.

12 And you yourselves may the Lord make to increase and abound in your love one toward another, and toward all, even as we also toward you:

13 To the end that he may stablish your hearts unblameable in holiness before God and our Father, at the coming of our Lord ¹Jesus with all his saints.

CHAPTER IV.

FURTHERMORE then, brethren, we beseech you and exhort you in the Lord Jesus, that as ye received of us how ye ought to walk and to please God, ¹even as also ye are walking, ye would abound yet more.

2 For ye know what commandments we gave you by the Lord Jesus.

3 For this is the will of God, your sanctification, to wit, that ye abstain from fornication:

4 That every one of you should know how to acquire his own vessel in sanctification and honour;

5 Not in the lust of carnal desire, even as the Gentiles which know not God:

6 That he should not go beyond and overreach his brother in the matter: because that the Lord is the avenger of all these things, as we also forewarned you and testified.

7 For God called us not for uncleanness, but in sanctification.

¹ *So all the most ancient MSS.*

8 He therefore that despiseth, despiseth not man, but God, who also gave unto you his Spirit, which is holy.

9 But as touching brotherly love ye need not that one write unto you: for ye yourselves are taught of God that ye should love one another.

10 And indeed ye do it toward all the brethren which are in the whole of Macedonia. But we beseech you, brethren, to abound yet more;

11 And to study to be quiet, and to do your own business, and to work with ²your hands, even as we commanded you;

12 That ye may walk becomingly toward them that are without, and may have lack of nothing.

13 But ³we would not have you to be ignorant, brethren, concerning them which are ⁴sleeping, that ye may not sorrow, even as the rest do which have no hope.

14 For if we believe that Jesus died and rose again, even so them also which fell asleep through Jesus will God bring together with Him.

15 For this we say unto you in the word of the Lord, that we which are living, who remain behind unto the coming of the Lord, shall in no wise gain an advantage over them which fell asleep.

16 Because the Lord himself shall come down from heaven with a shout, with the voice of the archangel, and with the

² *So most of the oldest MSS.*
³ *So all the oldest MSS.*
⁴ *So the three most ancient MSS*

trump of God : and the dead in Christ shall rise first :

17 Then we which are living, who remain behind, shall be caught up all together, with them, in the clouds, to meet the Lord, into the air : and so shall we be always with the Lord.

18 So then comfort one another with these words.

CHAPTER V.

BUT concerning the times and the seasons, brethren, ye have no need to be written unto.

2 For yourselves know perfectly that the day of the Lord so cometh as a thief in the night.

3 [1]When they say, Peace and safety; then sudden destruction cometh upon them, as the pang upon a woman with child; and they shall in no wise escape.

4 But ye, brethren, are not in darkness, that the day should overtake you as a thief.

5 [2]For ye are all sons of light, and sons of the day : we are not of the night, nor of darkness.

6 Therefore let us not sleep, as the rest do ; but let us watch and be sober.

7 For they that sleep sleep in the night ; and they that be drunken are drunken in the night.

8 But let us, being of the day, be sober, putting on a breastplate of faith and love ; and for an helmet, the hope of salvation.

9 For God appointed us not unto wrath, but to the obtaining of salvation through our Lord Jesus Christ,

10 Who died for us, that, whether we wake or sleep, we should live together, with Him

11 Wherefore comfort each other, and edify one another, even as also ye do.

12 But we beseech you, brethren, to know them which labour among you, and preside over you in the Lord, and admonish you ;

13 And to esteem them very highly in love for their work's sake. Be at peace among yourselves.

14 But we exhort you, brethren, admonish the disorderly, comfort the fainthearted, support the weak, be longsuffering toward all men.

15 See that none render evil for evil unto any one ; but ever follow after that which is good, both toward one another, and toward all.

16 Rejoice always,

17 Pray unceasingly,

18 In everything give thanks : for this is the will of God in Christ Jesus toward you.

19 Quench not the Spirit.

20 Despise not prophesyings,

21 But prove all things ; hold fast that which is good,

22 Abstain from every form of evil.

23 But may the God of peace himself sanctify you wholly ; and may your spirit and soul

---

[1] *So all the oldest authorities.*

[2] *For is omitted in the Alexandrine and Sinaitic MSS. and in the ancient Syriac version, and the most ancient Fathers: the Vatican and Claromontane MSS. read* But.

and body be preserved whole without blame in the coming of our Lord Jesus Christ.

24 Faithful is he that calleth you, who also will do it.

25 Brethren, pray for us.

26 Salute all the brethren with an holy kiss.

27 I adjure you by the Lord that this epistle be read unto all the holy brethren.

28 The grace of our Lord Jesus Christ be with you.[1]

[1] Amen *is omitted by some of the oldest MSS., and inserted by others*

THE SECOND EPISTLE OF PAUL THE APOSTLE
TO THE
THESSALONIANS.

CHAPTER I.

PAUL, and Silvanus, and Timothy, unto the church of Thessalonians in God our Father and the Lord Jesus Christ:

2 Grace unto you, and peace, from God [1]our Father and the Lord Jesus Christ.

3 We are bound to give thanks to God always for you, brethren, as it is meet, because that your faith increaseth exceedingly, and the love of every one of you all toward each other aboundeth ;

4 So that we ourselves make our boast of you in the churches of God for your patience and faith in all your persecutions and the afflictions that ye are enduring :

5 Which is a token of the righteous judgment of God, that ye may be counted worthy of the kingdom of God, for which ye are also suffering :

[1] *Some of the oldest MSS. read* the Father.

6 If so be that it is a righteous thing with God to recompense affliction to them that afflict you ;

7 And to you who are afflicted rest with us, at the revelation of the Lord Jesus from heaven with the angels of his might,

8 In flaming fire, bestowing vengeance on them that know not God, and on them that obey not the gospel of our Lord Jesus [2][Christ] :

9 The which shall be punished with everlasting destruction from the presence of the Lord, and from the glory of his power ;

10 When he shall come to be glorified in his saints, and to be admired in all them that [3]believed (because our testimony to you was believed) in that day.

11 To which end we pray

[2] *Some of the oldest MSS. omit* Christ.
[3] *So all the oldest MSS.*

also always for you, that our God may count you worthy of your calling, and may fulfil all good pleasure of goodness, and work of faith, with power :

12 That the name of our Lord Jesus Christ may be glorified in you, and ye in him, according to the grace of our God and the Lord Jesus Christ.

CHAPTER II.

BUT we beseech you, brethren, touching the coming of our Lord Jesus Christ, and our gathering together unto him,

2 That ye be not soon shaken from your mind, nor yet be troubled, neither by spirit, nor by word nor by letter, as by us, to the effect that the day of ¹the Lord is come.

3 Let no man deceive you in any way : for ²[that day shall not come,] unless there shall have come the apostasy first, and the Man of ³Sin shall have been revealed, the son of perdition ;

4 He that opposeth, and exalteth himself above every one called God, or an object of worship ; so that he⁴ sitteth down in the temple of God, shewing himself that he is God.

5 Remember ye not that, when I was yet with you, I told you these things ?

6 And now ye know what hindereth, that he might be revealed in his own time.

7 For the mystery of lawlessness doth already work, only until he that now hindereth be taken out of the way.

8 And then shall the Lawless One be revealed, whom the Lord ⁵Jesus shall consume with the breath of his mouth, and shall destroy with the appearance of his coming :

9 Whose coming is after the working of Satan in all power and signs and wonders of falsehood,

10 And in all deceit of unrighteousness for them that are perishing ; because they received not the love of the truth, that they might be saved.

11 And for this cause ⁶doth God send them the working of delusion, that they should believe the falsehood :

12 That they all of them may be judged who believed not the truth, but had pleasure in unrighteousness.

13 ¶ But as for us, we are bound to give thanks to God alway for you, brethren beloved of the Lord, ·because God chose you from the beginning to salvation in sanctification of the Spirit and belief of the truth :

14 Whereunto he called you by our gospel, to the obtaining of the glory of our Lord Jesus Christ.

15 Therefore, brethren, stand fast, and hold the traditions

---

¹ *So all the oldest authorities.*
² *These words are not expressed in the original.*
³ *The two most ancient MSS. read* Lawlessness.
⁴ As God *is omitted by all the most ancient MSS.*
⁵ *So most of the oldest MSS. versions, and Fathers.*
⁶ *So all the oldest MSS.*

which ye were taught, whether by word, or by our epistle.

16 But our Lord Jesus Christ himself, and God and our Father, which loved us, and gave us eternal consolation and good hope in grace,

17 Comfort your hearts, and stablish you in every good work and word.

CHAPTER III.

FINALLY, brethren, pray for us, that the word of the Lord may have free course, and be glorified, even as it is also with you:

2 And that we may be delivered from perverse and wicked men: for all have not the faith.

3 But the Lord is faithful, who shall stablish you, and keep you from evil.

4 Moreover we have confidence in the Lord touching you, that ye both are doing and will do the things which we command [1][you].

5 But may the Lord direct your hearts into the love of God, and into the patience of Christ.

6 Moreover we command you, brethren, in the name of our Lord Jesus Christ, that ye withdraw yourselves from every brother that is walking disorderly, and not after the tradition which [2]they received of us.

7 For yourselves know how ye ought to imitate us: because we behaved not ourselves disorderly among you;

8 Neither did we eat bread from any man without recompence; but in labour and toil working night and day, that we might not be burdensome to any of you:

9 Not because we have not power, but to make ourselves an example unto you to imitate us.

10 For also when we were with you, this we commanded you, that if any man will not work, neither let him eat.

11 For we hear that there are some walking among you disorderly, working at no business, but being busybodies.

12 Now them that are such we command and exhort in the Lord Jesus Christ, that working with quietness they eat their own bread.

13 But ye, brethren, be not weary in well doing.

14 But if any man obeyeth not our word by this epistle, mark that man, and keep no company with him, that he may be ashamed.

15 And count him not as an enemy, but admonish him as a brother.

16 But may the Lord of peace himself give you peace always in every way. The Lord be with you all.

17 The salutation of me Paul with mine own hand, which is a token in every epistle: so I write.

18 The grace of our Lord Jesus Christ be with you all.[3]

[1] *Omitted by some of the oldest MSS.*
[2] *So almost all the earliest MSS.: he received is in none of them.*
[3] *Amen is omitted by the most ancient MSS.*

THE FIRST EPISTLE OF PAUL THE APOSTLE
TO
TIMOTHY.

CHAPTER I.

PAUL, an apostle of ¹Christ Jesus according to the commandment of God our Saviour, and Christ Jesus our hope;

2 Unto Timothy, mine own child in the faith: Grace, mercy, peace, from God the Father and Christ Jesus our Lord.

3 Even as I besought thee to abide still at Ephesus, when I was on my way to Macedonia, that thou mightest command some not to be teachers of strange things,

4 Nor yet give heed to fables and endless genealogies, the which minister questions, rather than God's ²dispensation which is in faith.

5 But the end of the commandment is love out of a pure heart and a good conscience and faith unfeigned:

6 From which things some having swerved have been turned aside unto vain babbling;

7 Desiring to be teachers of the law, though they understand not either what they say, or of what things they make affirmation.

8 But we know that the law is good, if a man use it lawfully,

9 And be aware of this, that the law is not made for a righteous man, but for the lawless and insubordinate, for the ungodly and sinners, for the unholy and profane, for smiters of fathers and smiters of mothers, for manslayers,

10 For whoremongers, for them that defile themselves with mankind, for slavedealers, for liars, for perjured persons, and if there be any other thing that is contrary to the sound doctrine;

11 According to the gospel of the glory of the blessed God, with which I was entrusted.

12 ³I give thanks to him that put strength in me, even Christ Jesus our Lord, that he counted me faithful, appointing me to the ministry;

13 Though I was before a blasphemer, and a persecutor, and an insulter: yet I obtained mercy, because I did it ignorantly in unbelief.

14 But the grace of our Lord was exceeding abundant with faith and love which is in Christ Jesus.

15 Faithful is the saying, and worthy of all acceptation, that Christ Jesus came into the

---

¹ *So the oldest MSS.*
² *So some of the oldest MSS.: others having* edification, *but in differing forms, which makes it probable that it was an alteration to suit the apparent sense.*
³ *And* is omitted by the most ancient *MSS.*

world to save sinners; of whom I am chief.

16 Howbeit for this cause I obtained mercy, that in me first Christ Jesus might shew forth the whole of his longsuffering, for a pattern for them which should hereafter believe on him to eternal life.

17 But unto the King of the ages, the immortal, the invisible, the only ¹God, be honour and glory for ever and ever. Amen.

18 This commandment I commit unto thee, my child Timothy, according to the former prophecies concerning thee, that thou mayest war in them the good warfare;

19 Holding faith, and a good conscience; which some having thrust from them made shipwreck concerning the faith:

20 Among whom is Hymenæus and Alexander; whom I delivered over unto Satan, that they may be taught by chastisement not to blaspheme.

CHAPTER II.

I EXHORT then first of all, that supplications, prayers, intercessions, giving of thanks, be made for all men;

2 For kings, and all that are in authority; that we may lead a quiet and peaceable life in all godliness and gravity.

3 For this is good and acceptable in the sight of our Saviour, even God;

4 Who willeth all men to be saved, and to come unto the certain knowledge of the truth.

5 For there is one God, one mediator also between God and men, Christ Jesus, [himself] man:

6 Who gave himself a ransom for all, the matter to be testified in its own time.

7 Whereunto I was appointed an herald, and an apostle, (I speak the truth in Christ, I lie not;) a teacher of the Gentiles in faith and verity.

8 I will then that the **men** pray in every place, lifting up holy hands, without wrath and doubting.

9 In like manner also, that **women** adorn themselves in orderly apparel, with ²shamefastness and sobermindedness; not with braided hair and gold, or pearls, or costly apparel:

10 But (which becometh women professing godliness) by means of good works.

11 Let the woman learn in silence in all subjection.

12 But I suffer not the woman to teach, nor yet to rule over the man, but to be in silence.

13 For Adam was first formed, then Eve.

14 And Adam was not deceived, but the woman being taken by the deceit hath become a transgressor.

15 Notwithstanding she shall be saved through her childbearing, if they continue in faith and love and sanctification with sobermindedness.

CHAPTER III.

FAITHFUL is the saying, If a man seeketh for the

---

¹ *Wise is omitted by all the oldest authorities.*

² *Commonly printed wrongly* shamefacedness.

office of a bishop, he desireth a good work.

2 A bishop then must be irreproachable, the husband of one wife, vigilant, soberminded, orderly, hospitable, apt in teaching:

3 No brawler, no striker;[1] but forbearing, averse from contention, no lover of money;

4 Ruling well over his own house, having children in subjection with all gravity;

5 (But if a man knoweth not how to rule over his own house, how shall he take care of the church of God?)

6 Not a novice, lest being besotted with pride he fall into the judgment of the devil.

7 Moreover he must have a good report also from them which are without; lest he fall into [the] reproach and the snare of the devil.

8 Deacons in like manner must be grave, not doubletongued, not given to much wine, not greedy of gain;

9 Holding the mystery of the faith in a pure conscience.

10 And moreover let these also first be proved; then let them serve as deacons, if they be not under reproach.

11 The women in like manner must be grave, not slanderers, sober, faithful in all things.

12 Let the deacons be husbands of one wife, ruling well over children and their own houses.

13 For they that served well as deacons obtain for themselves a good standingplace, and great boldness in the faith which is in Christ Jesus.

14 These things write I unto thee, though I hope to come unto thee shortly:

15 But if I should tarry long, that thou mayest know how thou oughtest to behave thyself in the house of God, which is the church of the living God, the pillar and ground of the truth.

16 And confessedly great is the mystery of godliness, [2]who was manifested in the flesh, justified in the Spirit, seen of angels, preached unto the Gentiles, believed on in the world, received up in glory.

CHAPTER IV.

HOWBEIT the Spirit saith expressly, that in after times some shall depart from the faith, giving heed to seducing spirits, and doctrines of devils;

2 In the hypocrisy of speakers of lies; of men having their own conscience seared with a brand;

3 Forbidding to marry, [and commanding] to abstain from meats, which God created unto participation with thanksgiving for them that believe and have full knowledge of the truth.

4 Because every creature of God is good, and nothing is to be refused, if it be received with thanksgiving:

---

[1] *Not greedy of filthy lucre is omitted by all the ancient authorities: it probably came in from Tit. i. 7.*

[2] *So all the most ancient authorities, except one, which reads* which, *neuter gender.*

5 For it is sanctified through the word of God and intercession.

6 By setting forth these things to the brethren, thou shalt be a good minister of ¹Christ Jesus, training thyself in the words of the faith, and of the good doctrine, whose course thou hast followed.

7 But profane and old wives' fables decline, and exercise thyself rather unto godliness.

8 For bodily exercise profiteth for a little : but godliness is profitable unto all things, having promise of the life that now is, and of that which is to come.

9 Faithful is the saying and worthy of all acceptation.

10 For to this end we both toil and ²suffer reproach, because we have set our hope on the living God, who is the Saviour of all men, especially of believers.

11 These things command and teach.

12 Let no one despise thy youth; but become an example to the believers, in word, in conduct, in love,³ in faith, in purity.

13 Till I come, give attention to the reading, to the exhortation, to the doctrine.

14 Neglect not the gift that is in thee, which was given thee through prophecy, with the laying on of the hands of the presbytery.

15 Make these things thy care; in these things be employed; that thy progress may be manifest to all.

16 Give heed unto thyself, and unto the doctrine; continue in them, for in doing this thou shalt both save thyself, and them that hear thee.

CHAPTER V.

AN elder rebuke not sharply, but exhort him as a father; the younger men, as brethren;

2 The elder women, as mothers; the younger as sisters, in all purity.

3 Widows that are widows indeed take into consideration;

4 But if any widow hath children or grandchildren, let these learn first to shew piety to their own family, and to requite their parents : for this is ⁴acceptable before God.

5 But she that is a widow indeed, and desolate, hath set her hope toward God, and continueth in her supplications and her prayers night and day.

6 But she that is given to dissipation is dead while she liveth.

7 And these things command, that they may be irreproachable.

8 But if any provide not for his own, and specially for those of his own house, he hath denied the faith, and is worse than an unbeliever.

9 Let a woman be enrolled a widow, who is not less than threescore years old, the wife of one husband, being

---

¹ *So all the earliest MSS.*
² *Most of the earliest MSS for* suffer reproach *read* strive.
³ *In spirit is omitted by all the oldest authorities.*
⁴ *Good and is omitted by all the ancient authorities.*

10 Well reported of in good works; if she at any time brought up children, if she entertained strangers, if she washed the saints' feet, if she relieved the afflicted, if she followed after every good work.

11 But younger widows decline: for when they shall wax wanton against Christ, they desire to marry;

12 Bearing a judgment, because they made void their first faith.

13 And withal they learn to be idle, going round from house to house; and not only idle, but tattlers also and busybodies, speaking things which they ought not.

14 I will therefore that the younger widows marry, bear children, guide the house, give none occasion to the adversary for reproach.

15 For some have already turned aside after Satan.

16 If any ¹[man or] woman that believeth hath widows, let such person relieve them, and let not the church be burdened; that it may relieve them that are widows indeed.

17 Let the presbyters that rule well be counted worthy of double honour, especially they who labour in the word and doctrine.

18 For the scripture saith, Thou shalt not muzzle an ox while he is treading out the corn. And the labourer is worthy of his hire.

19 Against a presbyter receive not an accusation, except on the word of two or three witnesses.

20 ²Them that sin rebuke before all, that the rest also may fear.

21 I adjure thee before God, and ³Christ Jesus, and the elect angels, that thou observe these things without prejudice, doing nothing by partiality.

22 Lay hands hastily on no one, neither be partaker of the sins of others: keep **thyself** pure.

23 Drink no longer water, but use a little wine for thy stomach's sake and thine often sicknesses.

24 Of some the sins are openly manifest, going before them to judgment; and some again they follow after.

25 In like manner the good works also of some are openly manifest; and those [works] that are otherwise cannot be hid.

CHAPTER VI.

LET as many as are bondmen under the yoke count their own masters worthy of all honour, that the name of God and his doctrine be not blasphemed.

2 Those again that have believing masters, let them not despise them because they are brethren; but serve them all the more, because they who receive the benefit are faithful and beloved. These things teach and exhort.

---

¹ *These words are omitted by most of the ancient MSS., but contained in others, and in the ancient Syriac version.*

² *Some of the ancient MSS. read* But them that sin.

³ *So the oldest MSS.*

3 If any man is a teacher of other doctrine, and assenteth not to wholesome words, even the words of our Lord Jesus Christ, and to the doctrine which is according to godliness;

4 He is besotted with pride, knowing nothing, but doting about questions and strifes of words, whereof cometh envy, strife, railings, evil surmisings,

5 ¹Incessant quarrellings of men depraved in mind, and destitute of the truth, supposing that godliness is a source of gain:²

6 .But godliness with contentment **is** a great source of gain.

7 For we brought nothing into the world, ³because neither can we carry any thing out.

8 But having food and covering, we shall be therewith sufficiently provided.

9 But they that desire to be rich fall into temptation and a snare, and into many foolish and hurtful lusts, such as drown men in destruction and perdition.

10 For the root of all evils is the love of money, after which while some were lusting, they wandered away from the faith, and pierced themselves through with many sorrows.

11 But thou, O man of God, flee these things; and follow after righteousness, godliness, faith, love, patience, meekness.

12 Fight the good fight of the faith, lay hold on eternal life, whereunto thou wast called, and didst confess the good confession before many witnesses.

13 I command thee before God, who endueth all things with life, and before Christ Jesus, who before Pontius Pilate testified the good confession;

14 That thou keep the commandment without spot, irreproachable, until the appearing of our Lord Jesus Christ:

15 Which in his own seasons he shall shew, the blessed and only Potentate, the King of kings, and Lord of lords;

16 Who only hath immortality, dwelling in light unapproachable; whom never man saw, nor can see: to whom be honour and eternal might. Amen.

17 Them that are rich in this present world command not to be highminded, nor to set their hopes on the uncertainty of riches, but in ⁴God, who giveth us all things richly to enjoy;

18 To do good, to be rich in good works, free in distributing, willing to communicate;

19 Laying up in store for themselves a good foundation against the time to come, that they may lay hold on ⁵the true life.

20 O Timothy, keep the trust committed to thee, turning

---

¹ *So all the ancient authorities.*

² *The words* from such withdraw thyself *are omitted by all the oldest MSS.*

³ *So the two oldest MSS. The clause is very variously filled up to escape the difficulty.*

⁴ *The living is omitted by nearly all the most ancient MSS.*

⁵ *So all the oldest MSS.*

away from the profane babblings and oppositions of the falsely called knowledge:

21 Which some professing missed the mark concerning the faith. Grace be with thee. The grace [of God] be with thee.¹

¹ Amen *is omitted in the oldest MSS.*

THE SECOND EPISTLE OF PAUL THE APOSTLE
TO
TIMOTHY.

CHAPTER I.

PAUL, an apostle of ¹Christ Jesus by the will of God, according to the promise of life which is in Christ Jesus,

2 To Timothy, my beloved child: Grace, mercy, peace, from God the Father and Christ Jesus our Lord.

3 I thank God, whom I serve from my forefathers in pure conscience, how unceasingly I have remembrance of thee in my prayers night and day;

4 Longing to see thee, being mindful of thy tears, that I may be filled with joy;

5 Calling to remembrance the unfeigned faith that was in thee, such as dwelt first in thy grandmother Lois, and thy mother ²Eunice; but I am persuaded that also in thee.

6 For which cause I put thee in mind to stir up the gift of God, which is in thee through the laying on of my hands.

¹ *So the oldest MSS.*
² *Pronounce* Euníce.

7 For God gave us not the spirit of cowardice; but of power, and of love, and of correction.

8 Be not thou ashamed therefore of the testimony of our Lord, nor yet of me his prisoner: but rather suffer afflictions with me for the gospel according to the power of God;

9 Who saved us, and called us with an holy calling, not according to our works, but according to his own purpose and the grace which was given to us in Christ Jesus before eternal times,

10 But hath now been made manifest by the appearing of our Saviour Jesus Christ, who abolished death, but brought life and incorruption to light through the gospel:

11 For which I was appointed an herald, and an apostle, and a teacher of the Gentiles.

12 For which cause I also suffer these things: nevertheless I am not ashamed: for I

know whom I have trusted, and am persuaded that he is able to keep that which I have committed unto him against that day.

13 Take an example of the sound words, which thou heardest from me in faith and love which is in Christ Jesus.

14 The goodly trust committed unto thee keep through the Holy Ghost which dwelleth in us.

15 Thou knowest this, that all they which are in Asia turned away from me ; of whom are ¹Phygelus and Hermogenes.

16 The Lord give mercy unto the house of Onesiphorus, because he oft refreshed me, and was not ashamed of my chain :

17 Nay, when he came to Rome, he sought me out the more diligently, and found me.

18 The Lord grant unto him that he may find mercy of the Lord in that day : and in how many things he ministered at Ephesus, thou knowest better than I.

CHAPTER II.

THOU therefore, my child, be strengthened in the grace that is in Christ Jesus.

2 And the things that thou heardest from me among many witnesses, these commit thou to faithful men, such as shall be able to teach them to others also.

3 ²Suffer afflictions with me as a good soldier of ³Christ Jesus.

¹ *Pronounce* Phýgĕlus *and* Hermógĕnes.
² *So all the most ancient authorities.*
³ *So the most ancient MSS.*

4 No man serving as a soldier entangleth himself with the affairs of life ; that he may please him who chose him to be a soldier.

5 And if a man also strive in the games, he is not crowned, except he strive according to the rules.

6 The labouring husbandman ought to partake first of the fruits.

7 Understand what I say ; for the Lord shall give thee clear apprehension in all things.

8 Keep in remembrance Jesus Christ, raised from the dead, of the seed of David, according to my gospel,

9 In which I suffer trouble, even unto bonds as an evil doer ; but the word of God hath not been bound.

10 For this cause I endure all things for the sake of the elect, that they also may obtain the salvation which is in Christ Jesus with eternal glory.

11 Faithful is the saying : For if we died with him, we shall also live with him :

12 If we endure, we shall also reign with him : if we shall deny him, he also will deny us :

13 If we disbelieve, yet he remaineth faithful : ⁴for he cannot deny himself.

14 Of these things put them in remembrance, adjuring them before the Lord not to strive about words, a thing tending to no profit, to the subverting of the hearers.

15 Study to present thyself approved unto God, a work-

⁴ *So all the oldest authorities.*

man not ashamed, rightly laying out the word of the truth.

16 But shun profane babblings: for they will advance unto a greater measure of ungodliness.

17 And their word will eat as doth a cancer: of whom is Hymenæus and Philetus;

18 Who concerning the truth went astray, saying that the resurrection is past already; and overthrow the faith of some.

19 Nevertheless the firm foundation of God standeth, having this seal, The Lord knoweth them that are his: and, Let every one that nameth the name of ¹the Lord depart from iniquity.

20 But in a great house there are not only vessels of gold and of silver, but also of wood and of earth; and some to honour, and some to dishonour.

21 If then a man shall purify himself from these, he shall be a vessel unto honour, sanctified, meet for the master's use, prepared unto every good work.

22 But flee youthful lusts: and follow after righteousness, faith, love, ²peace with them that call on the Lord out of a pure heart.

23 But foolish and irregular questions decline, knowing that they gender strifes.

24 And the servant of the Lord must not strive; but be gentle unto all, apt to teach, patient of wrong,

25 In meekness correcting those that oppose themselves; if God peradventure will give them repentance in order to the knowledge of the truth;

26 And that they may return to soberness out of the snare of the devil, having been taken captive by him in pursuance of God's will.

CHAPTER III.

BUT know this, that in the last days grievous times shall come.

2 For men shall be lovers of their own selves, lovers of money, boasters, haughty, evil speakers, disobedient to parents, unthankful, unholy,

3 Without natural affection, implacable, slanderers, incontinent, fierce, haters of good,

4 Traitors, headlong, besotted with pride, lovers of pleasure more than lovers of God;

5 Having an outward form of godliness, but having denied the power thereof: from these also turn away.

6 For of these are they which creep into houses, and lead captive silly women laden with sins, led away with divers lusts,

7 Ever learning, and never yet able to come to the full knowledge of the truth.

8 Now as Jannes and Jambres withstood Moses, so do these also withstand the truth: men corrupted in their minds, reprobate concerning the faith.

9 Notwithstanding, they shall proceed no further: for their

---

¹ *So all the ancient authorities.*
² *Peace with them, &c. should be read together, not with a comma between, as in A.V.*

folly shall be fully manifest unto all, as theirs also was.

10 But thou wert a follower of my doctrine, manner of life, purpose, faith, longsuffering, love, patience,

11 Persecutions, sufferings, such as happened unto me at Antioch, at Iconium, at Lystra ; such persecutions as I endured : and out of all the Lord delivered me.

12 Yea, and all that will live godly in Christ Jesus shall suffer persecution.

13 But evil men and impostors shall wax worse and worse, deceiving, and being deceived.

14 But continue thou in the things which thou learnedst and wert assured of, knowing from what teachers thou didst learn them;

15 And that from a child thou ¹knowest the holy scriptures, which are able to make thee wise unto salvation through faith which is in Christ Jesus.

16 Every scripture inspired by God is also profitable for doctrine, for conviction, for correction, for discipline which is in righteousness :

17 That the man of God may be complete, throughly furnished unto every good work.

CHAPTER IV.

I ADJURE thee² before God, and Christ Jesus, who shall one day judge the quick and the dead, ³and by his appearing and his kingdom ;

2 Preach the word ; be urgent in season, out of season ; convict, rebuke, exhort in all longsuffering and teaching.

3 For the time will come when they will not endure the sound doctrine ; but after their own lusts they shall heap to themselves teachers, having itching ears ;

4 And they shall turn away their ears from the truth, and shall turn aside unto fables.

5 But be thou sober in all things, suffer affliction, do the work of an evangelist, fulfil thy ministry.

6 For I am already being poured out, and the time of my departure is at hand.

7 I have striven the good strife, I have finished my course, I have kept the faith :

8 Henceforth there is laid up for me the crown of righteousness, which the Lord, the righteous judge, shall award me at that day : and not only to me, but unto all them also that have loved his appearing.

9 Do thy diligence to come shortly unto me :

10 For Demas forsook me, loving this present world, and departed unto Thessalonica ; Crescens to Galatia, Titus unto Dalmatia.

11 Only Luke is with me. Take Mark, and bring him with thee : for he is profitable to me for the ministry.

12 But Tychicus I sent to Ephesus.

¹ *So the oldest MSS.*
² *So, omitting* therefore, *and the* Lord, *and reading* Christ Jesus, *all the earliest MSS*
³ *So all the oldest MSS.*

13 The cloak that I left at Troas with Carpus, when thou comest, bring with thee, and the books, especially the parchments.

14 Alexander the smith did me much evil: the Lord [1]shall reward him according to his works:

15 Of whom be thou ware also; for he greatly [1]withstood our words.

16 At my first defence no man stood forward with me, but all forsook me: may it not be laid to their charge.

17 But the Lord stood by me, and strengthened me; that through me the preaching might be fulfilled, and that all the Gentiles might hear: and I was delivered out of the mouth of the lion.

18 [2]The Lord shall deliver me from every evil work, and shall preserve me safe unto his heavenly kingdom: to whom be the glory for ever and ever. Amen.

19 Salute Prisca and Aquila, and the household of Onesiphorus.

20 Erastus abode at Corinth: but Trophimus I left at Miletus sick.

21 Do thy diligence to come before winter. [3]Eubulus greeteth thee, and Pudens, and Linus, and Claudia, and all the brethren.

22 The Lord Jesus Christ be with thy spirit. Grace be with you.[4]

[1] *So all the oldest MSS.*

[2] And *is omitted by all the oldest MSS.*

[3] *Pronounce* Eubúlus.

[4] Amen *is omitted in some of the oldest MSS.*

THE EPISTLE OF PAUL
TO
TITUS.

CHAPTER I.

PAUL, a servant of God, and an apostle of Christ Jesus, for the faith of God's elect, and the knowledge of the truth which is according to godliness;

2 In hope of eternal life, which God, that cannot lie, promised before eternal times;

3 But in its own seasons made manifest his word in the preaching, with which I was entrusted according to the commandment of our Saviour God;

4 To Titus, mine own child after the common faith: Grace [1]and peace from God the Fa-

[1] *So the majority of the oldest authorities.*

ther and ¹Christ Jesus our Saviour.

5 For this cause left I thee behind in Crete, that thou shouldest further set in order the things that are wanting, and appoint elders in every city, as I prescribed to thee:

6 If any be under no imputation, the husband of one wife, having believing children who are not accused of dissoluteness, or unruly.

7 For a bishop must be under no imputation, as being the steward of God; not selfwilled, not soon angry, not a brawler, not a striker, not greedy of gain;

8 But a lover of hospitality, a lover of goodness, soberminded, just, holy, temperate;

9 Holding fast the faithful word according to the teaching, that he may be able both to exhort in the sound doctrine, and to rebuke the gainsayers.

10 For there are many unruly vain talkers and deceivers, specially they of the circumcision:

11 Whose mouths must be stopped, seeing they subvert whole houses, teaching things which they ought not, for the sake of base gain.

12 One of themselves, a prophet of their own, said, The Cretans are alway liars, evil beasts, slothful bellies.

13 This witness is true. Wherefore rebuke them sharply, in order that they may be sound in the faith;

14 Not giving heed to Jewish

¹ *So all the oldest MSS.*

fables and commandments of men that turn themselves away from the truth.

15 Unto the pure all things are pure: but unto them that are defiled and unbelieving nothing is pure; but both their mind and their conscience is defiled.

16 They make confession that they know God; but in their works they deny him, being abominable, and disobedient, and unto every good work reprobate.

CHAPTER II.

BUT do thou speak the things which become the sound doctrine:

2 That the aged men be sober, grave, discreet, sound in their faith, in their love, in their patience.

3 The aged women likewise, that they be in behaviour as becometh holiness, not slanderers, not enslaved to much wine, teachers of good things;

4 That they may teach the young women to be sober, to be lovers of their husbands, lovers of their children,

5 Discreet, chaste, ¹workers at home, good, submitting themselves to their own husbands, that the word of God be not blasphemed.

6 The younger men in like manner exhort to be soberminded,

7 In all things shewing thyself a pattern of good works: in thy doctrine shewing uncorruptness, gravity,²

² *Sincerity is omitted by the oldest MSS.*

8 Sound speech, that cannot be condemned; that he that is of the contrary part may be ashamed, having no evil thing to say of ¹us.

9 Exhort slaves to submit themselves unto their own masters, in all things to give satisfaction; not contradicting;

10 Not purloining, but shewing all good fidelity; that they may adorn the doctrine of our Saviour God in all things.

11 For the grace of God was manifested bringing salvation to all men,

12 Disciplining us, in order that, denying ungodliness and worldly lusts, we should live soberly, and justly, and godly, in the present world;

13 Looking for that blessed hope, and the manifestation of the glory of the great God and of our Saviour Jesus Christ;

14 Who gave Himself for us, that he might redeem us from all iniquity, and purify unto himself a peculiar people, zealous of good works.

15 These things speak, and exhort, and rebuke with all authority. Let no man despise thee.

CHAPTER III.

PUT them in mind to submit themselves to governments, to authorities, to obey magistrates, to be ready to every good work,

2 To speak evil of no man, to be not quarrelsome, forbearing, shewing all meekness unto all men.

3 For we ourselves also were once foolish, disobedient, led astray, serving divers lusts and pleasures, living in malice and envy, hateful, hating one another.

4 But when the kindness and love towards men of our Saviour God was manifested;

5 Not by works wrought in righteousness which we did, but according to his mercy he saved us, through the font of regeneration, and the renewing of the Holy Spirit;

6 Whom he poured out on us richly through Jesus Christ our Saviour;

7 That being justified by his grace, we should become heirs according to the hope of eternal life.

8 Faithful is the saying, and concerning these things I will that thou affirm constantly, in order that they which have believed God may be careful to practise good works. These things are good and profitable unto men.

9 But avoid foolish questions, and genealogies, and contentions, and strivings about the law; for they are unprofitable and vain.

10 A man that is an heretic, after a first and a second admonition, avoid;

11 Knowing that such an one is thoroughly perverted, and sinneth, being self-condemned.

12 When I shall send ²Artemas unto thee, or Tychicus,

¹ *So the majority of the oldest MSS.*
² *Pronounce* Aftĕmas

give diligence to come unto me to Nicopolis: for there I have determined to winter.

13 Forward zealously on their journey Zenas the lawyer and Apollos, that nothing be wanting unto them.

14 Moreover, let our people also learn to practise good works for the necessary wants, that they be not unfruitful.

15 All that are with me salute thee. Salute them that love us in the faith. Grace be with you all.[1]

[1] Amen *is omitted by all the oldest MSS.*

THE EPISTLE OF PAUL
TO
PHILEMON.

PAUL, a prisoner of Christ Jesus, and Timothy our brother, unto Philemon our dearly beloved, and fellow-labourer,

2 And to Apphia our [1]sister, and Archippus our fellow-soldier, and to the church in thy house:

3 Grace to you, and peace, from God our Father and the Lord Jesus Christ.

4 I thank my God always, making mention of thee in my prayers,

5 Hearing of thy love, and the faith which thou hast toward the Lord Jesus, and toward all the saints:

6 That the communication of thy faith may become effectual unto [2]Christ in the knowledge of every good thing which is in [1]us.

7 For [1]I had much joy and consolation in thy love, because the hearts of the saints have been refreshed by thee, brother.

8 Wherefore, though I have much boldness in Christ to enjoin thee that which is fitting,

9 Yet for love's sake I rather beseech thee. Being such an one,—as Paul the aged, and now a prisoner of Christ Jesus,

10 I beseech thee for mine own child Onesimus, whom I begat in my bonds:

11 Which in time past was to thee unprofitable, but now profitable to thee and to me:

12 Whom I have sent back [1]to thee: [1]receive him, that is, mine own heart:

13 Whom I was purposing to retain with myself, that in thy

[1] *So all the oldest MSS.*
[2] Jesus *is omitted by the three oldest MSS.*

stead he might minister unto me in the bonds of the gospel:

14 But without thy consent I would do nothing; that thy good service should not be as of necessity, but of free will.

15 For perhaps he therefore departed for a season, that thou mayest receive him eternally;

16 No longer as a servant, but above a servant, a brother beloved, specially to me, but how much more unto thee, both in the flesh, and in the Lord.

17 If therefore thou countest me a partner, receive him as myself.

18 But if he hath wronged thee, or oweth thee ought, set that down on mine account;

19 I Paul have written it with mine own hand, I will repay it: that I say not unto thee how thou owest unto me even thine own self besides.

20 Yea, brother, let me have profit of thee in the Lord: refresh my heart in [1]Christ.

21 Having confidence in thy obedience, I have written unto thee, knowing that thou wilt do even more than I say.

22 But at the same time prepare me also a lodging: for I hope that through your prayers I shall be granted unto you.

23 Epaphras, my fellow-prisoner in Christ Jesus, saluteth thee;

24 Marcus, Aristarchus, Demas, Lucas, my fellow-labourers.

25 The grace of our Lord Jesus Christ be with thy spirit.[2]

[1] *So all the oldest authorities.*
[2] Amen *is omitted by some of the oldest MSS., and inserted by others.*

THE EPISTLE TO THE
HEBREWS.

CHAPTER I.

GOD, having in many [1]sayings and in divers manners spoken in time past unto the fathers by the prophets,

2 [2]At the end of these days spake unto us in his Son, whom he appointed heir of all things, by whom he also made the worlds;

3 Who being the brightness of his glory, and the express image of his substance, and upholding the universe by the word of his power, when he had [3]made purification of sins,

[1] *Literally,* portions.
[2] *So all the most ancient MSS.*
[3] By himself *and* our *are not found in the most ancient MSS.*

sat down on the right hand of Majesty on high;

4 Having become so much better than the angels, as he hath inherited a more excellent name than they.

5 For unto which of the angels said he at any time, Thou art my Son, this day have I begotten thee? And again, I will be to him as a father, and he shall be to me as a son?

6 But when he again hath introduced the firstbegotten into the world, he saith, And let all the angels of God worship him.

7 And of the angels indeed he saith, Who maketh his angels winds, and his ministers a flame of fire.

8 But unto the Son, Thy throne, O God, is for ever and ever: [1]and the sceptre of thy kingdom is the sceptre of righteousness.

9 Thou lovedst righteousness, and hatedst iniquity; therefore God, even thy God, anointed thee with oil of gladness above thy fellows.

10 And, Thou, Lord, in the beginning didst lay the foundation of the earth; and the heavens are works of thine hands:

11 They shall perish; but thou remainest: and they all shall wax old as doth a garment;

12 And as a vesture shalt thou fold them up, and they shall be changed: but thou art the same. and thy years shall not fail.

13 But to which of the angels hath he said at any time, Sit on my right hand, until I make thine enemies thy footstool?

14 Are they not all ministering spirits, sent forth for ministry on account of them who shall be heirs of salvation?

CHAPTER II.

THEREFORE we ought to give the more earnest heed to the things which we have heard, lest we be diverted from them.

2 For if the word spoken by angels became binding, and every transgression and disobedience received just recompence of reward;

3 How shall we escape, if we have neglected so great salvation; seeing that it, having begun to be spoken by the Lord, was confirmed unto us by them that heard it;

4 God also bearing witness to it, with both signs and wonders, and various miraculous powers, and distributions of the Holy Spirit, according to his own will?

5 For not unto angels did he put in subjection the world to come, whereof we speak.

6 But one in a certain place testified, saying, What is man, that thou art mindful of him? or the son of man, that thou visitest him?

7 Thou madest him a little lower than the angels; thou crownedst him with glory and honour:[2]

---

[1] *So all the most ancient MSS.*

[2] *The words*, and didst set him over the works of thy hands, *though inserted in many of the oldest MSS. (probably from the Psalm), are wanting in the Vatican MS. and others.*

8 Thou didst put all things in subjection under his feet. For in that he put all things in subjection to him, he left nothing that is not put in subjection to him. But now we see not yet all things put in subjection to him.

9 But him that is made a little lower than the angels, even Jesus, we behold, on account of his suffering of death, crowned with glory and honour; in order that he [1]by the grace of God should taste death for every man.

10 For it became him, for whom are all things, and by whom are all things, bringing, as he did, many sons unto glory, to make perfect through sufferings the author of their salvation.

11 For both he that sanctifieth and they who are sanctified are all of one: for which cause he is not ashamed to call them brethren,

12 Saying, I will declare thy name unto my brethren, in the midst of the assembly will I sing of thee.

13 And again, I will put my trust in him. And again, Behold I and the children which God gave me.

14 Forasmuch then as the children are partakers of blood and flesh, he himself also in like manner took part in the same things; that through his death he might destroy him that hath the power of death, that is, the devil;

15 And might deliver as many as through fear of death were all their lifetime kept under bondage.

16 For as we know, it is not angels that he helpeth, but it is the seed of Abraham that he helpeth.

17 Wherefore it behoved him in all things to be like unto his brethren, that he might become a merciful and faithful high priest in things pertaining to God, to make expiation for the sins of the people.

18 For he himself having been tempted in that which he hath suffered, he is able to succour them that are tempted.

CHAPTER III.

WHEREFORE, holy brethren, partakers of an heavenly calling, consider the Apostle and High Priest of our confession, [2]Jesus;

2 That he is faithful to him that made him, as also was Moses in all His house.

3 For this person hath been counted worthy of more glory than Moses, inasmuch as he who established the house hath more honour than the house.

4 For every house is established by some one; but he that established all things is God.

5 And Moses verily was faithful in all His house, as a servant, for testimony of those things which were to be spoken after;

---

[1] *Some ancient copies, versions, and Fathers have, instead of* by the grace of God, except God, *or without God. Origen (Cent. III.) mentions both readings.*

[2] Christ *is omitted by all the earliest MSS.*

6 But Christ as a son over His house; whose house are we, if we hold fast the confidence and the matter of boasting of our hope.[1]

7 Wherefore (as the Holy Spirit saith, To day if ye hear his voice,

8 Harden not your hearts, as in the provocation, at the day of temptation in the wilderness:

9 Where your fathers tempted, [2]in proving [me], and saw my works forty years.

10 Wherefore I was grieved with [3]this generation, and said, They do alway err in their heart; and they never knew my ways.

11 According as I sware in my wrath, They shall not enter into my rest.)

12 Take heed, brethren, lest there shall be in any one of you an evil heart of unbelief, in departing from the living God.

13 But exhort one another daily, while it is called To-day; lest from among you any one be hardened through the deceitfulness of his sin.

14 For we have become partakers of Christ, if we hold the beginning of our confidence stedfast unto the end;

15 For it is said, To-day if ye hear his voice, harden not your hearts, as in the provocation.

16 For who were they that heard and provoked? Nay, was it not all that came out of Egypt by Moses?

17 And with whom was He grieved forty years? was it not with them that sinned, whose carcases fell in the wilderness?

18 And to whom sware He that they should not enter into his rest, but to them that disobeyed?

19 And thus we see that they could not enter in because of unbelief.

CHAPTER IV.

LET us therefore fear, lest, a promise being still left us of entering into his rest, any one of you should seem to have come short of it.

2 For unto us have good tidings been preached, as well as unto them: but the word of hearing did not profit them, [4]unmingled as they were in faith with those that heard it.

3 For we who believed do enter into the rest, even as He hath said, As I sware in my wrath, if they shall enter into my rest: although the works were finished from the foundation of the world.

4 For He hath spoken in a certain place of the seventh day on this wise, And God did rest on the seventh day from all his works.

5 And in this place again, If they shall enter into my rest.

6 Seeing therefore it still re-

---

[1] Firm unto the end *is omitted by the Vatican MS. and some other authorities. It seems to have come in from ver. 14, where all read it.*
[2] *So all the oldest MSS.*
[3] *So most of the oldest MSS.*

[4] *So in the Alexandrine, Vatican, Parisian, and Claromontane MSS., &c. The Sinaitic MS. reads in meaning as the A. V., but has a different word for* mixed *from the others.*

maineth that some enter therein, and they to whom it was first preached entered not in because of disobedience:

7 Again, he limiteth a certain day, saying in David, after so long a time, To-day; as it hath been said before, To-day if ye hear his voice, harden not your hearts.

8 For if Joshua had given them rest, then would He not afterward speak of another day.

9 There is yet reserved therefore a keeping of sabbath for the people of God.

10 For he that entered into his rest, he himself also rested from his own works, as God from his own.

11 Let us therefore earnestly strive to enter into that rest, lest any man fall into the same example of disobedience.

12 For the word of God is living, and active, and sharper than any twoedged sword, piercing even to the dividing of soul and of spirit, both joints and marrow, and is a discerner of the thoughts and ideas of the heart.

13 Neither is there any creature that is not manifest in his sight: but all things are naked and lying open unto the eyes of him with whom we have to do.

14 Seeing then that we have a great high priest, that is passed through the heavens, Jesus the Son of God, let us hold fast our confession.

15 For we have not an high priest unable to sympathise with our infirmities; but rather one in all points tempted in like manner, yet without sin.

16 Let us therefore come boldly unto the throne of grace, that we may obtain mercy, and find grace to help while yet there is time.

CHAPTER V.

FOR every high priest, being taken from among men, is appointed for men in things pertaining to God, that he may offer both gifts and sacrifices for sins:

2 Being able to have compassion on the ignorant and erring, seeing that he himself also is compassed with infirmity.

3 And by reason hereof he must, even as for the people, so also for himself, offer for sins.

4 And none taketh to himself the honour; but [1]only when called of God, as indeed was Aaron.

5 Thus Christ also glorified not himself to be made high priest; but he that spake unto him, Thou art my Son, to-day have I begotten thee.

6 Even as he saith also in another place, Thou art a priest for ever after the order of Melchisedec.

7 Who in the days of his flesh, having offered up prayers and supplications with strong crying and tears unto him that was able to save him from death, and having been heard by reason of his reverent submission;

8 Though he was a Son, yet

[1] *So all the oldest MSS*

learned he his obedience from the things which he suffered;

9 And being made perfect, he became the cause of eternal salvation unto all them that obey him,

10 Being addressed by God as high priest after the order of Melchisedec.

11 Concerning whom what we have to say is much, and difficult of interpretation for us to speak, seeing ye are become dull of hearing.

12 For though for the time ye ought to be teachers, ye again have need that some one teach you the first principles of the oracles of God; and are become such as have need of milk, and not of solid food.

13 For every one that useth milk is unskilled in the word of righteousness: for he is a babe.

14 But solid food belongeth to them that are of full age, even those who by reason of use have their organs of sense exercised with a view to discernment of good and evil.

CHAPTER VI.

THEREFORE leaving discourse concerning the beginning of Christ, let us go on unto perfection; not laying again the foundation of repentance from dead works, and of faith on God,

2 Of the doctrine of washings and laying on of hands, and resurrection of the dead and eternal judgment.

3 And this ¹will we do, if God permit.

4 For it is impossible, in the case of those who have been once enlightened, and have tasted of the heavenly gift, and have been made partakers of the Holy Spirit,

5 And have tasted the good word of God, and the powers of the world to come,

6 And have fallen away,—to renew them again unto repentance; seeing they crucify to themselves afresh the Son of God, and put him to an open shame.

7 For land which hath drunk in the rain that cometh oft upon it, and bringeth forth herbage meet for them for whom it is also dressed, partaketh of blessing from God:

8 But if it bear thorns and thistles, it is rejected, and is nigh unto cursing; whose end is to be burned.

9 But, beloved, we are persuaded better things of you, and things that accompany salvation, even though we thus speak.

10 For God is not unjust, so as to forget your work and ²your love, which ye shewed toward his name, in that ye ministered to the saints, and still minister.

11 But we earnestly desire that every one of you do shew the same diligence with regard to the full assurance of your hope until the end:

12 That ye become not slothful, but followers of them who

¹ *Some of the oldest MSS. read* let us do.

² *So all the oldest authorities The words* labour of *have been inserted from* 1 *Thess.* i. 3.

through faith and patience inherit the promises.

13 For when God made promise to Abraham, because he could swear by no greater, he sware by himself,

14 Saying, Surely blessing I will bless thee, and multiplying I will multiply thee.

15 And thus, after he had patiently endured, he obtained the promise.

16 For men verily swear by the greater: and of all gainsaying an oath is to them an end for confirmation.

17 In which behalf God, willing more abundantly to shew unto the heirs of the promise the immutability of his counsel, interposed with an oath:

18 That by means of two immutable things, in which it is impossible for God ever to lie, we may have strong encouragement, who have fled for refuge to lay hold upon the hope set before us:

19 Which we have as an anchor of our soul, both sure and stedfast, and entering into the part within the veil;

20 Where as forerunner on our behalf Jesus entered, having become an high priest for ever after the order of Melchisedec.

CHAPTER VII.

FOR this Melchisedec, king of Salem, priest of God the most high, who met Abraham returning from the slaughter of the kings, and blessed him;

2 To whom also Abraham apportioned a tenth part of all; first being by interpretation King of righteousness, and after that [being] also King of Salem, which is, King of peace;

3 Without father, without mother, without genealogy, having neither beginning of days, nor end of life; but likened unto the Son of God; abideth a priest for ever.

4 But consider how great this man was, unto whom Abraham, even the patriarch, paid tithes from the best of the spoil.

5 And indeed they of the sons of Levi, when they receive the priesthood, have a commandment to take tithes of the people according to the law, that is, of their brethren, though they be come out of the loins of Abraham:

6 But he whose genealogy is never reckoned from them hath taken tithes of Abraham, and hath blessed him that hath the promises.

7 And without all contradiction the less is blessed by the better.

8 And here indeed men that die receive tithes; but there one, of whom it is witnessed that he liveth.

9 And as I may so say, even Levi also, who receiveth tithes, hath paid tithes by means of Abraham.

10 For he was yet in the loins of his father, when Melchisedec met him.

11 If again perfection were by the Levitical priesthood, (for on the ground of it the people hath received the law,) what further need was there that a

different priest should rise after the order of Melchisedec, and that he should be said to be not after the order of Aaron?

12 For if the priesthood is changed, there is made of necessity a change of the law also.

13 For he of whom these things are spoken pertaineth to a different tribe, of which no man hath ever given attendance at the altar.

14 For it is evident that our Lord hath arisen out of Judah; of which tribe Moses spake nothing concerning [1]priests.

15 And it is yet far more abundantly evident: seeing that after the similitude of Melchisedec there ariseth a different priest,

16 Who is made, not after the law of a carnal commandment, but after the power of an endless life.

17 For [2]this testimony is borne concerning him, Thou art a priest for ever after the order of Melchisedec.

18 For there is verily a disannulling of the commandment going before for the weakness and unprofitableness thereof,

19 (For the law made nothing perfect,) and [there is] a bringing in of a better hope, by which we draw nigh unto God.

20 And inasmuch as it was not without an oath:

21 (For they without an oath are made priests; but He with an oath by him that saith unto him, The Lord sware and will not repent, Thou art a priest for ever:[3])

22 Of so much better a testament also hath Jesus become surety.

23 And they truly are appointed priests in numbers, because they are not suffered to continue by reason of death:

24 But He, because he continueth ever, hath his priesthood unchangeable.

25 Wherefore he is able also to save them to the uttermost that come unto God through him, seeing he ever liveth to make intercession for them.

26 For such an high priest was also becoming for us, holy, harmless, undefiled, separated from sinners, and made higher than the heavens;

27 Who needeth not daily, as those high priests, to offer up sacrifices first for his own sins, and then for the people's: for this he did once for all, when he offered up himself.

28 For the law maketh men high priests, which have infirmity; but the word of the oath, which was after the law, maketh the Son, who is made perfect for evermore.

CHAPTER VIII.

NOW of the things which we are saying this is the chief: We have such an high priest, who sat down on the right hand of the throne of Majesty in the heavens;

2 A minister of the holy place, and of the true taber-

[1] *So all the oldest MSS.*
[2] *So most of the oldest MSS.*
[3] *The words* after the order of Melchisedec *are omitted in the oldest MSS.*

nacle, which the Lord pitched, and not man.

3 For every high priest is appointed to offer gifts and sacrifices: whence it is necessary that this man have somewhat also to offer.

4 [1]Yea, if he were on earth, he would not even be a priest, seeing that there are [1]those that offer the gifts according to the law:

5 Such as serve the delineation and shadow of the heavenly things, even as Moses was admonished of God when he was about to complete the tabernacle: for, See, saith he, that thou make all things according to the pattern shewed to thee in the mount.

6 But now hath he obtained a more excellent ministry, in proportion as he is also mediator of a better covenant, one which hath been established upon better promises.

7 For if that first covenant were faultless, then would not place be sought for a second.

8 For finding fault with them, he saith, Behold, the days come, saith the Lord, when I will accomplish upon the house of Israel and upon the house of Judah a new covenant:

9 Not according to the covenant that I appointed to their fathers in the day when I took them by the hand to lead them out of the land of Egypt; because they continued not in my covenant, and I regarded them not, saith the Lord.

10 For this is the covenant that I will establish to the house of Israel after those days, saith the Lord, to put my laws into their mind; and I will write them in their hearts, and will be to them for a God, and they shall be to me for a people:

11 And they shall not have to teach every man his [2]fellow-citizen, and every man his brother, saying, Know the Lord: because all shall know me, from the least to the greatest.

12 Because I will be merciful to their iniquities, and their sins[3] will I remember no more.

13 In that he saith, A new [covenant], he hath made the first old. But that which decayeth and waxeth old is ready to vanish away.

CHAPTER IX.

NOW accordingly the first covenant had also ordinances of divine service, and the worldly sanctuary.

2 For the tabernacle was established, the first, wherein was the candlestick, and the table, and the shewbread; that tabernacle, which is called the holy place.

3 But after the second veil, the tabernacle which is called holy of holies;

4 Having a golden censer, and the ark of the covenant overlaid round about with gold, wherein was a golden pot containing the manna, and Aaron's rod that budded, and the tables of the covenant;

---

[1] *So all the oldest MSS.*
[2] *So all the ancient authorities.*
[3] *And their iniquities is omitted by the best of the ancient authorities.*

5 And over it the cherubim of glory overshadowing the mercyseat; of which we cannot now speak particularly.

6 Now these things being thus, the priests enter always into the first tabernacle, accomplishing the service of God;

7 But into the second the high priest alone once every year, not without blood, which he offereth for himself, and for the ignorances of the people:

8 The Holy Spirit this signifying, that the way into the holy place hath not yet been made manifest, while the first tabernacle is as yet standing:

9 The which tabernacle is a parable for the time now present; according to which are offered both gifts and sacrifices, having no power to perfect in conscience him that serveth;

10 Consisting only in meats and drinks, and divers washings, ordinances of the flesh, imposed on them until the time of reformation.

11 But Christ having appeared an high priest of the good things to come, through the greater and more perfect tabernacle, not made with hands, that is to say, not of this creation;

12 Nor yet through the blood of goats and calves, but through his own blood he entered once for all into the holy place, and obtained eternal redemption for us.

13 For if the blood of goats and of bulls, and ashes of an heifer sprinkling the defiled, sanctifieth to the purity of the flesh:

14 How much more shall the blood of Christ, who through the eternal Spirit offered **himself** without fault to God, purify [1]our conscience from dead works to serve the living God?

15 And for this cause he is the mediator of a new covenant, in order that, death having taken place, for the propitiation of the transgressions under the first [2]covenant, they which have been called may receive the promise of the eternal inheritance.

16 For where a testament is, there must also of necessity be implied the death of him that made it.

17 For a testament is of force in the case of the dead, seeing that it is of no strength at all while he that made it is alive.

18 Whence neither hath the first testament been dedicated without blood.

19 For when Moses had spoken every precept to all the people according to the law, he took the blood of the calves and of the goats, with water, and scarlet wool, and hyssop, and sprinkled both the book itself, and all the people,

20 Saying, This is the blood of the [3] testament which God enjoined unto you.

21 Moreover he in like manner sprinkled with the blood the tabernacle, and all the vessels of the ministry.

22 And one may almost say,

---

[1] *So the weightier early testimony.*
[2] *Or,* testament. *The word is the same throughout.*
[3] *Or,* covenant.

that all things are according to the law purged with blood; and that apart from shedding of blood remission cometh not.

23 It was therefore necessary that the figures of the things in the heavens should be purified with these; but the heavenly things themselves with better sacrifices than these.

24 For Christ entered not into holy places made with hands, counterfeits of the true; but into heaven itself, now to be made manifest before the face of God for us:

25 Nor yet that he may offer himself often, as the high priest entereth into the holy place every year with blood of others;

26 For then it were necessary that he should oftentimes suffer since the foundation of the world: but now once at the end of the world hath he been manifested for the putting away of sin by His sacrifice.

27 And inasmuch as it is appointed unto men once to die, but after that, judgment:

28 So also the Christ, once having been offered to bear the sins of many, shall appear a second time without sin, to them that wait for Him, unto salvation.

CHAPTER X.

FOR the law having a shadow of the good things to come, not the very image of the things, can never year by year with the same sacrifices, which they offer continually, make perfect them that draw near.

2 For then would they not have ceased to be offered, because that the worshipper once purged should have no more conscience of sins?

3 But in those sacrifices there is a remembrance again made of sins year by year.

4 For it is not possible that the blood of bulls and of goats should take away sins.

5 Wherefore when he cometh into the world, he saith, Sacrifice and offering thou wouldest not, but a body didst thou prepare me:

6 In whole burnt offerings and sacrifices for sin thou hadst no pleasure.

7 Then said I, Lo, 1 am come (in the volume of the book it is written of me) to do thy will, O God.

8 Above when he saith, Sacrifices and offerings and whole burnt offerings and sacrifices for sin thou wouldest not, neither hadst pleasure therein; such as are offered by the law;

9 Then saith he, Lo, I am come to do thy will.[1] He taketh away the first, that he may establish the second.

10 In pursuance of which will we have been sanctified, through the offering of the body of Jesus Christ once-for-all.

11 And every [2]high priest standeth day by day ministering and offering oftentimes the same sacrifices, the which can never take away sins:

12 But He, after he had offered one sacrifice for sins,

[1] O God *is omitted by all the oldest MSS.*
[2] *So the oldest and best authorities*

for ever sat down on the right hand of God;

13 From henceforth expecting till his enemies be made his footstool.

14 For by one offering he hath perfected for ever them that are being sanctified.

15 And the Holy Spirit also is a witness to us: for after that he had said,

16 This is the covenant that I will make with them after those days, saith the Lord, putting my laws into their hearts, and on their mind will I write them;

17 And, Their sins and their iniquities will I remember no more.

18 Now where remission of these is, there is no more offering for sin.

19 Having therefore, brethren, boldness to enter into the holy place by the blood of Jesus,

20 By a new and living way, which he inaugurated for us, through the veil, that is to say, his flesh;

21 And having a great priest over the house of God;

22 Let us draw near with a true heart in full assurance of faith, having our hearts sprinkled from an evil conscience, and our body washed with pure water.

23 Let us hold fast the confession of our hope without wavering; for he is faithful that promised;

24 And let us consider one another to provoke unto love and to good works:

25 Not forsaking the assembling of ourselves together, as the manner of some is; but using exhortation: and so much the more, as ye see the day approaching.

26 For if we sin wilfully after that we have received the knowledge of the truth, there remaineth no more a sacrifice for sins,

27 But a certain fearful receiving of judgment, and a fiery indignation, which shall devour the adversaries.

28 He that hath despised the law of Moses dieth without mercy under two or three witnesses:

29 Of how much sorer punishment, suppose ye, shall he be found worthy, who trampled under foot the Son of God, and accounted common the blood of the covenant, wherewith he was sanctified, and insulted the Spirit of grace?

30 For we know him that said, Vengeance belongeth unto me, I will recompense, saith the Lord. And again, The Lord shall judge his people.

31 It is a fearful thing to fall into the hands of the living God.

32 But call ever to remembrance the former days, in which, when first enlightened, ye endured a great fight of afflictions;

33 Partly, in that ye were made a gazingstock both by reproaches and tribulations; and partly, in that ye became partakers with them that were so used.

34 For ye both had compas-

sion of ¹them that were in bonds, and took joyfully the spoiling of your goods, knowing that ye have ²of your own a better and an enduring substance.

35 Cast not away therefore your confidence, for it hath great recompence of reward.

36 For ye have need of endurance, that ye may do the will of God and receive the promise.

37 For yet a very little while, and he that is coming shall come, and shall not tarry.

38 But ³my just man shall live by faith : but if he draw back, my soul hath no pleasure in him.

39 But we are not of backsliding unto perdition ; but of faith unto the saving of the soul.

CHAPTER XI.

NOW faith is the confidence of things hoped for, the evidence of things not seen.

2 For therein had the elders testimony borne to them.

3 By faith we understand that the worlds were framed by the word of God, so that ⁴that which is seen was not made of things which do appear.

4 By faith Abel offered unto God a more excellent sacrifice than Cain, by which he obtained witness that he was righteous, God testifying of his gifts : and by it he being dead yet speaketh.

5 By faith Enoch was translated that he should not see death ; and was not found, because God translated him : for before his translation a testimony is borne to him, that he had pleased God.

6 But without faith it is impossible to please him : for he that cometh to God must believe that he is, and that he becometh a rewarder of them that diligently seek him.

7 By faith Noah, being warned of God of things not seen as yet, taking forethought, prepared an ark to the saving of his house ; by which he condemned the world, and became heir of the righteousness which is according to faith.

8 By faith Abraham, when called, obeyed, in going out into a place which he was afterwards to receive for an inheritance ; and he went out, not knowing whither he was going.

9 By faith he sojourned in the land of the promise, as in a strange country, dwelling in tents with Isaac and Jacob, the heirs with him of the same promise :

10 For he looked for the city which hath the foundations, whose builder and maker is God.

11 By faith Sarah herself also received strength to conceive seed ⁵even when she was past

---

¹ *This is the more probable reading: the ancient authorities are divided.*

² *So, and omitting* in heaven, *most of the early authorities.*

³ *So the earliest MSS.: one however, and the ancient Syriac version, join* my *to* faith.

⁴ *So the most ancient MSS.*

⁵ *So the oldest MSS.*

age, because she judged him faithful who had promised.

12 Therefore sprang there even of one, and him as good as dead, so many as the stars of the sky in multitude, and as the sand which is by the sea shore innumerable.

13 These all died in faith, not having received the promises, but having seen them afar off,[1] and greeted them, and confessed that they were strangers and sojourners on the earth.

14 For they that say such things declare plainly that they seek after a home.

15 And truly, if they were mindful of that from whence they came out, they might have had opportunity to return.

16 But now they desire a better home, that is, an heavenly: wherefore God is not ashamed to be called their God: for he prepared for them a city.

17 By faith Abraham, being tempted, hath offered up Isaac: and he that had accepted the promises offered up his only begotten son,

18 He to whom it was said, that in Isaac shall thy seed be called:

19 Accounting that God is able to raise up, even from the dead; from whence he also received him in a figure.

20 By faith Isaac blessed Jacob and Esau even concerning things to come.

21 By faith Jacob, when dying, blessed each of the sons of Joseph; and worshipped upon the top of his staff.

22 By faith Joseph, when he died, made mention of the departing of the sons of Israel; and gave commandment concerning his bones.

23 By faith Moses, when he was born, was hidden three months by his parents, because they saw that the child was comely; and they were not afraid of the king's commandment.

24 By faith Moses, when he was come to years, refused to be called the son of Pharaoh's daughter;

25 Choosing rather to suffer affliction with the people of God, than to enjoy the pleasures of sin for a season;

26 Esteeming the reproach of Christ greater riches than the treasures in Egypt: for he had respect unto the recompence of reward.

27 By faith he forsook Egypt, not fearing the wrath of the king: for he endured, as seeing him who is invisible.

28 By faith he hath kept the passover, and the sprinkling of the blood, that he that destroyed the firstborn should not touch them.

29 By faith they passed through the Red sea as by dry land: which the Egyptians assaying to do were drowned.

30 By faith the walls of Jericho fell down, after they were compassed about seven days.

31 By faith the harlot Rahab perished not with them that

---

[1] And were persuaded of them *is omitted apparently by all the authorities.*

were disobedient, because she had received the spies with peace.

32 And what shall I more say? for the time will fail me if I tell of Gideon, and of Barak, and of Samson, and of Jephthah ; of David also, and Samuel, and of the prophets :

33 Who through faith subdued kingdoms, wrought righteousness, obtained promises, stopped the mouths of lions,

34 Quenched the power of fire, escaped the edge of the sword, out of weakness were made strong, waxed valiant in fight, turned to flight armies of aliens.

35 Women received their dead raised to life again : but others were tortured, not accepting deliverance, that they might obtain a better resurrection :

36 Others again had trial of cruel mockings and scourgings, yea, moreover of bonds and imprisonment :

37 They were stoned, they were sawn asunder, were tempted, were slain with the sword : they wandered about in sheepskins and goatskins ; being destitute, afflicted, in misery ;

38 (Of whom the world was not worthy :) wandering in deserts, and mountains, and dens, and in the caves of the earth.

39 And these all, being borne witness to through faith, received not the promise :

40 God having provided some better thing for us, that they without us should not be made perfect.

CHAPTER XII.

WHEREFORE let us also, having so great a cloud of witnesses encompassing us, laying aside every weight, and sin, which doth naturally enwrap us, run with patience the race that is set before us,

2 Looking unto the author and perfecter of the faith, even Jesus ; who for the joy set before him endured the cross, despising shame, and is set down at the right hand of the throne of God.

3 For consider him that hath endured such contradiction at the hands of them that sinned against him, that ye be not wearied, fainting in your souls.

4 Ye have not yet resisted unto blood, striving against sin.

5 And ye have quite forgotten the exhortation which speaketh unto you as unto sons, My son, despise not thou the chastening of the Lord, nor faint when thou art rebuked of him :

6 For whom the Lord loveth he chasteneth, yea, and scourgeth every son whom he receiveth.

7 ¹It is for chastisement that ye are enduring : God is dealing with you as with sons ; for what son is he whom the father chasteneth not?

8 But if ye are without chastisement, whereof all have

¹ *So all the ancient MSS.*

been made partakers, then are ye bastards, and not sons.

9 Furthermore we once had the fathers of our flesh as chastisers, and we gave them reverence: shall we not much rather be in subjection unto the Father of our spirits, and live?

10 For they verily for a few days chastened us after their own pleasure; but he for our profit, that we may be partakers of his holiness.

11 Now no chastening for the present seemeth to be matter of joy, but of grief: nevertheless afterward it yieldeth the peaceable fruit of righteousness unto them which have been exercised thereby.

12 Wherefore lift up the hands which hang down, and the feeble knees;

13 And make straight paths for your feet, that that which is lame be not turned out of the way, but may rather be healed.

14 Follow peace with all men, and sanctification, without which no man shall see the Lord:

15 Looking diligently lest any man falling short of the grace of God,—lest any root of bitterness springing up,—trouble you, and thereby the greater number be defiled;

16 Lest there be any fornicator, or profane person, as Esau, who for one meal sold his own birthright.

17 For ye know how that afterward, when he would have inherited the blessing, he was rejected: for he found no place of repentance, though he sought it carefully with tears.

18 For ye have not drawn near unto the mount that might be touched, and that burned with fire, nor unto blackness, and darkness, and tempest,

19 And the sound of a trumpet, and the voice of words; which voice they that heard intreated that the word should not be spoken to them any more:

20 (For they could not endure that which was commanded, And if so much as a beast touch the mountain, it shall be stoned:[1]

21 And, so terrible was the sight, Moses said, I exceedingly fear and quake:)

22 But ye have drawn near unto mount Sion, and unto the city of the living God, the heavenly Jerusalem, and to an innumerable company, the whole host of angels,

23 And the assembly of the firstborn which are written in heaven, and to God the Judge of all, and to the spirits of just men made perfect,

24 And to the mediator of the new covenant, even Jesus, and to the blood of sprinkling, speaking better things than Abel.

25 See that ye refuse not him that speaketh. For if they escaped not for refusing him that spake on earth, much more

[1] Or thrust through with a dart *is not in any of the ancient MSS. It has been inserted from Exod.* xix. 13.

shall not we escape, if we turn away from him that speaketh from heaven:

26 Whose voice then shook the earth: but now he hath promised, saying, Yet once more I shake not the earth only, but also the heaven.

27 And this word, Yet once more, signifieth the removing of those things that are shaken, as of things that have been made, in order that those things which cannot be shaken may remain.

28 Wherefore we receiving a kingdom which cannot be shaken, let us have thankfulness, whereby let us serve God acceptably with reverent fear:

29 For indeed our God is a consuming fire.

CHAPTER XIII.

LET brotherly love continue.

2 Be not forgetful to entertain strangers: for thereby some entertained angels unawares.

3 Remember them that are in bonds, as if bound with them; and them which suffer adversity, as being yourselves also in the body.

4 Let your marriage be held in honour in all things, and let your bed be undefiled[1]: for whoremongers and adulterers God will judge.

5 Let your conversation be without covetousness; be content with such things as ye have. For he himself hath said, I will never leave thee, neither will forsake thee.

6 So that we ever boldly say, The Lord is my helper, and I will not fear: what shall man do unto me?

7 Remember them which had the rule over you, such as spoke unto you the word of God: the end of whose life considering, imitate their faith.

8 Jesus Christ is the same yesterday, and to-day, and for ever.

9 Be not carried [2]away with divers and strange doctrines. For it is a good thing that the heart be established with grace; not with meats, in which they who walked were not profited.

10 We have an altar, whereof they have no right to eat which serve the tabernacle.

11 For the bodies of those beasts, whose blood is brought into the sanctuary by the high priest,[3] are burned outside the camp.

12 Wherefore Jesus also, that he might sanctify the people through his own blood, suffered outside the gate.

13 Let us go forth therefore unto him outside the camp, bearing his reproach.

14 For we have not here an abiding city, but we seek that which is to come.

15 Through him therefore let us offer up a sacrifice of praise to God continually, that is, the fruit of lips giving thanks to his name.

16 But to do good and to communicate forget not: for

---

[1] *So most of the oldest MSS.*

[2] *So all the oldest MS.*

[3] *For sin is omitted or variously placed, by two of the oldest MSS*

with such sacrifices God is well pleased.

17 Obey them that have the rule over you, and submit to them: for they keep watch on behalf of your souls, as having to give account, that they may do it with joy, and not with lamentation, for that is unprofitable for you.

18 Pray for us: for we trust we have a good conscience, desiring in all things to behave ourselves with seemliness.

19 But I the more abundantly exhort you to do this, that I may be restored to you the sooner.

20 But the God of peace, that brought up from the dead, through the blood of the everlasting covenant, the great Shepherd of the sheep, even our Lord Jesus,

21 Make you perfect in every good work to do his will, doing in you that which is well-pleasing in his sight, through Jesus Christ; to whom be the glory for ever and ever. Amen.

22 But I beseech you, brethren, suffer the word of my exhortation: for I have written a letter unto you in few words.

23 Know ye that our brother Timothy is set at liberty: with whom, if he come shortly, I will see you.

24 Salute all them that have the rule over you, and all the saints. They from Italy salute you.

25 Grace be with you all. Amen.

THE GENERAL EPISTLE OF
JAMES.

CHAPTER I.

JAMES, a servant of God and of the Lord Jesus Christ, to the twelve tribes which are in the dispersion, greeting.

2 My brethren, count it all joy when ye fall into divers temptations;

3 Knowing this, that the proof of your faith worketh endurance.

4 But let endurance have a perfect work, that ye may be perfect and entire, in nothing deficient.

5 But if any of you is deficient in wisdom, let him ask of God, that giveth to all simply, and upbraideth not; and it shall be given to him.

6 But let him ask in faith, nothing doubting. For he that doubteth is like a wave of the sea driven with the wind and tossed.

7 For let not that man think that he shall receive any thing from the Lord.
8 He is a doubleminded man, unstable in all his ways.
9 Let the brother who is low glory in his exaltation :
10 But the rich [glorieth] in his humiliation : because as the flower of the grass he shall pass away.
11 For the sun arose with its heat, and dried up the grass, and the flower thereof fell away, and the beauty of the form of it perished : so also shall the rich man wither in his ways.
12 Blessed is the man that endureth temptation : for when he is approved, he shall receive the crown of life, which ¹He promised to them that love him.
13 Let no man say when he is tempted, I am tempted from God : for God is unversed in evil, and he tempteth no man :
14 But every man is tempted, when he is drawn away and enticed by his own lust.
15 Then lust having conceived, bringeth forth sin : and sin, when finished, bringeth forth death.
16 Do not err, my beloved brethren.
17 Every good gift and every perfect gift cometh down from above, from the Father of the lights of heaven, with whom is no variableness or shadow of turning.

¹ The Lord, *which is very variously read by those MSS. that contain it, is omitted altogether by the two oldest MSS.*

18 Of his own will begat he us with the word of truth, that we should be a kind of firstfruit of his creatures.
19 Ye know it, my beloved brethren ; but let every man be swift to hear, slow to speak, slow to wrath :
20 For the wrath of man worketh not the righteousness of God.
21 Wherefore putting off all filthiness and superabundance of malignity, receive with meekness the implanted word, which is able to save your souls.
22 But be ye doers of the word, and not hearers only, deceiving your own selves.
23 Because if any is a hearer of the word, and not a doer, he is like unto a man contemplating his natural face in a glass :
24 For he contemplateth himself, and departeth, and straightway forgetteth what manner of man he was.
25 But whoso hath looked into the perfect law of liberty, and continueth, he being not a forgetful hearer, but a doer of work, this man shall be blessed in his deed.
26 If any man among you thinketh that he is religious, and bridleth not his tongue, but deceiveth his heart, this man's religion is vain.
27 Pure religion and undefiled before Him who is our God and Father is·this, To visit the fatherless and widows in their affliction ; to keep himself unspotted from the world.

CHAPTER II.

MY brethren, have not the faith of our Lord Jesus Christ, the Lord of glory, with respect of persons.

2 For if there have come unto your assembly a man with gold rings, in gay clothing, and there have come in also a poor man in vile clothing;

3 And ye have respect to him that weareth the gay clothing, and say,[1] Sit thou here in a good place; and say to the poor, Stand thou there, or sit under my footstool:

4 Is not this to doubt within yourselves, and to become judges, of evil thoughts?

5 Hearken, my beloved brethren, Did not God choose out the *poor of [2] the world to be rich in faith, and heirs of the kingdom which he promised to them that love him?

6 But ye have despised the poor. Do not the rich oppress you, and is it not they which draw you before the judgment seats?

7 Is it not they which blaspheme the goodly name by the which ye were called?

8 Yet if ye fulfil the royal law according to the scripture, Thou shalt love thy neighbour as thyself, ye do well:

9 But if ye have respect to persons, ye commit sin, being convicted by the law as transgressors.

10 For whosoever [3] hath kept the whole law, and yet [3] hath offended in one point, hath become guilty of all.

11 For he that said, Do not commit adultery, said also, Do not commit murder. Now if thou committest no adultery, yet if thou committest murder, thou art become a transgressor of the law.

12 So speak ye, and so do, as being about to be judged by the law of liberty.

13 For the judgment shall be without mercy to him that wrought not mercy: [4] mercy rejoiceth against judgment.

14 What is the profit, my brethren, if a man say he hath faith, but have not works? can his faith save him?

15 If a brother or sister be naked, and destitute of daily food,

16 And one of you say unto them, Depart in peace, be warmed and filled; notwithstanding ye give them not those things which are needful to the body; what is the profit?

17 So also faith, if it have not works, is dead in itself.

18 But a man will say, Thou hast faith, and I have works: shew me thy faith without [5] works, and I will shew thee my faith by my works.

19 Thou believest that [6] God is one; thou doest well: the devils also believe, and tremble.

20 But wilt thou know, O

---

[1] Unto him *is omitted by all the oldest MSS.*
[2] So all the MSS.
[3] So all the oldest MSS.
[4] And *is omitted by the oldest MSS.*
[5] Thy *is omitted by the oldest MSS. and versions.*
[6] So the most ancient MSS.; others read as A. V.

vain man, that faith without works is idle?

21 Was not Abraham our father justified by works, when he offered Isaac his son upon the altar?

22 Thou seest that faith wrought with his works, and by works faith was made perfect;

23 And the scripture was fulfilled which saith, Abraham believed God, and it was reckoned unto him for righteousness: and he was called God's friend.

24 Ye see[1] that by works a man is justified, and not by faith only.

25 And in like manner was not Rahab the harlot justified by works, when she received the messengers, and thrust them forth another way?

26 For as the body without spirit is dead, so faith without its works is dead also.

CHAPTER III.

MY brethren, be not many teachers, knowing that we shall receive greater condemnation.

2 For oftentimes we all offend. If any man offendeth not in word, the same is a perfect man, able also to bridle the whole body.

3 [2]But if in the mouths of horses we put bits, that they may obey us; we turn about also their whole body.

4 Behold also the ships, though they be so great, and are driven by fierce winds, yet are turned about with a very small rudder, whithersoever the desire of the helmsman willeth.

5 So also the tongue is a little member, and boasteth great things. Behold, how great a forest is kindled by [2]how small a fire!

6 And the tongue is a fire, that world of iniquity: the tongue is that one among our members, which defileth the whole body, and setteth on fire the course of nature; and it is set on fire by hell.

7 For every nature of beasts, and winged things, and of creeping things, and things in the sea, is tamed, and hath been tamed by the nature of man:

8 But the tongue can no one of men ever tame; it is a restless mischief; it is full of deadly poison.

9 Therewith bless we [2]the Lord and Father; and therewith curse we men, which are made after the similitude of God.

10 Out of the same mouth proceedeth blessing and cursing. My brethren, these things ought not so to be.

11 Doth a fountain send forth out of the same clift the sweet and the bitter?

12 Can the fig tree, my brethren, bear olives? or a vine, figs? [2]neither can salt water bring forth sweet.

13 Who is a wise man and endued with knowledge among you? let him shew out of his good conduct his works in meekness of wisdom.

[1] Then *is omitted by all the oldest MSS.*
[2] *So all the oldest MSS*

14 But if ye have bitter envying and rivalry in your heart, boast not against and lie not against the truth.
15 This wisdom is not one descending from above, but earthly, sensual, devilish.
16 For where envying and rivalry is, there is confusion and every evil thing.
17 But the wisdom from above is first pure, then peaceable, gentle, easily persuaded, full of compassion and good fruits, without doubting, and without hypocrisy.
18 And the fruit of righteousness is sown in peace by them that work peace.

CHAPTER IV.

FROM whence come wars and fightings among you? come they not hence, even of your lusts that war in your members?
2 Ye lust, and have not: ye commit murder, and ye envy, and cannot obtain: ye fight and make war. ¹Ye have not, because ye ask not:
3 Ye ask and receive not, because ye ask amiss, that ye may spend it in your lusts.
4 Ye ²adulteresses, know ye not that the friendship of the world is enmity to God? whosoever therefore will be a friend of the world becometh an enemy of God.
5 Or do ye think that the scripture saith in vain, The Spirit that ³he placed in us jealously desireth us?
6 But he giveth the greater grace. Wherefore he saith, God resisteth the proud, but giveth grace unto the humble.
7 Submit yourselves therefore to God: but resist the devil, and he shall flee from you:
8 Draw near to God, and he will draw near to you. Purify your hands, ye sinners, and make chaste your hearts, ye doubleminded.
9 Be afflicted, and mourn and weep: let your laughter be turned into mourning, and your joy into humiliation.
10 Be humbled before the Lord, and he will exalt you.
11 Speak not one against another, brethren: he that speaketh against a brother, or judgeth his brother, speaketh against the law, and judgeth the law: but if thou judgest the law, thou art not a doer of the law, but a judge.
12 One is the lawgiver and judge, he who is able to save and destroy: but thou, who art thou that judgest ³thy neighbour?
13 Go to now, ye that say, To-day, or to-morrow, we will go into this city, and will spend there one year, and will traffic and get gain;
14 (Whereas ye know not what shall be on the morrow. For what is your life? For ⁴ye are a vapour, which appeareth for a little time, and then vanisheth away.)
15 Instead of your saying,

---

¹ *Thus all the MSS.*
² Adulterers and *is omitted by all the oldest MSS. The figure is that well-known one of God being husband of the soul, and departure from Him being adultery.*
³ *So all the oldest MSS.*
⁴ *So (probably) all the oldest MSS.*

If the Lord will, we shall both live, and shall do this or that.

16 But now ye boast in your vainglory: all such boasting is evil.

17 So that to him that knoweth to do good, and doeth it not, to him it is sin.

CHAPTER V.

GO to now, ye rich men, go weep, howling over your miseries which are coming on.

2 Your riches are corrupted, and your garments are become motheaten:

3 Your gold and your silver is rusted through: and the rust of them shall be for a testimony to you, and shall eat your flesh as fire. Ye laid up treasure in the last days.

4 Behold, the hire of the labourers who mowed your fields, which is held back, crieth out from you; and the cries of them that reaped have entered into the ears of the Lord of Sabaoth.

5 Ye lived in pleasure on the earth, ye were wanton: ye nourished your hearts in the day of slaughter.

6 Ye condemned, ye murdered the just man: he doth not resist you.

7 Be patient therefore, brethren, until the coming of the Lord. Behold, the husbandman waiteth for the precious fruit of the earth, being patient over it till it shall have received the early and latter [rain]:

8 Be ye also patient: establish your hearts, because the coming of the Lord is nigh.

9 Murmur not, brethren, one against another, that ye be not judged: behold, the judge standeth before the door.

10 Take, [2]brethren, as an example of affliction and of patience the prophets, who spoke in the name of the Lord.

11 Behold, we count them happy that have endured: ye [have] heard of the endurance of Job: [3]behold also the end of the Lord, for the Lord is very pitiful and merciful.

12 But above all things, my brethren, swear not, neither by the heaven, nor by the earth, nor by any other oath: but let your yea be yea, and your nay, nay: that ye fall not under judgment.

13 Is any among you afflicted? let him pray. Is any merry? let him sing praise.

14 Is any sick among you? let him call for the elders of the congregation, and let them pray over him, anointing him with oil in the name of the Lord,

15 And the prayer of faith shall save the sick man, and the Lord shall raise him up: even if he have committed sins, it shall be forgiven him.

16 Confess therefore one to another your transgressions,

---

[1] Rain *is not expressed in one of the oldest MSS. (the Vatican): the other (the Sinaitic) supplies* fruit instead. *This shews that originally no word was expressed.*

[2] My *is omitted in two of the oldest MSS.*

[3] *The testimony of the ancient MSS. is divided; but the imperative is the more probable reading.*

and pray for one another that ye may be healed. The supplication of a righteous man availeth much in its working.

17 Elijah was a man of like passions with us, and he prayed with prayer that it might not rain, and it rained not on the earth for three years and six months :

18 And again he prayed, and the heavens gave rain, and the earth brought forth her fruit.

19 Brethren, if any among you be seduced from the truth, and one convert him ;

20 Know, that he who converteth a sinner from the error of his way shall save a soul from death, and shall cover a multitude of sins.

THE FIRST EPISTLE GENERAL OF PETER.

CHAPTER I.

PETER, an apostle of Jesus Christ, to the elect strangers of the dispersion in Pontus, Galatia, Cappadocia, Asia, and Bithynia,

2 According to the foreknowledge of God the Father, in sanctification of the Spirit, unto obedience and sprinkling of the blood of Jesus Christ : Grace unto you, and peace, be multiplied.

3 Blessed be the God and Father of our Lord Jesus Christ, which according to his abundant mercy begat us again unto a living hope through the resurrection of Jesus Christ from the dead,

4 Unto an inheritance incorruptible, and undefiled, and that fadeth not away, reserved in heaven for you,

5 Who are kept in the power of God through faith unto salvation ready to be revealed in the last time.

6 In which time ye greatly rejoice, though now for a season, if need be, ye have been afflicted in manifold temptations :

7 That the proof of your faith, being much more precious than gold that perisheth, yet is tried with fire, may be found unto praise and glory and honour at the revelation of Jesus Christ :

8 Whom having not seen, ye love ; in whom, though now ye see him not, yet believing, ye rejoice with joy unspeakable and [already] glorified :

9 Receiving the end of your faith, even the salvation of souls.

10 Concerning which salva-

tion prophets enquired and searched diligently, even they who prophesied of the grace that should come unto you:

11 Searching to what, or what manner of season the Spirit of Christ which was in them did point, when it testified beforehand the sufferings regarding Christ, and the glories that should follow them.

12 Unto whom it was revealed, that not unto themselves, but unto you they did minister the things, which have now been reported unto you by them that have preached the gospel unto you with the Holy Spirit sent down from heaven; which things angels desire to look into.

13 Wherefore gird up the loins of your mind, being sober: hope perfectly for the grace that is being brought unto you in the revelation of Jesus Christ;

14 As children of obedience, not conforming yourselves to the lusts which were formerly in your ignorance;

15 But rather after the pattern of that holy One which called you, be ye yourselves also holy in all behaviour,

16 Because it is written, [1]Ye shall be holy, because I am holy.

17 And if ye call upon as your Father Him, who without respect of persons judgeth according to every man's work, pass the time of your sojourning in fear:

18 Knowing that not with corruptible things, silver or gold, were ye redeemed from your vain behaviour received by tradition from your fathers;

19 But with precious blood as of a lamb without blemish and without spot, even the blood of Christ,

20 Who verily hath been foreordained before the foundation of the world, but was manifested at the end of the times for you,

21 Who are through him [1]believers in God, that raised him up from the dead, and gave him glory; so that your faith and hope are in God.

22 Seeing ye have purified your souls in obeying the truth through the Spirit unto unfeigned love of the brethren, love one another from the [2]heart earnestly:

23 Being born again, not of corruptible seed, but of incorruptible, by the word of God, which liveth and abideth.[3]

24 For all flesh is as grass, and all the glory of man as the flower of grass. The grass withered, and the flower thereof fell away:

25 But the word of the Lord abideth for ever. And this is the word which by the gospel was preached unto you.

CHAPTER II.

WHEREFORE having laid aside all malice, and all guile, and hypocrisies, and envies, and all evil speakings,

2 As newborn babes, desire

---

[1] *So all the oldest MSS.*

[2] *Pure is omitted by the two oldest MSS.*

[3] *For ever is omitted in all the oldest MSS.*

the spiritual guileless milk, that ye may grow thereby:

3 If so be ye have tasted that the Lord is good:

4 To whom coming, a living stone, rejected indeed of men, but chosen of God, and had in honour,

5 Be ye also, as living stones, built up a spiritual house, ¹for an holy priesthood, to offer up spiritual sacrifices acceptable to God, through Jesus Christ.

6 ²Because it is contained in ³scripture, Behold, I lay in Sion a chief corner stone, elect, had in honour: and he that believeth on him shall not be ashamed.

7 Unto you therefore which believe is the honour: but unto them which be disobedient, the stone which the builders rejected, the same is made the head of the corner,

8 And a stone of stumbling, and a rock of offence, even to them which stumble, being disobedient to the word: whereunto also they were appointed.

9 But ye are a chosen generation, a royal priesthood, an holy nation, a peculiar people; that ye should shew forth the virtues of him who called you out of darkness to his marvellous light:

10 Which in time past were no people, but are now the people of God: which were unpitied, but now have obtained compassion.

11 Dearly beloved, I beseech you, as sojourners and strangers, to abstain from fleshly lusts, which war against the soul;

12 Having your behaviour comely among the Gentiles: that, in the matter in which they speak against you as evildoers, they may by your good works, which they behold, glorify God in the day of visitation.

13 Submit yourselves to every ordinance of man for the Lord's sake: whether it be to the king, as supreme;

14 Or unto governors, as unto them that are sent by him for vengeance on evildoers, and praise of them that do well.

15 For so is the will of God, that with well doing ye put to silence the ignorance of those foolish men:

16 As free, and not as using your liberty for a cloak of your maliciousness, but as the servants of God.

17 Honour all men. Love the brotherhood. Fear God. Honour the king.

18 Servants, ⁴[by being] subject to your masters with all fear; not only to the good and considerate, but also to the perverse.

19 For this is thankworthy, if a man for conscience toward God endure tribulations, suffering wrongfully.

20 For what glory is it, if, when ye do wrong, and are buffeted for it, ye shall take it patiently? but if, when ye do well, and suffer for it, ye

---

¹ *So all the oldest MSS.*
² *So, omitting also, all the MSS.*
³ *The is omitted in the oldest MSS.*
⁴ *Not expressed in the original.*

shall take it patiently, [it is glory,] ¹for this is thankworthy with God.

21 For hereunto were ye called: because Christ also suffered for ²you, leaving ²you a pattern, that ye should follow his steps:

22 Who did no sin, neither was guile found in his mouth:

23 Who, when he was reviled, reviled not again; when he suffered, he threatened not; but committed ³[them] to him that judgeth righteously:

24 Who his own self bare our sins in his own body on the tree, that we, having died to our sins, should live unto righteousness: by whose stripe ye were healed.

25 For ye were ⁴going astray as sheep; but are now returned unto the Shepherd and Bishop of your souls.

CHAPTER III.

IN like manner, ye wives, ⁵[by] being in subjection to your own husbands; so that even if any obey not the word, they also shall, ⁶without speech, be won by the behaviour of their wives;

2 When they have beheld your chaste behaviour coupled with fear.

¹ *So two of the oldest MSS.*
² *So all the ancient MSS. Some of later date have* suffered for us, leaving you: *but none read as the A. V.*
³ *Not expressed in the original.* Them, *i.e. his persecutors. See* Luke xxiii. 34.
⁴ *So all the oldest MSS.*
⁵ *Not expressed in the original. So all the ancient MSS.*

3 Whose adorning let it not be that outward adorning of plaiting the hair, and of wearing of gold, or of putting on of garments;

4 But let it be the hidden man of the heart, in the incorruptible ornament of the meek and quiet spirit, which is in the sight of God of great price.

5 For after this manner in the old time the holy women also, who hoped in God, adorned themselves, being in subjection unto their own husbands.

6 As Sarah obeyed Abraham, calling him lord: of whom ye have become children, if ye do well, and are not afraid of any sudden fear.

7 Ye husbands, in like manner, dwelling according to knowledge with the woman as with the weaker vessel, giving them honour as being also heirs with ⁷you of the grace of life: that your prayers be not hindered.

8 Finally, all being of one mind, sympathising, loving the brethren, compassionate, humbleminded:

9 Not rendering [to others] evil for evil, or reproach for reproach: but contrariwise blessing them; because ye were thereunto called, that ye should inherit a blessing.

10 For he that desireth to love life, and to see good days, let him refrain his tongue from evil, and his lips that they speak no guile:

11 Let him turn away from

⁷ *So the oldest MS. There is considerable variation in the others.*

evil, and do good; let him seek peace, and pursue it.

12 For the eyes of the Lord are upon the righteous, and his ears are ¹[open] unto their supplication: but the face of the Lord is ²against them that do evil.

13 And who is he that will harm you, if ye be followers of that which is good?

14 But if even ye suffer for righteousness' sake, happy are ye: and be not afraid with their terror, neither be troubled:

15 But sanctify Christ in your hearts as Lord: being ready always to give an answer to every man that asketh you a reason of the hope that is in you, ³but with meekness and fear:

16 Having a good conscience; that, in the matter in which ye ⁴are spoken against, they may be ashamed that falsely accuse your good conversation in Christ.

17 For it is better, if the will of God be so, that ye suffer for well doing, than for evil doing.

18 Because Christ also suffered for sins once; a just person for unjust persons, that he might bring us to God, being put to death in the flesh, but made alive in the spirit:

19 In which he also went and preached unto the spirits in prison;

20 Which were once disobedient, when the longsuffering of God was waiting in the days of Noah, while the ark was preparing, wherein few, that is, eight souls were saved by water.

21 Which, the antitype [of that], doth now save ⁵you also, even baptism: not the putting away of the filth of the flesh, but the enquiry of a good conscience after God, by the resurrection of Jesus Christ:

22 Who is gone into heaven, and is on the right hand of God; angels and authorities and powers being made subject unto him.

CHAPTER IV.

FORASMUCH then as Christ suffered⁶ in the flesh, arm yourselves likewise with the same mind: because he that suffered in the flesh hath ceased from sin;

2 That ye no longer should live the rest of your time in the flesh by the lusts of men, but by the will of God.

3 For the time past of our life may suffice us to have wrought out the will of the Gentiles, walking as ye have done in lasciviousness, lusts, excess of wine, revellings, banquetings, and abominable idolatries:

4 Wherein they think it strange that ye run not with them to the same slough of riot, speaking evil of you:

---

¹ *Not expressed in the original.*
² *Literally* upon, *as before.*
³ *So all the oldest MSS.*
⁴ *So the oldest MS.: the others reading as the A. V.*
⁵ *So the three oldest MSS.*
⁶ *For* us *is omitted by two of the oldest MSS.: the Sinaitic MS reads* for you.

5 Who shall give account to him that is ready to judge the quick and the dead.

6 For for this cause was the gospel preached to dead men also, that they might be judged according to men in the flesh, but live according to God in the spirit.

7 But the end of all things is at hand : be ye therefore sober, and watch unto prayer,

8 Above all things having your love towards one another fervent : because love ¹covereth a multitude of sins.

9 Using hospitality one to another without murmuring.

10 Each man even as he received a gift of grace, ministering it one to another, as good stewards of the manifold grace of God.

11 If any speaketh, ²[speaking] as oracles of God ; if any ministereth, ²[ministering] as of the ability which God bestoweth : that in all things God may be glorified through Jesus Christ, to whom be the glory and the might for ever and ever. Amen.

12 ¶ Beloved, think it not strange concerning the fiery trial which is to try you, as though some strange thing were happening unto you :

13 But in as far as ye are partakers of Christ's sufferings, rejoice ; that, at the revelation of his glory, ye may be glad also with exultation.

14 If ye be reproached for the name of Christ, happy are ye ; for the Spirit of glory and the Spirit of God resteth upon you :³

15 But let none of you suffer as a murderer, or as a thief, or as an evildoer, or as a prier into other men's matters.

16 Yet if any suffer as a Christian, let him not be ashamed ; but let him glorify God in this name.

17 Because the time is come that judgment must begin at the house of God : and if ²[it] first ²[begin] at us, what shall the end be of them that obey not the gospel of God ?

18 And if the righteous scarcely be saved, where shall the ungodly and sinner appear ?

19 Wherefore let also them that suffer according to the will of God commit the keeping of their souls in well doing ⁴unto a faithful Creator.

CHAPTER V.

THE elders ⁴therefore which are among you I exhort, who am also an elder, and a witness of the sufferings of Christ, and also a partaker of the glory which is about to be revealed :

2 Feed the flock of God which is among you, ²[overseeing it,] not by constraint, but willingly ;⁵ not for filthy lucre, but of a ready mind ;

3 Neither as being lords over your portions, but becoming examples to the flock.

---

¹ *So most of the ancient MSS.*
² *Not expressed in the original.*
³ On their part he is evil spoken of, but on your part he is glorified, *is omitted in all the oldest MSS. and versions.*
⁴ *So all the oldest MSS.*
⁵ *Two of the oldest MSS add* according to God.

4 And when the chief Shepherd shall be manifested, ye shall receive the amarantine crown of his glory.

5 In like manner, ye younger, submit yourselves unto the elders. Yea, all ¹gird on humility one to another: because God resisteth the proud, and giveth grace to the humble.

6 Humble yourselves therefore under the mighty hand of God, that he may exalt you in due time:

7 Casting all your anxiety upon him, because he careth for you.

8 Be sober, be vigilant; ²your adversary the devil, as a roaring lion, walketh about, seeking whom he may devour:

9 Whom resist stedfast in the faith, knowing that the very same sufferings are being accomplished in your brotherhood that are in the world.

10 But the God of all grace, who called ³you unto his eternal glory by Christ Jesus, after that ye have suffered a little while, ⁴shall himself make you perfect, stablish, strengthen, settle you.

11 To him be the ⁴might for ever and ever. Amen.

12 By Silvanus the faithful brother, as I reckon, I have written unto you in few words, exhorting, and testifying that this is the true grace of God: wherein ⁵stand ye.

13 She that is elected together with you in Babylon saluteth you; and so doth Marcus my son.

14 Greet ye one another with a kiss of charity. Peace be to you all that are in ⁴Christ.

---

¹ *So the oldest MSS.*
² *Because is omitted by two out of three of the oldest MSS.*
³ *So all the ancient MSS.*
⁴ *So two of the three oldest MSS.*
⁵ *So all the oldest MSS.*

THE SECOND EPISTLE GENERAL OF
PETER.

CHAPTER I.

SYMEON PETER, a servant and apostle of Jesus Christ, to them that have obtained like precious faith with us in the righteousness of our God and [our] Saviour, Jesus Christ:

2 Grace and peace be multiplied unto you in the knowledge of God, and of Jesus our Lord.

3 Seeing that his divine power hath given unto us all things that pertain unto life and godliness, through the

knowledge of him that called us [1]by his own glory and virtue,

4 Through which he hath given unto us his exceeding great and precious promises : that by means of these ye may become partakers of the divine nature, having escaped from the corruption that is in the world [2]through lust.

5 And for this reason, giving on your part all diligence, provide, in [the exercise of] your faith, virtue ; and in your virtue, knowledge ;

6 And in your knowledge, selfrestraint ; and in your selfrestraint, patience ; and in your patience, godliness ;

7 And in your godliness, brotherly kindness ; and in your brotherly kindness, love.

8 For these things, being in you, and multiplying, render you not idle nor yet unfruitful towards the perfect knowledge of our Lord Jesus Christ.

9 For he that lacketh these things is blind, shortsighted, having forgotten the purification of his former sins.

10 Wherefore the rather, brethren, give diligence to make your calling and election secure : for doing these things, ye shall never fall :

11 For so your entrance shall be richly ministered unto you into the eternal kingdom of our Lord and Saviour Jesus Christ.

12 Wherefore I will be [3]sure to put you always in remembrance of these things, though ye know them, and be established in the truth which is present [with you].

13 But I think it meet, as long as I am in this tabernacle, to stir you up, putting you in remembrance ;

14 Knowing that shortly I must put off my tabernacle, even as our Lord Jesus Christ shewed unto me.

15 Moreover I will endeavour that ye may on every occasion be able after my decease to have these things in remembrance.

16 For not in pursuance of cunningly devised fables did we make known unto you the power and coming of our Lord Jesus Christ, but having been eyewitnesses of his majesty.

17 For he received from God the Father honour and glory, when there was sent such a voice to him from the excellent glory, This is my beloved Son, in whom I am well pleased.

18 And this voice we heard sent from heaven, when we were with him in the holy mount.

19 And we have more secure the prophetic word ; whereunto ye do well that ye take heed, as unto a candle shining in a dark place, until the day shall dawn, and the morning star shall arise in your hearts :

20 Knowing this first, that no prophecy of the scripture cometh of private interpretation.

21 For prophecy was never sent after the will of man : but

[1] *So three of the four oldest MSS.*
[2] *Literally*, in.
[3] *So all the oldest MSS.*

men had utterance from God,[1] being moved by the Holy Spirit.

CHAPTER II.

BUT there were false prophets also among the people, even as there shall be false teachers likewise among you, which shall bring in heresies of destruction, even denying the Master that bought them, bringing upon themselves swift destruction.

2 And many shall follow their [2]licentious ways; by reason of whom the way of truth shall be evil spoken of.

3 And in covetousness shall they with feigned words make merchandise of you: for whom the sentence now of a long time lingereth not, and their destruction slumbereth not.

4 For if God spared not angels when they sinned, but cast them into hell, and delivered them unto [3]dens of darkness, being reserved unto judgment;

5 And spared not the old world, but preserved Noah the eighth person, a preacher of righteousness, bringing in the flood upon the world of ungodly men;

6 And burning the cities of Sodom and Gomorrah to ashes condemned them to be overthrown, laying down an example of those that should in after time live ungodly;

7 And delivered righteous Lot, vexed with the behaviour of the lawless in their licentiousness:

8 For the righteous man dwelling among them, in seeing and hearing, tormented his righteous soul from day to day with their lawless deeds;

9 The Lord knoweth how to deliver the godly out of temptation, and to reserve the unrighteous unto the day of judgment under punishment:

10 But chiefly them that go after the flesh in the lust of uncleanness, and despise government. Presumptuous, self-willed, they are not afraid to rail at [4]dignities.

11 Whereas angels, though they be greater in strength and might, bring not railing judgment against them before the Lord.

12 But these, as irrational animals, born to be taken and destroyed, speaking evil of the things that they understand not, shall even perish in their corruption,

13 Receiving the reward of unrighteousness: counting as pleasure that delicate living which is but for a day: spots and blemishes, sporting themselves in their deceits while they feast with you:

14 Having eyes full of [5]adultery, and that cannot be made to cease from sin: alluring unstable souls: having an heart exercised with covetous

---

[1] *The readings of the oldest MSS. are in a state of confusion, which can hardly be explained in English. That adopted in the text is found in the Vatican MS.*

[2] *So all the MSS. The reading pernicious has no authority whatever.*

[3] *So all the oldest MSS.*

[4] *Literally, glories.*

[5] *Literally, of an adulteress.*

practices: children of the curse:

15 Which have forsaken the right way, and are gone astray, following the way of Balaam ¹[the son] of Bosor, who loved the wages of unrighteousness;

16 But had a rebuke for his own iniquity: the dumb ass speaking with man's voice forbad the madness of the prophet.

17 These are wells without water, mists driven by a whirlwind; for whom the blackness of darkness is reserved.²

18 For by speaking great swelling words of vanity they allure with lusts, by wantonness of the flesh, those that ³are scarcely escaping ⁴from them who live in error,

19 Promising them liberty, while they themselves are the slaves of corruption: for by whatsoever a man is overcome, by the same he is also enslaved.

20 For if, having escaped the pollutions of the world in the knowledge of the Lord and Saviour Jesus Christ, but having again become entangled therein, they are overcome, their last state is worse than the first.

21 For it had been better for them not to have known the way of righteousness, than, after they have known it, to turn back from the holy commandment delivered unto them.

22 ⁵It is happened unto them according to the true proverb, The dog gone back to his own vomit; and the sow that was washed to wallowing in the mire.

CHAPTER III.

THIS second epistle, beloved, I now write unto you; in both which I stir up your pure mind by way of remembrance:

2 That ye may be mindful of the words spoken before by the holy prophets, and of the commandment of the Lord and Saviour ⁶given by your apostles:

3 Knowing this first, that there shall come in the last of the days scoffers ⁷in [their] scoffing, walking after their own lusts,

4 And saying, Where is the promise of his coming? for since the fathers fell asleep, all things continue thus from the beginning of the creation.

5 For this they willingly are ignorant of, that by the word of God the heavens were from of old, and the earth formed out of water and by means of water:

6 By which waters the world that then was, being overflowed with water, perished:

7 But the heavens and the earth which are now by ⁸the same word are kept in store,

---

¹ *Not expressed in the original.*
² *For ever is omitted in the two oldest MSS.*
³ *So all the oldest MSS.*
⁴ *So most of the oldest MSS. and versions.*
⁵ *But is omitted in the three oldest MSS.*
⁶ *So all the MSS. earlier than the fourteenth century.*
⁷ *So all the ancient MSS. and versions.*
⁸ *Or, by his word: the ancient MSS. are divided.*

reserved unto fire against the day of judgment and perdition of ungodly men.

8 But, beloved, be not ignorant of this one thing, that one day is with the Lord as a thousand years, and a thousand years as one day.

9 The Lord is not slack concerning his promise, as some count slackness; but is longsuffering to ¹you-ward, not willing that any should perish, but that all should come to repentance.

10 But the day of the Lord will come as a thief;² in which the heavens shall pass away with a rushing noise, and the heavenly bodies shall be scorched up and dissolved, the earth also and the works that are therein shall be burned up.

11 Seeing that all these things shall be ³thus dissolved, what manner of persons ought ye to be in all holy behaviour and godliness,

12 Looking for and hastening the coming of the day of God, by reason of which the heavens being on fire shall be dissolved, and the heavenly bodies shall be scorched up and melted with fervent heat.

13 But, according to his promise, we look for new heavens and a new earth, wherein dwelleth righteousness.

14 Wherefore, beloved, seeing that ye look for such things, strive diligently to be found in peace, without spot, and blameless in his sight,

15 And account the longsuffering of our Lord salvation; even as our beloved brother Paul also according to the wisdom given unto him wrote unto you;

16 As also in all his epistles, speaking in them of these things; in which ⁴epistles are some things hard to be understood, which the ignorant and unstable wrest, as they do also the other scriptures, unto their own perdition.

17 Ye therefore, beloved, seeing ye know beforehand, beware lest, being led away together with the error of the wicked, ye fall from your own stedfastness.

18 But grow in the grace and knowledge of our Lord and Saviour Jesus Christ. To him be the glory both now and for ever. Amen.

---

¹ *So all the ancient MSS.*
² *In the night is omitted in the three oldest MSS. It probably came in here from 1 Thess. v. 2.*
³ *So two of the oldest MSS.: the other two reading as the A. V.*
⁴ *So the three most ancient MSS., having the relative pronoun in the feminine: the other MSS. have it in the masculine (or neuter)*

THE FIRST EPISTLE GENERAL OF
JOHN.

CHAPTER I.

THAT which was from the beginning, which we have heard,—which we have seen with our eyes, which we looked upon, and our hands handled, —concerning the Word of life ;

2 (And the life was manifested, and we have seen it, and bear witness, and declare unto you that eternal life, which was with the Father, and was manifested unto us ;)

3 That which we have seen and heard declare we unto you [1]also, that ye also may have fellowship with us : and truly our fellowship is with the Father, and with his Son Jesus Christ.

4 And these things write we,[2] that [3]our joy may be full.

5 And this is the message which we have heard of him, and announce unto you, that God is light, and in him is no darkness at all.

6 If we say that we have fellowship with him, and walk in the darkness, we lie, and do not the truth :

7 But if we walk in the light, as he is in the light, we have fellowship one with another, and the blood of Jesus[4] his Son cleanseth us from all sin.

[1] Also *is found in the oldest authorities.*
[2] Unto you *is omitted in the two oldest MSS.*
[3] *So the two oldest MSS.*
[4] Christ *is omitted by the oldest authorities.*

8 If we say that we have no sin, we deceive ourselves, and the truth is not in us.

9 If we confess our sins, He is faithful and just to forgive us our sins, and to cleanse us from all unrighteousness.

10 If we say that we have not sinned, we make him a liar, and his word is not in us.

CHAPTER II.

MY little children, these things write I unto you, that ye may not sin. And if any man have sinned, we have an advocate with the Father, Jesus Christ the righteous :

2 And he is a propitiation for our sins : yet not for ours only, but also for [5][the sins of] the whole world.

3 And hereby we have the knowledge of him, if we keep his commandments.

4 He that saith, I have the knowledge of him, and keepeth not his commandments, is a liar, and the truth is not in him.

5. But whoso keepeth his word, in him verily is the love of God perfected : hereby know we that we are in him.

6 He that saith he abideth in him ought himself also so to walk, even as he walked.

7 [6]Beloved, I write no new commandment unto you, but

[5] *Not expressed in the original.*
[6] *So all the oldest authorities*

an old commandment which ye had from the beginning. The old commandment is the word which ye heard.[1]

8 Again, a new commandment I write unto you, which thing is true in him and in you: because the darkness is passing away, and the true light now shineth.

9 He that saith he is in the light, and hateth his brother, is in the darkness even until now.

10 He that loveth his brother abideth in the light, and there is none occasion of stumbling in him.

11 But he that hateth his brother is in the darkness, and walketh in the darkness, and knoweth not whither he goeth, because the darkness blinded his eyes.

12 I write unto you, little children, because your sins are forgiven you for his name's sake.

13 I write unto you, fathers, because ye know him that was from the beginning. I write unto you, young men, because ye have overcome the wicked one. I [2]have written unto you, children, because ye know the Father.

14 I have written unto you, fathers, because ye know him that was from the beginning. I have written unto you, young men, because ye are strong, and the word of God abideth in you, and ye have overcome the wicked one.

15 Love not the world, neither the things that are in the world. If any man love the world, the love of the Father is not in him.

16 For all that is in the world, the lust of the flesh, and the lust of the eyes, and the vainglory of life, is not of the Father, but is of the world.

17 And the world is passing away, and the lust thereof: but he that doeth the will of God abideth for ever.

18 Children, it is the last time: and as ye heard that antichrist cometh, even now have there arisen many antichrists; from whence we know that it is the last time.

19 They went out from among us, but they were not of us; for if they had been of us, they would have continued with us: but [3][they went out,] that they may be made manifest that all are not of us.

20 And ye have an anointing from the Holy One, and know all things.

21 I have not written unto you because ye know not the truth, but because ye know it, and because no lie is of the truth.

22 Who is the liar, but he that denieth that Jesus is the Christ? He is the antichrist, that denieth the Father and the Son.

23 Whosoever denieth the Son, neither hath he the Father: [4]he that confesseth the Son hath the Father also.

---

[1] From the beginning *is omitted by all the oldest authorities.*

[2] *So all the oldest authorities.*

[3] *Not expressed in the original.*

[4] *So all the earliest authorities.*

24. As for you, let that[1] abide in you, which ye heard from the beginning. If that which ye heard from the beginning abide in you, ye also shall abide in the Son, and in the Father.

25 And the promise that He himself promised unto us is this, even eternal life.

26 These things have I written unto you concerning them that deceive you.

27 And as for you, the anointing which ye received from him abideth in you, and ye need not that any one teach you: but as [2]his anointing teacheth you concerning all things, and is true, and is no lie, and even as He taught you, [3]abide in him.

28 And now, little children, abide in him; that, if he should be manifested, we may have confidence, and not shrink with shame from him at his coming.

29 If ye know that he is righteous, ye know that every one also that doeth righteousness is born of him.

CHAPTER III.

BEHOLD, what manner of love the Father hath bestowed upon us, that we should be called children of God: [4]and [5][so] we are: therefore the world knoweth us not, because it knew him not.

2 Beloved, now are we children of God, and it never yet was manifested what we shall be: [5][but] we know that, if it be manifested, we shall be like him; because we shall see him as he is.

3 And every man that hath this hope on Him purifieth himself, even as He is pure.

4 Whosoever committeth sin transgresseth also the law: and sin is the transgression of the law.

5 And ye know that he was manifested to take away our sins; and in him is no sin.

6 Whosoever abideth in him sinneth not: whosoever sinneth seeth him not, neither knoweth him.

7 Little children, let no one deceive you: he that doeth righteousness is righteous, even as he is righteous.

8 He that doeth sin is of the devil; because the devil sinneth from the beginning. For this purpose the Son of God was manifested, that he might destroy the works of the devil.

9 Whosoever is born of God doeth not sin, because his seed abideth in him: and he cannot sin, because he is born of God.

10 In this the children of God are manifest, and the children of the devil: whosoever doeth not righteousness is not of God, and he that loveth not his brother.

11 For this is the message that ye heard from the beginning, that we should love one another.

12 Not as Cain was of the wicked one, and slew his bro-

---

[1] *Therefore is omitted by all the oldest authorities.*
[2] *So the three oldest MSS.*
[3] *So all the oldest MSS.*
[4] *So all the ancient MSS.*
[5] *Not expressed in the original.*

ther. And wherefore slew he him? Because his own works were wicked, and his brother's righteous.

13 Marvel not, brethren, if the world hateth you.

14 We know that we have passed over from death into life, because we love the brethren. He that loveth not[1] abideth in death.

15 Every one that hateth his brother is a murderer: and ye know that no murderer hath eternal life abiding in him.

16 Herein have we the knowledge of love, that He laid down his life for us: and we ought to lay down our lives for the brethren.

17 But whoso hath this world's sustenance, and beholdeth his brother having need, and shutteth up his heart from him, how abideth the love of God in him?

18 Little children, let us not love with word neither with tongue; but in deed and in truth.

19 And herein [2]shall we know that we are of the truth, and shall persuade our hearts before him.

20 For if our heart condemn us, it is because God is greater than our heart, and knoweth all things.

21 Beloved, if our heart condemn us not, we have confidence toward God,

22 And whatsoever we ask, we receive from him, because we keep his commandments, and do those things that are pleasing in his sight.

23 And this is his commandment, That we should believe the name of his Son Jesus Christ, and love one another, as he gave us commandment.

24 And he that keepeth his commandments abideth in him, and he in him. And hereby we know that he abideth in us, by the Spirit which he gave us.

CHAPTER IV.

BELOVED, believe not every spirit, but try the spirits whether they are of God: because many false prophets are gone out into the world.

2 Herein know ye the Spirit of God: Every spirit that confesseth Jesus Christ come in the flesh is of God:

3 And every spirit that confesseth not Jesus [3][Christ come in the flesh] is not of God: and this is the [spirit] of antichrist, whereof ye have heard that it cometh; and now already is it in the world.

4 Ye are of God, little children, and have overcome them: because greater is he that is in you, than he that is in the world.

5 They are of the world: therefore speak they of the world, and the world heareth them.

6 We are of God: he that knoweth God heareth us; he that is not of God heareth not

---

[1] *His brother is omitted in the three oldest MSS.*
[2] *So all the oldest MSS.*
[3] *These words are omitted in the Alexandrine and Vatican MSS., but contained in the Sinaitic MS. and in the ancient Syriac version*

us. From this we know the spirit of truth, and the spirit of error.

7 Beloved, let us love one another, because love is of God; and every one that loveth is born of God, and knoweth God.

8 He that loveth not never knew God; because God is love.

9 In this the love of God was manifested in regard to us, that God hath sent his only begotten Son into the world, that we might live through him.

10 Herein is love, not that we loved God, but that he loved us, and sent his Son as a propitiation for our sins.

11 Beloved, if God so loved us, we also ought to love one another.

12 God hath no one beheld at any time. If we love one another, God abideth in us, and the love of Him is perfected in us.

13 Herein know we that we abide in him, and he in us, because he hath given us of his Spirit.

14 And we have beheld and do testify that the Father hath sent the Son as Saviour of the world.

15 Whosoever confesseth that Jesus is the Son of God, God abideth in him, and he in God.

16 And we have known and have believed the love that God hath in regard to us. God is love; and he that abideth in love abideth in God, and God in him.

17 Herein is love made perfect with us, that we have boldness in the day of judgment: because even as he is, so are we in this world.

18 Fear existeth not in love; nay, perfect love casteth out fear: because fear hath torment: and he that feareth is not made perfect in love.

19 We love,[1] because he first loved us.

20 If any say, I love God, and hate his brother, he is a liar: for he that loveth not his brother whom he hath seen, [2]cannot love God whom he hath not seen.

21 And this commandment have we from him, That he who loveth God love his brother also.

CHAPTER V.

EVERY one that believeth that Jesus is the Christ hath been begotten of God: and every one that loveth him that begat loveth him also that is begotten of him.

2 Herein we know that we love the children of God, when we love God, and do his commandments.

3 For this is the love of God, that we keep his commandments. And his commandments are not grievous, because

4 All that is begotten of God overcometh the world: and

---

[1] Him *is omitted by the Alexandrine and Vatican MSS.: the Sinaitic has* God *instead of it. This variety in the authorities which insert it shews that the original text did not contain it.*

[2] *So the two oldest MSS.*

this is the victory that hath overcome the world, even our faith.

5 Who is he that overcometh the world, but he that believeth that Jesus is the Son of God?

6 This is he that came by water and blood, even Jesus Christ; not in the water only, but in the water and in the blood. And the Spirit is that which beareth witness, because the Spirit is the truth.

7 For they that bear witness[1] are three,

8 The spirit, and the water, and the blood: and the three agree in one.

9 If we receive the witness of men, the witness of God is greater: for the witness of God is this, [2]that he hath borne witness concerning his Son.

10 He that believeth on the Son of God hath the witness in [3] him: he that believeth not God hath made him a liar; because he hath not believed in the witness that God hath borne concerning his Son.

11 And this is the witness, that God gave to us eternal life, and this life is in his Son.

12 He that hath the Son hath the life; he that hath not the Son of God hath not the life.

13 These things have I written unto you,[4] that ye may know that ye have eternal life; [5]even to you that believe on the name of the Son of God.

14 And this is the confidence that we have towards him, that, if we ask anything according to his will, he heareth us:

15 And if we know that he heareth us whatsoever we ask, we know that we have the petitions that we have asked of him.

16 If any see his brother sinning a sin not unto death, he shall ask, and shall give him life for them that sin not unto death. There is a sin unto death: concerning it I do not say that he should make request.

17 All unrighteousness is sin: and there is a sin not unto death.

18 We know that whosoever is begotten of God sinneth not; but he that hath been begotten of God, [6] it keepeth him, and the wicked one toucheth him not.

19 We know that we are of God, and the whole world lieth in the wicked one.

20 [7] Moreover we know that the Son of God is come, and hath given us an understanding, that we know the true

---

[1] *The words*, in heaven, the Father, the Word, and the Holy Ghost: and these three are one. And there are three that bear witness in earth, *are omitted by all Greek MSS. (till the sixteenth century); all the Greek Fathers; all the ancient versions; and most of the Latin Fathers.*

[2] *So all the oldest MSS.*

[3] *So most of the oldest MSS.*

[4] *So, omitting* that believe on the name of the Son of God, *all the oldest MSS.*

[5] *So the two oldest MSS.*

[6] *So the Vatican MS. and the Alexandrine (but in this latter the original scribe has corrected* him *to* himself). *The Sinaitic MS has* himself.

[7] *So the oldest MSS.*

One; and we are in the true One, in his Son Jesus Christ. This is the true God, and eternal life.

21 Little children, keep yourselves from idols.[1]

[1] Amen *is omitted by all the oldest authorities.*

THE SECOND EPISTLE OF
JOHN.

THE elder unto [1] the elect lady and her children, whom I love in truth; and not I only, but also all they that know the truth;

2 For the truth's sake, which abideth in us, and shall be with us for ever:

3 [2]There shall be with us grace, mercy, and peace, from God the Father, and from [3]Jesus Christ, the Son of the Father, in truth and love.

4 I rejoice greatly, that I have found of thy children walking in truth, according as we received commandment from the Father.

5 And now I beseech thee, lady, not as writing unto thee a new commandment, but that which we had from the beginning, that we love one another.

6 And this is love, that we walk according to his commandments. This is the commandment, even as ye heard from the beginning that ye should walk in it.

7 Because many deceivers went forth into the world, they who confess not Jesus Christ coming in the flesh. This is the deceiver and the antichrist.

8 Look to yourselves, that [4]ye lose not those things which ye wrought, but that ye receive reward in full.

9 Whosoever [5]goeth before you, and abideth not in the doctrine of Christ, hath not God: he that abideth in the doctrine,[6] he hath both the Father and the Son.

10 If any cometh unto you, and bringeth not this doctrine, receive him not into your house, neither bid him good speed:

[1] *Or,* Kyria the elect.
[2] *So all the oldest authorities, except the Alexandrine MS., which omits* there shall be with us *altogether.*
[3] The Lord *is omitted by the Alexandrine and Vatican MSS., but inserted by the Sinaitic MS*
[4] *So is the preponderance of authority. But the oldest MSS. vary: the Vatican has* that ye lose not the things which we wrought.
[5] *So all the oldest MSS.*
[6] Of Christ *is omitted by all the oldest MSS.*

11 For he that biddeth him good speed is partaker of his evil deeds.

12 Having many things to write unto you, I would not do so with paper and ink: but I hope to come unto you, and to speak face to face, that ¹your joy may be full.

13 The children of thy elect sister greet thee.²

---

¹ *So the Alexandrine and Vatican MSS.: the Sinaitic has* our.
² Amen *is omitted by all the oldest authorities.*

THE THIRD EPISTLE OF
JOHN.

THE elder unto Gaius the beloved, whom I love in the truth.

2 Beloved, I pray that thou mayest prosper in all things, and be in health, even as thy soul prospereth.

3 For I rejoiced greatly, when the brethren came and testified to thy truth, even as thou walkest in the truth.

4 I have no greater joy than this, that I hear of my children walking in the truth.

5 Beloved, thou doest faithfully whatsoever thou doest to the brethren, ¹who besides are strangers;

6 Which bore witness of thy charity before the church: whom if thou bring forward on their journey worthily of God, thou shalt do well:

7 Because that for ¹the Name's sake they went forth, taking nothing from the Gentiles.

¹ *So all the oldest MSS.*

8 We therefore ought to support such, that we may become fellow-workers for the truth.

9 I wrote ¹somewhat unto the church: howbeit Diotrephes, who loveth to have the preeminence among them, receiveth us not.

10 Wherefore, if I come, I will bring to mind his deeds which he doeth, prating against us with wicked speeches: and not content therewith, neither doth he himself receive the brethren, and forbiddeth them that would, and casteth them out of the church.

11 Beloved, imitate not evil, but good. He that doeth good is of God: but he that doeth evil hath not seen God.

12 Demetrius hath good testimony from all, and from the truth itself: yea, and we also bear testimony; and ¹thou knowest that our testimony is true.

13 I had many things to write ¹unto thee, but I am not willing with ink and reed to write unto thee:

14 But I hope immediately to see thee, and then we shall speak face to face. Peace be to thee. The friends salute thee. Salute the friends by name.

¹ *So all the oldest MSS.*

THE GENERAL EPISTLE OF
JUDE.

JUDE, a servant of Jesus Christ, and brother of James, to the called, ¹beloved in God the Father, and preserved for Jesus Christ:

2 Mercy unto you, and peace, and love, be multiplied.

3 Beloved, in giving diligence to write unto you of the common salvation, I found it necessary to write unto you forthwith, exhorting you to contend earnestly for the faith once for all delivered unto the saints.

4 For there crept in of old certain men, men before written down in prophecy for this judgment, ungodly men, turning the grace of our God into lasciviousness, and denying the only ²Master, and our Lord Jesus Christ.

5 I wish therefore to put you in remembrance, knowing as ye do all ³[these] things once for all, how that ⁴Jesus having saved the people out of the land of Egypt, ²secondly destroyed them that believed not.

6 And the angels which kept not their dignity, but left their own habitation, he hath reserved in everlasting chains under darkness unto the judgment of the great day.

7 And how that Sodom and Gomorrha, and the cities about them, giving themselves over to fornication, and going away after strange flesh, are in like manner to these set forth for an example, suffering the just punishment of eternal fire.

8 In like manner nevertheless these dreamers also defile the flesh, despise dominion, and speak evil of ⁵dignities.

9 Yet Michael the archangel, when contending with the

¹ *So all the oldest authorities.*
² *So all the oldest MSS.*
³ *Not expressed in the original.*

⁴ *The ancient authorities are divided; some reading* God, *some* the Lord, *but in various forms. The Alexandrine and Vatican MSS. read as in the text.*
⁵ *Literally,* glories.

devil he disputed about the body of Moses, durst not bring against him a railing accusation, but said, The Lord rebuke thee.

10 But these speak evil of whatever things they know not: but whatever things they know naturally, as the irrational animals, in these they corrupt themselves.

11 Woe unto them! for they went in the way of Cain, and ran greedily after the error of Balaam for reward, and perished in the gainsaying of Korah.

12 These are the rocks in your lovefeasts, when they feast with you without fear, pasturing their own selves: clouds they are without water, carried ¹away by winds; autumn trees without fruit, twice dead, plucked up by the roots;

13 Raging waves of the sea, foaming out their own shame; wandering stars, to whom is reserved the blackness of darkness for ever.

14 Yea, and Enoch, the seventh from Adam, prophesied of these, saying, Behold, the Lord came with ten thousands of his holy ones,

15 To execute judgment upon all, and to convict all the ungodly of all their ungodly deeds which they ungodly committed, and of all their hard speeches which ungodly sinners spoke against him.

16 These are murmurers, complainers, walking after their own lusts; and their mouth speaketh great swelling words, having men's persons in admiration for the sake of advantage.

17 But, beloved, remember ye the words which were spoken before by the apostles of our Lord Jesus Christ;

18 That they told you there should be mockers in the last time, walking after their own ungodly lusts.

19 These be they who separate themselves, sensual, not having the Spirit.

20 But ye, beloved, building up yourselves on your most holy faith, praying in the Holy Spirit,

21 Keep yourselves in the love of God, looking for the mercy of our Lord Jesus Christ unto eternal life.

22 And some ²indeed convict, ³when they contend with you;

23 But others save,⁴ pulling them out of the fire; ⁵and of others have compassion with fear, hating even the garment spotted by the flesh.

24 But unto him that is able to keep you from falling, and to present you faultless before the presence of his glory with exceeding joy,

25 To the only wise God our Saviour ³through Jesus Christ our Lord, be glory, majesty, dominion and power, ³before all time, and now, and to all ages. Amen.

¹ *So all the MSS.*

² *The ancient MSS. are divided, but that in the text is the more probable reading.*
³ *So all the oldest MSS.*
⁴ *With fear is omitted by all the oldest MSS.*
⁵ *So the three oldest MSS.*

THE REVELATION
OF
JOHN.

CHAPTER I.

THE Revelation of Jesus Christ, which God gave unto him, to shew unto his servants what things must shortly come to pass ; and he signified it sending by his angel unto his servant John :

2 Who testified the word of God, and the testimony of Jesus Christ, [1]as much as he saw.

3 Blessed is he that readeth, and they that hear the words of this prophecy, and keep those things which are written therein : for the time is at hand.

4 JOHN to the seven churches which are in Asia : Grace be unto you, and peace, from him which is, and which was, and which is to come, and from the seven Spirits which are before his throne ;

5 And from Jesus Christ, the faithful witness, the first begotten of the dead, and the Ruler of the kings of the earth. Unto him that [2]loveth us, and [3]washed us from our sins in his blood,

6 And he made us [a]a kingdom, even priests unto God and his Father ; to him be the glory and the dominion [4]for ever. Amen.

7 Behold, he cometh with the clouds ; and every eye shall see him, and they which pierced him : and all the tribes of the earth shall wail because of him. Yea, Amen.

8 I am the Alpha and the Omega,[5] saith the Lord [c]God, which is, and which was, and which is to come, the Almighty.

9 I John, [6]your brother, and companion in the tribulation and [7]kingdom and patience [8]in Jesus, was in the isle that is called Patmos, on account of the word of God, and [9]the testimony of Jesus.[10]

10 I was in the Spirit on the Lord's day, and heard behind me a great voice as of a trumpet,

11 Saying, [11]What thou seest, write in a book, and send unto the seven churches ;[12] unto

---

[1] *So, omitting* and, *all the MSS.*
[2] *So all the old MSS.*
[3] *Or,* loosed us: *the difference between the two words in Greek is only that of one letter.*
[4] *So the Alexandrine MS.*
[5] *The beginning and the ending is omitted in two out of the three oldest MSS. It has apparently been inserted from ch.* xxii. 13.
[6] *Also is omitted in all the old MSS.*
[7] *In the is omitted in all the old MSS.*
[8] *So two of the three oldest MSS.: others vary, but only one later MS. reads as the A. V.*
[9] *For is omitted by two of the oldest MSS.*
[10] *Christ is omitted by all the old MSS.*
[11] I am Alpha and Omega, the first and the last: and, *is omitted by all the old MSS. and versions.*
[12] *Which are in Asia is omitted by all the MSS. of every date.*

Ephesus, and unto Smyrna, and unto Pergamus, and unto Thyatira, and unto Sardis, and unto Philadelphia, and unto Laodicea.

12 And I turned to see the voice that spake with me. And being turned, I saw seven golden candlesticks;

13 And in the midst of the seven candlesticks one like unto the Son of Man, clothed with a garment down to the foot, and girt about the breasts with a golden girdle.

14 His head and his hairs were white as white wool, like snow; and his eyes as a flame of fire;

15 And his feet like unto fine brass,[1] as if they had been burned in a furnace; and his voice as the sound of many waters.

16 And having in his right hand seven stars: and out of his mouth going forth a sharp twoedged sword: and his countenance as the sun shineth in his strength.

17 And when I saw him, I fell at his feet as dead. And he laid his right hand upon me, saying,[2] Fear not; I am the first and the last, and the living One;

18 And I was dead, and, behold, I am alive for evermore;[3] and have the keys of death and of Hadés.

19 Write [4]therefore the things which thou sawest, and what things they are, and the things which shall be after these;

20 The mystery of the seven stars which thou sawest in my right hand, and the seven golden candlesticks. The seven stars are angels of the seven churches: and the seven candlesticks[5] are seven churches.

CHAPTER II.

UNTO the angel of the church[6] in Ephesus write; These things saith he that holdeth the seven stars in his right hand, he that walketh in the midst of the seven golden candlesticks;

2 I know thy works, and thy labour, and thy patience, and that thou canst not bear wicked persons: and thou didst try them which say they are apostles, and are not, and didst find them false:

3 [7]And hadst patience, and didst bear for my name's sake, and hast not been weary.

4 Nevertheless I have against thee that thou hast left thy first love.

5 Remember therefore from whence thou art fallen, and repent, and do the first works; or else I will come unto thee,[8] and will remove thy candle-

---

[1] *Literally,* chalcolibanus. *The precise meaning of the word is quite unknown.*
[2] Unto me *is omitted by all the old MSS.*
[3] Amen *is omitted by all the old MSS.*
[4] *So all the old MSS. and versions.*
[5] Which thou sawest *is omitted by all the oldest MSS.*
[6] *So all the MSS. of every date.*
[7] *So, slightly varying, all the MSS.: none reading as the A. V.*
[8] Quickly *is omitted by the oldest MSS.*

stick out of his place, if thou do not repent.

6 Notwithstanding, this thou hast, that thou hatest the works of the Nicolaitans, which I also hate.

7 He that hath an ear, let him hear what the Spirit saith unto the churches. To him that overcometh will I give to eat of the tree of life, which is in[1] the paradise of God.

8 And unto the angel of the church in Smyrna write; These things saith the first and the last, which was dead, and revived;

9 I know thy[2] tribulation, and thy poverty; nevertheless thou art rich; and the slandering of thee by them which say they are Jews, and are not, but are the synagogue of Satan.

10 Fear [3]not those things which thou art about to suffer: behold, the devil shall cast some of you into prison, that ye may be tried; and ye shall have tribulation ten days. Be thou faithful unto death, and I will give thee a crown of life.

11 He that hath an ear, let him hear what the Spirit saith unto the churches. He that overcometh shall not be hurt by the second death.

12 And to the angel of the church in Pergamus write; These things saith he which hath the sharp sword with two edges;

13 I know[4] where thou dwellest, even where Satan's throne is: and thou holdest fast my name, and didst not deny the faith of me even in the days of Antipas [5]my martyr, my faithful one, who was slain among you, where Satan dwelleth.

14 But I have a few things against thee, because thou hast there them that hold the teaching of Balaam, who taught Balak to cast a stumblingblock before the sons of Israel, to eat things sacrificed unto idols, and to commit fornication.

15 So hast thou also them that hold the doctrine of the Nicolaitans, [6]in like manner.

16 Repent [5]therefore, or else I will come unto thee quickly, and will fight against them with the sword of my mouth.

17 He that hath an ear, let him hear what the Spirit saith unto the churches. To him that overcometh will I give[7] of the hidden manna, and will give him a white stone, and on the stone a new name written, which none knoweth saving he that receiveth it.

18 And unto the angel of the church in Thyatira write; These things saith the Son of God, who hath his eyes like

---

[1] The midst of *is omitted by all the old MSS.*

[2] Works and *is omitted by two out of the three oldest MSS. It was probably put in from ver. 2 and ch. iii. 1, 8, 15.*

[3] *So two of the three oldest MSS., and the best of the later ones.*

[4] Thy works and *is omitted by all the oldest MSS.*

[5] *So two of the three oldest MSS.*

[6] *So all the MSS., none reading as the A.V.*

[7] To eat *is omitted by all the old MSS.*

unto a flame of fire, and his feet are like ¹fine brass;

19 I know thy works, and thy love, and thy faith, and thy service, and thy patience, and thy works; and the last to be more than the first.

20 Notwithstanding I have² against thee that thou sufferest ³thy wife Jezebel, which calleth herself a prophetess; ⁴and she teacheth and seduceth my servants to commit fornication, and to eat things sacrificed unto idols.

21 ⁵And I gave her time to repent, and she will not repent of her fornication.

22 Behold, I cast her into a bed, and them that commit adultery together with her into great tribulation, except they repent of ⁶her deeds.

23 And her children will I kill with death; and all the churches shall know that I am he which searcheth the reins and hearts: and I will give unto every one of you according to your works.

24 But unto you I say, ⁷unto the rest in Thyatira, as many as have not this doctrine, such as have not known the depths of Satan, as they call them;

I ⁸put upon you none other burden.

25 But that which ye have, hold fast till I come.

26 And he that overcometh, and he that keepeth my works unto the end, to him will I give authority over the nations

27 And he shall rule them with a rod of iron, as the vessels of a potter are broken to shivers: as I also have received of my Father.

28 And I will give him the morning star.

29 He that hath an ear, let him hear what the Spirit saith unto the churches.

CHAPTER III.

AND unto the angel of the church in Sardis write; These things saith he that hath the seven Spirits of God, and the seven stars; I know thy works, that thou hast a name that thou livest, and art dead.

2 Be watchful, and strengthen the things which remain, that were ready to die: for I have not found thy works perfect before ⁹my God.

3 Remember¹⁰[therefore] how thou hast received and heardest, and keep, and repent. If therefore thou shalt not watch, I will come¹¹ as a thief, and thou shalt not know what hour I will come upon thee.

4 ¹²Nevertheless thou hast a

---

¹ *See note on ch. i. 15.*
² *A few things is omitted by all the old MSS.: the Sinaitic MS. has I have much against thee.*
³ *The ancient MSS. are divided as to the insertion of thy, but on the whole it seems probable that it is genuine.*
⁴ *So all the MSS.*
⁵ *So most of the old MSS.*
⁶ *So all the old MSS., except the Alexandrine.*
⁷ *And is omitted by all the MSS.*
⁸ *So two of the three oldest MSS.*
⁹ *So all the oldest MSS.*
¹⁰ *Therefore is omitted in one of the three oldest MSS.*
¹¹ *On thee is omitted by two of the three oldest MSS.*
¹² *So all the MSS., none omitting Nevertheless.*

few names¹ in Sardis which have not defiled their garments; and they shall walk with me in white, because they are worthy.

5 He that overcometh, ²the same shall be clothed in white raiment; and I will not blot out his name out of the book of life; and I will confess his name before my Father, and before his angels.

6 He that hath an ear, let him hear what the Spirit saith unto the churches.

7 And to the angel of the church in Philadelphia write; These things saith ³the true One, the holy One, he that hath the key of David, he that openeth, and none ⁴shall shut; and shutteth, and none ⁵openeth;

8 I know thy works: behold, I have granted before thee an open door, which none can shut: because thou hast little power, and thou didst keep my word, and didst not deny my name.

9 Behold, I give ⁶[them] of the synagogue of Satan, which say they are Jews, and are not, but do lie,—behold, I will make them to come and worship before thy feet, and to know that I have loved thee.

10 Because thou didst keep the word of my patience, I also will keep thee from the hour of temptation, which is about to come upon all the world, to try them that dwell upon the earth.

11 ⁷I come quickly: hold fast that which thou hast, that no one take thy crown.

12 He that overcometh, I will make him a pillar in the temple of my God, and he shall nevermore go out: and I will write upon him the name of my God, and the name of the city of my God, the new Jerusalem, which cometh down out of heaven from my God,—and mine own new name.

13 He that hath an ear, let him hear what the Spirit saith unto the churches.

14 And unto the angel of the church ⁸in Laodicea write; These things saith the Amen, the faithful and true witness, the beginning of the creation of God;

15 I know thy works, that thou art neither cold nor hot: I would thou wert cold or hot.

16 So then because thou art lukewarm, and neither ⁹hot nor cold, I shall soon spue thee out of my mouth.

17 Because thou sayest, I am rich, and I have become wealthy, and have need of nothing; and knowest not that thou of all others art the wretched one, and ¹⁰the

---

¹ Even *is omitted by all the MSS.*
² *Or,* He that overcometh thus.
³ *This order is found in two out of the three oldest MSS.*
⁴ *So all the oldest MSS.*
⁵ *The Sinaitic MS. and some later ones read* shall open.
⁶ *Not expressed in the original.*

⁷ Behold *is omitted by all the old MSS.*
⁸ *So all the MSS.*
⁹ *So two of the three oldest MSS. and most of the later ones.*
¹⁰ *So the Alexandrine and the later MSS. The reading is in some con-*

pitiable one, and poor and blind and naked:

18 I counsel thee to buy of me gold fresh smelted from the fire, that thou mayest be rich; and white raiment, that thou mayest be clothed, and that the shame of thy nakedness may not be made manifest; and eyesalve [1] to anoint thine eyes, that thou mayest see.

19 As many as I love, I rebuke and chasten: be zealous therefore, and repent.

20 Behold, I stand at the door, and knock: if any man hear my voice, and open the door, I will come in to him, and will sup with him, and he with me.

21 He that overcometh, to him will I grant to sit with me in my throne, as I also overcame, and sat down with my Father in his throne.

22 He that hath an ear, let him hear what the Spirit saith unto the churches.

CHAPTER IV.

AFTER these things I saw, and, behold, a door set open in heaven: and the former voice which I heard as of a trumpet talking with me, saying, Come up hither, and I will shew thee things which must be hereafter.

2 And immediately I was in the spirit: and, behold, a throne was there in heaven, and one sitting upon the throne.

3 And he that sat, [2] in appearance like a jasper and a sardine stone: and a rainbow round about the throne, like the appearance of an emerald.

4 And round about the throne, four and twenty thrones: and upon the four and twenty thrones, [3] elders sitting, clothed in white raiment; and [4] on their heads crowns of gold.

5 And out of the throne proceed lightnings and [5] voices and thunderings: and [there were] seven lamps of fire burning before [6] the throne, which are [7] [the] seven Spirits of God:

6 And before the throne [1] as it were a sea of glass like unto crystal. And in the midst of the throne, and round about the throne, four beings full of eyes before and behind.

7 And the first being [was] like a lion, and the second being [was] like a steer, and the third being had a face as a man, and the fourth being [was] like a flying eagle.

8 And the four beings had each of them six wings. Around and within they are full of eyes: and they have no rest day and night, saying, Holy, holy, holy,[8] Lord God Almighty, which was, and

---

[3] *So, omitting* I saw, *nearly all the MSS., and all the versions.*

[4] They had *is omitted by all the MSS. and versions.*

[5] *Such is the order in all the old MSS. and versions.*

[6] *Many MSS. read* his throne.

[7] The *is omitted by most of the later MSS.*

[8] *This word is repeated* eight times *in the Sinaitic MS.;* nine times *in the later Vatican MS.:* in some others twice, six times, eight times. *In the Alexandrine MS., and many*

---

[2] fusion, *the other ancient MSS. being divided.*

[1] *So all the oldest MSS.* Was *is omitted by all the MSS.*

which is, and which is to come.

9 And whensoever those beings shall give glory and honour and thanks to him that sitteth upon the throne, who liveth for ever and ever,

10 The four and twenty elders shall fall down before him that sitteth upon the throne, and shall worship him that liveth for ever and ever, and shall cast down their crowns before the throne, saying,

11 Thou art worthy, [1]our Lord and God, to receive the glory and the honour and the might: because thou didst create all things, and by reason of thy will they [2]were, and were created.

CHAPTER V.

AND I saw on the right hand of him that sat upon the throne a book written within and on the back, sealed with seven seals.

2 And I saw a strong angel proclaiming with a loud voice, Who is worthy to open the book, and to loose the seals thereof?

3 And no one [3]in heaven, nor in earth, neither under the earth, was able to open the book, neither to look thereon.

4 And I wept much, because no one was found worthy to open[4] the book, or to look thereon.

5 And one of the elders saith unto me, Weep not: behold, the Lion which is of the tribe of Judah, the Root of David, conquered, [so as] to open the book, and[5] the seven seals thereof.

6 And I beheld[6] in the midst of the throne and of the four living-beings, and in the midst of the elders, a Lamb standing as if slain, having seven horns and seven eyes, which are the seven Spirits of God sent forth into all the earth.

7 And he came and took [7]it out of the right hand of him that sat upon the throne.

8 And when he took the book, the four living-beings and the four and twenty elders fell down before the Lamb, having each one [8]a harp, and golden vials full of incense, which are the prayers of the saints.

9 And they sing a new song, saying, Thou art worthy to take the book, and to open the seals thereof: for thou wast slain, and didst redeem

---

others, *and the versions, it occurs three times, as in our text.*

[2] *The ancient MSS. here differ widely. The Alexandrine and the later Vatican read as in our text; the later Vatican however, and some others, adding* the holy One: *the Sinaitic reads,* O Lord, who art our Lord and end.

[2] *So the two most ancient MSS.*

[3] *Many MSS. read* in heaven above.

[4] *And* to read *is omitted by all the oldest MSS.*

[5] *To loose is omitted by almost all the MSS. and versions: the Sinaitic MS. inserts it.*

[6] *And lo is omitted by most MSS. The Alexandrine MS. has,* and lo, and in the midst, &c., *omitting* I beheld. *Hardly any read as the A. V.*

[7] *So the two oldest MSS., and many others.*

[8] *So the three oldest and many other MSS.*

¹[us] to God by thy blood out of every kindred, and tongue, and people, and nation;

10 And didst make ²them ³[unto our God] ⁴a kingdom and ⁵priests: and ⁵they reign on the earth.

11 And I beheld, and I heard ⁶[as it were] a voice of many angels round about the throne and the living-beings and the elders: and the number of them was myriads of myriads, and thousands of thousands;

12 Saying with a loud voice, Worthy is the Lamb that hath been slain to receive the power and riches and wisdom and strength and honour and glory and blessing.

13 And every creature which is in the heaven, and on the earth, and under the earth, and upon the sea, and the things that are in them, heard I all saying, Unto him that sitteth upon the throne, and unto the Lamb be the blessing and the honour and the glory and the might for ever and ever.

14 And the four living-beings said, Amen. And the ⁷elders fell down and worshipped.⁸

CHAPTER VI.

AND I saw when the Lamb opened one of the ⁹seven seals, and I heard one of the four ¹living-beings saying, ¹⁰as it were the voice of thunder, Come.¹¹

2 And I saw, and behold a white horse: and he that sat on him having a bow; and a crown was given unto him: and he went forth conquering, and in order that he might conquer.

3 And when he opened the second seal, I heard the second living-being saying, Come.¹²

4 And there went out another horse, red: it was given to him that sat thereon to take away peace from the earth, and that they should kill one another: and there was given unto him a great sword.

5 And when he opened the third seal, I heard the third

---

¹ Us *is omitted by the Alexandrine MS.*

² *So all the MSS., except one of the fourteenth century, and that is only presumed to read as the A. V.: it has not been examined.*

³ Unto our God *is omitted by the Alexandrine MS.*

⁴ *So the two most ancient MSS. The Sinaitic also reads,* and a priesthood.

⁵ *So the Alexandrine and later Vatican MSS., and many others: the Sinaitic has,* they shall reign. *Hardly any read as the A. V.*

⁶ *So the Sinaitic MS., and many others: the Alexandrine and the rest omitting* as it were.

⁷ Four and twenty *is omitted by all the MSS. and versions.*

⁸ Him that liveth for ever and ever *is omitted by all the MSS. and versions.*

⁹ *So all the old MSS. The Sinaitic MS. omits* seals.

¹⁰ *So all the old MSS.*

¹¹ And see *is omitted by two out of the three oldest MSS., the Alexandrine and the Parisian, and by many others. The Sinaitic and the later Vatican and others have it, but in different words from the commonly received text, which circumstance marks it as a spurious addition.*

¹² *This time (see on ver.* 1) *the later Vatican also, and many more MSS., omit* and see.

living-being saying, Come.[1] And I saw, and lo a black horse; and he that sat on him having a balance in his hand.

6 And I heard [2]as it were a voice in the midst of the four living-beings, saying, A [3]measure of wheat for a [4]penny, and three [3]measures of barley for a [4]penny; and the oil and the wine hurt thou not.

7 And when he opened the fourth seal, I heard the voice of the fourth living-being saying, Come.[1]

8 And I looked, and behold a pale horse: and his name that sat on him was Death, and Hadés was following with him. And authority was given unto them over the fourth part of the earth, to kill with sword, and with famine, and with death, and by the beasts of the earth.

9 And when he opened the fifth seal, I saw under the altar the souls of them that have been slain for the word of God, and for the testimony which they bore:

10 And they cried with a loud voice, saying, How long, thou Master holy and true, dost thou not judge and avenge our blood on them that dwell on the earth?

11 And there was given unto every one of them [5]a white robe; and it was said unto them, that they should rest yet for a little season, until their fellow-servants also and their brethren, that should be killed as they were, should be fulfilled.

12 And I beheld when he opened the sixth seal, and[6] there was a great earthquake; and the sun became black as sackcloth of hair, and the [7]whole moon became as blood;

13 And the stars of the heaven fell unto the earth, as a fig tree casteth her unripe figs, when she is shaken of a mighty wind.

14 And the heaven parted asunder as a scroll when it is rolled together; and every mountain and island were moved out of their places.

15 And the kings of the earth, and the great men, [8]and the chief captains, and the rich men, and the mighty men, and every bondman, and every freeman, hid themselves in the caves and in the rocks of the mountains;

16 And said to the mountains and to the rocks, Fall on us, and hide us from the face of him that sitteth on the throne, and from the wrath of the Lamb:

17 For the great day of his wrath is come; and who is able to stand?

---

[1] *This time it is nearly as in ver. 1, on which see.*
[2] *So the three oldest MSS.*
[3] *Literally*, chœnix.
[4] *Literally*, denarius.
[5] *So all the old MSS., none being known to read as the A.V.*
[6] *Lo is omitted by two of the three oldest MSS., and by many others.*
[7] *So all the older MSS. and versions. The whole moon, i.e. the full moon.*
[8] *So all the older MSS.*

CHAPTER VII.

AND after ¹this I saw four angels standing on the four corners of the earth, holding the four winds of the earth, that the wind should not blow on the earth, nor on the sea, nor against any tree.

2 And I saw another angel coming up from the rising of the sun, having the seal of the living God: and he cried with a loud voice to the four angels, to whom it was given to hurt the earth and the sea,

3 Saying, Hurt ye not the earth, nor the sea, nor the trees, till we have sealed the servants of our God upon their foreheads.

4 And I heard the number of them which were sealed: an hundred and forty-four thousand were sealed of all the tribes of the sons of Israel.

5 Of the tribe of Judah were sealed twelve thousand. Of the tribe of Reuben,² twelve thousand. Of the tribe of Gad,² twelve thousand.

6 Of the tribe of Asher,² twelve thousand. Of the tribe of Naphtali,² twelve thousand. Of the tribe of Manasseh²ND, twelve thousand.

7 Of the tribe of Simeon,² twelve thousand. Of the tribe of Levi,² twelve thousand. Of the tribe of Issachar,² twelve thousand.

8 Of the tribe of Zebulon,² twelve thousand. Of the tribe of Joseph,³ twelve thousand. Of the tribe of Benjamin were sealed twelve thousand.

9 After this I beheld, and, lo, a great multitude, which no one could number, of all nations, and tribes, and peoples, and tongues, standing before the throne, and before the Lamb, clothed with white robes, and palms in their hands;

10 And they ⁴cry with a loud voice, saying, Salvation to our God which sitteth upon the throne, and unto the Lamb.

11 And all the angels stood round about the throne, and about the elders and the four living-beings, and fell before the throne on their faces, and worshipped God,

12 Saying, Amen: the blessing, and the glory, and the wisdom, and the thanksgiving, and the honour, and the power, and the might, be unto our God for ever and ever. Amen.

13 And one of the elders answered, saying unto me, What are these which are arrayed in white robes? and whence came they?

14 And I said unto him, ⁵My lord, thou knowest. And he said to me, These are they which come out of the great tribulation, and they washed their robes, and made them white in the blood of the Lamb.

15 Therefore are they before the throne of God, and serve

---

¹ *So all the old MSS.*
² Were sealed, *in these places, is omitted by all the old MSS.*
³ Were sealed *is omitted by all the old MSS.*
⁴ *So all the oldest MSS*
⁵ *So three of the four oldest MSS.*

him day and night in his temple: and he that sitteth on the throne shall spread his habitation over them.

16 They shall hunger no more, neither thirst any more; neither shall the sun light on them, nor any heat.

17 For the Lamb which is in the midst of the throne shall tend them, and shall lead them unto the fountains of the waters of life: and God shall wipe away every tear from their eyes.

CHAPTER VIII.

AND when he opened the seventh seal, there was silence in heaven about the space of half an hour.

2 And I saw the seven angels which stand before God; and to them were given seven trumpets.

3 And another angel came and stood over the altar, having a golden censer; and there was given unto him much incense, that he should mingle it with the prayers of all the saints upon the golden altar which was before the throne.

4 And the smoke of the incense ascended up to the prayers of the saints out of the angel's hand before God.

5 And the angel took the censer, and filled it from the fire of the altar, and cast it towards the earth: and there were [1]thunderings, and voices,

[1] *No old MSS. have the order as in the A. V.: the Alexandrine has* thunderings, and lightnings, and voices: *the Sinaitic and the later Vatican as in the text. Probably the changes were made to bring* thunderings *and* lightnings *together.*

and lightnings, and an earthquake.

6 And the seven angels which had the seven trumpets prepared themselves to sound.

7 And the [2]first sounded, and there was hail and fire mingled in blood, and it was cast upon the earth: [2]and the third part of the earth was burnt up, and the third part of trees was burnt up, and all green grass was burnt up.

8 And the second angel sounded, and as it were a great mountain burning with fire was cast into the sea: and the third part of the sea became blood;

9 And the third part of the creatures which were in the sea, and had life, died; and the third part of the ships were destroyed.

10 And the third angel sounded, and there fell a great star from heaven, burning as a lamp, and it fell upon the third part of the rivers, and upon the fountains of the waters;

11 And the name of the star is called Wormwood: and the third part of the waters became wormwood; and many men died of the waters, because they were made bitter.

12 And the fourth angel sounded, and the third part of the sun was smitten, and the third part of the moon, and the third part of the stars; that the third part of them might be darkened, and the day might not shine for a third part of it, and the night in like manner.

[2] *So all the oldest MSS.*

13 And I saw and heard ¹an ²eagle flying through the midst of heaven, saying with a loud voice, Woe, woe, woe, to the inhabiters of the earth by reason of the other voices of the trumpet of the three angels, which are about to sound!

CHAPTER IX.

AND the fifth angel sounded, and I saw a star fallen out of heaven unto the earth: and to him was given the key of the pit of the abyss.

2 And he opened the pit of the abyss; and there arose a smoke out of the pit, as the smoke of a great furnace; and the sun and the air were darkened by reason of the smoke of the pit.

3 And out of the smoke came forth locusts over the earth: and unto them was given power, as the scorpions of the earth have power.

4 And it was commanded them that they should not hurt the grass of the earth, neither any green thing, neither any tree; but only those men which have not the seal of God upon their foreheads.

5 And it was given to them that they should not kill them, but that they should be tormented five months: and their torment is as the torment of a scorpion, when it hath stricken a man.

6 And in those days shall men seek death, and shall not find it; and shall vehemently desire to die, and death shall flee from them.

7 And the shapes of the locusts were like unto horses prepared for war; and on their heads were as it were crowns like gold, and their faces were as the faces of men.

8 And they had hair as the hair of women, and their teeth were as the teeth of lions.

9 And they had breastplates, as it were breastplates of iron; and the sound of their wings was as the sound of chariots of many horses running to ²war.

10 And they have tails like unto scorpions, and stings in their tails: and in their tails was their power to hurt men five months.

11 ³They have as king over them the angel of the abyss, whose name in the Hebrew tongue is Abaddon, but in the Greek tongue he hath his name Apollyon.

12 One woe is past; behold, there come two woes more after these things.

13 And the sixth angel sounded, and I heard a voice from the ⁴[four] horns of the golden altar which is before God,

14 Saying to the sixth angel which had the trumpet, Loose the four angels which are

---

¹ *Literally,* one.
² *So all the oldest MSS.*
³ And *is omitted by all the oldest MSS.*
⁴ *The reading is uncertain. We have here but two very ancient MSS., and of those the Alexandrine omits* four, *while the Sinaitic omits altogether the words* from the four horns of: *reading,* I heard the voice of the golden altar, &c.

bound on the great river Euphrates.

15 And the four angels were loosed, which had been prepared against the hour, and day, and month, and year, that they might slay the third part of men.

16 And the number of the armies of the horsemen were two hundred thousand thousand: and I heard the number of them.

17 And after this manner I saw the horses in the vision, and them that sat on them, having breastplates red, as fire, and blue, as smoke, and yellow, as brimstone: and the heads of the horses are as heads of lions; and out of their mouths issueth fire and smoke and brimstone.

18 From these three [1]plagues were the third part of men killed, by the fire, and the smoke, and the brimstone, which issueth out of their mouths.

19 For the power of [2]the horses is in their mouth, and in their tails: for their tails are like unto serpents, and had heads, and with them they do hurt.

20 And the rest of men, which were not killed by these plagues, did not even repent of the works of their hands, that they should not worship devils, and idols of gold, and silver, and brass, and stone, and of wood: which neither can see, nor hear, nor walk:

21 Neither repented they of their murders, nor of their sorceries, nor of their fornication, nor of their thefts.

CHAPTER X.

AND I saw another strong angel coming down out of heaven, clothed with a cloud, and the rainbow upon his head, and his face as it were the sun, and his feet as pillars of fire:

2 And having in his hand a little book open. And he set his right foot upon the sea, and his left foot on the earth,

3 And cried with a loud voice, as a lion roareth: and when he cried, the seven thunders uttered their voices.

4 And when the seven thunders spoke,[3] I was about to write: and I heard a voice out of heaven saying unto me, Seal up the things which the seven thunders spoke, and write them not.

5 And the angel whom I saw standing upon the sea and upon the earth lifted up his [4]right hand to heaven,

6 And sware by him that liveth for ever and ever, who created the heaven and the things therein, and the earth

[1] *So all the oldest MSS., and almost all the rest: and all the versions, and the Fathers, Greek and Latin.*

[2] *So all the oldest MSS. (except that the Alexandrine reads* places instead of horses)*, and almost all the rest: with all the versions and Fathers.*

[3] *Their voices is omitted by all the MSS., versions, and Fathers. One MS. of the eleventh century contains the words, but not in the same order as the common text.*

[4] *So most of the oldest and other MSS. The Alexandrine MS. and a few others have as the A.V.*

and the things therein, and the sea and the things therein, that there shall be delay no longer:

7 But in the days of the voice of the seventh angel, when he is about to sound, the mystery of God is finished, as he declared the glad tidings to his servants the prophets.

8 And the voice which I heard from heaven, [I] again [heard] ¹speaking unto me, and ¹saying, Go take the book which is open in the hand of the angel which standeth upon the sea and upon the earth.

9 And I went unto the angel, and told him to give me the little book. And he said unto me, Take it, and eat it up; and it shall make thy belly bitter, but shall be in thy mouth sweet as honey.

10 And I took the little book out of the angel's hand, and ate it up; and it was in my mouth as sweet honey, and as soon as I had eaten it, my belly was embittered.

11 And ²they say unto me, Thou must prophesy again concerning peoples, and nations, and tongues, and many kings.

CHAPTER XI.

AND there was given me a reed like unto a rod, ³saying, Rise, and measure the temple of God, and the altar, and them that worship therein.

2 And the court which is without the temple cast thou out, and measure not it; for it was given unto the Gentiles: and the holy city shall they tread under foot forty and two months.

3 And I will give unto my two witnesses, and they shall prophesy a thousand two hundred and threescore days, clothed in sackcloth.

4 These are the two olive trees, and the two candlesticks which stand before the ⁴Lord of the earth.

5 And if any one is minded to hurt them, fire proceedeth out of their mouth, and devoureth their enemies: and if any one is minded to hurt them, he must in this manner be killed.

6 These have power to shut the heaven, that rain may not fall during the days of their prophecy: and they have power over the waters to turn them into blood, and to smite the earth with every plague, as often as they will.

7 And when they have finished their testimony, the wild-beast that cometh up out of the abyss shall make war against them, and shall overcome them, and kill them.

8 And their dead ⁵body ⁶[is] upon the open street of the great city, namely, that which spiritually is called Sodom and

¹ *So two out of the three most ancient MSS.*
² *So all the oldest MSS.*
³ *So, omitting* and the angel stood, *all the ancient MSS. For* saying, *which is the reading of the Alexandrine and most MSS., the Sinaitic as* he saith.
⁴ *So all the ancient MSS., and almost all others.*
⁵ *So two out of the three ancient MSS., and most of the others. The Sinaitic reads* bodies: *see below on ver. 9.*
⁶ *Not expressed in the original.*

Egypt, where also [1]their Lord was crucified.

9 And some from among the people and tribes and tongues and nations look upon their dead [2]body three days and an half, and [3]suffer not their dead bodies to be put in a tomb.

10 And they that dwell upon the earth, [4]rejoice over them, and make merry, and shall send gifts one to another ; because these two prophets tormented them that dwelt on the earth.

11 And after the three days and an half the Spirit of life from God entered into them, and they stood upon their feet ; and great fear fell upon them which beheld them.

12 And they heard a great voice out of heaven saying unto them, Come up hither. And they went up to heaven in the clouds ; and their enemies beheld them.

13 And in that hour there was a great earthquake, and the tenth part of the city fell, and in the earthquake were slain names of men seven thousand : and the remnant became affrighted, and gave glory to the God of heaven.

14 The second woe is past ; behold, the third woe cometh quickly.

15 And the seventh angel sounded ; and there were great voices in heaven, saying, The [5]kingdom over the world is become our Lord's, and of his Christ ; and he shall reign for ever and ever.

16 And the four and twenty elders, which sat before God on their thrones, fell upon their faces, and worshipped God,

17 Saying, We give thee thanks, O Lord God Almighty, which art, and wast ;[6] because thou hast taken thy great might, and hast reigned.

18 And the nations were angry, and thine anger came, and the time of the dead, to be judged, and to give their reward unto thy servants the prophets, and to the saints, and them that fear thy name, the small and the great ; and to destroy them which destroy the earth.

19 And the temple of God was opened in heaven, and the ark of his covenant was seen in his temple : and there were lightnings, and voices, and thunderings, and an earthquake, and a great hail.

CHAPTER XII.

AND a great sign was seen in heaven ; a woman clothed with the sun, and the moon under her feet, and upon

---

[1] *So two of the three ancient MSS., and almost all the rest, and the versions and Fathers. The Sinaitic, the third of the ancient MSS., has* the Lord.
[2] *So all the ancient MSS. here, and most of the others.*
[3] *So all the ancient MSS.*
[4] *So all the MSS., ancient and modern, except one of the thirteenth century, which however has the future in another form from the common text.*
[5] *So all the ancient MSS., and nearly all the rest, and all the versions and Fathers.*
[6] *And art to come is omitted by all the ancient MSS., and nearly all the rest.*

her head a crown of twelve stars:

2 And she being with child crieth, travailing in birth, and pained to be delivered.

3 And another sign was seen in heaven; and behold a great red dragon, having seven heads and ten horns, and upon his heads seven diadems.

4 And his tail draweth [down] the third part of the stars of heaven, and did cast them to the earth: and the dragon standeth before the woman which is ready to be delivered, that when she hath borne, he may devour her child.

5 And she brought forth a man child, who shall rule all the nations with a rod of iron: and her child was caught up unto God, and to his throne.

6 And the woman fled into the wilderness, where she hath a place prepared of God, that they may feed her there a thousand two hundred and threescore days.

7 And there was war in heaven: Michael and his angels fighting with the dragon; and the dragon fought and his angels,

8 And prevailed not; nor was even their place found any more in heaven.

9 And the great dragon was cast out, the old serpent, he that is called the devil and Satan, which deceiveth the whole world: he was cast out into the earth, and his angels were cast out with him.

10 And I heard a loud voice in heaven, saying, Now is come the salvation and the might and the kingdom of our God, and the power of his Christ: because the accuser of our brethren is cast down, which accuseth them before our God day and night.

11 And they overcame him because of the blood of the Lamb, and because of the word of their testimony; and they loved not their lives unto the death.

12 Therefore rejoice, ye heavens, and ye that dwell in them. Woe to ¹the earth and the sea! for the devil is come down unto you, having great wrath, because he knoweth that he hath but a short time.

13 And when the dragon saw that he was cast unto the earth, he persecuted the woman which brought forth the man child.

14 And to the woman were given [the] two wings of the great eagle, that she might fly into the wilderness, into her place, where she is nourished for a time, and times, and half a time, from the face of the serpent.

15 And the serpent cast out of his mouth after the woman water as a river, that he might cause her to be carried away by the river.

16 And the earth helped the woman, and the earth opened her mouth, and swallowed down the river which the dragon cast out of his mouth.

17 And the dragon was wroth with the woman, and departed to make war with the rest of her seed, which keep the com-

¹ *So all the old MSS. and versions.*

mandments of God, and have the testimony of Jesus.[1]

CHAPTER XIII.

AND [2]he stood upon the sand of the sea. And I saw a wild-beast coming up out of the sea, having ten horns and seven heads, and upon his horns ten crowns, and upon his heads the name of blasphemy.

2 And the wild-beast which I saw was like unto a leopard, and his feet were as the feet of a bear, and his mouth as the mouth of a lion: and the dragon gave to it his power, and his throne, and great authority.

3 And [3][I saw] one of its heads as it were wounded to death; and the stroke of its death was healed: and the whole earth wondered after the beast.

4 And they worshipped the dragon, because he gave his power unto the beast: and they worshipped the beast, saying, Who is like unto the beast? who is able to make war with him?

5 And there was given unto him a mouth speaking great and blasphemous things; and authority was given unto him to work forty-two months.

6 And he opened his mouth for blasphemies against God, to blaspheme his name, and his tabernacle, [4]which dwell in heaven.

7 And it was given unto him to make war with the saints, and to overcome them: and authority was given him over [5]every tribe and people and tongue and nation.

8 And all that dwell upon the earth shall worship him, [3][every one] whose name is not written in the book of life of the Lamb which is slain from the foundation of the world.

9 If any hath an ear, let him hear.

10 [6]If any is for captivity, into captivity he goeth: [7]if any to be slain with the sword, he must be slain with the sword. Here is the patience and the faith of the saints.

11 And I beheld another wild-beast coming up out of the earth; and it had two horns like a lamb, and it spake like a dragon.

12 And it exerciseth all the authority of the first beast in his presence, and causeth the

---

[1] Christ *is omitted by all the MSS. and versions: for* Jesus *the Sinaitic S. has* God.
[2] *So all the oldest MSS.*
[3] *Not expressed in the original.*
[4] And them *is omitted by all the oldest MSS.*
[5] *So all the ancient MSS.*
[6] *The readings in this passage are in great confusion. That in the text is, as far as can be gathered, that of all the ancient MSS. One confusing element is that in two, the Parisian and Sinaitic, the transcribers have passed by mistake from the first occurrence of* captivity *to the second. But no one of the most ancient MSS. reads as the A.V., and apparently, of the more modern, only that one out of which Erasmus constructed the present received text.*
[7] *The readings here also are confused. That in the text is found in the Alexandrine MS.*

earth and them which dwell therein to worship the first beast, whose deadly wound was healed;

13 And worketh great miracles, so that it even maketh fire come down ¹on the earth in the sight of men,

14 And deceiveth them that dwell on the earth, because of the miracles which it was given him to work in the sight of the beast; ordering them that dwell on the earth to make an image to the beast, which hath the wound by the sword, and did live.

15 And it was given him to give breath unto the image of the beast, that the image of the beast should even speak, and should cause that as many as worship not the image of the beast should be killed.

16 And he causeth all men, both small and great, rich and poor, free and bond, ²to receive a mark on their right hand, or on their forehead:

17 ³That no one should be able to buy or sell, save he that hath the mark, ⁴the name of the beast, or the number of his name.

18 Here is wisdom: let him that hath understanding calculate the number of the beast: for it is the number of a man; and his number is Six hundred and ⁵sixty-six.

CHAPTER XIV.

AND I saw, and, behold, ⁶the Lamb standing on the mount Sion, and with him an hundred and forty-four thousand, having ⁷his name and his Father's name written on their foreheads.

2 And I heard a voice out of heaven, as a voice of many waters, and as a voice of great thunder: and ⁸the voice which I heard [was] as of harpers harping with their harps:

3 And they sing as it were a new song before the throne, and before the four living-creatures, and the elders: and no one could learn the song but the hundred and forty-four thousand, which have been purchased from the earth.

4 These are they which were not defiled with women; for they are virgins. These are they which follow the Lamb whithersoever he goeth. These were purchased from among men as a firstfruit unto God and to the Lamb.

5 And in their mouth was

---

¹ From heaven *is omitted by two out of the three most ancient MSS., and almost all the rest.*

² *Literally,* that they give to them a mark, &c.

³ And *is omitted by two out of the three most ancient MSS.*

⁴ Or *is omitted by the Alexandrine MS., the later Vatican, and nearly all the later MSS. The Parisian MS. reads,* the mark of the name: *the Sinaitic,* the mark of the beast, or his name.

⁵ *The Parisian MS. (fifth century)* reads six hundred and sixteen. *This uncertainty has existed from the earliest times: Irenæus mentions it in the second, or beginning of the third century.*

⁶ *So all the ancient, and almost all the other MSS.*

⁷ *So all the oldest MSS., versions, and Greek and Latin Fathers.*

⁸ *So all the oldest authorities.*

found no falsehood : [1]they are blameless.[2]

6 And I saw an [3][other] angel flying in the midst of heaven, having the everlasting gospel to preach unto them that dwell on the earth, and to every nation, and tribe, and tongue, and people,

7 Saying with a loud voice, Fear God, and give glory to him ; for the hour of his judgment is come : and worship him that made the heaven, and the earth, and sea, and fountains of waters.

8 And another [4]second angel followed, saying, Babylon [5]the great is fallen, is fallen, which hath made all the nations drink of the wine of the wrath of her fornication.

9 And [6]another third angel followed them, saying with a loud voice, If any worshippeth the beast and his image, and receiveth the mark on his forehead, or upon his hand,

10 He also shall drink of the wine of the wrath of God, which is poured out without mixture in the cup of his indignation ; and he shall be tormented with fire and brimstone in the presence of the [7][holy] angels, and in the presence of the Lamb :

11 And the smoke of their torment ascendeth up for ever and ever : and they have no rest day nor night, who worship the beast and his image, and whosoever receiveth the mark of his name.

12 Here is the patience of the saints, [8]which keep the commandments of God, and the faith of Jesus.

13 And I heard a voice from heaven saying, [9]Write, Blessed are the dead which die in the Lord from henceforth : Yea, saith the Spirit, that they may rest from their labours ; [10]for their works do follow with them.

14 And I saw, and behold a white cloud, and upon the cloud one sitting like unto the Son of man, having on his head a golden crown, and in his hand a sharp sickle.

15 And another angel came out of the temple, crying with a loud voice to him that sat on the cloud, Put forth thy sickle, and reap : for the time [11]to reap is come ; for the harvest of the earth is [12]ripe.

16 And he that sat on the cloud thrust in his sickle upon the earth ; and the earth was reaped.

---

[1] For *is omitted by two out of the three oldest MSS.*
[2] Before the throne of God, *inserted in the ordinary text, is absolutely without any MS. authority.*
[3] Other *is omitted by the Sinaitic, and by most of the later MSS., but is contained in the Alexandrine and Parisian.*
[4] *Thus, or nearly thus, all the oldest MSS.*
[5] *Thus the oldest MSS. The Sinaitic omits from* another, ver. 8, *to* another, ver. 9.
[6] *Thus almost all the MSS. The common text has no MS. authority.*
[7] *One of the oldest MSS. omits* holy.
[8] *So, in sense, all the oldest MSS.*
[9] Unto me *is omitted by all the ancient MSS.*
[10] *So all the oldest MSS.*
[11] For thee *is omitted by all the ancient MSS.*
[12] *Literally,* dried.

17 And another angel came out from the temple which was in heaven, he also having a sharp sickle.

18 And another angel came out from the altar, he that hath power over the fire; and cried with a loud cry to him that had the sharp sickle, saying, Put forth thy sharp sickle, and gather the clusters of the vine of the earth; for her grapes are fully ripe.

19 And the angel thrust in his sickle into the earth, and gathered the vine of the earth, and cast into the great winepress of the wrath of God.

20 And the winepress was trodden outside the city, and blood came forth from the winepress, even unto the bits of the horses, to the distance of a thousand and six hundred furlongs.

CHAPTER XV.

AND I saw another sign in heaven, great and marvellous, seven angels having seven plagues, which are the last, because in them is filled up the wrath of God.

2 And I saw as it were a sea of glass mingled with fire: and the conquerors of the beast, and of his image, [1]and of the number of his name, standing on the sea of glass, having harps of God.

3 And they sing the song of Moses the servant of God, and the song of the Lamb, saying, Great and marvellous are thy works, Lord God Almighty;

[1] And of his mark *is omitted by all the ancient MSS.*

just and true are thy ways, thou King of [2]the nations.

4 Who shall not fear thee, O Lord, and glorify thy name? for thou only art holy: for all the nations shall come and worship before thee; because thy righteous acts have been made manifest.

5 And after these things I saw, and[3] the temple of the tabernacle of the testimony in heaven was opened:

6 And the seven angels came out of the temple, having the seven plagues, clothed in linen pure and shining, and girt about their breasts with golden girdles.

7 And one of the four living-creatures gave unto the seven angels seven golden vials full of the wrath of God, who liveth for ever and ever.

8 And the temple was filled with smoke from the glory of God, and from his might; and none was able to enter into the temple, till the seven plagues of the seven angels should be finished.

CHAPTER XVI.

AND I heard a great voice out of the temple saying to the seven angels, Go and pour out the [4]seven vials of the wrath of God into the earth.

2 And the first departed, and poured out his vial [4]into the earth; and there fell a noisome

[2] *Thus all the ancient MSS., except the Parisian, which reads* of the ages *(see* 1 *Tim.* i. 17). *The reading of the A.V. has no authority at all*
[3] Behold *is omitted by all the MSS*
[4] *So all the ancient MSS.*

and grievous sore upon the men which had the mark of the beast, and which worshipped his image.

3 And the second[1] poured out his vial into the sea; and it became blood, as of a dead man: and every living soul died, [of all] that were in the sea.

4 And the third[2] poured out his vial into the rivers and the fountains of the waters; and they became blood.

5 And I heard the angel of the waters saying, Thou art righteous,[3] which art and wast [4]holy, because thou didst judge thus.

6 For they shed the blood of saints and prophets, and thou hast given them blood to drink; [5]they are worthy.

7 And I heard [6]the altar saying, Even so, Lord God Almighty, true and righteous are thy judgments.

8 And the fourth poured out his vial upon the sun; and it was given unto it to scorch men with fire.

9 And men were scorched with great heat, and blasphemed the name of God, which hath power over these plagues: and they repented not to give him glory.

10 And the fifth poured out his vial upon the throne of the beast; and his kingdom became darkened; and they gnawed their tongues for pain,

11 And blasphemed the God of heaven because of their pains and their sores, and repented not of their works.

12 And the sixth poured out his vial upon the great river Euphrates; and the water thereof was dried up, that the way of the kings which come from the rising of the sun might be prepared.

13 And I saw [7][coming] out of the mouth of the dragon, and out of the mouth of the beast, and out of the mouth of the false prophet, three unclean spirits like frogs.

14 For they are spirits of demons, working miracles, which go forth unto the kings of the [8]whole world, to gather them to the war of the great day of God Almighty.

15 Behold, I come as a thief. Blessed is he that watcheth, and keepeth his garments, lest he walk naked, and they see his shame.

16 And they gathered them together to the place called in Hebrew [9]Harmagedon.

17 And the seventh poured

---

[1] *Angel is omitted by the oldest MSS.*
[2] *Angel is omitted by all the ancient MSS.: and so throughout.*
[3] *O Lord is omitted by all ancient, and almost all other MSS.*
[4] *So, or the holy One, all the ancient MSS. The A.V., and shalt be, has absolutely no Greek text whatever corresponding to it, and is a pure invention.*
[5] *For is omitted by all the old MSS.*
[6] *Another out of is omitted by all ancient MSS., and rests only on the authority of one MS. of the twelfth century.*

[7] *Not expressed in the original.*
[8] *Earth and of the is omitted by all ancient MSS.*
[9] *So (with one d) all the early MSS. The H is in the Hebrew name, and in many of our MSS (the ancient MSS. have no aspirates)*

out his vial ¹upon the air; and there came a great voice out of the temple,² from the throne, saying, It is done.

18 And there were ³lightnings, and voices, and thunders; and there was a great earthquake, such as was not since ⁴there was a man upon the earth, such an earthquake, so great.

19 And the great city was divided into three parts, and the cities of the nations fell: and Babylon the great was remembered before God, to give unto her the cup of the wine of the fierceness of his wrath.

20 And every island fled away, and there were found no mountains.

21 And a great hail, as of a talent in weight, cometh down out of heaven upon men: and men blasphemed God because of the plague of the hail, because exceeding great is the plague thereof.

CHAPTER XVII.

AND there came one of the seven angels which had the seven vials, and talked with me, saying unto me, Come hither; I will shew thee the judgment of the great harlot that sitteth upon [the] many waters:

2 With whom the kings of the earth committed fornication, and the inhabitants of the earth were made drunk with the wine of her fornication.

3 And he carried me away in the spirit into the wilderness: and I saw a woman sitting upon a scarlet coloured wild-beast, full of names of blasphemy, having seven heads and ten horns.

4 And the woman was arrayed in purple and scarlet colour, and gilded with gold and precious stones and pearls, having a golden cup in her hand full of abominations and filthiness of her fornication:

5 And [having] upon her forehead a name written, MYSTERY, BABYLON THE GREAT, THE MOTHER OF THE HARLOTS AND OF THE ABOMINATIONS OF THE EARTH.

6 And I saw the woman drunken with the blood of the saints, and with the blood of the witnesses of Jesus. And when I saw her, I wondered with great wonder.

7 And the angel said unto me, Wherefore didst thou wonder? I will tell thee the mystery of the woman, and of the wild-beast that carrieth her, which hath the seven heads and the ten horns.

8 The beast that thou sawest was, and is not; and shall ascend out of the abyss, and goeth into perdition: and they that dwell on the earth shall wonder, whose names are not written in the book of life from the foundation of the world, when they see the beast,

---

¹ *So all the ancient MSS.*
² Of heaven *is omitted by the Alexandrine MS.: the Sinaitic has* of God, *shewing that originally there was only as in the text.*
³ *So the Alexandrine MS.: the Sinaitic has* thunders, and lightnings, and voices, and thunders.
⁴ *So the Alexandrine MS.*

that he was, and is not, and ¹shall come again.

9 ²Here is the mind which hath wisdom. The seven heads are seven mountains, on which the woman sitteth.

10 And they are seven kings: the five are fallen, the one is, the other is not yet come; and when he cometh, he must continue a short space.

11 And the beast that was, and is not, even he is the eighth, and is of the seven, and goeth into perdition.

12 And the ten horns which thou sawest are ten kings, which have received no kingdom as yet; but receive power as kings one hour together with the beast.

13 These have one mind, and ³give their might and power unto the beast.

14 These shall make war with the Lamb, and the Lamb shall overcome them, because he is Lord of lords, and King of kings, and they that are with him, called, and chosen, and faithful.

15 And he saith unto me, The waters which thou sawest, where the harlot sitteth, are peoples, and multitudes, and nations, and tongues.

16 And the ten horns which thou sawest, ³and the beast, these shall hate the harlot, and shall make her deserted and naked, and shall eat her flesh, and shall burn her with fire.

17 For God put in their hearts to fulfil his will, ⁴[and to agree,] and to give their kingdom unto the beast, until the words of God shall be fulfilled.

18 And the woman which thou sawest is the great city, which reigneth over the kings of the earth.

CHAPTER XVIII.

⁵AFTER these things I saw another angel coming down out of heaven, having great power; and the earth was lightened with his glory.

2 And he cried⁶ with a strong voice, saying, Babylon the great is fallen, is fallen, and is become an habitation of demons, and an hold of every unclean spirit, and an hold of every unclean and hateful bird.

3 For all the nations have drunk of ⁷the wrath of her fornication, and the kings of the earth committed fornication with her, and the merchants of the earth waxed rich through the abundance of her luxury.

4 And I heard another voice out of heaven, saying, Come out of her, my people, that ye be not partakers in her sins, and that ye receive not of her plagues;

5 Because her sins have reached unto heaven, and God hath remembered her iniquities.

---

¹ *So all the ancient MSS.: some of the later have* and *is present; but none read as the A.V.*
² And *has no authority whatever.*
³ *So all the ancient MSS*

⁴ *Omitted by the Alexandrine MS.*
⁵ And *is omitted by all the ancient MSS.*
⁶ Mightily *is omitted by all MSS. whatever.*
⁷ The wine of *is omitted by all the most ancient MSS.*

6 Repay to her even as she repaid,[1] and double [2][unto her] double according to her works: in the cup which she mixed, mix for her double.

7 As much as she glorified herself, and lived in luxury, so much torment and sorrow give her: for she saith in her heart, I sit a queen, and am not a widow, and shall never see mourning.

8 Therefore in one day shall her plagues come, death, and mourning, and famine; and she shall be utterly burned with fire: because strong is the Lord God who hath judged her.

9 And there shall weep and mourn over her the kings of the earth, who committed fornication and lived luxuriously with her, when they see the smoke of her burning,

10 Standing afar off for the fear of her torment, saying, Alas, alas the great city, Babylon the strong city! for in one hour is thy judgment come.

11 And the merchants of the earth weep and mourn over her; for none buyeth their merchandise any more:

12 Merchandise of gold, and silver, and precious stones, and of pearls, and fine linen, and purple, and silk, and scarlet, and all citron wood, and every article of ivory, and every article of most precious wood, and of brass, and of iron, and of marble,

13 And cinnamon, and [3]amo-mum, and odours, and ointments, and frankincense, and wine, and oil, and fine flour, and wheat, and cattle, and sheep, and horses, and chariots, and slaves, and persons of men.

14 And thy harvest of the desire of thy soul is departed from thee, and all thy fat things and thy splendid things are [4]perished from thee, and [5]men shall find them no more at all.

15 The merchants of these things, which were made rich by her, shall stand afar off for the fear of her torment, weeping and mourning,

16 Saying, Alas, alas the great city, that was clothed in fine linen, and purple, and scarlet, and gilded with gold, and precious stones, and pearls:

17 For in one hour all that wealth is made desolate. And every pilot, and [6]every one who saileth any whither, and shipmen, and as many as trade by sea, stood afar off,

18 And cried when they saw the smoke of her burning, saying, Who is like unto the great city?

19 And they cast earth on their heads, and cried, weeping and mourning, saying, Alas, alas the great city, whereby all that have ships in the sea were made rich out of her costliness: for in one hour is she made desolate.

20 Rejoice over her, thou

---

[1] You *is omitted by all the ancient MSS.*
[2] *Not expressed in the original.*
[3] *So the most ancient MSS.*
[4] *So all the ancient MSS.*
[5] *So* [they shall find them] *the most ancient MSS.*
[6] *So all the most ancient MSS., the more recent ones being variously corrected.*

heaven, and ye ¹saints, and ye apostles and ye prophets; for God hath judged your judgment upon her.

21 And one strong angel took up a stone, great as a millstone, and cast it into the sea, saying, Thus with violence shall be thrown down the great city Babylon, and shall be found no more at all.

22 And the sound of harpers, and musicians, and of fluteplayers,· and trumpeters, shall be heard no more at all in thee; and no craftsman, of whatsoever craft, shall be found any more in thee; and the sound of the millstone shall be heard no more at all in thee;

23 And the light of a lamp shall shine no more at all in thee; and the voice of the bridegroom and the bride shall be heard no more at all in thee: for thy merchants were the great men of the earth; for with thy sorceries were all the nations deceived.

24 And in her was found the blood of prophets, and of saints, and of all that have been slain upon the earth.

CHAPTER XIX.

²AFTER these things I heard ³as it were a loud voice of a great multitude in heaven, saying, Hallelujah; ³the salvation and the glory⁴ belong unto our God:

¹ *So most of the ancient MSS.*
² *And is omitted by all the ancient MSS.*
³ *So all the ancient MSS.*
⁴ *And honour is omitted by all the ancient MSS. The Sinaitic omits* and the glory *also.*

2 For true and righteous are his judgments: for he hath judged the great harlot, which did corrupt the earth with her fornication, and hath avenged the blood of his servants at her hand.

3 And again they said, Hallelujah. And her smoke goeth up for ever and ever.

4 And the four and twenty elders and the four living-creatures fell down and worshipped God that sitteth on the throne, saying, Amen; Hallelujah.

5 And a voice came forth ⁵from the throne, saying, Praise our God, all ye his servants, [and] ye that fear him, both small and great.

6 And I heard as it were the voice of a great multitude, and as it were the voice of many waters, and as it were the voice of mighty thunderings, saying, Hallelujah: for the Lord God omnipotent reigneth.

7 Let us rejoice and exult, and give honour to him: for the marriage of the Lamb is come, and his wife hath made herself ready.

8 And it was given to her that she should be arrayed in fine linen, bright and pure: for the fine linen is the righteousness of the saints.

9 And he saith unto me, Write, Blessed are they which are called unto the marriage supper of the Lamb. And he saith unto me, These are the true sayings of God.

⁵ *So two of the three oldest MSS.: the Sinaitic reading,* voices came out of, *&c.*

10 And I fell at his feet to worship him. And he said unto me, See thou do it not: I am a fellow-servant of thine, and of thy brethren that have the testimony of Jesus: worship God: for the testimony of Jesus is the spirit of prophecy.

11 And I saw heaven opened, and behold a white horse; and he that sitteth upon him [is] ¹[called] Faithful and True, and in righteousness he doth judge and make war.

12 His eyes [were as] a flame of fire, and on his head were many diadems; having ²[names written, and] a name written, that no man knoweth, but he himself:

13 And clothed with a vesture dipped in blood: and his name is called The Word of God.

14 And the armies which are in heaven followed him upon white horses, clothed in fine linen, white and pure.

15 And out of his mouth goeth a sharp sword, that with it he may smite the nations: and he shall rule them with a rod of iron: and he himself treadeth the winepress of the fierceness ³of the wrath of Almighty God.

16 And he hath on his vesture and on his thigh a name written, KING OF KINGS, AND LORD OF LORDS.

17 And I saw an angel standing in the sun·; and he cried with a loud voice, saying to all the fowls that fly in midheaven, Come, gather yourselves together unto the ³great banquet of God:

18 That ye may eat the flesh of kings, and the flesh of captains of thousands, and the flesh of strong men, and the flesh of horses, and of them that sit on them, and the flesh of all men, both free and bond, both small and great.

19 And I saw the wild-beast, and the kings of the earth, and their armies, gathered together to make their war against him that sitteth on the horse, and against his army.

20 And the beast was taken, and ⁴ those that were with him, the false prophet that wrought the miracles in his presence, with which he deceived them that received the mark of the beast, and them that worshipped his image: these two were cast alive into the lake of fire which burneth with brimstone.

21 And the rest were slain with the sword of him that sitteth upon the horse, the sword which proceedeth out of his mouth: and all the fowls were filled with their flesh.

CHAPTER XX.

AND I saw an angel coming down out of heaven, having the key of the abyss and a great chain in his hand.

2 And he laid hold on the dragon, the old serpent, which

---

¹ *Omitted in the Alexandrine MS.*
² *These words are omitted by some of the most ancient MSS.*
³ *So all the ancient MSS.*
⁴ *So the Alexandrine MS. (the Parisian is here deficient). In the others the reading is very various.*

is the devil, and Satan, and bound him a thousand years,

3 And cast him into the abyss, and shut, and sealed over him, that he deceive the nations no more, till the thousand years shall be fulfilled: and after that he must be loosed a little season.

4 And I saw thrones, and they sat upon them, and judgment was given unto them: and I saw the souls of them that were beheaded for the witness of Jesus, and for the word of God, and which did not worship the beast, neither his image, neither received his mark upon their forehead and on their hand; and they lived and reigned with Christ a thousand years.

5 But the rest of the dead lived not again until the thousand years were finished. This is the first resurrection.

6 Blessed and holy is he that hath part in the first resurrection: on such the second death hath no power, but they shall be priests of God and of Christ, and shall reign with him a thousand years.

7 And when the thousand years are expired, Satan shall be loosed out of his prison,

8 And shall go forth to deceive the nations which are in the four corners of the earth, Gog and Magog, to gather them together to the war: the number of whom is as the sand of the sea.

9 And they went up on the breadth of the earth, and compassed the camp of the saints about, and the beloved city: and fire came down [1] out of heaven, and devoured them.

10 And the devil their deceiver was cast into the lake of fire and brimstone, where also are the wild-beast and the false prophet. And they shall be tormented day and night for ever and ever.

11 And I saw a great white throne, and him that sitteth on it, from whose face the earth and the heaven fled away; and there was found no place for them.

12 And I saw the dead, [2] the great and the small, standing before [3] the throne; and books were opened: and another book was opened, which is the book of life: and the dead were judged out of those things which were written in the books, according to their works.

13 And the sea gave up the dead which were in it; and death and Hadés delivered up the dead which were in them: and they were judged each according to their works.

14 And death and Hadés were cast into the lake of fire. This is the second death, [4] [even] the lake of fire.

15 And whosoever was not found written in the book of life was cast into the lake of fire.

[1] *From God is omitted by the Alexandrine MS., and variously inserted by those later MSS. which read it. The Sinaitic MS. omits from fire here to fire in the next verse.*
[2] *So the two oldest MSS.*
[3] *So the Alexandrine, and almost all other MSS. The Sinaitic reads* upon the throne.
[4] *So all the ancient MSS.*

CHAPTER XXI.

AND I saw a new heaven and a new earth: for the first heaven and the first earth were passed away; and the sea is no more.

2 And I[1] saw the holy city, new Jerusalem, coming down out of heaven from God, prepared as a bride adorned for her husband.

3 And I heard a great voice out of [2]the throne saying, Behold, the tabernacle of God is with men, and he [3]will dwell with them, and they shall be his people, and he shall be God with them, their God.

4 And [4][God] shall wipe away every tear from their eyes; and there shall be no more death, neither sorrow, nor crying, nor pain: for the former things are passed away.

5 And he that sitteth upon the throne said, Behold, I make all things new. And he saith,[5] Write: for these words are faithful and true.

6 And he said unto me, [6]They are fulfilled. I am the Alpha and the Omega, the beginning and the end. I will give unto him that is athirst of the fountain of the water of life freely.

7 He that overcometh shall inherit [7]these things; and I will be to him a God, and he shall be to me a son.

8 But the fearful, and unbelieving, and the polluted with abominations, and murderers, and fornicators, and sorcerers, and idolaters, and all liars, shall have their part in the lake which burneth with fire and brimstone, which is the second death.

9 And there came unto me one of the seven angels which had the seven vials and were full of the seven last plagues, and talked with me, saying, Come hither, I will shew thee the bride, the wife of the Lamb.

10 And he carried me away in the spirit to a great and high mountain, and shewed me [7]the holy city Jerusalem, coming down out of heaven from God,

11 Having the glory of God: and her brightness was like unto a stone most precious, as it were to a jasper stone clear as crystal;

12 Having a wall great and high, having twelve gates, and at the gates twelve angels, and names written thereon, which are the names of the twelve tribes of the sons of Israel:

13 On the east three gates; on the north three gates; on the south three gates; and on the west three gates.

14 And the wall of the city had twelve foundation stones and upon them the [7]twelve names of the twelve apostles of the Lamb.

---

[1] John *is omitted by all MSS. whatever.*
[2] *So the oldest MSS.*
[3] *The Sinaitic MS. has* dwelt.
[4] God *is omitted by the Sinaitic and many later MSS.*
[5] Unto me *is omitted by the Alexandrine and many later MSS.*
[6] *So the Alexandrine MS. The Sinaitic and many later MSS. read* merely, I am become the Alpha, &c.
[7] *So all the ancient MSS.*

15 And he that talked with me had ¹ for a measure a golden reed, to measure the city, and the gates thereof, and the wall thereof.

16 And the city lieth foursquare, and the length is as great as the breadth: and he measured the city with the reed, twelve thousand furlongs. The length and the breadth and the height of it are equal.

17 And he measured the wall thereof, an hundred and forty-four cubits, the measure of a man, which is, that of an angel.

18 And the masonry of the wall of it was jasper: and the city, pure gold, like unto clear glass.

19 And the foundations of the wall of the city were adorned with every precious stone. The first foundation was jasper; the second, sapphire; the third, chalcedony; the fourth, emerald;

20 The fifth, sardonyx; the sixth, sardius; the seventh, chrysolith; the eighth, beryl; the ninth, topaz; the tenth, chrysoprasus; the eleventh, jacinth; the twelfth, amethyst.

21 And the twelve gates were twelve pearls; every several gate was of one pearl: and the street of the city was pure gold, as it were transparent glass.

22 And I saw no temple therein: for the Lord God Almighty is the temple thereof, and the Lamb.

23 And the city hath no need of the sun, neither of the moon, to shine in it: for the glory of God did lighten it, and the Lamb is the light thereof.

24 And the nations ² shall walk by means of the light of it: and the kings of the earth do bring their glory ³ into it.

25 And the gates of it shall not be shut at all by day: for there shall be no night there.

26 And they shall bring the glory and honour of the nations into it.

27 And there shall in no wise enter into it any thing that defileth, or worketh abomination or falsehood: but only they which are written in the Lamb's book of life.

CHAPTER XXII.

AND he shewed me a ⁴river of water of life, bright as crystal, proceeding out of the throne of God and of the Lamb.

2 In the midst of the street of it, and on either side of the river, the tree of life, bearing twelve manner of fruits, and yielding her fruit every month: and the leaves of the tree were for the healing of the nations.

3 And there shall be no more curse: and the throne of God and of the Lamb shall be in it; and his servants shall serve him:

4 And they shall see his face; and his name shall be in their foreheads.

¹ *So all the ancient MSS*
² *So, omitting* of them that are saved, *all the ancient MSS.*
³ And honour *is omitted by all the ancient MSS.*
⁴ Pure *is omitted by all the ancient MSS*

5 And there shall be no ¹more night; and they need no ²[light of] lamp, neither light ²[of the sun]; because the Lord God shall shine upon them: and they shall reign for ever and ever.

6 And he said unto me, These sayings are faithful and true: and the Lord God of the ¹spirits of the prophets sent his angel to shew unto his servants what things must shortly come to pass.

7 ¹And behold, I come quickly: blessed is he that keepeth the sayings of the prophecy of this book.

8 And I John am he who heard these things, and saw them. And when I heard and when I saw, I fell down to worship before the feet of the angel which shewed me these things.

9 Then saith he unto me, See thou do it not: for I am a fellow-servant of thine, and of thy brethren the prophets, and of them which keep the sayings of this book: worship God.

10 And he saith unto me, Seal not the sayings of the prophecy of this book: for the time is near.

11 He that is unjust, let him be unjust still: and he which is filthy, let him be filthy still: and he that is righteous, let him ¹still do righteousness: and he that is holy, let him sanctify himself still.

12 ³Behold, I come quickly; and my reward is with me, to give every man according as his work ¹is.

13 I am the Alpha and the Omega, ¹first and last, the beginning and the end.

14 Blessed are they that ⁴wash their robes, that they may have power over the tree of life, and may enter in through the gates into the city.

15 Without are the dogs, and the sorcerers, and the fornicators, and the murderers, and the idolaters, and whosoever loveth and doeth falsehood.

16 I Jesus sent mine angel to testify these things unto you in the churches. I am the root and the offspring of David, the bright morning star.

17 And the Spirit and the bride say, Come: and let him that heareth say, Come: and let him that is athirst come: ³whosoever will, let him take the water of life freely.

18 ⁵I testify unto every one that heareth the sayings of the prophecy of this book, If any shall add unto ⁶them, God shall add unto him the plagues that are written in this book:

19 And if any shall take away from the sayings of the book of this prophecy, God shall take away his part out

---

¹ *So all the ancient MSS.*
² *The words in brackets are omitted in some of the principal MSS.*
³ *And is omitted by all the ancient MSS.*
⁴ *So the most ancient MSS., the later ones reading* do his commandments, *as the A.V.*
⁵ *So the Alexandrine and many later MSS. The Sinaitic has,* Or I testify. *No MSS. have* For.
⁶ *So most MSS., none reading as the A.V.*

of the ¹tree of life, and ²[out of] the holy city, ³which are written in this book.

20 He which testifieth these things saith, Surely I come quickly. Amen, come, Lord Jesus.

21 The grace of ⁴the Lord Jesus⁵ be with ⁶the saints. Amen.

---

¹ *So all the MSS., none reading as the A. V.*
² *Omitted by the Alexandrine MS., but inserted by the Sinaitic.*
³ *And from the things is omitted in almost all the MSS.*
⁴ *Hardly any MSS. read* our.
⁵ *Christ is omitted by the oldest MSS.*
⁶ *So the Sinaitic MS. The Alexandrine reads,* be with all *(and no more): the later MSS. read,* be with all the saints : *but no MS. reads as the A. V.*

THE END.

www.ingramcontent.com/pod-product-compliance
Lightning Source LLC
Chambersburg PA
CBHW051724300426
44115CB00007B/457